Special Education
FOR ALL TEACHERS

Fourth Edition

Ronald P. Colarusso
Georgia State University

Colleen M. O'Rourke
Georgia State University

KENDALL/HUNT PUBLISHING CO
4050 Westmark Drive   Dubuque, Iow

Book Team

Chairman and Chief Executive Officer *Mark C. Falb*
Director of National Book Program *Paul B. Carty*
Editorial Developmental Manager *Georgia Botsford*
Developmental Editor *Tina Bower*
Vice President, Production and Manufacturing *Alfred C. Grisanti*
Assistant Vice President, Production Services *Christine E. O'Brien*
Prepress Editor *Angela Puls*
Permissions Editor *Elizabeth Roberts*
Designer *Deb Howes*
Senior Vice President, College Division *Thomas W. Gantz*
Managing Editor, College Field *Gregory DeRosa*
Associate Editor, College Field *Kristin Tremblay*

Contents

Chapter 3
The Referral and Placement Process
Gwendolyn T. Benson and Harry L. Dangel

Chapter 4
Characteristics of Students with Behavior and Learning Challenges
L. Juane Heflin and Rebecca M. Wilson

Chapter 5

Characteristics of Students with Sensory, Communication, Physical, and Health Impairments

Kathryn Wolff Heller and Colleen M. O'Rourke

Chapter 6

Instructional Methods for Students with Mild Disabilities

David E. Houchins, Mary Beth Calhoon, and Harry L. Dangel

Chapter 7 OMIT

Reading Assessment and Instruction for Students At-Risk
Margaret E. Shippen, David E. Houchins, and Candace E. Steventon

Chapter 8   OMIT
Math Assessment and Instruction for Students At-Risk
David E. Houchins, Margaret E. Shippen, and Margaret M. Flores

Chapter 9
Students with Moderate and Severe Mental Retardation
Paul Alberto, Melissa Alldread Hughes, and Rebecca Waugh

Chapter 12

Collaboration with Families and Professionals

Peggy A. Gallagher and Debra Schober-Peterson

Chapter 13
Students Who Are Talented and Gifted
John E. Kesner, and Teresa Pawlick

Preface

This text book is written for all professionals who are interested in the education of students with special needs. The intent is to provide information and increase knowledge about these students in the hope that greater understanding will lead to the acceptance of them and their diverse needs in our schools and our society. It also is intended to provide instructional and management strategies for general education classroom teachers who interact with these students on a daily basis. This book is written to serve as a text for students enrolled in preservice courses addressing special education. In addition, it can serve as a supplemental text or resource for those professionals currently serving students with special needs. The goals of *Special Education for All Teachers* are:

- To present the philosophy of inclusion, and the application and implementation of laws related to the education of students with special needs;
- To discuss the identifying characteristics of students with special needs; and
- To provide practical information relative to:
  - the referral process
  - general instructional adaptations
  - strategies for teaching reading and math
  - the use of environmental adaptations and technology
  - behavior management
  - collaboration

It is our belief that every student has the right to a free appropriate education and that this education should occur in the least restrictive environment appropriate for each student's individual educational needs. For this belief to become a reality, educators must accept the responsibility for the education of all students regardless of their abilities or disabilities. Perhaps the greatest challenge to the classroom teacher is to meet the educational needs of the diverse student population in our schools today. Students with differing abilities contribute to the diversity in the classroom and there is no doubt that many of them will have special needs which must be addressed. We believe that good teachers have the desire and ability to accept the challenge of meeting the needs of some students with special needs in the general education classroom if they are provided with the appropriate knowledge and resources.

The classroom teacher must have the ability and willingness to make appropriate referrals and to integrate students with special needs into the general education program. But they cannot succeed alone. The successful education and integration of all students requires cooperation and collaboration among classroom teachers, special educators, parents, students, administrators, and other professionals.

This textbook focuses on relevant and practical issues in educating students with special needs and students who are at-risk for learning problems in the general education program.

Chapters 1 and 2: Introduce the concept of inclusion and the laws that impact the education of all students.

Chapter 3: Reviews the processes of referral, evaluation, and placement.

Chapters 4, 5 and 9: Present information about the characteristics and needs of special students.

Chapters 6, 7 and 8: Address the strategies and methods general educators can use for academic instruction of students who have, or are at-risk for, learning problems.

Chapters 10 through 12: Offer suggestions for environmental adaptations and technology use, strategies for behavior management, and ways to enhance collaboration with parents and other professionals.

Chapter 13: Presents information about the characteristics and needs of students who are gifted and talented and provides ideas for how the classroom teacher can enrich the general education curriculum for these students.

In this fourth edition of *Special Education for All Children,* all chapters address the newest law, the Individuals with Disabilities Education Improvement Act (IDEA 2004). Chapter 6 (instructional methods) has been significantly revised and Chapter 11 (behavior management) is an entirely new chapter.

It is our hope that the content of this text book will assist all teachers and school professionals in ensuring success for all students.

Ronald P. Colarusso
Colleen M. O'Rourke
2006

Acknowledgments

We wish to thank the authors for sharing their collective knowledge and expertise in this book. This text is a collaborative effort of the Special Education faculty at Georgia State University and we are pleased to have several new authors in this fourth edition. This book was written in response to a recognized need to provide teachers with information about how they might serve students with disabilities more effectively in the general education classroom. We appreciate the authors' commitment to this goal and their willingness to revise and expand their chapters.

To the instructors of the *Exceptional Children and Youth* course and the students enrolled at Georgia State University, we are grateful for your feedback and suggestions. You prompted the initial writing of this book and taught us some valuable lessons in writing an introductory textbook.

We are deeply indebted to Rebecca M. Wilson for her willingness to test the early draft of this book in her classes and we acknowledge the contributions of Marie C. Keel to our earlier editions.

R.P.C.
C.M.O'R.

Teaching Every Student, a Mandate for Today

Colleen M. O'Rourke and Ronald P. Colarusso

Chapter Objectives

- to define special education and describe its role in the educational system;
- to provide an overview of the characteristics and special needs of students with disabilities;
- to explore the controversy of labeling and the impact it can have on teachers and students;
- to examine the history of special education and the change in society's attitude towards individuals with disabilities;
- to present the educational options and service delivery models used in today's schools to meet the special needs of students; and
- to explore the issue of diversity and its relevance in the identification of students who need special education services.

Obtaining an education is the personal responsibility of all United States' citizens. This is evident in the existence of federal and state laws requiring children to be engaged in some form of education. Unfortunately, these federal and local laws mandating education have not always guaranteed the appropriate education for all citizens. Over the years, specific laws and lawsuits were needed to insure the provision of appropriate education for individuals from minority groups and those with disabilities. The sentiments behind these laws reflect Americans' values and our belief that all individuals should have an equal opportunity for an appropriate education. Today's classrooms reflect our society and its diversity. Students come to school with unique personalities, abilities, attitudes, and values, not to mention the diversity found in gender, race, religion, ethnic background, and socioeconomic status. Yet we have come to expect full participation in our educational system for all students.

Some students in our schools today need specialized instruction, or special education, if they are to have that equal opportunity for learning. In this chapter we will examine special education and the rationale for its existence as well as its history and current status. In addition, this chapter explores the issues of labeling and diversity as they relate to the provision of special education services.

Mr. Meyers, a middle school math teacher, was looking forward to the start of the new school year. He had just transferred to a new school and was excited to meet the other teachers and the new students. Teaching middle school students was always a challenge, but Mr. Meyers enjoyed it. Today was the first day of preplanning and Mr. Meyers began to review his students' permanent folders. Suddenly he stopped. "This must be a mistake" he thought. "This student has learning disabilities and should be in a special education class, not mine!" He set the student's folder aside, so he could talk to the principal about it. Mr. Meyers continued through his stack of folders. "Wait a minute" he said to himself. "Here are two more. This student has been classified as having a behavior disorder, and here's one with a hearing loss. They can't expect me to teach these students in my classes along with all the other students!"

Some general education teachers might be surprised to find students with disabilities in their classes. These teachers may understand the value of education for all students, but assume students with disabilities are the responsibility of special education teachers. As you will see in this chapter, the education of students with disabilities is the responsibility of everyone affiliated with the school: classroom teachers, special educators, administrators, and parents.

Defining Special Education

Education can be defined as the process of learning and developing as a result of schooling and other experiences. Through education we promote literacy, personal autonomy, and economic self-sufficiency. For a variety of reasons (cognitive, behavioral, communicative, or physical) students with disabilities may need special education to ensure they have the opportunity to participate fully in the educational process. Students with special needs must be identified accurately and provided with specific services if they are to reach their developmental and educational potential. **Special education** is defined in federal law as specially designed instruction to meet the unique needs of a student with a disability including instruction conducted in the classroom, in the home, in hospitals and institutions, and in other settings and instruction in physical education. "Special education is not a place, but a group of services tailored to the special needs of an individual student" (Kaplan, 1996, p. 36). As noted in the definition these services can be provided in many different places or environments; the general education classroom, a special classroom, or even at home. The decisions regarding when and where special education occurs should be made according to what is appropriate for the individual student.

Students with disabilities have the same needs as their peers, as well as different needs specific to their disabilities. As we look more closely at these students throughout this book, you will discover they have some similarities, but you also will find that they are a heterogeneous group. Students who have physical disabilities may require special desks and communication devices, but may not need any modification of the general education academic curriculum. In contrast, students with learning disabilities may not require any physical modifications of the classroom, but they may need their teachers to use specific teaching strategies. Even students with the same disability are unique individuals with different learning needs. One student with a learning disability may perform best on an exam given orally, and yet another score higher on a standard written test. Students usually are targeted to receive special education because they exhibit cognitive, behavioral, communication, sensory or physical differences from their peers. These differences will be examined briefly in this chapter. Chapters 4, 5 and 9 will explore the causes of these differences and more fully describe the characteristics of students with disabilities.

Cognitive Differences

Cognitive disabilities affect the student's ability to acquire and/or express knowledge and may be demonstrated by difficulties with attention, perception, memory, and the generalization of knowledge and skills. Cognitive differences may be exhibited in students with mental retardation[1], learning disabilities, or a traumatic brain injury. These students typically develop academic skills at a slower rate than other students; taking longer to perform academic tasks and requiring more practice and repetition. If the typical student can complete a worksheet of math problems in 20 minutes, the student with a cognitive disability may need twice that long to complete it. These students may not reach a developmental level that allows for abstract thinking and will need concrete objects and experiences to understand and remember concepts and skills.

The general education classroom is just one of many places special education services can be provided.

To ensure students with cognitive differences participate as fully as possible in general education classrooms, some modifications or adaptations of curriculum, materials, and/or instructional methods will be needed. Without this special education, these students generally experience steadily decreasing performance in all subjects. Many academic skills must be learned in a specific sequence. If students do not master one step in a sequence, or a prerequisite skill, they will not be able to acquire the ones which follow. A student who cannot recognize and remember the letters of the alphabet will not be able to read. These skill deficits are compounded as new skills continue to be taught and new tasks become more difficult. Students get behind academically and never catch up.

Behavioral Differences

Although behavioral differences among people are expected, some students, those with **behavior disorders or emotional disturbances,** will act in a way that is chronically, and significantly different from their peers. We are all unique individuals who act and react according to our personalities, our cultural backgrounds, and our life experiences. As long as our behavior is acceptable according to social standards, it is considered normal. Yet everyone has exhibited unacceptable or inappropriate behavior at some time. Teachers know that their students will not act in an acceptable manner at all times. Effective teachers use a variety of strategies to prevent misbehavior and encourage appropriate behavior in the classroom. However, some students may exhibit significant behavior problems. Their inappropriate behaviors are so severe as to interfere with their own learning and the learning of other students in the classroom. For example, a student who constantly bullies other students, or steals and destroys classmates' belongings will be a serious problem for the teacher. Other students with disabilities also may demonstrate mannerisms or behaviors which are considered unacceptable. For example, students who are blind may rock back and forth; students who are mentally retarded may display affection inappropriately; students who have experienced traumatic brain injury may act impulsively. All of these students need intervention programs, or special education, to learn new and acceptable behaviors. Students with serious behavior disorders who are not provided with assistance will be unable to function in the classroom and will be a constant disruption to both their teachers and their classmates.

---

[1]The term *mental retardation* is used in the federal law, however, many other terms may be encountered when reading about this disability. Terms such as *intellectual disability, mental handicap,* or *educational handicap* may be used in some states to describe this same population of individuals.

Communication Differences

Communication disorders are any disruption in an individual's ability to understand or express thoughts, feelings, and ideas. Most individuals take the ability to communicate for granted. Although communication styles, voices, and dialects may vary, we express our thoughts and listen to others with ease on a daily basis. We use oral and written communication to exchange ideas, learn, and build relationships. They are the basis of interpersonal interactions as well as the foundation of academic instruction in the classroom.

Speech and language impairments, or communication disorders, can have a significant impact on a student's academic performance and social interaction. Individuals with speech or language impairments may have difficulty producing speech sounds accurately and fluently. They may be unable to express their thoughts in a way others understand, or they may fail to understand the communication of others. They may have trouble learning to read and write. In some students, a communication disorder may accompany another disability; for example, students with learning disabilities, mental retardation, or hearing impairments often have language processing problems. These problems affect their ability to perform required school tasks such as reading and writing. Other students may exhibit communication disorders with no additional disability; they will have the same cognitive, behavioral, and physical abilities as their peers. Students with communication disorders need special services provided by speech-language pathologists to improve and facilitate their communication abilities. This special education assists students in their academic learning and in developing positive social interactions.

Sensory and Physical Differences

Sensory disabilities occur whenever any sensory system (vision, hearing, taste, touch, etc.) is impaired. **Physical disabilities** result from diseases or disorders which affect normal physical development or functioning. The most common sensory disabilities are vision and hearing impairments. Such sensory impairments may impose certain restrictions on students. For example, a visual impairment may prohibit the use of a standard print textbook. Large print textbooks, exams written in Braille, raised maps, and other modified materials may be needed for students with impaired vision. Students with a hearing loss may need amplification devices, sign language interpreters, note takers, and other adaptations for them to succeed in the classroom. Without these forms of special education, students with sensory disabilities would not be able to reach their full academic potential.

All students have varying levels of physical abilities, strength, and stamina. Some are better coordinated than others. While certain students may tire quickly, others never seem to run out of energy. Students with physical disabilities (orthopedic impairments or health problems) may have special needs with regard to their ability to function fully in the general education classroom setting. Students who use braces or wheelchairs require modifications in the school's physical environment to allow access to classes and activities. Other modifications that students with physical disabilities might require include augmentative communication devices, lap boards, oral examinations, adapted physical education activities, and modified restrooms.

Defining Disability

When is a difference, a disorder, or a condition considered a disability? Currently, schools define disabilities according to the guidelines and regulations established by their state. These state regulations are based on the federal law which defines disabilities and

TABLE 1-1

Disability Categories Specified in PL 108-446 (IDEA 2004)

- Specific learning disabilities
- Speech or language impairments
- Mental retardation
- Emotional disturbance
- Multiple disabilities
- Hearing impairments (including deafness)
- Orthopedic impairments
- Other health impairments
- Visual impairments (including blindness)
- Autism
- Deaf-blindness
- Traumatic brain injury

provides states with funding for students who qualify for special education services. As shown in **Table 1-1,** the federal law, Public Law 108-446, the Individuals with Disabilities Education Improvement Act of 2004 (IDEA 2004), defines students with disabilities as those with specific learning disabilities, speech or language impairments, mental retardation, emotional disturbance (behavior disorders), multiple disabilities, hearing impairments (including deafness), orthopedic impairments, other health impairments, visual impairments (including blindness), autism, deaf-blindness, or traumatic brain injury who need special education or related services as a result of the disability.

Other students who do not meet the eligibility criteria specified in IDEA still may qualify for special education services under Section 504 of the Vocational Rehabilitation Act of 1973. For example, attention deficit/hyperactivity disorder (ADHD) is not listed as a specific category of disability under IDEA. This could mean that these students would not be eligible for special education services and the federal government would not provide funds to serve them. However, the impact of ADHD on the ability of students to learn is widely recognized and these students are eligible for services under Section 504. The federal laws which mandate special education services will be discussed in Chapter 2. Students who are gifted and talented also may receive special services in schools but they are not protected by the same laws which mandate services to students with disabilities.

Prevalence

Currently in the United States, over 5.8 million children and youth ages 6 through 21 years receive special education services (U.S. Department of Education, 2003). This represents 12.1 percent of the public school population or more than 1 out of every 10 students. Comprehensive special education services were mandated by federal law beginning in 1975. Since that time, the number of students served by special education has increased each year as demonstrated in **Table 1-2** and **Table 1-3.**

The distribution of students receiving special education services by disability area is shown in **Table 1-3.** From the 1992–93 school year to the 2001–02 year three categories of disability have shown a dramatic increase in the numbers of students: other health impairments, autism, and traumatic brain injury. The increase in students served under

TABLE 1-2

Students Served By Special Education, School Years 1995–1996 Through 2001–02, Ages 6 Through 21.

School Year	Total Served
1995–1996	5,078,841
1996–1997	5,230,663
1997–1998	5,396,889
1998–1999	5,539,688
1999–2000	5,677,884
2000–2001	5,774,220
2001–2002	5,867,078

From U.S. Department of Education (2003). *Twenty-fifth annual report to Congress on the implementation of The Individuals with Disabilities Education Act.* Washington, DC: Author.

TABLE 1-3

Changes in Number of Students Ages 6 through 21 by Disability Category, School Years 1992–93 and 2001–02

Disability	1992–93	2001–2002
• Specific learning disabilities	2,366,233	2,887,115
• Speech-language impairments	998,023	1,093,581
• Mental retardation	532,348	605,267
• Emotional disturbance	401,644	477,627
• Multiple disabilities	103,275	128,552
• Hearing impairments	60,606	71,222
• Orthopedic impairments	52,576	73,821
• Other health impairments	66,055	338,658
• Visual impairments	23,534	25,845
• Autism	15,580	97,904
• Deaf-blindness	1,392	1,615
• Traumatic brain injury	3,960	20,743
• Developmental delay	N/A	45,128
• All disabilities	4,361,751	5,867,078

From U.S. Department of Education (2003). *Twenty-fifth annual report to Congress on the implementation of The Individuals with Disabilities Education Act.* Washington, DC: Author.

other health impaired is attributed to the increasing number of students with attention deficit/hyperactivity disorder receiving special education services under this category. The increases in the numbers of students with autism and traumatic brain injury may be attributed to these categories being added to IDEA in 1991 and better diagnoses of these conditions.

As can be seen, the highest percentage of students receiving special services in schools today (49%) have learning disabilities. Other categories of disabilities which are considered high prevalence, or **high incidence,** due to the large numbers of students requiring

FIGURE 1-1

Percentage of Students Served by Special Education, by Age Group, School Year 2001–02

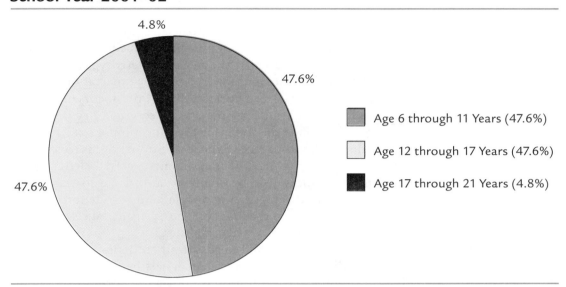

4.8%

47.6%

47.6%

■ Age 6 through 11 Years (47.6%)

□ Age 12 through 17 Years (47.6%)

■ Age 17 through 21 Years (4.8%)

From U.S. Department of Education (2003). *Twenty-fifth annual report to Congress on the implementation of The Individuals with Disabilities Education Act.* Washington, DC: Author.

services are speech or language impairment (18.6%), mental retardation (10.3%), and emotional disturbance (behavior disorder) (8.1%). Over 86% of students ages 6 through 21 receiving services under IDEA in 2001–02 were classified under one of these four high incidence categories. The remaining categories often are described as **low incidence** due to the limited number of students exhibiting those types of disabilities. Based on the prevalence figures, general education teachers certainly will find students with learning disabilities, speech or language impairments, mental retardation, and behavior disorders in their classrooms. Due to their lower incidence, students with physical or sensory disabilities, autism, traumatic brain injury, or other health impairments will be encountered less frequently. In addition, some of these students with low incidence disabilities (e.g., physical disabilities, health impairments) will function quite well in the general education classroom and will perform in academic areas at a level equal to their peers without disabilities.

The number of students who receive special education services is not equally distributed across the ages of 6 through 21 years. As seen in **Figure 1-1,** equal percentages of students ages 6 through 11 years and 12 through 17 years receive services, while a significantly smaller percentage of students ages 18 through 21 years receive them. There are also gender differences in the number of students receiving special education services; approximately 66 percent of these students are male and 34 percent are female.

The Controversy of Labeling

When it is determined that a student needs and is eligible for special education services, a label is placed on that individual: mental retardation, physical handicap, behavior disorder, etc. Unfortunately, most of the labels used to identify and categorize students for special education services have negative connotations. Labels can change the way a student is viewed by teachers, peers, and even family. Suddenly the biases, myths, and misperceptions associated with certain labels become attached to the student. We look for and expect certain behaviors (or misbehaviors) with certain labels. We become focused on the disability and not the ability of the individual. The actions and reactions of teachers, peers, and parents to these students can have a significant impact on students' attitudes towards school, their academic goals and performance, as well as their behavior and self-concept.

Educators have argued for many years whether we must label students in order to provide them with appropriate educational services. Opponents of labeling point to such problems as the potential mislabeling of students, the negative stereotypes associated with labels, the effects of labels on self-esteem, and lowered teacher expectations, as reasons not to assign labels (Ysseldyke, Algozzine, & Thurlow, 1992). Proponents of labeling counter that without labels students would not get the special services they need. The federal government provides special funds to the states for the education of students with disabilities. Labeling students allows schools to receive those additional funds to offer the special programs and services the students need. If no students were labeled, schools would not receive the special funding and would be unable to afford the special education programs and services. In addition, categorizing and labeling students provides opportunities for research in both medicine and education. Lastly, using labels can assist professionals in communicating about students with disabilities.

As teachers recognize the unique educational needs of all students in their classrooms, not just those with disabilities, the importance of labels becomes minimized. However, since an individualized approach to education is not yet the norm in all schools and classrooms, it is important to examine the impact of disabilities and labeling on teachers and students. How does a teacher react to students who have been labeled "special" or "different"? What do peers think of their classmates who are different?

Teacher Expectations

Teachers' expectations of their students can be influenced by a variety of factors. A student's gender, race, physical appearance, or performance in other classes, even comments from parents or fellow teachers can impact teachers' expectations of academic performance and behavior. Add to these factors, the effect of a label of exceptional ability or disability. If teachers are told a student is gifted, they assume outstanding ability and expect performance at a level above others in the class. If teachers are told a student is mentally retarded, they assume limited ability and expect performance below others in the class. These teacher attitudes and expectations can have a profound impact on teacher-student interaction (Doris & Brown, 1980; Foster, Ysseldyke, & Reese, 1975; MacMillan, Meyers, & Yoshida, 1978; Van Acker, Grant, & Henry, 1996) which in turn influences the students' own attitudes, expectations, and behaviors. This may result in positive outcomes when teachers' expectations are high for students. However, it is not difficult to envision the disastrous outcomes when teachers' expectations are low.

Peer Expectations

The attitudes of students toward their peers with disabilities have been examined by many researchers (Asher & Taylor, 1981; Drabman & Patterson, 1981; Goodman, Gottlieb, & Harrison, 1977; Horne, 1985; Prillaman, 1981). Such studies have reported conflicting results with some suggesting students view their peers with disabilities in a positive way, and others showing the students view these peers negatively. Many students enter school with misperceptions and stereotypic views of individuals who are different from the norm (Pang, 1991). This may be due to limited interaction with individuals who are different from them in any way (language, race, culture, disability, etc.) as well as the result of the influence of negative portrayals of persons with disabilities often seen in the media. It can be difficult for students without disabilities to get beyond labels and their negative connotations. The acceptance or rejection of students with disabilities may have more to do with their labels than with the students as individuals.

True of any type of diversity

The attitudes and behaviors of school personnel exert a powerful influence on the attitudes of students towards their peers (Fiedler & Simpson, 1987; Garrett & Crump, 1980). Students imitate the attitudes and behaviors they observe on a daily basis. Successful integration and acceptance of students with disabilities into the mainstream of general education requires the support of the entire educational system. Schools and classrooms must serve as models for the inclusion and acceptance of all individuals regardless of differences due to ability or disability.

The Delivery of Special Education Services

Examining the history of society's attitudes towards individuals with disabilities and the progression of educational options available to them provides a perspective for viewing today's approaches to identification and intervention. As our society has evolved, so has our social consciousness and our treatment of those who are perceived as different from the mainstream of society. Special students, who today receive the full benefit of our educational system, would have been willfully ignored or abused in earlier times. Federal laws not only prevent discrimination in education, housing, and employment based on disabilities, but also mandate free, appropriate education for all students, no matter how severe their disabilities or how limited their abilities.

History of Special Education

Prior to the late 1700s, disabilities and differences were viewed with fear and superstition. Physical disabilities and mental incompetence were thought to be curses from the gods. Emotional problems and seizures were believed to be the result of possession by demons or evil spirits. Infants with mental retardation or physical disabilities were abandoned or put to death, while adults with disabilities were ignored, abused, or exploited. Over time, the ethics of some religions espoused that society should care for its less fortunate members. Large institutions or asylums were built to house individuals who were considered different or deviant and to protect them from what many people perceived as a cruel world in which individuals with disabilities would not fit or survive. The asylums generally provided overcrowded, unsanitary living conditions and the residents received little food, clothing, or care. These asylums did keep persons whom society viewed as undesirable or physically unattractive out of the community at large (Kanner, 1964; Carlson, 1990).

Rare exceptions to this treatment are found in the actions of several religious and professional men during the 1700s. In 1760, the Abbe de l'Epee founded a school for the Deaf in Paris. A few years later in 1789, Valentin Huay opened the National Institution of Young Blind People. Phillippe Pinel (1745–1826) opposed the use of chains to restrain patients who were mentally ill and proposed occupational training for them. These individuals and some of their contemporaries became outspoken supporters for the humane treatment and education of children with disabilities (Pritchard, 1963; Winzer, 1986).

In the United States, the history of special education as described by Cruickshank (1958) begins in the nineteenth century. Physicians, ministers, educators, and social activists such as Samuel Gridley Howe, founder of the Perkins School for the Blind, Dorothea Dix, a retired teacher and advocate for persons with mental illness, and Thomas Hopkins Gallaudet, founder of the American School of the Deaf, were instrumental in establishing the first schools for children who were blind, mentally retarded, or deaf. These first schools in America were modeled after the European custom of educating students with disabilities in boarding or residential schools. The building of such schools reflected society's recognition that these individuals needed different or special treatment. However, the provision of the special services was relegated to isolated facilities, segregated from the mainstream of education and the community. Special services or classrooms in local public schools were virtually nonexistent at this time. From 1850 to 1920, there was a rapid increase in the number of special residential schools, with every state establishing some type of residential program for certain children with disabilities.

Public school programs for students with special needs began early in the 20th century and grew gradually until the middle of the century. As the country's population increased and people congregated in large cities, groups of children with disabilities were found in local communities. Parents resisted sending their children to residential schools which often were located a great distance from their community. Cities began to establish day school programs for these special children, particularly those with the most common disorder, mild or moderate mental retardation. These special education schools for the "educable mentally retarded" often were the sole source of special services in the local community. Later, special education classes were established in the local schools. It was not uncommon to find students who had disabilities other than mental retardation (e.g., learning disabilities, emotional disorders, hearing impairment, etc.) placed in these classes, although the services provided were neither appropriate nor adequate.

Special programs for some students with physical disabilities and various health problems (asthma, heart disease, etc.) became popular during this same period of time (Hardman, Drew, Egan, & Wolf, 1993). Public schools built adapted facilities on their campuses for these students where special education could be provided, but this resulted in the segregation of students from the rest of the school population.

Since students who were deaf or blind were fewer in number than students with other disabilities, public school programs were not commonly available for these children until later in the century. The residential and day school programs operated by states or private schooling typically were the only educational options for these students. Parents of children with severe physical and/or mental disabilities were encouraged to place them in residential care facilities, state institutions, or to care for them at home, since the prevailing attitude was that these children could not be educated.

Changing Attitudes

During the 1940s and 1950s, society's attitude toward disabilities was undergoing a dramatic change. World War I and World War II left thousands of individuals injured and disabled. Prior to their injuries, these people were respected and accepted members of their families and communities. When they returned from the War, their families and communities generally welcomed them back with continued respect and acceptance. Disabilities were being viewed in a more favorable light than ever before. This attitude of acceptance began to extend to children and others whose disabilities were not related to the War. Head traumas incurred during military service led to research and a better understanding of the brain and its relationship to learning. As medical explanations were discovered for Epilepsy, Cerebral Palsy, and other conditions, society's attitudes began to change and some of the myths and misperceptions about individuals with these disorders were dispelled (Cruickshank, 1958).

A powerful force in the evolution of educational services for students with disabilities has been parental concern and its resultant action. During the 1900s, parents began to form local, state, and eventually national and international organizations (Cruickshank, 1958; McCleary, Hardman, & Thomas, 1990). Initially these groups served as a forum for parents to discuss common problems and find sources for services. As they grew, these organizations became effective advocates for individuals with disabilities. They raised money for treatment centers and lobbied federal and state agencies to provide funding for research, professional training, and treatment. Parent and professional groups such as the Association for Retarded Citizens of the United States (ARC) and the Learning Disabilities Association of America (LDA) have had significant influence on the actions of local school boards, state legislatures, and even Congress in providing educational services to individuals with disabilities.

Moving into the Mainstream

Programs developed during the 1960s generally followed the model of segregating students with disabilities in separate, or self-contained, classrooms. There was little or no interaction between the students and teachers in these classrooms and the students and teachers in general education classrooms. Some schools during this period still did not offer any special education services. Parents were told to send their children to private schools, at their own personal expense, or to state operated schools or institutions.

Countering this common practice of segregated services, some parents and professional organizations were espousing the philosophy of normalization; one of the steps leading to current practices in special education. **Normalization** (Nirje, 1969) is the belief that individuals with disabilities should be integrated into the mainstream of society. They should live, learn, and work in environments as similar to the norm as possible having full access to the programs and services available to the community at large. In the schools, this would mean students with disabilities should have appropriate classrooms (not cramped quarters in the basement), access to the cafeteria, gym, etc. As will be discussed in Chapter 2, legislation and litigation were used to enhance the rights of individuals with disabilities and to achieve access to programs and services.

With the passage of Public Law 94-142, the Education for All Handicapped Children Act, in 1975, states were required to provide a free, appropriate, public education to all students with disabilities. The law further mandated that the education of these students take place in the **least restrictive environment** (LRE). The principle of least restrictive environment requires that students with disabilities be educated with their peers who do not have disabilities to the maximum extent appropriate, or in other words, in the mainstream of the general education setting. This led to wide spread use of the **resource room** as the model for educating students with disabilities. In this model, students received their special education in a separate class for the majority of the school day and were **mainstreamed** or participated in the same learning and social activities as their peers for the remainder of the day. This model is still used today. Parents and teachers, however, have examined the benefits and limitations of the resource room model and the current trend is for the full inclusion of students with disabilities in the general education classroom.

The Delivery of Special Education Services in Today's Schools

Classroom teachers play an important role in the identification of students with disabilities. A student does not receive special education services, however, simply because the classroom teacher thinks the student has a disability. Special education services only can be provided following a comprehensive assessment by a team of professionals who have determined the student is eligible for special education. Throughout the school year, classroom teachers will encounter students who experience difficulty in learning, behaving, or communicating. Not all of these students have disabilities. A student may have difficulty learning a new math concept, not due to a learning disability, but because the earlier, prerequisite skills were not taught. A student may refuse to speak in class, not due to a communication disorder, but out of fear of being teased by peers. A student may be talking back to the teacher and picking fights with classmates, not due to a behavior disorder, but as the result of a temporary conflict at home.

When a teacher encounters a student who is having difficulty in the classroom, the teacher naturally makes whatever modifications seem appropriate given the individual student's needs. Such strategies as meeting with the student to discuss the problem, providing additional instruction and practice, or speaking with the parents might help to resolve the problem. If the problem persists, and the teacher decides additional help is needed, the prereferral team is the next source for assistance.

The **prereferral team** (or the student support team or student study team) is a team of teachers and sometimes other school professionals (e.g., curriculum specialist, counselor, special education teacher, etc.) who can meet with the classroom teacher to devise additional strategies and modifications which might help the student succeed in the general education classroom. In some cases, even after implementing the prereferral team's recommendations, the problem still persists. At this point, the prereferral team will recommend a comprehensive assessment to determine if the student is eligible for special education services. The assessment is done by a multidisciplinary team composed of the parent and such specialists as a school psychologist, a special education teacher, and a speech-language pathologist. Although the classroom teacher will provide the multidisciplinary team with information about the student's academic performance and classroom behavior, the teacher is not responsible for the assessment. Upon completion of the assessment, the multidisciplinary team will determine if the student is eligible for special education services. The team also will decide what specific services are needed as well as how and where they will be delivered. The prereferral and assessment process is discussed in detail in Chapter 3.

Placement Options

As defined earlier, special education is instruction designed to meet the unique learning needs of students with disabilities. The form that the special education takes, modifications in curriculum or materials, specific instructional methods, or specialized equipment, will vary for each student. The environment in which the special education occurs also will vary. Some students' special needs can be met while the student remains in the general education classroom on a full-time basis. For other students, their needs may be best met by full-time placement in a special education classroom. Still others may benefit from a combination of general education classroom instruction and special education services. For example, some students will remain in the classroom for their academic instruction and receive additional tutoring or instruction in a resource room. The specific special education services and the environment in which they are provided will vary based on the nature of the disability and what is appropriate for the individual student. No two students are the same in abilities and in needs, even though they may share the same disability label. No label can fully describe a student's educational, social, psychological, or physical abilities and disabilities.

Inherent in the requirement of the least restrictive environment is the provision of a variety of educational placement options. States and school districts must offer a variety of educational settings for students with disabilities including residential programs, separate schools, separate or self-contained classrooms, and resource rooms, as well as the

FIGURE 1-2

Definitions of Educational Placement Settings

General Classroom	Students receive services in programs designed primarily for students without disabilities, provided the students with disabilities are in a separate room for less than 21% of the school day.
Resource Room	Students receive services in programs designed primarily for students without disabilities, provided the students with disabilities are in a separate room for 21 to 60% of the school day.
Separate Class	Students receive services in a separate program 61 to 100% of the school day.
Separate School	Students receive services in publicly or privately operated programs designed primarily for students with disabilities, that are not housed in a facility with programs for students without disabilities. Students receive special education and related services in the separate day school for greater than 50% of the school day.
Residential Program	Students are served in publicly or privately operated programs in which they receive care for 24 hours a day. This includes placement in public nursing home care facilities or public or private residential schools.
Homebound/Hospital Program	Students are served in either a home or hospital setting.

(U.S. Department of Education, 1997)

general education classroom. Homebound/hospital programs are additional settings which may be a required placement for some students with disabilities who cannot be in other school settings due to the nature of their disability. States and school districts will provide educational services to students in these settings. Federal law (IDEA) defines all of the possible educational settings as shown in **Figure 1-2.** The appropriate placement for any one student is determined by the multidisciplinary team and is based on the student's needs. The first choice of placement should always be the least restrictive setting in which the student's educational needs can be met with the option of moving to a more restrictive setting if needed. **Figure 1-3** shows the typical placement options on a scale from least restrictive to most restrictive.

Most students with disabilities are receiving academic instruction in the general education classroom for a significant portion of the school day and 96% of those students are served in regular school buildings (U.S. Department of Education, 2003). As shown in **Figure 1-3,** during the 2000–01 school year, almost half of students with disabilities are educated in the general education classroom for most of the school day.

When students with disabilities are placed in the general education classroom, special education teachers consult with the classroom teacher to provide support and assistance to ensure appropriate educational strategies and interventions are implemented. Over 76% of students with disabilities remained in the classroom for 40% or more of the school day during 2000–01. Some of these students left the classroom for periods of time to receive special academic instruction in a resource room or a separate class.

Some students with disabilities may leave the general education classroom during the school day to receive ancillary or support services which are services other than academic

FIGURE 1-3

Educational Placement Options from Least Restrictive to Most Restrictive

Least Restrictive

Most Restrictive

- General Education Classroom
- Resource Room
- Separate Class
- Separate School
- Residential Program

FIGURE 1-4

Educational Placements of Students with Disabilities Ages 6 through 21, School Year 2000–01

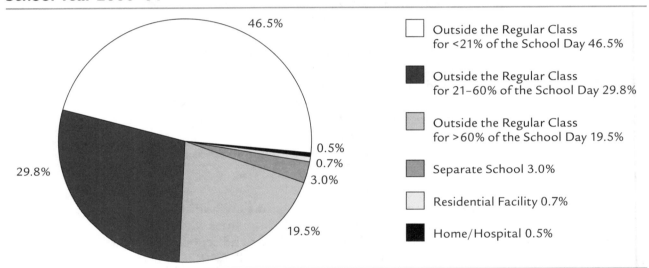

46.5%

29.8%

19.5%

0.5%
0.7%
3.0%

☐ Outside the Regular Class
   for <21% of the School Day 46.5%

■ Outside the Regular Class
   for 21–60% of the School Day 29.8%

▨ Outside the Regular Class
   for >60% of the School Day 19.5%

▦ Separate School 3.0%

☐ Residential Facility 0.7%

■ Home/Hospital 0.5%

From U.S. Department of Education (2003). *Twenty-fifth annual report to Congress on the implementation of The Individuals with Disabilities Education Act.* Washington, DC: Author.

instruction. Examples of support services are physical therapy for students with physical disabilities, mobility training for students with visual impairment, or speech-language therapy for students with communication disorders.

Some students whose instructional needs are significantly different from their peers may spend the majority of the school day in special classes or in some cases, in special schools. **Figure 1-4** shows that 20% of students with disabilities were served in separate classes in 2000–01, and only approximately 3% were in separate schools. Although some students are being educated in separate classes, they also will enter the mainstream of their schools for instructional and social activities whenever possible. Such inclusion might include instruction in selected academic subjects, instruction in nonacademic subjects such as art, music, or physical education, or participation in school sports, clubs, and extracurricular activities. The extent of participation will differ from student to student according to their individual needs and abilities.

The educational placements for students with disabilities vary according to the disability category (see **Table 1-4**). Students with speech or language impairments typically spend the least amount of time outside the general education classroom, followed

TABLE 1-4

Percentage of Students Ages 6 through 21 by Disability in Educational Placements

| | Served outside the general education class | | | |
Disability	<21% of school day	21–60% of school day	>60% of school day	Separate Environment
Specific learning disabilities	44.3%	40.3%	14.4%	1.0%
Speech-language impairments	85.6	8.4	5.1	0.9
Mental retardation	13.2	29.1	51.7	6.1
Emotional disturbance	26.8	23.4	31.8	18.1
Multiple disabilities	12.1	16.0	45.5	26.4
Hearing impairments	42.3	20.0	22.5	15.3
Orthopedic impairments	46.4	23.4	24.3	6.0
Other health impairments	45.1	33.9	16.7	4.4
Visual impairments	50.5	20.1	16.0	13.4
Autism	24.3	15.3	46.4	14.0
Deaf-blindness	18.1	9.9	34.2	37.8
Traumatic brain injury	32.3	27.9	29.4	10.4
Developmental delay	46.4	29.9	22.3	1.3

From U.S. Department of Education (2003). *Twenty-fifth annual report to Congress on the implementation of The Individuals with Disabilities Education Act.* Washington, DC: Author.

by students with specific learning disabilities. Given these are high-incidence disabilities and these students will spend the majority of their school day in the general education classroom, teachers will need to be particularly knowledgeable about these disability categories and the appropriate educational strategies for these students. Students with multiple disabilities, deaf-blindness, and mental retardation will spend the least amount of time in the general education classroom and are more likely to be educated in separate facilities (separate schools, residential facilities, or homebound or hospital environments) than students with other types of disabilities.

Differences in educational placement also are seen according to differences in the student's age. As shown in **Figure 1-5,** more students between the ages of 6 and 11 years are placed in the general education classroom for greater periods of time than are older students. The percentage of time spent in general education classrooms decreased for older students while the percentages of separate school placements increased.

The educational placement of students with disabilities has changed over the past 10 years with more students being served in less restrictive environments (U.S. Department of Education, 2003). Students with disabilities are spending more time in general education classrooms and less time in all of the other placement settings today when compared to 10 years ago. This reinforces the importance of general education classroom teachers having the knowledge and skills needed to teach students with disabilities.

Inclusive Classrooms

Recently, the term **inclusion** has been used to describe the process of educating students with disabilities in the mainstream of the general education setting. Advocates for what is labeled **full inclusion** believe that the general education classroom is the appropriate

FIGURE 1-5

Percentage of Students with Disabilities, by Age Group, by Educational Placement, School Year 2000–01

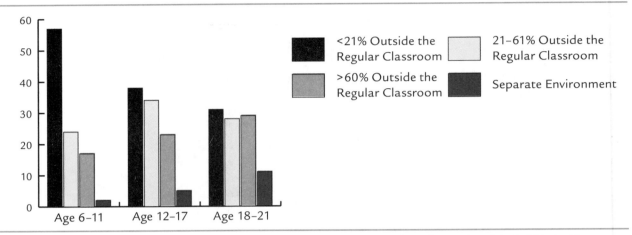

From U.S. Department of Education (2003). *Twenty-fifth annual report to Congress on the implementation of The Individuals with Disabilities Education Act.* Washington, DC: Author.

educational placement for all students with disabilities; not just those with mild disabilities, but also those with severe disabilities. They believe students should not leave the classroom to receive special services. Instead, any special service needed should be provided in the general education classroom through the collaboration and cooperation of the classroom teacher and special education professionals. Proponents of inclusion argue that pulling students from the classroom to receive special services fragments their education and inhibits communication and cooperation between the classroom teacher and the special educator.

The full inclusion movement seeks the elimination of a dual system of education, general education versus special education, and advocates that "the general education system assume unequivocal, primary responsibility for all students in our public schools" (Davis, 1989, p. 440). Proponents of full inclusion (Reynolds, Wang, & Walberg, 1987; Stainback & Stainback, 1992; Thousand & Villa, 1990) cite the cost of maintaining a dual educational system, the negative result of labeling some students as disabled or "deviant", and the benefits of individualized instruction for all students (disabled or not) as reasons to reform the current system of service delivery. They also argue that the educational strategies and techniques used by general and special education teachers are similar and can be implemented in the general education classroom.

This proposed restructuring of the current educational system and insistence on full inclusion are controversial issues among general and special educators and parents. Not all special education professionals and parents believe full inclusion, or a full-time placement in the general education classroom, will meet the educational needs of all students with disabilities (Kauffman, Gerber, & Semmel, 1988; Kavale & Mostert, 2003; Wiederholt, 1989). These educators generally support full inclusion as a placement option when it is appropriate for a student, but they are skeptical that it is the best model of service delivery for all students. Researchers have only begun to examine the academic progress of students in full inclusion classrooms. Klinger, Vaughn, Hughes, Schumm,

TABLE 1-5

Arguments For and Against Full Inclusion

Proponents of Full Inclusion Argue:	Opponents of Full Inclusion Argue:
• Labeling is de-emphasized. • Stigma of leaving class for special instruction is decreased. • Students remain with their peers full-time. • Social skills are improved. • Self-esteem is increased. • General education students benefit from interaction. • Interaction and cooperation among all school personnel is enhanced. • The realities of our society are faced.	• Classroom teachers, parents, and students are not prepared. • Class sizes are too large to allow teachers to meet all students' needs. • Quality of education to all students will decrease. • School personnel do not have the necessary collaborative skills. • Some students need instructional strategies and technology not available in the classroom.

and Elbaum (1998) studied the academic achievement of students with and without learning disabilities in six general education classrooms at one elementary school. They found that many of the students with learning disabilities as well as the high-achieving students made considerable gains during the academic year. However some students with learning disabilities and a number of low- and average-achieving students without disabilities made no significant improvement during the year, in spite of the substantial in-class support provided by special education teachers.

Classroom teachers are concerned about their ability to meet the diverse needs of the students currently in their classrooms (Fuchs & Fuchs, 1994). Will they be able to meet the needs of all the students currently receiving special education services as well? Many teachers, in both general and special education, fear that students with disabilities will be placed in general education classrooms on a full-time basis without adequate support, ensuring frustration and failure for both students and teachers. They note that the educational strategies and techniques needed to teach certain students cannot be implemented in the general education classroom, and that resource rooms or self-contained classrooms staffed by special education teachers are needed. Some parents and professionals are concerned that full inclusion will hurt the students it is proposed to help by eliminating placement options. There are benefits and drawbacks to inclusion as can be seen in **Table 1-5.** Both proponents and opponents of inclusion recognize there are problems with the current delivery of special education services and their common goal is to improve those services.

The current status of inclusion might be summarized best by the **Council for Exceptional Children (CEC),** the major professional organization in special education, in their policy statement on service delivery:

> "CEC believes that a continuum of services must be available for all children, youth, and young adults. CEC also believes that the concept of inclusion is a meaningful goal to be pursued in our schools and communities. In addition, CEC believes children, youth, and young adults with disabilities should be served whenever possible in general education classrooms in inclusive neighborhood schools and community settings. Such settings should be strengthened and supported by an infusion of specially trained personnel and other supportive practices according to the individual needs of the child." (Council for Exceptional Children, 1994, pp. 5–6).

Special Education Across the Lifespan

Although the discussion of special education services in this chapter has focused on students in elementary, middle, and secondary schools, it is important to note that many disabilities will affect individuals throughout their lifetime, not only during their school years. For example, mental retardation, deafness, or severe physical disabilities can have a significant impact on children's cognitive, physical, communicative, or social/emotional development long before they enter school. These disabilities and others also may affect an individual's ability to obtain employment or live independently in adulthood.

Educators and providers of social services have recognized the importance of providing services as early as a disability can be identified, in infancy if possible, and extending services beyond the typical age for completion of secondary school, 18 years. The federal laws which mandate special education services, target infants and toddlers with disabilities and their families for early intervention services. Providing both direct services to the young child and support services to the family can minimize the effect the disability will have on the child's early development and later learning. These laws also target adolescents and young adults through age 21 for **transition services.** Transition services are designed to assist students with disabilities in making the transition from living at home and attending school to independent living, employment, and community involvement. The laws which require early identification and mandate the provision of transition services will be discussed in Chapter 2.

The Issue of Diversity

Diversity is an issue that has been prominent in special education from its very beginning and remains in the forefront today. As a group, individuals with disabilities were considered different (or diverse) and were segregated from the mainstream of education in the past. They were placed in institutions, special schools, and self-contained classes. These segregated options still may be appropriate educational placements for some individuals, if these options are selected on an individual basis. However, when an entire group is segregated as a means of avoidance due to prejudice, then it is discrimination against a diverse group. The issue of diversity in relation to race, ethnicity, and culture also has played a role in special education. The number of minority students in special education is disproportionate to the general school population statistics (Artiles & Trent, 1994; Chinn & Hughes, 1987; U.S. Department of Education, 2001). If students belong to a minority group, they may be at risk for inappropriate placement in special education.

A major focus of this book is diversity: the diversity students with disabilities bring to the learning environment. These students may exhibit differences from (and similarities to) their peers in the classroom in their cognitive and learning abilities, behavior, communication styles, or physical and sensory capabilities. However, teachers must realize and accept the fact that all students, not just those with disabilities, bring their own unique competencies, attitudes, and learning styles to the classroom. For students with disabilities, the issue of diversity can become a complex one. In addition to the differences associated with their disabilities, these students may exhibit differences due to their ethnic, racial, or cultural backgrounds.

Cultural Diversity

Over time, educators have come to understand that students need a multicultural education to succeed in a nation and a world rich in cultural diversity. Today's classrooms reflect the variation in gender, race, religion, language, socioeconomic status, family

much later than previously predicted

structure, motivation, talents, and abilities found in the community at large. Based on U.S. Census data, it is predicted that by the year 2020, the U.S. population will be more than 35% racial and ethnic minorities and by 2050 what is now the majority will be the minority (U.S. Bureau of the Census, 1999). To be effective in the classroom, teachers must be prepared to consider the cultural values, lifestyles, and language of each student in their classes.

Culture can be defined as "the cumulative deposit of knowledge, experience, meanings, beliefs, values, attitudes, religions, concepts of self, the universe, and self-universe rela-

Multicultural education is based on the premise that all students benefit from exposure to different people, beliefs, and ideas.

tionships, hierarchies of status, role expectations, spatial relations, and time concepts acquired by a large group of people in the course of generations" (Porter & Samovar, 1976, p. 7). Culture pervades every aspect of our lives. It influences the way we view life, the way we think, and the way we behave. Culture has an impact on our dress and personal appearance, food preferences, work habits and play behaviors, attitudes towards health and education, learning styles, and religious beliefs. The values and beliefs we acquire from our cultural group guide us in social interactions, which affect our family and interpersonal relationships and the expectations we have of others (Saville-Troike, 1982).

Cultural pluralism is the belief that cultural differences and the contributions of various groups can strengthen and enrich society. **Multicultural education** is based on the premise that all students benefit from exposure to different people, beliefs, and ideas. It promotes the strength and value of cultural diversity as well as human rights and respect for those who are different from oneself.

Cultural differences may be mistaken for abnormality when one's own cultural group is viewed as setting the standard for all others. The dominant cultural group in a community or a nation generally considers itself the standard and views other groups as deviations. Cultural groups may vary markedly in their use of eye contact, physical proximity and contact, nonverbal communication, or verbal interaction with persons in positions of authority. As a teacher, I am speaking to a student who avoids eye contact with me. Do I assume the student is ignoring me, or doesn't care what I'm saying, or is showing disrespect? In some cultures, direct eye contact with adults in positions of authority is considered to be disrespectful. Teachers and students must realize that what they consider inappropriate or unacceptable behavior based on their own cultural beliefs and actions may be normal and standard in another cultural group.

Some cultures highly value group success and therefore encourage cooperative behavior over competitive behavior. Others value and foster individual success and achievement. One culture might encourage spontaneity and creativity in children, and yet another teach the importance of restraint in all behaviors. This disparity in values can result in differences in behavior which are viewed and judged as appropriate or inappropriate based on the viewer's cultural perspective. One teacher might perceive a student's shouting out of answers and ideas as disruptive, while another teacher sees it as a reflection of the student's interest and active participation in the learning process.

Individuals from different cultures often view the world from vastly different perspectives (Siccone, 1995).

Appreciation of one's own cultural heritage and acceptance of others is the key to success in multicultural classrooms and communities. Appreciation and acceptance of differences do not develop spontaneously. Most people fear and avoid what is different and unknown to them. Teachers must provide students with experiences that foster an acceptance and appreciation of diversity. The school curriculum and instructional materials must reflect the contributions of diverse individuals and groups to our world. With knowledge and understanding, differences due to culture or disability become less frightening and easier to accept.

Diversity and Disability

Educators must ensure that cultural differences are not mistaken for educational disabilities. Personal bias or prejudice might result in teachers judging students as disabled based on stereotypic assumptions, assuming that some individuals will learn or behave in certain ways. The percentage of students in special education from minority groups is disproportionately high given their percentage in the school-age population at large (Artiles & Trent, 1994). **Table 1-6** shows the percentage of students receiving special education services by disability and race/ethnicity for the 2001–02 school year. The distributions are very similar to those of previous years, however the racial/ethnic distribution differs from that of the school-age population (ages 6 through 21) at large (U.S. Department of Education, 2003). Asian/Pacific Islander students made up 3.8% of the school-age population, yet they constituted only 1.9% of the students receiving special education services. Black students with disabilities (20.5%) exceeded their representation among the general school population (15.1%) with the largest discrepancies in the categories of mental retardation (34%) and developmental delay (22.7%). The Hispanic student population at-large was 16.6%, while 14.6% were receiving special education services. The greatest discrepancy for white students was found in the category of other health impairments where they represent 74.1% of students in this category, but are 63.5% of the general school-age population. In gifted and talented programs, students from minority cultures, particularly African-American, Hispanic, and Native American, are underrepresented (Gollnick & Chinn, 1990).

Students' cultural values or customs, their linguistic ability, or their experiential background may set them apart from their peers. This diversity presents a unique challenge for educators in the areas of assessment, instruction, and socialization. If differences in culture or language are not considered when selecting assessment tools, instructional strategies, and social activities, the result may be academic failure, social isolation, and inappropriate referral to special education for students who are culturally different.

As cultural and linguistic diversity increases in the population at large, so too it increases in the population of individuals with disabilities. It is difficult for

President Bush's Reading First plan links federal funding to scientifically proven methods of reading instruction.

TABLE 1-6

Percentage of Students Served by Disability and Race-Ethnicity 2001–02 School Year, Ages 6 Through 21

Disability	American Indian/ Alaska Native	Asian/ Pacific Islander	Black (non-Hispanic)	Hispanic	White (non-Hispanic)
Specific learning disability	1.5	1.6	18.7	18.5	59.8
Speech/language impairment	1.2	2.6	15.9	14.6	65.7
Mental retardation	1.1	1.7	34.0	12.1	51.1
Emotional disturbance	1.2	1.2	28.2	9.5	59.9
Multiple disabilities	1.3	2.3	19.8	13.9	62.7
Hearing impairment	1.2	4.7	16.4	20.1	57.6
Orthopedic impairment	0.9	2.8	14.5	15.8	66.1
Other health impairments	1.1	1.4	14.9	8.5	74.1
Visual impairment	1.2	3.7	17.3	16.6	61.2
Autism	0.6	4.8	17.2	9.9	67.5
Deaf-blindness	1.9	3.6	13.5	18.0	63.0
Traumatic brain injury	1.2	2.3	18.4	11.1	67.0
Developmental delay	2.0	2.6	22.7	8.0	64.8
All disabilities	1.3	1.9	20.5	14.6	61.7
General population (ages 6–21)	1.0	3.8	15.1	16.6	63.5

From U.S. Department of Education (2003). *Twenty-fifth annual report to Congress on the implementation of The Individuals with Disabilities Act.* Washington, DC: Author.

any family to accept and adjust to having a special child. The family's attitude toward disabilities and their resultant behavior can be a major factor in the identification of the disorder and the implementation of an intervention program. Families from diverse cultural backgrounds may have beliefs about disabilities that differ significantly from the beliefs of the majority culture. Language differences between the family and school personnel may inhibit the communication of test results and recommendations as well as the expression of parental questions and concerns. Language differences often cause problems in the identification of students who are from diverse cultural or linguistic groups. These students are at greater risk for being mislabeled and receiving inappropriate or inadequate services.

Other Sources of Diversity

The differences associated with cultural background and with disability are not the only sources of classroom diversity. These students are simply one group in the school population who may have special needs which classroom teachers must address. The social and domestic conditions of poverty, malnutrition, inadequate health care, drug abuse, homelessness, and child abuse or neglect also contribute to the diverse needs of students in today's schools. All of these conditions can affect school attendance, motivation, and academic performance, placing many students **at-risk** for school failure.

Schools and teachers face the challenge of meeting the special needs of all students during a time of limited fiscal resources. Educators are expected to provide effective instruction to all students in spite of the diversity of their needs, learning styles, and other characteristics. Yet budgetary restraints often prohibit reductions in class size, hiring of additional teachers and aides, or the implementation of other strategies which might ensure the successful education of every student. According to the U.S. Department of Education (2003), it costs an average of $5,918 more per pupil to educate a student with a disability than it costs for a general education student. If the goal of meeting the educational needs of today's students is to be met, instructional practices must be changed to accommodate diversity, no matter what the source of that diversity. However, special education cannot be used to serve the needs of students from diverse backgrounds by labeling them disordered when in fact they simply are different. The instructional strategies presented throughout this book are not strategies to aid only students with disabilities. They are strategies which teachers can implement in their classrooms to meet the unique learning styles and needs of all students.

Summary

This chapter has examined the role special education plays and the students it serves in today's educational system. Teachers face a challenging task: to ensure that all students have the opportunity to learn and develop to their potential. When students in the general education classroom exhibit cognitive, behavioral, communicative, sensory, or physical differences from their peers, the task can appear overwhelming. It is only through the cooperation and collaboration of classroom teachers, special education professionals, and parents that the goal of full participation in the educational process to the extent most appropriate for each student will be met.

Discussion Questions and Activities

1. Which of the disabilities included in IDEA could be considered "invisible"? What might be the impact of having a disability that was "invisible" as compared to one that is "visible"?

   Specific L. D.

   misdiagnosed

   Often not served

2. List the reasons for the increasing numbers of students who receive special education services each year.

   Labeling, mandates, medical research, teacher expectations, changing attitudes, parental concern, identification of ADHD

3. From a teacher's point of view, discuss the pros and cons of labeling students. Now discuss the pros and cons of labeling from a parent's point of view.

4. How might general education teachers encourage a multicultural education in their classrooms and schools?

Provide experiences that foster appreciation of all cultures.

Appreciate ones own cultural heritage

5. Interview a friend or family member who attended elementary school prior to 1965. Focus your questions on issues of services to students with disabilities. For example, ask if there were services provided in the school this individual attended; if not, where did individuals with disabilities receive services?

6. Interview an individual who has a disability. Focus your questions on the individual's school experiences.

7. Contact your local school system and make arrangements to observe: a general education classroom in which students with disabilities are placed, a resource room, and a separate class for students with disabilities.

Internet Resources

Closing the Gap
www.closingthegap.com

Council for Exceptional Children (CEC)
www.cec.sped.org

Internet Resources for Special Children
www.irsc.org

National Center for Culturally Responsible Educational Systems
www.nccrest.org

National Information Center for Children and Youth with Disabilities (NICHCY)
www.nichcy.org

Office of Special Education and Rehabilitative Services
www.ed.gov/about/offices/list/osers/osep/index.html

Special Education Resources on the Internet (SERI)
www.seriweb.com

The National Institute on Disability and Rehabilitation Research
www.abledata.com

References

Anderson, J. A. (1988). Cognitive styles and multicultural populations. *Journal of Teacher Education, 39(1),* 2–9.

Artiles, A., & Trent, S. (1994). Overrepresentation of minority students in special education: A continuing debate. *Journal of Special Education, 27,* 410–437.

Asher, S. R., & Taylor, A. R. (1981). Social outcomes of mainstreaming: Sociometric assessment and beyond. *Exceptional Education Quarterly, 1,* 13–30.

Carlson, N. R. (1990). *Psychology: The science of behavior.* Boston: Allyn & Bacon.

Chinn, P. C., & Hughes, S. (1987). Representation of minority students in special education classes. *Remedial and Special Education, 8(4),* 41–46.

Council for Exceptional Children. (1994). CEC policies for delivering services to exceptional children. Reston, VA: Author.

Cruickshank, W. M. (1958). The development of education for exceptional children. In W. M. Cruickshank & G. O. Johnson (Eds.), *The education of exceptional children and youth* (pp. 3–42). Englewood Cliffs, NJ: Prentice-Hall.

Davis, W. E. (1989). The regular education initiative debate: Its promises and problems. *Exceptional Children, 55,* 440–447.

Doris, S., & Brown, R. (1980). *Toleration of maladaptive classroom behaviors by regular and special educators.* Fresno, CA: California State University. (ERIC Document Reproduction Service No. ED 211 456).

Drabman, R. S., & Patterson, J. N. (1981). Disruptive behavior and the social standing of exceptional children. *Exceptional Education Quarterly, 1,* 45–56.

Fiedler, C. R., & Simpson, R. L. (1987). Modifying the attitudes of nonhandicapped high school students toward handicapped peers. *Exceptional Children, 53,* 343–349.

Foster, G. G., Ysseldyke, J. E., & Reese, J. (1975). I wouldn't have seen it if I hadn't believed it. *Exceptional Children, 41,* 469–473.

Fuchs, D. S., & Fuchs, L. S. (1994). Inclusive schools movement and the radicalization of special education reform. *Exceptional Children, 60,* 294–309.

Garrett, M. K., & Crump, W. D. (1980). Rethinking the regular education initiative: Focus on the classroom teacher. *Remedial and Special Education, 11(3),* 7–16.

Gollnick, D. M., & Chinn, P. C. (1990). *Multicultural education in a pluralistic society* (3rd ed.). Columbus, OH: Merrill.

Goodman, H., Gottlieb, J., & Harrison, R. H. (1977). Social acceptance of EMRs integrated into a nongraded elementary school. *American Journal of Mental Deficiency, 76,* 412–417.

128271

Hardman, M. L., Drew, C. J., Egan, M. W., & Wolf, B. (1993). *Human exceptionality, society, school, and family* (4th ed.). Boston: Allyn & Bacon.

Horne, M. D. (1985). *Attitudes toward handicapped students: Professional, peer, and parent reactions.* Hillsdale, NJ: Lawrence Erlbaum Associates.

Kanner, L. (1964). *A history of the care and study of the mentally retarded.* Springfield, IL: Charles C. Thomas.

Kaplan, P. S. (1996). *Pathways for exceptional children: Home, school, and culture.* St. Paul, MN: West Publishing.

Kauffman, J. M., Gerber, M. M., & Semmel, M. I. (1988). Arguable assumptions underlying the regular education initiative. *Journal of Learning Disabilities, 21,* 6–11.

Kavale, K. A., & Mostert, M. P. (2003). River of ideology; islands of evidence. *Exceptionality, 11(4),* 191–208.

Klinger, J. K., Vaughn, S., Hughes, M. T., Schumm, J. S., & Elbaum, B. (1998). Outcomes for students with and without learning disabilities in inclusive classrooms. *Learning Disabilities Research & Practice, 13(3),* 153–161.

MacMillan, D. L., Meyers, C., & Yoshida, R. (1978). Regular class teachers' perceptions of transition programs for EMR students and their impact on the students. *Psychology in the Schools, 15,* 9–103.

McCleary, I. D., Hardman, M. L., & Thomas, D. (1990). International special education. In T. Husen & T. N. Postewaite (Eds.), *International encyclopedia of education: Research and studies* (pp. 608–615). New York: Pergamon Press.

Nirje, B. (1979). The normalization principle and its human management implications. In R. B. Kugel & W. Wolfensberger (Eds.), *Changing patterns in residential services for the mentally retarded.* Washington, DC: The President's Committee on Mental Retardation.

Pang, O. (1991). Teaching children about social issues: Kidpower. In C. Sleeter (Ed.), *Empowerment through multicultural education* (pp. 179–197). Albany, NY: State University of New York Press.

Porter, R. E., & Samovar, L. A. (1976). Communicating interculturally. In L. A. Samovar & R. E. Porter (Eds.), *Intercultural Communication: A Reader* (p. 7). Belmont, CA: Wadsworth.

Prillaman, D. (1981). Acceptance of learning disabled students in the mainstream environment: A failure to replicate. *Journal of Learning Disabilities, 14,* 344–346.

Pritchard, D. G. (1963). *Education and the handicapped: 1760–1960.* London: Routledge & Kegan Paul.

Reynolds, M. C., Wang, M. C., & Walberg, H. J. (1987). The necessary restructuring of special and regular education. *Exceptional Children, 53,* 391–398.

Saville-Troike, M. (1982). *The ethnography of communication: An introduction.* Oxford: Basil Blackwell.

Siccone, F. (1995). *Celebrating diversity: Building self-esteem in today's multicultured classrooms.* Boston: Allyn and Bacon.

Stainback, S., & Stainback, W. (1992). *Curriculum considerations in inclusive classrooms: Facilitating learning for all students.* Baltimore, MD: Paul H. Brookes.

Thousand, J. S., & Villa, R. A. (1990). Strategies for educating learners with severe disabilities within their local home schools and communities. *Focus on Exceptional Children, 23(3),* 1–24.

U.S. Bureau of the Census (1999). *Statistical Abstract of the United States: 1999* (119th ed.). Washington, D.C.: U.S. Department of Commerce.

U.S. Department of Education (1997). *Nineteenth annual report to Congress on the implementation of The Individuals with Disabilities Education Act.* Washington, DC: Author.

U.S. Department of Education (2003). *Twenty-fifth annual report to Congress on the implementation of The Individuals with Disabilities Education Act.* Washington, DC: Author.

Van Acker, R., Grant, S. B., & Henry, D. (1996). Teacher and student behavior as a function of risk for aggression. *Education and Treatment of Children, 19,* 316–334.

Wiederholt, J. L. (1989). Restructuring special education services: The past, the present, the future. *Learning Disability Quarterly, 12,* 181–191.

Winzer, M. A. (1986). Early developments in special education: Some aspects of Enlightenment thought. *Remedial and Special Education, 10(5),* 422–449.

Ysseldyke, J. E., Algozzine, B., & Thurlow, M. (1992). *Critical issues in special education.* Boston: Houghton Mifflin.

2

The Legal Foundation for Special Education

Colleen M. O'Rourke and Ronald P. Colarusso

Chapter Objectives

- to provide an overview of the legislative history that relates to the special education of students with disabilities;
- to define the key educational provisions required by law for students with disabilities.

Many special educators and parents of children with disabilities will agree that special education services exist in the public schools today because federal laws require them. Most also would say that the gains made in the provision of appropriate services were achieved through litigation and legislation occurring in the 1960s and 70s. As seen in Chapter 1, students with disabilities have not always had the same right to education and access to services as their peers.

The laws that ensure the rights of today's students with disabilities did not just happen. They were the result of the work and dedication of parents, advocacy groups, and professional organizations that serve individuals with disabilities. In large measure, these groups owe their success in achieving equality in education to minority groups and their struggle to guarantee civil rights for all citizens. As the civil rights movement entered the arena of public education, it resulted in court decisions and legislation that prevented discrimination in education based on race. These decisions and laws were the foundation for parental and professional action to prevent discrimination in education based on disability. Initial right to education litigation in the area of special education was based on *Brown v. Board of Education* (1954). In this civil rights case, the U.S. Supreme Court ruled that separate schools for black and white students were unequal and therefore unconstitutional. This case ended racially segregated public education and provided a legal precedent for the elimination of segregated public education based on disability.

This chapter outlines the legal foundation for special education. It addresses some of the important litigation and laws that have shaped and determined the rights and services available to individuals with disabilities today. Five laws will be discussed: Section 504 of the Vocational Rehabilitation Act of 1973 (Public Law 93-112); The Education for All Handicapped Children Act (Public Law 94-142); Education of the Handicapped Act, Amendments of 1986 (Public Law 99-457); The Individuals with Disabilities Education Act (IDEA) (Public Law 101-476), the 1997 Amendments (P.L. 105-17) and the 2004 Amendments (P.L. 108-446); and the Americans with Disabilities Act (ADA) (Public Law 101-336). Our focus will be on the special education requirements of these laws. Following the summary of these laws, IDEA (the current law) will be examined in detail. It is important that classroom teachers understand the provisions of this law since teachers play a key role in its implementation and the delivery of the services it mandates.

Litigation History

Parent activism was a significant factor in the growth and expansion of special education from 1950 to 1974 (Blackhurst & Berdine, 1993). The National Association for Retarded Children, now known as the Association for Retarded Citizens of the United States (ARC), was formed in the 1950s. Its members, many of whom were parents, began to pressure public schools for services. In the 1960s, the Association for Children with Learning Disabilities, now the Learning Disabilities Association of America (LDA), was formed and followed the precedent of the ARC. When schools denied services to students with disabilities, or provided inadequate services, parents and professional organizations began to file lawsuits and to lobby Congress.

Special education related litigation began to appear in the 1960s. These lawsuits played a prominent role in the development of current legislation. They led to laws that ensured educational services for individuals with disabilities. They also forced the clarification of the intent of the laws through interpretation by state courts, district courts, and the U.S. Supreme Court. The early lawsuits generally focused on the inadequacy of the education provided to students with disabilities. In some cases, parents sued school districts because no services were being provided to students with certain disabilities. By 1974, over 36 "right to education" lawsuits were filed in 25 states (Blackhurst & Berdine, 1993). Thomas and Denzinger (1993) document over 800 court cases that have impacted the education of students with disabilities. **Table 2-1** outlines several significant cases that have shaped the delivery of special education services.

The laws pertaining to the rights of individuals with disabilities grew out of constitutional amendments and acts of Congress. The first of these is the 14th Amendment to the U.S. Constitution which Congress ratified in 1868. This amendment forbids states to deny any person life, liberty, or property without due process of law, or to deny any person equal protection of the laws. **The Civil Rights Act of 1964,** which was based on the

TABLE 2-1

Rulings in Court Cases Relevant to Special Education

Case	Ruling
Hobson v. Hansen (1967)	• This suit challenged the practice of educational tracking, or ability grouping, based on standardized test scores. The practice was ruled to be unconstitutional as it discriminated against poor and minority students.
Diana v. State Board of Education (1970)	• Parents of Spanish-speaking students filed suit challenging placement of their children in classes for the mentally retarded. They alleged that intelligence tests were culturally biased and resulted in inappropriate labeling of their children. The result was the requirement for nondiscriminatory assessment and testing of students in their primary language.
Larry P. v. Riles (1972)	• Parents of African-American children filed suit challenging inappropriate placements of children in classes for the mentally retarded. The result was a ruling that a) Intelligence Tests cannot be the sole basis for placement, and b) that a test must be developed which is not culturally biased.

TABLE 2-1

Rulings in Court Cases Relevant to Special Education (continued)

Case	Ruling
PARC v. Commonwealth of Pennsylvania (1972)	• The Pennsylvania Association for Retarded Children (PARC) filed suit against the state of Pennsylvania to obtain access to public education for children with mental retardation. Although Pennsylvania provided special classes for some students with disabilities, students with moderate, severe or profound retardation could be excluded from public education. The case resulted in the provision of educational programs (beyond traditional academic programs) for students with mental retardation. The court also ruled that parents have the right to a hearing when they are dissatisfied with their child's placement. Many of the provisions of P.L. 94-142 were based on this case.
Mills v. District of Columbia Board of Education (1972)	• A group of parents in Washington, D.C. filed suit against the public schools for access to education for children with disabilities, including those with behavior problems. The court, which ruled in favor of the parents, expanded the ruling to include all students with disabilities and created a zero reject policy. The court also refused to allow schools to claim fiscal inability as an excuse for not providing appropriate services.
New York State Association for Retarded Children v. Carey (1979)	• This suit challenged the placement of children who were mentally retarded and had hepatitis-B (a disease that can be contained) in separate self-contained programs. The court ruled that the students' placement could not be made based soley on the existence of the disease.
Battle v. Commonwealth of Pennsylvania (1980)	• Parents of students with disabilities challenged the state of Pennsylvania to extend education services beyond the 180-day school year. The ruling found that some students with disabilities need an extended school year to prevent significant regression and requires the school to provide summer programming.
Rowley v. Hendrick Hudson School District (1982)	• Hendrick Hudson School District in New York provided a student with a hearing impairment a sign language interpreter plus six other things. They then terminated this service the following year because the student was doing so well. The due-process hearing officer, federal district court, and federal appellate court supported the parents by requiring the school to provide the interpreter ruling that it maximized the student's educational achievement. The U.S. Supreme Court reversed the ruling stating that Congress never intended for schools to "maximize" the educational progress of students with disabilities, but to make available an appropriate educational program. They established a two part standard for evaluating a "free appropriate public education": 1) the state must provide meaningful access to an education for each disabled child, and 2) sufficient supportive and related services must be provided to permit a child to benefit educationally from special instruction.

continued on next page

TABLE 2-1

Rulings in Court Cases Relevant to Special Education (continued)

Case	Ruling
Irving Independent School District v. Tatro (1984)	• In this case the family sought for the provision of catheterization services to allow their child to remain in school for the entire school day. The Court ruled that catheterization is a related service needed by some students to maintain access to education and that schools are required to provide related services that students need to remain in school.
Honig v. Doe (1988)	• Parents challenged that children with disabilities should not be expelled from school for inappropriate behavior that is due to the disability. The Court ruled that students cannot be expelled if the inappropriate behavior is related to the disability.
Daniel R. R. v. State Board of Education (1989)	• The Fifth Circuit Court of Appeals held that a segregated class was an appropriate placement for a student with Down syndrome. The Court established two factors for determining compliance with the requirement of least restrictive environment (LRE) for students with severe disabilities: 1) it must be determined if the student can make satisfactory progress and benefit educationally in the general education classroom with curriculum modifications and using supplementary aids and services; and 2) it must be determined if the student has been integrated to the maximum extent appropriate.
Timothy W. v. Rochester School District (1989)	• The First Circuit Court of Appeals established that students are entitled to a free and appropriate public education no matter the severity of the student's disability. Education was defined broadly to include functional skill instruction.
Oberti v. Board of Education of the Borough of Clementon School District (1992)	• The Court ruled that the school must offer placement in a general education classroom with supplementary aids and services to a student with disabilities before considering more segregated placements. The student cannot be denied placement in a general education classroom just because the curriculum and services would need to be modified.
Agostini v. Felton (1997)	• The U.S. Supreme Court reversed a ruling that banned the delivery of publicly funded educational services to students enrolled in private schools. This means that special educators can now provide services to students enrolled in parochial schools.
Cedar Rapids Community School District v. Garret F. (1999)	• The U.S. Supreme Court ruled on the issue of related services reaffirming that intensive and continuous school health care services (if not performed by a physician) that are necessary for a student to attend school can qualify as related services.
Schaffer v. Weast Superintendent of Montgomery County Schools (2005)	• The U.S. Supreme Court ruled that the burden of proof in an administrative hearing challenging an IEP is placed upon the party seeking relief. This means that if a student, represented by his or her parents, challenges an IEP the burden of proof is their responsibility. However, the rule applies with equal effect for the school system. Some states have laws or regulations that always put the burden of proof on the school district. The court chose not to address these state laws. No such law exists in Maryland where this case was located.

Commerce Clause of the Constitution and on the 14th Amendment, forbids discrimination on the basis of race, religion, sex, or national origin. Title IV of this act pertains to education. It mandated unitary school systems as opposed to dual (separate but equal) systems and eliminated the separation of students based on race. This law established a framework that led to a series of public laws directed to the rights of all individuals with disabilities. Some of these laws require access and services in broad terms while others relate specifically to education.

Section 504 of the Vocational Rehabilitation Act of 1973 (Public Law 93-112)

This act is considered to be the first federal civil rights law protecting the rights of persons with disabilities. The language of this law mirrors that of the Civil Rights Act of 1964. Section 504 states that:

> No otherwise qualified handicapped individual shall, solely by reason of his handicap, be excluded from participation in, be denied the benefits of, or be subjected to discrimination in any program or activity receiving federal financial assistance.

Under Section 504, an individual with a disability is defined as any individual who:

- has a physical or mental impairment which substantially limits one or more of such person's major life activities,
- has a record of such impairment, or
- is regarded as having such an impairment. (29 U.S.C. Sec. 706(8))

In addition, a physical or mental impairment is defined as:

- any physiological disorder or condition, cosmetic, disfigurement, or anatomical loss affecting one or more of the following body systems: neurological; musculoskeletal; special sense organs; respiratory; including speech organs; cardiovascular; reproductive; digestive; genito-urinary; hematic and lymphatic; skin; and endocrine; or
- any mental or psychological disorder, such as mental retardation, organic brain syndrome, emotional or mental illness, and specific learning disabilities. (34 Code of Federal Regulations Part 104.3)

The law applies to any private or government agency receiving federal funds. This includes not only state, county, and local governments, but also preschool programs, elementary and secondary schools, and institutions of higher education. These agencies and programs would lose all federal funding if they violated Section 504 by denying individuals with disabilities employment opportunities, benefits, or access to services or activities. As a result of Section 504, major changes have occurred not only in the accessibility of educational, vocational, and social services, but also in architectural accessibility for persons with disabilities. It required that existing structures be

Section 504 applies to any program receiving federal funding, including preschool programs.

modified so as to be accessible to persons with disabilities and that new facilities be designed and constructed to meet standards of accessibility.

Although Section 504 applies to individuals of all ages, school age individuals bene-fitted from its application to educational programs and school environments. It guaran-tees a free, appropriate education to all children, including those with handicapping con-ditions. Section 504 also requires that school districts bear the cost if the lack of appropriate facilities necessitates the transfer of a student to an alternative, appropriate placement. The law specifies that arrangements be made for participation by students with disabilities in non-academic and extracurricular activities "to the maximum extent appropriate to the needs of the handicapped person in question."

Many of the provisions of Section 504 were incorporated into later federal laws which addressed the education of students with disabilities. These later laws include The Educa-tion for All Handicapped Children Act of 1975 (Public Law 94-142) and The Individuals with Disabilities Education Act (IDEA) of 1990 (Public Law 101-476) and its later amend-ments. Even with these laws, Section 504 remains an important, comprehensive civil rights statement for students with disabilities. Although school systems must meet the mandates of IDEA, the current law governing special education, Section 504 is applied if a student's condition does not meet the criteria specified under IDEA but meets the crite-ria specified under this law. The most common use of Section 504 is in securing services for students with attention deficit/hyperactivity disorder (ADHD), an example of a disor-der not defined as a disability under IDEA. Most school systems have developed "504 Committees" to ensure that they are not discriminating against a student whose condi-tion meets the standards specified in this legislation. Some school systems follow the same procedures as IDEA and complete an IEP for 504 students.

The Education for All Handicapped Children Act (Public Law 94-142)

In the 1970s, parents and professional groups were dissatisfied with the services schools provided to students with disabilities. They sought action by Congress and in 1975 Pub-lic Law 94-142 was enacted. This law is a landmark in legislation for special education. It reflected Congress's belief that state and local educational agencies have the responsibil-ity to provide appropriate education to all children. By passage of the law and provision of federal funds, Congress asserted that the national interest is served by the federal gov-ernment's support of programs to meet the needs of students with disabilities.

With Public Law 94-142 Congress forced school systems to take affirmative action in the education of students with disabilities. In other words, school districts now had to take specific actions to educate these students, and in return, they would receive financial assistance specifically designated for the education of the handicapped. The law man-dated a free, appropriate public education (FAPE) with related services for students with disabilities ages 5 to 21. No longer could schools refuse to provide services that were needed for the appropriate education of students or provide them at an extra cost to the parents.

Public Law 94-142 addressed numerous issues in the identification and education of students with disabilities. It mandated a comprehensive, nondiscriminatory evaluation prior to special education placement as well as periodic reevaluation. A written, individu-alized education program (IEP) specifying goals and objectives was required for each stu-dent receiving special education services. The special education services had to be pro-vided in the least restrictive environment (LRE). The law also specified procedural safeguards to protect the rights of students and parents. Public Law 94-142 dramatically and permanently changed the delivery of services to students with disabilities. Not only would school systems be required to provide services, they would be held accountable for the appropriateness of those services.

The Education of the Handicapped Act Amendments of 1986 (Public Law 99-457)

When it becomes necessary to update a law or add new provisions to existing laws, Congress can add amendments to a current law. In 1986, Congress amended P.L. 94-142. The major provisions of the law were reaffirmed and several sections of the law were amended when Congress passed Public Law 99-457. The most significant changes were: (a) the extension of the rights and protections of P.L. 94-142 to children with disabilities ages 3 to 5 years; and (b) the provision of funds to assist states in planning, developing, and implementing a comprehensive, statewide system of early intervention for infants and toddlers (birth to age 3 years) with disabilities and their families.

While Public Law 94-142 required an individualized education program (IEP), P.L. 99-457 required an individualized family service plan (IFSP) for children birth to age three. Like the IEP, the IFSP describes the child's needs and the services to be provided to enhance development. The IFSP also addresses the family's needs and the services to be provided to ensure that the family understands the child's disability and is involved in the intervention program. In fact, if it is determined that services to the family are needed for the appropriate education of the child, those services will be provided even if the child does not need direct services.

The Individuals with Disabilities Education Act (IDEA) (Public Law 101-476)

With the passage of Public Law 101-476 in 1990, Congress again reauthorized Public Law 94-142. This amendment to P.L. 94-142, referred to as IDEA, introduced several significant modifications to the 1975 Act. IDEA updated the terminology used to describe this population and actually renamed the 1975 Act. The term *handicapped,* used previously, no longer was considered acceptable and was replaced with *disabled.* Since the law applies to persons with disabilities from birth through age 21, the label *children* was inappropriate and was changed to *individuals.* To reflect the sentiment that the disability should not define the person, the phrasing of the title of the Act was modified to place the emphasis on the person not the disability. The preferred phrasing became *individuals with disabilities* rather than *disabled individuals.* Thus the law known as *The Education for All Handicapped Children Act* became *The Individuals with Disabilities Education Act (IDEA).*

IDEA added two new categories of disability: autism and traumatic brain injury. These students had been receiving services prior to this law, but they were labeled under one of the other existing categories. Parents and professionals advocated for separate categories to ensure accurate identification and appropriate services. The law also defined transition services (services to ensure the progression from school to post-school activities) and required that these services be included on the student's IEP no later than age 16. In addition, IDEA defined assistive technology devices and services and required that students with disabilities have access to this technology if needed.

The Individuals with Disabilities Education Act Amendments of 1997 (IDEA 97) (Public Law 105-17)

After two years of discussion and debate in the Senate and House of Representatives President Clinton signed this bill into law on June 4, 1997. P.L. 105-17 reauthorized and amended the Individuals with Disabilities Education Act (IDEA) and is referred to as IDEA 97. IDEA 97 included several major changes and modified some procedures that were included in the previous laws. Students with disabilities now must be included, with accommodations when necessary, in State and district wide assessment programs. For example, when States or school districts administer the Iowa Test of Basic Skills to all students in certain elementary grades, students receiving special education services must be included in that assessment. In the past many of these students did not take these State or district wide assessments. States were required to develop alternative assessments for students who could not participate in regular assessments. IDEA 97 added additional specific requirements for an IEP, such as an explanation of the extent to which the student will not participate in the general classroom program.

A more significant role for parents in the decision making process was mandated by IDEA 97. Parents must be included on any team that makes decisions about their child's educational placement. Mediation was emphasized in resolving conflict between schools and the parents of a student with disabilities. States were required to create a mediation system and bear the cost of the process. The most controversial and complicated changes were in the area of discipline and alternative placement of students with disabilities.

The Individuals with Disabilities Education Act Amendments of 2004 (IDEA 2004) (Public Law 108-446)

The reauthorized *Individuals with Disabilities Education Act* (IDEA 2004) (PL 108-446) was signed into law on December 3, 2004, by President George W. Bush. The provisions of the act became effective on July 1, 2005, with the exception of some of the elements pertaining to the definition of a "highly qualified teacher" that took effect upon the signing of the act. Some major changes to the provisions of IDEA were made to align it with *No Child Left Behind,* the *Elementary and Secondary Education Act* (ESEA) of 1965. Major alignment was made with definitions of academic subjects, language proficiency and highly qualified teachers. The "core academic subjects" are defined as English, reading or language arts; mathematics; science; foreign languages; civics and government; economics; arts; history; and geography. An individual who is considered "limited English proficient" is one: whose language is other than English; who is a Native American, Alaska Native, or a native resident who comes from an environment where a language other than English has had a significant impact on the individual's level of English language proficiency; whose difficulties in speaking, reading, writing, or understanding the English language may be sufficient to deny the individual the ability to successfully achieve in classrooms where the language of instruction is English or to participate fully in society. To be "highly qualified" a special education teacher must obtain full state certification. Special education teachers who teach core academic subjects exclusively to students must also meet the certification requirements applied to elementary school teachers or in the case of instruction above the elementary level, have subject matter knowledge appropriate to the level of instruction being provided in all subjects they teach. A major change in the 2004 Amendment is that special education services must be provided by the local education agency (LEA) for students with disabilities who are enrolled in private elementary schools and secondary schools within the LEA. State and local funds must supplement and not supplant the proportionate amount of federal funds required. Additional amendments address evaluations, over-identification, private schools, discipline, IEPs, and procedural safeguards. Some of these changes are intended to eliminate unneeded requirements that require much time and paperwork. Because IDEA is the most comprehensive law governing the provision of special education services in the schools, the provisions of this law are described in greater detail later in the chapter.

The Americans with Disabilities Act (ADA) (Public Law 101-336)

The ADA, signed into law in 1990, prohibits discrimination on the basis of disability. It extends the civil rights protection mandated by Section 504 for persons with disabilities into the private sector. The ADA specifically prohibits discrimination in both public and private employment, accommodations (work place, hotels, restaurants, stores, etc.), transportation services (buses, trains, airplanes, etc.), and telecommunications.

Employers with 15 or more employees must make reasonable accommodations for persons with disabilities to avoid discrimination in hiring, firing, and promotions. Public facilities must be accessible. New vehicles for public transportation must be accessible, and transit services (e.g., specially equipped vans) must be available for individuals who cannot use existing transportation systems. Telephone companies must provide relay services and special telecommunication devices for individuals who are deaf or unable to communicate using the standard telephone system.

The provisions of the ADA enable individuals with disabilities to function more independently than ever before. However, the law is not without its critics. Some people argue that the ADA is too expensive to implement, and the federal government should not be involved in local issues. Proponents of the law counter that individuals with disabilities have been denied access to facilities and services for many years. Without federal intervention, the discrimination would continue.

Comparing Three Current Laws

Of the laws discussed here, three play a major role in the regulation of services provided by schools: IDEA 2004, Section 504, and the ADA. **Table 2-2** compares the major provisions of these three laws.

The federal laws passed in the 1970s and later (Section 504, P.L. 94-142, P.L. 99-457, IDEA, and ADA) had a significant impact on the rights of individuals with disabilities and the provision of services to these individuals. The framework for these laws often was set in prior legislation. **Table 2-3** summarizes a number of other public laws that are relevant to special education and have expanded the services available to students with disabilities.

TABLE 2-2

A Comparison of the Provisions of IDEA 2004, Section 504, and ADA

	IDEA 2004	Section 504	ADA
Title of Act	• The Individuals with Disabilities Education 2004 Act.	• Section 504 of the Vocational Rehabilitation Act of 1973, amended in 1986	• The Americans with Disabilities Act, 1990
Description	• Assures the right of all individuals with disabilities to a free appropriate public education.	• Anti-discriminatory statute, guarantees civil rights to qualified persons with disabilities.	• Civil rights law that enforces the non-discrimination of persons with disabilities.
Purpose	• To assure all children with disabilities have a free appropriate public education with special education to meet their individual needs.	• To eliminate discrimination on the basis of disability in any program or activity receiving federal financial assistance.	• To eliminate discrimination on the basis of disability in public or private employment, transportation, telecommunication, accommodations, or program accessibility.
Funding Provision	• Federal money based on number of students receiving special education adjusted for poverty rates in the state. Funds withdrawn for non-compliance.	• The loss of federal funds for non-compliance	• Fines for non-compliance
Age	• Birth to 21 years	• All ages	• All ages
Definition of Disability	• Individuals with disabilities are defined by category with criteria specified in the law.	• Any person who has a physical or mental impairment which substantially limits one or more major life activities.	• Individuals with physical or mental impairments that substantially limit one or more major life activities. Excludes users of alcohol and drugs.
Due Process	• A set of procedures with mediation as an option from local hearings to civil court.	• Civil court	• Civil court

TABLE 2-2

A Comparison of the Provisions of IDEA 2004, Section 504, and ADA (continued)

	IDEA 2004	Section 504	ADA
Type of Programs	• An individualized education plan that specifies the special education services to be provided and the location of these services.	• Schools are required to provide appropriate general or special education and related aids and services that meet the educational needs of the student with a disability as adequately as the needs of students without disabilities are met.	
Preschool	• Part C provides early intervention for infants birth to 2 yrs. and their families. Part B mandates special education for ages 3–5 and transition from early intervention to preschool.	• Requires that individuals with disabilities have the same opportunities as other individuals. In states where preschool is available to other children, children with disabilities must have the same opportunity.	
Vocational Training/ Transition	• Included and requires post-secondary and transitional goals as a part of the IEP by age 16 that address training, education, employment, and independent skills.	• Amended in 1986 to include supported employment.	
Accessibility	• Provides assistance to make schools accessible.	• Requires accommodations so that the individual may receive appropriate education.	• Accessibility codes for public and private entities to accommodate individuals with disabilities as employees and consumers.
Individual Education Plan	• A required team process with parent participation	• An individualized education program developed in accordance with IDEA.	

continued on next page

TABLE 2-2

A Comparison of the Provisions of IDEA 2004, Section 504, and ADA (continued)

	IDEA 2004	Section 504	ADA
Parental Involvement	• Parents have rights to participate fully in all aspects of the process from eligibility to program modification; due process procedures.		
Least Restrictive Environment	• Students shall be placed in the least restrictive environment where they can most benefit from their special education. Attempts to educate the student in the general education setting must be demonstrated before a segregated placement is chosen.	• Students shall be placed in the general educational environment unless it is demonstrated that the education of the student in the general educational environment with the use of supplemental aids and services cannot be achieved satisfactorily.	
Nondiscriminatory Evaluation	• It is required that students be tested in their native language and that the tests used do not discriminate.		

The No Child Left Behind Act of 2001 (Public Law 107-110)

The No Child Left Behind Act (NCLB) is the latest version of the Elementary and Secondary Education Act of 1965. It redefines the federal role in K–12 education to help improve the academic achievement of all students and to close the achievement gap between disadvantaged and minority students and their peers. Four main principles of the education reform plan are:

1. stronger accountability for results,
2. expanded flexibility at the local level,
3. expanded options for parents, and
4. an emphasis on teaching methods that have been proven to work.

This general education law will have an effect on the education of all students including those receiving special education services. The following are some of the major provisions that will have a significant impact on the education of all students at-risk for low achievement.

TABLE 2-3

Legislation Relevant to Special Education Prior to IDEA

Law	Summary
Public Law 83-531 (1957)	• Provided funding for research in mental retardation.
Public Law 88-164 (1963)	• Provided funds to train teachers of students with disabilities. Established research and demonstration projects.
Public Law 89-10 (1965)	• Provided funding to develop programs for students who were economically disadvantaged or had disabilities.
Public Law 89-313 (1965)	• Provided funding for the education of children with disabilities in state institutions and hospitals.
Public Law 89-750 (1966)	• Established the Bureau of Education for the Handicapped and a National Advisory Committee on the Handicapped.
Public Law 90-538 (1968)	• Established demonstration centers for preschoolers with disabilities.
Public Law 91-230 (1970)	• Consolidated existing legislation for students with disabilities. Recognized learning disabilities as a disability and emphasized the importance of services for students who were gifted and talented.
Public Law 92-424 (1972)	• Required 10% of Head Start enrollment be available to children with disabilities.
Public Law 93-380 (1974)	• Required services for students with disabilities. Many of its provisions are included in P.L. 94-142.
Public Law 95-561 (1978)	• Provided funds to states for planning and improving programs for gifted and talented students.
Public Law 96-88 (1980)	• Created the Federal Department of Education.
Public Law 98-199 (1983)	• Amended P.L. 94-142 and emphasized preschool, secondary, and postsecondary programs for students with disabilities.
Public Law 100-407 (1988)	• Established statewide assistive technology services.
Public Law 101-392 (1990)	• Required access to the full range of vocational education programs for students with disabilities.

Accountability

NCLB creates assessments in each state that measure what students know and learn in reading and math in grades 3 through 8. Student progress and achievement will be measured for every student, every year. The data will be available in annual report cards on school performance and in statewide progress reports. Statewide reports will include performance data for individual groups according to race, gender, and other criteria to demonstrate not only how well students are achieving overall but also the progress in closing the achievement gap between disadvantaged students and other groups of students.

Flexibility

To cut down on federal red tape, NCLB will reduce the overall number of Elementary and Secondary Education Act (ESEA) programs at the U.S. Department of Education from 55 to 45 and will offer most local school districts the freedom to allocate up to 50 percent of the federal dollars they receive among several education programs. It will allow for the creation of up to 150 local demonstration projects for school districts interested in obtaining the flexibility to consolidate all funds they receive from several programs in exchange for entering into an agreement holding them accountable for higher academic performance. A few states will have new flexibility in the use of some federal funds to coordinate their efforts with local school districts through state-local "flexibility partnerships" designed to make sure federal education funds are being used effectively to meet student needs.

Expanding Options

The parents of children from disadvantaged backgrounds who are attending failing schools would be allowed to transfer their child to a better-performing public or charter school immediately after a school is identified as failing. Federal money can be used to provide supplemental educational services such as tutoring, after school services, and summer school programs for students in failing schools. NCLB also expands federal support for charter schools by giving parents, educators and interested community leaders greater opportunities to create new charter schools.

Reading

To ensure that every student can read, NCLB authorizes an increase in federal funding for reading and links that funding to scientifically proven methods of reading instruction through President Bush's Reading First plan.

Teacher Quality

NCLB requires a highly-qualified teacher in every public school classroom by 2005. In addition to specific funds for teacher quality, NCLB will allow local schools freedom to spend up some additional federal funds for hiring new teachers, increasing teacher pay, and improving teacher training and development.

English Proficiency

NCLB consolidates the U.S. Department of Education's bilingual and immigrant education programs in order to focus support on enabling all limited English proficient (LEP) students to learn English as quickly and effectively as possible. All LEP students will be tested for reading and language arts in English after they have attended school in the United States for three consecutive years. Parents will be notified that their child demonstrates limited English proficiency and is in need of English language instruction. The new Act will focus on helping LEP students learn English through scientifically-based teaching methods.

Implementation of Federal Laws

The implementation of federal laws involves both federal and state agencies. Once laws are passed, detailed regulations are written as guidelines for implementation. These regulations describe the procedures which must be followed to comply with the laws. State laws and regulations tend to mirror the federal laws. This results in commonalities across states in their special education programs and procedures. However, differences exist among states in such areas as the language used, the criteria for defining a disability, and the approach to service delivery. Each state must present its plan for the delivery of special education services to the U.S. Office of Special Education Programs for approval. This provides evidence that the state is meeting the intent of the law to provide appropriate educational services to students with disabilities. Prior to submission of the plan, states must provide an opportunity for public review and comment on the plan.

At the local level, school districts and their boards of education are responsible for the delivery of special education services. These local districts must operate their special education programs according to the regulations established at the state and federal levels. Although there may be some degree of local control and autonomy, education is primarily a responsibility of the state. For this reason, teachers should be familiar with the rules and regulations of their local educational agency and state. A copy of your state's special education regulations can be obtained from your State Department of Education or Department of Public Instruction.

Federal funds are provided for the education of students with disabilities. These funds are awarded to each state that has an approved plan for the delivery of special education services. The funds are based on the number of students currently receiving special education services. While most of this money is passed from the state to the local education agency, additional local funds are needed to fully cover the cost of the special education services. Each state must monitor local education agencies to insure that their approved plan is being carried out, and the monies are being spent for special education services. The U.S. Office of Special Education Programs is responsible for monitoring each state.

In spite of the written federal and state regulations for implementation, the laws related to special education are complex. It is difficult to translate the full intent of the laws into regulations that anticipate all possible situations in the education of students with disabilities. Thus, the lawsuits and court decisions discussed earlier in this chapter have played an important role in interpreting the laws. Certainly lawsuits will continue to be filed in the future. The courts will continue to clarify and provide interpretation of the basic principles underlying the laws.

Major Provisions of the Individuals with Disabilities Education Improvement Act (IDEA 2004)

As noted previously in this chapter, The Individuals with Disabilities Education Improvement Act of 2004 (IDEA 2004) continues the national support for the public education of all students. The law requires that each state have an approved plan that describes the policies and procedures for the identification and education of all students with disabilities. Until this plan is approved, the state will not receive federal funds to support the education of students with disabilities.

Students with disabilities exhibit one or more of several specific conditions that result in their need for special education and related services to obtain an appropriate public education. General disability areas include cognitive, processing, emotional and behavioral, physical, sensory, and health related impairments. IDEA classifies these impairments under the following categories:

- Autism
- Deaf-Blind
- Emotional Disturbance
- Hearing Impairment
- Specific Learning Disabilities
- Mental Retardation
- Multiple Disabilities

- Orthopedic Impairment
- Other Health Impairment
- Speech or Language Impairment
- Traumatic Brain Injury
- Visual Impairment

IDEA mandates that state and local educational agencies identify, evaluate, and provide services to students who qualify under the definitions of these disability categories. Definitions and in-depth discussions of each exceptionality are presented in Chapters 4 and 5. It is important to remember that although IDEA has specific criteria for each of the above mentioned categories, ADA and Section 504 define disability in broad terms in relation to one's ability to function in our society. (See Table 2-2).

Public Law 94-142 included several fundamental components that were reaffirmed, clarified, modified and expanded by later amendments and now by IDEA 2004. They remain as guiding principles in the provision of special education services today. The major components of IDEA have implications for the education of students in all settings especially the general education classroom. In most cases, they involve general education classroom teachers and their role in the education of students with disabilities. A discussion of these provisions and how they must be implemented in educational settings follows.

Free Appropriate Public Education (FAPE)

All students with disabilities have the right to a free and appropriate education at public expense. The federal laws have ensured that these students will no longer be denied the right to attend school. Prior to the passage of P.L. 94-142, schools could claim that programs were not available or that certain students with disabilities could not be educated. As discussed in Chapter 1, this meant some students were turned away from public schools, and parents were forced to pay for any educational services themselves. Now public schools must provide appropriate education to all students at no cost to parents. The term "appropriate" is not defined in the law. Teachers, special educators, school officials, and parents must work together to determine what is appropriate for each student. This has led to a number of court cases to define the term and to determine if certain services are appropriate. Several of these cases were noted in Table 2-1.

Nondiscriminatory Evaluation and Placement

Special education services cannot be provided unless a student meets eligibility criteria based on the results of a comprehensive assessment by a multidisciplinary evaluation team. This assessment must be individualized and nondiscriminatory. The nondiscriminatory provision was added to eliminate errors in the classification and placement of students. It was believed that many students received unreliable and invalid assessments, and then were labeled inappropriately and placed in special education classrooms. School personnel must assure that they are using tests that are valid for the purpose they are used and that the testing and evaluation materials are fair and unbiased. It is required that states monitor and prevent the inappropriate overidentification of racial or ethnic minority students as having disabilities. This is due to the history of a disproportionate representation of students from minority groups in special education. States must collect data that determines if there is disproportionate representation by specific impairment, educational placement, or disciplinary actions, including suspensions and expulsions. The intent of this provision is to eliminate discrimination based on cultural background, race, or disability. In addition, IDEA requires that when assessing students suspected of having a disability:

- At least one member of the evaluation team be a specialist (usually a special education teacher) with knowledge in the area of the suspected disability.
- The parent of the student must be a member of the group making evaluation and placement decisions.
- All areas related to the suspected disability be evaluated, including health, vision, hearing, behavior, general intelligence, motor abilities, academic performance, and language abilities.
- Trained personnel select and administer the tests.
- The evaluation be done in the student's native language or other mode of communication (e.g., sign language).
- The results of the assessment reflect the student's aptitude or achievement, not the disability (e.g., sensory, physical, or communication impairment).
- The evaluation determines not only what disability a student might have, but also the most appropriate way to address the disability.
- Eligibility and placement cannot be determined on the basis of the results of a single test, such as a general intelligence test.

If the IEP team determines that an alternate assessment of achievement is appropriate for a student, the IEP must include a statement of why the student cannot participate in the regular assessment and why the particular alternate assessment selected is appropriate. The statement must explain how the alternate assessment is aligned to the student's alternate achievement standards and appropriate short-term objectives. A statement of any appropriate accommodations that are necessary to measure the academic achievement and functional performance must be included.

The most significant change in the evaluation process is the procedures for evaluating a student suspected of having a specific learning disability. A Local Education Agency (LEA) is not required to take into consideration evidence of a severe discrepancy between achievement and intellectual ability in oral expression, listening comprehension, written expression, basic reading skill, reading comprehension, mathematical calculation, or mathematical reasoning. An LEA may use a process that determines if the student responds to scientific, research-based intervention as a part of the evaluation procedures.

Individualized Education Program (IEP)

A major component of IDEA is the requirement that every student receiving special education services have an individualized education program (IEP). The IEP is a written statement of the plan designed to meet the student's special needs and to ensure that an appropriate education is provided. It is the product of the comprehensive assessment. The IEP is developed annually by an IEP team. The team members include the student's general education teacher, a special education teacher or supervisor of special education programs, the parents or surrogate, the student if appropriate, and other individuals as needed (e.g., psychologist, speech-language pathologist, physical therapist, etc.). The IEP must include a statement of the student's present levels of academic achievement and functional performance and a statement of measurable academic and functional annual goals. The IEP must include a description of how the student's progress toward meeting the annual goals will be measured. It must also include a statement of the special education and related services, supplementary aids and services, and any program modifications or supports for school personnel that will be provided for the student. Included in the IEP are:

- The student's present level of educational performance.
- The annual goals.
- Short-term instructional objectives for students who take alternative assessments.
- A statement of the specific educational services to be provided, who will provide them and where they will be provided.
- The starting date and expected duration of services.
- A statement of the extent to which the student will be able to participate in general education programming.
- An explanation of the extent to which the student will not participate with nondisabled students in the general class or in extracurricular and nonacademic activities.
- The evaluation plan and criteria to determine if the objectives are being met.
- Postsecondary goals and transition services beginning no later than age 16.

Under IDEA 2004, a transition plan is required for all students beginning no later than 16 years of age. The IEP must include appropriate measurable postsecondary goals based upon age-appropriate transition assessments related to training, education, employment and, where appropriate, independent living skills and the transition services (including courses of study) needed to assist the student in reaching those goals. This plan ensures that students' education is focused on the skills needed for employment and community living after they have left the public school environment.

The IEP documents the student's needs and the school's commitment of resources and services. It can be an evaluation device to determine a student's progress toward stated goals as well as a management tool to assure that special education services are provided. In cases of controversy, the IEP may be important as a legal instrument to provide evidence whether the requirements of the law have been met.

An IEP must be reviewed by the team annually or sooner if requested by the parent or teacher. In addition, a student's eligibility for special education services must be reevaluated every three years. IDEA 97 modified the procedures required in the reevaluation process. Previously, it was required that tests be administered in this process (e.g., IQ tests, academic achievement tests, etc.). Under the reauthorization of IDEA, the IEP team considers all available information in making a decision about the student's continued eligibility for special education services. The team may request the administration of specific tests when needed, but retesting is not required.

In the case of a student with a disability who transfers school districts within the same academic year and had an IEP that was in effect, the local education agency (LEA) shall provide the student with a free appropriate public education (FAPE) described in the previously held IEP until a new IEP is developed. If the transfer is to a school district in another state, the same rule applies until the LEA conducts an evaluation if determined to be necessary. To facilitate the transition, the new school must take reasonable steps to promptly obtain the student's records from the previous school in which the student was enrolled and the previous school must promptly respond to the request.

Changes to a student's IEP after the annual IEP meeting for a school year may be made without a meeting if the parent and the LEA agree. This can be done by amending the IEP rather than by redrafting the entire IEP. In addition, the parent and the LEA may agree to use alternative means of meeting participation, such as video conferences and conference calls.

Infants and toddlers who qualify for special education must have an individualized family service plan (IFSP). The significance of this plan is that the family may be offered direct services if they are needed for the child's development. In fact, a family may receive services and assistance even though the child does not receive any direct services. In addition IDEA 2004 requires that a school transition plan be developed to ensure the appropriate continuation of special education services.

Least Restrictive Environment (LRE)

Educating students with disabilities in the least restrictive environment (LRE) means that they should remain in the school environment with their nondisabled peers to the greatest extent possible and appropriate. The current law requires that before a student is removed from the general education classroom setting attempts be made to educate the student in the classroom with supplemental services and aids. Prereferral teams must plan and implement an intervention program for the general education classroom setting. The process of referral and the role of prereferral teams are discussed in Chapter 3. However, it must be demonstrated that specific interventions in the general education classroom were unsuccessful before the student is referred for special education. Only when the disability is severe enough that education in the general classroom is not effective, are schools allowed to remove students from the general education classroom. This provision is "based on the premise that many creative alternatives exist to help the regular educator serve children with learning or adjustment problems within the context of a regular class setting" (Wood, 1984, p. 11).

A common misperception is that the principle of LRE requires all students with disabilities to be educated solely in general education classrooms. In fact, the law requires that a continuum of placement options be available to students with disabilities. This continuum ranges from the totally integrated, general education classroom setting to a totally segregated, separate school as shown in **Figure 2-1.**

The appropriate placement for any student is determined by the IEP team based on the specific needs of that student. Even though students may have the same disability, the LRE that is appropriate for one, may be inappropriate for another. For the majority of students with disabilities, placement in the general education classroom for at least a part of the school day is appropriate.

Determining Appropriate Programming in the LRE

In 1989, as a result of a court action involving issues related to the educational placement of a student with significant mental retardation and language delays (Daniel R. R. v. State Board of Education), the Fifth Circuit Court of Appeals identified specific questions which must be asked in order to determine if programming is appropriate and in the least restrictive environment. These questions also were adopted by the Eleventh and Third Circuit Courts of Appeals and are used currently as guidelines by the courts when determining if appropriate programming placement decisions are made by school districts (Martin, 1993).

FIGURE 2-1

Educational Placement Options from Least Restrictive to Most Restrictive

Least Restrictive

Most Restrictive

- General Education Classroom
- Resource Room
- Separate Class
- Separate School
- Residential Program

1. Are modifications in the regular classroom and throughout the full continuum of services available?
2. What modifications does the one student being considered on the IEP require?
3. Having determined the necessary modifications, will those modifications actually produce benefits?
4. Now that we know what we are contemplating in the regular setting, would there be any foreseeable detriment to this one child under consideration?
5. Will the placement of this child, and all that his or her program entails, have a negative impact on other students in that setting?
6. If the IEP Committee decides not to have the child in all regular settings, how will the IEP Committee assure there are maximum opportunities for interaction with nondisabled peers?

The Daniel R. R. case also brought into question the educational benefits available in specific LRE placements for students with a severe disability. It provided four questions to ask when determining if a student could receive benefit from a placement in a general education class and the effect of that student's placement on other students and the system (Martin, 1993).

1. What educational benefits are available to the child in a regular classroom compared to the educational benefits of a special education classroom?
2. What nonacademic benefits will the child receive from interacting with nondisabled children?
3. What is the child's effect on the regular education teacher and other children in the regular education classroom?
4. What are the costs of the supplementary aids and services necessary to support the child in a regular education classroom?

The interpretation of IDEA by the U.S. Office of Special Education Programs in Washington, D.C. and recent court rulings have increased dramatically the number of students with disabilities included in general education classes. There is disagreement among both professionals and parents as to the benefits of inclusion for all students, as well as the student with disabilities. Some school systems have eliminated self-contained special classes and have adopted a model of full inclusion. This extreme position eliminates the continuum of services option. In this extreme inclusive model, the IEP is no longer the basis for placement, since all students with disabilities are placed in the general education classroom.

Regardless of the final outcome of the debate and controversy surrounding inclusion, more students with disabilities will spend a greater part of their school day in the general education school program. The philosophy of placement has shifted from that of initial placement in a restrictive environment and movement toward the mainstream, to that of initial placement in a least restrictive environment and movement toward a segregated environment if needed. As a result, all classroom teachers will interact with students with special needs. The responsibility for the education of all students will be shared by general education teachers and special education teachers. This shared responsibility will require additional skills for all teachers. Chapter 12 discusses the need for collaboration with families and professionals in sharing the responsibilities of educating students with disabilities.

Discipline and Placement in Alternative Educational Settings

Behavior and discipline have been controversial issues under IDEA, especially when determining whether a student with disabilities could be expelled from school for violating school rules (e.g., carrying a weapon) or must "stay put" in the student's current educational placement. IDEA 97 maintained the provision that students with disabilities may not be expelled for behaviors that are manifestations of their disabilities, even for violations which involve drugs and weapons. IDEA 2004 has changed this "stay put" provision for serious cases. School personnel may now consider any unique circumstances on a case-by-case basis when determining whether to order a change in placement for a student with a disability who violates a code of student conduct. A hearing officer may remove a student to an interim alternative educational setting for not more than 45 school days without regard to whether the behavior is determined to be a manifestation of the student's disability, in cases where the student has inflicted serious bodily injury upon another person while at school, on school premises, or at a school function. "Serious bodily injury" is a bodily injury that involves a substantial risk of death, extreme physical pain, protracted and obvious disfigurement, or protracted loss or impairment of the function of a bodily member, organ, or mental faculty.

Depending on the violation of school rule or law, school personnel may suspend a student with a disability for not more than 10 days. They also may change the student's placement to an appropriate interim alternative educational setting for not more than 45 days. If prior to the incident the IEP team did not conduct a functional behavioral assessment with a behavior intervention plan, the IEP team must develop an assessment plan to address the student's behavior within 10 days. If a behavior plan is in place, the team must review the existing plan and modify it as necessary within 10 days. A determination if the student's behavior is a manifestation of the disability is required if the action taken is for more than 10 days. In addition, a student not yet determined eligible for special education services may qualify for the protections of IDEA 97 if the school system had knowledge of the disability. Chapter 11, Behavior Management of Students addresses these issues in greater detail.

Related Services and Supplementary Aids

Each local school system must provide a free appropriate public education for students with disabilities who require special education services and any related services as specified in the student's IEP. Related services include, but are not limited to, specialized transportation and such developmental, corrective and other supportive services as are required to assist a student with a disability to benefit from special education. These may be assistive technology devices, assistive technology services, audiological services, counseling services (including rehabilitation counseling), early identification and assessment services, educational interpreting services, medical services for diagnostic or evaluation purposes, physical and occupational therapies, psychological services, and recreation services (including therapeutic recreation). Related services also include parent counseling and training, school health services, school nutrition services, and social work services in schools.

Supplementary aids and services include, but are not limited to, assistive technology devices, assistive technology services, educational interpreting services, note takers, preferential seating, provision of assignments in writing, or other such services required to assist a student with a disability to benefit from the general education program. This applies to any education program in which the student may participate including art, music, physical education, and vocational education.

Rights of Students with Disabilities and Their Parents

IDEA guarantees procedural safeguards for students with disabilities and their parents in all areas relating to identification, evaluation, and placement. At one time, it was common practice to evaluate students and make changes in their educational program without their parents' knowledge or consent. This law makes parents important participants in the planning and execution of the educational program for their child. Parents must be notified and give their consent before the student is assessed or the educational program is changed. IDEA establishes specific procedures which must be followed from evaluation through placement and programming to protect the rights of students and parents. Specific due-process requirements under IDEA are:

- Written notice must be provided to parents and written parental permission obtained for the evaluation of a student for special education services. Parent participation in eligibility decisions is required.
- Parents may refuse special education services for their child.
- Written parental permission must be obtained before the school initiates or changes the placement of a student in special education services. Parent participation in all placement decisions is required.
- Parental notices must provide a description of the proposed actions and be written in the native language of the home.
- All matters relating to the student must be held confidential.
- Parents have the right to obtain an independent assessment of their child at their expense. The assessment may be at the expense of the school if the school agrees, or if it is required by a hearing officer.
- Parents have the right to inspect and review all educational records of their child. This law expands the privacy rights of all students that were legislated by the Family Rights and Privacy Act of 1974 (Buckley Amendment) to protect the privacy of an individual's records.
- Parents have the right to have records amended if information is inaccurate, misleading, no longer relevant to the child's education, or violates any rights of the child.

School systems provide parents with in-depth information about their rights regarding the special education of their child. This is usually presented as a parent's rights statement. These statements include topics such as: records, confidentiality of information, independent evaluation, notification of meetings and actions, parental consent, hearings, evaluation procedures, least restrictive environment, private school placement, and alternative educational settings.

In most cases, parents and school officials are able to reach agreement on the appropriate placement and programming for students. Disagreements can arise due to honest differences in opinion as to what is best for the student. When the parents and school do not agree about any part of the special education program, either party may request a due-process hearing. IDEA emphasizes mediation as the first step in conflict resolution. States now are required to create a mediation system in which parents and schools may participate voluntarily at the State's expense. If mediation is not successful in resolving the dispute or if the parent or school choose not to participate, the next step is a due process hearing before an impartial officer during which parents and school officials present evidence to challenge the placement or provision of services. If mediation is successful, a formal agreement must be written and signed. The hearing officer will decide on the appropriateness of the educational program. During the hearing parents and school officials have the right:

- To have legal counsel
- To present evidence and call witnesses

- To a written or taped record of the hearing
- To a written decision of the disposition of the case.

The decision of the hearing officer must be implemented unless it is appealed to the civil courts at either the state or federal level. The parents have the right to take their case directly to court bypassing the due-process hearing. However, in most cases when this has happened, the court has referred the case back to the due-process hearing.

The needs of students with disabilities are best met when schools and parents work together. This partnership between parents and the school is not easily formed and maintained. Some parents may be reluctant to participate, believing they do not have the expertise needed. Others may view schools as adversaries rather than partners. Chapter 10 discusses the importance of parents as team members in the educational process and provides suggestions to facilitate their involvement.

Summary

This chapter has outlined the legal foundation for special education. The relevant court cases and laws that have determined the rights and services available to individuals with disabilities were reviewed. The discussion of The Individuals with Disabilities Education Improvement Act (IDEA) and its requirements offers classroom teachers the basic information needed to understand their role in the provision of services to students with disabilities. The education of students with disabilities is a shared responsibility between general and special educators in partnership with parents. The more knowledgeable each participant in the process is, the more effective the delivery of services will be.

Name: _____   Date: _____

Discussion Questions and Activities

1. As a teacher or other school professional, if you had a question regarding the federal law mandate special education services (or your state's plan for implementation of those laws resources are available to you?

Internet Resources listed on next page
state.tn.us/education (any state)

2. Why do you think IDEA 97 mandated greater parent participation in eligibility and placement decisions for students with disabilities? What impact does this have on schools?

3. Contact your local school system and find out what information and materials are provided to parents of children with disabilities regarding their legal rights in regard to their child's education.

4. What is transition? Why was it mandated by IDEA? Why do you think IDEA 2004 added a postsecondary plan requirement to the transition plan by age 16?   *p. 18 and p 377-78*

Requires long-term planning & systematic instruction
Work-Based Education
School to Work Programs
Fewer programs available for MR adults

5. Walk around your College or University campus. How accessible is it for individuals with disabilities? List the modifications or adaptations that you see.

6. Prior to IDEA 97 students with disabilities often were excluded from State and district wide assessments. Why might schools want to exclude these students from assessments? Why should these students be included in the assessments?

7. Federal funds are provided to States for the education of students with disabilities. These funds then are passed from the state to the local education agency. The trend in government programs in recent years has been to reduce federal control of programs and funds and to increase local control. What do you see as the pros and cons of reducing federal controls and increasing local controls in the delivery of special education services?

Internet Resources

IDEA 2004
www.ed.gov/policy/speced/guid/idea/idea2004.html

No Child Left Behind
www.ed.gov/nclb/landing.jhtml?src=ln
www.whitehouse.gov/news/reports/no-child-left-behind.html

Office of Special Education and Rehabilitative Services
www.ed.gov/about/offices/list/osers/osep/index.html

Parent Advocacy Coalition for Educational Rights
www.pacer.org

Section 504
www.hhs.gov/ocr/504.html
www.504idea.org/504resources.html

Special Education Law
www.wrightslaw.com

U.S. Department of Education
www.ed.gov

References

Blackhurst, A. E., & Berdine, W. H. (1993). *An introduction to special education* (3rd ed.). New York: Harper Collins.

Haring, N. G., & McCormick, L. (Eds.). (1990). *Exceptional children and youth* (5th ed.). New York: Merrill/Macmillan.

Individuals with disabilities Education Act Amendments of 2004, P.L. 108-446, 108th Congress.

Martin, R. (1993). A checklist of questions to ask in determining LRE. *The Special Educator, 8,* 2.

Thomas, S. B., & Denzinger, C. A. (1993). *Special education law: Case summaries and federal regulations.* Topeka, KS: National Organization on Legal Problems in Education.

Wood, J. W. (1984). *Adapting instruction for the mainstream: A sequential approach to teaching.* New York: Merrill/Macmillan.

The Referral and Placement Process

Gwendolyn T. Benson and Harry L. Dangel

Chapter Objectives

- to describe the responsibilities of the classroom teacher in determining whether a student is eligible for special education services;
- to describe the types of information that general educators should use in helping to decide if a student needs special education services;
- to specify the type of accommodations that might be provided within the general education classroom prior to special education referral;
- to list and describe the elements of an Individualized Educational Program;
- to describe the function of other service plans for special education, such as Individualized Transition Plans and Individualized Family Service Plans; and
- to specify the rights and roles of parents in the eligibility and staffing process.

In Chapter 2 you read about the laws and regulations that are in place for providing special education services for students with disabilities. In this chapter, you will read about how the special education regulations operate in real life. Chapter 3 will walk you through the stages of referring a student for special education services, including gathering information and planning a program. Much of the material in this chapter focuses on younger students because students typically are referred for assessment and determined eligible for special education services when they are in elementary school. The process is the same for students who are identified and placed in later grades.

Ms. Winters first noticed that Miguel, age 9, seemed to be in a world of his own. It was clear from his lack of response when she had asked him to read, that he would require special attention and effort. He also seemed to make no attempt to solve the mix of two-digit addition and subtraction problems that she assigned to her lowest math group, and he sat looking out of the window when other students were doing independent seatwork. Just what she needed—one more problem student!!

The problem with 12-year-old Tiffany wasn't that she was unable to do the work—in fact on rare occasions she gave insightful comments on issues of recycling and ecology in her seventh-grade Earth Science class. What concerned Mr. Taylor were the periods of withdrawal from class discussion and refusal to participate along with outbursts of anger and defiance.

For Ms. Johnson, it wasn't that Ray was a problem. He was just one of 125 adolescents she saw each day in her 10th grade American History classes. The problem was that Ray, who had been labeled as having a learning disability, was going to be reevaluated, and Ms. Johnson had been asked to provide information that would be part of the deliberations. She didn't know about disabilities and psychological testing—she was a history teacher.

Just like these three teachers, some day you will be faced with individual students who are having difficulty in class and, like these teachers, must decide what to do next about meeting the needs of such students. In spite of differences in the ages and specific needs of each, there are common steps to be followed in deciding whether each student who is **at-risk** for failure is eligible for special education services and for the planning which follows. This chapter will focus on the role of the classroom teacher in the referral and placement process.

Determining Eligibility for Services

When is a student who is having problems in the classroom eligible for special education services? What is the process for getting a student placed in a special program? Those are basic questions which confront many classroom teachers when faced with students such as the ones described above. When a student's instructional needs (whether due to physical, sensory, learning/intellectual, developmental, or emotional/behavioral causes) lie beyond what a teacher is able to provide within the context of the general education class, then we think of special education as a possible option. That is to say that a student is eligible for special education services, not because special education services can be helpful (one might assume that providing an individualized program would be helpful for any student), but that general education teachers and programs cannot meet the student's needs. The determination of whether a student is eligible for special education is based on the fact that the student has been appropriately evaluated and meets the requirements for one of the federally defined categories of disability (i.e., autism, deaf-blind, serious emotional disturbance, hearing impairment, specific learning disabilities, mental retardation, multiple disabilities, orthopedic impairments, other health impairments, speech or language impairment, traumatic brain injury, or visual impairment). The impairment must have had a negative impact on the student's educational performance, and special educational services are needed due to the impairment.

A student's eligibility for placement and service in a particular special education program is

Most students who are eligible for special education services are identified within the first five years of school.

dictated first by the federal laws, especially the Individuals with Disabilities Education Improvement Act of 2004 (IDEA), which were described in Chapter 2, then by the operational guidelines established by each state's department of education, and finally by the procedural provisions adopted by the individual school system. Eligibility for special education services is established by an evaluation team of school professionals who, through formal and informal assessment procedures, decide whether a student meets the established eligibility criteria. From a teacher's viewpoint, the eligibility for special education services is based on three factors:

1. The student's problem is **significant** enough to require special instruction not available in the general education class.
2. The student's problem is **persistent** to the extent that it interferes with school success from year to year.
3. The student's problem is **inherent to (i.e., based in) the student** rather than just the result of a temporary difficulty, such as a home problem or conflict with a teacher.

Most students who are eligible for special education services are identified within the first five years of school. Students whose need for special education services are based on a physical or medical problem frequently are identified before coming to school. This would include students with visual impairment, hearing impairment, orthopedic impairment, or those exhibiting more severe forms of mental retardation. In general, the more severe a student's disability, the younger the student will be when identified as eligible for special education services. Parents and physicians identify many physical and developmental disabilities and provide the initial referral for special services. Students with more mild or subtle disabilities (e.g., learning disabilities, mild mental retardation, and even many sensory disabilities) typically are first noticed by an observant elementary-level teacher. Occasionally a student with a disability may not be identified until later if the disability is mild or is the result of some sudden problem, for example, the result of an injury which impacts learning abilities (e.g., a traumatic head injury) that occurred in later school years.

Figure 3-1 outlines the referral and placement procedures for special education services. The process in schools typically begins when a teacher judges a student's achievement, behavior, or development to be of concern. However, concern may be triggered by a source outside the classroom (e.g., a parent, speech-language pathologist, psychologist, or physician).

FIGURE 3-1

Referral and Placement Procedures

Step 1. Concern/Reflection:
- Observation of student exhibiting problems in achievement, behavior, or development.

Step 2. Prereferral for Specialized Interventions and Modifications:
- Prereferral team develops intervention plan to be implemented in the general education classroom.

Step 3. Referral for Special Education Services:
- If the prereferral intervention plan is unsuccessful, the student is referred for evaluation by a multidisciplinary team to determine eligibility for services.

Step 4. Develop the Individualized Educational Program (IEP):
- If the student is eligible for services, the staffing team meets and plans goals, objectives, service delivery, and placement.

Concern and Reflection

Although general education teachers play a major role in each of the four steps of the Referral and Placement Procedures, the process of finding and identifying students who need special education service usually begins with an observant and concerned general education teacher. It is the general education teacher's awareness that a student has not been making the same progress as other students or whose social/emotional behaviors interfere with the student's learning or the learning of others that typically starts the process. When Ms. Winters first noticed Miguel's poor performance in reading and math classes, she started to ask herself some questions about the circumstances surrounding his performance. As was noted above, the student's problems need to be **significant, persistent,** and **inherent to the student.** The questions below are designed to help teachers decide whether a student's problems are significant and persistent.

The best frame of reference for any teacher to use in deciding that a student's problems are **significant** and **persistent** is to compare the classroom performance of that individual with the rest of the class in those areas that might typically indicate a disability. The most definitive of these are basic academic skills as indicated by the questions below:

1. **Does the student's past record indicate a pattern of consistently low academic performance?**

   To answer this, a teacher needs to review a student's permanent record file. This record of the history of a student's school performance will provide a starting point for judging the relative severity of the problem. The teacher should consider the following evidence:

   a. Has the student repeated any grade levels? For example, having to repeat second grade is an indication of a significant academic problem.
   b. What is the pattern of grades that the student has earned? If a student has, for example, always earned "Ds" and "Fs" in reading across the years, it would be evidence of a problem.
   c. What is the pattern of scores on standardized measurements of progress? If a student's scores on group achievement tests (e.g., Iowa Test of Basic Skills) or criterion-referenced tests that are given to measure individual and school-wide progress is consistently in the bottom 25% of the class in that grade level at the student's school (and also below grade level norms), the student has a significant academic problem. Note that it is recommended that the standard for this be the student's classmates to minimize the likelihood of low achievement being caused by the quality of the teaching or limitations of the curriculum.

2. **Does the student's current academic performance indicate a pattern of low academic performance?**

   Figure 3-2 lists the basic academic areas of reading, written expression, mathematics, content mastery and the student performance that would raise concerns in each area. By reviewing a student's classroom performance compared to classmates, a teacher can more accurately determine whether that performance is a matter of concern. The questions below ask the teacher to determine if a student is in the lower one-fourth of the class in specific areas that are critical for school success. That is to say, in a class of 24 other students, is this student's performance one of the six lowest? In this early stage of identification for possible special education services, the standard of lowest one-fourth is used to be relatively inclusive in identifying students having difficulty so as not to miss a student who should be referred for further evaluation.

FIGURE 3-2

Statement of Status Checklist

Academic Area	Observed Behaviors place student in the lower 1/4 of the class when performance is compared with classmates
BASIC READING SKILLS (the ability to recognize and decode words). Students should be in the second half of first grade or above to evaluate this section.	1. Word recognition of the reading material used in class is in lower ¼ of class. 2. Word recognition is below 90%. 3. Number of correct words per minute in oral reading is in lower ¼ of class.
READING COMPREHENSION (the ability to understand and relate information about what has been read). Students should be in the second half of first grade or above to evaluate this section.	1. Retelling information after reading it is in lower ¼ of class. 2. Accurately paraphrasing material after reading it is in lower ¼ of class. 3. Predicting unknown or missing word (cloze) from context is in lower ¼ of class.
WRITTEN EXPRESSION (the ability to express ideas in writing). This area is evaluated only after written composition skills have been taught, typically second grade or higher.	1. Communicates ideas when using written expression is in lower ¼ of class, i.e., meaningful, age-appropriate sentence or paragraph(s) (disregarding handwriting, capitalization, punctuation, spelling, and grammar). 2. Organization of written expression (e.g., idea development is logical) is in lower ¼ of class. Productivity in written expression (number of words, sentences, and words per sentence) is in lower ¼ of class.
MATHEMATICS (the ability to use basic arithmetic operations, to comprehend a problem statement and to determine what operations and numerals are necessary to solve this problem). Students should be in the second half of first grade or higher to evaluate this area.	1. Accuracy of daily assignments in arithmetic operations is in lower ¼ of class (to include those aspects of numeration, addition, subtraction, multiplication, division, fractions and decimals, etc. that have been introduced to the student). 2. Mastery of mathematical facts and operations for grade level is in lower ¼ of class. 3. Accuracy in solving mathematical word problems is in lower ¼ of class. 4. Mastery of the language of mathematics in lower ¼ of class, e.g. time, money, measurement, terms of quantitative relationships, geometry, etc.
CONTENT MASTERY (the ability to apply basic learning skills—listening, reading, writing—to content areas, e.g., science, social studies, health) Students should be in third grade or above to evaluate this area.	1. Understanding of content vocabulary is in lower ¼ of class. 2. Verbal contributions to class discussions are in lower ¼ of class, even when reading was not required for understanding. 3. Performance in relating concepts presented in class to real-world examples is in lower ¼ of class.

Adapted from Dangel & Ensminger, 1999

FIGURE 3-3

Concern and Reflection

Questions to Ask	Observations
Is it an opportunity issue?	• Has the student been present and attentive for the instruction? • Is the problem only with material that is newly presented? • Have this student's opportunities for success been as plentiful and systematic as for others?
Is it an issue related to the student's background?	• Does the student's language background differ from the predominant language used in the classroom and in classroom materials? • Do differences in the student's life experiences make it difficult to meet the expectations of the classroom?
Is it a performance issue?	• Does the student appear to make an appropriate effort to do the work? • Does a change in incentives/rewards correct the problem? • What if rewards are different, clearly available, immediately delivered?
Is it a situation issue?	• Does the problem occur with clearly defined times, places or with certain persons (e.g., before or after lunch, end or beginning of the day, group or independent activities)?
Is it a content issue?	• Does the problem occur in an isolated content area, such as math or social studies, or is the problem generalized across areas?
Is the apparent problem improving?	• Is the problem and the effect it has on the student getting better, worse, or staying the same?

After a teacher has established a concern, i.e., has determined that a student's classroom performance is significantly and persistently below classmates, it is important to gather additional information about the nature of the student's apparent problems. The next set of questions to be answered deal with why the apparent classroom performance problems are occurring. They are detailed in **Figure 3-3.**

A teacher answers the questions posed in **Figure 3-3** by reviewing the past and defining the present. Reviewing the past means that a teacher, such as Mrs. Winters, can get a great deal of valuable information about any student who is having difficulties by examining the information in the student's permanent record file. The patterns of attendance, achievement performances, promotions and reports of behavioral difficulties offer helpful information related to a teacher's concerns and reflections about a student's progress.

Reviewing the Past

Reviewing the student's background documents the extent to which a student's problem has been a persistent problem, offers insight as to the severity of the problem, and provides information as to whether the problem is inherent to the student. Although a student's background and past performance are, at best, imperfect indicators of current and future instructional needs, they should not be overlooked. Potentially valuable information may be available from parents or in a permanent folder (see **Figure 3-4**). By examining a student's past performance the teacher can answer questions about:

FIGURE 3-4

Defining Classroom Variables

Reviewing the Past

Opportunities to Learn	Parent information
	Good School Attendance
	Attended Preschool
Instruction	Previous grades
	Standardized tests
Curriculum	Previous instructional programs
Delivery of service	Retention
	Previous special programs

- What previous opportunities to learn have been provided?
- What is the pattern of success to previous instruction?
- What was the curriculum that was taught previously?
- What types of special provisions have been used to deliver the instructional program?

Conversing with a parent, whether a formal meeting or a telephone call, offers an opportunity to assess a student's or even a family's history of access to learning materials and school success. In the case of a young student, a parent's report gives an invaluable picture about developmental milestones and preschool opportunities. A parent can provide information on medical problems that might impact school success. A parent's response to questions about a student's per-

Contact with parents and the information they can provide regarding medical problems, educational history, and the student's perception of school is very important.

ception of school—such as favorite class activities—can give a different and sometimes important view of a student in school. In spite of the fact that a parent may present an overly positive view of a student and that the parents of students who are struggling in school may be the ones least likely to come to school, contacts with parents and the information they can provide are important.

Ms. Winters considers the following questions before meeting with Miguel's parents:

1. What does M. tell you that he likes most (or least) about school this year?

What do M.'s parents report about the classroom that he likes? Anything? Does it match with what you have observed? How might you use this information to work with M.?

2. What did M. say about school last year? What did he like?

How does the report of previous years in school match with this year's? Does the report seem accurate? Are there areas of interest that could be included in programming for M.?

3. What does M. enjoy doing in his free time? Does he ever look at magazines or books?

How does M. spend his time? Is there evidence of M. reading outside of school? Do there appear to be opportunities to interact with reading material?

4. Who are M.'s playmates? What do they do together?

Does M. interact with any other students from the class outside of school? Does he choose students of the same age or children who are younger? Does he appear to be involved in any organized activities? Does he play games in which he must follow rules and structure?

5. Are there any medical or physical problems of which I should be aware when working with M.?

Is there any information related to M.'s health that might help explain the lack of class involvement? Are there other professionals who have worked with M. who might be helpful?

Another source of information about a student's past school performance is the permanent record file. The permanent record is the accumulated information about a student's school performance. It can be used to help evaluate a student's previous access to learning materials and the pattern of previous school progress. The permanent record also can be used to corroborate information received from parents. **Figure 3-5** is a page from Miguel's permanent record file.

Ms. Winters can judge the extent to which he has had access to opportunities to learn by reviewing this information. She notes his preschool experiences (he attended both a preschool and kindergarten program), his age (he entered first grade at age 6 years-6 months—at about the same age as other students) his attendance (he has not missed more than four days of school in any year), and the extent to which he perhaps has been moved from school to school and as a result, had his education disrupted (he has been enrolled in the same school system for all of his school experiences).

This information is important because it confirms for Ms. Winters that Miguel has had appropriate opportunities to learn. Had he not had preschool experiences or been unusually young compared to other students, or been absent from school for extended periods, or moved frequently from one school to another (especially during the school year), some of his academic problems might be attributed to a lack of opportunity or disrupted opportunity to learn rather than to an inability to learn.

FIGURE 3-5

Permanent Record File—Miguel, page 1

Name	Jones, Miguel R.		*Parents/Guardian*	William and Martha Jones
Address	2342 Newton Street, Summerville, USA			
Phone	(770) 555-4321		*Date of Birth*	3-5-nine years ago

Date	*School*	*Placement*	*Days Present*	*Days Absent*
• 5 years ago	Private preschool	Preschool	na	na
• 4 years ago	Washington Elementary	Kindergarten	178	2
• 3 years age	Washington Elementary	1st grade	176	4
• 2 years ago	Washington Elementary	2nd grade	178	2
• last year	Washington Elementary	2nd grade	179	1
• this year	Washington Elementary	3rd grade		

Placement	*Reading* *Grd./Lev.*	*Arith.* *Grd./Lev.*	*Writing* *Grd./Lev.*	*Social* *Studies*	*Science* *Grd.*	*Conduct*	*Standard* *Text Results*
• First Grade	C 1.0	C 1.5	C 1.5	B	na	B	Total 1.2
• Second Grade	F 1.2	F 1.5	D 1.2	F	D	D	Not given
• Second Grade	C 1.5	D 2.0	C 1.8	B	C	B	Not given
• Third Grade	D 2.0	F 2.3	F 1.8	C	F	D	Total 1.8

The permanent record also allows Ms. Winters to review the extent of Miguel's academic progress and make a determination about the effectiveness of past instruction. She examines the pattern of grades (he did relatively well in first grade but started to earn failing grades in second grade), the pattern of performance on standardized tests (Miguel has been consistently well below average), and any indication of being retained in a grade (Miguel repeated second grade).

The pattern of academic progress in Miguel's permanent record is one of continuing difficulty. The near average grade performance in first grade is the only suggestion of possible average progress. Was this because that teacher saw some achievement progress that has since been lost, or was it because the teacher avoided giving a low grade and was waiting for him to "grow out of it"? Ms. Winters will need to interpret the achievement information based on what she knows about the school's achievement pattern and program in which Miguel is enrolled. If, for example, his below average academic performance on standardized achievement tests is within the range of what other students in his class have scored, Miguel would not be seen as "at-risk". If, however, other students who experienced the same instruction scored above average on standardized measures, Miguel would be considered "at-risk" and be more likely to need special education services.

Finally, Ms. Winters will review whether the curriculum or the delivery of services ever have been changed for Miguel. Sometimes a student, such as Miguel, who has been experiencing difficulty in school will have been given some special instruction. This may be done through a special general education program, such as Title 1 (a federally funded compensatory program for at-risk students), Reading Recovery (an intensive individualized reading program in general education), or special support from a trained paraprofessional. If Miguel has received any of these special services previously and is still having significant problems, we would consider him to be more at-risk for subsequent school failure.

FIGURE 3-6

Permanent Record File—Tiffany, page 1

Name	Bishop, Tiffany C.	*Parents/Guardian*	Bart and Betsy Bishop
Address	412 Walnut Drive, Summerville, USA		
Phone	(770) 555-1234	*Date of Birth*	7-22-twelve years ago

Date	*School*	*Placement*	*Days Present*	*Days Absent*
• 7 years ago	Washington Elementary	Kindergarten	178	2
• 6 years ago	Washington Elementary	Grade 1	177	3
• 5 years age	Washington Elementary	Grade 2	180	0
• 4 years ago	Washington Elementary	Grade 3	177	3
• 3 years age	Washington Elementary	Grade 4	163	17
• 2 years ago	Washington Elementary	Grade 5	151	29
• 1 year ago	Adams Middle School	Grade 6	148	32
• this year	Adams Middle School	Grade 7		

Placement	*Reading Grd./Lev.*	*Arith. Grd./Lev.*	*Writing Grd./Lev.*	*Social Studies*	*Science Grd.*	*Conduct*	*Standard Test Results*
• Kindergarten							
• Grade 1	B 1.8	C 1.5	B 1.9	C	na	B	Total 1.7
• Grade 2	B 2.7	C 2.1	B 2.6	C	C	B	Not given
• Grade 3	B+ 3.8	C 3.0	C 3.4	B	C–	B–	Total 3.4
• Grade 4	C 4.4	D 3.8	B 4.6	B	D	D	Not given
• Grade 5	B 5.5	D 3.2	A 5.7	C	F	D	Total 5.1
• Grade 6	A 6.6	F 3.4	B 6.7	B	F	F	Not given

In general, the longer a student is enrolled in school, the more potentially valuable information will be accumulated from attendance patterns, grades, standardized achievement measures, and teachers' observations. Thus, the permanent records of a middle school student would provide a richer source of school-related data than would the file of an elementary level student. Note in the example for Tiffany in **Figure 3-6,** the information Mr. Taylor might obtain about her behavior rather than academic problems.

Tiffany's permanent records indicate that when she got to fifth and sixth grades she missed nearly one day of school per week (based on a 180-day school year). What was the pattern of these absences? Did she miss several extended periods each year or were the absences scattered throughout the year? Her records also reveal that her achievement levels have gone up in nearly every subject (e.g., reading), except arithmetic, where they have been relatively flat for the past three years. Why did she make adequate progress in arithmetic for the first three years and none since? And then there are the conduct grades which have gone from "Bs" the first three years in school to "Ds" and an "F".

The Prereferral Process

After Ms. Winters had confirmed for herself that Miguel was clearly falling further behind the other students in her class, she decided that he (and for that matter—she) needed some additional help. She knew that in her school system the first step to getting special help for a student was to go to the prereferral team.

A **prereferral team** (sometimes called a student support team or student study team) is composed of those educators with information about a student who can plan, implement, and evaluate the effectiveness of various modifications and adaptations in a general education classroom. Although a prereferral team is not required by federal regulations, many states now require that students being referred for possible special education services go through the prereferral process prior to determining eligibility for special education (Kovaleski, Gickling, Morrow, & Swank, 1999; Rhodes, Ochoa, & Ortiz, 2005). The purpose of a prereferral team is to determine whether a student can be successful in a general education class if additional accommodations and modifications are made. The team typically includes the teacher who has identified a concern about a student and a group of other classroom teachers and support personnel. It is often helpful to have other teachers on the team who teach at the same grade level or in the same content area in which the student of concern is currently placed (e.g., other third-grade teachers or math teachers). In addition to teachers, support personnel such as a school counselor, a speech-language pathologist, or a special education teacher might be included to provide specific help.

The purpose of a prereferral team is to determine whether a student can be successful in a general education class if additional accommodations and modifications are made.

The prereferral team has been found to have several advantages (Craig, Hull, Haggart, & Perez-Selles, 2000; Kerr, Nelson, & Lambert, 1987; Strickland & Turnbull, 1990; Stump, 2002).

- Systematic prereferral intervention tends to reduce the number of inappropriate referrals to special education.
- Teams can reduce the overrepresentation of minority groups in special education.
- These teams gather information that can be used to evaluate a student for possible special education services.
- Teams can provide immediate intervention without waiting for eligibility to be established.
- Teams can promote the inclusion of culturally relevant curricular content.
- The approach takes advantage of the expertise of those teachers who have been working most closely with a student.
- Prereferral teams can help to refine vague or subjective referrals.
- Teams can promote cooperation between the general educator and the special educator.
- Teams help to promote acceptance and support within the general education program for students with disabilities.

The prereferral team answers the question of whether or not a student should be referred for evaluation for special education services by examining four aspects of schooling: **opportunities to learn, instruction, curriculum, and delivery of services** (see **Figure 3-7**). These four elements are not only components for providing special education services and the Individualized Educational Program (discussed later in this chapter), but also are factors for determining a student's eligibility for special services.

It is best to think of the decision about whether a student should be referred and placed in a special education program as a **dynamic** rather than a **static** assessment of

FIGURE 3-7

Prereferral Information

	Reviewing the Past	Defining the Present	Evaluating the Changes
Opportunities to Learn	• Parent information • Attendance • Preschool	• Sensory screening	• Provide access
Instruction	• Previous grades • Standardized tests	• Observations • Checklists	• Adapt instruction
Curriculum	• Previous programs	• Current program	• Adjust curriculum
Delivery of Service	• Retention • Special programs	• Define setting	• Alter delivery of services

learning and/or behavior. That is to say, a decision can be made more accurately from multiple sources of information about opportunities to learn, instruction, curriculum, and delivery of services which include a look at the student across time and settings. The difference between using multiple sources of information to develop a dynamic view of a student rather than a set of static scores is similar to the difference between learning about a child from a videotape as opposed to a snapshot. Because learning and behavior are active, rather than static concepts, a dynamic picture is needed (Adelman & Taylor, 1993; Stump, 2002).

The dynamic view of a student requires examining past performance and possible problems, a description of the present performance, and an evaluation of what has happened when access, instruction, curriculum, and delivery models have been changed. Using only a set of numbers or scores projects an image of a student's performance that is static or fixed in time.

Defining Present Performance

Carefully describing a student's classroom performance is a major component of the referral process because it helps determine how serious the problem might be. The more precisely we can describe what a student does in the classroom, the more useful the information can be for making placement decisions and ultimately for developing a program for that student. As with reviewing the past, the prereferral team will examine opportunities to learn, instruction, curriculum, and delivery of services in defining present performance.

To determine if a student has had **access to opportunities to learn,** vision and hearing screenings are conducted. Sometimes these screenings are done as part of the eligibility testing for placement in special education, but we recommend that they occur at the prereferral level to rule out sensory impairment. The sensory screening involves checking visual and auditory **acuity.** Acuity is the term used to define the clarity of sensory information. The screening is to determine whether the student can see and hear clearly enough to learn in the classroom. Visual acuity usually is established by having a student identify letters on the Snellen eye chart. Auditory acuity usually is measured by having students respond to tones produced by an audiometer. The vision and hearing screening are only gross indicators of acuity. If a student's acuity falls below the standards for acceptable performance, the parent is notified and requested to obtain a more in-depth evaluation from an appropriate professional. For example, what appears to be difficulty in following directions may actually be poor auditory acuity (i.e., the student couldn't hear the teacher). The acuity problem might be remediated through medical intervention rather than placement in a special education program.

Classroom observations are used to describe a student's present response to **instruction.** The observations and descriptions are critical to understanding a student's problems and should include these elements:

1. Use words that **describe observable behaviors** rather than words that make a judgement about behavior. For example, avoid words such as learn, know, and understand which are not clearly observable. Note how observable terms are used in place of these words:

> **NOT** *Miguel can't* ***learn his spelling words.***
> **BUT** *Miguel* ***writes his spelling words incorrectly.***
> **NOT** *Miguel doesn't* ***understand how to read.***
> **BUT** *Miguel* ***miscalls basic sight words.***

In each case the preferred form of reporting the student's classroom performance is a form that can be observed and confirmed by another professional. It is also preferable, when possible, to describe what the student does, rather than what the student doesn't do. For example:

> **NOT** *Tiffany will* ***not listen to the teacher.***
> **BUT** *Tiffany continued to* ***speak out of turn.***

2. It also is useful to **define the conditions** under which the student's behavior occurred. For example, it would help to have information that:

> Miguel writes his spelling words incorrectly **when the teacher dictates them for the Friday spelling test.**
> Miguel miscalls basic sight words **when orally reading from a graded text.**
> Miguel does not respond verbally **when asked his name.**
> Tiffany spoke out of turn **during a class discussion of the reading assignment.**

In each example the additional information about the conditions under which the behavior occurred helps to explain the behavior. The condition statement might include the content or materials being used, the action of the teacher, or the classroom setting. Frequently the behavior that is of concern is so prevalent that the statement of behavior serves as an example various situations or settings.

3. It is also helpful to provide some objective information regarding the **extent or frequency** of the behavior that is being described. Such a description can take the form of a percentage:

> Miguel writes his spelling words incorrectly **an average of 60% of the time** when the teacher dictates them for the Friday spelling test.
> Miguel miscalls basic sight words when orally reading from a graded text **50% of the time.**

Other times, a statement of **frequency** provides a better means of defining the extent to which a behavior occurs. For example:

> **Miguel does not respond verbally when asked his name 2 of 3 times.**
>
> **Tiffany spoke out of turn 12 times during a class discussion of the reading assignment.**

By specifying the percentage or frequency of a target behavior, a teacher can note both the circumstances under which the behavior occurs and detect any changes in the extent to which the behavior occurs.

4. The final component of reporting information about the instruction is to specify what positive reinforcers were used to promote the student's performance. Reinforcers are the positive consequences we provide students for their efforts to do something (e.g., a star on a completed assignment, free time after an exam, etc.). Ms. Winters must consider the following:

> - **Was a reinforcer provided to Miguel for working on his math assignment? An effective reinforcer will encourage him to try, although it won't enable Miguel to do work accurately if he hasn't mastered the skills.**
> - **Was Miguel aware of the reinforcer? What effect did it appear to have? Does Miguel make more of an effort when working for the reinforcer? If so, what reinforcer was used and when was it administered? If not, does his performance improve when a reinforcer is provided?**
> - **Does Miguel ever do the math work? Under what conditions?**

Defining present performance on **curriculum** and **delivery of service** involves specifying the content and skills that have been presented to the student and describing how instruction is presented, including the grouping of students. For example, Ms. Winters reports to her colleagues that Miguel is reading in the first-grade reader in their literature-based reading series, doing mixed addition and subtraction (first-grade level work at her school), using manuscript for printing his written work, and working with the rest of the students on their unit on the community. He is grouped with her lowest reading and math groups and shows little interaction with other students during student-directed unit activities. A student's work samples also offer a rich source of information about present levels of performance. Maintaining the set of spelling tests from week to week, for example, allows Ms. Winters to note that Miguel often spells phonetically regular words correctly, but misses those words which require "just remembering" silent letters or non-phonetic spelling. Math worksheets, samples of written expression, reading worksheets, and questions from the end of chapters in content areas offer insight into a student's work patterns. See **Figure 3-8** for examples of work samples.

The actual operation of a prereferral team during the review of past and present student information may be as formal or informal as necessary. It is highly recommended that careful notes are taken regarding what has been tried with a student and what seems to work or not to work.

FIGURE 3-8

Work Samples

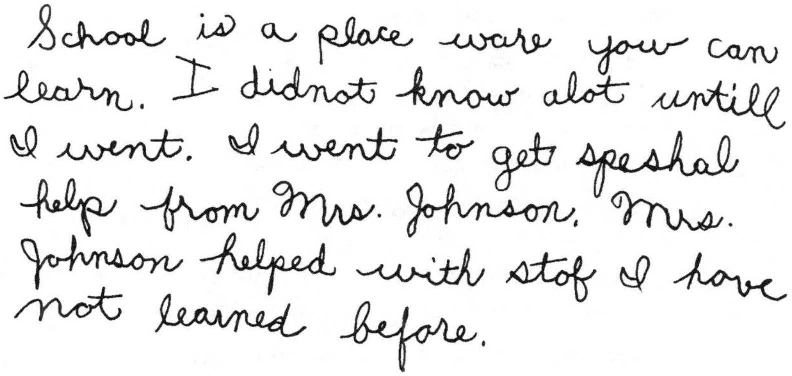

School is a place ware your can learn. I didnot know alot untill I went. I went to get speshal help from Mrs. Johnson. Mrs. Johnson helped with stof I have not learned before.

Marc spells words the way they sound.

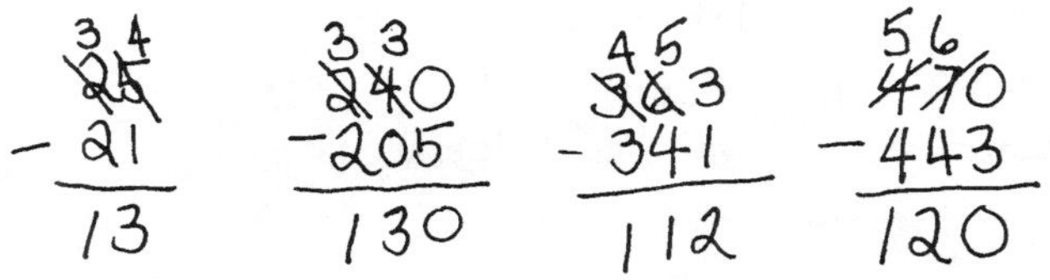

$$-\frac{\begin{array}{r}3\,4\\ \cancel{2}\cancel{5}\end{array}}{\begin{array}{r}21\\ \hline 13\end{array}}$$

$$\begin{array}{r}3\;3\\ \cancel{2}\cancel{4}0\\ -205\\ \hline 130\end{array}$$

$$\begin{array}{r}4\;5\\ \cancel{3}\cancel{8}3\\ -341\\ \hline 112\end{array}$$

$$\begin{array}{r}5\;6\\ \cancel{4}\cancel{7}0\\ -443\\ \hline 120\end{array}$$

Susan works left to right in subtraction

Evaluating Changes

One of the most important aspects of a prereferral team's intervention is an evaluation of the impact of modifications to materials, instruction, curriculum, and delivery of services. These interventions are designed, implemented, and evaluated by general educators in an attempt to determine whether making modifications to their classroom procedures results in improvements for the student (see **Figure 3-9**).

Modifying materials indicates that the team typically would plan to have the student who is at-risk use the same books, worksheets, learning centers, and other instructional materials as are used for the rest of the students in the class. **Modifying** instruction means that a teacher would be expected just to vary the same methods employed with the rest of the class for the referred student. Because the curriculum relates to the information, skills, and concepts that the teacher is expected to teach, **modifying** the curriculum at the prereferral level typically involves presenting less material in each activity (e.g., covering the social studies chapter one section at a time rather than all at once, or reducing the number of spelling words covered on each test). **Modifying** the delivery system involves staying in the general education classroom with age peers while perhaps changing the room arrangement, or grouping to evaluate its effect.

When Ms. Winters meets with her school's prereferral team, she brings a copy of Miguel's permanent record, examples of his work in her class, and the notes she has taken about what has bothered her about his classroom work. Although there are several areas in which Miguel needs help, the team decides to focus only on his work in math to see if a focused approach in one area will make a difference.

FIGURE 3-9

Prereferral Interventions

Examples of Prereferral Accommodations

Modifying Materials	• Highlight instructions • Separate worksheets into sections • Use transparencies of worksheets • Allow more time to complete work
Modifying Instruction	• Model how to do assignment • Provide additional practice • Provide immediate corrective feedback • Provide more frequent reinforcement
Modifying the Curriculum	• Reduce amount of information presented at one time • Isolate the type of problems • Prioritize critical skills
Modifying the Delivery of Services	• Change student's seat • Match student with peer helper

After meeting to examine Ms. Winters's report on Miguel, the prereferral team makes the following set of recommendations to help him improve his performance in arithmetic class:

- **Modifications** to learning materials are to be provided by dividing each page of problems into separate sections and having Miguel complete one section at a time, rather than doing the entire page.

- **Modifications** are to be made to the instruction by having Ms. Winters demonstrate how to do the first problem on each of the first three lines, giving Miguel feedback on his first problem on each line, and providing free time for getting 80% correct.

- **Modifications** are to be made regarding the curriculum by having Miguel first do only the addition problems, having those checked, and then trying the subtraction problems.

- **Modifications** are to be made in the delivery of services by moving Miguel to the front of the room to be seated next to Thomas, a friend who does well in arithmetic class.

None of these require Ms. Winters to teach different material or teach in a manner or set up conditions that are qualitatively different. Rather, she conducts the class and instructs her students in the same manner as before, except that Miguel, seated next to Thomas for help, works through the problems in a controlled fashion, and gets more direct instruction and feedback.

After four weeks of trying these modifications with Miguel, Ms. Winters is ready for the prereferral team to review the results. She collects all of his math worksheets and although Miguel seemed to enjoy the additional attention and he appeared to be trying his best to do the work that was assigned, he still is averaging only 47% correct. His performance remains far below that of his classmates. Ms. Winters reports to the team that she judges that Miguel needs more help. The prereferral team meets and concludes that they have documented that Miguel needs more than the accommodations that Ms. Winters can provide. The team recommends that he be referred for a special education evaluation.

Issues of Diversity

In the last quarter of the twentieth century, the profile of students in American public schools has changed significantly. In 2004, students with single parents usually (three-quarters of the time) had that parent working outside the home (Bureau of Labor Statistics, 2005) and in seven of the ten largest school systems, more that 25% of the students lived in homes that fell below the poverty level (National Center for Educational Statistics, 2003). During the reauthorization of the IDEA (1997), Congress examined research on the general profile and academic performance of students with disabilities in schools. The data indicated that students with disabilities were more likely than other students to come from families with low socioeconomic status and families whose parents had less formal education (U. S. Department of Education, 2004).

As noted in Chapter 1, the growing diversity of the school population and the tendency for students from nontraditional homes to sometimes experience learning and behavior difficulties in school requires special attention in the evaluation, labeling, and placement of at-risk students. Data on the educational performance of these students have indicated that they are achieving below their potential (Cartledge, 1999; U.S. Department of Education, 2002) and that a disproportionate number of them are inappropriately referred to, and placed in, special education (Artiles, 1998; Yates, 1998). When this happens repeatedly and primarily to one group of students in a school district, it results in a disproportionate percentage of group membership in special education. Overrepresentation occurs when the percentage of minority students in special education exceeds the percentage of these students in the total student population (Zhang & Katsiyannis, 2002). According to the Administrators Guide on Addressing Over-Representation of African American Students in Special Education (National Alliance of Black School Educators (NABSE) & ILIAD Project, 2002), when such disproportionality occurs, the entire school community, including teachers, administrators, school board members, community leaders, and family members, must ask the question, "Why is this group of students over-represented in special education?" In many cases, the answer will lead stakeholders to examine general education program practices and consider strategies, particularly those related to school climate, prereferral intervention practices, family involvement, and professional development, that may prevent and/or reduce the incidence of over-representation.

Federal guidelines require protection of the rights of students by ensuring that nondiscriminatory testing procedures be followed. IDEA 2004 has increased the protection for students with diverse backgrounds by adding safeguards to prevent misidentification of students with racial, ethnic, and language diversity (NICHCY, 2004). New requirements include collection and examination of data regarding disproportionality, including identification in accordance with a particular disability, placement in a particular educational setting, and incidence (suspension, expulsion) duration, and type of disciplinary actions. These will be discussed further in the section on Multidisciplinary Team evaluation procedures. For the prereferral team, sensitivity to the cultural background of each student needs to be considered in several areas. Language and communication skills are a direct product of an individual's background and experiences. Teachers need to consider these when evaluating whether an academic problem is due to a lack of opportunity to learn or is inherent to the student. For example, what appears to be a reading comprehension problem may be the result of a limited vocabulary due to English being the second language learned. A second factor is the influence of cultural differences on behavior. A student who is reluctant to ask for help and avoids the teacher's eye contact may be responding appropriately within the expectations of that student's culture. The student's teacher, however, may consider the student withdrawn. Third, there is evidence that some culturally diverse students experience more mobility and dislocation than students raised in majority culture homes (Smith & Lucksson, 1992). For example, some families of these students may be migrant workers, while in other cases, families may move frequently based on financial or family dynamics. Regardless of the reasons, frequent family moves from school to school can disrupt a student's schooling. The disruption can be severe enough to make it appear as if that student's academic or behavior performance is due to a disability.

An *"At-A-Glance"* reference sheet that describes what teachers should do at various phases prior to, during, and after the pre-referral team meets is provided for your convenience.

At-A-Glance Reference Sheet for Teachers

What teachers should do prior to referral to the Pre-referral Team:
1. Document difficulties the student may have with instruction and try to determine possible reasons for the problems.
2. Provide and document classroom modifications and/or other strategies.
3. Assess interventions (modifications and/or other strategies) to ensure that they are appropriate and successful.
4. Monitor the student's progress for a significant period of time.
5. Determine to what extent learning and/or behavioral difficulty persists in spite of interventions used.
6. Meet with parent/guardian if interventions were unsuccessful.

What teachers should do at the point of referral to the Pre-referral Team:
1. Become familiar with the possible roles of pre-referral team members.
2. Identify team members who have experience using and designing instructional techniques that address the individual needs of students.
3. Compile student performance data.
4. Continue to document classroom modifications and/or other strategies.
5. Maintain communication with parent/guardian.

What teachers should do after the first Pre-referral Team Meeting:
1. Implement and monitor the effectiveness of intervention strategies recommended by the Pre-referral Team.
2. Pay close attention to the length of time each intervention is attempted.
3. Maintain communication with parent/guardian.

What teachers should do if the student does not show progress and is not eligible for Special Education Services:
1. Continue to document classroom modifications and/or other strategies.
2. Continue to compile student performance data.
3. Seek additional assistance from educators with expertise in designing techniques that address the individual needs of students.
4. Consider whether the student would be eligible for Section 504 services (this determination should be facilitated by the pre-referral team).
5. Solicit support from school administrators and other teachers.

Referral for Special Education Services

The multidisciplinary team, sometimes called the special services team, has the responsibility for determining whether a student referred for possible special education placement, actually meets the eligibility requirements for special education as defined by federal and state regulations. They are the ones who collect and analyze the information about a student's referral for possible special education services. The team must include a school psychologist, a special educator, and a representative from general education. The provisions of IDEA 2004 specify the rights of students and parents that must be protected during the referral and evaluation process. These rights have been presented in Chapter 2.

As noted earlier, most of the students who are placed in special education programs are identified in elementary school. The probability that a student will be referred and receive service in learning disabilities, for example, is primarily due to the likelihood of the general educator making a referral (Colarusso, Keel, & Dangel, 2001). The decision of whether a student needs special education services must include information from a representative of general education, hopefully the classroom teacher, as well as from those specialists trained to evaluate and service students with special needs, that is school psychologists and special education teachers. The **general educator** is a key member of the team because of the important perspective this professional brings to the decision-making process.

> **Regarding Miguel, Ms. Winters might consider:**
>
> • **How does the typical second-grade student perform in my reading or math class and how is Miguel the same or different?**
>
> • **What has been the pattern of his progress in school?**
>
> • **What classroom-based evidence, such as work samples, is there that illustrate his typical school problems?**

The **special educator,** either a teacher or a specially trained diagnostician, can provide insight from observations of the student, especially when using structured checklists that might relate to classroom behaviors. Specific achievement test results usually are provided by a special educator, as well as information as to the type of interventions that might be needed for a particular student and the guidelines for eligibility. The **school psychologist** is trained to administer and interpret standardized tests, especially tests of intelligence. When appropriate, adaptive behavior (possible mental retardation) and personality assessments (possible emotional/behavior disorders) are administered by the school psychologist. In the case of a communication disorder, a **speech-language pathologist** would assess speech and language functioning. If a hearing loss is suspected, an **audiologist** would conduct an in-depth evaluation of hearing.

Children with more obvious disabilities, for example orthopedic impairments such as cerebral palsy, severe intellectual disabilities, or severe visual impairment, usually are identified by parents, physicians, or by preschool teachers before enrolling in school. A **Child Find** program is required by federal law in each state to help coordinate efforts of medical, social, and community agencies in identifying children with special needs who are not yet in public school programs. Additionally, a parent of a child, a state or local educational agency, or other state agency may initiate a request for an initial evaluation to determine if the child is a child with a disability (IDEA 2004).

FIGURE 3-10

Sources of Eligibility Information

Source	Information Provided
General Education Teacher	• progress records • intervention results • work samples
Special Educator	• achievement testing • observations • checklists
Psychologist	• intelligence testing • personality testing • adaptive behavior assessment
Other Specialists —Speech-Language Pathologist —Audiologist —Physician —Social Worker	• speech and language assessment • hearing assessment • medical information • information on home environment
Parents	• background information • information on development • interests and activities

Determining Eligibility

Today Ms. Winters really felt out of place. She was a member of the multidisciplinary eligibility team that was determining if Miguel was eligible for special education services. The other members of the team, Mrs. Parks, the special education teacher, and Mrs. Farber, the school psychologist, seemed more comfortable with what was happening than she did. Her friend, Mrs. Parks, assured Ms. Winters that her contribution would be important in determining whether or not Miguel would receive special education services. **Figure 3-10** shows the type of information typically provided by each member of a multidisciplinary eligibility team.

Mrs. Farber indicated that Miguel had scored slightly above average on the WISC-III *(Wechsler Intelligence Scale for Children-Third Edition),* and he had experienced relatively more difficulty with those subtests which were timed and required a degree of persistence. When Mrs. Farber asked if team members had any comments, Ms. Winters was able to add that she had frequently noticed that Miguel seemed to have trouble staying on task and seemed to give up easily, once he was frustrated. Then when Mrs. Parks described Miguel's low achievement test scores in Word Recognition and Reading Comprehension and his poor performance on Arithmetic Computation, Ms. Winters added that those conclusions matched his performance in her class. She went on to note, however, that even though Miguel had a problem getting the right answer to comprehension questions in reading, he appeared quite interested in the story she had been reading to the class after lunch and had demonstrated surprisingly good insight about the feelings of one of the characters. When asked, Ms. Winters elaborated on Miguel's progress during the year, the things she had tried both before and during the prereferral process. She concluded that although Miguel was a "sweet child who appeared to want to do well in school, he just seemed lost." She described how his efforts declined as the day went on, and how he had started to become a behavior problem—especially during math class. She also described Miguel's pattern of academic problems detailed in his permanent record folder and the comments of his mother. The team considers how information about Miguel's problems fit the eligibility criteria established within the definition of each disability area. **Figure 3-11** gives examples of three disability areas.

After each team member had shared information about Miguel, Mrs. Farber reviewed the information and lead the discussion of the possibility that Miguel was eligible for services in the area of learning disabilities. By the end of the meeting, the team had decided that Miguel should be eligible for services in learning disabilities for the following reasons:

1. Although his performance on the intelligence test indicated that he should be able to learn the skills and information in third grade, his academic achievement indicated a **severe** discrepancy between his ability to do the work and his actual achievement in basic reading skills, reading comprehension, and mathematical calculations (individual state regulations for eligibility specify the extent of the severe discrepancy in achievement). See **Figure 3-12** for commonly used assessment instruments.
2. The achievement problem Miguel displays has been a **persistent** problem for him since he entered first grade. The hope that he would "grow out of it" has not been realized.
3. After a discussion of the extent of Miguel's achievement problems, the team examined the possibility that his academic deficits were based on his learning problems as opposed to some external factor(s). They discussed how, in spite of his opportunities for success and apparent efforts to do the work, his **inherent** difficulty with attending to the task at hand and difficulty in organizing his work constantly frustrated his attempts to work at the level of his classmates.

By the end of the meeting, Ms. Winters realized that although determining Miguel's eligibility for services in learning disabilities was relatively straightforward, she, as the classroom teacher, had played a vital part. While the test scores and observations of the other professionals helped to add objectivity to the process, her observations of his patterns of work in her third-grade class provide the basis of reality for her colleagues to interpret their results. She understood that a low test score on arithmetic calculations was relevant only if it was confirmed by classroom information that a student did, in fact, perform poorly in arithmetic. On the other hand, if a student was doing well in the classroom but scored low on the test, the team must conclude that the test results were probably suspect—perhaps a student misunderstood directions, had become fatigued while completing the tests, did not feel well, or for some reason was not putting forth a best effort. The process of interpreting assessment data for the purpose of determining eligibility of a student referred for special education services requires the observations and work samples gathered by the classroom teacher to confirm the results of standardized testing.

FIGURE 3-11

Eligibility Decision Making

Disability Area	Severity	Persistence	Inherent to Student
Mental Retardation	IQ to establish "significant subaverage intellectual functioning" and measurement of deficit in adaptive behavior	Document that impairment "manifested during developmental period"	Yes
Visual Impairment	Acuity of 20/200 or less in the better eye	With best correction	Yes
Learning Disabilities	Discrepancy between IQ and achievement	"Disorder in basic psychological processing"	Yes

FIGURE 3-12

Assessment Instruments Used for Eligibility Decisions

Intelligence Tests
- Stanford-Binet Intelligence Scale—Revised
- Wechsler Intelligence Scale for Children III
- Wechsler Adult Intelligence Scale—Revised
- Wechsler Preschool and Primary Scale of Intelligence
- Kaufman Assessment Battery for Children

Individual Achievement Tests
- Kaufman Test of Educational Achievement
- Peabody Individual Achievement Test—Revised
- Wide Range Achievement Test—Revised
- Woodcock-Johnson Psychoeducational Battery
- Wechsler Individual Achievement Test

Group Achievement Tests
- California Achievement Tests
- Iowa Tests of Basic Skills
- Metropolitan Achievement Tests
- Stanford Achievement Tests

Reevaluating Students

For Ray's teacher, Ms. Johnson, the question of eligibility for special education services is quite different. Ray, as you may recall from the beginning of the chapter, is already being served as a student with a disability. The regulations of IDEA require periodic reevaluations to validate that the labeling and services remain appropriate. This process typically occurs about every three years or more. Ms. Johnson must help determine whether Ray should still receive special education services.

The reevaluation process is even more dependent on information from the general classroom than is the initial assessment for eligibility. Because a special educator has already been serving any student being reevaluated, such as Ray, and because general educators have been involved in special planning and instructional programming (the IEP process), there is significant classroom-based information available for determining eligibility. Consider the following questions when determining whether students should remain eligible for special education services.

- Are the goals of the general education curriculum appropriate for the student in the future?

- Consider both long-term goals (i.e., how appropriate are the general education options with regard to secondary school curricular options and graduation standards?) and more immediate goals (i.e., how appropriate are the general education curricular goals and standards for the next year?).

- How successful has the student been in meeting the expectations of the current curricular goals (i.e., classroom performance, grades, and standardized assessments)? How much, if at all, have these been modified from the goals of general education? Is it likely that future general education goals will need more or less modification?

- What level of instructional support has the student needed in order to make progress with the current curricular goals?

- Will the need for support be likely to increase or decrease in the future?

- What has been the degree of "least restrictive environment" that has been provided (e.g., has the student been most successful academically and socially in a general education setting or in pull-out settings)?

- To what extent does the student benefit from working with same age-peers?

- What is the pattern of the student's progress across the past several years?

- Do areas related to initial eligibility (e.g., a disability in reading or social withdrawal) show improvement or decline?

- Has relative standing on standardized tests provided evidence of improvement?

Once again, consider the question, "Should Ray (or any student who is currently eligible for special education services) continue to receive special education services?" The answers to the questions above provide more relevant information than do standardized test scores. This is because the questions deal more directly with those key elements of what is provided in special education services: adjusting the curriculum, altering the instruction, and modifying the delivery of service.

Developing Individualized Educational Programs

Once it has been determined that a student is eligible for special education services, an instructional plan is developed that is appropriate for the eligible student and specifies those persons, both general and special educators, who are responsible for providing each part of it. The Individualized Educational Program (usually referred to as the **IEP**) is required by law (IDEA) to assure that the special education services provided to a student are planned and implemented in the prescribed manner. You may want to refer back to Chapter 2 which outlines the specific legal requirements that must be followed when providing special education services to a student. IDEA 2004 includes the following changes related to the IEP:

1. Revises language, regarding members of the IEP Team to include, **not less than one** regular education teacher and **not less than one** special education teacher.
2. Identifies when the IEP Team meeting attendance is not necessary.
3. Authorizes excusals from IEP meetings.
4. Adds new provisions for making changes to the IEP, such as an agreement between the parent and the local educational agency not to convene an IEP meeting for the purposes of making changes, and instead developing a written document to amend or modify the student's current IEP.
5. Encourages consolidations of IEP meetings.
6. Authorizes alternative means of meeting participation, for example video conferences and conference calls.

Who Plans the IEP

The process of developing a student's special education program sometimes is referred to as a staffing and must include the student's parents or guardian, representation from general education, as well as appropriate special educators. The special educators would have expertise in those areas in which special services are anticipated to be needed. For example, for a third-grade student eligible for services in learning disabilities because of a disability in reading, the third-grade teacher who referred the student, the teacher of students with learning disabilities, and the parent(s) or guardian would be the minimum group required to develop and approve the IEP. It is conceivable that a school also might want to include a general education administrator (e.g., the principal or assistant principal), school support personnel (e.g., counselor, reading specialist, or social worker), and other special education specialists (e.g., a speech-language pathologist) as team members.

In the case of an older student with multiple disabilities, including orthopedic impairments, the meeting might include most of the individuals listed above plus the student, physical or occupational therapist, a vocational education specialist, and a specialist on transitional services. IDEA 2004 emphasizes the importance of including the parent and, when appropriate, the student (NICHCY, 2005).

What Does the IEP Include

IEP requirements emphasize the importance of 3 core concepts:

- The involvement and progress of each student with a disability in the general curriculum, including addressing the unique needs that arise out of the student's assessment;
- The involvement of parents and students, together with regular and special education personnel, in making individual decisions to support each student's educational success; and
- The preparation of students with disabilities for employment and other post-school activities.

Plan for Developing an IEP

When a prereferral team has been part of the process for determining eligibility, the IEP should evolve naturally from the information and documentation gathered by the prereferral and multidisciplinary eligibility teams in specifying the elements of the IEP. Ideally, the IEP committee works logically from describing the student's presenting problems in the context of the classroom (or present instructional setting) to what needs to be provided in an appropriate educational program. Specifically, the IEP committee:

- describes the student's **academic achievement and functional performance,**
- determines the **annual goals** that are appropriate, and helps the student to be involved in and progress in the general education curriculum,
- specifies the **instructional objectives** that are expected to be mastered as part of reaching the goals,
- develops **benchmarks,** aligned to alternate assessments and alternate achievement standards,
- describes the **special education services needed** and who is responsible for providing it, especially as related to helping the student with the general education curriculum,
- describes the extent to which the student will **participate in school-wide assessment programs,** including appropriate accommodations,
- determines whether the student shall take an alternate assessment on a particular state or district-wide assessment of student achievement and if so, includes a statement of why the student cannot participate in the regular assessment and why the alternate assessment is appropriate,
- specifies how **progress on the IEP is measured and communicated to parents or guardians,**
- indicates the **extent of time to be spent in general education,** and explains reasons for any nonparticipation in general education,
- describes the **projected dates for initiating services and dates to review annual progress,** and
- addresses requirements for students with disabilities transferring school districts within a state and between states.

Figure 3-13 relates the IEP components to the concerns of the committee.

What Is the Problem?

For many IEPs the description of a student's current level of performance can be developed from the information gathered by the prereferral team. The current level of performance should include information about the following general areas, as appropriate

FIGURE 3-13

IEP Components

IEP Committee Concern	IEP Components
• What is the problem?	• Current Level of Performance
• What does the student need to be able to do?	• Annual Goals and relationship to curriculum • Instructional Objectives
• How will the program be provided to help the student?	• Delineation of responsibility • Specifying time in general education • Specifying dates to initiate and review services • Assessment of student progress

for a particular student: academic performance relative to the school's curriculum, classroom working behaviors relative to the school's expectations, personal and social behaviors relative to expectations, and a description of particular disabilities which would interfere with school performance.

The statement of current level of educational performance would include a brief description of the student's strengths and weaknesses in the school curriculum. For example, "Reads fourth-grade material with 75% accuracy in word recognition."

The description of present levels of performance should be tied to the eligibility decision and help to put the eligibility into a school-based context. For example, a team writing a statement of current level of performance for a student eligible for services due to an emotional/behavior disorder would describe the impact of the emotional/behavior disorder on meeting the expectations of the school ("doesn't comply with teacher's directions to begin seatwork" or "has not established friendships with other classmates"). Likewise, for students with visual impairments, learning disabilities, or mental retardation, the team would describe current classroom difficulties in areas such as seeing words in the text, mastering basic academic skills, and developing appropriate adaptive behaviors respectively for each group.

The current level of performance might provide additional information about a student's problems as well as describing areas of relative strength. For example, describing other areas of school performance in which emotional/behavior skills might be noted ("follows the rules and competes appropriately with classmates during physical education periods"), or in which vision might be important ("difficulty copying letters even when model is at the desk" or "mastered basic addition facts using manipulatives"), or in which learning skills are needed ("language skills are comparable to classmates"). Other general information may be included in the current level of performance to help provide a context of strengths and weaknesses for individual students.

On the IEPs for most students, the current level of performance should be related to the major objectives of the school's curriculum. For example, if reading is part of a student's general education program, then a statement such as "reads grade-level reading material with 80% accuracy in word recognition" and "comprehends grade-level factual information at 50%" is important information because it compares the student's performance to the school's expectations for achievement. Information about skills in reading, mathematics, written expression, and language proficiency typically are included for students at the elementary level because these skill areas comprise the core of the academic curriculum. At the secondary level, academic areas also would reflect the school's curriculum, such as "the ability to use content area texts."

Classroom working behaviors would include a description of issues such as whether a student completes work on time, follows directions, brings the needed materials to class, and works cooperatively with others. Personal and social behaviors might include a description of self-help skills, self-concept, interactions with peers, and use of free time. Finally, if appropriate, any impact of disabilities not covered in the other items should be described. These might include a physical or sensory disability which affects classroom performance or stereotypic behavior which interferes with the ability to achieve in the classroom. In the case of preschool students or students with more severe disabilities, a description of the extent to which certain developmental markers have been achieved, such as mobility skills, self-help skills (feeding, toileting), and language skills are important components of the current level of performance.

As part of the revisions in IDEA 2004, there are several special factors that must be considered in preparing the information on current level of performance for the IEP. The IEP team must specify whether the student has behavior that interferes with learning or the learning of others. If so, the student's behavior must be assessed and a plan developed to manage the behavior. The IEP team also must indicate whether the student has limited proficiency in English or has some special communication needs. These needs must be described in the present level of performance statement and the student's language needs addressed in the IEP. The team must state whether the student is blind or visually impaired or deaf or hard of hearing and what services will be provided for these sensory problems. Finally, any need for assistive technology services or devices must be indicated (see Chapter 8 for more details).

> **Ms. Winters's role as the general education classroom teacher is to provide special information about the extent to which Miguel's behavior has interfered with his learning or the learning of others and whether there is evidence of any communication problems. She reflects on his off-task and out-of-seat behaviors as well as his relationships with his classmates. She considers whether there have been times when he had difficulty understanding her instructions or could not follow directions she gave to the class. Did he seem able to carry on conversations with her and his classmates?**

Two cautions are worth noting here. Use the description of the current level of performance to indicate both what a student does and does not do (i.e., positive and negative behaviors) and avoid relying heavily on standardized test scores to indicate the level of performance. While test scores may be helpful to summarize and communicate performance information, many times a test score obscures a clear image of what a student is able or unable to do. A 3.5 grade-level performance in math doesn't tell us whether a student has mastered the 4 times multiple tables or the concept of one-half.

What Does the Student Need to Be Able to Do?

The goals on the IEP should be developed from the areas of concern identified in the current level of performance and should be related, but not limited, to the general education curriculum and issues of the student's eligibility. That is to say, the IEP for students eligible for services in emotional/behavior disorders would have goals which relate to the problems such as "exhibited an inability to build or maintain satisfactory personal relationships with peers and teachers" (IDEA, 2004). IDEA 2004 makes several changes to the provisions governing IEPs. One of the most significant changes is the elimination of the requirement that a student's annual goal also contains short term objectives that are incremental steps toward the goals. Short term objectives are now a requirement in the IEPs of students with only the most significant cognitive disabilities. Local school districts have the option to continue to require all IEPs to include short term objectives.

How Will the Program Be Provided?

This part of the IEP specifies the responsibilities for providing the instruction and services for each element of the goals and objectives. The guiding legislation for special education requires students to receive services in the least restrictive environment (LRE), that is to minimize separation from peers of the same age in a neighborhood school. The issue of LRE involves who provides the services (general or special educators) and where the service is to be provided (in a special school, self-contained classroom, resource room, or the general education classroom). Remember, Special Education is a service, not a place. The question of how responsibility, or shared responsibility, is determined for a student in a special education program is a matter of continuing debate (see Chapter 1). Regardless of the formal designation of who provides the services to meet each IEP goal and objective, a student who is eligible for special education services remains the responsibility of all educators in the school, not just the responsibility of special education teachers.

We take the position that the least restrictive environment is not synonymous with only the general education classroom but includes the full continuum of services from special schools to the general education classroom. The key to determining the least restrictive environment for a particular student is that it must be the most effective environment for providing instruction and services. In the great majority of cases, the IEP would indicate times during the day when a student receiving special education services and general education students will be together. This shared responsibility is important because we believe students with disabilities, in order to be part of the general society after their schooling has ended, need to be educated with their age peers to the extent appropriate. The students in general education programs also need the opportunity to be educated with students with disabilities.

The IEP is to be written with the full participation of all those responsible for serving the student, as well as the student's parents or guardian, and even the student, if appropriate. This shared development helps to promote mutual trust and understanding among educators, related service specialists, and parents. Refer to the suggestions given in Chapter 12 for organizing and conducting the IEP meeting.

The IEP that was developed for Miguel is shown in **Figure 3-14.**

Note that Goals 1, 2, and 3 directly address his low performance level in reading and mathematics and are linked to the general education curriculum. They also are concerns because Miguel is eligible for services in learning disabilities due to achievement in these areas that is significantly below his ability. The IEP committee decides that Miguel will receive his reading instruction from Mrs. Parks in the resource room because she is using the kind of highly structured phonics-based program that would be most beneficial for him. Ms. Winters, with consultation help from Mrs. Parks, will be responsible for the arithmetic goal because his needs in this area seem reasonable within the program Ms. Winters already has established. The fourth goal focuses on increasing on-task behavior. This is **supportive** content because, although being on-task is not by itself a reason for being eligible for special education, it contributes to Miguel's low achievement in reading and mathematics. Miguel's mother, Mrs. Jones, had reported that Miguel says he enjoys going to school, but that he tells her little about his lessons. She indicates that he seldom looks at books or magazines at home and seems to prefer the company of younger playmates. This information is added to what the team has gathered from the school setting.

The IEP for Tiffany is shown in **Figure 3-15** and is structured to be implemented in her general education classes. This is because her behavioral problems occur within the context of the general education classes. Team teaching and consultation will be the way for special educators to assist the classroom teachers in working with Tiffany.

Reviewing and Revising IEPs

IDEA 2004 includes changes regarding who and by what method the various team members participate in drafting of the IEP. The law encourages the use of alternative ways of meeting, such as conference calls. The revised law also allows changes to the IEP without the need for the entire IEP Team to reconvene for a formal meeting. IDEA legislation also requires school personnel to document the progress of each student with an IEP. General educators are required to participate in the annual review of students' IEPs and to assist in the revisions that are made. The law requires the review to evaluate:

1. The progress or lack of progress to the IEP and, if included, general education goals,
2. Possible revisions of goals, placement, and responsibilities,
3. The results of assessments for the purpose of reevaluation,

FIGURE 3-14

Miguel's IEP

Annual Goal 1	**Placement**	**Person Responsible**	**Duration**
• Miguel will demonstrate mastery of sight vocabulary on second-grade material.	Resource room	Mrs. Parks	1 year

Instructional Objectives	**Start Date**	**Review Dates**	**Method**	**Criteria**
• 1.1 Given phonetically regular CVCC and CCVC words from second-grade reading book, M. will pronounce the words.	9-25	11-15, 1-15, 3-15, 5-15	Observation	90%
• 1.2 Given phonetically irregular words in context, M. will pronounce the words.				

Annual Goal 2	**Placement**	**Person Responsible**	**Duration**
• Miguel will demonstrate literal comprehension skills on second-grade material.	Resource room	Mrs. Parks	1 year

Instructional Objectives	**Start Date**	**Review Dates**	**Method**	**Criteria**
• 2.1 Given a selection from the second-grade reader, M. will answer 5 factual comprehension questions.	9-25	11-15, 1-15, 3-15, 5-15	Work samples	80%
• 2.2 Given a selection from the second-grade reader, M. will paraphrase the major theme and state 5 supporting details.				

Annual Goal 3	**Placement**	**Person Responsible**	**Duration**
• Miguel will increase fluency in solving addition and subtraction problems requiring regrouping.	Third Grade	Ms. Winters	1 year

Instructional Objectives	**Start Date**	**Review Dates**	**Method**	**Criteria**
• 3.1 Given worksheets of mixed two-digit addition and subtraction problems, M. will write the correct answer.	9-25	11-15, 1-15, 3-15, 5-15	Work samples	90%
• 3.2 Given probes of mixed two-digit addition and subtraction problems, M. will write the correct answer.				> 5 correct/ min.

Annual Goal 4	**Placement**	**Person Responsible**	**Duration**
• Miguel will increase his on-task behavior.	Third Grade	Ms. Winters	1 year

Instructional Objectives	**Start Date**	**Review Dates**	**Method**	**Criteria**
• 4.1 M. will complete 4 of 5 assignments within the time allotted.	9-25	11-15, 1-15, 3-15, 5-15	Work samples	80%

FIGURE 3-15

Tiffany's IEP

Annual Goal 1	Placement	Person Responsible	Duration
• Tiffany will reduce the incidences of defiant behavior.	Seventh grade class	Mrs. Douglas	1 year

Short-term Objectives	Start Date	Review Dates	Method	Criteria
• 1.1 Tiffany will exhibit fewer than two incidents of defiant behavior per week.	9–20	10–30, 12–15, 2–15, 4–12	Observation	< 2/week
• 1.2 Tiffany will exhibit less than one incident of defiant behavior per week.				< 1/week

Annual Goal 2	Placement	Person Responsible	Duration
• Tiffany will increase her level of class participation	Earth Science class	Mr. Taylor	1 year

Short-term Objectives	Start Date	Review Dates	Method	Criteria
• 2.1 Tiffany will volunteer information in class.	9–20	10–30, 12–15, 2–15, 4–12	Observation	4 days/wk
• 2.2 Tiffany will work cooperatively with classmates in small groups.			Observation	3 of 3 opportunities

Annual Goal 3	Placement	Person Responsible	Duration
• Tiffany will increase her assignment completion rate.	7th grade classes	Mr. Taylor, Ms. Jones & Matthews	1 year

Short-term Objectives	Start Date	Review Dates	Method	Criteria
• 3.2 Tiffany will turn in assignments on time	9–20	10–20, 11–20, 12–20	Work samples	3 of 4 days

4. Information provided by the parents and the student's anticipated needs, and
5. Other relevant information.

Some of the most common problems with IEPs are a lack of coordination with general educators (Lipsky & Gartner, 1996), the failure to include parents in the development of IEPs, and IEP goals and objectives that are not individually designed for a student's instructional needs (Drasglow, Yell, & Robinson, 2001). IDEA 2004 authorizes a new pilot program that will allow up to 15 states to offer parents the option of a multi-year IEP, not to exceed 3 years.

Individualized Transition Plan

The Individualized Transition Plan (ITP) was established by IDEA to supplement the services outlined in the IEP and focuses on the demands of the world outside of school. It assures that planning and services are available and coordinated to assist young adults with disabilities in moving from school to community-based programs, agencies, and services. The ITP is required to be part of the IEP for any student with disabilities beginning with the first IEP that will be in effect when the student turns 16 years of age or earlier if determined by the IEP Team. The plan should address issues of vocational preparation (career awareness, job training, placement, and follow-up), independent living skills (consumer skills, community travel, and supportive living), and leisure-time options

(Cronin & Patton, 1993). The ITP planning should involve the student and parents as well as the community agencies that will provide or coordinate the services.

The planning for a 14-year-old, therefore, would include additional concerns beyond what is included in the IEP of a younger student, such as Miguel. The ITP addresses the problems encountered by students preparing to leave school and has the intention of promoting independent living. That is to say, to assure that a student leaving school has:

- mastered the skills needed to function independently (e.g., speaking, listening, reading, and writing)
- general knowledge about the world (e.g., consumer information, health, community resources, and responsibilities related to citizenship
- knowledge of career options and the development of vocational skills
- the ability to apply personal and vocational skills and knowledge to promote self-determination and quality of life (Wiederholt & Dunn, 1995).

The development of a transition plan for Thomas, a 15-year-old who is classified as moderately mentally retarded, will bridge the gap between the school and community. Thomas's IEP indicates that he is to be served in general education exploratory classes in his middle school where he will rotate through home economics, wood working, and art classes with his age peers. During other times of the day, Thomas is receiving services in the self-contained special education program. This program includes a language arts class in which he learns basic reading and writing skills related to functioning successfully in his neighborhood and community; a functional mathematics program which focuses on mastering money, time, and measurement problems he will face outside of school; a course in citizenship; and a science course on environmental issues. Three additional goals (the ITP portion) have been included to facilitate Thomas's movement from school to the community.

The first of the ITP goals is to develop an awareness of vocational opportunities in the immediate community and involves instruction in identifying the types of jobs in his community, the skills and training needed for each, and the types of activities each job requires. This goal is met through instruction by his special education teacher, Mrs. Phillips, as part of the curriculum for all the students in his class. A second goal is to demonstrate ability to access and use the public transportation system which was selected to enable Thomas to have access to the facilities available throughout his city. For this goal, Mr. Shoemaker, the community-education specialist, works with a small group of students to teach them to identify the bus routes, scheduled departure times, and procedures for riding the bus (e.g., having the exact change for the fare and recognizing and signaling when to get off). The final ITP goal is to participate in a community-sponsored leisure activity. This goal is met when Mrs. Phillips contacted Mike Ward, Scoutmaster of a local Explorer Scout group, and enrolled Thomas in an urban scouting program, sponsored by a local church. The group not only participates in outdoor leisure activities, but has an active program of community service, such as assisting with food distribution programs and participating in a senior citizens' gardening program. Through the ITP, Thomas should make a smooth transition to the world beyond school.

Individualized Family Service Plan

While the IEP is the formal plan for serving school-aged students, the Individualized Family Service Plan (IFSP) is designed for infants and toddlers (P.L. 99-457). The IFSP has many similarities to the IEP for school-age students, such as specifying current functioning levels, identifying goals and objectives, indicating services and who will provide them, and indicating the time-frame for initiating and reviewing services. There are, however, several important differences. These include a broader approach with the family unit as the focal point for delivering service to the infant or toddler with disabilities and recognizing and building on each family's strengths in developing a service plan, naming a service manager to coordinate services, reviewing the service plan every six months, and indicating the method of providing transition to other services as the child grows older.

Additionally, IDEA 2004 requires changes regarding the IFSP including the following:

- New child find criteria with emphasis on at-risk populations;
- New provisions for early childhood transition;
- Additional dispute resolution options; and
- New members to State Interagency Coordinating Councils.

Section 504 of the Rehabilitation Act

Section 504 of the Rehabilitation Act of 1973 is a civil rights law that prohibits discrimination against individuals with disabilities. Though Section 504 ensures that a student with a disability has equal access to an education, it does not require the school to provide an individualized education plan (IEP) that is designed to meet the student's unique needs and provides the student with educational benefit. Fewer procedural safeguards are available for students with disabilities and their parents under Section 504 than under IDEA (Wright & Wright, 2001). A student with a disability does not automatically qualify for special education services under IDEA or may not need special education services. The student may, however, receive protections under Section 504 of the Rehabilitation Act. In order to be eligible for protections under Section 504, the student must have a physical or mental impairment that **substantially limits** at least one major life activity. Major life activities include walking, seeing, hearing, speaking, breathing, learning, reading, writing, performing math calculations, working, caring for oneself, and performing manual tasks.

In determining eligibility, Section 504 requires an evaluation and draws information from a variety of sources. The 504 Committee, which may be composed of the same persons who serve on the pre-referral team, should consider all available information including, medical, educational, and psychological records as appropriate. If a student is determined eligible to receive services under Section 504, a plan is developed that will address reasonable accommodations and modifications that are not available to students who do not have a disability (See **Figure 3-16**).

A reasonable accommodation in the school setting is a modification or adjustment of educational programs to afford students with disabilities equal opportunity to access programs. After the 504 Committee has determined the

This student may be eligible for protection under Section 504 for impairments such as ADD or diabetes.

FIGURE 3-16

The Components that Should Be Included in a 504 Plan

Section 504—Individual Accommodation Plan

Plan date: September 26, this year   **Projected review date:** May 28, next year

Student's Name: Marie Peterson   **DOB:** 8/22/95 **Age:** 7 yrs. 1 mo.
School: Carters Elementary School   **Grade:** 2nd
Parent/Guardian: M/M Joseph (Katelyn) Peterson   **Phone:** 404-777-1244 (W) 678-999-0122 (H)
Address: 124 Johnson Turner Road   **City:** Summerville
State: USA   **ZIP:** 30333

Committee Members Present:
Ms. Marjorie Majors, *Team Chairperson*
Mrs. Lucille McKee, *Recorder*
Ms. Joyce Smith, *Classroom Teacher*
Ms. Francis Murray, *Classroom Teacher*
Ms. Arlene Freeman, RN, *School Nurse*
Dr. Carolyn Jones, *School Psychologist*
Mr. Joseph Peterson, *Father*

Describe the student's physical or mental impairment, including prognosis if appropriate:
Marie has cerebral palsy that was diagnosed shortly after birth. Although her motor function has improved, it is expected that she will always require the use, minimally, of a walker. At times, the student will require a wheelchair for increased and eased mobility.

Describe the educational limitations experienced by the student as a result of this disability:
Currently, the student performs at the second grade level, and is able to progress along with the general classroom population. Her grades reflect average (C-B) assignment and test performance. She also scores in the average range on standardized measures. Therefore, there are no educational limitations known at this time.

Describe the medical limitations experienced by the student as a result of this disability:
Although the student rarely has elimination accidents, she does utilize personal hygiene undergarments on a daily basis. If an accident occurs, assistance will be required in changing the undergarment.

List any other limitations that may affect the student's activities while at school:
1. The student is not able to utilize the stairs.
2. At times, the student's hands become fatigued and she is not able to complete written assignments in expected amount of time.
3. The student has impaired mobility.
4. The student may experience some spastic movements when overly tired.

List the accommodations that are necessary for this student to participate in the educational program:
1. The student requires the use of the elevator to move between floors for lunch and physical education.
2. The student needs to arrive to the classroom five minutes prior to the other student's arrival. This will allow her to move at her own pace without the possibility of colliding with other students.
3. The student requires extended time to complete assignments and assessments.
4. The student requires assistance moving her lunch tray to and from the table.
5. The student should leave the classroom fifteen minutes prior to the other students leaving at the end of the school day. This will allow the student to move to the school bus without the possibility of colliding with other students.

continued on next page

FIGURE 3-16

The Components that Should Be Included in a 504 Plan (continued)

6. The student should be allowed liberal restroom breaks.
7. The student should be allowed to rest during periods of fatigue. If the fatigue is too great (the student will inform the teacher), the parents may be called in order for the student to go home and rest.
8. The adaptive physical education teacher should meet with the general physical education teacher in order to develop an appropriate physical education plan so that the student may participate during her regular scheduled physical education time.
9. The student should be allowed to sit close near the door, but away from the general flow of traffic in the classroom.

List any anticipated discipline problems that may result from the disability:
No discipline problems are anticipated. However, the teacher and classmates should be aware that when the student looses control of her extremities, when she becomes spastic, that she may hit others or objects unintentionally. Students and staff members should allow her space, as well as a place to rest during moments of fatigue.

Describe positive behavioral interventions that may be used to address this behavior:
Not applicable.

List consequences that may be used when this behavior occurs:
Not applicable.

Parent/Guardian Signature (if attending meeting)

Katelyn Peterson, Mother

accommodations that are necessary for a student, teachers are required to implement them. Failure to do so places the school district in violation of Section 504. Classroom teachers should be aware of the following examples of impairments that may entitle a student to 504 protection:

- Diseases such as AIDs, tuberculosis, or hepatitis B;
- Medical conditions such as chronic asthma, diabetes, heart disease, or seizure disorders; physical disabilities such as cerebral palsy or muscular dystrophy;
- Attention deficit disorder with or without hyperactivity;
- Alcohol/drug addicted students (does not protect students who are currently using drugs or alcohol);
- Students with temporary disabilities; and
- Students with pregnancy related complications.

It is important to remember that the presence of one of these conditions in itself does not qualify a student for Section 504 protection. The impairment must also cause a substantial limitation of a major life activity. Classroom teachers should consider the following three questions in determining whether a student's impairment substantially limits one or more major life activities:

1. What is the nature and severity of the impairment?
2. How long will it last or is it expected to last?
3. What is its permanent or long term impact or expected impact?

In developing a 504 Plan, the committee should include all of the student's teachers, the parent/guardian, an administrator, and other individuals as appropriate. The 504 Plan should be kept as part of the Student Support Team file and reviewed as needed. Though school systems develop their own formats for what a 504 Plan should look like, an example of areas that should be addressed is provided in **Figure 3-16.**

Summary

The process of determining that the responsibility for the education of a student should be shared by general and special education must be a thoughtful, systematic one. First, a teacher who is concerned about the progress of a student should attempt to identify and reflect on the exact nature of the problem. A series of modifications should be implemented in the classroom, either formally through a prereferral team or informally by the concerned teacher, to determine the extent of the problem and what type of interventions might be useful in resolving it. In the event of severe, persistent problems that are inherent to the student (as opposed to external factors involving the home or school) a referral for special education services is appropriate.

The classroom teacher plays a major role in collecting and reporting information and work samples about how the student responds to various instructional situations. This information becomes part of the assessment data used to establish whether a student meets the eligibility requirements for one of the special education categories described in IDEA 2004.

The final role of the classroom teacher is to help plan and implement the instructional program for the student. The instructional responsibility is a shared responsibility between general and special educators and, as such, requires continual planning and cooperation in order to provide quality instructional services.

Discussion Questions and Activities

In Chapter 3 you read about Miguel and the development of his Individualized Educational Program (IEP). As a future teacher, whether in general or special education, you will be required to provide input into the development of students' IEPs. Ms. Winters, Mrs. Parks, and Miguel's mother have agreed that he needs special help and modifications for his spelling. They have completed the goal below but not the instructional objective(s). Write two (2) objectives, 5.1 and 5.2, that would be appropriate for Miguel's annual goal in spelling. Remember to apply the guidelines discussed in the chapter for writing IEPs.

Annual Goal 5	Placement	Person Responsible	Duration
• Miguel will increase his spelling of second grade words.	Third Grade	Ms. Winters	1 year

Instructional Objectives	Start Date	Review Dates	Method	Criteria
• 5.1				

• 5.2

Internet Resources

A web site with IDEA 2004 and updated information about the legislation.
http://www.cec.sped.org/law_res/doc/law/index.php

A US Department of Education pdf file with detailed information about IEPs.
http://www.ed.gov/policy/speced/guid/idea/tb-iep.pdf

An article about involving parents in the IEP process.
http://ericec.org/digests/e611.html

A web site with information about students with learning disabilities.
http://www.ncld.org/

A web site with information about prereferral teams and their role in reducing disproportionate representation in special classes.
http://www.emstac.org/registered/topics/disproportionality.htm

A web site that brings together teachers and related services providers, in addition to supporting associations of educational leadership.
http://www.ideapractices.org

The Families and Advocates Partnership for Education (FAPE) at PACER Center links families, advocates, and self-advocates.
http://www.fape.org

The Policy-Maker Partnership (PMP) at the National Association of State Directors of Special Education increases the capacity of policymakers.
http://www.ideapartnership.org

References

Adelman, H. S., & Taylor, L. (1993). *Learning problems & learning disabilities: Moving forward.* Pacific Grove, CA: Brooks/Cole Publishing.

Artiles, A. J. (1998). The dilemma of difference: Enriching the disproportionality discourse with theory and content. *The Journal of Special Education, 32,* 32–36.

Bureau of Labor Statistics (2005). *Report on the American Workforce.* Washington DC: U.S. Bureau of Labor.

Cartledge, G. (1999). African American males and serious emotional disturbance: Some personal perspectives. *Behavior Disorders, 25,* 76–79.

Colarusso R., Keel, M., & Dangel, H. (2001). A comparison of eligibility criteria and their impact on minority representation in LD programs. *Learning Disabilities Research & Practice, 16(1),* 1–7.

Craig, S., Hull, K., Haggart, A. G., & Perez-Selles, M. (2000). Promoting cultural competence through teacher assistance teams. *Teaching Exceptional Children, 32(3),* 6–12.

Cronin M. E., & Patton J. R. (1993). *Life skills instruction for all students with special needs: A practical guide for integrating real-life content into the curriculum.* Austin, TX: PRO- ED.

Dangel, H. L., & Ensminger, E. E. (1999). *Statement of Status Checklist—Revised.* West-Metro GLRS: Atlanta, GA.

Drasglow, E., Yell, M. L., & Robinson, M. R. (2001). Developing legally correct and educationally appropriate IEPs. *Remedial and Special Education, 22,* 359–373.

Kerr, M. N., Nelson, C. M., & Lambert, D. I. (1987). *Helping adolescents with learning and behavior problems.* Columbus, OH: Merrill.

Kovaleski, J. F. Gickling, E. E., Morrow, H., & Swank, P. R. (1999). High versus low implementation of instructional teams: A case for maintaining program fidelity. *Remedial and Special Education, 20,* 170—183.

Lipsky, D. K., & Gartner, A. (1996). Inclusive education and school restructuring. In W. Stainback & S. Stainback (Eds.), *Controversial issues confronting special education: Divergent perspectives* (pp. 3–15). Boston: Allyn & Bacon.

National Alliance of Black School Educators (NABSE) & ILIAD Project (2002). *Addressing over-representation of African American students in special education: The prereferral intervention process—an administrator's guide.* Arlington, VA: Council for Exceptional Children and Washington DC: National Alliance of Black School Educators.

National Center for Educational Statistics (2003). *Digest of Education Statistics.* Washington, DC: U.S. Department of Education.

National Information Center for Children and Youth with Disabilities. (2005). IDEA 2004 *Training Manual.* Washington, DC: Author.

Rhodes, R., Ochoa, S., & Ortiz, S. (2005). *Assessing Culturally and Linguistically Diverse Students: A Practical Guide.* Guilford Press: New York, NY.

Smith, D. D., & Lucksson, R. (1992). *Introduction to special education: Teaching in an age of challenge.* Boston: Allyn & Bacon.

Strickland, B. B., & Turnbull, A. P. (1990). *Developing and implementing individualized education programs.* Columbus, OH: Merrill.

Stump, C., (2002). Prereferral: The first step in addressing your child's learning disability. SchwabLearning.org. A parent's Guide to Helping Kids with Learning Difficulties.

U.S. Department of Education (2003). *Twenty Third Annual Report to Congress on the Implementation of the Individuals with Disabilities Education Act.* Washington, DC: Author

Wiederholt, J. L., & Dunn, C. (1995). Transition from school to independent living. In D. D. Hammill & N. R. Bartel (Eds.), *Teaching students with learning and behavior problems: Managing mild-to moderate difficulties in resource and inclusive settings* (pp. 381–417). Austin, TX: PRO-ED.

Wright, P. W., & Wright, P. D. (2001). *Wrightslaw: From emotions to advocacy—the special education survival guide.* Harbor House Law Press: Hartfield, VA

Yates, J. R. (1998, April). The state of practice in the education of CLD students. Paper presented at the annual meeting of the Council for Exception Children. Minneapolis, MN.

Zhang, D., & Katsiyannis, A. (2002). Minority representation in special education: A persistent challenge. *Remedial and Special Education, 23(2),* 180–187.

4

Characteristics of Students with Behavior and Learning Challenges

L. Juane Heflin and Rebecca M. Wilson

Chapter Objectives

- to introduce the definitions and terminology associated with students with learning and behavior challenges;
- to describe the characteristics of students with the following disabilities:
  - Attention Deficit/Hyperactivity Disorder (ADHD)
  - Emotional Disturbance (ED)
  - Autism
  - Specific Learning Disabilities (SLD)
  - Mild Mental Retardation (MMR)
  - Traumatic Brain Injury (TBI)
- to provide information regarding the etiology of the learning and behavior differences; and
- to delineate educational issues related to learning and behavior challenges.

Changing family compositions and dynamics, educational reform movements, and changes in society are resulting in more students entering school with behaviors and learning abilities that are challenging to educators. Most students with behavior disorders, learning disabilities, mild mental retardation, and attention deficit/hyperactivity disorder start their school careers in general education classrooms. Their learning foundation is established while under the supervision of a general education teacher. With the implementation of the No Child Left Behind Act of 2001 (NCLB), inceasing numbers of students with behavior and learning challenges will be taught and assessed in general education settings. Fortunately, for the vast majority of students with behavior and learning challenges all that is required to succeed in school is a teacher who is able to make minor adjustments in the environment and assignments. A smaller number of these students will qualify as having a learning disability, emotional disturbance or mild mental retardation and will require partial or full-time specialized services to benefit from their educational experiences.

Students with behavior and learning challenges are described together in this chapter because they often occur together. Frequently, students with behavior challenges will have learning difficulties, and students with learning difficulties will demonstrate challenging behavior. When two or more disabilities occur in an individual, they are considered to **coexist.** When individuals have coexisting disabilities, the primary or most pronounced disability will be listed first in the eligibility code and given priority when determining appropriate educational services. For example, if a student has both learning disabilities and behavioral disorders, the student's eligibility team will decide which of the disabilities is most severe, will designate that as the primary disability, and list it first.

This chapter will provide an overview of students whose behavior and learning needs create unique challenges for teachers. Following a general description of etiology and classification systems, each of the disabilities will be discussed by first providing a definition based on IDEA 2004, followed by a description of the characteristics of a student with the disability. Next, the specific etiology of the condition will be presented along with the criteria which must be met when assessing the student for eligibility. Finally, issues for the classroom teacher will be discussed, covering specific concerns and recommendations that should be considered when working with a student who has the disability.

Etiology

When humans encounter anything that is different from the norm or from what is expected, the natural tendency is to wonder "Why?". Even though answering this question may not provide useful knowledge for the classroom teacher, an analysis of what has caused a disability or difference in learning or behavior is a consideration of its **etiology.** Differences are caused by a combination of biologic and environmental factors, and almost everyone has engaged in a "nature" versus "nurture" argument about which contributes more significantly. In some conditions, such as autism, biology makes the most significant contribution to an individual's unusual behaviors and preoccupations, but environmental factors certainly can alter the individual's actions (Prior, 1989). In other cases, such as depression, an individual may have the biologic components for the condition, but it may or may not appear, depending on what happens within the environment. The following is a brief description of these two contributors: biology and environment.

Biological Influences

Biology influences the neural, chemical, and functional aspects of the body and causes differences which are said to originate from within the individual. Biology accounts for traits and conditions which are **hereditary** and are transmitted to the child from the mother and the father. Biology also accounts for conditions which appear because of a physiologic change which occurs in the individual before birth **(prenatally),** during birth **(perinatally),** or at some time after birth **(postnatally).**

Heredity

Biologic influences occurring before birth include genetically transmitted conditions and predispositions. Just as eye color and height are inherited, so are certain conditions (See **Table 4-1**). Researchers are documenting that learning disabilities as well as mild mental retardation may be passed down from parents to their children, indicating a genetic component (Plomin & Kovas, 2005; Spinath, Harlaar, Ronald, & Plomin, 2004). One of the three causes of Down syndrome (which will be discussed in more detail later), is an abnormality on the 21st chromosome, clearly a genetic influence. Conditions such as depression, schizophrenia, and attention deficit/hyperactivity disorder occur more frequently in biologic families, so heredity is suspected as a primary influence. In other cases, genetic influences may result in a biologic predisposition that sets the stage for the appearance of a condition. For example, an inborn trait, such as temperament (Chess & Thomas, 1987), may predispose an infant to behave in certain ways. A child who is born with a difficult temperament may be inclined to be fussier, to awaken at different times, to take naps of varying lengths, and to have intense reactions.

TABLE 4-1

Examples of Genetically Influenced Conditions

- Learning Disabilities
- Down Syndrome
- Depression
- Schizophrenia
- ADHD
- Cystic Fibrosis
- Tuberous Sclerosis
- Phenylketonuria
- Fragile X
- Autism
- Mild Mental Retardation

Although certain conditions or predispositions clearly are inherited, controversy exists related to the influence of heredity on intellectual abilities. Sir Francis Galton in his 1869 book, *Hereditary Genius,* traced the hereditary connections of prominent men and determined intelligence is completely genetically determined at birth. In 1916, Louis Terman, a supporter of the hereditary nature of intelligence, published the Stanford-Binet Intelligence Scale, providing a way to identify children whose intellectual capacity varied from the average. These researchers believed that heredity was the sole determinant of intelligence, a controversial position that has been supported by some in recent years (Hernstein & Murray, 1994) but is strongly disputed by others (Haynes, 1995; Wahlsten, 1995), who view environmental factors as having a more powerful influence on intelligence.

Prenatal, Perinatal, and Postnatal Influences

During the prenatal period, a fetus may be exposed to diseases, such as maternal rubella, which may result in the infant being born with mental retardation or sensory impairments. Mothers who do not eat appropriately while they are pregnant deprive their unborn children of important nutrients which may cause later learning problems. Likewise, a woman who uses drugs or alcohol while she is pregnant will expose the fetus to toxins which can alter the developmental outcomes for the child. Other conditions which are present at birth and are therefore described as **congenital** include: cystic fibrosis, spina bifida, and cerebral palsy. Many of these conditions will be discussed in Chapter 5. Any of these conditions may affect learning and behavior.

Perinatal and postnatal changes in the individual often are caused by disease or physical trauma which result in neurologic impairments. During the perinatal period, brain damage may be caused by birth complications such as **anoxia,** which occurs when the oxygen supply is cut-off from the brain. Postnatally, brain damage may occur when the child is shaken severely or when the child is in an accident, such as a car wreck. The developmental outcomes from these insults will be discussed in the section on traumatic brain injury (TBI). Brain damage may be the result of disease such as encephalitis or from exposure to toxic substances such as lead. Behavior and learning also may be affected by the appearance of diseases such as cancer or muscular dystrophy. Prenatal, perinatal, and postnatal influences contribute to the development of learning and behavioral problems but do not necessarily cause them (Tramontana & Hooper, 1987). Biologic influences, both inherited traits and those which result in a physiologic change, contribute to the

TABLE 4-2

Factors Which May Influence the Development of B/LD

Prenatal

- poor maternal nutrition
- maternal rubella
- teratogens (e.g., nicotine, alcohol, drugs)
- incompatible Rh factor
- prematurity

Perinatal

- low birth weight
- anoxia
- meconium staining

Postnatal

- shaken baby syndrome/abuse
- disease
- neglect/lack of stimulation
- accidents
- teratogens (e.g., lead, mercury, toxic fumes, nicotine, drugs, poisons)
- poverty
- poor nutrition
- poor health care
- parental educational attainment

appearance of exceptional behavioral and learning characteristics. Environmental influences also contribute to differences in behavior and learning (See **Table 4-2**).

Environmental Influences

Culture

The culture in which we are born, reared, and live plays a powerful role in shaping how we perceive and respond to the world around us. Culture can even dictate when conditions require intervention. In their research, Weisz, Suwanlert, Chaiyasit, and Weiss (1988) demonstrate that Thais do not identify extreme shyness or frequent fighting as problematic and believe that such behaviors will improve over time. In contrast, Americans rated these behaviors as serious enough to warrant professional help. In addition to the broad influence of culture, society is fragmented into various ethnic groups and social classes that influence behavior and learning (Kniveton, 1989; Rotheram-Borus, 1993; Salett & Koslow, 1994). Each society defines what is deviant (different from the norm), the role of the person who behaves in deviant ways, and expectations for the person who has been labeled as being deviant (Scheff, 1966). Even so, a student from a culture that is different from the majority of students in a school should not qualify for special education services due to cultural differences. However, culturally sanctioned behaviors which differ from what schools or teachers expect, may present challenges. For example, some individuals are culturally socialized to keep their emotions to themselves, while other cultures encourage the expression of emotions (Rotheram-Borus, 1993).

TABLE 4-3

Parenting Styles

Authoritarian

- expects unquestioning obedience
- uses harsh discipline
- children not allowed to make choices or express themselves

Permissive

- allows total freedom
- few expectations
- imposes few consequences

Authoritative

- recognizes children's ability levels
- realistic expectations for behavior
- warm and nurturing
- applies consequences consistently and fairly

A number of factors, including cultural socialization, may contribute to under- or over-diagnosis of students from different race and ethnic groups. Contributing factors may include intentional or unintentional bias of professionals determining eligibility, mismatch between the values and behaviors of teachers and the students they serve, or institutional discrimination (Osher et al., 2004). It is recognized that, at higher socioeconomic levels, African American males are overrepresented as having mental retardation while Asian females are least likely to be identified with mental retardation (Oswald, Coutinho, Best, & Nguyen, 2001). Similarly, African American students are overrepresented in the category of emotional disturbance while Asian, Pacific Islander, and Hispanic students are disproportionately underrepresented (Cullinan & Kauffman, 2005). More research is needed to document the factors contributing to the disproportionate representation of students identified for special education services.

Home

The home and, in particular, parents have considerable influence on the development of behavior. Baumrind (1967, 1991) studied the parenting styles of the parents of young children and adolescents. She found noteworthy differences between the styles of parents of children who are aggressive, children who are conflicted, and children who are healthy. Baumrind (1973) describes three types of parenting styles which are presented in **Table 4-3.** The differences in levels of parental control and nurturance have been found to result in significant differences in child outcomes (Baumrind, 1993, 1994). For example, an authoritative parenting style produces children who are friendly, cooperative, independent, with high self-esteems, and a focus on achievement. Authoritarian and permissive parenting styles do not tend to produce children with these characteristics.

Different parenting styles involve different methods of discipline. Parents who are harsh, inconsistent with discipline, erratically express their anger, and use nagging to get compliance tend to produce children who are aggressive. When parents and children engage in coercive styles of interaction at home, teachers may discover that these children will try to be intimidating at school in order to get what they want. Negative interactions and ineffective communication in the home also have been linked to the development of psychotic disorders (Miklowitz, Velligan, Goldstein, & Nuechterlein, 1991). Differences in parenting styles of discipline and interaction may produce differences in children's behavior and motivation to learn (Burt, McGue, Krueger, & Iacono, 2005; Dishion, Patterson, Stoolmiller, & Skinner, 1991; Henry, Moffitt, Robins, & Earl, 1993). Interventions which change the ways in which parents interact with their children have produced positive changes in the children's behavior (Kazdin, 1987).

Additionally, economic pressures and marital problems experienced by the parents can affect children's behaviors and their ability to learn. Conger, Ge, Elder, and Lorenz (1994) indicate that parents who are stressed over having enough money experience more marital conflict and engage in more conflicts with their children. Cummings (1994) found that marital discord interferes with effective parenting and results in higher rates of aggression among children. Divorce has been found to contribute significantly to the development of behavior and learning disorders (Sirvanli-Ozen, 2005). The research findings on family influences are very complex. It is difficult to draw any firm conclusions about family influences; however, there is little doubt that family factors are important.

School

The school and, in particular, teachers can influence the development of learning and behavior problems. Teachers are largely from middle-class backgrounds, and students are from all social classes. Teachers and students may become involved in values conflicts, such as when a teacher requires eye-to-eye contact and specific verbal responses ("*Yes, Ma'am*" or "*No, Sir*") which students may not have been taught to value at home. These conflicts can contribute to behavior and learning problems. It is known that teachers respond differently to students based on their expectations of the students (Van Acker, Grant, & Henry, 1996). If a teacher expects a student to know the answer, the teacher will wait longer for the student to respond. If a teacher expects a student to fail, the pause for a response will be shorter, and the teacher's non-verbal communication will be more negative (Sadker, Sadker, Fox, & Salenta, 1994). Kounin (1970) identified specific teacher behaviors that elicit behavior problems and subsequent learning difficulties. Teachers who are boring, disorganized, unprepared, or easily side-tracked, as well as those who present material too fast or too slow, actually encourage students to misbehave or stop attending. To reduce behavior and learning problems, teachers can reduce student confusion and disinterest by demonstrating the following elements:

- comfortable classroom pace
- strong sense of purpose
- high expectations of achievement
- talks only as much as necessary
- focuses on academic tasks
- structured transitions
- maximizes instructional time (keeps distractions to a minimum).

Scott, Nelson, and Liaupsin (2001) indicate that there is a clear association between academic underachievement and behavior problems. This association suggests curriculum factors may influence behavior. Failure to individualize curricula can result in assignments that are too difficult or too easy, promoting misbehavior (Moore & Edwards, 2003; Umbreit, Lane, & Dejud, 2004). When students react to inappropriate curricula by behaving inappropriately, they typically are removed from the learning situation and consequently do not acquire the knowledge or skills being presented. This tends to cause the students to fall further behind in their learning which, in turn, increases the likelihood that they will demonstrate inappropriate behaviors because they are frustrated by the academic demands.

Finally, Preiser and Taylor (1983) discussed the possible role of the school's physical environment on behavior. Their suggestions support the earlier work of Kozol (1967) who described how a dilapidated and decaying school environment could have serious detrimental effects on students' behavior and learning.

Peers

The peer group is a major influence on behavior and learning, second only to parents as an agent of social-

The peer group can have a significant influence on attitudes and behavior.

ization (Kindermann, 1993). The peer group can have a significant influence on sexual attitudes, sexual behavior, expression of aggression, moral standards, and emotional security. The peer group plays an important role in shaping attitudes and behaviors affecting school performance and dropping out (Farmer et al., 2003). Finally, it has been determined that associating with antisocial peers generates higher levels of misbehavior (Dishion, 1995).

Impact of Environment on Learning

An individual's behavior and achievement are affected by culture, home, school, and peers because the individual learns to behave in ways consistent with those influences or as a response to them. Although genetically inherited predispositions may account for the emergence of some behavioral or learning differences, everyone, including students with disabilities, learns how to behave and respond. The two dominant theories that explain how we learn to react are **behavioral learning** and **social learning.** Behavioral learning theory (Skinner, 1953) emphasizes that individuals engage in behaviors that allow them to either get something they want or avoid something they don't want. For example, if you want to get a good grade in class, you will attend class meetings, study for tests, and demonstrate good social skills with your instructor. You have learned to exhibit these behaviors in order to get something you want (a good class grade). Likewise, you have learned to brush your teeth in order to avoid having the dentist put fillings in your teeth. Students are quick to learn that their behaviors can help them get something they want or avoid something they don't want. If students come from chaotic and deprived home environments, they may have learned that the only way they can have food to eat is to take it from someone else. It should come as no surprise then that they demonstrate the same behaviors in school. Students also learn that if they want to avoid doing math, all they need to do is pick a fight with a peer right before math class, and they will spend the period in the Principal's office, rather than in the dreaded math class. Or they may have learned to act "helpless" so that someone else will do their math work for them. Students may learn to give-up and act disinterested instead of attempting an assignment that they have not been able to do in the past. After all, who wants to put effort into something that has been graded "wrong" in the past?

Social learning theory suggests that humans learn to behave in certain ways based on what they observe others doing (Bandura, 1969). A student may observe someone they admire spitting on the floor and then will spit on the floor in order to be like that person. Likewise, students may observe someone else being punished for getting out of line in the hallway and will subsequently try to stay in line so that they won't be punished. Not all students have had the opportunity to observe appropriate models. For example, a student may never have received a positive response when saying "Good Morning" or may never have heard anyone say "Good Morning" to another person. A student may have learned how to sell drugs without being caught by observing others engaged in that activity. Behavioral and social learning theories substantiate that students demonstrate poor behaviors and learning strategies because they have learned to do so, whether through actual experience or observation.

Conclusion

Biology and environment combine to make each of us who we are. Many predispositions and conditions that affect behavior and learning are inborn. It is clear that many behavior and learning differences result from environmental factors which influence the developing person. To further complicate the issue, many biologic predispositions will not appear unless environmental factors elicit them. For example, women who smoke during pregnancy predispose their unborn children to having learning disabilities (Streissguth, 1986), and a mother who drinks during pregnancy may predispose a child to a host of behavioral and learning disorders such as hyperactivity, sporadic mastery of tasks, aggressive behaviors, and limited understanding of cause and effect (Fried, Watkinson, & Dillon, 1987; Jackson, 1990). However, if these children experience supportive environments which are effective in teaching them the basics of reading and writing, their predisposition for learning disabilities may never become evident. Infants who were prenatally substance exposed may not demonstrate any of the negative outcomes associated with the maternal drug use if the infants receive early intervention within supportive environments (Harping, 1990). Conversely, the environment may be able to create behavior and learning disorders even in the absence of a biologic predisposition. For example, a student who has no predisposition for learning problems may experience a series of traumatic school events which can cause the student to lose interest in learning. This loss of interest then may result in the student failing academic tasks. Children who were not prenatally substance exposed, but who were raised in postnatal environments where drugs were being used demonstrate behaviors very similar to those who have been prenatally substance exposed (Hays, 1988; Wilson, McReary, & Kean, 1979).

In conclusion, both biologic factors and environmental conditions may create a heightened risk for the development of behavioral or learning problems. Some disabilities, such as Down Syndrome, are more influenced by genetic contributions, while other disabilities, such as depression may be more affected by environmental factors. For the vast majority of students with mild learning and behavioral disorders, the etiology of the disability will never be known. Since the cause of a mild disability may never be pinpointed, teachers should focus their energies on providing appropriate instruction. To say that it doesn't matter what happens to children in school because they come from "bad homes" denies them any chance of success. Likewise, persistent efforts to blame the family will only increase hostility between schools and families and will divert the emphasis away from important instructional tasks. Before beginning the discussion of behavioral disorders and learning disabilities, we will discuss the two systems used to categorize them: the educational system and the psychiatric classification system.

Classification Systems

Educational System: IDEA 2004

As presented in Chapter 2, students in educational settings are classified according to categories defined in IDEA 2004. Each state uses federal definitions as guidelines to develop specific eligibility criteria for each of the twelve categories of disabilities. All of the definitions include the necessity for the disability to adversely affect educational performance before a student may be considered eligible for special education services. For example, students with a mild learning disability may not be identified during kindergarten because the disability has not affected their ability to benefit from their educational opportunities. However, as the students encounter more academic tasks, it will become apparent that the disability is affecting learning, and a referral for assessment for eligibility would be appropriate. The federal definitions are provided in this chapter under each specific behavioral and learning disability except for attention deficit/hyperactivity disorder (ADHD) which is not addressed in IDEA 2004. For a diagnosis of ADHD, individuals must turn to alternate sources such as Section 504 of Vocational Rehabilitation Act as discussed in Chapter 2 or a psychiatric classification system such as the one contained in the *DSM IV-TR,* the *Diagnostic and Statistical Manual of Mental Disorders* (4th ed., text revision) (APA, 2000). A discussion of the psychiatric classification system follows.

Psychiatric Classification System: *DSM IV-TR*

The *Diagnostic and Statistical Manual of Mental Disorders* (4th ed., text revision) (APA, 2000) is an approach to classifying disorders that is widely used by medical and mental health professionals. Whereas the educational system relies on disability definitions provided in IDEA 2004, most physicians, psychiatrists, and insurance companies rely exclusively on diagnoses made according to the *DSM IV-TR.* The *DSM IV-TR* provides time-frames and characteristics that must be present before an individual can be diagnosed as having a disorder. A *DSM IV-TR* diagnosis must be made by a physician, psychologist, psychiatrist, or specially trained counselor. Educational personnel (with the exception of a school psychologist) cannot make a *DSM IV-TR* diagnosis. Diagnoses enable professionals to speak a common language, plan treatments, and make insurance claims. The *DSM IV-TR* contains all of the same disability conditions as found in IDEA 2004, plus many more. A *DSM IV-TR* diagnosis does not qualify a student for special education services, and actually may exclude the student from services (e.g., a *DSM IV-TR* diagnosis of "conduct disorder" specifically excludes a student from special education in most states). *DSM IV-TR* diagnoses are frequently irrelevant for educational purposes and teachers must be cautious when encountering a *DSM IV-TR* diagnosis since they are not reviewed annually as are the diagnoses under IDEA 2004. However, since the *DSM IV-TR* is widely used among non-educational agencies, and must be used for diagnosing attention deficit/hyperactivity disorder (ADHD), this classification system will be referenced during the discussions of behavior and learning problems.

Categories of Students with Behavior and Learning Challenges

Every teacher has a set of expectations regarding behavior that must be present in order for teaching to occur. Some teachers expect students to stay seated at all times, work individually, and speak only after they have raised their hands and been called on. Other teachers allow students to move around the room as necessary in order to gather materials for completing collaborative work and allow questions to be asked without the raising of hands. When students demonstrate behaviors that differ from those expected by the teacher, the teacher will have to give special consideration to their management. Behavioral differences range from mild to severe, with the mild differences being considered nuisances and the severe differences requiring referral for eligibility as disorders. Similarly, students who demonstrate differences in the way they learn may have difficulty benefiting from typical school environments. Sometimes a change in the way material is presented and emphasized is sufficient to facilitate learning. For example, some individuals learn best when presented with visuals, such as pictures and printed material, to illustrate new information. However, some learning differences cannot be accommodated simply by modifying the manner of presentation.

Although it is recognized that individualized and intensive instruction may be necessary to promote academic and social achievement for students with behavior and learning challenges, it is not known if the instructional strategies vary according to the different eligibilities (Sabornie, Cullinan, Osborne, & Brock, 2005). What is known is that without intervention, individuals with behavior and learning challenges have a poor prognosis for success in post-school environments (Luftig & Muthert, 2005; Walker, Ramsey, & Gresham, 2004). For students with mild disabilities, a critical determinant of post-school success is proficiency with the general education curriculum. Indeed, the mandates of NCLB will require that the majority of students with behavior and learning challenges participate in general education assessments as a part of each school's accountability measure. To promote student achievement, teachers must understand the differences between the categories of behavior and learning challenges and must become proficient in implementing instructional strategies shown to be effective across the range of mild disabilities. The following categorical descriptions provide information useful for differentiating among students with mild disabilities and discuss unique issues for teachers. Discussions of effective instructional strategies appear in other chapters of this text. Information on categorical descriptions is ordered as follows: attention deficit/hyperactivity disorder (ADHD), emotional disturbance (ED), autism, specific learning disabilities (SLD), mild mental retardation (MR), and traumatic brain injury (TBI). For each of these categorical descriptions, a definition will be provided, followed by discussions of characteristics, specific etiological contributions, assessment considerations, and issues for classroom teachers.

Attention Deficit/Hyperactivity Disorder (ADHD)

Children naturally vary in such things as activity level, impulse control, and ability for sustained attention. As they grow older, most children develop an increased ability to inhibit and control their activity level, impulsivity, and attention. However, a small group of children have extreme problems in managing all three. Such children exhibit inattention, impulsivity, and overactivity. Many exhibit problems in learning and may not exhibit acceptable behaviors in most social situations, especially in school. Estimates of the prevalence of ADHD vary widely, but the Centers for Disease Control and Prevention (2005) suggests that approximately 7.8% of students aged 4–17 years, have been diagnosed as having ADHD.

Definition

Since IDEA does not define ADHD, parents must turn to the psychiatric classification system to establish a diagnosis. As mentioned previously, the Diagnostic and Statistical

Manual of Mental Disorders (4th ed., text revision) (APA, 2000), contains criteria for a number of disabling conditions, including ADHD. The *DSM IV-TR* definition of ADHD specifies that the condition requires evidence of inattention, hyperactivity, and impulsivity, as defined by the presence of a certain number of symptoms. The *DSM IV-TR* manual lists the specific symptoms which must be present. The symptoms must have been apparent before age seven, have occurred for at least six months, and be inconsistent with the child's developmental level. The behaviors must be present in two or more settings (e.g., school and home). In addition, the student must show significant impairment in social and academic functioning. Finally, the *DSM IV-TR* requires the following:

> The symptoms do not occur exclusively during the course of a Pervasive Developmental Disorder, Schizophrenia, or other Psychotic Disorder and are not better accounted for by another mental disorder (e.g., Mood Disorder, Anxiety Disorder, Dissociative Disorder, or a Personality Disorder). (APA, 2000, p. 93)

DSM IV-TR criteria classifies students with ADHD into the following categories:

- Predominantly inattentive
- Predominantly hyperactive/impulsive
- Combined type with inattentive and hyperactive.

According to the first category, an individual with ADHD can have problems with sustained attention without demonstrating hyperactivity (excessive motor movements). For example, students with the predominantly inattentive type of ADHD may be able to sit in their desks and look at the teacher, giving the appearance of listening to directions, but will fail to carry out the assignment given by the teacher. In contrast, students with the predominantly hyperactive/impulsive type of ADHD may fidget with their shoes, lean over the desk to talk to another student, and jump up to sharpen a pencil. Neither student will complete the assignment. Although differences in the diagnosis of ADHD relate to the level of hyperactivity, the educational outcomes are basically the same in that the students will not complete their assignments. In addition, students who demonstrate highly active behavioral levels create challenges for teachers trying to establish orderly, focused learning environments.

Various definitions of ADHD include the characteristics of inattention, impulsivity, motor restlessness, and differences in motivation. Parent and advocacy groups for ADHD lobbied to have ADHD as a discrete definition and category during the 1990 reauthorization of IDEA, but the issue was controversial. Parents of children with ADHD think the current disability categories are insufficient to include their children. Many professionals believe that these children can be served by existing programs and that creating too many categories would be counterproductive (Forness, 1993).

As a result of the efforts of advocates, the IDEA 2004 description of Other Health Impairment (OHI) specifies issues with attention and ADHD is listed as one of the chronic or acute health problems that could lead to an OHI eligibility. As stated in the law:

> Other health impairment means having limited strength, vitality or alertness, including a heightened alertness to environmental stimuli, that results in limited alertness with respect to the educational environment, that—
>
> (i) Is due to chronic or acute health problems such as asthma, attention deficit disorder or attention deficit hyperactivity disorder, diabetes, epilepsy, a heart condition, hemophilia, lead poisoning, leukemia, nephritis, rheumatic fever, and sickle cell anemia; and
>
> (ii) Adversely affects a child's educational performance.

Some students with ADHD will be found eligible for special education services under the category of OHI. Some students with ADHD will be served under another category of eligibility, such as ED or SLD, as determined by the eligibility team to reflect the most pronounced coexisting disability. Students with ADHD who do not qualify for special education services under one of the specific IDEA 2004 categories can receive accommodations under Section 504 of the Vocational Rehabilitation Act (1973). Indeed, most students with ADHD will be served according to the guidelines of Section 504 and a written plan will identify specific types of accommodations to allow them to benefit from their educational opportunities.

Characteristics

There are three major characteristics present in children with ADHD: inattention, impulsivity, and hyperactivity. **Inattention** is defined as an inability to focus or concentrate for age-appropriate amounts of time. It is indicated by chronic difficulty in sustaining attention to tasks or play, chronic careless mistakes in schoolwork, not listening when spoken to directly, not following directions, having cluttered and disorganized materials, losing books and other materials, and being easily distracted by external stimuli not affecting other students. Setley (1995) discusses the misnaming of attention deficit disorder and suggests other possibilities such as "Attention Focusing Disorder," "Attention Fluctuation Disorder," or "Attention Surplus Disorder." **Impulsivity** is the inability to control one's behaviors and reactions on a reflective level. It is characterized by a tendency to blurt out answers, answering a question before the question is completely asked, not waiting for turns, chronically interrupting others, and failing to finish work. Teachers may describe impulsivity as a tendency to act first and think later. **Hyperactivity** is defined as excessive motor movement. It includes such behaviors as excessive fidgeting, squirming in seat, leaving seat while others remain seated, running about and climbing when such activity is clearly inappropriate, and seeming to be continuously in motion. Bloomingdale, Swanson, Barkley, and Satterfield (1991) describe hyperactivity as an excess of activity that is not task related, and others have suggested that this overactivity has erroneously been the focus of adult concern when the other components have more negative implications for learning (DuPaul, Guevremont, & Barkley, 1991). In addition, current research indicates that individuals with ADHD not only have difficulties with attention, impulsivity, and hyperactivity, but also deficits in **motivation** (Barkley, 1990). It is this last key element which explains why students with ADHD have difficulty focusing on school or social tasks but seem to have little difficulty playing video games for prolonged periods of time.

Thirty to fifty percent of students labeled as ADHD also exhibit conduct disorders or oppositional defiant disorder (Conners, 1993). Students with conduct disorders (CD) exhibit aggression toward people or animals, destruction of property, stealing, chronic lying, and severe rule violations. Oppositional defiant disorder (ODD) involves "a recurrent pattern of negativistic, defiant, disobedient, and hostile behavior toward authority figures that persists for at least six months" (*DSM IV-TR*, 2000, p. 100). Clearly, ADHD and CD or ODD can coexist, creating a condition where a student may be at risk of engaging in antisocial

Inattention is an inability to concentrate for age-appropriate amounts of time, and is one of the characteristics in children with ADHD.

behavior. In fact, studies show a significantly higher incidence of involvement with the law by coexisting ADHD/CD students (Crowley, Milkulich, MacDonald, Young, & Zerbe, 1998). Yet, it should be noted that not all students with ADHD have antisocial tendencies.

In addition to ever increasing numbers of children being identified as having ADHD, more adults are being diagnosed with the disorder. Individuals with ADHD typically do not outgrow the disability. Due to the growing awareness that adults can have the disorder, one of the large parent and professional organizations, Children with Attention Deficit Disorder (CH.A.D.D.), has changed its name to "*Children and Adults with Attention Deficit Disorders.*" Whereas school systems are responsible for identifying all students with disabilities, adults with disabilities, such as ADHD, must self-identify in order to receive accommodations in post-secondary education or the workplace according to ADA.

Specific Etiology

Those who view ADHD as having a pure biologic etiology have different explanations for its cause than do those who insist that ADHD results from environmental influences. Historically, it was believed that individuals who suffered minor damage to the brain would become hyperactive, inattentive, and impulsive, and the term minimal brain dysfunction (MBD) was used to describe them (Strauss & Lehtinen, 1947). Although today's researchers do not describe students with ADHD as having brain damage, they do believe that the condition may be caused by brain differences due to an underlying biological cause (Voeller, 2004). The disorder may occur due to a chemical imbalance in the neurologic system or a deficiency of neurotransmitters in the brain (Thapar, O'Donovan, & Owen, 2005). Zametkin et al. (1990) concluded that the brain of a person with ADHD uses less glucose than the brain of a person who does not have ADHD, further describing a brain difference. Others have suggested that ADHD occurs more frequently among biologic relatives; therefore, there must be a genetic predisposition (Sprich, Biederman, Crawford, Mundy, & Faraone, 2000).

Some researchers suggest that changes in society have created generations of students who have short attention spans. Chemical and environmental toxins have been identified as contributing to the development of ADHD (Feingold, 1975; Waldman, 1991). Additionally, it has been suggested that increased television viewing and the popularity of fast-paced video games have resulted in diminished attention spans and a preference for activities which are quick with immediate consequences. Poverty and deprivation also appear to create a heightened risk for ADHD in children (Werry, Elkind, & Reeves, 1987).

Proponents for both the biologic and environmental arguments present plausible causes for ADHD. However, the etiology of ADHD is unknown, with an explanation involving a combination of factors being the most reasonable. The etiology debate is further complicated by those who insist that ADHD is not a unique condition, but rather a component of other disabilities, therefore caused by whatever led to the emergence of the original disability.

Assessment for Eligibility

A noneducational diagnosis of ADHD by someone, such as a psychologist or psychiatrist, using the *DSM IV-TR* can lead to a student being deemed eligible for special services under Section 504. Students with ADHD who need accommodations as guaranteed by Section 504, will receive those services in the general education classroom. Students with ADHD, who are eligible for services under IDEA 2004, will have an IEP which specifies the support they will need to benefit from their educational opportunities.

Behavior rating scales are often used to document the symptoms of ADHD. Both parents and teachers use methods of direct observation and different rating scales to support the existence of symptoms across settings. **Figure 4-1** provides examples of the teacher version and the parent version of the Conners' Rating Scales (Conners, 1993).

Issues for the Classroom Teacher

There is general agreement that students with ADHD require highly structured home and school environments. In addition, a significant number of students with ADHD have been prescribed a variety of medications to help improve academics and enhance social functioning. **Stimulant medications** such as Ritalin, Dexadrine, and Cylert are prescribed by physicians, with Ritalin being the most common. When stimulant medications were first prescribed for students, they were described as having a paradoxical effect. The paradox occurs because a stimulant would excite an adult, but has the opposite effect on children. We now know that this is untrue. Stimulants stimulate children just as they do adults. However, our understanding of ADHD has changed considerably. It is now believed that the parts of the brain that control motivation, attention, and inhibition are underactive in persons with ADHD. Therefore, the stimulants do what they should: stimulate the under-stimulated parts of the brain, resulting in greater attention and control of behavior.

As with all human behavior, the relationship between medication and improvement, or lack thereof, appears to be complex. Medication alone constitutes an inadequate form of intervention. Academic and environmental modifications definitely will be needed for students receiving stimulant medication. Teachers working with students who demonstrate the characteristics associated with ADHD must create carefully structured environments which incorporate behavior management techniques as described in Chapter 11.

To conclude, the causes of ADHD are still unknown although biologic and environmental factors have been identified which can lead to the manifestation of the disorder. IDEA 2004 does not contain a discrete eligibility category for students with ADHD, although provisions have been made for students with the disability to be served under the label OHI if a medical professional has diagnosed the presence of the condition. Stimulant medications have been found to be helpful for reducing the motor activity of students with ADHD, but the use of such drugs has been controversial. Teachers will be challenged to structure the environment and academic tasks so that students with ADHD will be able to succeed in school. **Figures 4-2a** and **4-2b** provide examples of the performance on a spelling test of a 10-year-old male diagnosed with ADHD. The sample in **Figure 4-2a** was written while the student was not taking medication. Notice that he did not begin the test until the teacher was on number seven. The test in **Figure 4-2b** reflects his performance after medication was initiated. **Figure 4-3** presents a description of a student with ADHD.

Emotional Disturbance (ED)

All teachers will encounter students with challenging behaviors. Students come to class with many personal issues and needs. Most of these will spill over into the classroom and affect the student's potential for learning. Not all challenging behaviors will be extreme. Teachers are accustomed to working with students who sulk or who are less than thrilled about an assignment at hand. It is developmentally appropriate for students to go through phases where they orchestrate mini-rebellions (*"At 11:00, everyone drop your pencil."*) or are more interested in interacting with their peers than they are in complying with adult directives. However, some students' inappropriate behaviors and emotional reactions occur with greater intensity and frequency than the behaviors and reactions of

Samples of Rating Scales to Document ADHD

Conners' Teacher Rating Scale - Revised (S)
by C. Keith Conners, Ph.D.

Child's Name:_____ Gender: M F

Birthdate:____/____/____ Age:_____ School Grade:_____
      Month Day Year

Teacher's Name:_____ Today's Date:____/____/____
                                         Month Day Year

Instructions: Below are a number of common problems that children have in school. Please rate each item according to how much of a problem it has been in the last month. For each item, ask yourself, "How much of a problem has this been in the last month?", and circle the best answer for each one. If none, not at all, seldom, or very infrequently, you would circle 0. If very much true, or it occurs very often or frequently, you would circle 3. You would circle 1 or 2 for ratings in between. Please respond to each item.

	NOT TRUE AT ALL (Never, Seldom)	JUST A LITTLE TRUE (Occasionally)	PRETTY MUCH TRUE (Often, Quite a Bit)	VERY MUCH TRUE (Very Often, Very Frequent)
1. Inattentive, easily distracted	0	1	2	3
2. Defiant	0	1	2	3
3. Restless in the "squirmy" sense	0	1	2	3
4. Forgets things he/she has already learned	0	1	2	3
5. Disturbs other children	0	1	2	3
6. Actively defies or refuses to comply with adults' requests	0	1	2	3

Conners' Parent Rating Scale - Revised (S)
by C. Keith Conners, Ph.D.

Child's Name:_____ Gender: M F

Birthdate:____/____/____ Age:_____ School Grade:_____
      Month Day Year

Parent's Name:_____ Today's Date:____/____/____
                                         Month Day Year

Instructions: Below are a number of common problems that children have. Please rate each item according to your child's behavior in the last month. For each item, ask yourself, "How much of a problem has this been in the last month?", and circle the best answer for each one. If none, not at all, seldom, or very infrequently, you would circle 0. If very much true, or it occurs very often or frequently, you would circle 3. You would circle 1 or 2 for ratings in between. Please respond to each item.

	NOT TRUE AT ALL (Never, Seldom)	JUST A LITTLE TRUE (Occasionally)	PRETTY MUCH TRUE (Often, Quite a Bit)	VERY MUCH TRUE (Very Often, Very Frequent)
1. Inattentive, easily distracted	0	1	2	3
2. Angry and resentful	0	1	2	3
3. Difficulty doing or completing homework	0	1	2	3
4. Is always "on the go" or acts as if driven by a motor	0	1	2	3
5. Short attention span	0	1	2	3
6. Argues with adults	0	1	2	3

FIGURE 4-2A

Spelling Test of a Student with ADHD While Not on Medication

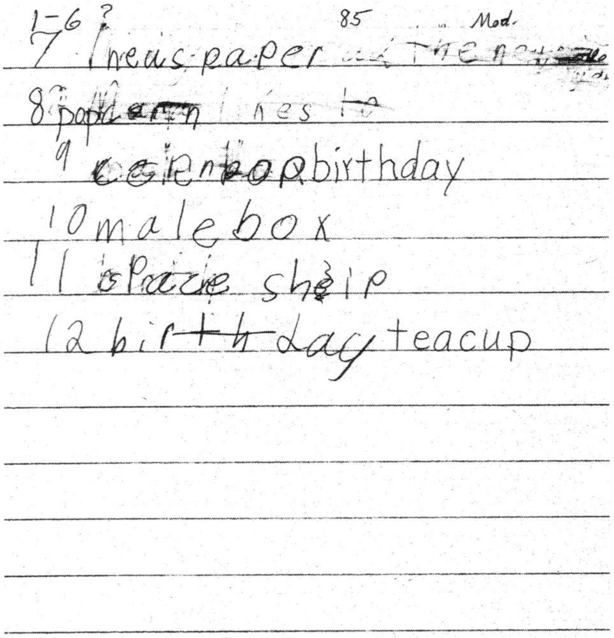
1–6 ? 85 Mod.
7 newspaper
8 popcorn
9 birthday
10 malebox
11 ship
12 teacup

FIGURE 4-2B

Spelling Test of the Same Student as in Figure 4-2A While on Medication

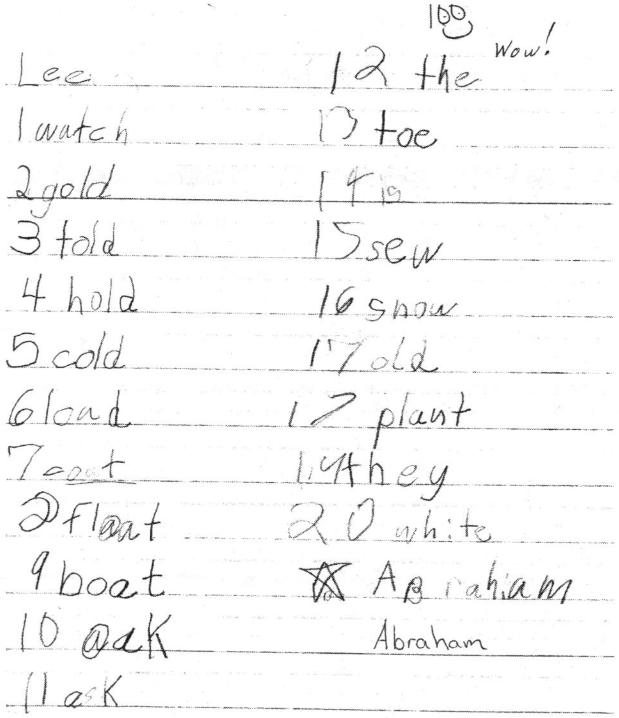
100 Wow!
Lee
1 watch
2 gold
3 told
4 hold
5 cold
6 load
7 coat
8 float
9 boat
10 oak
11 ask
12 the
13 toe
14 is
15 sew
16 snow
17 old
18 plant
19 they
20 white
Abraham
Abraham

FIGURE 4-3

Description of a Student with ADHD

Jessie's parents married later in life than most of their friends. They also waited until the perfect time to have children. It had taken quite a long time and many doctors' visits before Jessie was conceived. The birth of a healthy boy was a joyous and celebrated occasion. The baby was the center of attention, and attention he demanded! Feeding an infant on demand and giving the long awaited only child that attention didn't seem out of line to his doting parents.

During his preschool years, Jessie was demanding, easily frustrated, and often destructive. When other children began to make friends and invite each other over, Jessie was left out. Around other children, Jessie's behavior became intolerable. He was possessive, reckless, and never satisfied. Special occasions, such as birthdays or parties, became a nightmare for anyone around Jessie. He would become overstimulated, scream, cry, and throw tantrums.

The preschool teacher talked at length to Jessie's parents about his behavior. His language skills and memory were advanced when compared to his peers. However, his fine motor skills were below expectation for his age; he had great difficulty cutting and coloring. During activities, Jessie would demand his turn, then rush through carelessly, and race to whatever caught his eye.

Jessie's parents, agreeing with the teacher's assessment, scheduled an appointment with their pediatrician. Dr. Smalley had a personal interest in ADHD and had received additional training in the identification and treatment of this disability. It was determined that Jessie's parents should attend a course he was teaching and try some of the behavioral techniques they learned. Although the strategies could not stop Jessie's behavior, his parents gained valuable insight into minimizing his out-of-control behaviors. His parents also became more comfortable managing Jessie's behavior by using non-emotional and consistent responses.

In school, additional problems began to appear. Jessie knew all the answers to the questions his teacher posed to the class and did not hesitate to blurt out his response, even when the inquiry was made to a reading group of which he was not a member. Jessie spent a great deal of time at the pencil sharpener, the window, and in time-out. His papers were almost impossible to read due to his illegible handwriting, erasures, and the way he rushed through the task. His parents continued to consult with Dr. Smalley and provided him with information regarding Jessie's classroom behavior. It was decided that an in-depth evaluation needed to be done.

Jessie's parents and his teacher completed questionnaires specific to his behavior. Additional tests were given to assess his cognitive abilities, language skills, and academic achievement levels. After reviewing all the documentation, Dr. Smalley diagnosed Jessie as having ADHD. Before prescribing medication, Dr. Smalley instructed both the parents and the teacher to collect information for two weeks. At home, his parents were told to record food intake, number of hours sleeping, and outbursts of screaming and crying. At school, the teacher was to record the number of times Jessie was out of his seat, how many papers he completed legibly, altercations with his peers such as pushing incidents, shouting out of answers, and overall classroom participation. After the two-week observation period, Dr. Smalley prescribed Ritalin. Jessie's parents and his teacher were requested to continue collecting information on Jessie's behavior to determine if the medication was beneficial. Since there was no indication of additional disabilities, Jessie could be provided accommodations and adaptations under Section 504.

After many years of continued medication and behavior management, Jessie is now in middle school. His grades are excellent, and he exceeds academically. His behavior remains a challenge to everyone: teachers, parents, grandparents, scout leaders, and friends. He has not overcome his compulsive need to be first, interrupt conversations, have his say, or tell others what to do. Interactions are difficult because of his lack of control, and he does not have many friends. Although he always will have difficulty with relationships, Jessie will be able to earn a college degree and select a career that he finds rewarding. Jessie's ADHD can be managed, but it cannot be cured.

FIGURE 4-4

Robot drawn by a 15-year-old male with EBD to destroy all humans because they are imperfect

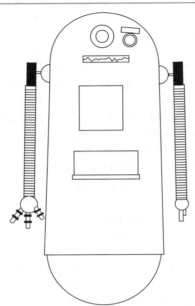

their peers. These students' behaviors may differ so significantly that they are labeled as having **emotional disturbances (ED). Figure 4-4** displays a picture drawn by a student with an emotional disturbance.

Definition

Until IDEA 97, the federal category for students who meet the eligibility being discussed here was "serious emotional disturbances" (SED). The legislative concession to the on-going pressure to change the definition of SED (see below) was to drop the word "seri-ous". IDEA 97 specifies that the term "emotional disturbances" (ED) will be used instead of SED. Nothing was changed in the actual definition for ED.

The federal definition of ED was taken from the work of Bower (1960) who was designing criteria to determine which California school children were in need of mental health services. Bower's criteria were incorporated, with some critical changes, into the definition that became a part of IDEA. According to federal law, ED is defined as:

(i) The term means a condition exhibiting one or more of the following characteristics over a long period of time and to a marked degree, which adversely affects educa-tional performance:

  (A) An inability to learn which cannot be explained by intellectual, sensory, or other health factors.

  (B) An inability to build or maintain satisfactory interpersonal relationships with peers and teachers.

  (C) Inappropriate types of behavior or feelings under normal circumstances.

(D) A general, pervasive mood of unhappiness or depression.

(E) A tendency to develop physical symptoms or fears associated with personal or school problems.

(ii) Emotional disturbances includes schizophrenia. The term does not apply to children who are socially maladjusted, unless it is determined that they have an emotional disturbance.

The definition in P.L. 94-142 (1975) originally included children with autism under section (ii), but autism was moved into the category of "Other Health Impaired" in 1981 and finally established as a discrete category under IDEA in 1990.

The federal definition of ED contains components which are controversial and inhibit the provision of services to students with challenging behaviors and emotional disorders. Questions have been raised as to what is meant by "a marked degree" and "a long period of time" and how that should be measured. The exclusion of students who are socially maladjusted seems to contradict criteria (B) and has led to the conclusion that we should be able to differentiate between students who choose to act out and those whose behavior is not under their control (Weinberg, 1992). This conclusion has been challenged repeatedly (Merrell & Walker, 2004). Some cite lack of remorse as evidence against eligibility for EBD (Gacono & Hughes, 2004) since emotion is not involved. However, lack of remorse should be viewed as one of the strongest indicators of a disturbance in emotion. Additionally, social maladjustment is comorbid with internalizing disorders such as depression (Davis, Sheeber, & Hops, 2002). Finally, Nelson, Rutherford, Center, and Walker (1991) argue that the public schools have an obligation to serve all students, including those with social maladjustments, and that it is in society's best interest to serve these students and hopefully prevent many of them from becoming a social burden.

Most researchers and authors in the field use the term **emotional behavioral disorders (EBD)** rather than ED. Some states, such as Georgia, use the new label (EBD) with the ED definition. In essence, a student must qualify for the label EBD according to ED criteria. For the remainder of this section, the preferable term, emotional/behavioral disorders (EBD) will be used instead of ED.

Characteristics

Emotional/behavioral differences may be directed outward, as in the case of students who are verbally or physically aggressive, or may be directed inward, as in the case of students who become very depressed or develop extreme fears **(phobias).** The behaviors and emotions that are directed outward are called **externalizing,** and the ones directed inward are called **internalizing** (Quay, 1986). Students with EBD can demonstrate externalizing behavior disorders, internalizing behavior disorders, or a combination of both. Since students with externalizing behavior disorders are those who act out, educators tend to notice them before they notice students with internalizing behavior disorders. Students with internalizing behavior disorders may be withdrawn and call little attention to themselves, but may need specialized interventions just as much as the students who are acting out (Bucy, 1994). **Figure 4-5** describes a student who exhibits EBD characteristics.

Quay and Peterson (1987) categorize behaviors using a behavioral dimensions classification system. According to their system, emotional/behavioral disorders may be divided into six classifications. These classifications and examples of typical behaviors are as follows:

1. **Conduct Disorder (CD):** antisocial, acting-out, disruptive, temper tantrums, uncooperative, negative, argumentative, bully, blames others, selfish, cruel.

2. **Socialized Aggression (SA):** also called socialized delinquents; associates with "bad" companions, may belong to a gang, steals, cheats, lies, truant, runs away from home, thinks highly of others who break laws or violate moral codes.

FIGURE 4-5

Description of a Student Exhibiting Characteristics of an Emotional Behavioral Disorder

Tamika was born to an upper-middle-class family in a suburban area. As their first born, Tamika's parents had high expectations for her and reinforced her for perfect performance in all areas. Although they did not punish her when her performance was less than perfect, Tamika could sense that her parents were disappointed, which made her feel badly about herself. Frequently, Tamika would work on tasks much longer than necessary, until the finished product met her standards.

Tamika did well in school until her third-grade year. As the work became more challenging, Tamika discovered that she could not complete assignments perfectly within the given amount of time. Her previous teachers had provided Tamika with multiple copies of handouts, so that her assignments would be turned in with no mistakes or erasures. Her third-grade teacher, in addition to expecting her to finish her work in the same time that it took the others, refused to give her extra copies of worksheets so that she could have a perfect product. In addition, Tamika's tolerance for the mistakes made by her peers diminished, and she openly criticized their efforts.

As the year progressed, Tamika began to get more and more anxious about making mistakes and felt physically ill when her teacher gave an assignment. She attempted to structure herself so that there was little deviation in her routines and kept her desk and locker highly ordered.

Tired of her criticism and what they perceived to be an uppity attitude, her peers began to torment her by moving things in her desk and "accidentally" marking on her papers. Tamika rarely spoke to anyone and bottled her turmoil inside of her until one day she exploded.

As the teacher was passing back test papers, Tamika was thinking about her current unfinished assignment, full of erasures and mistakes, wadded up in her book bag. She was further dismayed to see the 87 that glared at her in red ink at the top of her test. At the same time, one of her peers bumped her desk on the way back to his seat and laughed. Tamika grabbed her pencil and lunged at the boy, stabbing him in the arm.

Tamika's teacher described her as uncontrollably violent when her parents arrived to pick her up from the principal's office. When Tamika returned to school following a brief suspension, her interactions with peers and teachers became increasingly aggressive and abusive. It finally became apparent that Tamika's long-standing beliefs were interfering with her ability to be a part of and benefit from the educational environment.

3. **Attention Problems-Immaturity (AP):** short attention span, distractible, impulsive, inattentive, acts younger than they are, has trouble following directions.
4. **Anxiety-Withdrawal (AW):** anxious, avoids, self-conscious, sensitive, depressed, fearful, believes they will always fail, difficulty making decisions, complains of feeling sick.
5. **Psychotic Behavior (PB):** difficulty differentiating between reality and fantasy, hallucinations, delusional thinking; e.g., childhood schizophrenia.
6. **Motor Excess (ME):** hyperactive, difficulty sitting still, fidgety, appears nervous, jumpy.

These six categories of behavior are useful in describing students who have emotional behavioral disorders. As you think logically about these six categories, you will see that they can be grouped to create two behavioral profiles (undersocialized aggressive and socialized aggressive) and one emotional profile. The difference between the two behavioral profiles is awareness. Students who fit the profile of having an undersocialized aggressive conduct disorder, appear to be unaware of behavioral expectations and do not appear to be aware of how to behave. These are students who demonstrate behaviors which fit in the categories of CD, AP, and ME. On the other hand, students who fit the profile of having a socialized aggressive conduct disorder appear to be aware that their

TABLE 4-4

Categories of Emotional Behavioral Disorders According to Quay and Peterson

Behavioral Disorders (externalizing)	Emotional Disorders (internalizing)
Undersocialized Aggressive Conduct Disorder	
• Conduct Disorder	• Anxiety-Withdrawal
• Attention Problems—Immaturity	• Psychotic Behavior
• Motor Excess	
Socialized Aggressive Conduct Disorder	
• Socialized Aggression	

behaviors are inappropriate and try to hide them or engage in them secretly. These are students who demonstrate behaviors described in the second category, socialized aggression (SA) (Quay, 1986). Whereas undersocialized aggression and socialized aggression are behavioral disorders, the behaviors described in the fourth category, anxiety-withdrawal (AW), are considered emotional disorders. Psychotic behaviors (PB) also may result from emotional disorders and are included in that profile. Although this distinction between behavioral and emotional disorders seems fairly clear-cut, the difficulty comes when one attempts to separate the emotions from the behavior or vice versa (Tankersley, 1993). **Table 4-4** provides a graphic depiction of the types of emotional/behavioral disorders and their corresponding Quay and Peterson (1987) categories.

Note that using the classification system provided by Quay and Peterson (1987) or the classifications provided in the *DSM IV-TR* may actually prevent a student from being deemed eligible for special education services. Specifically, if classified as having a conduct disorder (CD) according to either source, the student will be automatically excluded from special education eligibility according to IDEA 2004. In addition, classifying a student as demonstrating socialized aggression according to Quay and Peterson often creates barriers for being able to consider whether or not the student is eligible for special education because of the perceived association with social maladjustment.

Specific Etiology

Emotional and behavioral disorders may be attributed to genetic predispositions, environmental factors, or a combination of the two. Some researchers suggest that the tendency for engaging in criminal behavior may be inherited, as well as the predisposition for depression and schizophrenia (Gottesman, 1991; Quinsey, Skilling, Lalumiere, & Craig, 2004). Others emphasize the role of parents in the development of aggressive or antisocial behaviors and depression (Burt et al., 2005; Counts, Nigg, Stawicki, Rappley, & von Eye, 2005). Finally, Goldstein (1988) suggests that some students are genetically inclined to be schizophrenic, but that the disorder will be demonstrated only if the environmental conditions bring it out and suggests the same for individuals who demonstrate disorders of affect.

The social and behavioral learning theories discussed previously in this chapter explain how most students with EBD learn to behave inappropriately. Students with EBD may have been reinforced by getting their way when they hit or yell at someone, so they continue to use this tactic to get what they want. Students with EBD may have observed someone they admire using profanity and choose to cuss to be like that person. Or they may kick box to be as macho as actors in movies. Similarly, a student who demonstrates behavior that creates chaos in a classroom may have never been told NOT to push another person or touch someone else in an inappropriate manner. Or perhaps they were punished one time when they stole an item but received no consequence the next time they took something that did not belong to them. Inconsistent discipline confuses students about which behaviors are acceptable and which are not.

Assessment for Eligibility

Determining the eligibility of students who might have emotional behavioral disorders can be difficult. This is the most subjective of all disability areas in that it relates directly to teacher tolerance. Teachers who expect rigid conformity to a set of permissible behaviors, as they have defined them, will refer more students for consideration of EBD than will teachers who have a high tolerance for behavioral variations (Kauffman & Wong, 1991; Nelson, 1991). For example, teachers who expect students to stay in their seats unless given permission to do otherwise, raise their hands before speaking, and work quietly on an assignment until it is finished, will experience a higher number of students who do not behave "appropriately" than will the teacher who allows students to speak at will, move about the classroom, and make decisions about the order in which tasks are to be completed. Teacher tolerance relates not only to the rules established in a classroom, but also to a teacher's preferences. Some teachers do not mind higher noise levels or students balancing back on two legs of a chair. These same behaviors will be so distracting to other teachers that they will spend large amounts of time and energy trying to change these behaviors. Some behaviors, such as fighting, verbal assault, and sexual acting-out are clearly unacceptable in school environments and will be perceived by all teachers as intolerable.

Once unacceptable behaviors have been identified, professionals will need to document their occurrence. Direct observation may be used in which the teacher counts the number of times a behavior occurs (frequency) and/or how long a behavior lasts (duration). Simple tallying may be used to record the frequency of a behavior, such as when a teacher makes a mark on a piece of paper or clicks a golf-counter whenever a student talks without raising her hand. The duration of time that a student is out of his seat and wandering around the room may be measured by using a stop watch or the second hand on a wall clock. It also is important to determine if there is a pattern in when the behavior occurs (e.g., only during math class).

Another method of determining the degree of inappropriateness of a student's behavior is to assess the student on a behavior rating scale. There are several behavior rating scales available for use. To use a rating scale, someone who knows the student fairly well will mark behavioral items by indicating if

Teachers who expect students to remain in their seats quietly working usually experience a higher number of students who do not behave "appropriately."

they are characteristic of the student being rated. For example, one item on a rating scale might be "Fights". The rater would decide if fighting is not a problem, a mild problem, or a severe problem for the student being rated (Quay & Peterson, 1987). Some scales ask the observer to rate a student on a continuum between two opposite behaviors. For example, the observer would rate the student between "outgoing" and "withdrawn" (Bullock & Wilson, 1989). There are no right or wrong answers on rating scales; they simply indicate how students behave in relation to their peers. Once a student has been rated on a scale, the rater will follow the directions on the scale to determine a score. The score will indicate how different from the norm the student's behavior is and usually will provide scores in different subscale areas to help identify where the student has the most behavioral trouble. For example, the Revised Behavior Problem Checklist (RBPC) (Quay & Peterson, 1987) provides subscale scores in: Conduct Disorders, Socialized Aggression, Attention Problems, Anxiety Withdrawal, Psychotic Behavior, and Motor Excess. A student's subscale scores may indicate that the student has little problem with psychotic behavior, but significant problems with socialized aggression. The Behavior Dimensions Rating Scale (BDRS) (Bullock & Wilson, 1989) provides subscale scores in: Aggressive/Acting Out, Irresponsible/Inattentive, Socially Withdrawn, and Fearful/Anxious. **Figure 4-6** provides excerpts from the RBPC and the BDRS. Behavioral rating scales and/or direct observation may be used to substantiate the five criteria for EBD as specified in the law in order to help determine eligibility.

In addition to evaluating a student's behavior to determine eligibility, multidisciplinary school personnel must evaluate cognitive development, academic performance, physical abilities, and communication skills. To be eligible for classification as having an EBD, students must have an IQ test with a score above 70. With an IQ score below 70, the student probably will be considered eligible for special education services under the category of mental retardation. In addition, physical abilities must include adequate vision and hearing, or the student would be considered for eligibility as having a visual or hearing impairment. The presence of health conditions (such as diabetes, narcolepsy, seizures) might force the consideration of the student as having a health impairment (OHI) and exclude the consideration for classification as EBD. A discrepancy between academic achievement (performance) and IQ (potential) might suggest a learning disability and not EBD, particularly if the student has not responded to previous intervention. Although most professionals agree that disability conditions can coexist, EBD will not be the preferred label if any other condition is present. Professionals will use another label (e.g., LD, OHI, MR) if it applies, since EBD is considered the most stigmatizing of all labels (Osher et al., 2004).

Before a student is referred for assessment for special education services due to an emotional behavioral disorder, teachers must document that they have tried a number of strategies in the general education classroom and that these strategies have been unsuccessful. Prereferral strategies are described fully in Chapter 3 of this book and might include establishing a behavioral management plan, seating the student in an area free from distraction, and reducing the potential for frustration (which often leads to acting out) by shortening assignments, giving tests orally, and providing students with their own copies of material so that they do not have to copy from the board.

Issues for the Classroom Teacher

One of the most challenging issues for classroom teachers who are working with students with emotional behavioral disorders is the management of distracting and disruptive behaviors. Teachers who implement a sound classroom management plan for the entire class will reduce the number of challenging behaviors (Emmer & Stough, 2001). Chapter 11

FIGURE 4-6

Samples of Behavior Rating Scales

Behavior Dimensions Rating Scale (Bullock & Wilson, 1989)

1. _____ hurts others	∗ ∗ ∗ ∗ ∗ ∗ ∗	praises others _____ 1.
2. _____ self-conscious	∗ ∗ ∗ ∗ ∗ ∗ ∗	confident _____ 2.
3. _____ short attention span	∗ ∗ ∗ ∗ ∗ ∗ ∗	long attention span _____ 3.
4. _____ nondisruptive	∗ ∗ ∗ ∗ ∗ ∗ ∗	disruptive _____ 4.
5. _____ outgoing	∗ ∗ ∗ ∗ ∗ ∗ ∗	withdrawn _____ 5.
6. _____ possessive	∗ ∗ ∗ ∗ ∗ ∗ ∗	sharing _____ 6.
7. _____ talkative	∗ ∗ ∗ ∗ ∗ ∗ ∗	quiet _____ 7.
8. _____ shy	∗ ∗ ∗ ∗ ∗ ∗ ∗	sociable _____ 8.
9. _____ likes classmates	∗ ∗ ∗ ∗ ∗ ∗ ∗	dislikes classmates _____ 9.
10. _____ observes rules	∗ ∗ ∗ ∗ ∗ ∗ ∗	breaks rules _____ 10.
11. _____ distractible	∗ ∗ ∗ ∗ ∗ ∗ ∗	stays on task _____ 11.
12. _____ tense	∗ ∗ ∗ ∗ ∗ ∗ ∗	tranquil _____ 12.
13. _____ bold	∗ ∗ ∗ ∗ ∗ ∗ ∗	timid _____ 13.

Revised Behavior Problem Checklist (Quay & Peterson, 1987)

1. Restless; unable to sit still	0	1	2
2. Seeks attention; "shows-off"	0	1	2
3. Stays out late at night	0	1	2
4. Self-conscious; easily embarrassed	0	1	2
5. Disruptive; annoys and bothers others	0	1	2
6. Feels inferior	0	1	2
7. Steals in company with others	0	1	2
8. Preoccupied; "in a world of his own;" stares into space	0	1	2
9. Shy, bashful	0	1	2
10. Withdraws; prefers solitary activities	0	1	2
11. Belongs to a gang	0	1	2
12. Repetitive speech; says same thing over and over	0	1	2
13. Short attention span; poor concentration	0	1	2
14. Lacks self-confidence	0	1	2
15. Inattentive to what others say	0	1	2
16. Incoherent speech, what is said doesn't make sense	0	1	2

describes considerations for creating a positive, focused atmosphere which encourages appropriate behaviors and discourages inappropriate behaviors.

Most teachers can relate to the challenges associated with managing disruptive behaviors, but an emerging management issue for teachers is how to help students with internalizing disorders. These are the students who are depressed, anxious, possibly suicidal, and who may engage in self-destructive behaviors (anorexia, bulimia, substance abuse). Often these students do not want to attract the attention of an adult and will be extraordinarily obedient and compliant in school, even though their disorders are just as serious as the disorders of students who act out. Teachers should be aware of the tell-tale signs of depression and potential suicide as well as the indicators of self-destructive behaviors. **Table 4-5** lists some of the common signs that students are depressed and may be experiencing suicidal ideation (thoughts about ending one's life). School counselors are trained to recognize the signs and indicators and are a good resource for teachers.

The most dangerous thing that educators do is ignore the warning signs, thinking that the youth will grow out of a "stage". All too often, educators who think that the student is just going through a phase or who see the suicide threats as attention-seeking behavior, end up attending a funeral wondering what went wrong. The most helpful thing that educators can do is support the student without minimizing the depth of the

TABLE 4-5

Warning Signs of Depression and Potential Suicide

1. Verbal threats
2. Changes in behavior (withdrawal, aggression, hyperactivity) including mood swings
3. Unusual purchases (items used in suicide attempts OR bizarre, out of character items)
4. Difficulty concentrating and staying on task (includes indecisiveness)
5. Changes in appetite, sleep, weight or affect
6. School problems (drop in grades, absences, tardies, disruptions, cheating)
7. Final arrangements (giving away prized possessions, making a will, cleaning out room)
8. Death themes in conversation, writings, drawings, etc.
9. Use of drugs or alcohol
10. Sudden, unexpected happiness (relief, energy)
11. Frequent accidents
12. Prolonged grief after a loss
13. Neglect of personal hygiene and appearance
14. Previous suicide attempts

student's experience. For example, rather than tell a student that "it's not the end of the world", empathize with and actively listen to the student's perceptions. Attempts to convince the student that suicide is morally wrong are usually counterproductive. Never promise that you won't tell anyone. Rather, promise the student that you will be very selective about who you tell and that you will only tell the people who need to know in order to help. Being supportive also includes helping students recognize what they have to look forward to, not only in life, but also in the near future. A game, concert, holiday, and so forth can be more motivational for withstanding daily dilemmas than the promise of a career. Finally, for students who are suicidal, never leave them alone, especially when they say they "just need to go to the bathroom". Teachers are not usually trained as counselors, but can actively listen to a student until trained help arrives.

Another issue facing teachers is how to manage students who have gone beyond disruptive and distracting behaviors and are demonstrating behaviors that threaten the safety of others. Violence in the classroom has become one of the major issues impacting education (Sautter, 1995). In an attempt to reduce the number of violent incidents, schools have taken measures such as installing metal detectors and hiring security officers. Schools also are developing anti-violence curricula which emphasize problem solving and peaceful alternatives to violent behavior. Just as with students who are threatening suicide, students who are threatening to harm someone else must be taken very seriously. Each school should develop a set of procedures for how to address threats of violence. The most ineffective actions that a school can take in addressing threats of violence are to suspend or expel the student. If the student has threatened violence in order to get kicked out of school, it worked. The student got exactly what was desired. Guess what the student will do again when the suspension is up? If the student has threatened violence in order to get attention, it worked again. The student not only got the attention from school staff when the violence was threatened, but probably got some sort of peer attention and approval while out of school. The procedures developed by a school to address threats of violence must take into consideration what life events have brought the student to this action and how more effective problem solving strategies can be taught so the student doesn't resort to the same threats in the future. For the morale of the intended victim(s), students who make threats should be considered for placement in alternate environments that can provide additional supervision, structure, and instruction in peaceful problem solving. If the student is receiving special education services, it will be up to the IEP team to decide which alternatives are most appropriate.

Autism

Definition

Although the characteristics of persons with autism have remained constant since Kanner's (1943) original description, the definition has changed considerably. Much of the change in definition has occurred as we have developed a clearer understanding of the etiology. Since autism originally was considered an emotional disturbance, the disability was included in P.L. 94-142 (1975) within the Seriously Emotionally Disturbed (SED) category. Due to the efforts of advocacy groups, autism was moved out of SED and into Other Health Impaired (OHI) in 1981. Although students with autism will require interventions similar to those used with students with ED, the advocates were attempting to clear up the myth that autism was an emotional disturbance. The inclusion of autism under OHI, although less stigmatizing, did little to help clarify the nature of the disability and the appropriate intervention. In 1990, during the reauthorization of P.L. 94-142, autism was again moved, this time out of OHI and into its own discrete category. According to IDEA 2004:

> Autism means a developmental disability significantly affecting verbal and nonverbal communication and social interaction, generally evident before age 3, that adversely affects educational performance. Other characteristics often associated with autism are engagement in repetitive activities and stereotyped movements, resistance to environmental change or changes in daily routines, and unusual responses to sensory experiences. Autism does not apply if a child's educational performance is adversely affected primarily because the child has a serious emotional disturbance. A child who manifests the characteristics of autism after age three could be identified as having autism if the criteria . . . are satisfied.

This definition reminds us that autism is a developmental disability (it occurs during the developmental years) and must be evident before the age of three (APA, 2000). It is not uncommon for parents of children with autism to first learn that the disorder may be present when they take their young children in for hearing screening because the children do not respond to hearing their names called. Although they may not realize that their child has unusual patterns of behavior until the child is four years of age or older, the parents must be able to document unusual behaviors prior to the age of three for a diagnosis of autism.

Characteristics

The term "autism" was coined by Leo Kanner (1943) who created the word from the Greek word "autos" which means "self". Kanner used the term to describe the behaviors of a group of children whom he thought to be so self-centered that they could not relate to the world around them. Another term, **pervasive developmental disorder (PDD)** also is used to identify persons with autism. PDD is a broader term established by the American Psychiatric Association in their *DSM* editions. Autism is a more specific classification under the umbrella PDD category. If the professional evaluating the student is unsure as to whether or not the student has classic autism, another of the PDD diagnoses may be preferred. Other autism-related disorders which fall under the category of PDD in the *DSM IV-TR* are Rett syndrome, Childhood Disintegrative disorder, Asperger syndrome, and PDD - Not Otherwise Specified (NOS).

Before describing some of the behaviors that are characteristic of autism, it is important to understand that autism ranges from mild to severe (Lord, Cook, Leventhal, & Amaral, 2000). This means that some people may demonstrate extreme forms of the behaviors characteristic of autism while others may be only mildly affected. In addition, as evidenced by the different classifications listed in the *DSM IV-TR*, there are a number of subtypes or variations of autism. An individual's behavior may be very different depending on the severity of the disorder and the actual subtype present. For this reason, the term autism spectrum disorders (ASD) is now being used by parents, professionals and advocates instead of the term autism. Autism spectrum disorders captures that there are dramatic variations among individuals with this disability. Rather than say, "if you've seen one child with autism, you've seen them all," it is commonly stated, "if you've seen one child with autism, you've seen one child with autism." The term autism will continue to be used throughout this chapter, because that is the eligibility category in IDEA 2004, but the reader is reminded to view the term as the shortened version of "autism spectrum disorders" and think of the condition as highly unique to a given individual and multifaceted in the way it is manifest.

Individuals with autism have difficulties in three major areas of functioning: communicating, relating, and adapting. Individuals with autism demonstrate communication patterns that are different from what is expected (Wetherby et al., 2004). They typically fail to make eye contact and instead may prefer to use peripheral vision. Lack of eye contact hinders the efforts of others to initiate and maintain communication. In addition, an individual with autism may fail to develop oral language or may not to use it if it has developed. These individuals may rely on nonverbal language (gestures or pointing) to indicate preferences. When oral language is demonstrated, it may have unusual intonation or pitch and may sound like machine-generated speech (Kanner, 1943). The exception to machine-sounding speech occurs when a person with autism repeats something he has heard. The repetition of others' oral speech may sound like an echo and is called **echolalia.** During echolalia, the speech may mimic exactly the original speaker, including the intonation and pitch. Echolalia may occur right after the original words are spoken (e.g., when asked *"What is your name?"* the person with autism may say *"What is your name?", "Your name?"* or simply *"Name?"*) or the echolalia may be delayed as in the case when a newscast heard the previous night or months prior is repeated verbatim. Persons with autism may talk to themselves, demonstrating that they can speak (Volden & Lord, 1991) but may have difficulty using verbal communication in an interactive manner.

In addition to lack of interactive communication, individuals with autism have difficulty relating to the world, including people, objects, and events that are encountered. Regarding relationships with other people, infants with autism may not be cuddly and may actively resist being held. As these infants grow older, they may not seek out others for interactions and may not go to another person even for comfort or help when hurt. An individual with autism may appear to be oblivious to the feelings of others and may not acknowledge the presence of another person.

This inability to relate to other humans extends to objects as well. A child with autism may not show an awareness of the purpose of a toy and instead may play with it in an unusual manner. For example, rather than rolling a toy truck across the floor, a child with autism may turn the toy over and spin the wheels. Rather than playing a xylophone, a person with autism may flip the string that is attached to the front of the toy.

A person with autism may not relate to events as we would expect but may react much differently. When confronted with a sad event, the person with autism may react by laughing. Students with autism may cry for no apparent reason. A person with autism may not be afraid of things that typically produce fear (e.g., heavy traffic) but may express terror at things that usually are not fear-producing (e.g., flushing toilets, noise from fish aquariums). These unusual ways of relating may continue for prolonged periods of time, and they lead us to a discussion of the third area of difficulty: adapting.

Individuals with autism are characterized by an inability to adapt to change. They may insist that appearances and routines are always the same. For example, if a chair is moved from one spot to another or if a different route is taken when driving to the store, a person with autism may be noticeably upset. This person may insist on wearing a t-shirt without a coat even when the temperature drops below freezing or insist on sitting in the same seat on a bus every time. When this insistence on sameness extends into activities it is called **perseveration.** A person with autism may perseverate on one activity, such as flipping the string on the toy xylophone, for hours at a time. An individual with autism may demonstrate perseveration by repeating the same word over and over or by engaging in the same motor motion, such as touching each floor tile once, for extended periods of time. Because of their insistence on sameness and their tendency to perseverate, persons with autism are not very adaptable. In fact, the insistence on sameness and perseveration may lead to behaviors that appear almost ritualistic. For example, one young girl with autism always started her school day by taking barrettes out of a baggie that she brought from home and lining them up in one corner of a room. If she was prevented from engaging in this activity (e.g., a piece of heavy equipment had been placed in that particular corner of the room) or was interrupted during this activity (e.g., if there was a fire drill or another student took one of her barrettes), she would become upset and throw a tantrum. It can be challenging to work with a student who wants everything to stay the same and insists on engaging in specific activities at specific times.

Besides the difficulties in communicating, relating, and adapting that have been described, persons with autism may demonstrate **self-stimulating behaviors** and **self-injurious behaviors.** Self-stimulating behaviors, also called "stimming," are repetitious actions that serve no apparent purpose. For example, persons with autism may "stim" by rocking back and forth on their heels or by flapping their hands quickly in front of their eyes (Epstein, Taubman, & Lovaas, 1985). Interestingly, infants between 9 and 12 months of age with developmental delays may demonstrate higher rates of self-stimulatory behavior than infants who are later diagnosed with autism (Baranek, 1999).

Although self-stimulating behaviors do not appear to serve a useful purpose, research is indicating that such behaviors are biologically necessary and actually may decrease stress levels while increasing awareness. For these reasons, all humans engage in self-stimulating behaviors, even college students (Rago & Case, 1978). The difference is that you have learned to self-stimulate in socially acceptable ways whereas a person with autism has not. For example, when you sit in class and begin to get bored, you engage in self-stimulating behaviors to increase your awareness and stay awake. You may flip your foot, twist your hair, or doodle on your paper. When you get stressed or upset, you may self-stimulate by walking, eating, or rubbing the back of your neck, thereby lowering your stress level. A person with autism may not have learned socially acceptable ways of self-stimulating and may jump up and down, or flap their arms, or blow on their fingers.

Self-injurious behaviors (SIBs) are those behaviors which seem to be directed at causing injury to a person's own body. SIBs include banging one's head against a wall, hitting oneself in the ear, and biting or scratching oneself (Bachman, 1972). These behaviors become serious when they are repeated over and over, posing a threat of tissue damage, brain damage, and even death. It is believed that SIBs are committed for one of two reasons. One reason is to exert control over the environment, and the other is as a response to a biologic defect (de Catanzaro, 1978; Guess & Carr, 1991). Most SIBs will be demonstrated in order to control the environment by manipulating others. For example, if a person does not want to write his name on a paper, he may have learned that if he screams, the adult asking him to write his name will leave him alone. At some point, however, the person doing the screaming to get out of the task will encounter someone who doesn't care if he screams. Then the person will have to do something more drastic, such as scream and roll around on the floor, in order to get out of the task. This behavioral progression will continue until the person is demonstrating SIBs to manipulate others and control events in the environment. Once the person has learned that banging his head against the wall is effective for getting him something that he wants or helping him avoid something that he doesn't want, the person will choose that behavior as the quickest means of getting a desired outcome and will not even bother starting with the lesser behavior, screaming.

In a smaller percentage of cases, SIBs will occur, not to manipulate, but as a result of a biologic defect which causes a need for deep pressure or results in uncontrollable motor activity (Bakke, 1990; Baumeister, 1991; Cataldo & Harris, 1982). Individuals with disorders other than autism engage in high rates of SIBs. SIBs are seen in persons with Lesch-Nyhan syndrome (Zirpoli & Lloyd, 1987), mental retardation (Kobe, 1994), and Tourette syndrome (Jeffery, 1994), as well as other disabilities.

Before leaving this discussion of the characteristics of persons with autism, it is important to point out that individuals can demonstrate any of the behaviors mentioned and not have autism. For example, individuals with severe mental retardation will engage in self-stimulating behaviors and self-injurious behaviors. Many of us insist on sameness by sitting in the same seat in a classroom or theater. An infant with a difficult temperament may not want to be cuddled (Chess & Thomas, 1987). In order to diagnose autism a clear pattern must exist across behaviors and the specific criteria, as mentioned in the *DSM IV-TR*, must be met. **Table 4-6** summarizes the characteristics associated with autism.

TABLE 4-6

Behavioral Characteristics Commonly Associated with Autism Spectrum Disorders

- difficulty relating to others
  - may not demonstrate typical patterns of affection
  - may not initiate social interaction
  - oblivious to other's feelings/mood
- difficulty relating to objects
  - unusual attachments (collects sticks, straws, gum wrappers, etc.)
  - odd play that goes on and on (picks fuzz off chairs, used staples off floor, etc.)
- unusual reactions to events
  - insistence on sameness
- unusual communication
  - little direct eye contact
  - delayed language
  - use of behaviors to communicate
  - unusual intonation and pitch when language present
  - echolalia
- abnormal responses to sensations
  - hyper- or hyposensitive to touch, smell, taste, sound
  - affect does not match situation
- self-stimulation (stims)
- self-injurious behaviors (SIBS)

Post-school outcomes for persons with autism once were described as extremely poor, as the majority of adults with autism were unable to live independently or productively and required residential care. This outlook has changed considerably due to more appropriate school programming and a heightened awareness of the needs of individuals with autism. Programs that emphasize the acquisition of useful skills in the vocational, recreational, and social realms and the provision of supported employment opportunities have demonstrated positive outcomes for adults with autism (Smith, 1995).

Specific Etiology

When Kanner (1943) was first systematically studying a group of children with autism, it was believed that autism was caused when the child chose to withdraw from the world around him. This withdrawal was thought to occur as the child responded to feeling unloved or unwanted by his mother. The mothers of children with autism were described as being cold and unloving, and the term "refrigerator mother" appeared (Bettelheim, 1967). This absence of love and warmth later was extended to involve both the mother and the father as equally to blame for their child's withdrawal.

Inconsistencies were noted, however, in the fact that the family might have other children who did not have autism, and therefore could not have caused the disorder in only one child. A theory evolved in which deprivation in the environment was blamed for the appearance of autism. It was explained that the child was in an unstimulating environment and chose to withdraw into a place that was more stimulating. Again, inconsistencies were noted as the environments of children with autism were examined and most found to be sufficiently appealing and stimulating.

After these false starts, it is now accepted that autism is caused by a neurologic dysfunction or difference that is congenital (present at birth) (Pickett & London, 2005). There have been several suggestions as to the exact type of neurologic dysfunction. Researchers have noted differences in the structural composition, the chemical levels, and the functioning of the brain. Structurally, the brain of persons with autism may be different from others, particularly in the density of the cerebellum or in the appearance of the cerebral cortex (Courchesne, 1995). Chemically, researchers have noted higher levels of neurotransmitters, particularly serotonin (Anderson & Hoshino, 1987) and opioid peptides (Zingarelli, 1992) in the brains of persons with autism. Functionally, researchers have noted that a person with autism and a person who does not have autism may complete identical tasks but use different parts of their brains as documented by brain scans (Bachsbaum, 1992). To summarize, autism is caused by differences in the neurologic system. These differences may be due to:

- structural differences in the brain
- chemical differences
- differences in the way the brain functions as a whole

Although it is now recognized that the etiology of autism is a difference in neurologic functioning, it is still unclear as to what causes the neurologic difference in the first place. A number of factors point to the genetic basis for the neurological differences in autism and there appear to be ten or more genes interacting to produce autism (Wassink, Brzustowicz, Bartlett, & Szatmari, 2004). Additional support for the genetic basis includes the higher rates of autism in males than in females and the recognition that extended biological families of children with autism often report histories of language, learning, or social problems (Dawson et al., 2002; Piven et al., 1994) including psychiatric issues such as obsessive compulsive disorders, depression, schizophrenia, social phobia and bipolar disorder (Ghaziuddin, 2005). Genetic influences may weaken the immune system, predisposing a child to be vulnerable to toxins that could detrimentally influence neurological development. This leads to the theoretical link between autism and toxins in the environment. Vaccines, and more specifically some of the compounds in the vaccines (i.e., ethylmercury, thimerosal), have been blamed for causing autism. For the scientific community, the link has been refuted (DeStefano et al., 2004; Hviid, Stellfeld, Wohlfahrt, & Melbye, 2003), but much speculation still appears on the Internet. Although rare complications from a vaccine cannot be ruled out, scientists suggest that the likelihood of a child contracting a fatal childhood disease if not vaccinated is much greater than the likelihood that the child will develop autism if given vaccinations. Research continues to examine the possible causes of the neurological differences that lead to autism, and most of that research focuses on the genetic possibilities.

Assessment for Eligibility

Since autism is a pervasive disorder that is evident at a young age, the diagnosis usually is made by a pediatrician or multidisciplinary team working in a medical context. A diagnosis of autism given by a qualified professional using the criteria in the *DSM IV-TR* does not automatically qualify students for special education services in their local school systems. Such a diagnosis can contribute to an understanding of the student, but according to IDEA 2004, the school system has to undertake its own evaluation process to determine if autism is adversely affecting the student's educational performance.

To determine eligibility, school system personnel across a number of disciplines will conduct a variety of evaluations. Parents may provide the results of independent assessments, including *DSM IV-TR* diagnoses, if available. Many of the younger students may arrive at school with diagnoses of autism, CDD, Rett's Disorder, or PDD-NOS. A diagnosis of Aspergers is usually not given until around age 11 (Howlin, 2003), so school systems may be integrally involved in providing documentation that may lead to that diagnosis.

There are a number of behavioral assessments specifically designed to evaluate behavior characteristic of students with autism. For example, the Autism Diagnostic Observation Schedule (ADOS; Lord, Rutter, DiLavore & Risi, 1999) provides a standardized protocol for observation of social and communicative behavior and is considered to be the best of the diagnostic tools. In addition to collecting data using instruments designed to identify the presence or absence of autism, school psychologists or other diagnosticians will attempt to measure IQ/cognitive functioning/developmental level, academic level, and adaptive behavior. Speech-language pathologists (SLPs) will conduct assessments of language and communication, including articulation, oral-motor coordination, language comprehension, expressive language, conventional and non-conventional non-verbal behavior. Occupational therapists may be needed to assess the students' functional adaptations and evaluate their sensory performance. Physical therapists, education specialists, and others may also conduct evaluations as necessary. Many districts have personnel who are specialists in autism and they may supervise specialized assessments.

Each of the professionals is trained to know which assessments are necessary and most likely to provide valid and reliable information for eligibility determination and identification of present levels of performance. The choice of which evaluations to conduct depends on the unique needs of the student. The school system's purpose for conducting the evaluations is to get as accurate a picture as possible of the child's current level of functioning and areas of need in order to determine eligibility and develop an appropriate program.

Issues for the Classroom Teacher

Classroom teachers will be challenged to manage the unusual behaviors demonstrated by students with autism. Teachers will need to be aware of their students' strengths and preferences and incorporate them into the daily routine. A student with autism will benefit from high levels of structure and routine in the class setting. Establishing a consistent routine and delineating appropriate expectations will help reduce disruptive and distracting behaviors. Once the student can function within an established routine, the teacher will be able to carefully plan the introduction of deviations into the schedule. Therefore, critical educational components for promoting appropriate learning opportunities for students with autism include:

- carefully structured environment
- predictable routines
- visual cuing
- implementing a communication system
- emphasizing communication, socialization, and functional academics in the curriculum

Classroom teachers may become involved in the controversy surrounding differing opinions regarding the best method to educate persons with autism. A number of options are available, and all have been found to be successful with at least a few students with autism. For school systems, the choice of intervention approaches must be made according to which approach has a substantial research base (NRC, 2001). Some approaches, such as the one created by Ivar Lovaas at UCLA, require intensive one-on-one instruction using specially trained persons over a long period of time (Lovaas, 1987) and are therefore difficult and expensive to implement in school settings (Chambliss & Doughty, 1994). In addition, the one-on-one therapy is not compatible with the trend towards inclusive education. Other approaches incorporate techniques that make exaggerated claims about their effectiveness, yet have not been proven effective. Educators need to be aware of current "fads" in the treatment of autism so that they do not seem uninformed when parents request a particular intervention. However, research supports that the most effective programs are those that involve the family in the development of an individually tailored plan providing systematic instruction within structured environments which take a functional approach to addressing problem behavior (Iovannone, Dunlap, Huber, & Kincaid, 2003). School programs need to incorporate a relevant curricula which include functional academics, vocational preparation, and the explicit teaching of necessary life skills (Berkell, 2005).

Obviously, classroom teachers will be challenged to support positive behavioral adaptations for students with autism to replace some of the odd or unusual behaviors associated with the disability. Providing the student with a means of communication will help reduce the demonstration of inappropriate behaviors (Durand, 1992). Developing IEP goals and objectives that are individualized for the student also will be critical. Students with autism need to have an IEP written for them which emphasizes their greatest areas of need: communication and socialization. Unfortunately, this clarity of need often is clouded when IEP teams focus on the student's "**splinter skills**". Splinter skills are defined as those skills which seem to indicate specific areas of competence or ability. For example, it is not uncommon for students with autism to demonstrate **hyperlexia,** the ability to decode any print material. Students with hyperlexia can read aloud almost anything that is placed in front of them and can usually spell and reproduce words, even difficult words. However, this is a splinter skill. The students have no comprehension of what they are reading and writing. The tendency is then for IEP teams to capitalize on this special skill in the writing of goals and objectives. It is not unusual to see a goal written that a 5-year-old child will improve his decoding ability from the 11th to 12th grade level. This is unfortunate as such a goal ignores the child's more pressing needs: the ability to initiate interactions, the ability to communicate needs and wants, and even the ability to demonstrate comprehension at the first grade level. A very real issue for the classroom teacher is how to promote the writing of chronologically age appropriate goals and objectives that focus on communication and socialization (the two major deficit areas in autism) when others on the IEP team may be wanting to place the child in algebra or calculus.

Having a student with autism in your classroom can be a tremendously rewarding experience. Even if you do not have a student with autism, the chances are high that you will have students who have some neurologic differences that result in behaviors that are borderline autistic. Remembering to focus on structure, routine, predictability and clear visual signals will help all students, not just those who meet the eligibility for autism. Emphasizing effective communication and appropriate socialization also will be important. It is the school's role to teach students the skills they need to facilitate their post-school independence and self-determination, not to provide interventions that treat symptoms or promote splinter skills.

Specific Learning Disabilities (SLD)

Society places a high emphasis on quick, efficient thought and reactions. For some individuals, the ability to interpret symbols (as in language) and nuances (occurring in social situations) is inhibited. Although of normal or superior intelligence, such individuals are at a disadvantage because of their inability to decode symbols or perceive meaning. If this disadvantage causes a significant impairment, the individual may have difficulty learning the things that are expected at school. Such students are considered to have a learning disability. Often, a teacher cannot discern a student with a learning disability from other students until the student is asked to complete an academic task. A student with a learning disability may be indistinguishable from a same age peer when they are playing or interacting but may be unable to read aloud when asked. This situation is further complicated by the fact that a student can have a learning disability related to one area, such as reading, and perform as expected in another area, such as math. Students with learning disabilities account for the largest percentage of students receiving special education services and also are the most diverse group of students since the disability can affect specific areas of learning and perception which are unique to the individual. **Figure 4-7** provides activities to simulate a learning disability.

Learning disabilities affect an individual's ability to understand and use language and to discriminate differences. If you think about it, you'll realize that almost every school task incorporates language. Listening, thinking, speaking, reading, writing, and spelling all involve language. Even calculations must be taught using language and rely on an understanding of mathematical symbols for their completion. Understanding specific learning disabilities has been as challenging for teachers and parents as for the students themselves. Terms that have been used in the past to describe learning disabilities include perceptual handicaps, brain injury, minimal brain dysfunction, dyslexia, central processing disorder, word blindness, and developmental aphasia. The term specific learning disability has replaced these other terms.

Definition

Significant controversy has surrounded the creation of an acceptable definition for learning disabilities. The federal definition is cited most often and is considered a consensus definition because it represents a compromise; however, it is not endorsed by all professionals and advocate groups. The federal definition of learning disabilities from IDEA 2004 is as follows:

> Specific learning disability means a disorder in one or more of the basic psychological processes involved in understanding or in using language, spoken or written, that may manifest itself in the imperfect ability to listen, think, speak, read, write, spell, or to do mathematical calculations, including

Activities to Simulate a Learning Disability

To imagine what it would be like to have a learning disability related to decoding written symbols, read the following two paragraphs. Try to read them aloud while maintaining the same even flow you typically use with reading.

In mobern soceity an inbivibual's ytiliba to be self-sufficient is usually encouraqed fron childhood. By eht tine we are adults, we are uspposed to have learmed to debend upon ourselves, to de as puick on the ward as the next persom and to be ready to dolh our own in a more of less ilesoht world.

Inbequenbence is also comsidered inbortamt so that eno is mot a durben on srehto. This atttiued quts tremendous pressure no the norimyiit mith disapilitiez. Trying to keep threi self-respect im a society that equates inbequenbemce with physical well-being nakes an already tluciffid situation almost elbarelotni, for the bersom with a disability thinks the sane way. Me neeb to chanqe this boint of viem. It's inportamt to realize that on individual can really tsixe alone. We are all interbeqendent, amd at best, physical deinpendence is variable. Everyome experiences sdoirep of debenqence: illness and dlo age are undiscrinimating. Moral inqebendence, on the other hand, is elbitcurtsedni. (Hale, 1979)

To envision what it might be like to have a learning disability related to math, here is a simple equation. The math symbol rules are: "÷" means subtract; "+" means to multiply; "−" means to divide; and "×" means to add. Now, cover the rules and find the solution.

$$6 \div 2 + 1 \times 4 - 2 = ?$$

Did you arrive at four as the answer? Well that's wrong. The rules changed again while you were working. Also, that first number is a 9. For some individuals with learning disabilities, it appears as if the rules are constantly changing and that symbols are fluid.

conditions such as perceptual disabilities, brain injury, minimal brain dysfunction, dyslexia, and developmental aphasia. Specific learning disability does not include learning problems that are primarily the result of visual, hearing, or motor disabilities, of mental retardation, of emotional disturbance, or of environmental, cultural, or economic disadvantage. (34 CFR, Ch. III, Sec. 300.7)

The federal definition is criticized for being too vague and for failing to reflect the fact that learning disabilities persist into adulthood. The definition also uses numerous terms, such as basic psychological processes, which can be interpreted in various ways and have no agreed upon definitions themselves. Strong concern has been raised due to the implied insistence that learning disabilities cannot occur with sensory impairments, emotional disturbances, or distinct disadvantages. The federal definition does emphasize the language-based nature of learning disabilities.

Although there is general recognition that students can have learning disabilities that affect their learning and socialization, professionals and advocates cannot agree upon one definition. The definition used in IDEA 2004 is so vague that the process of implementation has resulted in different criteria being used across the nation. This results in the situation where a student may qualify as having a learning disability in one school district but not another, depending on how each district has chosen to define the general federal guidelines. The difficulty in establishing a unified definition will become more apparent as the reader considers the challenges of measuring the characteristics described in the next section.

Characteristics

Students with specific learning disabilities can have deficits in any or all of the following **basic psychological processes:** short- or long-term memory, auditory, visual, and haptic discrimination, sequencing, attention, organization, psychomotor skills/visual-motor integration, conceptualization/reasoning, and social perception. These deficits can appear in the classroom as problems of listening, writing, or speaking. Such deficits may interfere with any school subject, but most often there are difficulties in reading. Even if the student is on grade level in reading, there may be specific failures in mathematics or writing or in any activity that requires using the deficient skill. For example, oral instructions may be misunderstood, while written instructions are comprehended easily. The reverse may be the case for other students with learning disabilities where oral understanding is intact but there is difficulty in comprehending written instruction. Specific examples of classroom problems students may experience in each area are presented in **Table 4-7.**

Some students with learning disabilities may understand oral instruction better than written instruction.

Teachers must keep in mind that all children may experience difficulty in one or more of these areas at some point in their school career. For the student with learning disabilities, these problems persist across time and typically are more severe than those of the other students in the class.

By far, the most distinguishing characteristic of individuals with specific learning disabilities is academic underachievement. Students with learning disabilities may show deficits in one or more of the following areas: oral expression, listening comprehension, written expression, basic reading skills, reading comprehension, mathematics computation, and mathematics reasoning. Each of these areas is defined and classroom indicators are provided in **Table 4-8.**

As with psychological processes, teachers must remember that most students will exhibit problems in one or more of these areas at some point in their school careers. It is the persistent problems in specific areas that suggest whether or not a student should be assessed for special education services.

Students with learning disabilities may become frustrated with their own inability to perform as well as their peers who seem to be able to learn so easily. Frustration often translates into anger, nervousness, impulsiveness, and hyperactivity. Students may choose to act out rather than call attention to their inability to complete a task. Or, they may choose the opposite route and withdraw themselves from the learning situation by sleeping, daydreaming, and losing interest. Such students often are misunderstood by their teachers and may be accused of being lazy or unmotivated. Unfortunately, they have real learning problems that are much more complicated than a lack of motivation.

Students learn to compensate for their learning disabilities but they cannot outgrow them or be cured of them. Fortunately, there are more post-secondary options for students with learning disabilities than ever before. Attendance at colleges and universities has become possible as federal statutes protect the rights of individuals with learning disabilities to enroll and receive appropriate modifications. As with individuals with ADHD, persons with learning disabilities must contact the institution's office of disability services and identify themselves as having a disability. Once this step is taken, the office is responsible for assisting the student and faculty regarding required modifications within federal guidelines.

TABLE 4-7

Classroom Indicators of Basic Psychological Processing Deficits

Basic Psychological Process	Classroom Indicators
Memory (Short- and Long-Term)	• Makes excuses for things not remembered • Can't recall facts about stories read or TV programs • Can't remember a sequence of letters or numbers • Can't remember where he or she stopped, if interrupted • Overly attentive to detail • Unable to recall sight vocabulary • Can't repeat sentences, numbers, or letters
Auditory Discrimination	• Doesn't pay attention to speech • Unable to locate source of sound • Difficulty assigning voices to people • Can't identify common environmental sounds • Can't discriminate between similar speech sounds • Can't follow oral directions • Can't do oral math problems • Doesn't spell phonetically • Confuses meaning of similar words • Can't blend or sequence speech sounds • Requests things to be repeated
Visual Discrimination	• Reverses, inverts, and confuses letters and words • Omits words and lines while reading • Disregards punctuation • Focuses attention on minor details • Unable to trace designs • Unable to catch a ball • Unable to match shapes and symbols
Haptic Discrimination	• Difficulty locating body parts • Lacks rhythm • Poor handwriting • Can't manipulate scissors, utensils, etc. • Poor athletic ability • Constantly in motion • Slow motor responses
Sequencing	• Cannot correctly sequence items along a dimension such as smallest to largest, lightest to darkest • Cannot follow directions in sequence • Cannot retell a story in sequence • Has poor sense of time
Attention	• Can't concentrate • Shifts attention at inappropriate times • Doesn't finish work on time • Unable to block out background activity • Can't respond to multiple commands or directions • Can't shift from one activity to another • Daydreams

TABLE 4-7

Classroom Indicators of Basic Psychological Processing Deficits (continued)

Basic Psychological Process	Classroom Indicators
Organization	• Sloppy • Attends to irrelevant details • Difficulty recognizing missing parts • Poor directional concepts • Loses things • Unable to "get ready" for a task • Careless • "Jumps in" before thinking • Reads word-by-word
Psychomotor Skills/ Visual-Motor Integration	• Can't copy from the blackboard • Can't trace or copy designs • Appears clumsy • Can't write or draw between lines • Grips pencil awkwardly • Hand trembles with fine motor tasks • Unable to align numbers or letters vertically or horizontally • Improper orientation of words or drawings on a page • Difficulty in running, hopping, skipping
Conceptualization/ Reasoning	• Lacks vocabulary • Can't follow directions • Talks in incomplete sentences • Can't grasp the main ideas of paragraphs • Doesn't see things as a whole • Doesn't recognize cause-effect relationships • Can't draw conclusions or infer • Poor sense of time
Social Perceptions	• Misinterprets the behavior of his peers • Misinterprets the meaning of gestures and facial expressions • Unable to size up social situations • Unable to make decisions • Lacks common sense

Specific Etiology

There are four possible medical reasons why students may experience learning problems (Mercer, 1997):

    acquired trauma
    genetic or hereditary influences
    environmental influences
    biochemical abnormalities

Central nervous system (CNS) damage due to acquired trauma before, at, or during birth may contribute to the learning problems experienced by some students. Before

TABLE 4-8

Academic Skill Deficit Areas for Students with Specific Learning Disabilities

Area	Definition	Classroom Indicators
Oral Expression	Ability to use spoken language to communicate ideas (as opposed to speech disorders).	• Difficulty labeling. • Difficulty relating information in sequence. • Difficulty exchanging meaningful conversation.
Listening Comprehension	Ability to understand spoken language at a level that is age-appropriate.	• Difficulty defining words that are used correctly in conversation. • Difficulty following basic and multi-step directions. • Difficulty retaining what someone has just said. • Difficulty recalling information from orally read stories. • Difficulty recalling information from oral lectures. • Difficulty understanding humor.
Basic Reading Skills	Ability to use word attack and sequencing skills in the process of decoding written symbols.	• Difficulty remembering what sounds are made by different letters. • Difficulty breaking words into component parts. • Difficulty recognizing words in isolation. • Difficulty in discriminating similar words (e.g., what/that). • Slow reading rate.
Reading Comprehension	Ability to process and understand the meaning of written language.	• Difficulty remembering what has been read. • Difficulty retelling stories in sequence. • Difficulty answering questions about material that has been read.
Math Calculation	Ability to process numerical symbols to derive results, including spatial awareness of symbol placements and sequence algorithms for operations.	• Difficulty recognizing numbers. • Difficulty remembering basic facts. • Difficulty with place value. • Difficulty with column alignment. • Difficulty with remembering steps in algorithm (e.g., regrouping, long division).
Math Reasoning	Ability to understand logical relationships between mathematical concepts and operations, including correct sequencing and spatial and symbolic representation.	• Difficulty determining if solution is correct. • Difficulty determining which operation to use in word problems. • Difficulty judging the size of objects. • Difficulty reading maps and diagrams. • Difficulty with time, money, and measurement concepts.
Written Expression	Ability to communicate ideas in writing with appropriate language (as opposed to merely poor spelling or grammatical errors or poor handwriting).	• Difficulty with organization and structure of ideas in writing. • Difficulty with writing mechanics. • Difficulty in generating ideas for writing. • Difficulty with spelling words in written context that can be spelled in isolation.

birth, or prenatally, the CNS can be injured due to maternal alcohol or drug consumption and use of tobacco products. Fetal alcohol syndrome may result from excessive maternal alcohol intake. Characteristics of this syndrome include academic difficulties, hyperactivity, and attentional problems (Smith, 1989). Children whose mothers use illicit drugs such as crack cocaine and PCP typically experience problems during infancy such as low birth weight, irritability, and low rates of social interaction (Van Dyke & Fox, 1990). Long-term studies have not been reported for these children. Maternal use of tobacco products also is related to academic learning problems and hyperactivity (Lovitt, 1989). During the birth process, children may suffer from traumas such as prolonged labor, anoxia (lack of oxygen to the brain), and injury from medical instruments, such as forceps (Mercer, 1997). The primary postnatal cause of learning disabilities is childhood head injury. Traumatic brain injury was added as a separate eligibility category under IDEA in 1990. Other postnatal causes include exposure to lead, high fevers, encephalitis, and meningitis.

There is growing support that learning disabilities often can be found in families (Smith, 1992). Learning disabilities occurs more often in males than females with fathers reporting similar learning difficulties in the school setting. Learning disabilities also are linked to several chromosomal abnormalities, such as Klinefelter syndrome and Fragile X syndrome in males and females and Turner syndrome in females.

Although research strongly suggests that learning disabilities are caused by neurologic differences which are present at birth, some environmental conditions may contribute to the emergence of these disabilities. Diseases, severe and prolonged deprivation of nutrition or stimulation, abuse, and environmental toxins may heighten the risk of learning disabilities. A final area of medical concern is biochemical abnormality, involving imbalances in the production of neurotransmitters, the brain chemicals that allow neural impulse transmission in the brain (Mercer, 1997).

Another possible cause of learning disabilities is "poor teaching." This covers a broad spectrum of possible circumstances such as problems with the curriculum not matching the student's needs, inappropriate teaching strategies, lack of classroom management resulting in the loss of instructional time, or inappropriate materials for learning. Limitations in assessment cannot distinguish a student with a specific learning disability from a student who is a victim of poor teaching.

Assessment for Eligibility

The procedures described in Chapter 3 are used to determine if a student is eligible for special education services due to a learning disability. To review, the student first will be referred for prereferral interventions. Different states use different names for the group of people who develop prereferral interventions including Student Support Team, Student Study Team and 504 Committee. The team attempts to provide techniques for resolving the learning problems within the context of the general education classroom. If, after a trial period, there is no evidence of improvement, the student is referred by the team and formally evaluated to determine eligibility for special education services. The assessment must evaluate the student in any area of suspected disability which may include: oral expression, listening comprehension, written expression, basic reading skills, reading comprehension, mathematics calculation, and mathematical reasoning. Deficits in one or more of these seven areas must be validated by at least two measures of performance. At least one of these measures must be from a standardized individually-administered test specifically designed to evaluate achievement in mathematics, reading, and language arts. A second measure of achievement can be either a group or individually administered test.

In addition, a measure of cognitive abilities (an individual test of intelligence) must be included in the assessment battery. The latter must be administered by a qualified psychological examiner. All information accumulated in the assessment process must be current.

SLD eligibility requires that the individual have normal or above normal intelligence. Historically, determination of eligibility for SLD was based on demonstration of a severe discrepancy between ability (IQ indicators of basic ability) and achievement scores. States were allowed to define "severe discrepancy" and a commonly used criterion was 20+ standard score points between ability and achievement (for example, an IQ score of 100 and achievement score in basic reading skills of 72 would constitute a 28 point discrepancy and would qualify as "severe"). However, according to IDEA 2004, eligibility determination for SLD does not require the establishment of a severe discrepancy but supports the documentation of failure to respond to research based interventions as sufficient for a student to be eligible as having SLD. Currently no accepted model exists to document "failure to respond" to intervention as a part of the identification process. Final regulations for IDEA 2004 may provide some guidance but more likely than not, individual states will be expected to establish their own procedures for documenting failure to respond. As with all eligibility decisions, a committee of knowledgeable professionals and the student's parents meet to decide if the student is eligible for special education services and what those services should be.

Issues for the Classroom Teacher

Often the classroom teacher is the first person to notice a student's learning problem since a learning disability generally is not identified before the child enters the academic setting. During the kindergarten year, many of these problems are thought to be a problem of maturation. The student may begin to struggle when the demands of reading are increased in subsequent grades. The transition into middle school or junior high is another difficult time period for the student with a learning disability. Often the changes of classes and teachers during the day can be overwhelming. This is an indication that teachers at all grade levels should be observant of their students in order to refer a student at any grade.

Teachers must be aware of some tell-tale signs of learning disabilities. Common classroom signs of deficits in psychological processes were presented in **Table 4-7** and academic deficits were presented in **Table 4-8.** Teachers should observe closely students who demonstrate persistent and severe problems in one or more of these areas. These students may be referred to the student support team and may require eligibility assessment for learning disabilities. Again, many students will exhibit deficits in one or more of these areas at some point in their school careers; care must be taken to avoid inappropriately referring students whose problems are minor and/or transitory.

Students with learning disabilities are typically in general education settings for many of their academic subjects such as science and social studies (Taylor & Larson, 2000). During elementary and middle school years, students tend to receive more support from a core group of teachers who are familiar with their learning differences. As the students move into high school, the curricular expectations become more stringent as end of term tests, graduation tests, and Carnegie units needed for graduation become priority concerns. With NCLB, the emphasis on having content-specific teachers providing instruction tends to create a focus on acquisition of content rather than the acquisition of learning strategies. Unfortunately, the emphasis on content acquisition and the threat of high stakes testing can shift the emphasis away from the unique challenges experienced by students with learning disabilities. Many students with learning disabilities will have been exposed to strategy instruction in previous grades but may have difficulty applying those skills in the rigorous curriculum. In the high school setting, difficulties with basic learning strategies such as note-taking can have a detrimental effect on the comprehension and retention of content information. High school students with learning disabilities may need assistance in understanding how to apply basic learning strategies such as reading in content areas, note-taking, test taking and written expression across content areas in order to promote their academic achievement (Boyle & Weishaar, 2001).

There are a number of strategies teachers can use to enhance the performance of students with learning disabilities. Providing a highly structured environment will help students develop routines, and the habits involved with following the routines will provide boundaries for their behavior. Another teaching strategy involves creating modified time schedules for these students so that you are checking on their progress more frequently and reminding them of what needs to be done next. In addition, teachers need to be aware of possible problems in social interactions as some students with learning disabilities fail to understand social cues and nuances. These students may benefit from specific social skills training.

To summarize, students with learning disabilities will benefit from:

- structured environments
- predictable routines
- more frequent progress checks
- structured methods of reminding students of what happens next
- direct teaching of social skills
- academic modifications specific to the area of disability (e.g., computers for composing/writing, spell checkers, books on tape, calculators)

The issue of "fairness" in the use of adaptations for the student with learning disabilities often is difficult for the general education teacher. Since a learning disability is a "hidden" disability, other students in the classroom may feel that the teacher is being "unfair" by making accommodations for the student with learning disabilities. Addressing this in the classroom can be difficult. Teachers must approach this issue with all the students and their families through open dialogue. Specific strategies for remediating the academic problems of students with learning disabilities are presented in Chapters 6, 7 and 8.

Mild Mental Retardation (MMR)

There are many labels used in referring to students with mental retardation. Labels such as "a student with intellectual disabilities" or "a person who is mentally challenged" are preferred (American Psychological Association, 1994). At this time, the term mental retardation continues to be used in the definition found in IDEA and will be used in this text. In this chapter information describing students with mild mental retardation will be presented. Chapter 9 provides an in-depth look at students with moderate and severe mental retardation.

Definition

Mental retardation is defined in IDEA 2004 as follows:

> Mental retardation means significantly subaverage general intellectual functioning, existing concurrently with deficits in adaptive behavior and manifested during the developmental period that adversely affects a child's educational performance.

The term **significantly subaverage intellectual functioning** describes information regarding a person's intelligence. This information is typically assessed using a standardized intelligence test such as the *Wechsler Intelligence Scale for Children-Third Edition (WISC-III)* or the *Stanford Binet IV.* After years of testing thousands of individuals researchers found that scores from these tests fell along a continuum and created a bell shaped curve. **Figure 4-8** displays the distribution of scores from intelligence testing and the percentages of the population that fall within these ranges. The calculations of means and standard deviations are made using statistical procedures during the development of the various tests.

Significantly subaverage intellectual functioning is defined as two or more standard deviations from the numerical mean of an individualized intelligence test. For example, the most commonly used intelligence tests have a mean of 100 with a standard deviation of 15 or 16. For example, the Wechsler tests have a mean of 100 and a standard deviation of 15. A score of 85 would be one standard deviation below the mean and a score of 70 would be two standard deviations below the mean. Standard deviations also go above the mean. A score of 115 would be one standard deviation above the mean and a score of 130 would be two standard deviations above the mean. Standard deviations above the mean are considered when assessing a student's needs for gifted programs. However, to be considered for eligibility under the category of mental retardation, the score on the Wechsler would have to be 70 or below. As shown in **Figure 4-8,** students who score between two and three standard deviations below the mean (55–70) could be considered for eligibility as having mild mental retardation.

According to AAMR (1992), it is critical that the student have significant deficits in adaptive behavior in addition to the significantly subaverage intellectual functioning. **Adaptive behavior** is defined by Grossman (1983) as "the effectiveness or degree with which individuals meet the standards of personal independence and social responsibility expected for age and cultural group" (p. 1). According to the American Association on Mental Retardation (1992), skill areas included in adaptive behavior are:

- communication
- self-care
- home living
- social skills

FIGURE 4-8

Theoretical Distribution of IQ Scores Based on a Normal Curve; Mild Mental Retardation on the Normal Curve

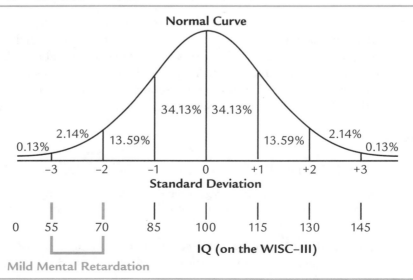

- community use
- self direction
- health and safety
- functional academics
- leisure
- work

Deficits in adaptive behavior address the student's difficulty in communicating, taking care of personal needs such as hygiene and dressing appropriately, functioning in the home and social setting, utilizing community agencies and services, planning and carrying out personal plans, managing their health and other safety issues, using academics in daily living applications such as purchasing clothing, and participating in leisure, recreational and work activities.

Currently a new definition of mental retardation has been adopted by the AAMR, but schools continue to follow the definition found in IDEA. Rather than focusing on the degree of mental retardation (i.e., mild, moderate, severe, and profound), this new definition focuses on the intensity of support needed by the individual to function in society. These levels of support include intermittent, limited, extensive, and pervasive. Future implications of the definition of mental retardation may prove to change current service provision to students and adults.

Characteristics

Physical characteristics of students with mild mental retardation do not differ significantly from the general population. Beirne-Smith, Patton, and Ittenbach (1994) report some differences in motor development, growth rate, and sensory defects. However, students diagnosed with specific syndromes, genetic conditions, or chromosomal abnormalities such as Down syndrome, Fetal Alcohol syndrome, or Fragile X syndrome will have distinct physical features and related medical problems (Batshaw & Perret, 1992). For example, students with Down syndrome often have heart conditions and upper respiratory problems.

There are strong trends in the demographic characteristics of students with mild mental retardation. More males than females have mild mental retardation. This can be attributed to factors such as syndromes associated with sex-linked genetic disorders, role expectations of male students, and the behavior of male students in the school setting that results in referral for special education services. Students from minority cultures and low socio-economic backgrounds are over-represented in the population of students with mild mental retardation (Oswald et al., 2001). Yeargin-Allsopp, Drews, Decoufle, and Murphy (1995) report that African American students are more likely to be labeled mildly mentally retarded than Caucasian

Physical characteristics of students with mild mental retardation do not differ significantly from the general population.

American students. Additional studies found that regardless of race or socioeconomic level, a student whose mother has less than a high school education is four times more likely to be labeled mildly mentally retarded (Drews, Yeargin-Allsopp, Decoufle, & Murphy, 1995).

Students with mild mental retardation demonstrate differences in cognitive development, learning, communication, motivation and adaptive behavior. These differences can lead to challenges in the classroom for both the teacher and student. **Table 4-9** delineates some of these differences.

TABLE 4-9

Characteristics of Mild Mental Retardation

Characteristics	Definition/Description	Classroom Indicators
Cognitive Development	The ability to perceive, understand and process information within an academic and functional setting. Cognition develops at a slower rate and a lower level than same age peers.	• Performs best in concrete operations rather than abstract operations. • Reads significantly below grade level—highest level expected is fourth to sixth grade. • Can perform basic math calculations of addition, subtraction, multiplication and division up to three digits. • Understands the basic concepts of science and social studies. • Comprehension of written information and abstract concepts are extremely difficult.
Learning	The ability to process information in an attempt to gain new information or skills. Significant learning problems in many areas.	
• Attention	Inability to discriminate relevant from irrelevant information. Short attention span.	• Difficulty recognizing color, size or shape of objects and symbols (letters and numbers). In a functional setting does not recognize the size or color of a key to match the door lock. • Difficulty concentrating for entire class sessions.
• Mediation	Inability to cognitively sort or evaluate alternatives in learning new information.	• Difficulty organizing, creating images, attaching meaning and classifying new information (e.g., fails to use the technique of crunching together into groups the first three and second four digits in a phone number or not using addition to correct subtraction).
• Memory	Problems of storing information in the brain's short term memory.	• Forgetting facts and other information within seconds after the presentation—using repetition and additional practice increases the likelihood of storing information in long term memory.
• Generalization	Difficulty taking skills and information and applying them in new situations.	• Problems calculating the discount percentage price in the classroom versus calculating it in the local clothing store.
Communication	The ability to send and receive messages with others. Communication skills are significantly below age peers.	• Fifty percent of the students have an articulation problem noticed when pronouncing their words during conversation. • May not follow directions or use vocabulary that is adequate to the lesson. Other examples would include the use of shorter sentences, speaking infrequently and misunderstanding questions.

TABLE 4-9

Characteristics of Mild Mental Retardation (continued)

Characteristics	Definition/Description	Classroom Indicators
Motivational	Factors that affect the use of skills and knowledge to learn or function in society. Poor motivation interferes with learning.	• Tend to have an external locus of control so that they will blame others or situations without realizing their responsibility or role (e.g., "My Mom worked late last night so I couldn't do my homework") • A debilitating fear of failure prevents students from attempting new activities. What appears to be a lazy student is often covering for a "Why try, I'll only fail the task" attitude. • A sense of outer-directedness causes students to distrust themselves and look to others to tell them what to do.
Adaptive Behavior	The ability to meet the expectations of one's age, gender, culture and environment including school, home and community. Significant deficits in two or more of the following areas:	
	communication	• Difficulty communicating personal information when lost or in need of help.
	self-care	• Lack the skills to meet hygiene standards such as wearing appropriate clothing that is clean and neat or maintaining the cleanliness of their body and hair.
	home living	• Difficulty in managing the financial aspects and maintenance of a home like paying bills, cooking nutritional meals, and organizing clutter.
	social skills	• Typically have poor social skills that cause them to be socially isolated by behaving like a young child using temper tantrums or crying to control the situation.
	community use	• Utilizing community resources such as the bank, mall, library, laundry, recreational facilities, etc. create a significant challenge due to the requirements of traveling independently and continuous decisions that must be made.
	self direction	• Determining life goals and projecting the necessary skills to meet those goals is an ongoing struggle.
	health and safety	• Knowledge of basic first aid, accessing medical assistance and maintaining good health becomes overwhelming and may create risky situations.
	functional academics	• Applying basic math skills to money management, time and measurement are difficult. Reading the newspaper, mail, contracts, applying concepts such as directionality remain a lifelong challenge.
	leisure	• Participation in, being a spectator at, or just understanding the rules of various sports; learning skills and obtaining equipment or materials needed for a hobby; and financing activities such as going to the movies or out to eat become a barrier to the quality of life.

As adults, persons with mild mental retardation are capable of holding down jobs, living independently, and enjoying recreational and leisure activities within the community. Job placements often include repetitive factory work, maintenance, and fast food restaurants. Many adults with mild mental retardation live independently with supervision provided by social workers or family members, on an as needed basis. Other adults need more closely supervised living arrangements and live in supervised apartments or group homes. Limitations to adult endeavors are imposed by the lack of community support and not by the characteristics of these persons. However, adults with mild mental retardation continue to be unemployed or underemployed, with fewer opportunities for independent living, community involvement, and social interactions (Keogh, Bernheimer, & Guthrie, 2004; Luftig & Muthert, 2005).

Specific Etiology

For the majority of students with mild mental retardation the causes are unknown. However there are many syndromes, genetic disorders, and chromosomal abnormalities that result in various degrees of mental retardation (Kozma & Stock, 1993). Three of the most commonly known causes of mental retardation are Fetal Alcohol syndrome, Down syndrome, and Fragile X syndrome. These syndromes have specific physical characteristics and medical conditions that are identified by medical personnel.

As discussed at the beginning of the chapter, mental retardation may be caused by many biological factors. Such factors include birth injuries, poor health and nutrition of the mother during pregnancy, prenatal exposure to alcohol or drugs, infections, environmental conditions, or a combination of factors. Baumeister, Kupstas, and Woodley-Zanthos (1993) propose that students living in poor socioeconomic homes often are exposed to a number of factors that may impact their development. Such factors include poor nutrition, poor parenting, a void of communication interactions, and a denial of "hope" for their future. Children of teenage parents are at a high risk for being labeled as mildly mentally retarded because they often lack educational opportunities, suffer health problems, and receive inadequate medical care. No one environmental factor causes mental retardation, and the vast majority of children who experience the conditions described above are not mildly mentally retarded.

Assessment for Eligibility

Teachers will identify students in the classroom who are experiencing significant difficulties in learning in addition to experiencing problems adequately functioning in the home, school, and community settings. These students should be referred to the prereferral or student support team according to the procedures outlined in Chapter 3. The team may recommend a comprehensive assessment based on their observations and discussions.

Students suspected of mild mental retardation will be assessed by a multidisciplinary team of professionals, with additional information obtained from parents and teachers. This team generally will consist of a psychologist, educational diagnostician, speech-language pathologist, and others if needed given the nature of the student's problems. Specific information regarding the student's intellectual abilities, academic achievement, adaptive behavior, and speech-language skills will be obtained. The student must complete physical, hearing, and vision screenings first to determine if problems identified in any of these areas must be addressed before other assessment can be initiated.

The assessment of a student for mild mental retardation will focus on two major areas: intellectual abilities and adaptive behavior. **Significant deficits** must be found in both areas. In the area of intellectual abilities, a psychologist will administer an individual intelligence test that will result in numerical scores. To be eligible for services in the category of mild mental retardation, the student must score between 55–70 on the intelligence test. There is a five-point standard error of measurement that will allow for some variation.

A significant deficit in intellectual abilities alone will not qualify a student as mildly mentally retarded. There must be significant deficits in adaptive behavior as well. For years, students who had significant deficits in their academics were placed in special education programs for students with mental retardation. However, these students functioned without problems in the community and at home. More often than not, these students were over-represented from minority populations. Deficits that focus on the student's ability to function outside of the school setting are measured using tests that assess how the student is performing in various areas of adaptive behavior. This information often is obtained through interviewing the student's parents and teachers. In general the interviewer will ask the informant to describe how the student performs certain tasks. For example, the parent would be asked to describe how a student would eat dinner that included a slice of roast beef. The interviewer would be listening to determine if the student had specific skills such as using a fork, cutting with a knife, etc. to score this item. The scores are calculated according to the various test directions to determine if significant deficits are found compared to the norm for the student's age.

Additional assessment in the areas of speech, language, academic achievement, and any motor or physical concerns are completed to identify additional strengths and weaknesses of the student. This information will be used to further document eligibility and assist in planning the student's individual education program (IEP).

Issues for the Classroom Teacher

Due to the degree of learning difficulties and adaptive behavior problems exhibited by students with mild mental retardation, one major issue for the classroom teacher is determining appropriate curriculum objectives and placement. At the elementary level, students with mild mental retardation often receive instruction in academic content areas in general education settings (Taylor & Larson, 2000). Given the mandates of IDEA 2004 and NCLB, students with mild mental retardation will be expected to participate in the general curriculum and high stakes testing. The teacher must decide what specific components of a lesson or skill should be critical for students with mild mental retardation in terms of their performance on the assessments as well as their long-term prognosis as independent adults. To enable students with mild mental retardation to acquire the important information, teachers may need to adapt materials and teaching strategies. For example, for fifth grade students studying the differences between vertebrate and invertebrate animals in the general education setting, the teacher should identify the basic essential information needed to discriminate between the categories. While students without disabilities expand on the discrimination with in-depth detail of the content, students with mild mental retardation are taught to focus on the essential differences and exposed to repetition of the elements in various modalities such as lecture, video, and hands-on activities. Then, appropriate accommodations on high stakes testing allow students with mild mental retardation to demonstrate their mastery of the content and promote school success in meeting adequate yearly progress. Such adaptations can be time-consuming as well as procedurally difficult for teachers. Use of technology and collaboration strategies discussed in later chapters may be helpful in addressing some of these procedural challenges.

There has been a dramatic shift in curricular expectations in regard to reading instruction for students with mild mental retardation (Conners, Atwell, Rosenquist, Sligh, 2001). The emphasis has moved from teaching basic sight words to a phonetic approach to teach decoding. Developmentally, students with mild mental retardation may have difficulty acquiring phonetic understanding in kindergarten and first grade but may be more capable of accomplishing the task if introduced later. Unfortunately, by the time students with mild mental retardation are ready to benefit from a phonetic approach, it is no longer being taught as a part of the general curriculum. Consideration may need to be given to retaining students with mild mental retardation in early grades to allow exposure to instruction that will be beneficial for subsequent acquisition of reading skills.

At the high school level, instruction for students with mild mental retardation heavily emphasizes functional outcomes. Criteria for selecting learning objectives should focus on how **functional** the skill will be for the student. A functional skill is determined by assessing the need for the skill or information being taught in relation to the student's current or future need for that skill or information. Secondary reading instruction should focus on applying skills already learned to understand information that will assist the person to live as independently as possible. For example, being able to read signs that provide directions, letters that contain information, phone books, and notes from relatives would be functional in contrast to reading novels that can now be purchased on tape. In math, the outcome for students with mild mental retardation is to be able to calculate measurement, costs of items, wages, and to manage money. At the high school level, an emphasis on post-school employment shifts the priority toward inclusive vocational instruction in order to promote independent living, community involvement, and social interactions (Luftig & Muthert, 2000).

Another major concern for the classroom teacher is the social inclusion of the student with mild mental retardation. Due to their difficulties making and sustaining friendships, as well as their inappropriate behavior, these students often are socially isolated. In general, students with mild mental retardation may act in an immature way. Behaviors such as pouting in response to not having things go their way or acting silly when it is time to be focused are common. Such behaviors can create a challenge for the teacher in trying to integrate the students and maintain the respect and dignity of everyone in the class (Cullinan, Sabornie, & Crossland, 1992). Often parents of other students in the class are concerned with the impact this student may have on the behaviors of their children. Social integration of the student with mental retardation requires students, parents, and teachers to use problem solving techniques to create a variety of strategies for success. **Figure 4-9** presents a description of a student with mild mental retardation.

In addition to addressing the issues of academic standards and social inclusion, the classroom teacher must decide how to grade the student with mild mental retardation. Often this issue is embedded in the teacher's sense of fairness. Questions concerning the meeting of curriculum standards, reducing the requirements for the student with mental retardation, or altering the grading procedures by including such things as effort, or using pass-fail instead of numerical/letter grades may depend on the teacher's understanding of the disability (Bursuck, Polloway, Plante, Epstein, Jayanthi, & McConeghy, 1996). For students with mental retardation to succeed in the general education class, there is no question that accommodations must be made. How teachers make these decisions and how comfortable they feel regarding them becomes a very personal matter.

Traumatic Brain Injury (TBI)

With the addition of the category of traumatic brain injury (TBI) to IDEA in 1990, an increase in attention and research has been given to the challenge of educating students with TBI (Bergland & Hoffbauer, 1996). This disability is unique in that in addition to

FIGURE 4-9

A Description of a Student with Mild Mental Retardation

David's Mom was a nurse in the neonatal intensive care unit so that a baby born with medical problems was a common occurrence in her life. But when the prenatal tests identified the extra chromosome that was the major indicator for Down syndrome, her life significantly changed. Her husband, the band director at the high school, was supportive in her decision not to abort the fetus. To David's Mom, it was like saying that a child with Down syndrome was something less than a person and did not deserve to live. Yet the unknown for the child and his future were difficult to envision.

David was born with a slight heart problem that was corrected at one month of age. Since his pediatrician was aware of the Early Intervention Program available for infants and toddlers, David began to receive services at three months from a physical therapist and a special education early interventionist. Since David's parents worked different hours, his Mom worked the evening shift and his Dad taught during the day, the intervention visits were scheduled at different times so that both Mom and Dad received the training that would assist in David's progress. During his first three years of life David met his developmental milestones such as walking and talking with only a slight delay. The family added a second and then a third child, so that life around the house was very busy.

At three years of age, David began preschool at the Montessori School nearest home. Through daily interactions with the adults and other children in the program, he was very sociable and school was the highlight of his day. Since David was progressing and accomplishing the goals that had been outlined in his IEP, the special education teacher from the local school system only served as a consultant to the teacher. One particular area that needed special attention was communication. So a speech-language pathologist was brought in to work with the teacher to focus on specific problems.

On the home front, life remained hectic. Keeping up with three preschool boys consumed everyone's time and energy. It was very important to David's Mom and Dad that he would be treated no differently from other children and that the community would treat him no differently. The family attended church and David participated in all of the programs offered, such as choir and Sunday School, At five years of age, David joined the T-ball team in the summer and he played on the soccer team in the fall.

For some unknown reason, the elementary school where David began kindergarten, thought that he would be served best in a separate special education class. David's parents met with school administrators, the principal, and the special education teacher. FINALLY, it was agreed that David would be given a chance to attend school in the general education class. To everyone's delight, David adjusted well to school and continued to make progress in his skill areas. With his teachers and his parents working together, David mastered the skills needed to begin first grade.

In the first grade, it became apparent that David would need direct instruction in reading. The school used the whole language approach to reading, so it became necessary for David to attend the special education resource room for reading. In the resource room, the teacher used the *SRA Reading Mastery Series* for instruction. This provided the instruction that David needed to learn to read. By the end of the year, David was reading just below a first-grade level. Math was a struggle, and David remained in the lowest math group in the general education class. At night his Mom and Dad would alternate assisting him with practice drills in both reading and math. By middle school, David attended the resource room for both reading and math. However, with the extra help from his parents and adaptations of the testing procedures, David remained in general education for science and social studies.

The family continued the extracurricular activities. By now all the boys were playing sports in the city leagues. David's first love became soccer and his interest in music began to appear. It was the drums! He had perfect rhythm and he would spend hours in the evening accompanying the music on the radio. At church he belonged to the youth group and participated in the service activities as well as the "fun" stuff.

David is now in high school and made the high school band playing the drums. His Dad spends the extra time to insure he knows the show for Friday night. He is enrolled in the work-study program at school so that he is off-campus for three hours each day training on various jobs. At school he is enrolled in a basic biology class and the required physical education class for all students. He hopes to have nine separate work experiences listed on his resume by the time he completes high school and continue to work part-time while attending the vocational/technical school in the county to become an apprentice in the construction business.

the rehabilitation of the injury, the student, family, friends, and teachers must adapt and cope with the sudden onset of the disability, as well as the changes in the student after the injury.

Definition

Traumatic brain injury (TBI) is defined in IDEA 2004 as follows:

> Traumatic brain injury means an acquired injury to the brain caused by an external physical force, resulting in total or partial functional disability or psychosocial impairment, or both, that adversely affects a child's educational performance. Traumatic brain injury applies to open or closed head injuries resulting in impairments in one or more areas, such as cognition; language; memory; attention; reasoning; abstract thinking; judgement; problem solving; sensory, perceptual, and motor abilities; psychosocial behavior; physical functions; information processing; and speech. Traumatic brain injury does not apply to brain injuries that are congenital or degenerative, or brain injuries induced by birth trauma.

The definition of TBI focuses on students who have sustained an injury caused by an external force. These injuries typically fall into two categories. A **closed head injury** occurs when the trauma does not cause a puncture to the skull or protective covering of the brain. It might be caused by hitting a windshield during an accident or when an infant is shaken violently. An **open head injury** causes some type of puncture to the protective covering of the brain such as a gunshot wound. In comparison to a traumatic injury, a student can experience a non-traumatic head injury. This includes brain damage from a stroke or near drowning. Students with non-traumatic head injuries are served under other disability categories according to their specific needs (Kelly & Filley, 1994; Savage & Ross, 1994).

Characteristics

Students with traumatic brain injury (TBI) often exhibit variable sequelae and deficits in several major areas of functioning (Taylor, 2004). These include physical abilities, cognitive processes, language skills, behavioral and emotional conduct, and social relations (Kelly & Filley, 1994; Lehr, 1990). Often the degree of disability is related to the severity of the brain injury, the length of time spent in a coma following the injury, and the specific area of the brain that was injured (Voogt & Voogt, 1994). Neuropsychologists describe recovery from a brain injury as a process that continues to present challenges over time. Problems that emerge immediately after a brain injury evolve during the maturation of the student and may actually become worse over time, particularly in terms of behavior (Taylor, 2004). TBI that occurs at an earlier age often results in greater impact and deficits than brain injuries occurring in older students (Gil, 2003). According to Bergland and Hoffbauer (1996), Hooper et al. (2004), Kelley & Filley (1994), Sosin, Sniezek, and Thurman (1991) unique characteristics of students with traumatic brain injury include the following:

- Typically male
- Member of ethnic/racial minority from urban settings
- Before age 10 and between ages 15 and 24
- Often with prior history of special education services (ADHD and BD most common)
- Sudden onset of the disability
- Loss of prior abilities or functions
- Inability to learn due to cognitive or processing deficits
- Inappropriate behavior resulting in a disruption of socialization

In cases of mild TBI, students complain of headaches, fatigue, and sleep disorders long after the injury has occurred (Hooper et al., 2004). Possible physical problems associated with moderate and severe TBI include loss of consciousness; fine and gross motor problems involving activities such as walking, talking, running, and writing; seizures; hydrocephaly; and paralysis; among others. Depending on the specific area of the injury, the student may have sensory impairments that include vision and hearing problems. These impairments will impact on the future educational needs of the student. Motor problems may affect speed and coordination, particularly when the task is complex (Lehr, 1990). Often physical impairments have a good prognosis for remediation with intensive rehabilitation programs (Kelly & Filley, 1994; National Information Center for Children and Youth with Disabilities, 1993).

In the area of cognitive processes, TBI may produce effects on concentration, memory, and executive functioning. Impairments in concentration and attention may make the student appear easily distracted or off-task. This in turn will significantly slow down the student's ability to process information. Memory deficits most often affect long-term storage and retrieval particularly of verbal material. Since memory skills are, to a large extent, developmental, the effects of TBI on memory may vary depending on the age at which a head injury occurs. Executive functioning deficits interfere with students' ability to organize, plan, and carry out their plans (Keyser-Marcus et al., 2002).

While language impairments generally are less severe in children than in adults with brain injuries, there may be effects on speech and articulation as well as subtle effects on language functioning. The impact on language functioning most likely will be evident in academic performances involving written language. Some initial problems with language may be an inability to recall names or bits of information, **mutism** (not talking), and/or not initiating conversation. According to Lehr (1990), there are great expectations for a positive recovery of language and speech skills, unless the injury has damaged the specific area of the brain that controls language and speech functioning.

In general, the effects on behavior may include an increase in the variability of behavior and an exaggeration of behavior patterns already present at the time of injury. The overall appearance is a reduced level of control over behavior which makes the student's behavior appear less predictable. Specific effects that might be observed include hyperactivity (overly active) or hypoactivity (under active), less frustration tolerance, an increase in irritability, aggressiveness and impulsiveness, a greater susceptibility to fatigue, and a reduction in motivation (Lehr, 1990).

In the area of social/emotional behavior, deficits are described by family, teachers, and friends as a change in the student's personality. There may be a reduction in social perception and judgment, exaggerated emotional expression, social ineptitude and social insensitivity, an increase in demands on others, and a decrease in compliance with the demands of others. Students may describe themselves as feeling out of control. It is possible that these inappropriate behaviors are rooted in the student's anger or in a perception of who they used to be. Students may act out sexually in response to the social isolation that is occurring (Lehr, 1990). **Figure 4-10** presents a description of a student with a traumatic brain injury.

Specific Etiology

TBI is the most common cause of death and injury to children, with approximately one million brain injury cases reported annually (National Information Center for Children & Youth with Disabilities (NICHCY), 2000). Three major causes of traumatic brain injury are (Hooper et al., 2004):

accidents
sports
violence/abuse

FIGURE 4-10

A Description of a Student with a Traumatic Brain Injury

Jamaal really enjoyed all sports, but was not particularly great at any one sport. His favorite afternoon activity was a basketball game on the driveway. His grades were above average and his favorite class was science. He looked forward to the days when there was an experiment to conduct in the science lab. Once the teacher had instructed the students to dissect a cow's eye. Now that was a great class!

It was a typical Saturday evening as a group of the guys gathered to drive around town and find where everyone was hanging out. It was six weeks before Jamaal's 16th birthday and the rite of passage into adulthood when he would receive his driver's license. This was the first opportunity for Jamaal's best friend to drive the guys around in the old pick-up truck his father had saved for him. When the guys arrived at the mall where everyone had gathered, they stopped to visit the girls. After a brief visit, it was decided that everyone would ride over to the drag strip for some fun. Everyone piled in and the truck sped off. Just as the truck made its lunge forward, Jamaal tumbled off the tailgate and landed on his head.

It was months later before Jamaal emerged from the rehabilitation center. He had spent three weeks in a coma and two months in the intensive care unit. From there it was hours and hours of physical therapy, occupational therapy, and speech therapy. It was a slow and painful process, and although Jamaal regained his ability to walk and talk, it was not a total recovery. It was obvious when he walked that Jamaal's gait was abnormal, and when he talked his speech was slurred. But Jamaal and his family were ecstatic with his recovery.

Upon returning to school, it was a shock to find that so much of what he knew before the accident was gone or fragmented. It was impossible to start where he had left off at the time of his accident. Jamaal began special education classes at the high school in the 11th-grade. Jamaal could learn, it just took him longer. He did not take notes but listened very intently to the information being presented. Often the information would have to be repeated or explained in a different way. He needed to have his tests read aloud, but was able to pass them. These changes required a tremendous emotional adjustment for Jamaal and his friends.

Progress continued at a slow pace and it took an additional two years for Jamaal to graduate. It was a great accomplishment, but his social life was never what one would expect for a teen-ager. Often Jamaal's interactions were inappropriate. His questions to females were out of line and he would attempt to touch them inappropriately. He was unable to perceive subtle hints regarding typical interactions. This would result in peers rejecting him.

Jamaal completed college, majoring in rehabilitation counseling. It has been a long and difficult road, but his hard work has paid off. However, his social interactions continue to be very depressing and frustrating for him. What is so difficult is that Jamaal remembers and realizes the way he used to be, but he cannot change the way he is.

Vehicle-related accidents are the most common cause of TBI, especially among adolescents. According to statistics, young children are more likely to be injured in a fall. Also in the United States, there is an increase in the number of gunshot wounds causing TBI in the younger population. Although technology has allowed us to protect students involved in sports with padding and helmets, a significant number of closed head injuries continue to occur during sporting events.

As mentioned earlier, nontraumatic brain injuries can be caused in a number of ways. **Anoxic injuries** occur due to a lack of oxygen to the brain. Possible causes of anoxic injuries include drownings, strangulation, and choking. Infections such as encephalitis and meningitis also are possible causes of nontraumatic brain injuries as are strokes, poisonings, and metabolic disorders (Savage & Ross, 1994).

Traumatic brain injuries continue to be a puzzle to the medical profession. Children who suffer such an injury rehabilitate differently than adults with the same type injury. Due to the fact that the brain of a child or adolescent is not fully developed when the injury occurs, the outcome can be affected by the continuing development of the brain. Other factors that contribute to the outcome include the severity of the injury and whether the injury affects a specific area of the brain or if it is global in nature (Savage & Ross, 1994).

Assessment for Eligibility

The actual diagnosis of a traumatic brain injury is made by a physician. However for educational purposes, assessment of students with traumatic brain injury requires a multidisciplinary team composed of professionals from a variety of areas, as well as family, teachers, and friends of the student (Keyser-Marcus et al., 2002). When possible, a pediatric neurologist completes a comprehensive neurological examination. Other professionals such as the speech-language pathologist, occupational therapist, physical therapist, and educational diagnostician will assess their specific areas of concerns. It is critical that the family, teachers, and friends contribute information concerning how the student functioned before the injury, and how the student is currently functioning in the home, school, and community environments (Lehr, 1990; Savage & Ross, 1994).

During the assessment process, it is important to obtain information about the abilities of the student before the injury occurred, as well as the student's current strengths and weaknesses. Previous learning skills will give the team members insight as to the strengths and particular ways of learning the student used previously. Recommendations for future programming will take this information into account in the rebuilding of lost skills. For example, if the student was a strong auditory learner (learned very quickly when listening to lectures), the use of materials with an auditory component may be a way to regain information that was lost.

Professionals will assess the student using many of the standardized test instruments available. Typically, an intelligence test and other achievement tests will be given. These tests will provide information regarding how the student problem solves, organizes information, recalls information, and will determine specific reading, math, and writing skills. Several speech and language tests will be administered by the speech-language pathologist to obtain information concerning the student's expressive and receptive language, as well as the student's speech production. The occupational and physical therapists will conduct an assessment of the student's fine and gross motor skills providing information on the student's motor abilities such as balance, gait, movement, and dressing, as well as the ability to use utensils such as a pencil or fork. Behavioral/personality tests will be given to assess the student's current social behavior including activity levels, self control, interactions, and emotionality (Kelly & Filley, 1994; Keyser-Marcus et al., 2002; Lehr, 1990; Savage & Ross, 1994).

An assessment of a student with TBI always should include observation of how the student functions in the home, school, and community settings (Savage & Ross 1994). The standardized test information is important, but it is limited in regard to how the student performs in daily living situations. Since appropriate performance in every day settings is the ultimate goal, information regarding how the student processes information or behaves in the school, home, and community is critical. Gil (2003) recommends ongoing educational assessments as students with TBI continue to develop. Family, teachers, and friends play an important role in observing and reporting this information.

Issues for the Classroom Teacher

A major issue related to the disability of traumatic brain injury is the adjustment of the student, family, teachers, and friends to the loss of the student's skills and the change in personality (National Information Center for Children and Youth with Disabilities, 1993). By the time the student returns to school, the medical aspects of the injury will be resolved, so that the person "looks" the same as before. When learning, behavioral, and social problems occur, it is difficult for teachers and peers to understand because the expectation is that the student is the same as before. More often than not, students with TBI remember how they were before the injury and feel frustration and anxiety, which only adds to the problems. Family, teachers, and friends also become frustrated with the situation, adding to the difficulties.

Another major challenge for students with traumatic brain injuries occurs as they continue to grow and develop. There is ample research to support the positive recovery of physical, cognitive, language, and behavior in students with TBI; however, as the student develops, additional problems may occur and cause a developmental lag (Gil, 2003). This is especially true of the behavioral and emotional characteristics. As social demands increase with adolescence, new behavioral problems may appear. A functional behavior assessment (see Chapter 11) may be critical for addressing behavioral challenges (Bowen, 2005).

With regard to the actual teaching of students with traumatic brain injury, the technology, teaching strategies, and behavior management techniques discussed in later chapters will assist in planning and implementing the day-to-day instruction. The use of palm pilots, color coding, graphic organizers, and mnemonic strategies can assist students with TBI organize and retain information (Keyser-Marcus et al., 2002). Close attention to noise, light, and activity will be important (Bowen, 2005). Knowledge of the specific strengths and weaknesses of the student will allow the teacher to select the appropriate technology, strategies, and techniques that will enhance the success of the student with a traumatic brain injury. It would be of benefit for the teacher to obtain information regarding the specific type of brain injury that the student has experienced. This will allow the teacher to better understand what to expect in regard to behavior and learning. Current written information, direct contact with the student's physician, or a contact with one of the national organizations listed at the end of this chapter will be beneficial to the teacher.

Information gained from these sources will aid in the teacher's understanding of the need to revise the IEP more frequently during the first few years following the injury. Progress in all of the areas of concern may render the IEP out of date before the typical annual revision is needed. Also the issue of transition should be a major focus of the IEP due to the fact that transitions and change often trigger a need for additional support for the student with a traumatic brain injury.

Summary

Students with behavior and learning challenges, such as those who are identified as having ADHD, EBD, autism, SLD, MR, and TBI can benefit from appropriately planned educational services in general education classrooms. Federal legislation reflects an awareness that the most promising post-school outcomes are associated with an education that aligns with the general education curriculum. IDEA 2004 and NCLB mandate that students with behavior and learning disabilities receive their education in the same settings as their peers without disabilities to the maximum extent appropriate and participate in the same assessments. With few exceptions, students with mild disabilities are required to participate in the same high stakes testing as their peers without disabilities.

Teachers may be overwhelmed at first when faced with some of the unique needs presented by students with behavior and learning challenges. Students with ADHD, who may be eligible for special education support under the category of OHI, will have difficulty sustaining attention on the relevant aspects of instruction and may also exhibit problems controlling their impulses. Students with EBD may demonstrate behaviors that interfere with their learning and the learning of others in the instructional environment. Students functioning at the higher end of the autism spectrum present tremendous challenges for general education teachers as their underlying neurological differences create for them a world that is very different from that experienced by other students in the classroom. An incredible quantity of research and unprecedented amounts of funding are resulting in rapid evolution of the understanding of autism spectrum disorders and new information appears frequently. Students identified with LD present a unique profile of strengths and weaknesses that create as much frustration for teachers as they do for the students. The inconsistent and sporadic mastery of tasks evident in students with SLD create daily challenges in instruction. Similarly, the proposed change in eligibility determination for students with SLD in IDEA 2004 will challenge professionals to document their implementation of evidence-based strategies for accurate decision making. Students with mild mental retardation, with their limitations of intellectual functioning, may need a high degree of support and accommodation to be successful in general education classrooms. Although very few students will be identified with TBI, the sudden discrepancy between their current functioning and how they functioned prior to the injury create psychological and practical challenges for teachers, the students, their peers, and the students' families. Students with TBI present additional challenges as their functioning is not stable but will continue to change over the course of their development. Teachers may need to be more vigilant about recognizing social altercations among some of their students without disabilities and those with mild disabilities, as students with LD, autism, and MR are more likely to be victims of teasing and bullying while those with externalizing EBD are more likely to bully and tease.

All students with mild disabilities will participate to some degree in general education settings and have academic goals aligned with the general education curriculum. Understanding the differences between the categories of mild disability will enable teachers to be more aware of the behavior and learning differences of all students. Although initially an intimidating prospect, general education teachers possess the content knowledge and pedagogy to successfully educate students with mild disabilities. Incorporating instructional strategies effective for students with mild disabilities will likely produce collateral benefit for all students. All students with mild disabilities as per IDEA 2004 will receive some level of additional support. Collaboration between general education teachers and special education teachers is the key to the most favorable post-school prognosis for students with ADHD, EBD, autism, LD, MR, and TBI.

Discussion Questions and Activities

1. Individually or in groups, discuss how different biological and environmental factors can contribute to the development of behavioral and learning disabilities. Are there any preventative actions that could reduce or minimize the ability of the factors to contribute to the development of disabilities?

2. What are the differences between the *DSM IV-TR* classification of disabilities and the eligibility categories in IDEA 2004? Why are there two different systems? *p. 105   vs   p. 5*
   ADHD covered under Section 504
   see p. 37

3. Individually or in groups, compare and contrast the characteristics and eligibility requirements of students with mild mental retardation, specific learning disabilities and emotional/behavioral disorders. Which academic and behavioral characteristics will be similar and which will be specific to each category?

4. Individually or in groups, identify two behaviors that a teacher might see in the classroom for each of the following disabilities. Describe implications specific to these behaviors.

   a. ADHD *p. 111*

   b. EBD *p. 115*

   c. Autism *p. 123*

   d. SLD *p. 129*

   e. MR *p. 139*

   f. TBI *p. 145*

5. Individually or in groups, discuss the eligibility issues regarding students with ADHD. Under what situations would a student with ADHD qualify for special education services?
   Now identified almost exclusively under Sec 504, because must be identified by a medical professional & served under OHI to be under IDEA 2004 —   p. 108

6. Individually or in groups, describe three characteristics of a student with autism and give two critical components that will support the student's learning in your classroom.

7. Individually or in groups, identify the possible associated difficulties for students with TBI and their families. What are the implications for supporting the students with TBI in your classroom?

8. Interview a general education teacher in your preferred content area (e.g., secondary biology, elementary art, early childhood, etc.) and ask about accommodations that are used for students with behavior and learning disabilities.

9. Talk with an administrator of a local school and ask what the procedures are for the following:

   a. Intervening with students who have suicidal ideation.

   b. Handling students who threaten school personnel.

   c. Reporting suspected abuse or neglect.

10. Locate a Physician's Desk Reference and look up the following medications which are commonly prescribed to children with behavior and learning disabilities. Write down the reasons for prescribing, impact on learning/behavior, and associated side-effects for each medication.

Web Scape
Web mD
websites p.155

   a. Ritalin

   b. Dexedrine

   c. Cylert

   d. Tegretol

   e. Prozac

   f. Wellbutrin

   g. Anafranil

   h. Risperdal/Risperidone

11. Parker T. is an 11-year-old boy who has been promoted to middle school this year. Records in Parker's cumulative folder indicate that he has never been a star student but has always plugged along and marginally passed his academic subjects. Early in his school career, teachers commented that Parker was very distractable and hyperactive. He was recommended for prereferral interventions in the second grade and was provided a study carrel, a self-monitoring sheet, frequent breaks and reduced assignment lengths. When Parker passed into the third grade, his teacher, who used high structure; short, hands-on presentations; immediate feedback; and a well-defined behavioral system discovered that Parker was performing adequately. Although the third grade teacher noted that Parker relied on peers in his cooperative learning groups to read materials to him and that Parker struggled with his individual reading and writing assignments, the teacher reported to the prereferral team that he had made progress and the decision was made that Parker no longer needed support from that team. Parker received average grades during his third grade year. When Parker transitioned to the fourth grade, the veteran teacher primarily used lecture format with lengthy, rote assignments. Parker once again had difficulty attending and began to clown around to get his peers' attention and to escape the assignments. The fourth grade teacher routinely sent Parker to the back of the room to copy words out of the dictionary, in order to reduce his misbehavior. Parker spent most of his fourth grade year sleeping. Parker barely passed to the fifth grade. The fifth grade teacher had been forewarned by the fourth grade teacher that Parker was "a lazy trouble maker", so she started out the year by recommending Parker for prereferral consideration. The team recommended the same strategies that had been used in the second grade. Unfortunately for Parker, the fifth grade work was much more demanding than before and he had missed out on much of the fourth grade instruction. Parker had difficulty reading the assignments and could not keep up with the demand for the production of written products. He began to fail in language arts, science, and social studies but maintained passing grades in math, P.E., art and music. Parker's attitude toward school began to change during this time. He had been bored in fourth grade but now was frustrated in most of his fifth grade classes. His teacher noticed that Parker would be sullen and oppositional during the classes he was failing, but would be more cooperative in math, P.E., art and music. After several weeks of on-going communication with Parker's mother, the fifth grade teacher requested a conference with Parker and his mom to discuss the possibility that the prereferral interventions that had been agreed upon were inadequate. Both Parker and his mother believed that more needed to be done, so a conference was set up with the prereferral team. At this meeting, Parker's mother consented to a comprehensive evaluation for consideration of IDEA eligibility. With a score of 95 on the IQ test given, a 60 on the standardized written expression test, and a 70 on the reading decoding test, Parker met the eligibility criteria for SLD in basic reading skills and written expression. At the middle school, Parker will receive language arts instruction for two periods daily in the resource class.

A. How would you prepare for Parker's arrival to your class if you were his:

   1) Sixth grade math teacher

   2) Sixth grade science teacher

3) Sixth grade social studies teacher

4) Sixth grade physical education teacher

B. In hindsight, what could have been done differently during Parker's elementary school years to have identified his disability earlier and minimized the impact that it has had on his educational progress?

Internet Resources

ADHD Report. Newsletter published six times a year available from:

Guilford Press
72 Spring Street
New York, NY 10012
(800) 365-7006
www.guilford.com

American Association on Mental Retardation
444 North Capitol Street, N.W, Suite 846
Washington, DC 20001-1512
1-800-424-3688
www.aamr.org

Autism Hotline
Autism Services Center
P.O. Box 507
Huntington, WV 25710-0507
(304) 525-8014
www.autismservicescenter.org

Autism Society of America
7910 Woodmont Avenue, Suite 300
Bethesda, MD 20814 - 3067
(301) 657-0881 or (800) 328-8476
www.autism-society.org

Brain Injury Association
8201 Greensboro Dr., Suite 611
McLean, VA 22102
(800) 444-6443
www.biausa.org

CH.A.D.D. (Children and Adults with Attention Deficit Disorders)
8181 Professional Place,
Suite 150,
Landover, MD 20785
1-800-233-4050
www.chadd.org

Council for Children with Behavior Disorders
P.O. Box 24246
Stanley, KS 66283
913-239-0550
www.ccbd.net

Division TEACCH
(resources for teaching students with autism)
www.teacch.com

LD On-Line
www.ldonline.org

Learning Disabilities Association of America
4156 Library Road
Pittsburgh, PA 15234 - 1349 (412) 341-1515
www.ldanatl.org

National Resource Center for Traumatic Brain Injury
www.neuro.pmr.vcu.edu

The ARC/U.S.
1010 Wayne Avenue, Suite 650
Silver Spring, MD 20910
(301) 565-3842
www.thearc.org

References

American Association on Mental Retardation. (1992). *Mental retardation: Definition, classification, and systems of supports* (9th ed.). Washington, DC: Author.

American Psychiatric Association. (2000). *Diagnostic and statistical manual of mental disorders* (4th ed., text revision). Washington, DC: Author.

American Psychological Association. (1994). *Publication manual of the American Psychological Association* (4th ed). Washington, DC: Author.

Anderson, G. M., & Hoshino, Y. (1987). Neurochemical studies of autism. In D. J. Cohen & A. Donnellan (Eds.), *Handbook of autism and pervasive developmental disorders* (pp. 166–191). New York: Winston.

Association for Children with Learning Disabilities. (1986, September–October). ACLD description: Specific learning disabilities. ACLD Newsbriefs, pp. 15–16.

Bachman, J. A. (1972). Self-injurious behavior: A behavioral analysis. *Journal of Abnormal Psychology, 80,* 211–224.

Bachsbaum, M. S. (1992). Attention performance in autism and regional brain metabolic rate assessed by positron emission tomography. *Journal of Autism and Developmental Disorders, 22,* 115–125.

Bakke, B. L. (1990). *Self-injury: Answers to questions for parents, teachers, and caregivers.* Minneapolis, MN: Minnesota University Institute for Disabilities Studies.

Bandura, A. (1969). *Principles of behavior modification.* New York: Holt, Rinehart, and Winston.

Baranek, G. T. (1999). Autism during infancy: A retrospective video analysis of sensory-motor and social behaviors at 9–12 months of age. *Journal of Autism and Developmental Disorders, 29,* 213–224.

Barkley, R. A. (1990). *Attention-deficit hyperactivity disorder: A handbook for diagnosis and treatment.* New York: Guilford Press.

Batshaw, M., & Perret, Y. (1992). *Children with disabilities: A medical primer.* Baltimore, MD: Paul H. Brookes.

Baumeister, A. A. (1991). Expanded theories of stereotype and self-injurious responding: Commentary on "Emergence and maintenance of stereotype and self-injury." *American Journal on Mental Retardation, 96,* 321–323.

Baumeister, A. A., Kupstas, F. D., & Woodley-Zanthos, P. (1993). *The new morbidity: Recommendations for actions and an updated guide to state planning for the prevention of mental retardation and related disabilities associated with socioeconomic conditions.* Washington, DC: U.S. Department of Health and Human Services.

Baumrind, D. (1967). Child care practices anteceding three patterns of preschool behavior. *Genetic Psychology Monographs, 75,* 43–88.

Baumrind, D. (1973). The development of instrumental competence through socialization. In A. Pick (Ed.), *Minnesota symposium on child psychology, Vol. 7* (pp. 3–46). Minneapolis, MN: University of Minnesota.

Baumrind, D. (1991). The influence of parenting style on adolescent competence and substance use. *Journal of Early Adolescence, 11(1),* 56–95.

Baumrind, D. (1993). The average expectable environment is not good enough: A response to Scarr. *Child Development, 64,* 1299–1317.

Baumrind, D. (1994). The social context of child maltreatment. *Family Relations, 43,* 360–368.

Beirne-Smith, M., Patton, J. & Ittenbach, R. (1994). *Mental Retardation.* New York: Merrill.

Berkell, D. E. (2005). *Autism: Identification, education, and treatment.* (2nd ed.) Hillsdale, NJ: Erlbaum.

Bettelheim, B. (1967). *The empty fortress: Infantile autism and the birth of the self.* London: Collier-Macmillan.

Bergland, M., & Hoffbauer, D. (1996). *New Opportunities for Students With Traumatic Brain Injuries: Transition to Postsecondary Education. Teaching Exceptional Children. 28 (2),* 54–56.

Bloomingdale, L., Swanson, J. M., Barkley, R. A., & Satterfield, J. (1991, March). *Response to the ADD notice of inquiry by the Professional Group for ADD and Related Disorders.* Scarsdale, NY: Professional Group for ADD and Related Disorders.

Bowen, J. M. (2005). Classroom interventions for students with traumatic brain injuries. *Preventing School Failure, 49,* 34–41.

Bower, E. M. (1960). *Early identification of emotionally handicapped children in the schools.* Springfield, IL: Charles E. Thomas.

Boyle, J. R. & Weishaar, M. (2001). The effects of strategic notetaking on the recall and comprehension of lecture information for high school students with learning disabilities. *Learning Disabilities Research and Practice, 16,* 133–141.

Bucy, J. E. (1994). Internalizing affective disorders. In R. J. Simeonsson (Ed.), *Risk resilience and prevention: Promoting the well-being of all children.* Baltimore, MD: Paul H. Brookes.

Bullock, L. M. & Wilson, M. J. (1989). *BDRS: Behavior dimensions rating scale.* Chicago, IL: Riverside.

Bursuck, W., Polloway, E. A., Plante, L., Epstein, M. H., Jayanthi, M., & McConeghy, J. (1996). Report card grading and adaptations: A national survey of classroom practices. *Exceptional Children, 62(4),* 301–318.

Burt, S. A., McGue, M. Krueger, R. F., & Iacono, W. G. (2005). How are parent-child conflict and childhood externalizing symptoms related over time? Results from a genetically informative cross-lagged study. *Development and Psychopathology, 17,* 145–165.

Callahan, M. (1987). *Fighting for Tony.* New York: Simon & Schuster.

Cataldo, M. R., & Harris, J. (1982). The biological basis for self-injury in the mentally retarded. *Analysis and Intervention in Developmental Disabilities, 2,* 21–40.

Center, D. (1990). Social maladjustment: An interpretation. *Behavioral Disorders, 15(3),* 141–148.

Centers for Disease Control and Prevention. (2005). Prevalence of diagnosis and medication treatment for attention-deficit/hyperactivity disorder—United States, 2003. *MMWR, 54,* 842–847.

Chambliss, C., & Doughty, R. J. (1994). *Parental response to Lovaas treatment of childhood autism.* Paper presented at the 9th Annual University of Scranton Psychology Conference, Scranton, PA. (ERIC Document Reproduction Service No. ED 370 340)

Chess, S., & Thomas, A. (1987). *Origins and evolution of behavior disorders: From infancy to early adult life.* Cambridge, MA: Harvard University Press.

Cline, D. (1990). A legal analysis of policy initiatives to exclude handicapped/disruptive students from special education. *Behavioral Disorders, 15(3),* 159–173.

Conger, R., Ge, X., Elder, G., & Lorenz, F. (1994). Economic stress, coercive family process, and developmental problems of adolescents. *Children and Poverty, 65(2),* 541–561.

Conners, C. (1993). *Attention Deficit Hyperactivity Disorder.* North Tonawanda, NY: Multi-Health Systems.

Conners, F. A., Atwell, J. A., Rosenquist, C. J. & Sligh, A. C. (2001). Abilities underlying decoding differences in children with intellectual disability. *Journal of Intellectual Disability Research. 45 (4),* 292–299.

Counts, C. A., Nigg, J. T., Stawicki, J. A., Rappley, M. D., & von Eye, A. (2005). Family adversity in *DSM IV-TR* ADHD combined and inattentive subtypes and associated disruptive behavior problems. *Journal of the American Academy of Child and Adolescent Psychiatry, 44,* 690–698.

Courchesne, E. (1995). New evidence of cerebellar and brainstem hypoplasia in autistic infants, children and adolescents: The MR imaging study by Hashimoto and Colleagues. *Journal of Autism and Developmental Disorders, 25,* 19–22.

Crowley, T. J., Milkulich, S. K., MacDonald, M., Young, S. E., & Zerbe, G. O. (1998). Substance-dependent, conduct-disordered adolescent males: Severity of diagnosis predicts 2-year outcomes. *Drug & Alcohol Dependence, 49,* 225–237.

Cullinan, D. & Kauffman, J. M. (2005). Do race of student and race of teacher influence ratings of emotional and behavioral problem characteristics of students with emotional disturbance? *Behavioral Disorders, 30,* 393–402.

Cullinan, D., Sabornie, E. J., & Crossland, C. L. (1992). Social mainstreaming of mildly handicapped students. *The Elementary School Journal, 92,* 339–352.

Cummings, E. (1994). Marital conflict and children's functioning. *Social Development, 3(1),* 16–36.

Davis, B., Sheeber, L., & Hops, H. (2002). Coercive family processes and adolescent depression. In J. B. Reid, G. R. Patterson, & J. J. Snyder (Eds.), *Antisocial behavior in children and adolescents: A developmental analysis and model for intervention* (pp. 173–192). Washington, DC: American Psychological Association.

Dawson, G., Webb, S., Schellenberg, G. D., et al. ((2002). Defining the broader phenotype of autism: Genetic, brain, and behavioral perspectives. *Developmental Psychopathology, 14,* 581–611.

deCatanzaro, D. A. (1978). Self-injurious behavior: A biological analysis. *Motivation and Emotion, 2,* 45–65.

DeStefano, F., Bhasin, T. K., Thompson, W. W., Yeargin-Allsopp, M., & Boyle, C. (2004). Age at first measles-mumps-rubella vaccination in children with autism and school-matched control subjects: A population-based study in metropolitan Atlanta. *Pediatrics, 113,* 259–266.

Dishion, T. (1995). Antisocial boys and their friends in early adolescence: Relationship characteristics, quality, and interactional process. *Child Development, 66,* 139–51.

Dishion, T., Patterson, G., Stoolmiller, M., & Skinner, M. (1991). Family, school, and behavioral antecedents to early adolescent involvement with antisocial peers. *Developmental Psychology, 27(1),* 172–180.

Drews, C. D., Yeargin-Allsopp, M., Decoufle, P., & Murphy, C. C. (1995). Variation in the influence of selected sociodemographic risk factors for mental retardation. *American Journal of Public Health, 85, (3),* 329–334.

DuPaul, G. J., Guevremont, D. C., & Barkley, R. A. (1991). Attention-deficit hyperactivity disorder. In T. R. Kratochwill & R. J. Morris (Eds.), *The practice of child therapy* (2nd ed., pp. 115–144). New York: Pergamon.

Durand, V. M. (1992). New directions in educational programming for students with autism. In D. E. Berkell (Ed.), *Autism: Identification, education, and treatment* (pp. 273–294). Hillsdale, NJ: Erlbaum.

Emmer, E. T., & Stough, L. M. (2001). Classroom management: A critical part of educational psychology, with implications for teacher education. *Educational Psychologist, 36,* 103–112.

Epstein, L. J., Taubman, M. T., & Lovaas, O. I. (1985). Changes in self-stimulatory behaviors with treatment. *Journal of Abnormal Child Psychology, 13,* 281–294.

Farmer, T. W., Estell, D. B., Leung, M., Trott, H., Bishop, J., & Cairns, B. D. (2003). Individual characteristics, early adolescent peer affiliations, and school dropout: An examination of aggressive and popular group types. *Journal of School Psychology, 41,* 217–232.

Feingold, B. R. (1975). *Why your child is hyperactive.* New York: Random House.

Forness, S. (1993, November). *The Balkanization of Special Education.* Paper presented at the meeting of the Severe Behavior Disorders Conference, Tempe, AZ.

Freeman, B. J. (1997). Guidelines for evaluating intervention programs for children with autism. *Journal of Autism and Developmental Disorders, 27,* 641–651.

Fried, D. A., Watkinson, B., & Dillon, R. F. (1987). Neonatal neurological status in a low-risk population after prenatal exposure to cigarettes, marijuana, and alcohol. *Developmental and Behavioral Pediatrics, 8,* 318–326.

Gacono, C. B., & Hughes, T. L. (2004). Differentiating emotional disturbance from social maladjustment: Assessing psychopathy in aggressive youth. *Psychology in the Schools, 41,* 849–860.

Ghaziuddin, M. (2005). A family history of Asperger syndrome. *Journal of Autism and Developmental Disorders, 35,* 177–182.

Gil, A. M. (2003). Neurocognitive outcomes following pediatric brain injury: A developmental approach. *Journal of School Psychology, 41,* 337–353.

Goldstein, M. (1988). The family and psychopathology. *Annual Review of Psychology, 39,* 283–299.

Gottesman, I. I. (1991). *Schizophrenia genesis: The origins of madness.* New York: W. H. Freeman.

Grossman, H. J. (Ed.). (1983). *Classification in Mental Retardation.* Washington, DC: American Association on Mental Deficiency.

Guess, D., & Carr, E. (1991). Emergence and maintenance of stereotype and self-injury. *American Journal on Mental Retardation, 96,* 299–319.

Hale, G. (Ed.). (1979). *Sourcebook for the disabled.* New York: Paddington.

Harping, J. (1990). *Cocaine babies: Florida's substance-exposed youth.* Tallahassee, FL: Office of Policy Research and Improvement.

Haynes, N. (1995). How skewed is "the bell shaped curve"? *Journal of Black Psychology, 21(3),* 275–292.

Hays, J. S. (1988). Newborn outcomes with maternal marijuana use in Jamaican women. *Pediatric Nursing, 14,* 107–110.

Henry, B., Moffitt, T. Robins, L., & Earls, F. (1993). Early family predictors of child and adolescent antisocial behavior: Who are the mothers of delinquents? *Criminal Behaviour and Mental Health, 3(2),* 97–118.

Hernstein, R. J., & Murray, C. (1994). *The Bell Curve.* New York: Free Press.

Hinshaw, S. (1992). Externalizing behavior problems and academic underachievement in childhood and adolescence: Causal relationships and underlying mechanisms. *Psychological Bulletin, 111(1),* 127–155.

Hooper, S. R., Alexander, J., Moore, D., Sasser, H., Laurent, S., King, J., Bartel, S., & Callahan, B. (2004). Caregiver reports of common symptoms in children following a traumatic brain injury. *NeuroRehabilitation, 19,* 175–189.

Howlin, P. (2003). Outcome in high-functioning adults with Autism with and without early language delays: Implications for the differentiation between Autism and Asperger syndrome. *Journal of Autism & Developmental Disorders, 33,* 3–13.

Hviid, A., Stellfeld, M., Wohlfahrt, J., & Melbye, M. (2003). Association between thimerosal-containing vaccine and autism. *Journal of the American Medical Association, 290,* 1763–1766.

IDEA: Individuals with Disabilities Education Act of 1990, 15, 20 U.S.C. 1401 (1990).

Individuals with Disabilities Education Improvement Act of 2004, 20 U. S. C. § 1400 *et seq.* (2004) (reauthorization of the Individuals with Disabilities Act of 1990)

Iovannone, R., Dunlap, G., Huber, H., & Kincaid, D. (2003). Effective educational practices for students with autism spectrum disorders. *Focus on Autism and Other Developmental Disabilities, 18,* 150–165.

Jackson, S. (1990). Crack babies are here! Can you help them learn? *CTA Action, 29(3),* 1–3.

Jeffery, K. (1994). *Tourette syndrome and stigma: A place from which parents advocate.* Special project in Sociology/anthropology. (ERIC Document Reproduction Service No. ED 378 761)

Kanner, L. (1943). Autistic disturbances of affective contract. *Nervous Child, 2,* 217–250.

Kauffman, J. M., & Wong, K. L. (1991). Effective teachers of students with behavioral disorders: Are generic teaching skills enough? *Behavioral Disorders, 16,* 225–237.

Kazdin, A. E. (1987). Treatment of antisocial behavior in children: Current status and future directions. *Psychological Bulletin, 102,* 187–203.

Kelly, J. P., & Filley, C. M. (1994). Traumatic brain injury in children. In C. Simkins (Ed.), *Analysis, Understanding and Presentation of Cases Involving Traumatic Brain Injury* (pp. 37–52). Washington, DC: National Head Injury Foundation.

Keogh, B., Bernheimer, L. P. & Gughrie, D. (2004). Children with developmental delays twenty years later: Where are they? How are they? *American Journal on Mental Retardation, 109,* 219–230.

Keyser-Marcus, L., Briel, L., Sherron-Targett, P., Yasuda, S., Johnson, S., & Wehman, P. (2002). Enhancing the schooling of students with traumatic brain injury. *Teaching Exceptional Children 34,* 62–67.

Kindermann, T. (1993). Natural peer groups as contexts for individual development: The case of children's motivation in school. *Developmental Psychology, 29(6),* 970–977.

Kniveton, B. (1989). Peer models and classroom misbehavior: A study of socio-economic differences. *School Psychology International, 10(2),* 105–112.

Kobe, F. (1994). Nonambulatory persons with profound mental retardation: Physical, developmental, and behavioral characteristics. *Research in Developmental Disabilities, 15,* 413–24.

Kounin, J. (1970). *Discipline and group management in classrooms.* New York: Holt, Rinehart and Winston.

Kozma, C., & Stock, J. S. (1993). What is mental retardation? In R. Smith (Ed.), *Children with mental retardation* (pp. 1–49). Rockville, MD: Woodbine House.

Kozol, J. (1967). *Death at an early age: The destruction of the hearts and minds of Negro children in Boston public schools.* Boston: Houghton-Mifflin.

LaVigna, G., & Donnellan, A. (1986). *Alternatives to punishment: Solving behavior problems with nonaversive strategies.* New York: Irvington.

Lehr, E. (1990). *Psychological management of traumatic brain injuries in children and adolescents.* Rockville, MD: Aspen.

Lord, C., Cook, E. H., Leventhal, B., & Amaral, D. G. (2000). Autism spectrum disorders. *Neuron, 28,* 355–363.

Lovaas, O. (1987). Behavioral treatment and normal educational and intellectual functioning in young autistic children. *Journal of Consulting and Clinical Psychology, 55,* 3–9.

Lovitt, T. C. (1989). *Introduction to learning disabilities.* Boston: Allyn & Bacon.

Luftig, R. L., & Muthert, D. (2005). Patterns of employment and independent living of adult graduates with learning disabilities and mental retardation of an inclusionary high school vocational program. *Research in Developmental Disabilities, 26,* 317–325.

Maag, J., & Howell, K. (1992). Special education and the exclusion of youth with social maladjustments: A cultural-organizational perspective. *Remedial and Special Education, 13(1),* 47–54, 59.

Mercer, C. D. (1997). *Students with learning disabilities* (5th ed.). Upper Saddle River, NJ: Merrill.

Merrell, K. W., & Walker, H. M. (2004). Deconstructing a definition: Social maladjustment versus emotional disturbance and moving the EBD field forward. *Psychology in the Schools, 41,* 899–910.

Miklowitz, D., Velligan, D., Goldstein, M., & Nuechterlein, K. (1991). Communication deviance in families of schizophrenic and manic patients. *Journal of Abnormal Psychology, 100(2),* 163–173.

Moore, J. W., & Edwards, R. P. (2003). An analysis of aversive stimuli in classroom demand contexts. *Journal of Applied Behavior Analysis, 36,* 339–348.

National Information Center for Children and Youth with Disabilities. (1993). *Traumatic Brain Injury* [Fact Sheet]. Washington, DC: Author.

National Information Center for Children and Youth with Disabilities (NICHCY). (2000, March). Fact Sheet Number 18 (FS18) [Online article]. Available: http://www.nichcy.org/pubs/factshe/fs18txt.htm

National Joint Commission on Learning Disabilities. (1983). Learning disabilities definition. *Learning Disabilities Quarterly, 6,* 42–44.

National Research Council. (2001). *Educating children with autism.* Committee on Educational Interventions for Children with Autism. Division of Behavioral and Social Sciences and Education. Washington, DC: National Academy Press.

Nelson, C. M. (1991). Serving troubled youth in a troubled society: A reply to Maag and Howell. *Exceptional Children, 58,* 77–79.

Nelson, C., Rutherford, R., Center, D., & Walker, H. (1991). Do public schools have an obligation to serve troubled children and youth? *Exceptional Children, 58(1),* 406–415.

No Child Left Behind Act of 2001, 20 U. S. C. 70 § 6301 *et seq.* (2002)

Osher, D., Cartledge, G., Oswald, D., Sutherland, K. S., Artiles, A. J., & Coutinho, M. (2004). Issues of cultural and linguistic competency in disproportionate representation. In R. B. Rutherford, M M. Quinn, & S. R. Mathur (Eds.), *Handbook of research in emotional and behavioral disorders* (pp. 54–77). New York: Guilford.

Oswald, D. P., Coutinho, M. J., Best, A. M. & Nguyen, N. (2001). Impact of sociodemographic characteristics on the identification rates of minority students as having mental retardation. *Mental Retardation, 39,* 351–367.

Pickett, J., & London, E. (2005). The neuropathology of autism: A review. *Journal of Neuropathology and Experimental Neurology, 64,* 925–935.

Piven, J., Wzorek, M., Landa, R., Lainhart, J., Bolton, P., Chase, G. A., & Folstein, S. (1994). Personality characteristics of the parents of autistic individuals (preliminary communication). *Psychological Medicine, 24,* 783–795.

Plomin, R., & Kovas, Y. (2005). Generalist genes and learning disabilities. *Psychological Bulletin, 131,* 592–617.

Preiser, W., & Taylor, A. (1983). The habitability framework: Linking human behavior and physical environment in special education. *Exceptional Educational Quarterly, 4(2),* 1–15.

Prior, M. (1989). Biological factors in childhood autism. *NIMHANS Journal, 7(1),* 91–101.

Quay, H. (1986). Classification. In H. C. Quay & J. S. Werry (Eds.), *Psychopathological disorders of childhood* (3rd. ed.). New York: Wiley.

Quay, H. C., & Peterson, D. R. (1987). *Manual for the revised behavior problem checklist.* Odessa, FL: Psychological Assessment Resources.

Quinsey, V. L., Skilling, T. A., Lalumiere, M. L., & Craig, W. M. (2004). *Juvenile delinquency: Understanding the origins of individual differences.* Washington, DC:American Psychological Association.

Rago, W., & Case, J. (1978). Stereotyped behavior in special education teachers. *Exceptional Children, 44,* 342–344.

Ritvo, E. R., & Freeman, B. J. (1977). National Society for Autistic Children definition of the syndrome of autism. *Journal of Pediatric Psychology, 2(4),* 142–145.

Rotheram-Borus, M. (1993). Multicultural issues in the delivery of group interventions. *Special Services in the Schools, 8(1),* 179–188.

Sabornie, E. J., Cullinan, D., Osborne, S. & Brock. L. (2005). Intellectual, academic, and behavioral functioning of students with high-incidence disabilities: A cross-categorical meta-analysis. *Exceptional Children, 72,* 47–63.

Sadker, M., Sadker, D., Fox, L., & Salata, M. (1994). Gender equity in the classroom: The unfinished agenda. *College Board Review, 170,* 14–21.

Salett, E. P., & Koslow, D. R. (Eds.). (1994). *Race, ethnicity, and self: Identity in multicultural perspective.* Washington, DC: National Multicultural Institute.

Sautter, R. C. (1995). Standing up to violence. *Phi Delta Kappan, 76,* K1–K12.

Savage, R. C., & Ross, B. (1994). School-age children with traumatic brain injuries. In C. Simkins (Ed.), *Analysis, understanding and presentation of cases involving traumatic brain injury* (pp. 53–64). Washington, DC: National Head Injury Foundation.

Scheff, T. (1966). *Being mentally ill.* Chicago, IL: Aldine.

Scott, T., M., Nelson, C. M., & Liaupsin, C. J. (2001). Effective instruction: The forgotten component in preventing school violence. *Education and Treatment of Children, 24,* 309–322.

Setley, S. (1995). *Taming the dragons: Real help for real school problems.* St. Louis, MO: Starfish.

Sirvanli-Ozen, D. (2005). Impacts of divorce on the behavior and adjustment problems, parenting styles, and attachment styles of children: Literature review including Turkish studies. *Journal of Divorce & Remarriage, 42,* 127–151.

Skinner, B. F. (1953). *Science and human behavior.* New York: Macmillan.

Smith, M. D. (1995). *A guide to successful employment for individuals with autism.* Baltimore: Paul H. Brookes.

Smith, S. M. (1989). Congenital syndromes and mildly handicapped students: Implications for special education. *Remedial and Special Education, 10(3),* 20–30.

Smith, S. (1992). Familial patterns of learning disabilities. *Annals of Dyslexia, 42,* 143–158.

Sosin, D. M., Sniezek, J. E., & Thurman, D. J. (1991). Incidence of mild and moderate brain injury in the United States. *Brain Injury, 10,* 47–54.

Spinath, F. M., Harlaar, N., Ronald, A., & Plomin, R. (2004). Substantial genetic influence on mild mental impairment in early childhood. *American Journal on Mental Retardation, 109,* 34–43.

Sprich, S., Biederman, J., Crawford, M. H., Mundy, E., & Faraone, S. V. (2000). Adoptive and biological families of children and adolescents with ADHD. *Journal of the American Academy of Child and Adolescent Psychiatry, 39,* 1432–1437.

Strauss, A. A. & Lehtinen, L. E. (1947). *Psychopathology and education of the brain injured child.* New York: Grune and Stratton.

Streissguth, A. P. (1986). Smoking and drinking during pregnancy to offspring learning disabilities: A review of literature and development of a research strategy. In M. Lewis (Ed.), *Learning disabilities and prenatal risk* (pp. 28–67). Urbana, IL: University of Illinois.

Tankersley, M. (1993). Classification and identification of internalizing behavioral subtypes (behavioral disorders, emotional disorders). *Dissertation Abstracts International, 54(06),* 2118. (University Microfilms No. AAC 9324904)

Taylor, H. G. (2004). Research on outcomes of pediatric traumatic brain injury: Current advances and future directions. *Developmental Neuropsychology, 25,* 199–225.

Taylor, H. E. & Larson, S. M. (2000). Teaching elementary social studies to students with mild disabilities. *Social Education, 64,* 232–236.

Thapar, A., O'Donovan, M., & Owen, M. J. (2005). The genetics of attention deficit hyperactivity disorder. *Human Molecular Genetics, 14,* R275–R282.

Tobin, T. (1994). Recent developments in functional assessment: Implications for school counselors and psychologists. *Diagnostique, 19,* 5–28.

Tramontana, M., & Hooper, S. (1987). Discriminating the presence and pattern of neuropsychological impairment in child psychiatric disorder. *International Journal of Clinical Neuropsychology, 9(3),* 111–119.

Umbreit, J., Lane, K. L., & Dejud, C. (2004). Improving classroom behavior by modifying task difficulty: Effects of increasing the difficulty of too-easy tasks. *Journal of Positive Behavior Interventions, 6,* 13–20.

U. S. Department of Education. (1991). *Clarification of policy to address the needs of children with attention deficit disorders within general and/or special education.* Washington, DC: Author.

Van Acker, R., Grant, S. B., & Henry, D. (1996). Teacher and student behavior as a function of risk for aggression. *Education and Treatment of Children, 19,* 316–334.

Van Dyke, D. C., & Fox, A. A. (1990). Fetal drug exposure and its possible implications for learning in the preschool and school-aged population. *Journal of Learning Disabilities, 23,* 160–163.

Volden, J., & Lord, C. (1991). Neologisms and idiosyncratic language in autistic speakers. *Journal of Autism and Developmental Disorders, 21,* 109–130.

Voogt, R. D., & Voogt, K. R. (1994). Emotions and traumatic brain injury. In C. Simkins (Ed.), *Analysis, understanding and presentation of cases involving traumatic brain injury* (pp. 23–35) Washington, DC: National Head Injury Foundation.

Waldman, S. (1991, July 15). Lead and your kids. *Newsweek,* 42–48.

Wahlsten, D. (1995). Increasing the raw intelligence of a nation is constrained by ignorance, not its citizens genes. *Alberta Journal of Educational Research, 41(3),* 257–264.

Walker, H. M., Ramsey, E, & Gresham, F. M. (2004). Antisocial behavior in school: Evidence-based practices (2nd ed.). Belmont, CA: Wadsworth.

Wassink, T. H., Brzustowicz, L. M., Bartlett, C. W., & Szatmari, P. (2004). The search for autism disease genes. *Mental Retardation and Developmental Disabilities Research Reviews, 10,* 272–283.

Weinberg, L. A. (1992). The relevance of choice in distinguishing seriously emotionally disturbed from social maladjusted students. *Behavioral Disorders, 17,* 99–106.

Weisz, J., Suwanlert, S., Chaiyasit, W., & Weiss, B. (1988). Thai and American perspectives on over and undercontrolled child behavior problems: Exploring the threshold model among parent, teachers and psychologists. *Journal of Consulting and Clinical Psychology, 56(4),* 601–609.

Werry, J. S., Elkind, G. S., & Reeves, J. C. (1987). Attention deficit, conduct, oppositional and anxiety disorders in children: Laboratory differences. *Journal of Abnormal Child Psychology, 15,* 409–428.

Wetherby, A. M., Woods, J., Allen, L., Cleary, J., Dickinson, H., & Lord, C. (2004). Early indicators of autism spectrum disorders in the second year of life. *Journal of Autism and Developmental Disorders, 34,* 473–493.

Wilson, G. W., McReary, D., & Kean, J. (1979). The development of preschool children of heroin-addicted mothers: A controlled study. *Pediatrics, 63,* 135–141.

Yeargin-Allsopp, M., Drews, C. D., Decoufle, P., & Murphy, C. C. (1995). Mild mental retardation in Black and White children in metropolitan Atlanta: A case-control study. *American Journal of Public Health, 85(3),* 324–328.

Zametkin, A., Mordahl, T. E., Gross, M., King, A. C. Semple, W. E., Rumsey, J., Hamburger, S., & Cohen, R. M. (1990). Cerebral glucose metabolism in adults with hyperactivity of childhood onset. *New England Journal of Medicine, 323,* 1361–1366.

Zingarelli, G. (1992) Clinical effects of naltrexone on autistic behavior. *American Journal on Mental Retardation, 97,* 57–63.

Zirpoli, T. J., & Lloyd, J. W. (1987). Understanding and managing self-injurious behavior. *Remedial and Special Education, 8(5),* 46–57.

5

Characteristics of Students with Sensory, Communication, Physical, and Health Impairments

Kathryn Wolff Heller and Colleen M. O'Rourke

Chapter Objectives

- to describe the most common etiologies of sensory, communication, physical, and health impairments;
- to provide an overview of the types of special education professionals and related service professionals and their roles in providing services to students with these disabilities;
- to define and describe the educational impact of visual impairments, hearing impairments, communication disorders, physical impairments, and health impairments; and
- to discuss effective management strategies for classroom teachers and special educators when teaching students with these disabilities.

Many students with sensory, communication, physical, or health impairments can be found in general education classes, following the general academic curriculum. In some instances, the disability may not be noticeable. In other cases, it results in severe limitations regarding sensory input, communication, movement, and/or activity. In either case, the impairment typically results in the need for the classroom teacher to plan collaboratively with a special education teacher for the use of assistive devices and teaching adaptations to allow the student to learn effectively.

Knowing the characteristics associated with these disabilities will give the classroom teacher the foundation to provide appropriate education. Students with vision or hearing loss often miss vital information due to the impact of the sensory impairment. Students with communication disorders may be unable to ask questions effectively. Students with physical impairments often have difficulty accessing material due to physical limitations. Students with health impairments may have conditions which affect stamina, resulting in fatigue during the school day. When teachers are responsible for the education of students with these types of disabilities, an understanding of the impairment and its implications will allow them to make the appropriate modifications for school success. This chapter will provide an overview of sensory, communication, physical, and health impairments to assist teachers in understanding these disabilities and their educational implications.

Etiologies

There are numerous causes (etiologies) of sensory, communication, physical, and health impairments. These disabilities typically are due to either biologic factors or environmental factors which can occur anytime from before birth through adulthood. The etiologies can be divided as occurring during three time periods:

(a) prenatally (before birth),
(b) perinatally (during or shortly after birth),
(c) postnatally (after birth).

There are several **prenatal** factors which can result in impairments. The most common factors are chromosomal and genetic defects, prenatal infections, congenital abnormalities, and environmental factors. Chromosomal and genetic defects refer to any of the several hereditary disorders which are passed from the parent(s) to the child. These hereditary defects may result in specific impairments, or syndromes (which include combinations of physical, sensory, communication, and health impairments). For example, two hereditary disorders are muscular dystrophy, which is a physical impairment, and sickle cell anemia, which is a health impairment. An example of a syndrome is Usher syndrome which includes both deafness and a visual impairment known as retinitis pigmentosa. Some of the manifestations of these hereditary disorders may be present at birth, while others may not become apparent until childhood or adolescence.

There is a group of prenatal infections which can result in physical, sensory, communication, and health disorders. These are referred to as the **STORCH** infections. STORCH is an acronym for: **S**yphilis, **T**oxoplasmosis, **O**ther, **R**ubella, **C**ytomegalovirus, and **H**erpes. When a pregnant woman has a STORCH infection, the infection may be transmitted to the fetus. If this occurs, physical impairments (e.g., cerebral palsy, paralysis, etc.), communication disorders, visual impairment, hearing impairment, or health impairments (e.g., heart defects, kidney defects, intestinal tract defects, etc.) may occur (Andersen, 2004). Whether the child will be affected in these areas and the severity of the impairment will depend upon the type of infection and the trimester of pregnancy during which the infection occurred.

Congenital abnormalities may occur during prenatal development and result in disability. For example, in the case of spina bifida, the neural tube (which forms the spinal cord and brain) does not close properly and results in an outpouching of the spinal cord and subsequent disability. Another congenital abnormality is a limb deficiency in which an infant is born with part of an arm or leg missing. In this instance, something occurred prenatally which interrupted the normal development of an anatomical structure.

There are several environmental factors which may result in impairments. When the fetus is exposed to radiation or drugs which the mother (or possibly the father) has taken, disabilities may occur. Complications of pregnancy or a lack of oxygen can result in damage to the brain with subsequent impairments in physical, communication, sensory, and/or health areas.

Perinatal factors and **postnatal** factors also may result in various impairments. During birth the infant may be exposed to infection, trauma, or a lack of oxygen, all of which may cause disability. After birth, the infant, child, or adolescent may have an accident which affects the eyes, ears, spinal cord, brain, or limbs (arms or legs). This can result in such conditions as vision loss, hearing loss, communication disorders, or physical disability. Infections and disease, such as meningitis and AIDS, may result in physical, sensory, and health impairments. Environmental causes, such as malnutrition, also may result in disability.

Identification and Eligibility for Services

Due to the visibility of many sensory, communication, physical, and health impairments, most students will be identified as having these impairments before they enter school. However, the teacher needs to be alert to some of the milder forms of these impairments which may go unidentified or impairments which may not manifest themselves until the school years. The teacher may be the first person to recognize that the student has a vision or hearing impairment. Physical impairments, such as scoliosis, often are detected in school during routine screening exams. Health impairments such as seizures also may be detected initially by a teacher. Knowing the characteristics of these conditions will assist the teacher in identifying possible impairments and referring the student for further assessment.

Assessments documenting a sensory, communication, physical, or health impairment usually involve medical personnel. They will provide a full medical examination using such evaluation measures as a physical exam, lab work, X-rays or scans, and specialized tests. However, when a sensory, communication, physical, or health impairment is diagnosed and documented, it does not automatically qualify a student for special education services. The impairment must impact on the student's educational performance to result in the qualification for services in the school setting.

Special Education and Related Service Professionals

In addition to the classroom teacher, the parent(s), and student, there are several professionals who may be part of the educational team for students with sensory, communication, physical, or health impairments. Which professionals participate on the team will vary depending upon the type of impairment and the student's educational needs. Some of these professionals include a special education teacher, physical therapist, occupational therapist, speech-language pathologist, audiologist, optometrist, nurse, and physician.

The **special education teacher** has knowledge and expertise in providing instructional strategies, adaptations, and curriculum modifications for students with exceptional needs. In many states special education teachers are certified in specific disability areas, such as visual impairments, hearing impairments, or physical and health disabilities. As seen in **Table 5-1,** special education teachers who are certified in specific disability areas have specialized knowledge regarding the education of students with particular disabilities.

Students who have visual impairments may have an **orientation and mobility (O&M) instructor.** The O&M instructor has specialized training in mobility and travel. This training often occurs in specific environments such as home, school, community, work, leisure settings, and public transportation. Instruction may include learning to use a cane and/or electronic mobility devices.

Students with physical impairments may receive services from a **physical therapist (PT)** or an **occupational therapist (OT).** The PT provides essential input to the team regarding optimal physical functioning in age-appropriate instructional activities, particularly as they relate to gross motor skills, proper positioning, and movement. The OT provides input regarding these same activities as they relate to fine motor skills, visual-motor skills, and self-care activities. The PT and OT consult with teachers, parents, and

TABLE 5-1

Specific Types of Special Education Teachers

Teachers Certified in Visual Impairments

- Special education teachers who are certified in visual impairments (VI Teachers) have knowledge of the educational implications of visual impairments and blindness and appropriate teaching strategies needed to serve this population. Some of the areas of expertise include adapting material, enhancing visual functioning, conducting educationally oriented functional vision exams and learning media assessments, teaching the use of assistive devices, teaching computer use with voice output or screen enlargement and keyboard skills, teaching reading and writing braille, teaching social skills, teaching the use of low vision devices, promoting concept development, and instruction in academic and nonacademic areas.

Teachers Certified in Hearing Impairments

- Special education teachers who are certified in hearing impairments (HI Teachers) have specific knowledge in hearing impairments and deafness. Some areas of expertise include teaching sign language, teaching concept development, adapting materials and instruction, selection and use of assistive devices, teaching the use of residual hearing, and teaching academic and nonacademic areas

Teachers Certified in Physical and Health Disabilities (also known as Orthopedic Impairments)

- Special education teachers who are certified in physical and health disabilities specialize in meeting the unique needs of students who have physical disabilities. Some areas of expertise include adaptations to instruction and material to accommodate for limitations in physical movement, selection and implementation of assistive devices, knowledge of educational implications of physical impairments, training in physical health care procedures, promoting communication through the use of augmentative and alternative communication systems, feeding techniques, positioning and handling techniques, and teaching academic and nonacademic skills.

other team members to provide training and to make recommendations for adaptations or construct devices for use in the learning environment.

Students who have difficulty in the areas of speech and/or language will receive services from a **speech-language pathologist (SLP).** The SLP provides input to the educational team regarding communication programming in age-appropriate functional activities targeted for instruction. The SLP also provides training to the student on methods of communication and speech and/or language skills, and selects or constructs devices to facilitate a student's communication and socialization skills. Many SLPs have experience and training in the areas of feeding skills and alternative augmentative communication (AAC), specially designed devices which allow individuals who cannot speak to communicate.

The **audiologist** is trained to identify the type and amount of hearing loss or dysfunction. The audiologist provides guidelines to the team on equipment (such as hearing aids) as well as procedures (such as environmental adaptations) to assist students in compensating for their hearing impairment. Depending on the individual's hearing loss, the audiologist also may be involved with aural rehabilitation, techniques to teach the individual to use whatever hearing remains (residual hearing) to its fullest. The school audiologist must have training and experience with a variety of alternative, nontraditional assessment procedures in order to work effectively with students with a wide range of disabilities.

The **optometrist** is trained to provide a regular eye exam and prescribe corrective lenses. Some optometrists have additional training in low vision. These optometrists will assess the student's need for low vision devices, prescribe the appropriate devices, and provide some training on their use. Low vision devices such as magnifiers and telescopes may assist the student with a visual impairment in seeing close images, such as print, or far images, such as a distant building.

The **nurse** can be a valuable information source for the educational team concerning a student's physical or medical condition and its effects on the student's educational program. Nurses may perform specialized medical procedures the student requires, such as tube feeding, catheterization, suctioning, or administration of medicines. They also may train other team members to perform these procedures. Training of parents or professionals on emergency procedures is part of the nursing role, as well as acting as a liaison between the educational team and the medical community.

Various types of **physicians** may be included on the educational team, depending on the individual student's needs. Most common to the team is the pediatrician. However, physicians with specialized knowledge of the student's specific disability also may be part of the educational team. Some of these include orthopedists (bone and muscle), neurologists (nervous system), ophthalmologists (eye), otorhinolaryngologists or ENTs (ear, nose and throat), urologists (urinary system), gastroenterologists (digestive system), pulmonologists (lung), and cardiologists (heart).

Visual Impairments

Students with visual impairments comprise a small percentage (0.5%) of the students receiving special education services. They vary as to the type of vision loss, the severity of the loss, and the impact this sensory loss has on functioning. Certain types of visual impairments will affect how clearly a student sees while others may affect how much a student can see at one time. Having an understanding of the common terms used in this field, the anatomy of the eye, the common conditions causing visual impairments, and general characteristics of students with visual impairments, will assist the teacher in better understanding the effects of visual impairments.

In the educational setting, visual impairment is defined by its impact on educational performance. Under IDEA, a student is defined as having a visual disability if the visual impairment, even with correction, adversely affects educational performance. There are several specific terms used to describe visual impairments.

- **Visual Impairment.** This term covers a wide range of vision loss which can include any visual deficit.

- **Blind.** Individuals who are totally without vision or who have light perception only are said to be blind. In education, this term refers to students who use other senses (i.e., hearing and touch) as primary channels for learning or receiving information.

- **Legal Blindness.** A person who is legally blind has a visual acuity of 20/200 or less in the better eye with correction or a visual field that is no greater than 20 degrees. The term visual acuity refers to the finest detail that the eye can distinguish. In this definition, the term 20/200 means that the person with the visual impairment can see an object or symbol at 20 feet that a person with unimpaired vision can see at 200 feet. Field of vision refers to the ability to see objects in the periphery of one's vision when looking straight ahead. Individuals with unimpaired vision can see objects within a 180 degree arc when looking straight ahead.

- **Low Vision (partially sighted or partial vision).** This term refers to individuals who have significant visual impairments with best correction, but still have usable vision.

Vision is used as the primary channel for learning or receiving information. Visual functioning may increase with the use of low vision devices, environmental modifications, and/or training (Corn, DePriest, & Erin, 2000). Less used terms include partially sighted or partial vision which tend to refer exclusively to distance vision with an acuity between 20/70 and 20/200.

Anatomy of the Eye

The eye is a complex sensory system that receives light rays and converts them to electro-chemical impulses to send to the brain for processing. As seen in **Figure 5-1,** the eye consists of several structures which are similar to the inner workings of a camera.

The outer protective layer of the eye is the white part of the eye which wraps around five-sixths of the eyeball and is known as the **sclera.** The sclera is a tough, dense, connective tissue that serves to protect the inner parts of the eye, similar to the outer casing of a camera. The remaining one-sixth of the outer portion of the eye is composed of a transparent tissue known as the **cornea.** The cornea often is called "the window of the eye" because light first passes through the cornea as it travels to the inner structures of the eye. This is similar to the extra protective lens put on the camera through which light first passes. The cornea, however, also bends the light rays to promote focusing of the image.

FIGURE 5-1

Anatomy of the Eye

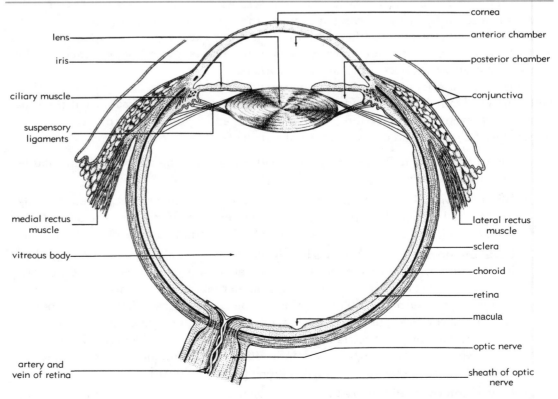

© Kendall/Hunt Publishing Company

After the light passes through the cornea, it goes through a liquid substance, the **aqueous humor,** and enters a hole in the eye, the **pupil.** The pupil appears black and is surrounded by the colored part of the eye, the **iris.** When someone says they have blue eyes, they are referring to the color of the iris. The iris causes the pupil to change size, which regulates how much light enters the eye. This is similar to the function of the F-stop on a camera. After the light travels through the pupil, it passes through the lens. As the lens of the camera focuses the light, the lens of the eye also focuses the light to the back portion of the eye. The light then passes through a transparent liquid known as the **vitreous humor** which gives the eyeball its round shape. Finally, the light is focused on the **retina** at the back of the eye which is similar to the film in the camera.

The retina contains approximately 125 million photoreceptors, categorized as **rods** and **cones** that convert light rays to electrical impulses (Ward, 2000). The rods are sensitive to low intensity illumination (dim light) and can detect gross form and movement. Rods are primarily responsible for peripheral vision and night vision. The cones are sensitive to high intensity illumination (daylight) and detect fine detail and colors. On the retina, there is a small central area in which most of the cones are located. This area is known as the **macula.** The macula is responsible for central vision. The remainder of the retina is responsible for peripheral vision.

After the image has been converted into electro-chemical impulses by the retina, the impulses travel to the **optic nerve** and exit the eye through the optic nerves located behind each eyeball. From there they travel to the **visual cortex,** in the occipital lobe of the brain. The visual cortex, in addition to other areas of the brain, allows an individual to interpret what is being seen.

Impairments Affecting Visual Functioning

When there is a visual impairment, the functioning of the eye may be affected in several different ways. These include: (a) poor visual acuity, (b) visual field deficits, (c) eye movement abnormalities, (d) light and color reception impairments, and (e) abnormalities of visual perception and brain functions (Corn, DePriest, Erin, 2000).

Poor Visual Acuity

Visual acuity refers to how clear or sharp an image appears. Poor visual acuity is caused most commonly by the refractive errors of hyperopia (farsightedness), myopia (nearsightedness), and/or astigmatism (blurred vision). These often can be corrected by wearing corrective lenses.

Visual Field Deficits

A person's field of vision is the entire area that can be seen without shifting one's gaze. Defects in visual fields may occur in a person's central field of vision, peripheral field of vision, or both as shown in **Figure 5-2.**

Central vision refers to the direct line of vision, which is essential for discerning details. A student with a central vision loss may be unable to read print, discern facial features, or perceive objects when looking straight at them (Riordan-Eva, Asbury, & Whitcher, 2003). These individuals must direct their gaze off to the side to see the desired item or person using their peripheral (side) vision. This is known as eccentric viewing.

Peripheral vision refers to the ability to perceive the presence of objects outside the direct line of vision. When a peripheral field loss exists, the student is unable to see objects in part or all of the peripheral vision. One of the common types of peripheral vision losses involves the loss of vision in a ring shape along the periphery which results

FIGURE 5-2

Field of Vision Deficits

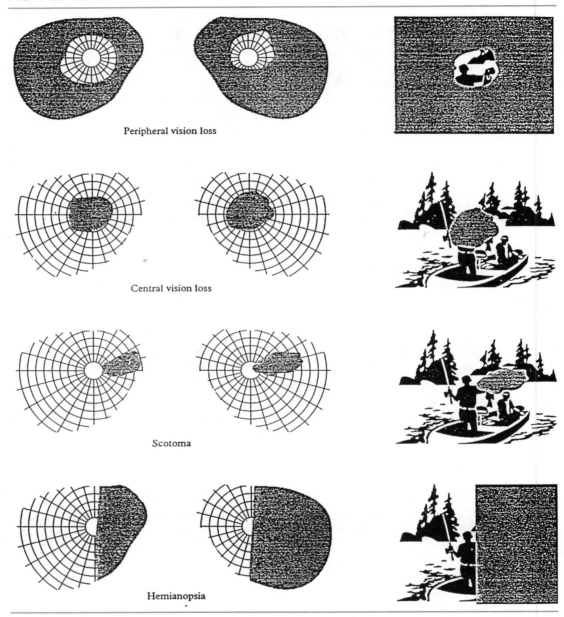

Peripheral vision loss

Central vision loss

Scotoma

Hemianopsia

From *Understanding Physical, Sensory and Health Impairments* by Heller, Forney, Alberto and Schwartzman. Copyright © Wadsworth Publishing Company. Reprinted by permission.

in a narrower visual field (i.e., like looking through a tunnel as depicted in the term "tunnel vision"). Since the rods are located primarily in the periphery, and they permit seeing in dim light, a peripheral field loss may be accompanied by loss of night vision. Other field deficits include blind spots (non-seeing area in the visual field) or loss of entire sections of the field of vision (e.g., loss of one half of the visual field).

Eye Movement Abnormalities

Problems in eye movement may occur from abnormalities of the six muscles surrounding each eye, the nerves innervating these muscles, or the brain. Three common impairments associated with problems in eye movement are strabismus, amblyopia, and nystagmus.

Strabismus is an unequal pull of the muscles surrounding the eye. This results in the eyes not being in correct alignment. One or both eyes may turn inward, outward, upward, or downward. This often can be corrected by surgery. When it is not corrected, the eyes are not in correct alignment, and double vision can occur. When a double image occurs, the brain often will suppress one image so that only one visual image will be seen instead of a double image.

The suppression of one image by the brain can lead to the inability to see clearly (or in extreme cases to see at all) through the eye with the suppressed image. When this occurs, the condition is referred to as **amblyopia,** or lazy eye. To correct amblyopia, the good eye may be patched to force the use of the "weak" eye.

Nystagmus is involuntary, rhythmic eye movements which may occur in a horizontal, vertical, diagonal, or rotary motion. The student with nystagmus may have poor visual acuity in the affected eye, although binocular vision also may be impaired. Individuals with nystagmus usually will perceive objects as stationary, with the brain adjusting perceptually for the movement. However, students may lose their place while reading and often can benefit from using an index card or typoscope (paper with rectangular hole cut out of it) to help keep their place.

Impairment in Color and Light Reception

The primary impairment in color reception is color blindness. Students who are color blind usually cannot see certain colors due to missing or damaged cones (color receptors) in the eye. This is typically a sex-linked genetic abnormality and results from absence of color genes on the X chromosome. The most commonly occurring congenital color defect is a red-green color defect in which red and green appear the same color (Gordon, 1998).

Lighting conditions also may impact on a student's visual functioning. Some students may be sensitive to light **(photophobia);** they may be uncomfortable in normal lighting conditions and need to wear sunglasses or a visor (or cap) indoors. Other students may need increased lighting to improve visual functioning. Still other students may be unable to see in dim light and may have difficulty going from the bright sunlight to a darkened hallway.

Abnormalities of Visual Perception and Brain Function

Students with impairment of the occipital lobe or other areas of the brain may have problems with depth perception, estimating distances, and spontaneous visual learning. In some conditions, objects may not be perceived (Ward, 2000).

Common Eye Conditions

There are several eye conditions which may result in poor visual acuity, visual field deficits, eye movement abnormalities, light and color reception impairments, and abnormalities of visual perception and brain functions. It is important to know the type of eye impairment a student has and possible educational implications of the condition. **Table 5-2** provides examples of conditions affecting different parts of the eye as well as general educational implications of each condition.

TABLE 5-2

Examples of Eye Conditions

Glaucoma

- Glaucoma is an abnormal increase in intraocular pressure in one or both eyes which can damage the eye. The increase in intraocular pressure is due to an imbalance between production and outflow of aqueous humor. If left untreated, the increase in pressure causes damage to the optic nerve fibers in the back of the eye. This results in restricted visual fields and eventual blindness. It is treated by medication and/or surgery. Low vision devices and sunglasses may be prescribed since photophobia and decreased visual acuity occur in glaucoma.

Cataract

- A cataract is clouding of the lens of the eye. A cataract's effect on vision varies depending on the size, position, and density of the cloudy area. Some cataracts involve pinpoint areas which do not interfere with vision while others may be centrally located and so dense that blindness results. Often decreased visual acuity and difficulty seeing in bright light is present. Cataracts typically are treated by surgical removal of the lens. Special glasses may be worn after surgery or in older individuals, artificial lenses may be implanted in the eye. If the cataract has not been surgically treated, lighting may be adjusted to reduce glare. Also, if the cataract is positioned centrally in the lens, unusual head positions may be observed, since the person is "looking around the cataract." Occasionally magnification may be helpful to improve vision.

Congenital Macular Dystrophies

- Macular dystrophies refer to a wide variety of disorders in which there are abnormalities of the macula (the part of the eye responsible for central vision and clear, distinct vision). Macular dystrophies range in severity from a reduction of visual acuity to a loss of central vision. There is no effective treatment at this time; however, to improve visual functioning, some individuals may use eccentric viewing or magnification.

Retinitis Pigmentosa

- In retinitis pigmentosa, there is a gradual loss of vision, beginning in the periphery and progressing towards the center of the field of vision. The condition begins with a peripheral field loss and night blindness. As it progresses, tunnel vision results and eventually central vision may be affected as well. There is no effective treatment at this time for retinitis pigmentosa. To assist with visual functioning, several optical devices may be helpful, such as magnifiers, hand telescopes, closed circuit television, and infra-red devices for use at night.

Retinoblastoma

- Retinoblastoma is the most common malignant childhood tumor of the eye. It occurs in about one in 15,000 to one in 30,000 live births and is life-threatening. The tumor is in both eyes in approximately 20–30% of the cases (Beers & Berkow, 1999). Small retinoblastomas may be treated effectively with radiation, along with chemotherapy or cryotherapy. Larger retinoblastomas require removal of the eye (enucleation). This is successful if the cancerous tumor is confined to the eye and has not spread to other parts of the body.

Cortical Visual Impairment

- Cortical visual impairment (CVI) refers to damage to the visual pathways or cortex of the brain. The resulting visual impairment may range from poor visual acuity to blindness, depending on the cause, the location, and the severity of the damage. Visual functioning may fluctuate during the day resulting in the student sometimes being able to see an object while other times not being able to see it. There is no specific medical treatment at this time, except treating underlying causes when possible. In individual students, it is difficult to determine whether visual functioning will improve or remain static.

TABLE 5-3

Screening Checklist for Visual Impairments

A. Eye Appearance

_____ Eyes red
_____ One eye turns in, out, up, or down
_____ Eyes in constant motion (nystagmus)
_____ Tears excessively
_____ Eyelid crusted

B. Visual Abilities

_____ No blink reflex
_____ Pupils do not react to light
_____ Does not fixate on object
_____ Cannot track object
_____ Does not scan for object
_____ Cannot follow moving object toward nose (converge eyes)

C. Behaviors

_____ Rubs eyes frequently
_____ Squints eyes
_____ Blinks frequently
_____ Closes one eye doing certain tasks
_____ Does not look straight at an object (looks from side)
_____ Turns or tilts head
_____ Approaches items by touch rather than sight
_____ Holds items (e.g., book) too close or too far

D. Verbal Complaints

_____ Complains of eye pain, headaches
_____ Complains of seeing double
_____ Complains of not being able to see well

E. Academic Work

_____ Cannot copy off the blackboard
_____ Makes frequent errors reading letters which are shaped similarly
_____ Rereads or skips words or lines when reading
_____ Uses hand to keep place
_____ Writes uphill or downhill on paper

Visual Assessment

There are several different types of assessments to evaluate a student's visual functioning. Assessments can be divided into various categories: visual screening, ophthalmologic or eye exam, low vision exam, and functional vision exam.

Some students will display certain behaviors which may indicate a visual problem as shown in **Table 5-3.** Teachers need to be alert for possible vision problems and refer the student for further testing if a vision impairment is suspected. To help detect a vision problem, schools use routine screening exams. These usually are performed by a school nurse or other trained personnel. Often they include reading an eye chart and visually locating objects. Typically this type of screening only detects problems in how clearly someone sees (acuity) from a distance and can miss other types of impairments.

An eye exam by an ophthalmologist or optometrist is designed to detect eye disease and problems in visual functioning. Eye disease is detected through close examination of the structure of the eye using a variety of instruments, as well as various tests. For example, a slit-lamp is used to examine the front part of the eye while an ophthalmoscope is used to examine the back structure of the eye. Several assessments will be used to determine how well the eye is functioning. The most common assessment involves using eye charts to determine how clearly a person sees and prescribing eye glasses when there is a problem in refraction (how clearly a person sees an object). Other assessments may include checking visual fields (how much a person sees), eye movement, color vision, and eye reflexes (e.g., blink reflex).

A low vision exam is performed by an optometrist trained in low vision. The primary purpose of this exam is to determine if the person would benefit from low vision devices. Low vision devices include such items as magnifiers (which are used for reading print) and telescopes (which are used for seeing distant items).

An educationally oriented functional vision exam usually is performed by the teacher certified in visual impairment (VI teacher). The focus of this exam is to determine how well the student is using vision and what modifications or teaching strategies are needed. The exam includes checking for visual abilities (e.g., tracking) as well as determining what environmental changes improve visual functioning (e.g., more light or contrast). The need for adaptations, such as using dark lined paper, also will be determined. A functional media assessment typically is included as a part of the exam. This assessment determines if the student can see standard print or would benefit from large print, braille, or a combination of these.

Management of Visual Impairments

Students with visual impairments comprise a diverse group of individuals who will need various amounts and types of adaptations to assist them in school. The educational team, with the lead of the vision teacher, will determine the types of modifications needed. Modifications for students with visual impairments can be divided into seven main areas:

1. use of assistive technology,
2. use of a person,
3. changes in the physical environment,
4. changes in student response,
5. changes in teacher instruction,
6. alteration in material, and
7. alteration in activities and/or curriculum (See **Table 5-4**) (Heller, Dangel, & Sweatman, 1995).

Students with visual impairments often will require assistive technology. Assistive technology refers to any item, piece of equipment or product that is used to increase or maintain the functional capabilities of individuals with disabilities. Low vision devices are a type of assistive device. These consist of such items as magnifiers, which enlarge print which is close to the student, and telescopes, which enlarge items at a distance. Machines such as CCTV (closed circuit televisions) enlarge books and other materials onto a large screen for the student to see. Other types of assistive devices include those for mobility. Canes, guide dogs, braille compasses, and electronic mobility devices may be used to assist the student in moving from one location to another. Students with visual

TABLE 5-4

Managing Visual Impairments

	Visual Impairment
Assistive Technology	• Low vision devices (e.g., magnifier)
Use of Person	• Peer teaming
Physical Environment	• Position student in relation to activities • Lighting • Contrast
Student Response	• Alternate response forms (e.g., braille) • More time
Teacher Instruction	• Use of verbal description
Alter Material	• Alter material so student can use it regardless of visual loss (e.g., enlarge material, use tactile models)
Alter Activity	• Modify activity to compensate for sensory loss
Alter Curriculum	• Learn additional specialized skills (e.g., mobility training)

From *Understanding Physical, Sensory, and Heath Impairments* by Heller, Forney, Alberto and Schwarteman. Copyright © Wadsworth Publishing Company. Reprinted by permission.

impairments may also use various types of assistive technology to provide access to school activities, including computer use (e.g., voice output word processors, braille printers (embossers), screen reading software). (See Chapter 10 for additional information on assistive devices).

A second type of modification involves using another person. Peer assistance may be used in which a peer assists the student in activities which require additional description or assistance in locating certain items. Peer teaming or working in groups also may be used. This not only allows additional assistance to the student with the visual impairment, but also provides this student the opportunity to assist peers on parts of the tasks which do not require a visual component.

The third type of modification is arrangement of the physical environment. Some students with visual impairment may need to be seated near the front of the room in order to see the board. Other options may be placing the student where there is less glare or where the lighting is appropriate for the student's needs. Sometimes there may be so much visual clutter in the room that it is difficult for the student to see what is important. In this case the teacher will need to make some modification regarding what is on the classroom walls. (See Chapter 10 for further discussion of classroom arrangement).

A fourth modification is student response. Some students with visual impairments will be using braille as their primary form of written communication and may do some of their classwork in braille. The teacher certified in visual impairments will be able to translate the braille into print for the teacher. Other response modifications include extending time limits for assignments or tests since reading braille or large print requires more time than reading standard print.

A fifth modification is teacher instruction. The teacher typically will not need to modify the instructional strategies used in the class. However, it is important that the

Books and handouts can be translated to braille for students with severe visual impairments.

teacher provides ample verbal description of what is being displayed or demonstrated so that the student with a visual impairment will understand and follow the discussion.

A sixth modification is adapting the material. Students with visual impairments or blindness may need material in braille, large print, or on audio cassette. The special education teacher will assist in obtaining large print books or braille books as well as putting material into braille. It also is important that the student be provided with concrete objects and tactile models representing what is being taught. For example, when teaching counting the students would benefit from using concrete objects to count. In geometry class it will be important to use models of the geometric shapes. When teaching anatomy in biology class, anatomical models which can be touched by the student are helpful.

In some instances an activity or curriculum modification is needed for the student with a visual impairment. Due to the lack of the most important distance sense used for learning, the student with a visual impairment may have several incomplete or incorrect concepts. A student who has only touched part of a fire truck may not fully understand its size or shape. Providing activities in which the student may touch and experience the concept being taught will promote a better understanding of the material. Additional areas may be added to the student's curriculum, such as teaching braille, mobility, and vocational and independent living skills in order to meet the student's needs.

Hearing Impairments

Just like students with visual impairments, students with hearing impairments are considered low incidence since they comprise only 1.3% of the population of students receiving special education services. They also will vary as to the type of hearing loss, the severity of the loss, and the impact the loss has on their ability to communicate and learn. Knowledge of the terminology associated with hearing loss, as well as the basic anatomy of the ear, types of hearing loss, and characteristics of students with hearing impairment, will increase the teacher's understanding of the effects of hearing impairment.

The term hearing impairment is a general term which includes all amounts and types of hearing loss, from mild, temporary hearing loss to profound, permanent losses. Individuals with a hearing impairment often are categorized as either deaf or hard-of-hearing. Under IDEA, the terms are defined as follows:

> Deaf: a hearing impairment which is so severe that the child is impaired in processing linguistic information through hearing, with or without amplification, which adversely affects educational performance.
>
> Hard of hearing: a hearing impairment, whether permanent or fluctuating, which adversely affects a child's educational performance, but which is not included under the definition of "deaf".

There are other definitions for these two categories of hearing impairment; however, there is a commonality among them. Individuals who are **hard-of-hearing** have sufficient auditory acuity and skills to learn speech and language through hearing when assisted by amplification devices. Like individuals with normal hearing, persons who are hard-of-hearing rely on hearing and listening for communicating and learning. In contrast, individuals who are **deaf** have such limited auditory acuity and skills, that they generally must rely on systems other than their hearing for communicating and learning. They will use systems which are visually based and may use sign language as their primary mode of communication. Individuals who are deaf also can be classified as **Deaf** or **deaf.** The use of the capital "D" indicates an identification with deaf culture and use of American Sign Language while the small "d" indicates individuals who primarily use oral communication.

Anatomy of the Ear

The ear is a complex sensory system that receives and processes sound. As can be seen in **Figure 5-3,** the ear is divided into three sections: the outer ear, the middle ear, and the inner ear.

The **outer ear** consists of the **pinna** and the **external auditory canal.** These structures collect the sound waves and direct them towards the middle ear.

The **middle ear** is a cavity at the end of the external auditory canal. It is separated from the outer ear by the **eardrum** (or **tympanic membrane**). Three small bones called the **ossicles** are located in the middle ear cavity: the **malleus** (hammer), the **incus** (anvil), and the **stapes** (stirrup). Sound waves travel down the ear canal and strike the eardrum setting it into vibration. This vibration is transmitted through the chain of bones ending at the last of them, the stapes.

The stapes fits into an opening, called the **oval window,** which leads to the inner ear. The **inner ear** is a series of fluid filled chambers that include both the **vestibular** (balance) mechanism (consisting of the **semicircular canals** and **vestibule**) and the hearing mechanism (consisting of the **cochlea**). Thus the inner ear contains sensory cells for both balance and hearing. As the ossicles vibrate, the stapes moves in and out of the oval window, setting the fluids of the cochlea into motion. The resulting fluid waves stimulate the sensory cells for hearing located in the cochlea. The stimulation or activation of the sensory cells triggers a complex electrochemical reaction which results in an electrical impulse being sent down the **auditory nerve (VIIIth cranial nerve).** The electrical signal travels through the brainstem and then on to the **auditory cortex** of the brain.

Hearing Assessment

There are different assessments which may be done to evaluate a student's hearing. These assessments can be divided into screenings and diagnostic evaluations. Most parents or caregivers notice severe hearing loss early in a child's life. The infant does not respond to noises in the environment and/or is not developing speech and language as expected. The parents seek help from their physician or a community health clinic. The family then is referred to an audiologist for testing and to a physician who specializes in the ear (otologist or otorhinolaryngologist) for the diagnosis of the problem.

Many students with less severe hearing losses, or hearing losses that are fluctuating in nature, are not identified as hearing impaired until school age. Their losses may be identified first in school-wide hearing screening programs or by astute classroom teachers. **Table 5-5** summarizes some of the student behaviors teachers might observe which could indicate a hearing loss.

If these behaviors are noted, the teacher should refer the student for a hearing screening. The screening typically is performed in the school by a speech-language pathologist, nurse, or other trained personnel.

When students fail the hearing screening, they will be referred to the audiologist for a complete hearing evaluation to determine both the degree and type of hearing loss. The audiologist will use an audiometer to present tones of various pitches and loudness to measure the student's hearing acuity. In addition, the student's ability to hear and

FIGURE 5-3

Anatomy of the Ear

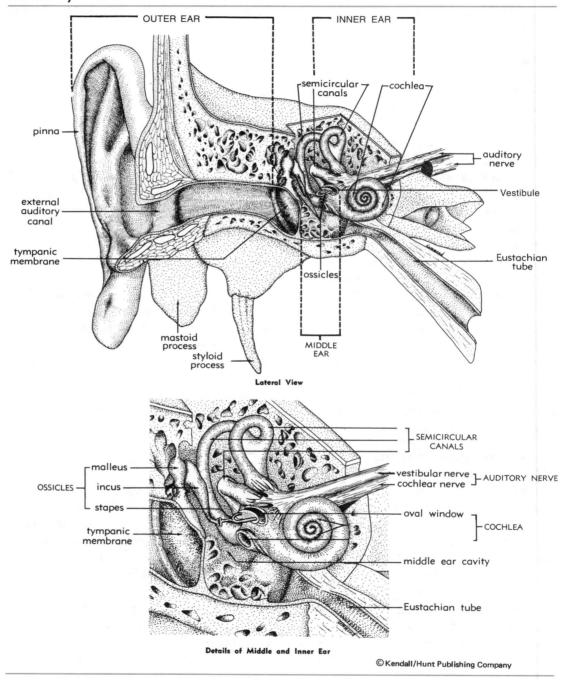

Lateral View

Details of Middle and Inner Ear

© Kendall/Hunt Publishing Company

understand speech will be assessed. Special testing techniques also may be used to determine if ear infections are present (immittance testing) or to assess very young children
(auditory brainstem response testing or otoacoustic emission testing). Depending on the
results of the assessment, the student may be referred to an otologist for medical evaluation and treatment.

TABLE 5-5

Screening Checklist for Hearing Impairments

A. Ear Appearance

_____ Discharge or drainage from ear
_____ Outer ear is red or swollen

B. Auditory Abilities

_____ Is unaware of sounds in the environment that others can hear
_____ Cannot localize sound (determine its location by listening)
_____ Does not startle or respond to very loud noises
_____ Does not turn or respond when called

C. Behaviors

_____ Is inattentive
_____ Scratches or pulls at ears frequently
_____ Frowns when listening
_____ Leans toward speaker or turns one ear toward speaker
_____ Concentrates on speaker's face and lip movements
_____ Turns volume on tape players, TV, or radios unusually high
_____ Exhibits delays in speech or language development
_____ Omits sounds at the end of words when speaking
_____ Omits or mispronounces high pitch speech sounds ("s", "t", "sh")
_____ Uses an excessively loud or soft voice
_____ Has frequent colds, allergies, or ear infections

D. Verbal Complaints

_____ Complains of ear aches, pain, tenderness, or itching
_____ Complains of ear noises (ringing or buzzing)
_____ Complains others "mumble" or speak too softly
_____ Complains of not being able to hear well

E. Academic Work

_____ Misinterprets questions or instructions and responds incorrectly.
_____ Asks for repetition of information, questions, and directions presented auditorily
_____ Waits to see what classmates are doing before beginning a task or responding
_____ Has difficulty in language arts (especially vocabulary, grammar, reading)

Degree of Hearing Loss

The degree or amount of hearing loss is determined by measuring an individual's hearing acuity to a series of tones of various pitches. The results are recorded on an **audiogram.** An audiogram is a graph which plots the faintest intensity levels or thresholds (as measured in decibels), at which a person can hear tones of specific pitches or frequencies (as measured in Hertz or Hz). **Figure 5-4** presents an audiogram with familiar sounds displayed on it according to their loudness and pitch.

An individual with normal hearing should be able to detect all of the frequencies tested (usually 250 Hz through 8000 Hz) in the intensity range of 0 to 25 decibels (dB). Since young children have more acute hearing than adults, the normal hearing range for

Audiogram of Familiar Sounds

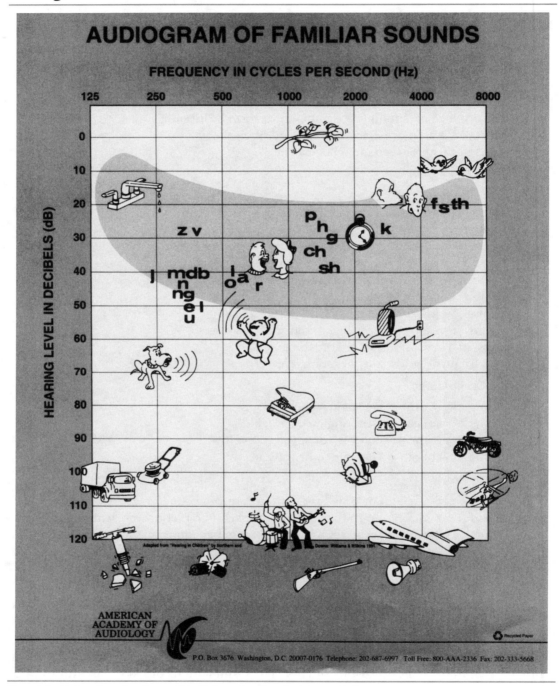

Copyright © American Academy of Audiology. Reprinted with permission.

children is considered to be between 0 and 15 dB. The louder the tone must be for someone to hear it, the greater the hearing loss. **Table 5-6** shows a commonly used classification system for degree of hearing loss and the psychosocial and educational impact of the loss.

Types of Hearing Loss

Hearing loss can result from damage to any part of the auditory system. If the hearing loss is the result of damage to the outer or middle ear, the loss is called **conductive.** For example, a large plug of wax or an object trapped in the ear canal would block the sound waves entering the ear and would cause a hearing loss. A hole in the eardrum or broken ossicles would prevent the vibrations from being conducted normally through the middle ear and result in a hearing loss. These hearing losses all would be conductive in nature. Most conductive type hearing losses are not permanent; they can be treated. Wax can be removed from the ear canal. A hole in the ear drum can be patched. Broken ossicles might be replaced surgically. In most of these cases, hearing will be restored. The most common cause of conductive hearing loss in children is middle ear infection (otitis media). This disorder is discussed in **Figure 5-5.**

If a hearing loss is the result of damage to the sensory cells or nerve fibers in the ear (inner ear damage), the loss is called **sensory** (or **sensorineural**). If the loss is due to injury to the auditory cortex of the brain, or the brainstem pathways leading to the brain, the term **central** hearing loss may be used to describe it. Sensory losses can result from many of the conditions or infections noted earlier in the chapter (heredity, STORCH infections, lack of oxygen at birth, postnatal infections, etc.). Generally, sensory losses are permanent. Once damaged, the sensory cells and/or nerve fibers cannot be restored or repaired. Today there is great concern over the increasing presence of sensory hearing loss in youngsters due to exposure to loud noise. See **Figure 5-6** for a discussion of this problem.

Hearing loss may affect both ears **(bilateral)** or it may affect only one ear **(unilateral).** Even unilateral losses can have a significant impact on a student's ability to hear and listen. A hearing loss in one ear makes it difficult to locate the source of sounds (localize) and to listen when background noises are present. In other words, a unilateral hearing loss can make it difficult to hear in typical classroom conditions.

Effects of Hearing Loss

The effects of a hearing loss will depend on many factors: the type and severity of the loss; whether the loss is unilateral or bilateral; the age at which the loss is acquired; the age at which the loss is identified; the hearing status of the parents; and the presence of additional disabilities (intellectual, sensory, or physical). Generally, the more severe the hearing loss, the greater its impact on communication and learning. If a loss is acquired before the development of language **(prelingual),** significant delays and difficulties are anticipated in speech and language development. When the loss occurs after a child has acquired speech and language **(postlingual),** the child may have the foundation for good oral communication skills. The loss still can have a significant impact on academic performance and social interaction.

Students with hearing impairment often lag behind their normal hearing peers in academic achievement (Bess, Dodd-Murphy, & Parker, 1998; Brackett & Maxon, 1986). Research has demonstrated significant deficits in reading ability, with many secondary students reading only at the fourth grade level (Quigley & Paul, 1989; Wolk & Allen, 1984). These deficits exist despite cognitive abilities comparable to that of individuals

TABLE 5-6

Relationship of Degree of Long-Term Hearing Loss to Psychosocial Impact and Educational Needs

Degree of Hearing Loss*	Possible Effect of Hearing Loss on the Understanding of Language and Speech	Possible Psychosocial Impact of Hearing Loss	Potential Educational Needs and Programs
Minimal (Borderline) 16–25 dB HL	May have difficulty hearing faint or distant speech. At 15 dB student can miss up to 10% of speech signal when teacher is at a distance greater than 3 feet and when the classroom is noisy, especially in the elementary grades when verbal instruction predominates.	May be unaware of subtle conversational cues which could cause child to be viewed as inappropriate or awkward. May miss portions of fast-paced peer interactions which could begin to have an impact on socialization and self concept. May have immature behavior. Child may be more fatigued than classmates due to listening effort needed.	May benefit from mild gain/low MPO hearing aid or personal FM system dependent on loss configuration. Would benefit from soundfield amplification if classroom is noisy and/or reverberant. Favorable seating. May need attention to vocabulary or speech, especially with recurrent otitis media history. Teacher requires inservice on impact of hearing loss on language development and learning.
Mild 26–40 dB HL	At 30 dB can miss 25–40% of speech signal. The degree of difficulty experienced in school will depend upon the noise level in classroom, distance from teacher and the configuration of the hearing loss. Without amplification the child with 35–40 dB loss may miss at least 50% of class discussions, especially when voices are faint or speaker is not in line of vision. Will miss consonants, especially when a high frequency hearing loss is present.	Barriers beginning to build with negative impact on self-esteem as child is accused of "hearing when he or she wants to," "daydreaming," or "not paying attention." Child begins to lose ability for selective hearing, and has increasing difficulty suppressing background noise which makes the learning environment stressful. Child is more fatigued than classmates due to listening effort needed.	Will benefit from a hearing aid and use of a personal FM or soundfield FM system in the classroom. Needs favorable seating and lighting. Refer to special education for language evaluation and educational follow-up. Needs auditory skill building. May need attention to vocabulary and language development articulation or speechreading and/or special support in reading. May need help with self esteem. Teacher inservice required.
Moderate 41–55 dB HL	Understands conversational speech at a distance of 3–5 feet (face-to-face) only if structure and vocabulary controlled. Without amplification the amount of speech signal missed can be 50% to 75% with 40 dB loss and 80% to 100% with 50 dB loss. Is likely to have delayed or defective syntax, limited vocabulary, imperfect speech production and an atonal voice quality.	Often with this degree of hearing loss, communication is significantly affected, and socialization with peers with normal hearing becomes increasingly difficult. With full time use of hearing aids/FM systems child may be judged as a less competent learner. There is an increasing impact on self-esteem.	Refer to special education for language evaluation and for educational follow-up. Amplification is essential (hearing aids and FM system). Special education support may be needed, especially for primary children. Attention to oral language development, reading and written language. Auditory skill development and speech therapy usually needed. Teacher inservice required.

*Based on modified pure tone average (500–4000 Hz)

Note: All children with hearing loss require periodic audiologic evaluation, rigorous monitoring of amplification and regular monitoring of communication skills. All children with hearing loss (especially conductive) need appropriate medical attention in conjunction with educational programming.

TABLE 5-6

Relationship of Degree of Long-Term Hearing Loss to Psychosocial Impact and Educational Needs (continued)

Degree of Hearing Loss*	Possible Effect of Hearing Loss on the Understanding of Language and Speech	Possible Psychosocial Impact of Hearing Loss	Potential Educational Needs and Programs
Moderately Severe 56–70 dB HL	Without amplification, conversation must be very loud to be understood. A 55 dB loss can cause child to miss up to 100% of speech information. Will have marked difficulty in school situations requiring verbal communication in both one-to-one and group situations. Delayed language, syntax, reduced speech intelligibility and atonal voice quality likely.	Full time use of hearing aids/FM systems may result in child being judged by both peers and adults as a less competent learner, resulting in poorer self concept, social maturity and contributing to a sense of rejection. Inservice to address these attitudes may be helpful.	Full time use of amplification is essential. Will need resource teacher or special class depending on magnitude of language delay. May require special help in all language skills, language based academic subjects, vocabulary, grammar, pragmatics as well as reading and writing. Inservice of mainstream teachers required.
Severe 71–90 dB HL	Without amplification may hear loud voices about one foot from ear. When amplified optimally, children with hearing ability of 90 dB or better should be able to identify environmental sounds and detect all the sounds of speech. If loss is of prelingual onset, oral language and speech may not develop spontaneously or will be severely delayed; if hearing loss is of recent onset speech is likely to deteriorate with quality becoming atonal.	Child may prefer other children with hearing impairments as friends and playmates. This may further isolate the child from the mainstream; however, these peer relationships may foster improved self concept and a sense of cultural identity.	May need full-time special aural/oral program for deaf children with emphasis on all auditory language skills, speechreading, concept development and speech. As loss approaches 80–90 dB, may benefit from a Total Communication approach, especially in the early language learning years. Individual hearing aid/personal FM system essential. Participation in regular classes as much as beneficial to student. Inservice of mainstream teachers essential.
Profound 91 dB HL or more	Aware of vibrations more than tonal pattern. Many rely on vision rather than hearing as primary avenue for communication and learning. Detection of speech sounds dependent upon loss configuration and use of amplification. Speech and language will not develop spontaneously and is likely to deteriorate rapidly if hearing loss is of recent onset.	Depending on auditory/oral competence, peer use of sign language, parental attitude, etc., child may or may not increasingly prefer association with the deaf culture.	May need special program for deaf children with emphasis on all language skills and academic areas. Early use of amplification likely to help if part of an intensive training program. May be cochlear implant or vibrotactile aid candidate. Requires continual appraisal of needs in regard to communication and learning mode. Part-time in regular classes as much as beneficial to student.

continued on next page

TABLE 5-6

Relationship of Degree of Long-Term Hearing Loss to Psychosocial Impact and Educational Needs (continued)

Degree of Hearing Loss*	Possible Effect of Hearing Loss on the Understanding of Language and Speech	Possible Psychosocial Impact of Hearing Loss	Potential Educational Needs and Programs
Unilateral One normal hearing ear and one ear with at least a permanent mild hearing loss	May have difficulty hearing faint or distant speech. Usually has difficulty localizing sounds and voices. Unilateral listener will have greater difficulty understanding speech when environment is noisy and/or reverberant. Difficulty detecting or understanding soft speech from side of bad ear, especially in a group discussion.	Child may be accused of selective hearing due to discrepancies in speech understanding in quiet versus noise. Child will be more fatigued in classroom setting due to greater effort needed to listen. May appear inattentive or frustrated. Behavior problems sometimes evident.	May benefit from personal FM- or soundfield FM system in classroom. CROS hearing aid may be of benefit in quiet settings. Needs favorable seating and lighting. Student is at risk for educational difficulties. Educational monitoring warranted with support services provided as soon as difficulties appear. Teacher inservice is beneficial.

References

Olsen, W. O., Hawkins, D. B. VanTassell, D. J. (1987). Representatives of the Longterm Spectrum of Speech. *Ear & Hearing. Supplement 8*, pp. 100–108.

Mueller, H. G. & Killion, M. C. (1990). An easy method for calculating the articulation index. *The Hearing Journal, 43, 9,* pp. 14–22.

Hasenstab, M. S. (1987). *Language Learning and Otitis Media.* College Hill Press, Boston, MA.

Developed by Karen L. Anderson, Ed. S. & Noel D. Matkin, Ph.D. (1991)

Adapted from: Bernero, R. J. & Bothwell, H. (1966). Relationship of Hearing Impairment to Educational Needs. Illinois Department of Public Health & Office of Superintendent of Public Instruction. Peer Review by Members of the Educational Audiology Association, Winter 1991

with normal hearing. The IQ distribution of the deaf population mirrors that of the hearing population (Moores, 1996; Ottem, 1980) with the deaf displaying the same diversity in IQ scores and an average performance IQ score nearly the same (96.89) as the norm (100) for hearing individuals (Braden, 1985). Academic performance, however, relies not only on cognitive abilities, but also on language skills. Most students with hearing impairment have significant and persistent delays and deficits in verbal language skills. These deficits are exhibited in their language expression (speaking and writing) as well as their language reception (listening and reading). Successful performance in the typical classroom depends on the ability to hear and understand the teacher, follow lectures, understand classroom discussions, and hear questions from peers. It is easy to see why the student with a hearing impairment is at a disadvantage.

Communication Systems

Students with hearing loss will develop and rely on different modes of communication depending on a variety of factors. These factors include, but are not limited to the amount of hearing loss, the individual's ability to use whatever hearing remains, the age at the onset of the loss, the mode of communication preferred by the family, and the availability of services and training. In general, the communication systems used by students with hearing impairment can be divided into **auditory/oral systems, manual systems,** and a combined or **total communication system.** The benefits and limitations of

FIGURE 5-5

Otitis Media

Otitis media is an inflammation of the middle ear cavity resulting from eustachian tube malfunction which typically is accompanied by an accumulation of fluid in the middle ear. It often is associated with colds, allergies, and upper respiratory infections. The incidence of otitis media is much higher than parents and teachers realize. The number of cases has increased significantly in recent years (Schappert, 1992) and it has been estimated that 85% to 90% of all children have at least one episode of otitis media by age six (Grundfast & Carney, 1987). As a medical condition, parents and teachers recognize the importance of accurate diagnosis and treatment of otitis media. Many individuals, however, are unaware of the significance of the mild hearing loss which accompanies this condition. Children who are otitis prone (having six or more episodes of otitis media before age six) are having recurrent bouts of otitis media which results in fluctuating hearing levels during a significant portion of their development. This fluctuation can have a serious impact on the child's auditory, speech-language, cognitive, and social development. These children are not "good listeners" due to the inconsistent auditory input they have received as their hearing fluctuates with the otitis media. It may be difficult for parents and teachers to detect a hearing loss since the child appears to hear normally at times (in quiet listening situations, when close to the person speaking, etc.). They often believe that the child's lack of response at times (when background noise is present, when called from a distance, etc.) is due to inattention or "not wanting to hear" rather than the result of a mild hearing loss.

Students with a history of repeated bouts of otitis media often show a delayed response to sounds, frequently say "*Huh?*" or "*What?*", and may not respond when called, appearing to be in their own world. Teachers should be alert for problems with auditory processing, difficulty listening in noisy situations, and a short attention span when information is presented auditorily.

FIGURE 5-6

Hearing Loss from Noise Exposure

Hearing and Noise

The fact that hearing loss can result from exposure to loud noise has been well documented. For many years the federal government has required safeguards in the occupational environment to protect workers' hearing. However, noise induced hearing loss is not restricted to the working, adult population. Recreational, as well as occupational, noise exposure is becoming widespread for both children and adults. Firearms, power tools, firecrackers, snowmobiles, go-karts, motorcycles, stereo system loudspeakers and headphones, and concerts all produce sound levels high enough to cause permanent damage to the ear.

The hearing loss associated with prolonged exposure to noise has a gradual onset and affects the listener's ability to hear high frequency, or high pitch, sounds. Individuals who are exposing themselves to high levels of noise often are not aware of changes in their hearing because the loss of sensitivity occurs gradually over time. Until there is a significant loss of hearing, the individual may blame others for speaking too softly or "mumbling".

Studies have documented an increase in the incidence of hearing loss from noise exposure in school-age children (Montgomery & Fujikawa, 1992; Peppard & Peppard, 1992). The good news is that most hearing loss from exposure to noise, both in job and recreational settings, is preventable. Teachers need to take the lead in educating their students about the hazard of loud noise and the importance of using of ear protection (ear plugs or muffs specially designed to reduce noise).

each system have been debated for many years by the advocates of each of the various systems (Moores, 1996). No single system can meet the needs of all students who are hearing impaired. More important than which specific system is used, is the development of good communication skills in these students.

Auditory/oral systems focus on the use of **residual hearing** (the usable hearing an individual has) to develop speech and language. Hearing aids, training in listening skills **(auditory training),** and lipreading (or **speechreading**) are used to develop the student's ability to understand and produce spoken English. **Cued speech** is a unique communication system that is speech-based, emphasizing the oral production of language. It incorporates a set of hand signals or cues to help the users in speechreading English sounds that are not highly visible on the lips (Cornett, 1975).

Manual systems do not rely on auditory input and oral output for communication, but use a system of hand symbols or movements to convey ideas or words. **Fingerspelling** is a form of manual communication in which each letter of the English alphabet is represented by a single hand and finger position. Words are spelled using this system. **American Sign Language (ASL)** is another form of manual communication in which whole words and complete thoughts can be expressed by a systematic combination of hand movements. ASL is only one of several sign languages that are used in the world. It is the most widely used manual communication system among deaf adults in this country. It is a unique language with its own structure, grammar, and rules, not a word for word translation of English language (Schein, 1984). Some manual communication systems, such as **Signing Exact English** and **Signed English,** are English language based and follow the grammar and syntax of spoken English.

The third system of communication is referred to as total communication. It is based on the premise that simultaneously using a combination of signs and speech will allow students with hearing impairment to use whatever mode possible to acquire language. True total communication systems incorporate and emphasize every possible mode for learning language and communication. This includes hearing, speechreading, speech, signing, fingerspelling, reading, and writing. Most public schools report that a total communication system is being used to educate their students who are hearing impaired. The teachers of the hearing impaired in these schools, however, will admit they do not give equal emphasis and training to all communication modes. They rely primarily on manual communication systems.

Management of Hearing Impairments

Because hearing loss has a profound impact on the development of speech and language, and on academic performance, special services will be required to assist these students in school. Students with hearing impairments are a diverse group of individuals and the specific services, adaptations, or modifications needed will vary. These modifications can be divided into the same seven categories as described earlier for students with visual impairments (Heller et al., 1995):

1. use of assistive technology,
2. use of a person,
3. changes in the physical environment,
4. changes in student response,
5. changes in teacher instruction,
6. alteration in material, and
7. alteration in activities and/or curriculum (see **Table 5-7**).

Students with hearing impairments typically will use amplification devices to improve their auditory functioning. With the implementation of the Americans with Disabilities Act of 1990, the public is becoming more aware of amplification devices and

TABLE 5-7

Managing Hearing Impairments

	Hearing Impairment
Assistive Technology	• Amplification and alerting devices
Use of Person	• Peer teaming, interpreter, or notetaker
Physical Environment	• Position student in relation to activities • Noise • Vision
Student Response	• Use of interpreter
Teacher Instruction	• Repeat announcements, questions from peers • Work with speech-language pathologist and teacher certified in hearing-impairment
Alter Material	• Use supplemental visual aids
Alter Activity	• Provide written instructions and assignments
Alter Curriculum	• Learn additional specialized skills (e.g., speechreading, manual communication)

the assistance available for individuals with hearing loss. Public telephones with amplifiers, televisions with closed captioning, modified alarms and alerting devices, and churches and movie theaters with specialized listening devices are becoming common place in our society. Individuals with impaired hearing rely on such assistive devices in addition to personal hearing aids to improve their ability to communicate.

Most students with a hearing impairment can benefit from, and will wear, hearing aids. Hearing aids are personal amplification devices consisting of a **microphone,** an **amplifier,** and a **receiver.** The microphone picks up sound in the environment and converts it to an electrical signal. The intensity of the electrical signal is first increased by the amplifier, and then converted back to sound by the receiver. The resulting amplified sound is directed into the ear of the hearing aid user. Hearing aids come in various forms as shown in **Figure 5-7.**

The **all-in-the-ear** model houses the microphone, amplifier, and receiver in a small plastic case which is molded to fit completely in the ear of the user. The **behind-the-ear** model is worn behind the user's ear and the sound is directed from the receiver to the ear via a plastic tubing and ear mold which fits into the user's ear. Of these two models, the behind-the-ear-aid is the one most often worn by school-age individuals.

A common misperception is that hearing aids can restore normal hearing to the user, much like glasses can restore vision to normal acuity. Hearing aids cannot restore normal hearing. These devices simply increase the loudness of the sound which enters the ear. Individuals with sensory hearing loss are the primary users of hearing aids. For them, sounds not only are inaudible, but also are distorted due to the loss of sensory cells and nerve fibers in the ear associated with this type of hearing loss. Hearing aids will allow these individuals to detect and hear many sounds which were inaudible without the amplification; however, the sounds often remain distorted. A recent development in amplification is a device called the **cochlear implant.** This device is described in **Figure 5-8.**

In the classroom setting, students with hearing impairments often utilize an amplification device known as an **FM (frequency modulated) system.** With this system, the classroom teacher wears a small microphone which picks up the teacher's voice. The voice is transmitted via a radio frequency carrier wave to a special receiver worn by the student

FIGURE 5-7

Types of Hearing Aids

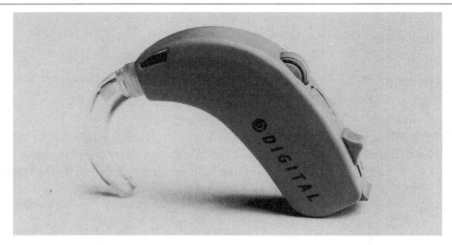

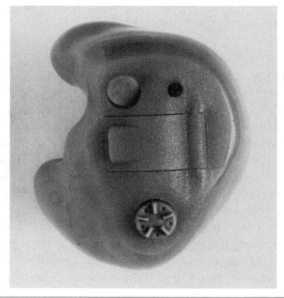

Copyright © by Bernafon-Maico Inc. Reprinted by permission.

or students in the class who are hearing impaired. The receiver sends the signal to earphones or to the students' own hearing aids, allowing for improved reception of the teacher's voice in noisy classrooms.

The second category of modifications, using another person, includes peer teaming and using interpreters and notetakers. Students with hearing impairments can benefit from cooperative learning strategies which involve peer teaming or group work. These strategies allow students with hearing impairment to benefit from the assistance of other students on some tasks and to offer assistance to their peers on other tasks. Students who rely on manual communication systems and are mainstreamed in the general education classroom often require interpreter support. A certified interpreter will accompany the student to classes to translate the teacher's and peers' spoken English into the manual communication system the student uses. The interpreter also may translate the student's questions and comments into spoken English if the student's speech is not under-

FIGURE 5-8

Cochlear Implants

The cochlear implant is a device deigned for individuals with profound hearing loss who cannot benefit from the use of conventional hearing aids. This amplification system is shown below. It consists of a microphone and processor worn behind the user's ear which picks up the sounds in the environment and converts them to an electrical signal. The amplified signal is sent to a transmitter, worn behind the ear. The transmitter relays the signal to a receiver which has been surgically implanted in the skull, behind the ear. The signal travels into the cochlea through electrodes which also have been implanted. Thus, the cochlear implant delivers an electrical signal directly to the inner ear, the cochlea.

Some individuals have shown significant improvement in their hearing and speech production abilities through the use of the cochlear implant. However, these devices are a point of great controversy in the medical, audiological, and Deaf communities. Some professionals believe the cochlear implant represents an appropriate use of technology to improve the hearing of individuals who are profoundly deaf, providing them with communication options. Others argue that the cochlear implant is an unnecessary, experimental, and invasive surgical procedure being used by surgeons and parents who are unfamiliar with the Deaf culture to "cure" the condition of deafness. These opponents do not view deafness as an "illness" or condition which needs to be "cured".

Auria™ sound processor, part of the Bionic Ear System cochlear implant, courtesy of Advanced Bionics Corp.

standable. No matter which communication system students with hearing impairment use, they will be using their visual and/or auditory skills to focus on understanding what is being said to them. They may be unable to take adequate notes in the classroom. For this reason, fellow classmates may serve as notetakers. Notetakers can use two-part, pressure-sensitive paper when taking their own notes, and then provide the additional copy to the student with the hearing impairment.

The third type of adaptation which may be needed for students with hearing impairments is the modification of the physical environment. These students should be seated where they can maximize the use of auditory and visual input. This generally means away from noisy hallways or windows and in close proximity to the teacher. However, most teachers do not remain stationary when teaching. They present information from different locations in the classroom during different activities. In this case, an exchange of

A student using the Nucleus 24 cochlear implant. Picture courtesy of Cochlear Corporation.

seats between the student with the hearing impairment and a peer with normal hearing can be prearranged if needed.

The fourth modification, student response, may be needed for students using manual communication systems. If the student's speech skills are limited, the student may sign responses to questions posed by the teacher or by classmates to an interpreter. The interpreter then relays the student's response in spoken English.

Significant modifications of teacher instruction, or instructional strategies, generally are not needed for students with hearing impairments. Since these students often rely on speechreading, teachers should remember not to speak when their back is turned to the class (e.g., when writing on the board). In addition, announcements over the public address system, or questions and comments from classmates seated behind a student with a hearing loss are difficult, if not impossible, for the student to hear. The teacher will need to repeat these announcements and questions. Many students with a hearing impairment have language skills below their peers and will receive additional services from the speech-language pathologist or the teacher certified in hearing impairment. If the classroom teacher discusses upcoming lessons with these professionals, it will allow them to prepare the students for key concepts and vocabulary words prior to their use in the classroom.

Some alteration of the materials used in teaching may be needed by students with hearing impairment. These students may miss or not understand information that is presented only auditorily. Using visual aids when teaching (overheads, diagrams, models, handouts, etc.) and being certain videos shown in class are captioned (the text is printed at the bottom of the screen) will help students with hearing loss succeed in the classroom.

Lastly, activity or curriculum modifications may be needed for the student with impaired hearing. If the student cannot hear instructions and assignments given orally, the teacher will need to have them available in written form. Additional areas may be added to the student's curriculum depending on the individual's needs. These areas might include instruction in manual communication, auditory training, speechreading, and/or

TABLE 5-8

Suggestions for Teachers of Students with Hearing Impairments

Provide favorable seating. The student should be seated close to the teacher and away from background noise. Flexibility in arranging seating during various activities allows the student an opportunity to observe and participate in classroom activities. Students with hearing aids should be seated to make maximum use of the aids.

Group activities may pose special problems. The student may not be able to see all the members in the group for speechreading. Also group activities may cause higher than normal levels of background noise.

Face the student when speaking and be sure that the student is looking at you. Other students may be able to listen while looking at their work, taking notes, or while you are facing the board, but students with hearing impairment need to watch the speaker when they listen.

Provide written instructions and summaries. Put lesson outlines, key vocabulary words, and assignments in handouts or on the board to assist the student in staying focused on the lesson.

Speak clearly but naturally. To help remember critical factors in speaking to students, Garwood (1987) suggested S-P-E-E-CH as a mnemonic device:

S = State the topic to be discussed.
P = Pace conversation at a moderate speed, allowing occasional pauses to aid comprehension.
E = Enunciate clearly without exaggerated lip movements.
E = Enthusiastically communicate, using body language and natural gestures.
CH = Check comprehension before changing topics. Ask the student questions to evaluate
      understanding. Do not simply ask "Do you understand?" and rely on a nod or a "yes". The
      student may not be willing to admit a problem understanding the material. Be alert to signs of
      confusion, such as blank stare or errors in following directions.

Rephrase and restate instructions and directions. This is especially important when it is apparent that the student is having trouble understanding. Some words contain sounds which are difficult to recognize by a student with a hearing loss. Changing the wording of your statement or question may help the student hear and understand.

Use a "Preteach-Teach-Postteach" strategy. (Reynolds & Birch, 1988) In this approach, the teacher discusses upcoming lessons with other professionals who may be working with the student (hearing impaired teacher or speech-language pathologist). That professional then insures that the student understands key words and concepts to be used in the coming class presentation. The teacher presents the lesson and reports back to the other professional any apparent difficulties the student experienced. The other professional then reviews the concepts with the student. This strategy is an excellent way to coordinate the efforts of several professionals.

Adapted from Haynes, W. O., Moran, M. J., & Pindzola, R. H. (1994). *Communication disorders in the classroom* (2nd ed.). Dubuque, IA: Kendall/Hunt.

speech and language therapy. This specialized instruction would be provided by the appropriate professionals (the speech-language pathologist, the audiologist, the teacher certified in hearing impairment), and would not be the responsibility of the classroom teacher.

The classroom teacher is the key to the success of students with hearing impairment. Using assistive devices and other support personnel as well as slightly modifying the environment and adapting teaching strategies can have a significant impact on the academic performance of these students. **Table 5-8** summarizes suggestions for the classroom teacher.

Communication Disorders

Among the various disability categories, students with communication disorders, or speech and language impairments, are second in prevalence in the schools only to students with learning disabilities. Because over 87% of students with communication disorders are educated exclusively in the general education classroom (U.S. Department of Education, 2002), it is important for classroom teachers to have an understanding of the nature and impact of these disorders. While hearing impairments often are considered a type of communication disorder, they are also a type of sensory deficit and have been discussed previously. The American Speech-Language-Hearing Association (ASHA, 1993) defines a **communication disorder** as follows:

> an impairment in the ability to receive, send, process, and comprehend concepts or verbal, nonverbal and graphic symbols systems (p. 40).

Communication disorders may be developmental or acquired and can range from mild to severe. They may be the result of the conditions or infections discussed earlier in the chapter and may accompany other disabilities in students, such as intellectual disabilities, hearing impairment, and physical impairment. But many students with communication disorders have no other disabilities and have the same cognitive, sensory, and physical abilities as their peers. Under IDEA, speech or language impairment means a communication disorder such as stuttering, impaired articulation, a language impairment, or a voice impairment that adversely affects a student's educational performance. To understand communication disorders, we first must consider the process of communication.

Communication

The ability to communicate is a skill most of us take for granted. We exchange information, opinions, and feelings by speaking, listening, reading, and writing on a daily basis. Only when the ability to communicate becomes impaired do we realize what an important and complex process it is. Humans communicate in many ways: verbally and nonverbally. The tools for communication can include facial expressions, body posture, hand gestures, even art and music. We will focus on two elements of communication: language and speech.

Language

Language can be defined as a code or a system shared by a group of people which gives meaning to sounds, gestures, or other symbols and enables those people to communicate (Heward & Orlansky, 1992). Rules govern language systems and users of any language system must learn to use the rules of their language to communicate effectively. **Expressive** language refers to the sending of information or messages to others, while **receptive** language refers to the receiving of messages from others.

Before considering language disorders, it is important to understand the components or elements of normal language. The components relate to its form (phonology, morphology, and syntax), its content (semantics), and its use (pragmatics). **Phonology** is the sound system of a particular language and the rules for combining sounds. Not all languages utilize the same sound system. Some sounds used in the spoken English language are not found in other languages, just as other languages use sounds not found in spoken English. These differences in sound systems can make learning and speaking a second language difficult for some students. **Morphology** refers to the rules for the structure of words, for example, the rules that we follow when we convert a word to a plural form or to a past tense. **Syntax** is the rule system which specifies word order for sentence structure. The two sentences "Mark gave Keesha the book" and "Keesha gave Mark the book" have very different meanings. The meaning is determined by the order of the names in the sentences. We understand the meaning of those sentences if we know the syntactical rule to apply when we decipher them. **Semantics** refers to the meanings of words and sentences, the content of the language we use. Many words, phrases, and sentences can have multiple meanings. The sentence "Maria was cold" could mean that Maria was physically cold or that she behaved in an uncaring manner. **Pragmatics** refers to the way language is used rather than the way it is structured. It involves the way we vary our language depending on the audience and the situation. For example, we change our vocabulary, phrasing, and length of sentences depending on whether we are speaking to a friend in a social setting, a supervisor at work, or a child playing.

Speech

Speech is the process of producing the vocal sounds associated with an oral language. Speech production involves several processes. **Respiration,** the inhalation and exhalation of air, provides the exhaled air stream that powers the voice. The vocal folds, found in the larynx above the trachea (see **Figure 5-9**), are set into vibration as air is exhaled during respiration.

This results in **phonation,** the actual production of voice. **Resonation** occurs as the vibrating air stream passes through the vocal tract, the cavities above the larynx, and the

FIGURE 5-9

The Vocal Tract

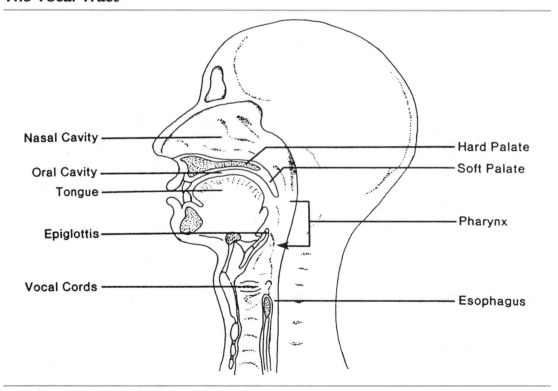

From The Biology Experience Lab Manual, 7th Edition by Dearing, Eckerlin & Wolfe. Copyright © 1989 by Kendall/Hunt Publishing Company. Used with permission.

richness of the sound is enhanced. The tongue, teeth, lips, and palate accomplish the final shaping or **articulation** of the sound to produce the sounds of our language.

The process of producing speech involves the complex coordination of all the structures and muscles of the respiratory system, the larynx, the oral cavity, and the face. Injury to any of these regions (e.g., lung cancer, laryngitis, cleft palate), or damage to the neurologic systems which control these regions (e.g., cerebral palsy, traumatic brain injury) can have a significant impact on speech production. Some students with severe disabilities may never be able to produce understandable or intelligible speech, and alternative systems of expressive language must be used such as sign language and communication boards.

Communication Disorders Assessment

Some school districts screen students for communication disorders prior to school enrollment while others screen selected grades, most commonly the elementary grades. Screenings are conducted by the speech-language pathologist using both informal and formal measures. When students fail a screening, they will be referred for a comprehensive speech and language evaluation. Although screenings are successful in identifying severe communication disorders, they may miss mild speech and language problems. Some students may have communication disorders that are subtle (e.g., difficulty with the appropriate use of language) or variable (e.g., a voice disorder associated with cheerleading). These disorders may be noted only when observed over a period of time by the classroom teacher. For this reason, the speech-language pathologist relies on referrals from classroom teachers regarding potential communication disorders. In some school districts, school-wide screening programs for communication disorders have been eliminated, and the identification of disorders relies solely on teacher and parent referrals. The speech-language pathologist may provide teachers and parents with a communication skills checklist like the one in **Table 5-9** to assist in the identification of potential disorders.

The classroom teacher is the person most aware of the student's communication abilities and difficulties in the school setting. It is important that teachers and speech-language pathologists work cooperatively in the identification, assessment, and treatment of communication disorders.

If it is determined that a student needs a comprehensive speech and language assessment, the methods and test materials used will vary depending on the age of the student and the type of suspected disorder. The speech-language pathologist may begin with an examination of the oral speech mechanism, looking for structural abnormalities or muscle incoordination. A hearing screening to detect potential hearing loss generally is included in the evaluation process. Specific tests will be administered to assess the student's articulation (pronunciation) of speech sounds, fluency of speech, voice quality, and language comprehension and expression. Depending on the results of the testing and on the history of the disorder, the speech-language pathologist may recommend additional evaluation by the audiologist, otorhinolaryngologist, psychologist, or special education teacher.

Common Communication Disorders

Communication disorders can be divided into **speech disorders** (problems with the production of oral language) and **language disorders** (problems with the comprehension or use of spoken or written language). These two types of communication disorders are not always discrete disorders; some students exhibit both speech and language disorders.

TABLE 5-9

Teacher Checklist for Communication Disorders

A. Receptive Language (Comprehension)

1. Does the student appear to understand what is heard in conversation and in classroom activities?	Yes	No	N/A
2. Does the student hear sounds (in words) appropriately? (e.g., you say "Wash the dog", and the student hears "Watch the dog")	Yes	No	N/A
3. Does the student follow verbal directions?	Yes	No	N/A
4. Does the student repeat simple sentences verbatim?	Yes	No	N/A
5. Does the student remember what was heard the previous day, week, or month?	Yes	No	N/A
6. Does the student understand basic concepts: opposites, categories, sequencing, etc.?	Yes	No	N/A
7. Does the student generalize knowledge of new concepts in a meaningful way?	Yes	No	N/A

B. Expressive Language

1. Is the student nonverbal (doesn't talk)?	Yes	No	N/A
2. Does the student use a minimum of five words (average) in a sentence during conversation?	Yes	No	N/A
3. Does the student use age-appropriate vocabulary?	Yes	No	N/A
4. Does the student use age-appropriate grammar?	Yes	No	N/A
5. Does the student respond appropriately to questions?	Yes	No	N/A

C. Articulation

1. Is the student who is functioning at the four-year-old level mispronouncing p, b, t, d, k, g, f, m, n, ng, h, w, or v?	Yes	No	N/A
2. Is the student who is functioning at the five-year-old level mispronouncing s, z, zh (as in beige), ch, dz (as in joke), l, sh, or any of the sounds listed in number 1?	Yes	No	N/A
3. Is the student who is functioning at the six-year-old level mispronouncing th (voiceless as in thin and voiced as in then), r (er), or any of the sounds listed in numbers 1 and 2?	Yes	No	N/A
4. Is the student using mainly vowel sounds when talking?	Yes	No	N/A
5. Is the student leaving the final consonant sound off of words?	Yes	No	N/A
6. Is the student concerned about his/her speech?	Yes	No	N/A
7. Are the student's parents concerned about his/her speech?	Yes	No	N/A
8. Are there any physical problems with the oral structures (e.g., cleft palate, missing teeth, etc.)?	Yes	No	N/A

D. Voice

1. Is the student's voice always hoarse?	Yes	No	N/A
2. Is the pitch of the student's voice abnormally high or low?	Yes	No	N/A
3. Is the student's voice breathy?	Yes	No	N/A
4. Is the loudness of the student's voice appropriate?	Yes	No	N/A
5. Does the student abuse his/her voice (loud talking, yelling, singing, excessive throat clearing, etc.)?	Yes	No	N/A
6. Is the student's voice too nasal?	Yes	No	N/A
7. Is the student's voice lacking in nasality?	Yes	No	N/A

E. Fluency

1. Does the student repeat, hesitate, or draw out sounds?	Yes	No	N/A
2. Does the student repeat, hesitate, or draw out syllables?	Yes	No	N/A
3. Does the student repeat, hesitate, or draw out words?	Yes	No	N/A
4. Does the student repeat, hesitate, or draw out phrases?	Yes	No	N/A
5. When speaking, does the student appear to struggle to get the words out (e.g., clench jaw, blink eyes, tense neck muscles, etc.)?	Yes	No	N/A
6. Is the student concerned about his/her disfluency?	Yes	No	N/A
7. Are the student's parents concerned about his/her disfluency?	Yes	No	N/A

TABLE 5-10	
Average Age for Mastery of Speech Sounds	
Speech Sound	**Age of Mastery**
p, b, t, d, k, g, f, m, n, ng, h, w	3 years
v	3 years, 6 months
s, z, zh (as in beige), ch, dz (as in joke), l	4 years
sh	4 years, 6 months
th (voiceless as in thin), th (voiced as in then), r (er)	5 years

From Arlt, P. B., & Goodban, M. T. (1976). A comparative study of articulation acquisition as based on a study of 240 normals, aged three to six. *Language, Speech, and Hearing Services in Schools, 7,* 173–180.

Speech Disorders

A speech disorder is an impairment of articulation, voice, or fluency (ASHA, 1993). Of these, **articulation disorders** are the most common. The ability to correctly articulate the sounds of a language depends on many factors including the student's age and physical abilities. The production of speech sounds follows a developmental pattern with some sounds being spoken accurately at a younger age than others. For example, a four-year-old child should be able to produce such sounds as "m", "n", "p", and "z", but may have difficulty producing the "th" and "r" sounds. By the age of five years, most youngsters should be able to produce correctly all of the sounds of our language. **Table 5-10** shows the average age estimates for the mastery of speech sounds.

Misarticulations, or errors of articulation may occur when students have abnormalities of the oral structures (e.g., missing teeth or a cleft palate). They also may occur when the student has damage to the parts of the brain or the nerve fibers that control the musculature of the speech mechanism (e.g., cerebral palsy or traumatic brain injury). Errors of articulation also occur when there is no biological reason. They may be the result of limited opportunity to learn and practice appropriate speech, or they may have no identifiable cause.

Voice disorders involve the attributes of the pitch, loudness, resonance, duration, and quality of the voice (ASHA, 1993). Teachers may notice that a student's voice seems too high or too low in pitch. They may consider it abnormally soft or loud, or unusually breathy or harsh. If these characteristics of the voice are significantly different from what is expected given a student's age and gender and are abusive to the larynx or negatively impact on communication, a voice disorder is present. Some voice disorders may be temporary, for example, the hoarseness associated with laryngitis or the lack of nasal resonance due to a cold. Other persistent disorders may be the result of more serious medical problems, for example, growths on the vocal folds, nerve damage resulting in paralysis of the vocal folds, or a cleft palate. A significant number of voice disorders in students are the result of vocal abuse (Herrington-Hall, Lee, Stemple, Niemi, & McHone, 1988). Frequent loud talking and yelling in school, especially during free time and sports activities, can become a habit for some students. These behaviors can lead to calloused growths on the vocal folds known as vocal nodules. The presence of nodules results in chronic hoarseness of the voice.

Fluency disorders is the third category of speech disorders. As speakers, we all exhibit occasional disfluencies, or interruptions in the flow of our speech. We pause in the middle of expressing a thought, we stumble over a word, we repeat a phrase, we use

TABLE 5-11

Aspects of Stuttering

1. Stuttering is universal. The disorder has existed throughout recorded history and is found among all peoples of the world.

2. Stuttering almost always begins in childhood, usually before age six. Ages three and four are particularly common periods for the onset of stuttering.

3. Stuttering occurs more often among males than females. Reports of sex ratio vary from 3:1 to as high as 6:1.

4. Stuttering tends to run in families. Family studies have shown that the risk of stuttering in relatives of a person who stutters is increased over that of the general population. Furthermore, the pattern of transmission in families is consistent with predictions derived from genetic models, yet genetic components of stuttering have not been proved.

5. The amount of stuttering varies widely with situations. Persons who stutter often report excessive speech difficulties when they are excited or feel under pressure. Saying their name, talking on the telephone, ordering in a restaurant, talking to a person in authority (e.g., a teacher), and talking in front of a group (as in a classroom) also are situations which elicit much stuttering. Additionally, persons who stutter have good days and bad days meaning that the frequency and severity of their stuttering fluctuates.

6. For those who do not outgrow it, stuttering tends to change—and even worsen—as the person matures. What began as a speech problem evolves into not only a speech problem but also a personal-social-psychological problem.

7. Stuttering need not hold a person back from achieving full potential. Many famous, brilliant, and talented people stuttered, such as: Winston Churchill, Moses, Marilyn Monroe, Sommerset Maugham, Isaac Newton, Mel Tillis, Bob Newhart, and James Earl Jones.

From *Communication Disorders in the Classroom*, 2nd edition by Haynes et al. Copyright 1994 by Kendall/Hunt Publishing Company. Used with permission.

fillers such as "uh" and "uhm". Some disfluency also is common in young children learning language (Culatta & Leeper, 1987). It is when these disruptions are so frequent that they draw extraordinary attention to the person's speech or interfere with communication, that a fluency disorder is present. A fluency disorder can be defined as an interruption in the flow of speaking, involving abnormal rate, rhythm, and repetitions. It may be accompanied by excessive tension and struggle behavior (ASHA, 1993). The most common fluency disorder is stuttering. When stuttering, students may exhibit whole-word repetitions, part-word repetitions (b-b-boy), or prolongations of sounds (mmmmmy). Students may seem to get stuck on sounds, unable to get the sound out. Their speech may be accompanied by struggle behaviors such as gestures, facial contortions, or squinting. Individuals who stutter typically display abnormal disfluency between the ages of two and five years. While spontaneous recovery may occur in some youngsters, many will need the assistance of a speech-language pathologist to attain fluent speech. Some individuals never attain fluent speech, continuing to stutter throughout their lives, in spite of attempts at intervention or treatment. Stuttering has many interesting aspects as shown in **Table 5-11.**

Language Disorders

Language disorders can include the absence of language, delayed language development, deviations in language development, and language problems acquired after language has developed. A language disorder is an impairment in the comprehension and/or use of spoken, written and/or other symbol systems. It may involve the form of language (phonology, morphology, or syntax), the content of language (semantics), and/or the function of language (pragmatics) (ASHA, 1993).

In some students, language disorders may be associated with other disabilities such as intellectual disabilities, learning disabilities, hearing impairment, autism, or emotional disorders. Other language disorders may be acquired after normal language has developed due to brain damage from head injury, tumors, or serious illness. Some students may exhibit language disorders that are the result of limited opportunity to learn language, while for other students the cause of their language disorder is never determined. No matter what the cause, language disorders can have a significant impact on the academic performance and social skills of students. Language is the foundation of instruction and interaction in the classroom. Students with language disorders may have difficulty following directions, understanding lectures, reading and comprehending their textbooks, asking questions, and participating in conversations.

Certain groups of school-age individuals are considered to be "at risk" for language disorders. These groups include: (a) students with a history of preschool language delay, (b) students with learning and/or reading disabilities, and (c) students who are earning poor grades, are being retained in a grade, or are not receiving special services (Haynes, Moran, & Pindzola, 1994). Classroom teachers should be particularly alert to signs of possible language disorders in these students. In addition to the checklist of communication skills in Table 5-9, the common symptoms of language disorders presented in **Table 5-12** may assist teachers in identifying language problems in the classroom.

Communication Variations

Regional, ethnic, and racial dialects of the English language are common in this country. These dialects are differences in the patterns of speech or the use of language found in a given region of the country, in certain social groups, or in specific cultural/ethnic groups. The linguistic variations may involve any aspect of speech and language, including: vocabulary (calling carbonated beverages "*soda*", "*pop*", or "*coke*"), sound pronunciation, word order, sentence structure, use of pronouns, and even the cadence of speech. These linguistic variations are considered language differences, not language disorders. For this reason, students who speak a dialectical variation of English generally do not receive direct services from the speech-language pathologist. Some professionals (Delpit, 1988; Foster, 1986) argue that although these students do not have disorders, they must acquire the skills they need to communicate effectively as judged by the dominant culture. If they don't, these students will be denied equal educational and employment opportunities. These professionals advocate that students be allowed, and encouraged, to retain their regional, ethnic, or racial dialects since it is an important part of their culture. Yet, such students also should be taught Standard English to ensure they will have equal social, economic, and educational opportunities.

The use of augmentative or alternative communication systems also is considered a communication variation. Some students may be unable to communicate through speech due to physical disabilities. For these students sign language, gestures, communication boards, or electronic devices may replace speech as their primary mode of expressive communication. (See Chapter 10 for additional discussion).

TABLE 5-12

Common Symptoms of Language Disorders in Older Children

Semantics

- word finding/retrieval deficits
- use of a large number of words in an attempt to explain a concept because the name escapes them (circumlocutions)
- overuse of limited vocabulary
- difficulty recalling names of items in categories (e.g., animals, foods)
- difficulty retrieving verbal opposites
- small vocabulary
- use of words lacking specificity (thing, junk, stuff, etc.)
- inappropriate use of words (selection of wrong word)
- difficulty defining words
- less comprehension of complex words
- failure to grasp double word meanings (e.g., can, file, etc.)

Syntax/Morphology

- use of grammatically incorrect sentence structures
- simple, as opposed to complex, sentences
- less comprehension of complex grammatical structures
- prolonged pauses while constructing sentences
- semantically empty placeholders (e.g., filled pauses, "uh", "er", "um")
- use of many stereotyped phrases that do not require much language skill
- use of "starters" (e.g., "you know . . .")

Pragmatics

- use of redundant expressions and information the listener has already heard
- use of nonspecific vocabulary (e.g., thing, stuff) and the listener cannot tell from prior conversation or physical context what is referred to
- less skill in giving explanations clearly to a listener (lack of detail), less skill in explaining something in a proper sequence, less conversational control in terms of introducing, maintaining, and changing topics (may get off track in conversation and introduce new topics awkwardly)
- rare use of clarification questions (e.g., "I don't understand", "You did what?")
- difficulty shifting conversational style in different social situations (e.g., peer vs teacher, child vs adult)
- difficulty grasping the "main idea" of a story or lecture (preoccupation with irrelevant details)
- trouble making inferences from material not explicitly stated (e.g., "Sally went outside. She had to put up her umbrella." Inference: It was raining.)

From *Communication Disorders in the Classroom*, 2nd edition by Haynes et al. Copyright 1994 by Kendall/Hunt Publishing Company. Used with permission.

Management of Communication Disorders

Most students with speech and/or language impairments benefit from direct intervention or direct services provided by the speech-language pathologist. The specific objectives and treatment approaches will vary depending on the student's age, as well as the type and severity of the disorder. The intervention might focus on improving the articulation of speech sounds or the fluency of speech, changing voice characteristics, or improving language use and understanding. When providing direct services, the speech-language pathologist may work with students in small groups in the classroom or in a separate office or treatment room located in the school building.

The majority of students with communication disorders are educated in the general education classroom. Many are capable of full participation in all instructional activities without any adaptations or modifications. Other students may require modifications to ensure maximum learning and full participation. Five of the modifications described for students with sensory deficits (visual and hearing impairments) can be applied to students with communication disorders. These include:

1. use of assistive technology
2. use of a person
3. changes in student response
4. changes in teacher instruction
5. alteration in activities and/or curriculum (see **Table 5-13**).

As noted previously, some students with communication disorders, particularly those who have physical impairments, may be unable to communicate with speech or oral language. These students may use communication boards, electronic devices, or other assistive devices for communication as described in Chapter 10.

Peer teaming and working in groups provide students with communication disorders an opportunity to practice speaking and listening skills. Peers can model appropriate speech, and small groups may be less intimidating to students who are self-conscious about their speech. Students with poor receptive language skills may benefit from a "listening buddy," a classmate who assists with oral instructions and assignments.

Changes in the student response might be needed in some situations. If a student uses an augmentative communication device, it may take longer for that student to respond to a question. Similarly, students with receptive or expressive language disorders may need

TABLE 5-13

Managing Communication Disorders

	Communication Disorders
Assistive Technology	• Augmentation communication devices
Use of Person	• Peer teaming
Student Response	• Allow more time
Teacher Instruction	• Model appropriate speech and language • Provide practice opportunities
Alter Activity	• Alter language level of instructions and assignments
Alter Curriculum	• Direct and/or collaborative services from speech-language pathologist

additional time to process questions and formulate their answers. Students who stutter may be uncomfortable responding in class or may need more time for oral responses.

Students who exhibit speech or language disorders typically do not require significant modifications in teacher instruction. Teachers should be certain the language level of their instruction is appropriate for students who exhibit language disorders. The classroom provides natural opportunities for communication and for generalization of the skills being targeted in speech-language therapy. Teachers should model appropriate speech and language and encourage the learning and practice of communication skills. Speech and language impairments can be barriers to social interaction and may have a negative impact on a student's self-esteem. Teachers should strive to promote a positive classroom environment that encourages and facilitates communication. Emphasis on quick responses or competition may cause stress for students with communication disorders and result in decreased participation in the classroom. Small group activities, large group discussions, oral reports, active listening, and role playing are instructional strategies which can benefit all students, including those with speech or language impairments.

Modification of activities and/or curriculum may be necessary for some students. If students have limited language skills, the language level of classroom activities and assignments may need to be altered to ensure that students can participate. Direct services from the speech-language pathologist typically are added to the curriculum for students with communication disorders. The speech-language pathologist may ask to observe the student in the classroom to assess more accurately the effectiveness of intervention strategies. Both the classroom teacher and the speech-language pathologist play a role in the development of communication and literacy skills (oral language, vocabulary, reading, writing, etc.). Students with speech and language impairments benefit from the development of common goals and the implementation of collaborative treatment programs. Although direct speech-language services are important for many students, collaborative and cooperative service delivery models also are appropriate and important for these students. Speech-language pathologists are spending more time in classrooms, working with teachers to plan and deliver lessons that develop and enhance speech, language, and literacy skills in all students.

Physical Impairments

Students with physical impairments, although few in number, comprise one of the most diverse group of exceptional individuals, due to the many types of diseases and disorders which interfere with the normal functioning of the muscles or bones. Physical impairments are also referred to as orthopedic impairments. According to IDEA, orthopedic impairments are defined as follows:

> Orthopedic impairments means a severe orthopedic impairment that adversely affects a child's educational performance. The term includes impairments caused by congenital anomaly (e.g., clubfoot, absence of some member, etc.), impairments caused by disease (e.g., poliomyelitis, bone tuberculosis, etc.), and impairments from other causes (e.g., cerebral palsy, amputations, and fractures or burns that cause contractures). (34 CRF, Ch. III, Sec. 300.7)

Basic Anatomy

When a student has a physical impairment, various anatomical structures may be affected. In some forms of physical impairments, such as cerebral palsy, spinal cord injury, and spina bifida, the brain or spinal cord is damaged. The location of the damage will determine the type of condition.

The central nervous system consists of the brain and the spinal cord. The brain is a complex structure in which certain parts have specialized functions. One area of the brain

FIGURE 5-10

The Motor Strip

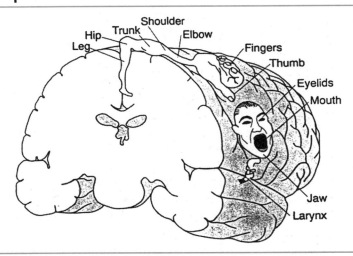

From *Neuroscience for the Study of Communicative Disorders* by Bhatnager. Reprinted by permission of Lippincott, Williams & Wilkins.

is known as the motor strip. Different parts of the motor strip correspond to different parts of the body (see **Figure 5-10**).

For example, nerve cells on the motor strip responsible for leg movement are located near the top of the motor strip, while nerve cells responsible for arm movement are located near the bottom of the motor strip. When a person wants to move an arm, electro-chemical impulses are sent from the motor strip to the spinal cord. The spinal cord acts like a super-highway in which impulses travel between the brain and the body. After the impulse travels down the spinal cord, it then exits along nerves which go to specific parts of the body (see **Figure 5-11**).

Nerves which exit near the top of the spinal cord travel to the upper part of the body. Nerves which exit near the bottom of the spinal cord travel to the lower part of the body. In the example of arm movement, the impulse exits through the nerves near the top of the spinal cord and travels through the nerves in the body to the muscles of the arm. The electro-chemical impulses cause the muscles of the arm to contract and move the arm. If there is damage to the motor strip (or other motor areas of the brain), movement will be abnormal. If there is damage to the spinal cord, the impulses from the brain cannot travel past the level of injury. This results in paralysis from the level of injury down through the rest of the body. If there was injury to the top part of the spinal cord, then paralysis would occur in both the upper body and the lower body.

Damage to other parts of the body result in other types of physical impairments. For example, in muscular dystrophy, the muscles of the body are damaged and interfere with movement. In osteogenesis imperfecta, the bones themselves have abnormalities, and in arthritis, the joints usually are affected.

Physical Assessment

Most physical impairments are readily apparent, and diagnosis will be made by a physician. Usually a physician who specializes in the specific area of disability, such as a neurologist or an orthopedist, will be involved. Physical examination, laboratory tests, and specialized tests for the specific disability will be performed to arrive at a diagnosis.

FIGURE 5-11

The Spinal Cord and Spinal Nerves

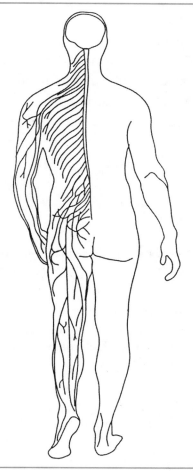

From *Neuroscience for the Study of Communicative Disorders* by Bhatnager. Reprinted by permission of Lippincott, Williams & Wilkins.

Further assessment will be made by a physical therapist, occupational therapist, speech-language pathologist, and teacher certified in orthopedic impairment, as appropriate. The type of support and modifications which the student needs will be decided by the educational team, based on their assessments of the student's physical and academic functioning. Some students with physical impairments will need support from special education, while others will not.

Common Physical Impairments

Cerebral Palsy

Cerebral palsy refers to a variety of nonprogressive disorders of voluntary movement and posture. It is caused by a malfunction of the motor areas of the brain occurring before birth, during birth, or within the first few years of life (Heller et al., 1996; Singer, 1998). Students with cerebral palsy typically have abnormal and uncoordinated motor movement. The cerebral palsy may be very mild and result in minimal or no limitation in physical activities. For example, a student's mild cerebral palsy may only be noticeable when

TABLE 5-14

Classification of Cerebral Palsy by Limb Involvement

Monoplegia: one limb is affected

Paraplegia: both legs are affected

Hemiplegla: one arm and one leg on the same side are affected

Triplegia: three limbs are affected (usually two legs and one arm)

Quadriplegia: all four limbs are affected equally

Diplegia: all four limbs are affected with legs more affected

TABLE 5-15

Different Types of Cerebral Palsy

Spastic Cerebral Palsy

- In spastic cerebral palsy, affected muscles have increased tone with increased resistance to movement. Movement is often slow and jerky with a decreased range of motion.

Athetoid Cerebral Palsy

- In athetoid cerebral palsy, there is fluctuating muscle tone resulting in slow, abnormal writhing movements in which the limb rotates back and forth. There are usually extra, purposeless movements which makes it difficult to move the limb to the intended location.

Ataxia

- In ataxia, there is an incoordination of voluntary muscle movement, with poor balance and equilibrium. Children often walk with feet wide apart, trunk weaving back and forth, and arms held out.

Mixed

- Many individuals with cerebral palsy have a combination of the above types of cerebral palsy.

running. At the other extreme, the cerebral palsy may be very severe. The student may be unable to perform the usual activities of daily living unless there are extensive adaptations. A student with severe spastic cerebral palsy may be unable to make the coordinated arm movements needed for eating, to coordinate legs to walk, and to articulate clearly when talking. Due to the differing limb involvement, cerebral palsy may be classified by which limb is affected as shown in **Table 5-14.** Several different types of cerebral palsy which have differing motor characteristics are described in **Table 5-15.**

Students with cerebral palsy often have additional impairments, such as visual impairments and seizures. Teachers will need to adapt for the physical impairment (e.g., use of adapted pencils or pointing devices) as well as the secondary conditions (e.g., use of low vision devices).

Spinal Cord Injury

Damage to the spinal cord can be caused by a wide range of disorders (e.g., spinal tumors) and traumatic events (e.g., car accidents). Depending on the location and type of spinal

FIGURE 5-12

Myelomeningocele

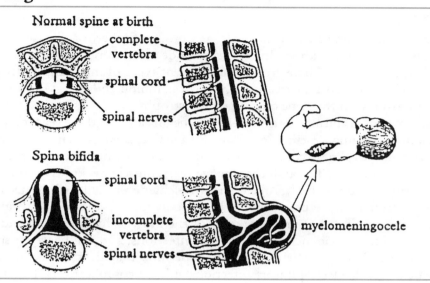

cord injury, the student may have symptoms ranging from weakness of a limb to paralysis of all parts of the body below the neck with ventilator-assisted breathing. The top part of the spinal cord relays nervous impulses to control movement and detect sensation to the arms and upper part of the body. Damage at this level would result in paralysis and loss of sensation from the upper body and arms down to the feet. Damage to the lower portion of the spinal cord may affect only the legs and urinary and bowel function, or only urinary and bowel function (since the nerves affecting bladder and bowel function are below the nerves affecting the legs). Additional problems of pressure sores (skin breakdown from having sustained pressure on a part of the body), respiratory insufficiency (from paralysis of the muscles which aid in breathing), and adjustment problems (such as depression) may occur as well. Physical and occupational therapies usually are prescribed, and psychological counseling may be of benefit.

Spina Bifida

Spina bifida is a defective closure of the bony vertebral column, occurring in the first 28 days of gestation. There are three types of spina bifida which differ in the severity of the defect: **spina bifida occulta, meningocele,** and **myelomeningocele.** In spina bifida occulta and meningocele, there usually is no functional impairment, while in myelomeningocele, functional impairments are common.

Myelomeningocele is the most common type of spina bifida. In this condition, the spinal cord is not completely surrounded by the spine. The infant is born with a sac like protrusion on the back which contains the spinal cord and its membranes as shown in **Figure 5-12.**

Surgery will be performed to remove the sac, but this will not correct the paralysis and lack of sensation which occur below the area of spinal cord damage. The area which is affected will depend upon where the outpouching occurred. In most instances, the myelomeningocele will occur in the lower section of the spinal cord. This results in total or partial leg paralysis, loss of sensation in the legs, and bowel and bladder problems. Adaptations and assistive devices will be needed by the student. The student may perform clean intermittent catheterization (insertion of a small tube into the bladder) to drain the urine at specific times during the day.

In many students with spina bifida, there may be a blockage in the flow of cerebral spinal fluid in the brain, resulting in a fluid accumulation in the brain, known as hydrocephalus. A shunt (tube) is usually put in place to drain the fluid.

Muscular Dystrophy

Muscular dystrophy can be defined broadly as a group of inherited diseases characterized by progressive muscle weakness due to primary degeneration of muscle fibers (Finkel, 2002; Heller, et al., 1996). There are several different types of muscular dystrophy, which vary as to their prognosis and severity. The most common childhood form is Duchenne muscular dystrophy. In this type of muscular dystrophy, weakness begins in the legs and progresses upwards. Typically, muscle weakness begins around three years of age with difficulty walking, running, or climbing stairs. By age five, there is a characteristic gait and calf enlargement. Weakness continues to progress, and a wheelchair often is needed by ten to twelve years of age. Through the teenage years, muscle weakness occurs in the muscles of the arms and upper body. An electric wheelchair eventually will be needed. Muscle weakness continues to the point that it is difficult for the adolescent to maintain an upright head position. Due to the weakness of the muscles for breathing and coughing, there is an increased incidence of respiratory infections, and the heart muscle often is affected. Most individuals with Duchenne type muscular dystrophy will die around twenty years of age due to respiratory infections or heart complications. The student with muscular dystrophy will need to be assessed and monitored continually to determine appropriate adaptations and physical assistance as the disease progresses. This disease results in a physical degeneration, not a mental one. Counseling regarding issues of death and dying often are needed to assist the student with a degenerative, terminal illness.

Limb Deficiency

A limb deficiency refers to any number of skeletal abnormalities in which the limbs (arms and legs) are partially or totally missing. Limb deficiencies include those types in which the end part of the limb is missing (such as in an amputation) as well as those which have the middle part of the limb missing (such as when a hand is attached to the shoulder or elbow region). There are several types of prosthetic devices (artificial limbs) which may be used to assist the individual with a limb deficiency in optimum functioning. Artificial legs may be used to walk or run, or a prosthetic hand may be used to pick up items. However, children born with limb deficiencies often are able to compensate for the deficiency by using the remaining part of the limb or by using a different limb. Children missing their arms, for example, may compensate by using their feet for a variety of tasks the missing hands would do (e.g., writing). In these cases, the individual may use a prosthesis for only cosmetics reasons, or may elect not to use one at all.

Management of Orthopedic Impairments

Management of the orthopedic impairment will vary depending upon the type of orthopedic impairment and its severity. The educational team, including the teacher certified in orthopedic impairment, physical therapist, occupational therapist, speech-language pathologist, family, and other educational personnel will determine the types of modifications needed. Modifications for students with orthopedic impairments can be divided into six main areas:

1. use of assistive technology
2. use of a person
3. changes in the physical environment

TABLE 5-16

Managing Physical Impairments

	Physical Impairment
Assistive Technology	• Devices to compensate for physical impairment (e.g., clay wrapped pencil, adapted computer)
Use of Person	• Peer teaming
Physical Environment	• Modify to allow access (e.g., wider aisles, lowered chalkboard)
Student Response	• Alternate response forms (e.g., eye gaze response, giving answers orally rather than in writing) • Allow more time
Teacher Instruction	• Allow student to feel material
Alter Material	• Alter material so student can physically use it (e.g., material larger so it can be manipulated, material placed in multiple choice format)
Alter Activity	• Change activity to compensate for physical disability
Alter Curriculum	• Add to curriculum specialized skills (e.g., use of technology)

4. changes in student response
5. alteration in material
6. alteration in activities and/or curriculum (See **Table 5-16**) (Heller et al., 1996).

Students with orthopedic impairments often will need to use assistive technology. There are many different types of assistive technology which may be used. Some of the types of assistive technology address positioning, hand and arm use, communication, mobility, and access to school activities. Proper position is imperative for students with physical impairments in order to optimize the movement and range of motion they have. Several positioning devices may be used, such as special chairs, trays and cut out tables, which optimize the student's ability to move. Assistive devices for hand and arm use may range from a student using a clay wrapped pencil, which can be grasped easily, to using a switch to control a computer which scans possible selections. Augmentative communication devices also may be used to allow the student to communicate effectively with others. Specialized wheelchairs, scooters, and other mobility devices may be needed to allow the student to move independently or with assistance. Many other assistive technology devices may be used to support computer access (e.g., enlarged keyboard, joysticks) and access to school activities (e.g., Smart Board for note taking).

A second type of modification involves using another person. Peer assistance may be used to help the student in activities that require additional physical movement the student is unable to perform. Peer teaming or working in groups also may be used. This not only allows additional assistance to the student with an orthopedic impairment on the parts of the task that require physical movement, but it also provides the student an opportunity to assist peers on parts of the tasks which do not involve a physical component.

The third type of modification is arrangement of the physical environment. Aisles may need to be widened to allow a student in a wheelchair to move freely about the classroom. Blackboards, light switches, and bulletin boards may need to be lowered so the student can access them. (See Chapter 10).

A fourth modification is student response. Students with severe physical impairments may be unable to write using a pad and paper. They may use a computer to write their responses or answer questions orally. Students may tire easily when their impairment is severe, so homework and tests may need to be shortened to minimize fatigue. Time limits often need to be extended for students who are slow due to their impairment or their use of augmentative devices.

A fifth modification is teacher instruction. The teacher typically will not need to modify the instructional strategies used in class. However, it is important that the teacher allows the student to feel or touch what is being discussed. Some students with physical impairments may have missed opportunities to feel what the item is like due to limitation in mobility and have incorrect information regarding the item.

A sixth modification is adapting the material. Students with physical impairments may provide their answer in any number of ways which will require modifying the material. Material often will need to be rewritten and spaced appropriately for a student to eye-gaze an answer. Students who have limited responses may need items placed in multiple choice format in order to respond. Other students may need material adapted for the computer in order to access it.

In some instances an activity or curriculum modification is needed for the student with a physical impairment. Due to the lack of motor movement, students may need some activities adapted. For example, frog dissection would be possible using a computer program, but not in the laboratory. Additional areas may be added to the student's curriculum, such as teaching the use of adapted devices, teaching the student to independently perform any physical health care procedures such as clean intermittent catheterization, and adaptations to vocational and independent living skills.

Health Impairments

There are several different types of health impairments which may interfere with a student's functioning at school. When this occurs, the students are classified as having other health impairments (OHI). Other health impairments are defined under IDEA as follows:

> Other health impairments means having limited strength, vitality, or alertness, due to chronic or acute health problems such as a heart condition, tuberculosis, rheumatic fever, nephritis, asthma, sickle cell anemia, hemophilia, epilepsy, lead poisoning, leukemia, or diabetes, that adversely affects a child's educational performance. (34 CRF, Ch. III, Sec. 300.7).

Some states add to their definition of other health impairments such conditions as AIDS and Attention Deficit/Hyperactivity Disorder.

Assessment of Health Impairments

Health impairments are diagnosed through the use of physical examination, blood work, and specialized tests for the specific type of impairment. Additional assessments may be made by the educational team to determine how the student is performing academically and whether modifications and support from special education are needed. Often these students require few modifications in the classroom. The teacher will need to be knowledgeable about the specific health impairment and any special procedures needed should an emergency situation arise. Based on the student's condition and assessment of the student's needs, a plan of action should be written out by the physician or nurse and known by all the educational staff working with the student in case an emergency occurs.

Common Health Impairments

Seizure Disorder (Epilepsy)

A seizure is a brief, temporary change in the normal functioning of the brain's electrical system due to excessive, uncontrolled electrical activity in the brain. A seizure disorder, also known as epilepsy, refers to a condition in which a person has recurrent seizures. The most common treatment for seizures is medication. However, in some instances medication may not be able to completely stop seizures from occurring, but only decrease their frequency.

There are many different types of seizures with varying characteristics. Some students will see flashing lights or experience some type of sensation immediately prior to the seizure, but many students will have no warning that a seizure is about to occur. Most seizures will involve a loss of consciousness, or altered consciousness, in which the student will miss information and not know what has occurred during the seizure. Some seizures will be very obvious, and others will be subtle. The most obvious type of seizure is the convulsive type known as a **generalized tonic-clonic** seizure. In this seizure, the student loses consciousness, and the body initially becomes very stiff, followed by a rhythmic jerking motion. Other seizures are not as noticeable, such as the **absence** seizure in which the student often stares blankly for a few seconds. Other types of seizures, such as **myoclonic** and **complex partial** seizures involve very different types of motor movements and may not appear to be a seizure to those unfamiliar with seizure disorders. **Table 5-17** describes the common types of seizures.

Teachers play a major role in seizure treatment, documentation, and identification. Teachers need to know what type of seizures the student has, and what to do if a seizure occurs. Often no treatment is needed, but for tonic-clonic seizures, the teacher will need to know what steps to take if one occurs as described in **Table 5-18.**

Accurate documentation of the occurrence of seizures (including a description of the seizure, how long it lasted, and time of day it occurred) will assist the physician in diagnosis and treatment. Seizures such as absence seizures are so subtle that teachers are often the first people to suspect that the student is having this type of seizure. Teachers will need to make a medical referral if a seizure is suspected.

Diabetes

The most common form of diabetes in children, known as type I diabetes, occurs when the pancreas produces little or no insulin. Without sufficient insulin, glucose (sugar) cannot be transported from the bloodstream into the cells of the body where it is needed for energy. This results in abnormally high levels of glucose in the blood while the cells of the body are starving for glucose. If not treated, this can be life threatening.

It is very important for a student with diabetes to eat lunch and snacks on a regular schedule.

TABLE 5-17

Common Types of Seizures

Tonic-Clonic Seizure (also known as grand mal seizure)

- **Characteristics:** When a tonic-clonic seizure occurs, the student suddenly loses consciousness and falls to the floor (and may be injured during the fall). In the first part of this seizure, the student will become very stiff. This is followed by a rhythmic jerking of the body. During this time, the tongue may be bitten causing blood and saliva to come out of the mouth. Breathing may be shallow which can cause the lips and fingernails to turn a bluish color. The person may lose bowel and/or bladder control during the seizure. Usually the seizure lasts only a few minutes, after which the student regains consciousness. At this time, the student experiences some confusion and is very tired.
- **Actions:** Know the steps to take if one occurs in the classroom (see Table 5-18). Allow the student to rest after the seizure is over.

Absence Seizure (also known as petit mal seizure)

- **Characteristics:** In this seizure, the student suddenly loses consciousness, stops whatever activity was being done, and either stares straight ahead or rolls the eyes upwards. There usually is no movement or change in posture, except possibly some eye blinking or mouth twitching. This type of seizure lasts a few seconds, and at its completion, the student will resume the previous activity as if nothing occurred. Absence seizures can occur only a few times a day or as frequently as hundreds of times a day.
- **Actions:** There is no specific first aid for this seizure. However, this type of seizure often interferes with learning since the student is missing information each time the seizure occurs. Pairing the student with another student may be helpful, so that the peer may show the student where they are in the book or lesson after a seizure occurs. Teachers also need to be alert to identify this subtle type of seizure which is often mistaken for daydreaming.

Myoclonic Seizure

- **Characteristics:** This seizure appears as a sudden, uncoordinated body jerk of all or part of the body. Sometimes the student may drop something, fall against something, or fall to the floor.
- **Actions:** There is no specific first aid for this seizure unless injury occurs.

Atonic Seizure (also known as a drop attack)

- **Characteristics:** This seizure involves the student suddenly collapsing or falling. Recovery typically occurs after ten seconds to one minute.
- **Actions:** There is no specific first aid for this seizure unless injury occurs in the fall.

Complex Partial Seizure (also known as psychomotor or temporal lobe seizure)

- **Characteristics:** This seizure consists of random purposeless activity in which the student appears dazed and may walk around, pick up objects, pick at clothes, or perform some other type of complex motor sequence. The student cannot control motor movements and will not remember what happened when the seizure is over.
- **Actions:** The teacher should remain with the student until the seizure is over, guiding the student away from any hazards.

TABLE 5-18

What to Do for a Tonic-Clonic Seizure

1. Stay calm and glance at a watch near the start of a seizure to determine how long it lasts.
2. Put the student in a lying position, move furniture out of the way to avoid injury.
3. Put student on his or her side to allow saliva to drain from mouth and prevent aspiration.
4. Shirt collars can be loosened, and something soft, such as a jacket, should be placed under the student's head.
5. Do not restrain the student's movements and do NOT put anything in the student's mouth since this may cause injury.
6. If seizure continues for more than five minutes or there are multiple seizures occurring immediately one after the other, call an ambulance (Epilepsy Foundation, 2001). This is because the student may need intravenous medication to stop the seizure.
7. If the seizure stops, but the student is not breathing, give mouth to mouth resuscitation. (This is very rare).
8. After the seizure is over, the student will not remember what happened and should be reassured and informed of what occurred.
9. The student should be assessed as to whether any injury occurred. If there was a blow to the head when the student fell, the student should be seen by a nurse or other medical personnel.
10. The student will be exhausted after the seizure and should be allowed to sleep.
11. It is important that the student's dignity be protected during and after the seizure. If the clothes were soiled, arrangements should be made to change them.
12. Document the occurrence of the seizure, including a description of the seizure, the time it occurred, the length of the seizure, if the student fell and had any injuries, what first-aid was given (if any), and whether the parents were notified.

Treatment for diabetes usually consists of the student maintaining a balance between medication, diet, and exercise. Insulin is taken by the student to replace the insulin missing from the body. Diet and exercise impact on the amount of glucose in the body and must be controlled so that the amount of insulin taken will correspond to the amount of glucose. This typically is not a problem unless excessive sugar is eaten, a meal is skipped, or the amount of exercise is altered significantly.

Usually the student with diabetes will need no special changes in the classroom routine. An exception is that the student may need to eat a snack to control the levels of glucose and insulin. It is very important that the student eats snacks and lunch on a regular schedule so that a reaction does not occur. Also, if excessive exercise is planned (such as during a field day), notify the parents in advance in case the amount of insulin needs to be adjusted for that time. The teacher should be alert for any reactions which may occur and know what actions to take. These are described in **Table 5-19.**

Asthma

Asthma is the most common lung disease of childhood. With asthma, there are acute attacks of shortness of breath and wheezing due to airway inflammation and airway

TABLE 5-19

Emergency Conditions in Diabetes

Condition	Caused By	Symptoms	Actions
Hyperglycemia (too much sugar)	Missed insulin dose. Noncompliance with diet.	Gradual onset • frequent urination, eating, & drinking; fatigue; nausea; vomiting; fruity odor on breath; rapid, deep breathing; unconscious.	Needs insulin. Follow emergency plan.
Hypoglycemia (too little sugar)	Missed a meal. Strenuous exercise. Took too much insulin.	Quick onset • headache; irritability; shaking; sweating; behavior change; weakness; slurred speech; confusion; shallow breathing; unconscious.	Needs sugar. Follow emergency plan.

obstruction (Beers & Berkow, 1999). A student with asthma has normal breathing until contact is made with a substance or situation which triggers the asthma attack. The trigger may be a specific allergen (i.e., substances to which the person is allergic such as dust mites or pollen), respiratory infections, inhalation of irritating substances (e.g., fumes, gases), environmental factors (e.g., air pollution, exercise), or emotional factors (Nettina, 2001). When the asthma attack occurs, the student will have difficulty breathing, as seen by shortness of breath, coughing, wheezing, labored breathing, and complaints of difficulty breathing.

Teachers who have students with asthma need to know how to decrease the occurrence of asthma attacks and what to do when one occurs. Teachers should be aware of the specific causes of an asthma attack for specific students and try to avoid those causes or triggers when possible. For example, if being close to the school rabbit causes an asthma attack or exercising is a factor, then modifications can be made to decrease contact with the rabbit or adapt the exercise program. When an asthma attack occurs, the student needs medication immediately. Medication usually is in the form of a spray which is inhaled and opens up the airway to improve breathing. The teacher needs to be sure the medication is always accessible (e.g., is taken on any field trips) and be familiar with proper administration as well as emergency procedures. Although it is very rare for an asthma attack to be fatal, the importance of proper treatment cannot be overstressed (Stemple & Redding, 1992).

Cystic Fibrosis

Cystic fibrosis is a genetic disease in which there is an abnormal secretion of mucous and electrolytes in the exocrine glands (glands which secrete fluid outside the body or to a body cavity which will empty to the outside). The effects of cystic fibrosis are especially present in the respiratory system, digestive system, and within the sweat. In the respiratory system, there is an abnormal amount of mucous, which is characterized by frequent coughing and increased respiratory infections. In regard to the digestive system, medication is taken to replace a pancreatic enzyme needed for digestion, and an increased caloric intake is usually required. Students with cystic fibrosis will have an increase of salt and chloride in their sweat. Most individuals with cystic fibrosis remain fairly healthy during their childhood and adolescence. Respiratory infections are common, resulting in increased school absences. However, cystic fibrosis is a progressive, terminal disease in which individuals usually die of respiratory complications. If diagnosed early, individuals will usually live until about thirty years of age, although some individuals live into their forties and fifties (Behrman, Kleigman, & Jenson, 2000).

Some modifications may be needed for students with cystic fibrosis. The most obvious sign of cystic fibrosis is a frequent cough. Classmates may avoid a student with cystic fibrosis for fear of catching an infection. The student with cystic fibrosis may try to suppress the coughing due to social embarrassment. The teacher should explain that coughing is important to clear unwanted secretions and that suppressing the cough is harmful. The teacher also will need to stress that the cough is not infectious. In the area of exercise, there may be some restrictions. In some cases, exercising on hot days may result in a dangerous loss of electrolytes in the sweat, which may require the student to take additional salt.

Modifications may need to be made for lunch and restroom use. Because of the loss of calories in the stools, students with cystic fibrosis need to be able to eat as much as they want at lunch (seconds, thirds, and fourths) in order to obtain sufficient caloric intake. Students with cystic fibrosis also need to go to the restroom frequently, requiring the student to leave class more often than peers. Since bowel movements tend to have a foul odor, teachers are encouraged to be sensitive to this since other students may make fun of the student. Arrangements often are made to allow the student to use the teacher restroom so that the student will be more at ease. A deodorizer may be made available.

Sickle Cell Anemia

Sickle cell anemia is an inherited disorder in which some of the red blood cells are abnormally shaped like a sickle (crescent) due to the presence of abnormal hemoglobin in the red blood cell. These sickle shaped cells do not survive as long as normal shaped red blood cells survive which results in fewer red blood cells and, hence, anemia. Students with sickle cell anemia often experience fatigue due to the anemia. They also may experience "sickling crisis" in which an increased number of cells sickle and become wedged in small capillaries due to their sickle shape. This will stop the flow of oxygen to the tissues below the block, and tissue death will occur. The sickling crisis may be brought on by anything which results in a decrease of oxygen. This includes dehydration, strenuous physical exercise, extreme fatigue, infection, or altitude change (Nettina, 2001). The student will experience pain wherever the blockage is occurring.

The teacher needs to be aware that students with sickle cell anemia may experience fatigue and short attention span due to the anemia. Planning more difficult work early in the day or in short segments may be helpful. If the student has a sickling crisis, the main symptom will be pain, and an emergency plan must be followed. Often students with sickle cell anemia have frequent or extended absences due to the sickling crisis. The teacher must ensure that arrangements are made to assist the student in making up missed work.

Childhood Cancer

Cancer refers to a condition in which certain cells have the trait of unregulated, excessive growth. These cells invade tissues and organs of the body and interfere with their normal functioning. There are several types of cancers, some of which are curable. Depending upon the type of cancer, treatment options include surgery, chemotherapy, and radiation.

Teachers need to be familiar with the type of cancer the student has and the type of treatment. Some students may experience fatigue, nausea, and hair loss due to the treatment. Students with cancer may have good and bad days and frequent absences. Modifications in the quantity of work the student is required to complete may be necessary. Emotional support often is needed for the student, classmates, and teachers, due to the potential severity of this condition.

AIDS

Acquired immune deficiency syndrome (AIDS) is one of the newest chronic illness of childhood. It is caused by the human immunodeficiency virus (HIV) which destroys the immune system. Transmission usually occurs in one of three ways: 1) sex with an infected partner, 2) sharing of contaminated needles during IV drug use, or 3) when the infected mother passes the infection on to the baby. The infection cannot be obtained through casual contact.

As HIV multiplies in the body, it destroys certain cells of the immune system (e.g., CD4 cells). Due to the injured immune system, the student with AIDS can acquire various types of infections which the body is unable to fight. The individual with AIDS usually dies of these infections. When a student has an injured immune system, it is important to maintain proper infection control. Infection control involves good handwashing, washing surfaces with a bleach, and sending sick students home. This will minimize the risk of infection from others to the student with AIDS, as well as insure proper infection control for all students.

Initially, the teacher will not need to make modifications for the student who is infected by HIV. However, as the infection continues, modifications may be required because of fatigue and frequent absences. Psychological support should be provided due to the terminal nature of this infection, as well as the hysteria and social stigma which surrounds it. Teachers may need to provide emotional support and dispel misconceptions regarding the disease to school personnel, as well as maintain strict confidentiality.

Management of Health Impairments

A diverse group of conditions comprise the category of other health impairments. Most students will have normal intelligence and may not appear ill. However, in many of these conditions, students will have periodic episodes of extreme distress. The teacher must be alert for these signs of distress and know what to do when they occur. For this reason, a plan of action in emergency situations should be developed with the physician and family, and then shared with the education team. Often students with these conditions have frequent absences due to their health-related problems. The teacher will need to assist the student in making up work. In certain instances, hospital or home bound instruction will be appropriate. In some of these conditions, fatigue and just not feeling well may impact negatively on the student's performance.

Modifications for students with other health impairments typically fall into four categories:

1. assistive technology and medical technology
2. use of a person
3. modification of physical environment
4. adaptation to the curriculum (See **Table 5-20**) (Heller et al., 1995).

Students with other health impairments may require certain health procedures during the school day, such as testing for the level of glucose in the blood to determine insulin dosage. Assistive devices or equipment, such as the glucose monitoring machine and other similar equipment may be needed for the particular type of health impairment. A person may be required to assist with the procedure. The student should be provided

TABLE 5-20

Managing Health Impairments

	Health Impairment
Assistive Technology	• Use of items used in health procedures
Use of Person	• Individual may assist student with health procedure
Physical Environment	• Arrange for a private area to perform procedure
Alter Curriculum	• Add to curriculum student learning how to do physical procedure

with an appropriate secluded physical environment, such as the nurse's office, to perform the procedure. Lastly, the curriculum may be altered to include teaching the student how to perform the health care procedure, recognize the signs which indicate distress, and understand the actions to take when a health problem occurs.

Summary

This chapter has reviewed a variety of sensory, communication, physical, and health impairments which students may experience. Students with these disabilities may encounter barriers to their success in the classroom which are unique to the disabilities. It is not possible to provide an in-depth discussion of each disability in an introductory textbook; however, it is important that the classroom teacher have a general understanding of these impairments and the modifications which may be needed. The responsibility for these modifications should be a shared one, with the classroom teacher playing a major role on the educational team that meets the needs of these students.

Discussion Questions and Activities

1. When you have a student with a sensory impairment in your general education classro___ be the role of the related service staff and special education teachers?

2. A student with a physical impairment is going to be placed in your general education classroom. What do you need to know about the student's physical impairment? How will you get this information? (What if the student were to have a health impairment rather than a physical impairment?).

3. Currently some Deaf adults are expressing concern that the move towards full inclusion of students with deafness in the general education classroom is not allowing these students to achieve to their fullest academic potential. In addition these students are not provided with an opportunity to learn about the Deaf culture. Advocates are calling for a separate educational system for these students (i.e., separate classes and/or schools). Discuss the pros and cons of a separate educational system for students who are deaf.

p 221 internet resources

individual research & experience

4. You teach in an inclusive general education classroom and among your students are several who have sensory, communication, physical, and health impairments. The parents of another student in your class (one who does not have any disability) have called and have expressed their displeasure that their child is in your classroom. They are concerned that their child will be held back in her learning because you will have to slow down your teaching and spend so much time with these students who have disabilities. How will you handle this situation?

Individual answers

5. Conduct a short lesson with the students using simulators to determine how much information they miss and what adaptations would be helpful. Vision impairment simulators may be purchased or made. To construct simulators, buy protective goggles (from a hardware store) and place construction paper over them. If construction paper is placed completely over the goggles, this will simulate total vision loss. If a hole is placed in the center of the construction paper, this will simulate a peripheral field loss. Placing only a circle of construction paper over the direct line of vision simulates a central field loss. Placing scotch tape over the goggles, instead of construction paper, will simulate light perception only. It should be stressed that since the college students actually have sight, the simulators do not give them an idea of what it would be like not having vision from birth. The simulators give only a general idea of the types of vision losses, but can prove helpful in understanding how lessons, environments, and materials may need to be modified. Ear plugs can be used to simulate a mild to moderate hearing loss.

6. Have an interpreter, speech-language pathologist, special education teacher, or related service provider (physical therapist, occupational therapist, etc.) come to class and discuss their role in the educational setting.

7. Contact your local school system and make arrangements to observe a teacher of students with visual impairments, a teacher of students with hearing impairments, a speech-language pathologist, an audiologist, a physical therapist, or an occupational therapist as they provide services to students with disabilities.

8. Peter is a ten-year-old boy who enjoys playing computer games and talking with his friends on the Internet. He was born with spastic quadriplegia cerebral palsy and a seizure disorder. Peter later developed asthma which results in frequently missing school in the winter months. He uses an electric wheelchair for mobility and is able to maneuver quite well around the school. His speech is not understandable so he uses an augmentative communication device with voice output which he accesses by slowly pointing to the symbols with his right hand. Peter does most of his work on the computer using an adapted keyboard. He is in general education classes for four periods a day and receives special education services for two periods a day. Peter successfully finished third grade last year, although he is one grade level behind in reading. Peter is now entering fourth grade and will be in Ms. Jones's class. Ms. Jones has never had a student with such severe physical and health impairments in her class. Although she understands that Peter has normal or near normal intelligence, she is very concerned about how she will teach him in her class. Prior to the start of school, the special education teacher, Ms. Daniels has scheduled a meeting with Ms. Jones, to discuss Peter.

a. What does Ms. Jones need to know about Peter's health and physical condition?

b. What are some possible modifications that you would expect Peter would need?

c. What are some of the issues that should be covered in the meeting?

d. What other professionals may be providing services to Peter?

e. What should be the role of the special education teacher throughout the academic year?

9. Marsha is a fifteen-year-old student in tenth grade who has been getting mostly "B" grades and has been very active in sports. She is very popular and enjoys socializing with her peers. However, lately she has been doing poorly in her school work. Marsha does not appear to be interested in her classwork and often appears to be daydreaming. Her math teacher attributed this to her age and her interest in boys. However, her basketball coach has found that Marsha is performing very poorly in the sport and has noticed that she keeps bumping into her teammates and is not making the easy shots. Mr. Tuttle, Marsha's English Literature teacher, also is concerned about her behavior and noticed that she rubs her eyes frequently, and rereads or skips words or lines when reading. Marsha also seemed to be oblivious to the work on the blackboard when it was not read aloud.

a. What type of impairment does Mr. Tuttle suspect and what should Mr. Tuttle do?

b. What type of medical exams should Marsha receive?

c. What would qualify Marsha for special education services?

d. If Marsha qualifies for special education services, what would be the role of the special education teacher?

e. What would Marsha's general education teachers need to know and what type of modifications would be discussed?

Internet Resources

Alexander Graham Bell Association for the Deaf
3417 Volta Place NW
Washington, DC 20007-2778
202-337-5220 (V/TTY)
www.agbell.org

American Speech-Language-Hearing Association
10801 Rockville Pike
Rockville, MD 20852-3279
1-800-638-8255
www.asha.org

Epilepsy Foundation of America
4351 Garden City Dr.
Landover, MD 20785-2267
1-800-EFA-1000
www.efa.org

National Association of the Deaf
814 Thayer Ave.
Silver Spring, MD 20910-4500
301-587-1788
301-587-1789 (TTY)
www.nad.org

NIDCD Clearinghouse (National Institute on Deafness and Other Communication Disorders)
1 Communication Ave.
Bethesda, MD 20892-3456
1-800-241-1044
1-800-241-1055 (TTY)
www.nidcd.nih.gov

The National Organization for Rare Disorders, Inc. (NORD)
P.O. Box 8923
New Fairfield, CT 06812-8923
1-800-999-6673
www.rarediseases.org

References

American Speech-Language-Hearing Association. (1993). Definitions of communication disorders and variations. *Asha, 35,* (Suppl. 10), 40–41.

Andersen, R. A. (2004). *Infections in children: A sourcebook for educators and child care providers.* Austin, TX: Pro-Ed.

Arlt, P. B., & Goodban, M. T. (1976). A comparative study of articulation acquisition as based on a study of 240 normals, aged three to six. *Language, Speech and Hearing Services in Schools, 7,* 173–180.

Beers, M. H., & Berkow, R. (1999). *The Merck manual of diagnosis and therapy* (17th ed.). Hoboken, NJ: John Wiley & Sons.

Behrman, R. E., Kleigman, & Jenson (2000). *Nelson textbook of pediatrics.* Philadelphia: W. B. Saunders.

Bess, F., Dodd-Murphy, J., & Parker, R. (1998). Children with minimal sensorineural hearing loss: Prevalence, educational performance, and functional status. *Ear and Hearing, 19(5),* 339–354.

Bhatnagar, S. C., & Andy, O. (1995). *Neuroscience for the Study of Communicative Disorders.* Baltimore, MD: Williams & Wilkins.

Brackett, D., & Maxon, A. B. (1986). Service delivery alternatives for the mainstreamed hearing-impaired child. *Language, Speech and Hearing Services in Schools, 17,* 115–125.

Braden, J. P. (1985). The structure of nonverbal intelligence in deaf & hearing subjects. *American Annals of the Deaf, 130,* 496–501.

Corn, A. (1983). Visual function: A theoretical model for individuals with low vision. *Journal of Visual Impairment and Blindness, 77,* 373–377.

Cornett, R. O. (1975). Cued speech and oralism: An analysis. *Audiology and Hearing Education, 1(1),* 26–33.

Culatta, R., & Leeper, L. (1987). Disfluency in childhood: It's not always stuttering. *Journal of Childhood Communicative Disorders, 10,* 157–171.

Delpit, L. D. (1988). The silenced dialogue: Power and pedagogy in educating other people's children. *Harvard Educational Review, 58(3),* 280–298.

Epilepsy Foundation. (2001). *First aid for generalized tonic clonic (grand mal) seizures.* Landover, MD: Author.

Finkel, R. S. (2002). Muscular dystrophy and myopathy. In B. L. Maria (Ed.) *Current management in child neurology.* (pp. 360–367). Hamilton: BC Decker.

Foster, H. L. (1986). *Ribin', jivin', and playin' the dozens* (2nd ed.). Cambridge, MA: Ballinger.

Garwood, V. P. (1987). Audiology in the public school setting. In F. N. Martin (Ed.), *Hearing disorders in children* (pp. 427–467). Austin, TX: PRO-ED.

Gordon, N. (1998). Colour blindness. *Public Health, 112(2),* 81–85.

Grundfast, K., & Carney, C. J. (1987). *Ear infections in your child.* Hollywood, FL: Compact Books.

Haynes, W. O., Moran, M. J., & Pindzola, R. H. (1994). *Communication disorders in the classroom* (2nd ed.). Dubuque, IA: Kendall/Hunt.

Heller, K. W., Alberto, P. A., Forney, P. E., & Schwartzman, M. N. (1996). *Understanding physical, sensory, and health impairments: Characteristics and educational implications.* Pacific Grove, CA: Brooks/Cole Publishers.

Heller, K. W., Dangel, H., & Sweatman, L. (1995). Systematic selection of adaptations for students with muscular dystrophy. *Journal of Physical and Developmental Disabilities, 7(3),* 253–265.

Herrington-Hall, B. L., Lee, L., Stemple, J. C., Niemi, K. R., & McHone, M. M. (1988). Description of laryngeal pathologies by age, sex, and occupation in a treatment-seeking population. *Journal of Speech and Hearing Disorders, 53,* 57–64.

Heward, W. L., & Orlansky, M. D. (1992). *Exceptional children. An introductory survey of special education* (4th ed.). New York: Macmillan.

Montgomery, J. K., & Fujikawa, S. (1992). Hearing thresholds of students in second, eighth, and twelfth grades. *Language, Speech and Hearing Services in Schools, 23,* 61–63.

Moores, D. F. (1996). *Educating the deaf: Psychology, principles, and practices* (4th ed.). Boston: Houghton Mifflin.

Nettina, S. (2001). *The Lippincott manual of nursing practice.* Philadelphia: J. B. Lippincott.

Ottem, E. (1980). An analysis of cognitive studies with deaf subjects. *American Annals of the Deaf, 125,* 564–575.

Peppard, A. R., & Peppard, S. B. (1992). Noise-induced hearing loss: A study of children at risk. *The Hearing Journal, 45(3),* 33–35.

Quigley, S., & Paul, P. (1989). English language development. In M. Wang, M. Reynolds, & H. Walberg (Eds.), *The handbook of special education: Research and practice* (Vol. 3) (pp. 3–21). Oxford, England: Pergamon.

Reynolds, M. C., & Birch, J. W. (1988). *Adaptive mainstreaming: A primer for teachers and principals.* New York: Longman.

Riordan-Eva, P., Asbury, T., & Whitcher, J. P. (2003). *Vaughan & Asbury's general ophthalmology.* Hightstown, NJ: McGraw-Hill.

Schappert, S. M. (1992). Office visits for otitis media: United States, 1975–1990. Advance data from vital and health statistics, No. 214, Hyattville, MD: National Centers for Health Statistics.

Schein, J. D. (1984). *Speaking the language of sign: The art and science of signing.* Garden City, NY: Doubleday.

Singer, H. W. (1998). Movement disorders in children. In J. Jankovic & E. Tolosa (Eds.) *Parkinson's disease and movement disorders.* (pp. 729–753). Philadelphia: Lippincott, Williams, & Wilkins.

Stemple, D. A., & Redding, G. J. (1992). Management of acute asthma. *Pediatric Clinics of North America, 39,* 1311–1325.

U. S. Department of Education. (2002). *Twenty-fourth annual report to Congress on the implementation of the Individuals with Disabilities Education Act.* Washington, DC: Author.

Ward, M. (2000). The visual system. In M. C. Holbrook & A. J. Koenig (Eds.) *Foundations of education, Vol 1. History and theory of teaching children and youths with visual impairments* (pp. 77–110). New York: AFB Press.

Wolk, S., & Allen, T. E. (1984). A five-year follow-up of reading comprehension achievement of hearing-impaired students in special education programs. *Journal of Special Education, 18,* 161–176.

6

Instructional Methods for Students with Mild Disabilities

David E. Houchins, Mary Beth Calhoon, and Harry L. Dangel

Chapter Objectives

- to identify considerations that should be taken into account when adapting the curriculum for students with mild disabilities;
- to describe the three levels in the elementary and secondary Planning Pyramids;
- to provide an overview of the characteristics of effective instruction and describe their importance in educating all students;
- to describe a model for preparing lessons;
- to describe specific instructional strategies to assist students across content areas;
- to identify ways that materials can be adapted to assist students in meeting the content demands of the general education classroom; and
- to describe how classroom teachers can address the specific needs of students with mild disabilities by adapting the way instruction is delivered.

Students with mild disabilities often are served in the general education classroom for most of the instructional day. To meet their special instructional needs, the general education teacher may need to make adaptations to curriculum, instruction, materials and assignments. These adaptations are based on principles of effective instruction derived from studies of effective teachers in both general and special education. The special education teacher who is responsible for the student is usually available to assist the classroom teacher in selecting the most appropriate strategies and adaptations.

This chapter provides specific strategies for adapting curriculum, instruction, materials, and assignments. You also will learn about making decisions about planning instruction and making adaptations to the curriculum. Then you will read about basic principles of effective instruction and apply them to instruction. You will learn specific techniques for adapting instruction across a variety of academic content areas. Finally, you will learn to adapt materials for students with mild disabilities and identify instructional delivery adaptations that can be made in the general education classroom.

Adapting the Curriculum

Nearly all students with learning difficulties will require the curriculum to be adapted to achieve success in the general education classroom. As you will recall from Chapter 3, the curriculum is the information and skills that are to be taught. The need for teachers to adapt the curriculum is apparent when one considers that students with mental retardation or specific learning disabilities, even when provided with adapted instruction, require more time than average learners to master the same curriculum. Because the school day has a limited amount of time in it, teachers are faced with either trying to cover the identical curriculum and expect lower levels of mastery from students with learning difficulties or selectively emphasizing the most important components of the curriculum that should be taught to mastery. It is expected that all learners, including those with disabilities, will be able to meet curriculum standards established by states and professional organizations (Erickson, Ysseldyke, Thurlow, & Elliott, 1998). In this section you will learn what you need to consider when making adaptations to the curriculum for students with learning difficulties. You will also learn how to plan for instruction using the Planning Pyramid as a framework for making instructional decisions. Examples of curricula in several areas are provided.

Planning daily lessons that meet the needs of all students is an ongoing challenge to the teacher. A good place to start in planning is to review the student's IEP. The goals and objectives provide a general framework of the skills needed to be taught. Teachers not only have to address the issue of planning for a student with learning difficulties, but also the issue of how to provide instruction to that student along with meeting the demands of 23 other third graders.

These issues are often addressed by the model followed by the prereferral team that organized each student's problems into adapting **What** to teach, **How** to teach it, and **Who** should be responsible (described in Chapter 3). The definition of "What is to be learned by students" is another way of defining the word **curriculum.** "The general education curriculum may be defined as a set of curricular expectations for students to achieve at each grade and level" (Raymond, 2000, p. 338). The general education curriculum identifies the competencies expected of adults in that community. The curriculum, in practical terms, is the instructional goals that have been defined by the schools as reflected in the knowledge and skills taught in the books and the materials used in the classrooms.

The first step in planning for students with disabilities is to examine the IEP and identify the adaptations of the curriculum that it specifies be used. When reading a student's IEP, teachers should think about how the IEP goal and objectives reflect the unique needs of the student. Consider how the IEP goals and objectives are enabling the student to better access the general education curriculum (Bateman & Linden, 1998). The IEP should not be cluttered with goals and objectives for all content standards in the general curriculum. An example of an annual goal and a short-term objective that addresses the unique spelling problems Miguel is having is provided below.

Annual Goal 5: Miguel will increase his spelling vocabulary

Short-term Objectives:

5.1   Given spelling words in isolation M. will write 100 second-grade spelling words correctly 3 out of 4 days.

5.2   M. will write 75 second-grade spelling words correctly when using them in sentences.

The curriculum for the student in special education whose problems are defined as mild, like Miguel, typically has adapted goals and objectives based on the curriculum used for the regular population of students. This would include goals focusing on the general education curricular outcomes of mastering academic skills (e.g., Miguel's goal of mastering spelling words on a second grade level is identical to the expectations of younger, average achievers). Using the curriculum of general education might include elements such as demonstrating the ability to meet course requirements in content areas (e.g., passing the U.S. History course), and passing standard competency tests (e.g., high school graduation tests).

The curriculum and instructional procedures discussed in this chapter are based on what is expected within general education classrooms. For students with mild disabilities, curricular options are guided by school competency testing policies, such as high school graduation tests, core curriculum course requirements, and the materials selected by educators to define the daily instructional content (Erickson, et al., 1998). Students for whom the curriculum needs to be modified to emphasize community-based skills and self-help skills are typically those who have moderate or severe disabilities. The needs of these students are discussed in Chapter 9. Of course, the line that separates these groups is not clear and the needs of any one student may include a combination of general education goals and community-based, functional goals (York, Doyle, & Kronberg, 1992).

Adapting the curriculum can include planning for an individual lesson, for a unit, or for an entire school year. Because instructional planning occurs on an ongoing basis, teachers need effective tools to assist them in deciding what to teach. The Planning Pyramid is one tool for teachers in planning lessons and units and making decisions about *how* to accommodate the diverse learners in the classroom (Vaughn, Bos, & Schumm, 1997; Lenz, 2004). The Planning Pyramid is based on the concept of scope of content. The teacher first identifies the most important concepts to be learned in each lesson or unit. The Pyramid assists the teacher to examine the content to be taught and to prioritize the most important concepts in each instructional unit. The Planning Pyramid recognizes that all students are capable of learning; however, not all students will learn all of the content that is covered.

There are two types of Planning Pyramids: elementary and secondary (see **Figures 6-1** and **6-2**). The base of the Elementary Planning Pyramid is considered the foundation of the lesson. The teacher identifies the essential information that all students need to learn. This section of the Pyramid is directed by the question, "What do I want *all* students to learn?" The middle section of the Pyramid represents information that *most* students are expected to learn. At this level of the Pyramid, the teacher would include supplementary

FIGURE 6-1

Elementary Planning Pyramid

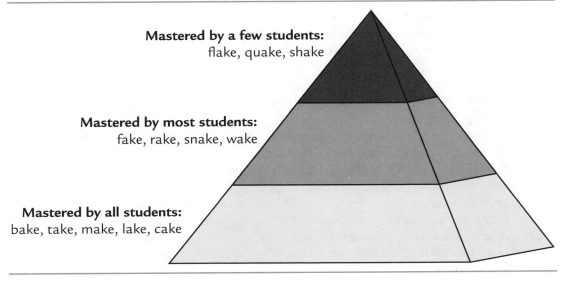

Mastered by a few students:
flake, quake, shake

Mastered by most students:
fake, rake, snake, wake

Mastered by all students:
bake, take, make, lake, cake

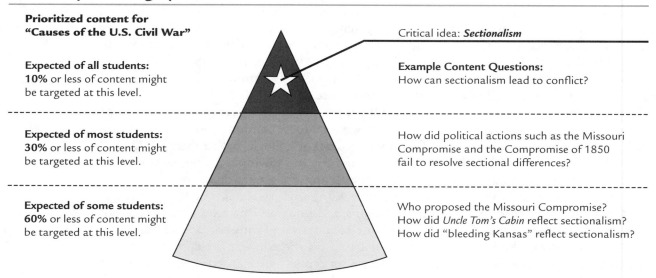

FIGURE 6-2

Secondary Planning Pyramid

**Prioritized content for
"Causes of the U.S. Civil War"**

Critical idea: *Sectionalism*

Expected of all students:
10% or less of content might
be targeted at this level.

Example Content Questions:
How can sectionalism lead to conflict?

Expected of most students:
30% or less of content might
be targeted at this level.

How did political actions such as the Missouri
Compromise and the Compromise of 1850
fail to resolve sectional differences?

Expected of some students:
60% or less of content might
be targeted at this level.

Who proposed the Missouri Compromise?
How did *Uncle Tom's Cabin* reflect sectionalism?
How did "bleeding Kansas" reflect sectionalism?

From Lenz, K. (2001). Smarter Planning: Considering Curriculum in Light of Standards-Based Reform. *Stratenotes,* 10. Lawrence, KS: University of Kansas.

facts and information about the concept introduced at the first level of the Pyramid. This section is directed by the question "What do I want *most* students to learn?" The top part of the Pyramid includes information that will expand the basic concepts and facts about the initial concept introduced. This information is geared towards those learners who demonstrate the desire to learn more about the concept. This section of the Pyramid is directed by the question "What information will a *few* students learn?"

The Secondary Planning Pyramid is the inversion of the Elementary Planning Pyramid. The pyramid is inverted since what is taught at the secondary level increasingly becomes more personalized. Students who master the critical ideas and content at the top level could be considered to be achieving "C" work. Those who master information at the middle and top level are thought of as attaining "B" work. Finally, students who achieve mastery of material at all levels are accomplishing "A" work.

The purpose of the Planning Pyramid is to assist teachers in organizing instructional lessons and identifying the Big Ideas to meet the needs of all learners. Teachers are cautioned to avoid using the Pyramid as a mechanism for segregating students into a particular level based on their academic ability. Additionally, all students should have equal access to information presented at all levels within the Pyramid (Vaughn, Bos, & Schumm, 1997). Figure 6-2 illustrates a Secondary Planning Pyramid using sectionalism as the content information.

Ms. Winters provides a spelling example using the elementary planning pyramid. She examines the set of 12 spelling words that will be presented to her students this week: bake, cake, fake, flake, lake, make, quake, rake, shake, snake, take, and wake. She identifies five of the words that every student, including her three students served in special education, will be expected to spell. These words are selected because they are common words within each student's spoken vocabulary and because each word consists of the -ake base and a single consonant. In addition to these five words, the class, with the exception of the students in special education, is expected to spell four additional words correctly. The additional words include ones that are less familiar, including one (snake) that introduces a consonant cluster. For six students who are more capable spellers,

FIGURE 6-3

Adapting the Curriculum

	Questions Regarding Curriculum Adaptation—Spelling	Examples
Select Level	Is the general education spelling curriculum appropriate for this student with regard to outcome knowledge and skills?	Use a set of spelling words from a lower grade in the general education series compared to an alternative set of materials.
Significance	Are the resources and instructional time required to master a curriculum element worthwhile for this student?	Skip selected words from the spelling lists because the student is unlikely to use them in everyday writing.
Supplement	Does the available curriculum provide sufficient appropriate activities for this student?	Supplement a student's spelling list with a couple of words that were misspelled when writing a story.
Size	Is the amount of curriculum content presented at one time appropriate for what this student can learn?	Reduce the number of spelling words on the weekly list from ten to five.

Ms. Winters presents three additional (bonus) words that are more abstract in meaning and require consonant clusters.

Although Miguel's goal in spelling is similar to a younger, average achiever, the general education teacher must consider how to incorporate the curriculum within her class. One approach teachers can use in deciding what to teach is to remember four basic ways of adapting the curriculum—the Four "Ss" (see **Figure 6-3**).

The initial phase of the Four Ss involves teachers making decisions on how to work through curriculum planning issues in determining what to teach students with mild disabilities. In regards to Miguel in spelling, the teacher decided not to *select* the same spelling words taught in the general education program. This was because Miguel had achieved little previous success in spelling and apparently had experienced a good deal of frustration learning new words. Instead, the teacher elected to choose a set of words he had used in his daily writing in her room because these words obviously had some functional importance to Miguel (note—the teacher also could have selected an appropriate commercially-developed spelling program to remediate Miguel's difficulties in spelling). An example of a traditional scope and sequence of curricular goals in spelling is shown in **Figure 6-4.**

Although teachers may not attend consciously to all four of the "Ss" for curriculum adaptation in deciding what to teach, their role is evident in planning. In the situation with Miguel, the teacher *selects* words such as "there" and "went" from his errors, rather than "Camp Wachahoochee" because of the *significance* of the words in everyday writing (she may want to include one or two of the words that Miguel thinks are significant). The teacher decides to start his list with words he uses the most and that he nearly gets correct. She further determines that five words at a time is an appropriate *size* for Miguel's spelling list. She notes which letter sounds or word structure are important for him to learn at this time. **Figure 6-5** shows an example of curriculum adaptation for a U.S. History lesson.

FIGURE 6-4

Curriculum Goals

Second-Grade Curricular Goals in Spelling

- Use correct spelling for frequently used sight vocabulary.
- Spell one-syllable words with short vowels (crack, split, splash).
- Spell one-syllable words that follow the silent-e pattern (plate, name, spoke).
- Spell one-syllable words with long-vowel combinations (rain, meat, boat).
- Use suffixes to make structural changes (s or es, ing, d or ed, er, est).

FIGURE 6-5

Curriculum Adaptation of a History Lesson

Example of Curriculum Planning in a U. S. History Class

The prospect of team teaching "Survey Level" ninth-grade U. S. History was going to present a new set of challenges to Mrs. Thomason. Her colleague, Jo Williams, the teacher of students with learning disabilities, was seated across the table from her, and now they had to decide on what was reasonable to teach to their class of 27 students—a combination of general curriculum (non-college preparatory) and special education adolescents. As they reviewed the text used by the other ninth-grade U. S. History classes, they discussed whether to select an alternative text for some or all of their students. Most history texts have very similar organizations (and a few actually come with multiple readability levels), so the teachers could have reasonably comparable groups while using two texts. On the other hand, they knew that even though both books would have a similar chapter structure, their students would be very aware of who was using the "dummy book" and who had the real text. They opted to maintain the same text. Also, upon reviewing the adopted text, they decided that the material was **structured** and presented in a sufficiently clear manner that they could adjust the content to fit their students. They did agree on several curricula adjustments which seemed appropriate. They decided that the size of the chapters was too long for most of their students to handle easily, so they planned to present segments of 5–6 pages at a time and to require mastery of only those sections of each chapter that were of **significance** to the overall mastery of the course objectives.

This would permit more able students to be exposed to the full range of content while holding the entire class responsible for the critical elements of the curriculum. This would reduce the **size** of the curricular content and allow them to emphasize mastery of the most important content as opposed to cursory coverage of the whole book. They also decided to **supplement** the text with a vocabulary study sheet for each chapter segment. The supplemental vocabulary sheet became a study sheet for preparing for quizzes on each segment.

Adapting Instruction

A critical component of providing instruction to students with mild disabilities in the general education classroom is the teacher's use of instructional principles that have been identified as contributing to student achievement. Effective instruction encompasses several broad areas:

- a focus on planning for instruction,
- increasing academic learning time,
- providing explicit instruction,
- attending to the students' current stage of learning.

Planning for Instruction

There is an increasing amount of knowledge in the world. It is easy for teachers to plan instruction in a manner that all too often leaves the student without having a good understanding of the information. As Pat Cross at the University of California, Berkley said "If it weren't for students impeding our progress in our race to the end of the term, we could certainly be sure of covering the material. The question, however, is not whether we as teachers can get to the end of the text or the end of the term, but whether our students are with us on that journey." The goal of teachers should be to determine what is most important to teach and to teach it well. One way teachers can remember how important it is to plan well is to use the **SMARTER** mnemonic (Lenz & Scanlon, 1998). The **SMARTER** mnemonic has teachers focus on what is most important to teach, to teach in an effective manner, and to reflect on what and how they taught.

- **S**elect critical content outcomes
- **M**ap out the content structures
- **A**nalyze learning difficulties
- **R**each enhancement decisions
- **T**each strategically
- **E**valuate content enhancements
- **R**eevaluate outcomes

There are numerous methods teachers can use to plan for instruction. Content Enhancement Routines have been validated as one such method general education and special education teachers can use to plan and adapt their instruction to meet the diverse needs of students. Content Enhancement Routines should be integrated into daily instruction of teachers. There are three types of Content Enhancement Routines (Deshler, Schumaker, Lenz, Bulgren, Hock, Knight, & Ehren, 2001):

1. organizing routines,
2. understanding routines,
3. recall routines.

All of the Content Enhancement Routines have graphic organizers, mnemonics to guide instruction, and are packaged for purchase. Many of the Content Enhancement Routines require the teacher to be trained by personnel associated with the Center for Research on Learning at the University of Kansas (www.kucrl.org). An example of each type of Content Enhancement Routines is provided below.

Organizing routines give teachers a way to arrange instruction around the "big picture" ideas and concepts. These routines provide students with a framework for understanding content, establishing relationships within the content, connecting content with previous and future content, and allowing students to self-monitor while learning. Organizing routines assist teachers in planning and developing lesson, unit, and course plans. The Unit Organizer Routine (Lenz, Bulgren, Schumaker, Deshler, & Boudah, 1994) is used to develop unit plans that focus student attention on the big ideas in a unit and how concepts within the unit relate to one another. The mnemonic device to teach the Unit Organizer Routine is **CRAFT:**

- **C**reate a context
- **R**ecognize content structures
- **A**cknowledge unit relationships
- **F**rame unit questions
- **T**ie content to tasks

"**C**reating a context" involves examining how the content in the unit is related to previous and future learning. "**R**ecognizing content structures" addresses how to conceptualize a structure to the unit information. "**A**cknowledge unit relationships" is concerned with exploring important relationships (i.e., compare and contrast) within the unit. "**F**raming the unit questions" deals with developing a list of essential questions that students should be able to answer after the unit has been taught. "**T**ie content to tasks" requires teachers to create a schedule of tasks to be completed during the unit and indicate how they connect to the unit content. **Figure 6-6** is a science example of a Unit Organizer.

Understanding Routines provide teachers with a means to make difficult concepts easier for students to understand. These routines allow teachers to assist students in comprehending and acquiring new content. One example is the Concept Mastery Routine (Bulgren, Deshler, & Schumaker, 1997). The Concept Mastery Routine allows teachers to better define, summarize, and explain key concepts in lessons. The mnemonic device for the Concept Mastery Routine is **CONCEPT:**

- **C**onvey the targeted concept
- **O**ffer the overall concept
- **N**ote key words
- **C**lassify characteristics
- **E**xplore examples and non-examples
- **P**ractice with a new example
- **T**ie down a definition

"**C**onvey the target concept" has teachers indicating the concept to be taught. A concept is a group or class into which happenings, thoughts, or items can be placed. "**O**ffer the overall concept" is the group or class into which the lesson concept can be placed. "**N**ote keywords" has the students and teachers brainstorm words associated with the lesson concept. "**C**lassify the characteristics" indicates where students group the characteristics which are related to the concept as always present, sometimes present, and never present. "**E**xplore examples and non-examples" requires students to identify instances that fit or do not fit. Examples are a word or phrase that can be described as possessing all of the always characteristics, none of the never characteristics, but could have some of the sometimes characteristics. Non-examples are a word or phrase that do not have all of the always characteristics and/or have one or more of the never characteristics. "**P**ractice with the new example" is a testing ground where the teacher can place a word or phase to carry out as an example or non-example. "**T**ie down the definition" has students list the lesson concept, the overall concept, and all of the always present characteristics. **Figure 6-7** is a math example of the Concept Mastery Routine.

FIGURE 6-6

The Unit Organizer

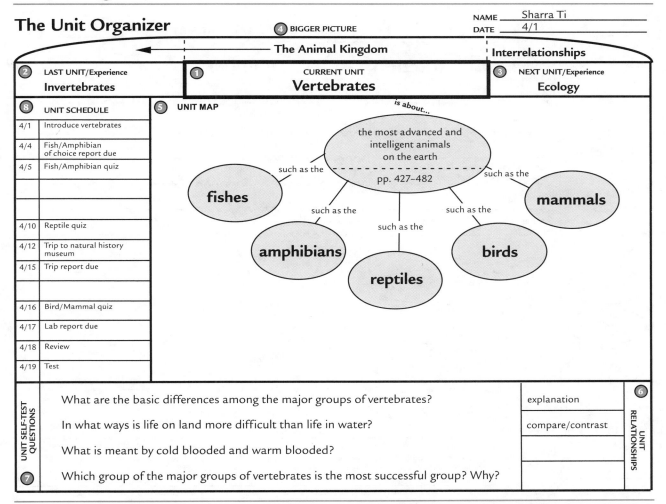

From Lenz, K. Bulgren, J.A., Schumaker, J.B., Deshler, D.D., & Boudah, D.A. (1994). *The Unit Organizer Routine.* Lawrence, KS: Edge Enterprises, Inc. Used with permission.

Recall Routines give teachers a method to increase student retention of critical content knowledge. An example of a recall routine is the Framing Routine (Ellis, 1998). The Framing Routine provides students with a method to take an abstract main idea and key topics into concrete representations. The mnemonic device for the Framing Routine is: **FRAME:**

- **F**ocus on the topic
- **R**eveal main ideas
- **A**nalyze details
- **M**ake a "So What?" statement
- **E**xtend understanding

"**F**ocus on the topic" has the students identify the key topic to be studied and provide a brief explanation of it. "**R**eveal main ideas" allows the students to identify subtopics

The Concept Mastery Routine

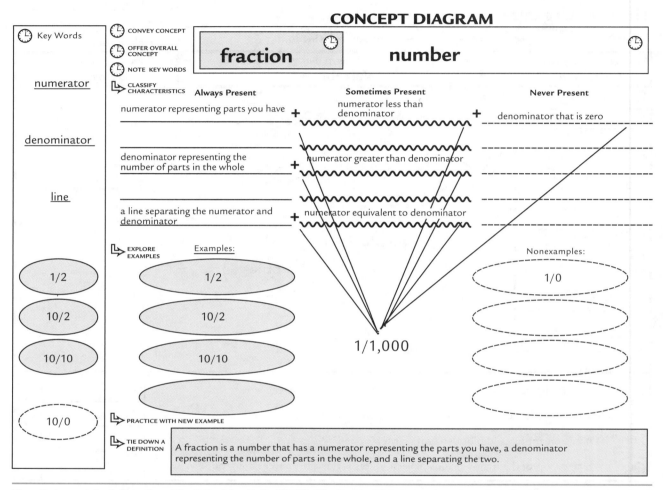

From Bulgren, J.A., Schumaker, J.B., & Deshler, D.D. (1998). *The Concept Mastery Routine.* Lawrence, KS: Edge Enterprises, Inc. Used with permission.

that comprise the key topic. The precise number of main ideas varies from one key topic to the next. "**A**nalyze the details" has students list the essential details to know and remember for each main idea. "**M**ake a so what statement" permits students to make a statement about how the current topic relates to the overall unit and how the topic might be used to understand real-world issues. "**E**xtend understanding" has students think about how the information might be connected with information beyond the current lesson. **Figure 6-8** is a social studies example of the FRAMING Routine.

Academic Learning Time

In preparing to work with students with mild disabilities, the key to promoting achievement among these students is the concept of Academic Learning Time (Berliner, 1987). Academic Learning Time means making certain that students are working on something that is directly related to what they need to learn and making the highest rate of correct responses possible during the time they are working on academic activities (Berliner, 1987; Walberg, 1988). Emphasis during planning and teaching is on having students

FIGURE 6-8

The FRAMING Routine

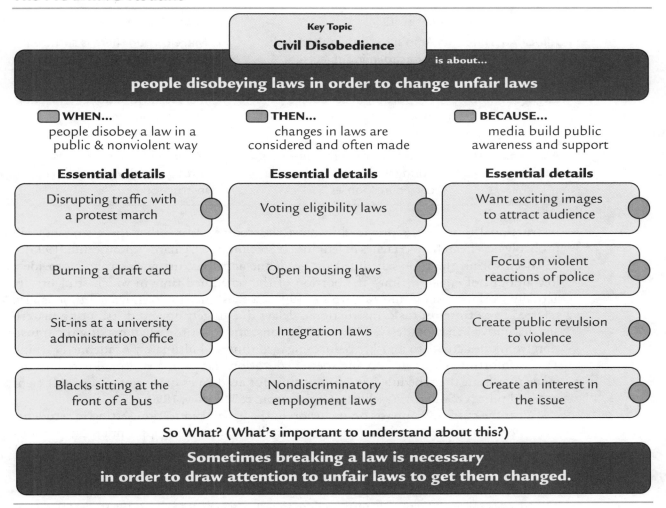

Key Topic
Civil Disobedience

is about...

people disobeying laws in order to change unfair laws

WHEN...
people disobey a law in a
public & nonviolent way

THEN...
changes in laws are
considered and often made

BECAUSE...
media build public
awareness and support

Essential details

Disrupting traffic with
a protest march

Burning a draft card

Sit-ins at a university
administration office

Blacks sitting at the
front of a bus

Essential details

Voting eligibility laws

Open housing laws

Integration laws

Nondiscriminatory
employment laws

Essential details

Want exciting images
to attract audience

Focus on violent
reactions of police

Create public revulsion
to violence

Create an interest in
the issue

So What? (What's important to understand about this?)

**Sometimes breaking a law is necessary
in order to draw attention to unfair laws to get them changed.**

From Ellis, E.S. (1998). *The Framing Routine.* Lawrence, KS: Edge Enterprises, Inc. Used with permission.

produce as many active, correct responses as possible to maximize academic achievement. With some students, special instructional procedures are needed to help them in making a high rate of correct responses. Some strategies used are appropriate for both general and special education classes.

Academic Learning Time (ALT) has several components (see **Figure 6-9**). One simple way to increase ALT is to assure sufficient time has been scheduled for the academic skill areas of concern. While it seems to be self-evident that teachers would plan most of the day to be devoted to academic activities, studies have revealed that students spend from 50 percent to 70 percent of class time allocated to instruction doing independent, non-teacher-directed (hand-off) activities (Adams, 1990). Classrooms that had an academic focus in which teachers actively instructed, frequently tested, and held students responsible for their work tended to result in higher achievement (Rosenshine, 1997). Unfortunately, in many classrooms nonacademic activities (e.g., activity periods, lunch counts, announcements, and planning nonacademic school activities) take away from the time allocated for academics (Baker & Zigmond, 1990). When the additional instructional needs of students with academic problems are considered, the limited amount of

FIGURE 6-9

Academic Learning Time

	What is it?	How can I increase it?
Allocated Time	• Amount of time scheduled for academic subjects.	• Make certain there is sufficient time scheduled for academic knowledge and skills.
Engaged Time	• Proportion of scheduled time in which students are on-task.	• Increase instructional efficiency through routines and management strategies.
Academic Learning Time	• Portion of the time-on-task during which students make correct responses.	• Maximize student success through briskly-paced direct instruction.

instructional time that is provided in most classrooms assures that these students will probably never catch up (Haynes & Jenkins, 1986; Simmons, Chard, & Kameenui, 1995).

Even within the time scheduled for academic activities, many classrooms provide a low amount of engaged time—the portion of the scheduled time in which students are actually working (Kameenui & Carnine, 1998; Rosenshine, 1997). Engaged time is also referred to as **time-on-task.** Instructional delays due to getting and distributing materials, disruptive behavior, delays in starting lessons, and lost time when making the transition from one activity to another reduce engaged time and ultimately Academic Learning Time. Unfortunately, even in many special education classes, instructional decisions are made that limit the scheduled amount of time for academics or do not ensure sufficient engaged time (O'Sullivan, Ysseldyke, Christenson, & Thurlow, 1990).

With the current emphasis on inclusion in the general education setting for students with special needs, teachers must possess the skills to implement appropriate adaptations of the classroom environment and instructional arrangements to increase academic engaged time. Montague, Bergeron, and Lago-Delello (1997) recommend the following strategies to increase academic engaged time for students with special needs:

1. provide explicit and direct instructions prior to task assignment to ensure the student understands the task directions;
2. provide frequent positive and corrective feedback during academic activities to monitor students' progress;
3. reduce task requirements and assign academic tasks that are commensurate with the students' ability levels to increase academic success and task completion; and
4. reinforce and reward students for task completion.

Finally, employing a systematic instructional approach that increases the students' rate of making active, correct responses promotes Academic Learning Time (Christenson, Ysseldyke, & Thurlow, 1989). The twin components of this idea, active and correct responding, are both important. Although many times classrooms are organized so that it appears an academic focus has been scheduled, and students are engaged, the at-risk learners may not be receiving effective instruction. A closer analysis of an apparently well-run class often reveals that some students working independently on worksheets or reading silently are unable to do the required work. As a result, in spite of appropriate scheduling and what appears to be on-task behavior, there are few correct responses, and in some cases, few responses at all. These students frequently are practicing errors, becoming increasingly frustrated and losing confidence in their ability to do the work. Yet in most classes, the core of the instructional day is set by teachers slavishly following the textbook (Simmons, Chard, & Kameenui, 1995).

Providing Explicit Instruction

Teachers who work effectively with students with disabilities frequently use an explicit instruction model of teaching that includes three main components:

1. demonstration and modeling,
2. guided practice, and
3. independent practice.

The explicit instruction model is considered a teacher-directed approach where the student is provided with specific instruction and guidance to learn the academic skills. To ensure that students are capable of producing correct responses, teachers first demonstrate exactly what the students are to do. They then help the student produce correct responses through ample opportunities for guided practice, and finally, they provide independent practice (Smith, 1989). When working with students with mild learning and behavior problems, what sets the special educator apart from regular educators, is the consistent, systematic manner in which instruction is delivered using the explicit instruction model. Three example lessons using explicit instructional components are presented in **Figures 6-10a, 6-10b,** and **6-10c.**

An explicit instructional model requires the teacher be actively involved in the presentation of instruction and checking student performance through both guided and

FIGURE 6-10A

Beginning Instruction on a Strategy to Study Spelling Words

Steps	What the teacher does . . .	What the student does . . .
Demonstration	The first thing I do when I begin to study a word is to look at the word, say the word, then say the word slowly as I trace my finger over each part of it. Watch and listen, "The word is **remember, re-mem-ber.**" I do this at least three times and then turn the paper over and write the word from memory. I check it by putting a line under each correct letter and repeat.	Points to the word with the teacher. Says the word with the teacher and traces word with the teacher. Then watches as the teacher writes it and checks each letter in the spelling.
Guided Practice	"Now look at the next word—member. You trace it three times and say it aloud while I come around to check how you are doing. Then see if you can write it correctly on the back of your paper. We will check it together." When everyone has finished the teacher says, "Now put a line under each letter as we check the spelling—m-e-m-b-e-r."	Students say "mem-ber" while tracing it. They repeat tracing and saying it three times and then write it from memory on the back of their paper. When the class is ready they underline each letter of the word they have written as the teacher says the letters.
Independent Practice	"Now, I want each of you to practice the rest of your spelling words by saying the word to yourself as you trace over the letters. Write the word on the back of your paper and check each letter."	The students trace the letters of each additional spelling word while saying the word to themselves, write the word, and check each letter.

FIGURE 6-10B

Beginning Instruction on Finding the Main Idea in Reading

Steps	What the teacher does . . .	What the student does . . .
Demonstration	Says, "When I look for the main idea of a paragraph, I first read the paragraph and then ask myself: • Is the first sentence the main idea because main ideas often come at the beginning? • Does the first sentence tell about the whole paragraph? • If not, can I find another sentence that might tell me the main idea?	Follows along pointing with a finger as the teacher reviews each sentence.
Guided Practice	After adequate demonstration, tell the student, "Now you try it. I will help you." The teacher checks understanding and guides the student as needed.	After reading a paragraph the student repeats what the teacher seemed to be saying, "I read the paragraph and then look at the first sentence to see if it's the main idea." The student continues through the paragraph.
Independent Practice	After sufficient correct responses, guided and corrected by the teacher, a work sheet containing independent work is assigned.	After guided practice, the student finds the main idea independently.

FIGURE 6-10C

Middle School Lesson on Remembering the Order of Doing Calculations

Steps	What the teacher does . . .	What the student does . . .
Demonstration	Teacher writes the mnemonic **Please My Dear Aunt Sally** on the overhead projector and then describes how the first letters of each word will help decide the order for doing computations, i.e., **P** = work inside the Parenthesis; then **M** = Multiply; then **D** = Divide; then **A** = Add; and finally **S** = Subtract. Then the teacher solves the problem.	Students write "Please My Dear Aunt Sally" at the top of the paper. Then students copy this problem: $(4 + 1) + 3 + (2 \times 4)$ and write the teacher's answer—"16".
Guided Practice	Observes students solving a parallel problem which requires the same order of operations as the demonstration problem. Gives corrective feedback when needed.	Works the problem assigned by the teacher numbering each step in order.
Independent Practice	Assigns a small set of practice problems with self-checking for the correct answers.	After guided practice, students work the practice problems while checking for accuracy.

independent practice. These steps are explained in the section that follows. Effective teachers begin lessons for students with disabilities by **telling** them the goal of each day's lesson and by relating how the new lesson applies to what had been learned previously (Englert, Tarrant & Mariage, 1992). This is done by reviewing the previous lesson, reflecting on why each lesson is important, and describing what the students should be able to do as a result of mastering the knowledge and skills to be presented. The teacher then makes connections with previously mastered content and may use an organizational framework to help **engage** their students (Ellis, Deshler, Lenz, Schumaker, & Clark, 1991). Engaging students also has a motivational aspect. It helps to ensure that students understand how this lesson will be important to them. By engaging each student, a teacher endeavors to promote the extent to which students value what is to be learned in the lesson and increase students' expectations of success (Adelman & Taylor, 1993).

As the actual teaching begins, effective teachers use strategies and techniques that support students in **acquiring** knowledge and skills. To do this a teacher needs to select teaching strategies that will maximize the probability of student success. Teachers do this by modeling or demonstrating the skills or how to access and use new knowledge. Often the instruction is multisensory so that learners have the opportunity to see real-life representations of what they are learning. For example, the teacher would show students how to count change beginning with adding the quarters first before expecting students to attempt the task. Teachers help students **acquire** knowledge and skills when they demonstrate the steps for doing a task or describe the thought processes they use when completing a task presented in the lesson (Smith, 1989). Active student responding, briskly paced activities with a high success rate (Rosenshine & Stevens, 1986) and corrective feedback (Englert, Tarrant, & Mariage, 1992) are used to ensure students' mastery (i.e., high Academic Learning Time) when acquiring new knowledge and skills.

As students begin working with new knowledge or on developing a new skill the effective teacher constantly **checks** on student performance and provides corrective feedback to guide students to make the correct responses. Through careful monitoring, a teacher both intervenes as soon as students experience difficulty as well as documents progress. The careful monitoring also allows the teacher to provide appropriate and immediate consequences—reinforcers or rewards for effort and success. Continued progress through an instructional sequence requires students to expect and value the consequences associated with doing the required work (Adelman & Taylor, 1993). Whether the consequences are externally controlled by the teacher (e.g., praise, tokens, or free time) or are intrinsically embedded within the task (e.g., the satisfaction of completing a story or solving a problem), teachers of students with disabilities must constantly examine whether the available consequences match individual student needs.

Finally, the teacher must consider the **hindrances** or difficulties to learning that might be unique to each student. A student's pattern of responses reveals how information is interpreted, and the observant teacher uses this information to plan for that student's special needs (Howell, & Nolet, 2000). The insight into what a student's errors indicate is a rich source of information about how to provide for individual instructional needs. One way to remember the steps for providing explicit instruction is to recall the letters that make up the key words in each step:

Tell the goal and purpose,
Engage the student in the learning, promote
Acquiring knowledge and skills, using effective teaching strategies,
Check student progress and provide appropriate
Consequences, and plan for
Hindrances in learning.
When the steps are put together, they spell TEACH.

FIGURE 6-11

TEACHing a History Lesson

TEACH Step	Activity in a history class
• Tells	"As we read this first section of our text on the pioneers moving west, I want you to understand what life was like on the trail for these settlers."
• Engage	"Before we begin to read, pretend that you are making the trip west across the frontier and list three things that you currently own that you would take with you. Take things that you want to have with you on the western frontier."
• Acquisition	"For my own list, I will write it and project it on the overhead projector."
• Checking and Consequences	"Brett, tell me what three items you wrote, and I will write them beside my list and show them on the overhead. Raise your hand for each item that matches the list that you made."
• Hindrances	"Don't worry about your spelling on the list, just put down your ideas."

Figure 6-11 shows an example of a **TEACH** lesson with a middle school student in a United States History class. Notice how the teacher demonstrates how he would start the assignment to help his students successfully do their work.

Providing Implicit Instruction

Implicit instruction is a self-regulated instructional approach where students are viewed as learners who actively help to set their own goals, monitor their classroom progress, use learning strategies, and reflect on and evaluate their progress and learning effectiveness. This approach is considered a student-directed approach where students are more responsible for their own learning in terms of self-monitoring and self-instruction. Learning is achieved by constructing new personal knowledge through linking prior knowledge with the new knowledge. To facilitate student learning, students make connections with authentic classroom activities and real-world problem solving (Schunk, 2000). The teacher's role is to provide learning situations that allow students to participate in connecting new knowledge to previous learning and to construct individual meanings. The effective teacher will provide meaningful learning experiences that are assessed with authentic (real life) assessments, provide the appropriate amount of support and guidance (often called scaffolding) through teaching, questioning, and explaining concepts necessary for students to build their own understanding.

Providing a Continuum of Instructional Choices

Today's classrooms include students with mild disabilities, high achievers, average achievers, low achievers, and culturally diverse learners. To address the needs of all students in a single classroom, teachers need to provide instruction along a continuum of explicit and implicit instruction. This continuum of instruction is based on the idea that effective teaching is a collaborative endeavor where the teacher provides students the support and guidance they need to achieve a goal efficiently. The combination of explicit and implicit instruction might range from having the teacher demonstrate how to do a task (more explicit), providing an outline of how to do a task, having students work in teams to do a task, providing students with a set of questions to guide doing a task to having students work independently on a task and then report back on what they discovered that was effective (more implicit) (Mercer & Mercer, 2006).

When selecting an instructional approach, Howell and Nolet (2000) suggest using an implicit approach when students have significant prior knowledge of the concept and have demonstrated consistent success with content. The implicit approach is useful when the task is well-defined, simple, and can be completed by a general problem-solving strategy with which the student is familiar. An explicit approach is more appropriate when the task is more complex, poorly defined, missing information, or requires a task-specific strategy for understanding. Additionally, explicit instruction should be used when the content is critical as a prerequisite skill for subsequent learning or when mastery learning is priority. Typically, our goal as teachers is to move students from more explicit (dependent on the teacher) to more implicit (student independence) teaching approaches.

Specific Instructional Adaptations

Students with mild disabilities may need adapted instruction in the areas of reading, written expression, and math. There are many research-based instructional strategies that are consistent with the model of effective instruction presented earlier in this chapter. Several of these strategies are described in this section of the chapter. The extent to which general educators make adaptation to accommodate the needs of students with mild disabilities (as well as other at-risk learners) is based primarily on how well the teachers view an intervention as fitting in the day-to-day classroom routine (Gersten & Woodward, 1990; Whinnery, Fuchs, & Fuchs, 1991). The degree of acceptability is based on several considerations:

- the perceived appropriateness of the intervention to the classroom,
- the amount of teacher time required,
- the teacher skill level required, and
- the possibility of any negative effects on other students.

Based on these considerations, a model has been provided for selecting interventions that takes into account three factors: Content, Control, and Efficiency. These three factors must be taken into account as decisions are made concerning appropriate interventions for students with mild disabilities in inclusive classrooms.

Focus of Interventions

When selecting interventions for students with mild disabilities, teachers must consider several questions. First, is the concern a management problem or an instructional problem? Management problems are those concerned with classroom behavior, social skills, and task completion. Instructional problems stem from students' difficulties in acquiring, maintaining, and generalizing academic skills. This review includes strategies for dealing with instructional problems. Readers who are interested in classroom management strategies should review the concepts in Chapter 11 Behavior Management of Students.

Control

Once the content of the problem has been determined, the teacher may choose to use interventions that are primarily either teacher-directed or student-directed. Teacher-directed interventions place the teacher at the center of the intervention. The teacher makes decisions regarding the strategy to be used, provides models and demonstrations of the strategy, directs students in practice, and monitors students' successful use of the strategy. These interventions are most appropriate when used at the acquisition stage of learning and have been demonstrated to be effective with students with mild disabilities (Mercer & Mercer, 2006).

Student-directed interventions place the student at the center of the intervention in which students are taught to use self-regulation procedures. Graham, Harris, and Reid (1993) define self-regulation as an individual's ability to regulate his or her own behavior. Self-regulation training is an appealing means of promoting independent academic and behavioral improvement in inclusive settings (Garner, 1992). Learning to use self-regulation procedures often increases task engagement, which in turn facilitates learning and also may decrease off-task behavior (Harper, Maheady, Mallette, & Karnes, 1999). More importantly, self-regulation techniques enable learners to monitor and regulate their own academic performance.

Efficiency

The final factor to be considered when selecting interventions is efficiency. Efficiency is a principal concern in the general education environment due to the large number of students served in the classroom. Interventions that require implementation with individual students are extremely time-intensive for the teacher and may need to be considered as a last resort. Interventions that are either small-group or whole-class centered typically provide a more efficient means of instruction. The decision regarding the choice between individual, small-group, or whole-class interventions often depends on the severity of the problem. As teachers determine whether to implement teacher-directed or student-directed strategies, they must also determine the appropriateness of implementing the strategies with the whole class, a small group, or individually (Keel, Dangel, & Owens, 1999).

Teacher-Directed vs. Student-Directed Interventions

The choice to use teacher-directed (explicit) or student-directed (implicit) approaches need not be an either/or decision. Typically the most effective approach for students with learning problems is to start with a blend of relatively more teacher-directed interventions followed by those with a more student-directed emphasis. The research evidence shows that teacher-directed methods are powerful tools for teaching and managing students with learning and behavior problems (Gersten, 1998). These must be included in the arsenal of techniques used in inclusive settings. There also is a complimentary role for student-directed techniques. Teacher-directed interventions emphasize how teachers think about, adapt, and present critical content to all students in a learner-friendly approach. Student-directed interventions include the skills and strategies needed to learn the content (Deshler, Schumaker, Lenz, Bulgren, Hock, Knight, & Ehren, 2001). When practice beyond initial mastery and generalization to other tasks is important, student-directed techniques are a viable option in providing focused practice and drill. Peer tutoring, technology-mediated instruction, and self-regulation strategies offer useful procedures for application that incorporate a student-centered focus.

Educators should be guided in their selection of these tools by their knowledge of the instructional principles that have proven to be effective for students with disabilities. For example, a review of validated practices for teaching students with mild disabilities by Fisher, Schumaker, and Deshler (1995) provides an excellent foundation for examining and selecting instructional procedures for promoting learning in inclusive settings. These authors identified validated inclusive practices that benefit most, if not all, students in a class, which can be embedded within the general education curriculum, and are practical in terms of time and implementation. Such characteristics should be part of both teacher-directed and student-directed programs.

Teacher-Directed Interventions

There are many teacher-directed interventions that have been demonstrated to be effective with students with mild disabilities and those identified as at-risk for disabilities. As stated earlier, few studies have actually been conducted in inclusive classrooms; therefore, this section reviews interventions that may be appropriately used in inclusive classrooms. The interventions reviewed here may be implemented either with the whole class or in small groups. The teacher-directed interventions described below are appropriate for general application for students with learning problems. Other teacher-directed interventions are presented in Chapters 7 and 8.

Direct Instruction

Direct Instruction is a system of teaching that has been demonstrated to be effective with a range of students (Adams & Engelmann, 1996) including those who have been considered to be disadvantaged and those with mild disabilities (Darch, 1991; Kozioff, LaNunziata, Cowardin, & Bessellieu, 2001). The components of direct instruction include explicit step-by-step teaching procedures that account for student mastery, immediate feedback, practice, and a gradual fading from teacher direction. Direct instruction programs are available across a wide variety of subject areas including reading, mathematics, written language and reasoning skills, oral language, and spelling. See Chapters 7 and 8 for a detailed discussion of direct instruction.

Story Maps

Story mapping is a technique used to provide or build upon prior knowledge to assist students in interpreting and comprehending new information (Mathes, Fuchs, & Fuchs, 1997). This technique can effectively guide students through text and assist in reading comprehension by providing an organization of text structure. Mathes, et al. (1997) successfully used story maps to teach reading comprehension of narrative stories within cooperative learning groups. Each cooperative learning group is comprised of four students with varying skill levels ranging from low achieving to high achieving. During the initial class session, all students read the same story. In subsequent class sessions, students work in groups to map the story. The first two minutes of the mapping activity are devoted to skimming the story silently to remind the students of the details of the story. The next 15 to 20 minutes are devoted to completing the maps in cooperative groups.

The maps are comprised of identifying the main character, setting, problem, and outcome. Each student in the group is assigned to be the "leader" for one of the story elements to be identified. Students are taught the "leader routine" using a prompt card with cues for each step of the routine. The routine consists of five steps:

1. *Tell*—the leader tells the answer first for a specific story part,
2. *Ask*—the leader asks other students to share their answers,
3. *Discuss*—the leader guides the group members to discuss the story part,
4. *Record*—the leader records the group's answer, and
5. *Report*—the leader reports the group's answer to the rest of the class.

It is very important to prepare students by familiarizing them with the purpose of the story map and how to correctly use the tool. The teacher may spend a number of days reading narratives, stopping at points in the stories that pertain to the individual components of the story map. The teacher can then ask students to identify which component the particular portion of the text relates to, thus allowing for immediate feedback. Eventually, students will independently fill out the story map with decreased prompting. A sample story map is displayed in **Figure 6-12.**

FIGURE 6-12

Story Map

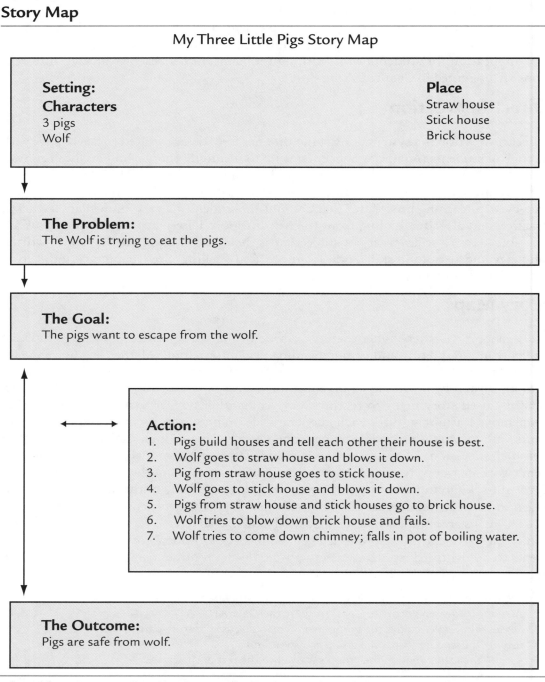

My Three Little Pigs Story Map

Setting:
Characters
3 pigs
Wolf

Place
Straw house
Stick house
Brick house

The Problem:
The Wolf is trying to eat the pigs.

The Goal:
The pigs want to escape from the wolf.

Action:
1. Pigs build houses and tell each other their house is best.
2. Wolf goes to straw house and blows it down.
3. Pig from straw house goes to stick house.
4. Wolf goes to stick house and blows it down.
5. Pigs from straw house and stick houses go to brick house.
6. Wolf tries to blow down brick house and fails.
7. Wolf tries to come down chimney; falls in pot of boiling water.

The Outcome:
Pigs are safe from wolf.

Adapted from Group story mapping: A comprehension strategy for both skilled and unskilled readers. By L. Idol, 1987, *Journal of Learning Disabilities,* 20, p. 199.

FIGURE 6-13

Math Concept Map

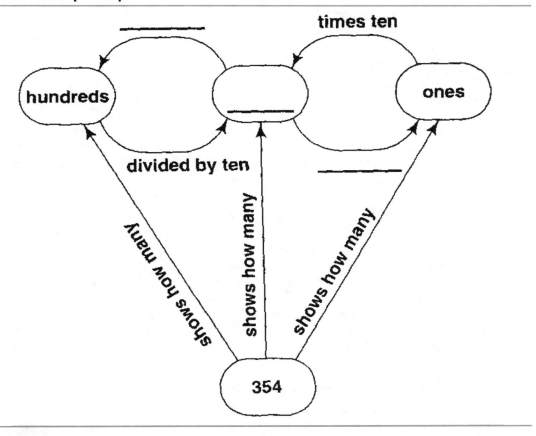

Concept Mapping

Additionally, concept mapping and graphic organizers are useful in helping students with disabilities demonstrate mathematics knowledge while requiring fewer verbal skills. Concept mapping requires the student to write a concept on paper then show relationships with lines by linking words (usually verbs) (Ashlock, 2005). **Figure 6-13** demonstrates a teacher-made concept map. It is important for students to describe their mathematical thinking on paper not only for diagnosis of improper thinking, but it aids in focusing the student on relationships.

Advance Organizers

An advance organizer is a verbal or written technique used to provide students with an overview or preview of material to be presented. It is intended to activate prior knowledge concerning a particular topic as well as provide information concerning the material that is to be presented (Ausubel, Novak, & Hanesian, 1978). When teachers use advance organizers there is an increase in comprehension of critical concepts during content area instruction (Darch & Gersten, 1986). An effective advance organizer

- informs the student of the purpose of the organizer;
- clarifies the actions of both the teacher and student;

- identifies and explains the topics;
- identifies subtopics and concepts that need to be addressed;
- provides background information;
- provides rationales for teaching the lesson;
- introduces unfamiliar terms or words;
- provides an organizational framework; and
- states desired results of the lesson.

An example of using an advance organizer is this example called a "concept diagram" (Bulgren, Schumaker, & Deshler, 1988). First, the teacher selects a specific idea or concept to be taught (e.g., mammal). Next, the teacher prepares a list of critical words or phrases directly related to the concept (i.e., warm-blooded, fur/hair, live births, etc.). Then the items are categorized into non-examples and examples of the key concept (horses, chickens, frogs, people). Finally, the teacher completes a Concept Diagram by inserting these items into the appropriate areas on the diagram. This routine includes providing an advance organizer; allowing students to supply a list of key words in relation to the lesson; naming and defining the concept; discussing "always (has hair)," "sometimes (has a tail)," and "never (has scales)" characteristics of the concept; discussing one example and one non-example of the concept; linking each to the characteristics; evaluating possible examples and non-examples to decide if they are components of the concept; and providing a post-organizer.

Advance organizers can assist students in activating their prior knowledge about a topic, provide information about the topics and tasks to be covered during a lesson, and provide structure for the class period (Lenz, Alley, & Schumaker, 1987). There are twelve components that may be incorporated in effective advance organizers:

- Inform the learner of the purpose of the advance organizer.
- Clarify the task's physical parameters in terms of actions to be taken by the teacher.
- Clarify the task's physical parameters in terms of actions to be taken by the student.
- Identify the topic of the learning task.
- Identify subtopics related to the task.
- Provide background information.
- State the concepts to be learned.
- Clarify the concepts to be learned.
- Motivate students through rationales.
- Introduce or repeat new terms or words.
- Provide an organizational framework for the learning task.
- State the outcomes desired as a result of engaging in the learning activity (p. 56).

Advance organizers may be either verbal or written. For example, when introducing a unit on safety in the home, one teacher might use a verbal advance organizer: *"Today, we will begin a unit on safety in the home. We will talk about several different topics: first, we'll talk about common household accidents and how to prevent them, second, we'll talk about ways to keep your home safe from intruders, and finally we'll discuss safe ways to exit your home in case of a fire. During each topic area, you'll apply the information we discuss to your own house. At the end of the unit, you will have a household safety manual specifically designed for your own home."* Another teacher might provide the advance organizer in the form of an outline of main topics. Students fill in the outline with information gained from the lectures and discussions.

Mastery Learning

The concept of mastery learning was proposed as a means of assuring that student achievement served as the criterion to move ahead with instruction (Bloom, 1982). The concept of mastery learning contends that nearly all students can meet the instructional demands of the curriculum *if given sufficient time.* While it seems self evident that the teacher should not go on to new material until the students have mastered the lessons that have been presented, there is much current evidence that teachers plan instruction based on covering the material rather than on making certain that students have learned the material (Vaughn, Bos, & Schumm, 1997). Teachers who implement a mastery learning approach carefully monitor students' progress with regular progress checks. This is done by using either testing or homework, modifying the pace of instruction based on student progress, and planning for more opportunities for instruction and practice for students who appear to need more instructional time. The difficulty faced by teachers who use a mastery learning approach is learning to juggle the additional time needed by students who are less efficient learners with the pressures to get through the book in a fixed amount of time. One way to use mastery learning in a general education classroom is to combine it with the Planning Pyramid, described earlier in this chapter.

> **Although Ms. Winters only expects Miguel to master five of the new spelling words (compared to the 12 words expected of her most capable students), she has him continue to practice those words until they have been mastered (rather than just spending a week on each set of words regardless of the level of mastery).**

Student-Regulated Interventions

In contrast to teacher-directed interventions, student-directed interventions focus on helping students learn to plan and evaluate the effectiveness of their classroom performance. Factors such as the ability to set realistic goals and plans, to deal with frustration, to overcome problems, and to be persistent are related to successful post-school adjustment (Spekman, Goldberg, & Herman, 1992; Werner, 1993). To assist students in developing a more self-directed outlook, educators and students might benefit from considering the following recommendations:

- begin by focusing on a content area which the student is committed to improving;
- establish with the student a well-defined goal that is easily monitored;
- emphasize self-monitoring some part of behavior related to the goal;
- establish and teach a routine for working on the goal that includes responses that are correct with abundant repetition to promote early success;
- assist students in over-learning the steps of the routine to assure application;
- teach routines that are content specific with clear applications to the student problem to ensure the likelihood of generalization;
- reduce the content difficulty during the initial stages of establishing the program so the student can focus on aspects of self-regulation, such as self-monitoring and self-instruction, rather than the curriculum; and
- include a focus on attribution from the beginning of the student's work by emphasizing the link between commitment, effort, and progress (Schunk, 2000).

Student-Regulated Task Engagement

Effective student-directed interventions in task engagement involve skills related to having students stay on task and complete their work. The skills fall into five areas:

- goal setting,
- self-management,
- self-instruction,
- self-monitoring or self-recording, and
- self-reinforcement (see **Figure 6-14**) (Nelson, Smith, Young, & Dodd, 1991).

A key aspect of what a student learns to do is to postpone an immediate reward in return for a more appropriate (and hopefully more satisfying) reward at a later time. Self-regulation of behavior involves identifying behavioral alternatives (continuing to work), choosing reinforcers for the behavioral alternatives, and managing the delivery of delayed consequences (teacher praise or a good grade).

Self-monitoring and self-recording have been demonstrated in a number of studies to improve classroom behavior of students in special education programs. For example, self-monitoring has been shown to increase on-task behavior of students served in programs for mild disabilities. This was done for three separate groups of four students each within a special class. The teacher used a set of audiotapes to cue students to record whether or

FIGURE 6-14

Student-regulated Strategies

Student-regulated Strategies	Characteristics of Strategies
• Goal setting	• Students are given the option of setting personal goals for accuracy and often prioritize objectives.
	• For example, "My goal is to improve from 65% to 80% correct on the weekly spelling test."
• Self-management	• Students organize themselves by identifying elements that are difficult and easy.
	• For example, "I think I know all 6 times tables, but I need to practice the 7 times tables some more."
• Self-instruction	• Students use "self-talk" steps in learning how to do a procedure.
	• For example, "To help me follow directions, first I read the directions to myself, then I underline the words that tell me what to do, then when I finish, I check to be sure that I did it correctly."
• Self-monitoring and recording	• Students identify the frequency with which target behaviors occur and use charts and graphs to show changes in performance.
	• For example, "I will color in the bar graph that shows the number of facts I got correct on my timed math drill."
• Self-reinforcement	• Students accept responsibility for rewarding themselves for the occurrence of target behaviors.
	• For example, "Because I met my goal of 80% on the spelling test, I will choose to do my new words on the computer."

not they were on task. The cues consisted of the verbal cue "Record" and were provided at approximately 10-minute intervals. During the intervention phases, students marked a monitoring sheet with a "+" or "0" to indicate whether they had been on-task. The teacher checked on-task performance at intervals between the verbal cues. Students' on-task behavior increased to between 80 percent and 91 percent for the students in this study (Blick & Test, 1987).

The efficacy of a self-recording strategy has been demonstrated when applied to a broader array of behaviors. Four middle school students who were receiving special educational services in a resource room were taught to use a self-recording procedure to promote a set of discrete behaviors (Clees, 1994–95). General education mathematics teachers identified the students as not meeting the teachers' expectations for appropriate behavior and having deficient organization skills. Specific target behaviors were developed with the assistance of general educators in social studies and science and included on a brief checklist:

- Brings necessary materials to class,
- Begins class on-task,
- Turns in completed homework,
- Completes all class work, and
- Writes homework in assignment book.

Students were trained to self-record whether their behavior in class had met the teacher's expectation statement. Training took 10 to 15 minutes per student. After the training students were instructed to keep track of what they needed to do by taking the form containing the schedule of teachers' expectations to each class and completing it and turning it in to the special education teacher at the end of the day. Students simply marked "yes" or "no" as to whether each of the five expectations was met. The attractiveness of this self-recording approach is its effectiveness and efficiency. Not only did the students' behavior improve across general education classes on behaviors that the general educators themselves identified as problems, but the procedure also required little training time, maintained the behavior change after the intervention was ended, and required only minimal participation by general educators (see **Figure 6-15**).

Self-monitoring, self-evaluation/self-reinforcement, and self-instruction have been used to reduce inappropriate verbalizations with junior high students. Self-monitoring involved making tally marks on one side of an index card for appropriate verbalizations and on the other side for inappropriate verbalizations. The self-evaluation/self-reinforcement strategy required students to ask, "How is this working out? How am I doing?" When students thought they were doing well, they were instructed to tell themselves, "I'm doing a great job." Self-instruction training involved the teacher first demonstrating for students and then having students overtly then covertly repeat a series of self-instruction commands (i.e., "Do I understand what I'm working on? What don't I understand? Should I raise my hand or talk out loud?"). The resultant drop in inappropriate verbalizations indicated the training was effective. Combining self-monitoring and self-instruction enhanced the improvement for these students (DiGangi & Maag, 1992).

Self-monitoring also can be used to improve academic performance. For example, students with learning problems used a student-directed intervention to improve spelling in a general education class. They listened to their spelling words using cassette players with headsets while they looked at the words printed in a column. The students then folded the column so the words could not be seen, listened to the tape with the words again, and stopped the tape while attempting to write each word in the second column. At the end of the list, the students checked whether each word in the second column was

FIGURE 6-15

Sample Self-monitoring Charts

Did I remember to:	Mon	Tue	Wed	Thu	Fri
Arrive at class on time?	✓	✓	✓		
Bring my books and pencil?	✓	—	✓		
Complete my homework?	✓	✓	✓		
Sit in my assigned seat?	—	✓	✓		
(Your choice)					

In doing my math did I . . .	Yes/No
Check the operation sign before starting?	✓
Line up the numbers in my columns?	✓
Begin solving in the ones column?	✓
Check my work?	—
Write my numbers neatly?	✓

spelled correctly and used proofreading marks to correct each error and write the corrected spelling in the third column. Words spelled correctly in the second column were given a checkmark in the third column. Students continued to practice spelling and self-correcting their work until the end of the period. This self-directed procedure resulted in more words spelled correctly and higher grades on the weekly spelling test when using the self-directed method. The students indicated they preferred this approach to the traditional method of study (Wirtz, Gardner, Weber, & Bullara, 1996).

Another form of student-directed work is to have students sort elements to be learned in groups. This self-management strategy can be done in several ways. For work that involves discrete elements (e.g., vocabulary words or names of presidents), putting the material to be learned on cards and grouping it into hard and easy piles helps students to focus more attention on the difficult ("hard") work (Dangel, 1989). The same sorting can be done for those elements that are relatively more or less important or more or less familiar. The emphasis here is to assist students to direct themselves to focus more effort on the parts of a task that are difficult and less on the task elements that are easy—something that efficient learners already do.

Another way to monitor individual student progress is the use of **student-directed strategies.** A student-directed (or self-mediation) strategy is one in which students are taught to take responsibility for monitoring and recording their own progress. Students may be taught self-directed strategies to monitor their work habits in class, checking their work, and monitoring and charting the progress (see **Figure 6-15**).

In addition to self-monitoring, students record and chart the results of their work to show themselves (and their teacher) the progress they have made in working toward their goal. Charts might show the number of things a student remembered to do, the number of words spelled correctly, or the percent of problems answered correctly. Once taught, these strategies also should assist students to function more independently in the regular education classroom.

Student-Regulated Instruction

There are other self-regulation interventions implemented within general education that can effectively promote the achievement of students with disabilities. These include Self-Regulated Strategy Development (SRSD), ITFITS, PLEASE, RPF-HECC, TELLS Fact or Fictions, and Learning Strategies from the Center for Research on Learning (Danoff, Harris, & Graham, 1993).

Self-Regulated Strategy Development (SRSD) is a cognitive strategy instructional program in which elements of self-regulation (i.e., goal setting, self-instruction, self-monitoring, and self-evaluation) are taught within the context of instruction in story writing. The instruction is intended for the whole class with emphasis on learning and applying a multi-step strategy involving generating a story, including specific story elements, and putting the story on paper. A mnemonic guides students to include important story elements: **Who** (main character), **When** (timeframe for the story), **Where** (location), **What=2** (What does the main character want and What happens?), and **How=2** (How does it end and How does the character feel?). Explicit instruction and modeling of the strategy are critical elements in the program. Students are led from a teacher-directed format to one in which they work collaboratively, then independently, set goals and use self-instruction and self-monitoring to practice and master the strategy (Danoff, Harris, & Graham, 1993).

A teaching approach such as SRSD is important for several reasons. First, it is a systematic strategy that is introduced and taught within a general education classroom in the context of the general education curriculum. Second, students with disabilities and their normally achieving classmates who are taught the strategy have demonstrated significant improvement in their ability to compose stories. Third, the self-regulation skills and strategy are taught within a content area so that no separate instruction is needed to apply these skills in an isolated instruction context, such as a resource room. Teachers using SRSD have been successful at promoting the goal of systematically moving from effective teacher-directed instruction to student-directed instruction. Teachers begin by explicitly modeling and teaching how to write, teaching strategy use, correcting written work, and gradually withdrawing direct teacher instruction as students become increasingly independent with each part of the writing process (Graham & Harris, 1994). The process moves from an emphasis on teacher-directed multiple opportunities for correct responses and students memorizing steps in the strategy to student-directed strategy implementation and self-monitoring.

Another example of applying strategies to content areas is called **IT FITS.** This strategy has been used to help students in special education learn science terms and definitions when using the keyword mnemonic approach IT FITS. Groups of students are taught to:

- **I** (Identify the term),
- **T** (Tell the definition of the term),
- **F** (Find a keyword),
- **I** (Imagine the definition by doing something with the keyword),
- **T** (Think about the definition doing something with the keyword), and
- **S** (Study what you imagined until you know the definition).

Students learn and retain more definitions when taught the terms and definitions in a systematic manner (King-Sears, Mercer, & Sindelar, 1992).

The **PLEASE** strategy is used to improve students' ability to write paragraphs (Welch, 1992). This strategy is effective in increasing understanding of written expression for student with learning difficulties. The strategy teaches students to:

- **P** (Pick a topic, audience, and appropriate textual format);
- **L** (List ideas concerning the topic);
- **E** (Evaluate the list);
- **A** (Activate the paragraph using a topic sentence);
- **S** (Supply sentences to support the topic);
- **E** (End the paragraph with a concluding sentence) and **E** (Evaluate the finished product)).

A different view of training self-regulation skills comes from research on developing strategies for solving problems in mathematics and shows that middle school students can successfully use the strategy to solve multiple-step word problems. The cognitive strategy **RPV-HECC** includes direct instruction on these steps:

- **Read** (for understanding),
- **Paraphrase** (your own words),
- **Visualize** (a picture or diagram),
- **Hypothesize** (a plan to solve the problem),
- **Estimate** (predict the number),
- **Compute** (do the arithmetic), and
- **Check** (make sure everything is right).

TELLS Fact or Fiction is a guided comprehension tool used to prepare students for approaching reading assignments. In teaching students to use TELLS Fact or Fiction, the teacher trains them to study these elements:

- **T** (Title);
- **E** (Examine the text to determine the theme);
- **L** (Look for words that appear to be important);
- **L** (Look for words that appear to be difficult);
- **S** (Identify the Setting);
- and finally, to decide whether the story is **Fact or Fiction.**

For example, before reading a passage, the teacher might have the students answer a question concerning one of the previous steps, such as "What does the title tell you about the story?" The teacher continues in this fashion until each step is completed. According to Sorrell (1990), a teacher may need to reserve approximately 15 minutes for this portion of the lesson.

SQ3R often is taught to students working in content area texts, such as science or social studies. Students talk themselves through the steps of the SQ3R strategy. It assists students in identifying key points and vocabulary, paraphrasing reading passages, and identifying the overall theme of text content. First, the students **S**urvey the chapter by scanning the chapter to understand what the chapter is about. Secondly, the students rephrase the headings in the chapter as **Q**uestions. At the **R**ead stage, students read the chapter to answer the questions they posed. They then focus on **R**eciting back to themselves the answers to their own questions without referring back to the passage. Lastly, during the **R**eview step the students review the material to ensure retention of information (Robinson, 1961). By using this self-instructional strategy, the student can work more independently of the teacher.

Learning Strategies, like Content Enhancement Routines discussed earlier in this chapter, have been developed and packaged by professors at the Center for Research on Learning (Schumaker & Deshler, 2005). Numerous learning strategies have been developed to help students acquire, store, and express or demonstrate their knowledge. Specifically, strategies have been developed for reading, studying and remembering information, writing, improving assignment and test performance, effectively interacting with others, motivation, and math. All of the strategies follow a common instructional sequence:

- Pretest and make commitments
- Describe the strategy
- Model the strategy
- Verbal elaboration and rehearsal
- Controlled practice and feedback
- Advanced practice and feedback
- Confirm acquisition and make generalization commitment

The **"pretest and make commitments"** stage requires the teacher to motivate students to learn the strategy and establish a baseline of student knowledge. This necessitates that the teacher assesses the student's current way of learning through a pretest, explain to the student why the strategy is needed, and has the student commit to learning the strategy. The **"describe the strategy"** stage involves teaching the overt and covert processes and steps of the new learning strategy. During this stage, the students compare the new strategy to the old strategy they were using while the teacher describes the overall strategic processes and steps used. The **"model the strategy"** stage has the teacher demonstrate the cognitive behaviors and overt physical responses in the strategy. During this stage, the teacher models the strategy by "thinking aloud" for the student and showing how the strategy is used. The **"verbal elaboration and rehearsal"** stage focuses on ensuring the comprehension of the strategy. Students verbally practice the strategy and the associated mnemonic to an automatic level. The **"controlled practice and feedback"** stage provides students with an opportunity to practice the strategy using below grade level materials with the goal of building confidence and fluency. At this stage, the responsibility for the strategy is gradually shifted to the student. The **"advanced practice and feedback"** stage gives students strategy practice using grade-appropriate materials. This provides students with the first step toward increasing their access to the general education curriculum. The **"post-test"** stage allows the teacher to confirm what the student has learned. The data from the pretest is compared to the posttest. The **"confirm acquisition and make generalization commitment"** stage requires students to take the knowledge they have learned to other settings like the general education classroom. During this stage students make a commitment to use the strategy in other settings and adapt it as needed. See **Figure 6-16** for a visual depiction of these instructional strategies.

Below are examples of three strategies that have been developed. Acquisition, storage, and expression and demonstration strategy examples are provided. A mnemonic is provided for each that summarizes the steps that students learn for each strategy.

An example of an acquisition strategy is the **Word Identification Strategy** (Lenz & Hughes, 1990). This strategy gives students an effective and efficient method to decode and identify unknown words. The strategy is based on the idea that the English language is made up of common prefixes, suffixes, and stems. The mnemonic for this strategy is **DISSECT:**

FIGURE 6-16

8-Step Instructional Procedure Diagram

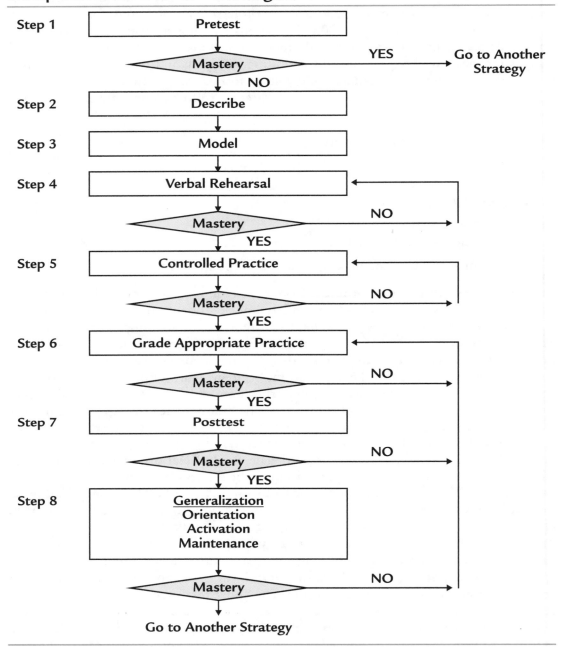

From Ellis, E.S., Deshler, D.D., Lenz, B.K., Schumaker, J.B., & Clark, F.L. (1991). An instructional mode for teaching learning strategies. *Focus on Exceptional Children, 23* (6), 1–24.

- **D**iscover the context of the word
- **I**solate the prefix
- **S**eparate the suffix
- **S**ay the stem
- **E**xamine the stem
- **C**heck with someone if unsure
- **T**ry the dictionary if needed

An example of a storage strategy is the **FIRST-Letter Mnemonic strategy** (Nagel, Schumaker, & Deshler, 1986). This strategy helps students who need to study large amounts of information for mastery. Students develop a list of information to learn, produce labels for each set of information, create a mnemonic for each set of information often based on the first letter of the word, place the information on a card, and then use the cards to study. The mnemonic for this strategy is **FIRST:**

- **F**orm a word from the sets of information
- **I**nsert a letter(s) in the word if needed
- **R**earrange the letters from the sets of information if needed
- **S**hape (make) a sentence if steps 1–3 were not effective
- **T**ry combinations of steps 1–4

An example of an expression and demonstration strategy is the **Test-taking Strategy** (Hughes & Schumaker, 1991). This strategy is used while students take tests in their classrooms. Students learn to manage their time, set priorities for taking the test, read test questions carefully, make educated guesses, and monitor their own test behavior. The mnemonic for this strategy is **PIRATES:**

- **P**repare to succeed by allotting time and starting in 2 minutes
- **I**nspect the instructions by underlining what to do and where to respond
- **R**ead the whole question, remember what you studied, reduce the choices
- **A**nswer the question or abandon it for the moment
- **T**urn back to questions skipped
- **E**stimate or guess in an educated manner
- **S**urvey the test for mistakes

Collaborative Strategies

Most teaching in general education classrooms is focused on the students as a single group, rather than addressing the needs of individual students (Schumm & Vaughn, 1992). This tendency is especially true in middle schools and high schools where teachers often view their responsibility as conveying content (i.e., history, science, English, or mathematics) rather than instructing students (Nolet & Tindal, 1994). The tendency to focus on group instruction and delivering content results in serious instructional risks for students

1. who learn more slowly,
2. who lack the background necessary to readily understand and apply the instruction, due to social or cultural reasons,
3. who are not as motivated as others to learn what is taught, due to previous school failures or background experiences, and
4. who may learn in a different manner than the large group model in which the teacher talks and students listen.

There are several ways in which classroom teachers can modify how instruction is delivered. The procedures move from large group strategies to one-on-one approaches. **Figure 6-17** summarizes these procedures.

Collaborative strategies, such as cooperative learning and peer tutoring are recommended as a means to increase achievement of students with academic difficulties by promoting interdependence among a group of heterogeneous students (Harper, Mallette, Maheady, Parkes, & Moore, 1993; Slavin, 1996). Cooperative learning strategies require

FIGURE 6-17

Student Grouping Options

Instructional Delivery	Advantages	Disadvantages
Whole class grouping	Easiest way to teach. Sense of teacher control.	Least effective, especially for students with learning difficulty.
Collaborative student groups	More effective in promoting student learning than whole class teaching.	Must train students in how to collaborate. Classroom is more active and noisy.
Peer Tutoring (one-to-one students)	More learning, especially for students with learning difficulties. Better able to monitor student progress.	Requires training of tutors. Is most effective in learning skills subjects, e.g., reading words, math facts.
One-to-one teacher-directed grouping	Maximizes probability of student learning, especially students with learning difficulties.	Very inefficient. Shifts teacher's time away from more capable learners.

groups of students to work together, usually grouped so that higher-achieving group members can assist students who are experiencing academic difficulties.

Cooperative learning models offer a way to promote the progress of individual students. These models have students of heterogeneous achievement levels assigned to groups of four or five for the purpose of promoting the learning of all group members as they work toward a common goal, such as passing the test at the end of the chapter. There are group rewards for evidence of progress in learning by the members of the group, as opposed to only rewarding top individual students in traditional classrooms. Cooperative learning models have been recommended for use to include students with diverse backgrounds and to promote the achievement of students with academic difficulties (Johnson & Johnson, 1994; Slavin, 1996).

An example of a cooperative learning tool is the Student Teams-Achievement Division model (Slavin, 1990). After a traditional presentation of the material, students meet in assigned groups to review the material as a means of preparing for a quiz. In cooperative learning situations, students have to rely on each other to achieve a common goal, thus rewards are based on group performance (Peck, 1989). Several cooperative learning strategies will be reviewed in this section.

Jigsaw is a cooperative learning strategy in which students are responsible for a portion of the learning and teaching. Students are asked to independently research a particular portion of the lesson and be prepared to share with their classmates (Brown, 1994). In this way, each student shares responsibility for a piece of the puzzle. Before presenting the jigsaw lesson, Brown (1994) suggests that teachers work closely with specialists within the domain of interest. After selecting a topic, it is divided into subtopics and distributed among members of each group. Each member is responsible for becoming an "expert" in the assigned area. The students later regroup and share their findings. For example, the teacher may assign a topic on life in Brazil. One member of the group may choose to research the sports and recreational activities found in Brazil. Another student may choose to learn about the types of food found in Brazil. A third student may learn about the traditions and cultures of Brazil. After the students obtain the necessary information, they share the information with the rest of the group members. If absenteeism is a concern, students may work in pairs to ensure the work is completed. Johnson and Johnson

(1994) modified the Jigsaw format to create interdependence among the group members. In the Johnson model the teacher assigns specific students within the group to assume the role of the "checker," "recorder," "observer," etc. The purpose of the roles is to encourage teambuilding to help one another succeed.

Peer tutoring, a form of cooperative learning, has one student serve as a teacher/ monitor of a student who needs additional instruction or practice. Students with learning problems can benefit from the help given by a peer tutor, as well as benefit from serving as a tutor for a younger student who might be having difficulty (Scruggs, Mastropieri, & Rickter, 1985). Peer tutors are effective when used to provide drill and practice after the teacher has given the initial instruction. Peer tutors must have clearly defined roles, and they should be trained to follow a well defined instructional procedure, give corrective feedback when an error is made, reinforce correct responses, and keep track of their pupil's progress (Keel, Dangel, & Owens, 1999).

An instructional strategy that provides both an increase in practice opportunities with immediate feedback and delivery of instruction in small groups is classwide peer tutoring (CWPT). Classwide Peer Tutoring is a system in which all class members are organized in tutor-tutee pairs and work together, rather than independently or in small groups (Greenwood & Delquadri, 1995). This strategy has been shown to be effective for teaching academic and social skills to students with mild disabilities (Calhoon & Fuchs, 2003; Topping & Ehly, 1998; Wehby, Falk, Barton-Arwood, Lane, & Cooley, 2003). For example, Greenwood (1999) reported that at-risk low-achieving students using CWPT in general education spent more time academically engaged and had higher achievement on standardized tests in reading, mathematics, and language than students in a comparable school not using CWPT. The CWPT approach, developed by the Juniper Gardens Children's Project, has been used with low-achieving minority, disadvantaged, and students with mild disabilities to improve academic performance (Delquadri, Greenwood, Whorton, Carta, & Hall, 1986). Unlike other types of peer tutoring, which involve upper-grade or higher-skilled students from other classes, CWPT is implemented within an intact classroom and has classroom peers tutor one another in a reciprocal fashion on academic skills. Structured, teacher-directed lessons are presented to students prior to implementation of CWPT. During a CWPT session, students work in pairs and tutor one another on the same material presented by the teacher for 15 to 30 minutes. Students are provided instruction on proper reinforcement procedures for correct responses and for correcting errors. Systematic instructional procedures include explicit presentation format, contingent point earning, systematic error correction procedures, and public display of student performance, and are implemented to ensure the integrity of the procedures and student participation (Greenwood & Delquadri, 1995).

Classwide peer tutoring is considered an effective instructional procedure because of the many benefits associated with using the procedures. First, the structured interaction between a well-trained tutor and a tutee promotes positive classroom management, and also increases efficient use of academic time. Second, peer tutoring encourages teachers to design lessons that follow clear, specific procedures. It also encourages active monitoring of students' progress and understanding. Finally, peer tutoring provides extended individual instructional support and increased opportunities to respond.

Peer Assisted Learning Strategies (PALS) (Fuchs & Fuchs, 2001), a reading comprehension strategy program, is based on a CWPT model (Delquadri et al., 1986) and is typically used as a supplement to existing reading programs. During PALS students participate in three essential reading comprehension activities while reading aloud from narrative text:

1. Partner Reading,
2. Paragraph Shrinking,
3. Prediction Relay.

All three activities provide students with explicit, systematic practice in reviewing and sequencing, summarizing and stating main ideas, and predicting story outcome (Fuchs, Mathes, & Simmons, 1997). Research on PALS in grades K-5 found increases in reading fluency and comprehension in students with disabilities, as well as in low-, average-, and high-achieving students (Allor, Fuchs, & Mathes, 2001; Fuchs, Fuchs, Thompson, Al Otaiba, Yen, Yang, et al., 2002). At the high school and middle school level, PALS significantly increased reading comprehension skills of students with RD in comparison to a contrast group of students with RD (Calhoon, 2005; Fuchs, Fuchs, & Kazdan, 1999). Furthermore, PALS uses effective structures for implementation of a CWPT mathematics program that includes both coaching and practice (Calhoon & Fuchs, 2003; Fuchs, Fuchs, Hamlett, Phillips, & Karns, 1995). In investigations of the effectiveness of PALS in K-6 general education and high school special education classrooms on learning computation and concept/application skills, tutor and tutee (or coach and player in this investigation) worked together in a 30-minute block. They progressed through an introduction, coaching (using a series of prescribed questions appropriate for the material to be learned), transition to practice, independent practice (both coach and player complete and score the practice worksheets), and completion. An important part of the coaching process was the correction that coaches gave to players who made errors. The coach circled each correct digit; incorrect digits were corrected by the player, and then marked with a triangle by the coach. If the third in a series of problems was answered correctly, the player proceeded to work on additional problems while the coach monitored with an answer sheet and, if there was an error, intervened with the prescribed questions to lead the player to the correct answer. The clearly structured coaching/correction procedure in the these peer tutoring studies applies the principles of effective instruction by having lessons that follow clear, specific procedures; provide individual instructional support; ensure sufficient academic time is used efficiently; provide high opportunities to respond; and active monitoring of student's progress and understanding (Greenwood, et al., 1995). In this sense, "student-directed" refers to "others-directed" rather than self-directed. This approach is most appropriate for students who have difficulty attending, who need guided practice and re-teaching, and who have trouble monitoring their responses and making decisions on how to restructure a task following an incorrect or inappropriate response. Activities that are appropriate for peer-direction are those requiring considerable repetition and practice along with corrective feedback which may be effectively provided by a peer who has been trained to present, evaluate, correct, and record the responses of a classmate.

Selecting and Adapting Materials

Selecting and adapting appropriate materials is critical to the success of students with mild disabilities in academic content courses. Selection may involve locating materials at the classroom or district level. At the classroom level, teachers may be given money to select supplemental materials. At the district level, a classroom teacher usually has minimal influence on the materials selected. If district level materials are not appropriate for students with diverse academic needs, teachers may need to adapt the materials. Adapting materials involves changing the way the student obtains or provides information without changing the overall learning objective. This section provides information on how to select materials and adapt materials.

Principles of Selecting Materials

Universal design is a principle where the curriculum is appropriate for all students, to the greatest extent possible, before being used in the classroom. The need for additional adaptations to the curriculum in the classroom is limited since the curriculum developers considered the strengths, weaknesses, and learning styles of diverse students prior to publishing the materials. The Center for Applied Special Technology (*www.cast.org*) is an organization working on universal design. They suggest that universal design should allow for

(a) multiple means of representation where the students are given multiple ways of acquiring information and knowledge,
(b) multiple means of expression where the students have different ways to demonstrate what they know, and
(c) multiple means of engagement where students are involved in the learning process differently to increase motivation.

Universal design is gradually being used by curriculum publishers. Unfortunately, universal design is not a common practice. Still, teachers should be aware of universal design as it increasingly becomes more widespread.

When selecting materials for students, teachers should take into consideration **six curriculum design principles.** Those principles include (Kameenui & Simmons, 1999):

(a) big ideas,
(b) conspicuous strategies,
(c) mediated scaffolding,
(d) strategic integration,
(e) judicious review,
(f) primed background knowledge.

All of the design principles should be woven throughout the materials students use. **Big ideas** focus the ideas, concepts, principles, and rules that are essential for students to learn. They allow the students to apply what they learn in multiple situations, generalize the knowledge, and expand upon it. **Conspicuous strategies** provide the students with planned, purposeful, and explicit instruction. Providing obvious methods of learning is most important during initial instruction. **Strategic integration** involves considering what and how students have learned earlier. Meaningful relationships among concepts and ideas should be made with previous information that has been taught. **Judicious review** takes into consideration that learning is not a "one shot" deal. Learning is provided in sufficient amounts of practice that is distributed over time, cumulative, and varied with emphasis on mastery and retention of knowledge.

Principles of Adapting Materials

Many texts used in general education classrooms, particularly in secondary classrooms, exceed the readability level of the grade level in which they are used (Schumaker & Deshler, 1984). Not only is the readability level often too high, but Armbruster and Anderson (1988) described the writing style of common textbooks as "inconsiderate." They described "considerate" texts as "user-friendly" or ". . . relatively easy to read, understand, and learn from" (p. 47). They indicated three problem areas that had been observed in textbooks: a) structure, b) coherence, and c) audience appropriateness.

Unfortunately, many content area teachers do not have the luxury of selecting their own textbooks. In this case, it is important to determine supplementary methods and materials for assisting students in understanding the content. Adapting text can be time consuming to teachers; therefore adaptations should be considered only when it would help students meet curriculum goals and objectives. Generally, text adaptations are unnecessary for the most able or average students. However, Horton and Lovitt (1994) found text adaptations are required for students performing below average or students with learning disabilities. Teachers should consider the simplest adaptations that require the least resources when selecting the type of adaptations to use.

Prior to adapting materials, teachers should ask themselves several questions to determine if an adaptation is appropriate. Teachers can use the **FLEXIBLE** mnemonic to make this decision (Schumm, 1999). First, the teacher should conclude whether the adaptation is **feasible.** Adaptations that work can reasonably be used in the classroom. When determining if an adaptation is feasible, the teacher can ask when the adaptation will fit into the daily schedule of the student. Also, the teacher should examine the resources necessary to implement the adaptation and whether those resources are accessible. If they are not accessible, the teacher will have to determine what steps can be taken to obtain the resources.

Second, the teacher should establish if the adaptation will be **lively.** Adaptations are successful when they are engaging, interesting, and worthwhile to students. When determining if an adaptation will be lively, the teacher should ask how the adaptation will be used to increase active learning. Adaptations should be as interesting and enjoyable as possible. Also, the teacher should consider what actions will be necessary to increase the chances the adaptation will be used over time.

Third, the teacher should determine if the adaptation can be **eliminated** over time. Many adaptations should be gradually faded over time to increase the independence of students. When determining if the adaptation can be eliminated over time, the teacher should ask what actions will be required to fade the adaptation over time. The teacher will have to determine if there will be time for instruction that can be used to eliminate the adaptation. Also, the teacher should decide if the adaptation has a good probability of being incorporated into the repertoire of the student or not. The adaptation is of no benefit unless the student uses it.

Fourth, the teacher should decide if the adaptation will be **explicit.** Adaptations that work are purposeful, obvious, and apparent to the student and parents. When determining if the adaptation is explicit, the teacher should determine the overall purpose of the adaptation. The overall purpose should be directly told to parents, students, and other teachers.

Fifth, the teacher should make a decision if the adaptation will be **intentional.** Successful adaptations are woven into the student's comprehensive educational plan. When determining if the adaptation is intentional, the teacher should decide how it will be integrated with the student's IEP goals and objectives. Also, the teacher should determine how the adaptation will impact district and state high stakes testing.

Sixth, the teacher should determine whether or not the adaptation will be **beneficial** to the student. Appropriate adaptations enhance the learning of all students. When determining if the adaptation is beneficial, the teacher should indicate how the adaptation will benefit the student and potentially other students in the classroom. Also, the teacher should determine if the adaptation will be a distraction to others or not.

Seventh, the teacher should indicate whether or not the adaptation puts the student in the **limelight.** Adaptations should not embarrass students or single them out. When determining if the adaptation will put the student in the limelight, the teacher should decide if the adaptation will cause undue attention or embarrassment for the student. The setting for the adaptation should be taken into consideration because it might directly influence whether it is embarrassing or not.

Eighth, the teacher should decide if the success or failure of the adaptation can be **evaluated.** Quality adaptations are evaluated over time and on an ongoing basis. When determining if the adaptation can be evaluated, the teacher should determine if it can be documented. The impact of the adaptation must be observable. The impact of the adaptation on the social status of the student should be considered. Parents might be helpful in deciding the impact of the adaptation. Ultimately, the teacher must determine whether or not the adaptation makes the student more independent.

Once it has been determined that a curriculum adaptation is needed, the teacher can take nine steps to implement an adaptation (Lenz & Schumaker, 1999).

1. **Construct a plan for adapting the materials.** When planning adaptations it is important to determine who will be responsible for preparing the adaptation and how much time and money it will take. Parents and administrators should support the use of the adaptation. Without their support, the adaptation might not be successful. Also, it is important to consider whether the adaptation is a one-time adaptation or something that will be needed over a long period of time.

2. **Identify and assess the demands students are not meeting.** The purpose of this step is to define what problem is being addressed. Different types of problems may be identified. The student might be having issues with obtaining information, remembering the information, or demonstrating competence.

3. **Establish instructional goals.** Once a problem has been identified, the teacher should determine the intensity of the intervention. The adaptation should be individualized. The length of the adaptation is dependent on the needs of the student and the degree to which it makes the student an independent learner. Some adaptations may not be sufficient enough. More intensive instruction may be needed.

4. **Decide whether content adaptations or format adaptations are needed.** Content adaptations should only be made if the IEP indicates the need. In most cases, the content stays the same. With format adaptations the arrangement, design, or layout of the information is changed without altering the content. Format adaptations should compensate for student's learning differences.

5. **Determine what aspects of the material should be adapted.** Common design problems that present a mismatch between the student and the materials include their (a) abstractness, (b) organization, (c) relevance, (d) interest to students, (e) the skills students need to use them, (f) the strategies students have to use with them, (g) the background knowledge of the students, (h) complexity, (i) quantity of information, (j) level of activities required, (k) related outcomes, and (l) student responses. **Table 6-1** provides a detail description of the design problems, short-term design adaptations, and long-term instructional goals.

6. **Determine the specific adaptation that will allow the student to meet the academic demands.** Adaptations may require that the teacher alter the existing materials. This might involve rewriting or reorganizing the materials. The teacher may also have to provide additional materials to support the student. This might involve providing the student with a study guide or outline of a chapter. Finally, the teacher might need to pick alternative materials. The materials the student is using might be so poorly designed that other resources might be necessary. When selecting alternative materials for students, the teacher should be careful that the materials do not make the student stand out. For example, some alternative materials may be in a softback format while the other materials in hardback. Such an arrangement might be rejected by students. Adaptations can be grouped according to five areas: acquisition, storage, retrieval, organization, expression, and assessment. A list of adaptations and modifications can be found at:
   http://www.sabine.k12.la.us/standards/CSmchecklis.htm#Modifications%20And%20Adaptations

7. **Inform the student and parents about the adaptation.** Decisions about adaptations should be made during the IEP meeting. The more students and parents are partners in determining the adaptations, the more likely it is that the adaptation will be implemented. Students should know why the adaptation is being provided and how it will be faded over time.

8. **Implement, evaluate, and adjust the adaptation.** The teacher should evaluate the implementation of the adaptation. Adjustments should be made as needed. This requires monitoring by the teacher. The student also should feel empowered to indicate if the adaptation is appropriate or not.

9. **Fade the adaptation if possible.** The adaptation should be gradually removed if possible. This will increase the independence of the student. In some cases, the adaptation may need to be continued. The adaptation should not be removed until the student has the skills and abilities to manage without it.

TABLE 6-1

Design Problems in Curriculum Materials and Possible Solutions

Design Problem	Short-Term Design Adaptation	Long-Term Instructional Goal
1. Abstractness. The content appears too conceptual, hypothetical, and impractical.	Provide students with more concrete examples, analogies, interpretations, or experiences.	Teach students how to seek more examples, explanations, and interpretations through questioning and research.
2. Organizations. The organization is not clear or is poorly structured.	Make the organization explicit for students by creating graphic organizer and reading guides and inserting cues that focus attention.	Teach students how to survey materials and identify text organization, read to confirm organization of ideas, and reorganize information for personal understanding and use.
3. Relevance. The information does not appear to have any relationship to students or their lives.	Make the connections between the information and students' lives explicit by building rationales and tying information to student experiences.	Teach students to ask appropriate questions about relevance, search for personal connections, and explore ways to make content relevant when given material that appears irrelevant to their lives.
4. Interest. The information or presentation of the information is boring.	Present information an assignment in ways that build on students' attention spans, participation, strengths, and interests.	Teach students self-management strategies for controlling attention in boring situations and how to take advantage of options and choices provided in assignments to make work more interesting.
5. Skills. The information is written at a level that assumes and requires skills beyond those possessed by students.	Present information in ways that use the skills students have.	Provide intensive instruction in basic skills required for basic literacy to middle—school students who are unprepared for secondary school content.
6. Strategies. The information is presented in ways that assume that students know how to approach tasks effectively and efficiently in strategic ways.	Provide instruction in learning strategies to students who do not know how to approach and complete tasks.	Cue and guide students in how to approach and complete learning and performance tasks by leading them through complex tasks.
7. Background. Understanding information usually requires critical background knowledge, but students often lack the experiences and concepts (or cannot make connections to personal background experiences) to make new information meaningful.	Present information in ways that provide background experiences or make background linkages clear.	Teach students how to become consumers of information from a variety of information sources and how to ask questions of these sources to gain background knowledge and insights.

TABLE 6-1

Design Problems in Curriculum Materials and Possible Solutions (continued)

8. Complexity. The information or associated tasks have many parts or layers.	Break down the information or tasks and present them explicitly and in different ways so that students can learn and perform.	Teach students how to "chunk" tasks, represent complex information graphically, ask clarifying questions, and work collaboratively in teams to attack complex tasks.
9. Quantity. There is a lot of difficult or complex information that is crucial to remember	Present the information in ways that facilitate remembering.	Teach strategies for chunking, organizing, and remembering information.
10. Activities. The instructional activities and sequences provided do not lead to understanding or mastery.	Provide students with scaffold learning experiences that include additional or alternative instructional activities, activity sequences, or practice experiences to ensure mastery at each level of learning before instruction continues.	Teach students to independently check and redo work, review information, seek help, ask clarifying questions, and inform others when they need more or different types of instruction before instruction in more content begins.
11. Outcomes. The information does not cue students how to think about or study information to meet intended outcomes.	Inform students about expectations for their learning and performance.	Teach students how to identify expectations and goals embedded in materials or to create and adjust goals based on previous experiences with similar materials.
12. Responses. The material does not provide options for students to demonstrate competence in different ways.	Provide opportunities to students to demonstrate what they know in different ways.	Teach students how they can best demonstrate competence, identify and take advantage of performance options and choice when they are offered, and request appropriate adaptations of tests and competency evaluations.

Taken from: Lenz, B. K. & Schumaker, J. B. (1999). *Adapting language arts, social studies, and science materials for the inclusive classroom*, pp. 12–13. Reston, VA: Council for Exceptional Children.

Specific Strategies for Adapting Materials

Dyke (1999) suggests five options for adapting text:

a) bypass reading,
b) decrease reading,
c) support reading,
d) organize reading, and
e) guide reading.

One simple type of adaptation that requires few resources is to **bypass reading.** This is accomplished by having the teacher read aloud the text, pairing the student with the reading deficit with a peer reader, use audiotape of the text, or use computer text-to-speech technology. When considering reading aloud to a student, the student's learning style must be considered. For example, many students with learning disabilities and especially students with attention deficit disorders have difficulty attending to spoken words. In this case, oral reading may not be effective for these students. Bypass reading can help engage the student during oral reading exercises as follows:

- "place a copy of the text in front of the listener
- encourage the listener to follow along as much as possible
- encourage the listener to ask you to stop whenever the message is unclear
- read with expression
- emphasize important points with voice intonation" (p. 7)

One easy method for **decrease reading** is to select a different text written on an earlier grade level that provides information on the same topic. One source for identifying alternative readings is the textbook publishers who often times provide parallel textbooks. Additionally, teachers can purchase commercially prepared materials such as *Cliff Notes* that provide abridged versions of text. Another option to decrease reading is highlight portions of the text. This technique is appropriate for the struggling reader who is unable to finish the required amount of reading in the allotted time. In order to adjust the amount of reading required, the teacher should first determine the student's reading rate. The following guidelines are suggested for correlating the student's reading rate and reading assignments.

- Select a representative sample of the text (excluding charts and lists) and have the student read aloud for one minute. Count the number of words read correctly to calculate words per minute (wpm).
- Obtain a normal reading rate by having all of the students in the class read silently for one minute and count the number of words read. Rank order the reading rates and calculate the median rate for the class.
- Determine the portion of the text the student can read in the allotted amount of time.
- Identify the portions of the text the student is to read, emphasizing the most important information to learn.

A final option for decreasing reading is to remove any distracting elements within the text. This can be achieved by covering up pictures or permanently removing the distractions from workbook pages. Eliminating supplementary information and colorful pictures enhances the student's ability to focus on relevant information.

- The **support reading** procedure is to assist students having difficulties comprehending text information when unfamiliar vocabulary or technical terms are used. The teacher can provide definitions for unfamiliar vocabulary either on a separate sheet of paper or written within the margins of the texts. Another option is for the teacher to provide a prompt that signals to the student to look up the term in the glossary. The page number could also be provided where the term can be located in the glossary to assist the student. Additionally, teachers can add questions embedded within the text written on sticky notes to have students reflect on what they have read.

For students who experience difficulty in comprehending definitions provided in the glossary, the teacher can provide a graphic concept map to define terms. Concepts maps contain a definition of the term, a description, key attributes of the term, and examples to enhance comprehension. **Figure 6-18** is an example of a Science Concept Map.

FIGURE 6-18

Science Concept Map

Definition: A mammal is a warm-blooded vertebrate that has hair and nurses its young

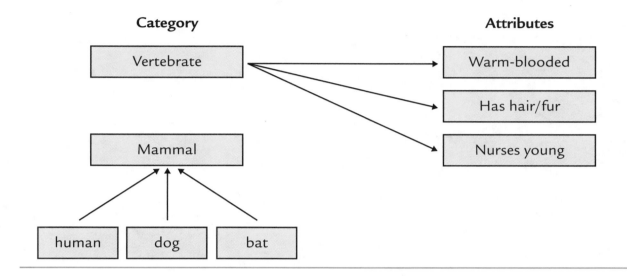

Students with attention problems may be able to read the text, but become frustrated because of the amount of reading required from a text. The use of **study guides** can redirect students to the essential information and enhance their ability to recall essential information. Study guides can enhance the comprehension of students with mild disabilities in content area classes. Masters, Mori, and Mori (1993) provide the following recommendations for developing study guides:

- Identify vocabulary words for the material to be read or discussed.
- Direct the student's attention to the most important information by writing focus statements that follow text or handout material.
- Use open-ended questions that follow the sequence of the written material.
- Develop questions about the charts, graphs, and pictures in reading material.
- Develop brief essay questions that require various types of responses, for example, compare/contrast, and cause/effect.
- Identify previous study guides that contain information related to the study guide in use.

Another option for adaptation is for teachers to prepare a preview and summary of the text chapter. The preview would consist of a review of prior knowledge that relates to the topic, the main idea of the chapter, and explanation of key terms. The summary presents the main ideas of the text chapter in a condensed form.

Summary

The teaching considerations for students with mild disabilities who are served in general education classrooms are an extension of the prereferral considerations discussed in Chapter 3. Teachers should adapt the curriculum, instruction, materials, and delivery of instructional services. It is important to use a model for effective instruction when planning any of these adjustments or adaptations. In addition to the strategies that promote student achievement that teachers manage, there are a number of well-documented strategies that students-direct. Student-directed strategies enhance task engagement (attending and responding), as well as achievement. Finally, the strategies described in this chapter are appropriate for all students, not just those with disabilities.

Name: _____   Date: _____ *OMIT*

Discussion Questions and Activities

1. Using the Planning Pyramid, choose a specific grade level and content area to develop a daily lesson plan. Include specific content area concepts to be taught at each of the three levels of the Pyramid.

2. Think about the information presented and the structure of one of the class periods in this course. Design an advance organizer that indicates (a) the goals of the class period, (b) the main points that were covered, (c) the activities that took place during the class period, and (d) the expectations the instructor had for the students.

3. Select 5 terms and definitions in the content area of your choice. Follow the IT FITS Keyword Mnemonic method to develop picture cards using the keyword method in learning vocabulary words. The picture cards should include all of the components of the IT FITS method.

4. Develop a rubric for evaluating curriculum based on the curriculum design principles and the FLEXIBLE mnemonic. Locate a curriculum at a specific grade level and content area of your choice. Evaluate the curriculum based on your rubric.

5. Interview a classroom teacher who has one or more students with mild disabilities. What academic instruction is the general classroom teacher responsible for? The special education teacher? What adaptations does the classroom teacher make for the students with mild disabilities?

6. Observe a classroom in which peer tutoring is taking place. What skills are being taught or practiced? Is the peer tutoring providing reinforcement for correct answers? Corrective feedback for errors? What is the teacher doing while peer tutoring is occurring? Ask the teacher what was done to train tutors to work with other students.

Internet Resources

World Wide Web sites for teachers
Education World
http://www.education-world.com/

The Educator's Reference Desk
http://www.eduref.org/

Home page of the Council for Exceptional Children
http://www.cec.sped.org/

Office of English Language Acquisition, Language Enhancement,
and Academic Achievement for Limited English Proficient Students
http://www.ncela.gwu.edu/

School-wide resources
http://school.aol.com/

Strategies for teaching students with disabilities
http://curry.edschool.virginia.edu/go/specialed/

What Works Clearinghouse
http://www.whatworks.ed.gov/

Federal Government Resources for Teachers
http://www.ed.gov/free/

Web-based resources on research on teaching
http://idea.uoregon.edu/~ncite/
http://cftl.org/

Web-based resources for teachers and parents of students with learning disabilities
http://www.ldonline.org/

References

Adams, M. J. (1990). *Beginning to read: Thinking and learning about print.* Urbana-Champaign, IL: University of Illinois, Center for the Study of Reading.

Adams, G. L., & Engelmann, S. (1996). *Research on direct instruction: Twenty-five years beyond DISTAR.* Seattle: Educational Achievement Systems.

Adelman, H. S., & Taylor, L. (1993). *Learning problems and learning disabilities: Moving forward.* Pacific Grove, CA: Brooks/Cole.

Allor, J. H., Fuchs, D., & Mathes, P. G. (2001). Do students with and without lexical retrieval weaknesses respond differently to instruction? *Journal of Learning Disabilities, 34,* 264–275.

Armbruster, B. B., & Anderson, T. H. (1988). On selecting "considerate" content area textbooks. *Remedial and Special Education, 9,* 47–52.

Ashlock, R. B., (2005). *Error Patterns in Computation: Using error patterns to improve instruction* (9th ed.). Upper Saddle River: New Jersey, Pearson Merrill Prentice Hall.

Ausubel, D. P., Novak, J. D., & Hanesian, H. (1978). *Educational psychology: A cognitive view* (2nd ed.). New York: Holt, Reinhart and Winston.

Baker, J. M., & Zigmond, N. (1990). Are regular education classes equipped to accommodate students with learning disabilities? *Exceptional Children, 56,* 515–526.

Bateman, B. & Linden, M. (1998). *Better IEPs* (3rd ed.). Longmont, CO: Sopris West.

Berliner, D. C. (1987, January). *Effective classroom teaching.* Paper presented at the fourth annual School Effectiveness Workshop, Phoenix, AZ.

Blick, D. W., & Test, W. (1987). Effects of self-recording on high-school students' on-task behavior. *Learning Disability Quarterly, 10,* 203–213.

Bloom, B. S. (1982). *All our children learning.* New York: McGraw Hill.

Brown, A. L. (1994). The advancement of learning. *Educational Researcher, 23(8),* 4–12.

Bulgren, J. A., Deshler, D. D., & Schumaker, J. B. (1997). Use of a recall enhancement routine and strategies in inclusive secondary classes. *Learning Disabilities Research & Practice, 12* (4), 198–208. Brown, A. L. (1994). The advancement of learning. *Educational Researcher, 23* (8), 4–12.

Bulgren, J., Schumaker, J. B., & Deshler, D. D. (1988). Effectiveness of a concept teaching routine in enhancing the performance of LD students in secondary-level mainstream classes. *Learning Disabilities Quarterly, 11,* 3–17.

Calhoon, M. B., (2005). Effects of a peer-mediated phonological skill and reading comprehension program on reading skill acquisition for middle school students with reading disabilities. *Journal of Learning Disabilities,* 38, 424–433.

Calhoon, M. B., & Fuchs, L. S. (2003). The effects of peer-assisted learning strategies and curriculum-based measurement on the mathematics performance of secondary students with disabilities. *Remedial and Special Education, 24,* 235–245.

Christenson, S. L., Ysseldyke, J. E., & Thurlow, M. L. (1989). Critical instructional factors for students with mild handicaps: An integrative review. *Remedial and Special Education, 10(5),* 21–31.

Clees, T. (1994–95). Self-Recording of students' daily schedules of teachers' expectancies: Perspectives on reactivity, stimulus control, and generalization. *Exceptionality, 5,* 113–129.

Dangel, H. L. (1989). The use of student-directed spelling strategies. *Academic Therapy Quarterly, 25,* 43–51.

Danoff, B., Harris, K., & Graham, S. (1993). Incorporating strategy instruction within the writing process in the regular classroom: Effects on the writing of students with and without learning disabilities. *Journal of Reading Behavior, 25,* 295–322.

Darch, C. (1991). Comprehension instruction for high school learning disabled students. *Research in Rural Education, 5,* 43–49.

Darch, C., & Gersten, R. (1986). Direction-setting activities in reading comprehension: A comparison of two approaches. *Learning Disability Quarterly, 9,* 235–243.

Deshler, D. D., Schumaker, J. B., Lenz, B. K., Bulgren, J. A., Hock, M. F., Knight, J., & Ehren, B. (2001). Ensuring content-area learning by secondary students with learning disabilities. *Learning Disabilities Research & Practice, 16,* 96–108.

DiGangi, S., & Maag, J. (1992). A component analysis of self-management training with behaviorally disordered youth. *Behavioral Disorders, 17,* 281–290.

Dyke, N. (1999). *How to adapt text for struggling readers.* Lawrence, KS: Curriculum Solutions.

Ellis, E. *The Framing Routine* (1998). Lawrence, KS: Edge Enterprises.

Ellis, E. S., Deshler, D. D., Lenz, B. K., Schumaker, J. B., & Clark, F. L. (1991). An instructional model for teaching learning strategies. *Focus on Exceptional Children, 23(6),* 1–24.

Englert, C. S., Tarrant, K. L., & Mariage, T. V. (1992). Defining and redefining instructional practice in special education: Perspectives on good teaching. *Teacher Education and Special Education, 15(2),* 62–86.

Erickson, R. N., Ysseldyke, J. E., Thurlow, M. L., & Elliott, J. L. (1998). Inclusive assessment and accountability systems: Tools of the trade in educational reform. *Teaching Exceptional Children, 31,* 4–9.

Fisher, J. B., Schumaker, J. B., & Deshler, D. D. (1995). Searching for validated inclusive practices: A review of the literature. *Focus on Exceptional Children, 27,* 1–28.

Fuchs, D., & Fuchs, L. S. (2001). Peer-assisted learning strategies in reading: Extensions for kindergarten, first grade, and high schools. Remedial and Special Education, 22(1), 15–22.

Fuchs, L., Fuchs, D., Hamlett, C., Phillips, N., & Karns, K. (1995). General educators' specialized adaptation for students with learning disabilities. *Exceptional Children, 61,* 440–459.

Fuchs, D., Fuchs, L. S., Karns, K., & Phillips, N. (1993). *Peabody peer-assisted learning strategies (PALS): Math methods.* (Available from Dr. Lynn S. Fuchs, Box 328, Peabody College, Vanderbilt University, Nashville, TN 37203).

Fuchs, D., Fuchs, L. S., & Kazdan, S. (1999). Effects of peer-assisted learning strategies on high school students with serious reading problems. Remedial and Special Education, 20, 309–318.

Fuchs, D., Fuchs, L. S., Mathes, P. G., & Simmons, D. C. (1997). Peer-assisted learning strategies: Making classrooms more responsive to academic diversity. *American Educational Research Journal, 34,* 174–206.

Fuchs, D., Fuchs, L. S., Thompson, A., al Otaiba, S. A., Yen, I., Yang., N. J. et al. (2002). Exploring the importance of reading programs for kindergartners with disabilities in the mainstream classroom. Exceptional Children, 68, 295–311.

Garner, R. (1992). Self-regulated learning, strategy shifts, and shared expertise: Reactions to Palincsar and Klenk. *Journal of Learning Disabilities, 5,* 226–229.

Gersten, R. (1998). Recent advances in instructional research for students with learning disabilities: An overview. *Learning Disabilities Research and Practice, 13,* 162–170.

Gersten, R., & Woodward, J. (1990). Rethinking the Regular Education Initiative: Focus on the classroom teacher. *Remedial and Special Education, 11,* 7–16.

Graham, S., & Harris, K. (1994). The role and development of self-regulation in the writing process. In D. H. Schunk and B. J. Zimmerman (Eds.), *Self-regulation of learning and performance: Issues and educational applications* (pp. 203–228). Hillsdale, NJ: Erlbaum.

Graham, S., Harris, K. R., & Reid, R. (1993). Developing self-regulated learners. In E. L. Meyen, G. A. Vergason, & R. J. Whelan (Eds.), *Educating students with mild disabilities* (pp. 127–149). Denver, CO: Love Publishing.

Greenwood, C. R. (1999). Reflections on a research career: Perspective on 35 years of research at the Juniper Gardens Children's Project. *Exceptional Children, 66,* 7–21.

Greenwood, C. R. & Delquadri, J. (1995). Classwide peer tutoring and the prevention of school failure. *Preventing School Failure, 39,* 21–26.

Harper, G. F., Maheady, L. Mallette, B., & Karnes, M. (1999). Peer tutoring and the minority child with disabilities. *Preventing School Failure, 43,* 45–51.

Haynes, M. C. & Jenkins, J. R. (1986). Reading instruction in special education resource rooms. *American Educational Research Journal, 23,* 161–190.

Howell, K. W., & Nolet, V. (2000). *Curriculum-based evaluation: Teaching and decision-making* (3rd ed.). Belmont, CA: Wadsworth/Thomson Learning.

Hughes, C. A., & Schumaker, J. B. (1991). Test-taking strategy instruction for adolescents with learning disabilities. *Exceptionality, 2,* 205–221.

Johnson, D. W., & Johnson, R. T. (1994). *Learning together and alone: Cooperative, competitive, and individualistic learning* (4th ed). Boston: Allyn & Bacon.

Kameenui, E., & Carnine, D. (1998). *Effective teaching strategies that accommodate diverse learners.* Upper Saddle River, NJ: Merrill/Prentice Hall.

Kameenui, E., & Simmons, D. (1999). *Toward successful inclusion of students with disabilities: The architecture of instruction.* Reston, VA: Council for Exceptional Children.

Keel, M. C., Dangel, H. L., & Owens, S. H. (1999). Selecting instructional interventions for students with mild disabilities in inclusive classrooms. *Focus on Exceptional Children, 31,* 1–16.

King-Sears, M. E., Mercer, C. D., & Sindelar, P. T. (1992). Toward independence with keyword mnemonic: A strategy for science vocabulary instruction. *Remedial and Special Education, 13(5),* 22–33.

Kozioff, M. A., LaNunziata, L., Cowardin, J., & Bessellieu, F. B. (2001). Direct instruction: Its contributions to high school achievement. *High School Journal, 84,* 54–72.

Lenz, B. K., Alley, G. R., & Schumaker, J. B. (1987). Activating the inactive learner: Advance organizers in the secondary content classroom. *Learning Disability Quarterly, 10,* 53–67.

Lenz, B. K., Bulgren, J. A., Schumaker, J. B., Deshler, D. D., & Boudah, D. A. (1994). *The unit organizer routine.* Lawrence, KS: Edge Enterprises, Inc.

Lenz, B. K., & Hughes, C. A. (1990). A word identification strategy for adolescents with learning disabilities. *Journal of Learning Disabilities, 23* (3), 149–158, 163.

Lenz, B. K., & Scanlon, D. (1998). SMARTER teaching: Developing accommodations to reduce cognitive barriers to learning for individuals with learning disabilities. *Perspectives, 24* (3), 16–19.

Lenz, B. K. & Schumaker, J. B. (1999). *Adapting language arts, social studies, and science materials for the inclusive classroom.* Reston, VA: Council for Exceptional Children.

Masters, L. F., Mori, B. A., & Mori, A. A. (1993). *Teaching secondary students with mild learning and behavioral problems.* Austin, TX: PRO-ED.

Mathes, P. G., Fuchs, D., & Fuchs, L. S. (1997). Cooperative story mapping. *Remedial and Special Education, 18,* 20–27.

Mercer, C. D., & Mercer, A. R. (2005). *Teaching students with learning problems* (7th ed.). Upper Saddle River, NJ: Prentice-Hall.

Montague, M., Bergeron, J., & Lago-Delello, E. (1997). Using prevention strategies in general education. *Focus on Exception Children, 19(8),* 1–12.

Nagel, D. R., Schumaker, J. B., & Deshler, D. D. (1986). *The FIRST-letter mnemonic strategy.* Lawrence, KS: Edge Enterprises.

Nelson, J. R., Smith, D. J., Young, R. K., & Dodd, J. M., (1991). A review of self-management outcome research conducted with students who exhibit behavioral disorders. *Behavioral Disorders, 16,* 169–179.

Nolet, V., & Tindal, G. (1994). Curriculum-based collaboration. *Focus on Exceptional Children, 27(3),* 1–12.

O'Sullivan, P. J., Ysseldyke, J. E., Christenson, S. L., & Thurlow, M. L. (1990). Mildly handicapped elementary students' opportunity to learn during reading instruction in mainstream and special education settings. *Reading Research Quarterly, 25,* 131–146.

Raymond, E. B. (2000). *Learners with mild disabilities: A characteristics approach.* Boston: Allyn & Bacon.

Robinson, F. P. (1961). *Effective study.* New York: Harper & Row.

Rosenshine, B. V. (1997). Advances in research on instruction. In J. W. Lloyd, E. J. Kameenui & D. Chard (Eds.), *Issues in educating students with disabilities.* Mahwah, NJ: Lawrence Erlbaum.

Rosenshine, B. V., & Stevens R. (1986). Teaching functions. In M. C. Wittrock (Ed.), *Handbook of research on teaching* (3rd ed., pp. 376–391). New York: MacMillan Publishing.

Schumaker, J. B., & Deshler, D. D. (In prep. 2005). *Teaching Adolescents to be Strategic Learners.*

Schumaker, J. B., & Deshler, D. D. (1984). Setting demand variables: A major factor in program planning for the LD adolescent. *Topics in Language Disorders, 4(2),* 22–40.

Schumm, J. (1999). *Adapting reading and math materials for the inclusive classroom.* Reston, VA: Council for Exceptional Children.

Schumm, J. S., & Vaughn, S. (1992). Reflections on planning for mainstreamed special education students: Perceptions of general classroom teachers. *Exceptionality, 3,* 121–126.

Schunk, D. (2000). Learning theories: An educational perspective (3rd ed.). Upper Saddle River, NJ: Prentice-Hall.

Scruggs, T. E., Mastropieri, M. M., & Rickter, L. L. (1985). Peer tutoring with behaviorally disordered students: Social and academic benefits. *Behavior Disorders, 10,* 283–294.

Simmons, D. C., Chard, D., & Kameenui, E. J. (1995). Translating research into basal reading programs: Applications of curriculum design. *LD Forum, 19(4),* 9–13.

Slavin, R. E. (1990). *Cooperative learning: Theory, research and practice.* Englewood Cliffs, NJ: Prentice-Hall.

Slavin, R. E. (1996). Research on cooperative learning and achievement: What we know, what we need to know. *Contemporary Educational Psychology, 21,* 43–69.

Smith, D. D. (1989). *Teaching students with learning and behavior problems* (2nd ed.). Englewood Cliffs: Prentice-Hall.

Sorrell, A. L. (1990). Three reading comprehension strategies: TELLS, story mapping, and QARs. *Academic Therapy, 25,* 359–368.

Spekman, N. J., Goldberg, R. J., & Herman K. L. (1992). Learning disabled children grow up: A search for factors related to success in the young adult years. *Learning Disabilities Research and Practice, 7,* 161–170.

Topping, K. & Ehly, S. (1998). *Peer-assisted Learning.* Mahwah, NJ: Erlbaum.

Vaughn, S., Bos, C. S., & Schumm, J. S. (1997). *Teaching mainstreamed, diverse, and at-risk students in the general education classroom.* Boston: Allyn & Bacon.

Walberg, H. J. (1988). Synthesis of research on time and learning. *Educational Leadership, 45,* 76–85.

Wehby, J. H., Falk, K. B., Barton-Arwood, S., Lane K. L., & Cooley, C. (2003). The impact of comprehensive reading instruction on the academic and social behavior of students with emotional and behavioral disorders. *Journal of Emotional and Behavioral Disorders, 11,* 225–239.

Welch, M. (1992). The PLEASE strategy: A metacognitive learning strategy for improving the paragraph writing of students with learning disabilities. *Learning Disabilities Quarterly, 15,* 119–128.

Werner, E. E. (1993). Risk and resilience in individuals with learning disabilities: Lessons learned from the Kauai longitudinal study. *Learning Disabilities Research and Practice, 8,* 28–34.

Whinnery, K. W., Fuchs, L. S., & Fuchs, D. (1991). General, special, and remedial teachers' acceptance of behavioral and instructional strategies for mainstreaming students with mild handicaps. *Remedial and Special Education, 12(4),* 6–17.

Wirtz, C. L., Gardner, R., Weber, K., & Bullara, D. (1996). Using self-correction to improve spelling performance of low-achieving third graders. *Remedial and Special Education, 17(1),* 48–58.

York, J., Doyle, M. B., & Kronberg, R. (1992). A curriculum development process for inclusive classrooms. *Focus on Exceptional Children, 25(4),* 1–16.

7

Reading Assessment and Instruction for Students At-Risk

Margaret E. Shippen, David E. Houchins, and Candace E. Steventon

Chapter Objectives

- to define literacy and describe how it develops in students;
- to describe the importance of reading as part of the literacy process;
- to identify and describe the five "big ideas" in reading;
- to describe the problems that students with disabilities and students at-risk for reading difficulties experience within the context of each "big idea;"
- to describe specific instructional strategies that promote learning of each "big idea;" and
- to identify appropriate assessment procedures to document student progress and/or need for further instruction within the context of each "big idea."

In the previous chapters, you learned about characteristics of students with disabilities and students at-risk for academic failure and the legal supports, instructional procedures, and educational resources that are in place to support these students' academic success. In this chapter, you will read about the most recent findings regarding effective reading instruction for students with disabilities and students at-risk for reading difficulties. In addition, you will read about the "big ideas" in beginning reading instruction that form the foundational concepts, essential components, and unifying curriculum activities necessary for effective beginning reading instruction for students with diverse learning needs (Kameenui, 1998). The five "big ideas" in reading reported in this chapter have been adapted from the work of Kameenui and colleagues at the National Center to Improve the Tools of Educators (NCITE) at the University of Oregon (Kameenui et al., 2001) and the findings of the National Reading Panel (NRP) (2000). Specifically, they are: phonological awareness, alphabetic principle, fluency, vocabulary/background knowledge, and comprehension. **Table 7-1** provides a brief explanation of each of the five big ideas in beginning reading instruction.

Teaching reading is a complex process. It requires extensive training, practice with supervision, and considerable experience (Moats, 1999). Therefore, this chapter is an introduction to and overview of concepts and practices that have proven to be successful for many students experiencing reading failure.

TABLE 7-1

The Big Ideas of Reading Instruction

Big Idea	A Brief Definition	Characteristics
1. Phonological Awareness	The ability to perceive spoken words as a sequence of sounds (phonemes) and to manipulate sounds in words.	Phonemic awareness Phonemic identification Phonemic manipulation Spoken language awareness
2. Alphabetic Principle	The ability to understand that letters (graphemes) represent sounds and words are comprised of letter strings and sound patterns.	Letter-sound correspondence Left to right progression of text Letter combinations and word patterns
3. Fluency	The ability to read text quickly and accurately with proper expression.	Rate and accuracy Error monitoring Reading with prosody
4. Vocabulary Knowledge	The ability to understand (receptive) and use (expressive) words to form meaning in oral and textual tasks.	Background knowledge Life experience Exposure to text
5. Comprehension	The ability to orchestrate complex cognitive and meta-cognitive processes to gain meaning from text.	Metacognition Self-regulation

Overview of Literacy

What is literacy and why is it important? There are many ways to define literacy. For the purpose of this chapter, literacy is the ability to read, write, spell, listen, and speak in ways that enable communication, promote understanding of ideas, and enrich lives (Moats, 2000; Glaeser, Lenz, Gildroy, & McKnight, 2000). Literacy is the most important educational goal for which teachers are responsible (Moats). Academic success, employment, and personal health depend upon individuals' ability to use and understand their culture's language system. For example in the United States, the following statistics are cause for alarm (Moats, 1999):

- Approximately 20% of our elementary students have significant reading problems.

- Between 60 to 70% of our nation's students who are African-American, Hispanic, limited-English speaking, or poor are experiencing reading difficulties.

- 25% of adults in this country lack the basic literacy skills required for gainful employment.

- Approximately one-third of students with poor reading skills are from college-educated parents (p. 7).

In addition, the National Institute of Student Health and Human Development views literacy and reading failure in the United States as a national health crisis (Lyon, 1999).

How does literacy develop? Literacy development is the combination of an individual's developmental processes and language and life experiences (Glaeser et al., 2000). Literacy and language skills develop over many years from birth through adulthood, yet a child's early literacy, or emergent literacy, normally develops prior to formal schooling and is crucial for that child's future success in school and society (Glaeser et al.). The foundation of literacy begins at birth when parents and family members are the primary providers of literacy awareness and instruction (McCardle, Cooper, Houle, Karp, & Paul-Brown, 2001). For example, Hart and Risley (1995) found in their longitudinal study that students from families with middle-to-high incomes experienced *4 million* verbal utterances per year as opposed to students in families with low incomes who experienced only *250,000* utterances a year. In addition, these researchers discovered that parents who conversed with their children in an interactive manner and who used rich language and vocabulary, produced students who could understand the English alphabetic code for reading and comprehend what is read. As a result, students come to school with differing life experiences, vocabularies, and world knowledge that set the stage for academic success or failure.

Reading: An Important Aspect of Literacy

Why is reading an important aspect of literacy? The ERIC Clearinghouse on Disabilities and Gifted Education (1996) reported the following:

> No other skill taught in school and learned by school students is more important than reading. It is the gateway to all other knowledge. If students do not learn to read efficiently, the path is blocked to every subject they encounter in their school years. (p. 1)

Reading difficulties are the primary cause of school failure (Carnine, Silbert, & Kameenui, 1997). Reading difficulties impede the ability to get at the meaning of written language (Snow, Burns, & Griffin, 1998). Students must acquire well-developed reading skills in order to access and participate in classroom learning.

While most students acquire language in a natural, developmental manner, their ability to acquire basic reading skills is not a natural process (Greene, 1998; Lyon, 1999; Moats, 2000). Teachers encounter students who come to school with environmental, experiential, and individual differences. More importantly, the total act of reading is affected if students are weak in just one reading skill (Chall, Jacobs, & Baldwin, 1991). For example, weak word recognition skills negatively affect a student's ability to read in an effortless manner. Lack of fluent reading tends to lower a student's motivation to continue to read. Limited reading practice limits a student's vocabulary knowledge and comprehension that results in poor academic achievement and limited literacy skills. Stanovich (1986) borrowed the biblical concept, the "Matthew Effect," that describes a rich-get-richer and poor-get-poorer phenomenon when applied to reading. In other words, those students who have limited access to the meaning of printed words fall behind their peers with average to above reading skills, resulting in an increasingly widening performance gap as they progress through school and life. Thus, reading holds cognitive consequences that limit one's quality of life.

Students at-risk for learning difficulties tend to differ from their average-achieving peers in the areas of language processing, memory, learning strategies, and vocabulary (Kameenui & Carnine, 1998). The remaining portions of this chapter will take a closer look at:

(a) the essential components, the "big ideas," of good reading instruction (See **Table 7-1**);
(b) the issues faced by students with disabilities and reading difficulties;
(c) specific strategies and methods teachers need to know in order to prevent and minimize reading difficulties; and
(d) assessment techniques that promote effective instructional decision-making to meet individual students' needs.

Phonological Awareness: The *First* Big Idea

Phonological awareness is a broad term that refers to one's ability to notice, hear, and manipulate the sounds in **spoken** words. This ability is distinct from one's ability to make sense of **written** language. In addition, phonological awareness focuses on the phonological structure of words as opposed to the meanings of words (Gildroy & Francis, 1999; Kameenui et al., 2001). The scope of phonological skills includes identifying and manipulating larger parts of spoken language, such as words and syllables, as well as phonemes (Armbruster, Lehr, & Osborn, 2001). Phonological awareness is a strong predictor of future reading and spelling achievement.

Within the realm of phonological awareness is the subcategory of **phonemic awareness.** Phonemic awareness is the ability to identify and manipulate sounds within words. Phonemes are the smallest units of spoken language. Phonemic awareness has gained significant attention among researchers and educators. Researchers have identified phonemic awareness as a strong predictor of how well students will learn to read during the first two years of school (National Reading Panel, 2000). The results of the meta-analysis (a synthesis of several research studies) conducted by the National Reading Panel found that teaching students to manipulate phonemes was highly effective with a variety of learners across a range of grade and age levels. In addition, the panel reported that teaching phonemic awareness to students significantly improved their reading more than instruction that did not include phonemic awareness activities.

Students Who Have Difficulties with Phonological Awareness

There is evidence that phonological processing ability distinguishes good and poor readers (Kameenui et al., 2001). Students who cannot identify words that comprise compound words, syllables within words, similar and dissimilar sounds of words, rhyming words, and individual sounds within words will have a difficult time understanding that letters within printed words represent sounds (Kameenui et al., 2001). Students who have difficulty with sounding out words or putting sounds together to make words will have trouble with decoding unfamiliar words in print.

Compounding the problem is the structure of the English language. The 26 letters in the English alphabet represent approximately 40 phonemes, or sound units. These phonemes generate over 250 graphemes or spelling combinations (e.g., /f/ as in ph, f, gh, ff) (Kameenui et al., 2001; Moats, 2000). Students who do not understand this letter-phoneme-grapheme relationship will have trouble with word reading.

Struggling readers have not learned how to think about spoken words as representing sequences of phonemes. One of the most consistent findings is that students who experience reading difficulties have significantly poorer phonemic awareness than do their successfully reading peers (Gildroy, 1999). Fortunately, researchers have continued to investigate interventions that provide effective instruction of phonemic awareness and phonological skills. Teachers now have available a variety of methods and strategies to help the majority of their students within the general classroom setting. The following section will introduce you to critical features and examples of effective phonological instruction.

Phonological instruction is most effective when delivered to small groups of students.

Strategies/Methods in Phonological Awareness

Providing systematic instruction of phonological skills during the first two years of kindergarten and first grade is critical. This instruction does not constitute a complete reading program. In fact, phonological instruction takes no more than 15 to 20 minutes per day and is most effective when delivered to small groups of students. Kameenui et al. (2001) suggested the following phonological awareness development curriculum for kindergarten and first grade. These skills progress from easier to more difficult phonological tasks.

- Word comparison—discriminating words that are similar or different (e.g., man/man=same; man/mat=different).
- Rhyming—identifying whether words rhyme (e.g., man and pan).
- Sentence segmentation—identifying the number of words in a sentence (e.g., The man had a tan=5 words).
- Syllable segmentation and blending—breaking apart and putting together syllables in words (mon-key).
- Onset-rime blending and segmentation—putting together the initial consonant with the remaining part of a one-syllable word (m-an) and identifying the first sound in a one-syllable word (/m/ in man).
- Blending and segmenting individual phonemes—putting together individual sounds in words (e.g., m-a-n: man) and breaking apart the individual sounds in words (e.g., man: /m/ /a/ /n/).
- Phoneme deletion and manipulation—identifying a word after removing, adding, or changing individual sounds (phonemes) within the word (e.g., removing /m/ from man=an; adding /t/ to rain=train; changing /m/ man to /p/ pan).

Activities in kindergarten should focus on the simpler tasks of rhyming, matching words with beginning sounds and blending sounds into words (Kameenui et al., 2001). In addition, listening-type games necessary to sharpen students' ability to attend to sounds and the introduction of letters and spellings to initiate the relation of letters to speech sounds should begin at the kindergarten level (Adams, Foorman, Lundberg, & Beeler, 1998). Most importantly, these skills need to be taught explicitly. Teachers must show students what they are expected to do. They must *model* skills they want students to demonstrate. The following examples of phonological skills instruction are adapted from Kameenui et al. (2001).

Sound and Word Comparisons

For sound and word comparisons, ask students to tell whether pairs or sets of words/sounds are the same or different. Here are some examples:

- The teacher says, "hat, fat, hat" and asks the students which word is different.
- The teacher says the sounds, "sss, k, sss" and asks the student which sound is different.
- The teacher says the word pairs, "fat/fat" and "fat/far" and asks if each word pair is the same or different.

Rhyming

To teach rhyming skills, the teacher can ask students to identify whether or not words rhyme (e.g., hat/cat; swing/ring). A higher-order rhyming skill is to ask students to produce words that rhyme with a model word (e.g., "A word that rhymes with **bat** is **cat.** Tell me another word that rhymes with **bat.**").

Blending and Segmenting

The auditory tasks of *blending* and *segmenting* are the two most critical skills that must be taught (Carnine, Silbert, & Kameenui, 1997). Effective phonological awareness programs

TABLE 7-2

Format for Telescoping Sounds

Teacher	Students
1. (Teacher gives instructions.) Listen, we're going to play a say-the-word game. I'll say a word slowly, then you say the word fast.	
2. (Teacher says the word slowly, then students say it fast.) Listen. (Pause.) iiifff. What word?	"if"
3. Teacher repeats step 2 with four more words: sat, Sid, am, fit.	
4. Teacher repeats the set of words until students can respond correctly to all the words, making no errors.	
5. Teacher gives individual turns to several students.	

From *Direct Instruction Reading, 3rd Edition* by Carnine/Silbert/Kameenui, © 1997. Reprinted by permission of Pearson Education, Inc., Upper Saddle River, NJ.

should focus on segmenting and blending skills starting with larger linguistic units such as words and syllables and proceeding to the smaller linguistic units of phonemes (Kameenui et al., 2001). Blending and segmenting skills constitute the preskills for sounding out words. Carnine and his colleagues refer to blending skills as "telescoping," which prepares students for later sounding-out exercises that require blending of printed letters into words. The teacher says a series of blended sounds. The students translate this series of sounds into a word said at a normal rate ("mmmaaannn" becomes *man*). Teachers should be aware of correct and consistent sound production techniques. *Continuous sounds,* those that are said without distortion, should be held for one to two seconds (e.g., /mmm/). *Stop sounds,* those that cannot be held without changing the sound, should be said in a quick manner (e.g., /k/). In summary, *telescoping* allows students an extended opportunity to hear that words are composed of smaller units of speech or phonemes.

The second skill, *segmenting,* is described by Carnine et al. (1997) in a slightly different manner than the most common usage of segmenting found in the literature. That is, segmenting is taught as "not stopping between sounds." The literature on phoneme segmentation generally refers to isolating the phonemes within a word. For example, *man* becomes /m/ /a/ /n/ instead of "mmmaaannn." The segmenting procedure involves the teacher modeling saying the word slowly. Then the students say the word slowly. Specific teaching procedures (*formats*) for teaching telescoping and segmenting are presented in **Tables 7-2** and **7-3** (Carnine et al., 1997).

Additional blending activities involve orally blending compound words (base-ball), syllables (tur-key) and onsets (the part of the word before the first vowel, e.g., /m/ in man) and rimes (the part of the word including the vowel and what follows it, e.g., /an/ in man) into a whole word. Additional segmenting activities include clapping or counting words in a 3 to 5 word sentence, clapping or counting syllables in words, and isolating initial, final, and medial (middle) sounds in one-syllable words. Students should demonstrate the ability to isolate, blend, and segment sounds within words by the middle of first grade (Kameenui et al., 2001).

Phoneme Deletion and Manipulation

The more difficult skills, phoneme deletion and manipulation, involve students being able to recognize words when a phoneme is removed (*man* without the /m/ is *an*), when phonemes are added to an existing word to form a new word (/s/ added to *pit* makes *spit*),

TABLE 7-3

Format for Segmenting

Teacher	Students
1. We're going to say words slowly.	
2. First word: sad. I'll say it slowly. Listen. (Pause) Sssaaad. You say it slowly. Get ready. (Teacher signals each time students are to switch to the next sound.)	"Sssaaad"
3. Teacher repeats procedure in step 2 with 3 more words.	
Next word: me. I'll say it slowly. Listen. (Pause) Mmmeee.	
You say it slowly. Get ready. (Signal.)	"Mmmeee"
Next word: mom. I'll say it slowly. Listen. (Pause) Mmmooommm.	
You say it slowly. Get ready. (Signal.)	"Mmmooommm"
Next word: fit. I'll say it slowly. Listen. (Pause) Fffiiit.	
You say it slowly. Get ready. (Signal.)	"Fffiiit"
4. Teacher repeats the set of words until students can say every word slowly, making no errors.	
5. Teacher gives individual turns to several students.	

From *Direct Instruction Reading, 3rd Edition* by Carnine/Silbert/Kameenui, © 1997. Reprinted by permission of Pearson Education, Inc., Upper Saddle River, NJ.

and when one phoneme is substituted for another to make a new word (word *pan* is changed to *man* by substituting a /m/) (Armbruster et al., 2001). Teachers should introduce letter-sound correspondence to students when they are learning to manipulate individual phonemes. The NRP (2000) reported that phonemic awareness training was most effective when students were taught to manipulate phonemes with letters. Teaching sounds with letters is important because it helps to see how phonemes relate to reading, spelling, and writing of words. For example, phoneme blending can progress as follows (Armbruster et al., 2001):

Teacher: What word is /m/ /a/ /n/?
Students: /m/ /a/ /n/ is *man*.
Teacher: Now we will write the sounds in *man*; /m/, write m; /a/, write a; /n/, write n.
Teacher: (Writes *man* on the board.) Now we are going to read the word *man*.

Likewise, phoneme segmentation and manipulation activities can progress from students separating sounds in a word, to saying each sound as they tap or clap, to writing each sound and reading the whole word.

Classroom Assessment in Phonological Awareness

Instruction in phonological awareness is effective only when you know *which* students need *what* type and *how much* instruction. As Torgesen (1998) so aptly stated, "The best solution to the problem of reading failure is to allocate resources for early identification and prevention" (p. 32). The NRP (2000) reported that students who possess phonological skills do not exhibit difficulties with later word reading and comprehension skills. Weaknesses in phonological awareness can be measured easily by a variety of nonreading tasks (Torgesen). Mercer and Mercer (2001) presented a general framework for examining the progression of phonological skills (see **Figure 7-1**).

FIGURE 7-1

General Hierarchical Framework of Phonological Awareness Language Components and Tasks

Language Components

Least Difficult ←————————————————————————————→ Most Difficult

		Word	Syllable	Onset and Rime	Phoneme
Preschool/Kindergarten	Word Oddity	Select odd word			
	Sentence Segmentation by Words	Count words heard			
	Sentence Segmentation by Syllables		Clap or count syllables in a word		
	Sound Matching				Match initial phoneme Match final phoneme
Kindergarten	Blending				Blend the sounds /d/ /o/ /g/ in "dog"
	Word Manipulation	Say "baseball" without saying "ball" ("base")	Say "winter" without saying "ter" ("win")	Say "mat" without saying /m/ ("at")	
	Syllable Splitting			Hear pair, say onset (/p/) Hear pair, say rime ("air")	
First Grade	Phoneme Segmentation				Hear *sat*, tap out phonemes (/s/, /a/, /t/,)
	Phoneme Manipulation				Say "monkey" without saying /k/ ("money")

Tasks (Least Difficult ↑ to Most Difficult ↓)

Most Difficult

From *Direct Instruction Reading, 3rd Edition* by Carnine/Silbert/Kameenui, © 1997. Reprinted by permission of Pearson Education, Inc., Upper Saddle River, NJ.

Mercer and Mercer (2001) explained phonological awareness as being comprised of four hierarchical language components: word, syllable, onset and rime, and phoneme. They suggested informal assessment tasks that teachers could design and administer. The following suggestions have been adapted from their work.

To assess the *word level* of phonological awareness, have a student recognize spoken words as a unit of language and compare similarities and differences among three to four spoken words. The student is asked which word does not belong. This assessment can test for differences in initial, medial, or final sounds in a set of words. Sentence segmentation by words requires a student to listen to the number of words spoken in a sentence. The student keeps track of how many words are in a sentence by clapping or tapping for each word heard. Finally, having a student delete a word segment and say what is left assesses word manipulation, a more difficult word skill. The use of compound words is suitable for this task.

Syllable awareness within words can be assessed using tasks similar to the word assessments. A student is asked to count the number of syllables heard in a word, to delete syllables from words, and then say the remainder of the word. The onset and rime level requires higher-order phonemic skills. A student must be able to delete individual phonemes and say what remains. For example, the student is asked to say "dinner" without saying "d." In addition to phoneme deletion, requiring a student to "split" syllables assesses onset and rime skills. The student is asked to break off or isolate the first phoneme (onset) of a syllable or to say the remaining part of the syllable (rime).

Phoneme awareness tasks are the most difficult tasks within the realm of phonological awareness and require some formal reading instruction before most students are able to demonstrate these skills. The successful completion of these tasks is a strong predictor of beginning reading acquisition (Adams, 1990); therefore, it is crucial that these skills be assessed in kindergarten and first grade. Phoneme segmentation requires a student to break a spoken syllable into its component phonemes. For example, the teacher may say "fat" and the student must tap or clap once for each phoneme (/f/ /a/ /t/). This task is more difficult than it seems, as many phonemes do not produce discrete sounds within words. Some phonemes spill into the next phoneme (e.g., *strap*). Finally, the most difficult phoneme awareness task is the ability to manipulate individual phonemes and regenerate a word or nonword. For example, a student is asked to delete a phoneme at the beginning, the end, or in the middle of the word and say what remains. In addition, the student is asked to reorder phonemes by saying syllables backwards (e.g., say *pit* backwards = *tip*).

Although formal measures of phonological awareness are available and can document progress against an established norm, teachers can assess and constantly monitor student progress with informal tests that mirror classroom instruction and require less administration time. Kameenui et al. (2001) suggested benchmarks for student performance of phonological skills. By mid-year, kindergarten students should be able to produce 25 first sounds per minute. By the end of kindergarten, students should be able to produce 35 sound segments per minute. By mid-year of first grade, students should be able to produce 35–45 first sounds per minute.

Finally, teachers who incorporate letters of the alphabet during phonological awareness activities will enhance students' concepts of print (i.e., knowing that marks on a page represent words that convey meaning). Mercer and Mercer (2001) suggested that concepts of print fall under the realm of emergent literacy skills, and teachers should assess these skills. They suggested that a teacher select an age-appropriate book for the student and ask the student to perform the following skills:

- Point out the front and back of the book.
- Demonstrate awareness that print contains a message.
- Indicate where to start reading on a page.
- Point to a single word and to two words.
- Indicate the direction to read words (i.e., left to right).
- Indicate that at the end of a line you sweep left to the next lower line.
- Demonstrate an understanding of the concepts of *first* and *last*.

- Indicate that you read the left page before the right page.
- Indicate that you stop at a period.
- Indicate that you pause at a comma.
- Count words in a line.
- Point to one letter.
- Point to an uppercase letter.
- Point to the top and the bottom of a page.
- Point to the top and the bottom of a picture. (p. 293)

Phonological awareness instruction coupled with reading meaningful connected texts to promote concepts of print are necessary preskills for students' understanding of the next "big idea," the alphabetic principle.

The Alphabetic Principle:
The *Second* Big Idea

The alphabetic principle consists of alphabetic understanding and phonological recoding. *Alphabetic understanding* is the awareness that the left-to-right spellings of printed words represent their phonemes. *Phonological recoding* is the ability to use letter-sound correspondences to pronounce an unknown printed string of letters to form words (Kameenui et al., 2001). The English language is an alphabetic system that is not perfectly alphabetic (i.e., the letters of the English words do not always map one-on-one to phonemes) (Adams, 1990); therefore, good readers must have a strategy that unlocks the code to the alphabetic principle. Decoding, the process of using letter-sound correspondences, is essential to the recognition of the English alphabet (Kameenui et al., 2001). Phonics instruction is an effective strategic instruction that helps students decode words and understand the alphabetic principle (Armbruster et al., 2001). Armbruster and colleagues summarized the findings of the NRP report (2000) on effectiveness of phonics instruction as:

- Systematic and explicit phonics instruction is more effective than nonsystematic or no phonics instruction.
- Systematic and explicit phonics instruction significantly improves kindergarten and first-grade students' word recognition and spelling.
- Systematic and explicit phonics instruction is particularly beneficial for students who are having difficulty learning to read and who are at-risk for developing future reading problems.
- Systematic and explicit phonics instruction is most effective when introduced early. (pp. 13–15)

What is "systematic and explicit" phonics instruction?

Systematic phonics instruction involves the direct teaching (explicit) of a carefully sequenced set of letter-sound relationships (systematic) (Armbruster et al., 2001). In addition, teachers model tasks and use brief and consistent wording to make the instruction explicit (Kameenui et al., 2001). This differs from the older version of phonics instruction of the 1960s. Foorman and Torgesen (2001) explained that phonics instruction at that time did not teach the *identity* of phonemes and the *systematic links* among phonemes (sounds) and graphemes (letters). Instead, teachers taught simple sounding-out procedures that involved no overt relationship to the letters of the alphabet.

Students Who Have Difficulties with the Alphabetic Principle

Kameenui et al. (2001) described students who lack alphabetic understanding as those who cannot

1. understand that words are composed of letters.
2. associate an alphabetic character (i.e., letter) with its corresponding phoneme or sound.
3. identify a word based on a sequence of letter-sound correspondence (e.g., that "mat" is made up of three letter-sound correspondences /m/ /a/ /t/).
4. blend letter-sound correspondences to identify decodable words.
5. use knowledge of letter-sound correspondences to identify words in which letters represent their most common sound.
6. identify and manipulate letter-sound correspondences within words.
7. read pseudowords (e.g., tup, with reasonable speed). (pp. 1–2)

As you readily can deduce from the list of difficulties, many students require systematic and explicit instruction that integrates phonemic awareness and the alphabetic principle. Teachers can use and have been using systematic and explicit phonics instruction successfully to integrate the big ideas of phonological awareness and the alphabetic principle. Burkhardt (as cited in Flesch, 1981) aptly stated, "When students are taught to read in a structured, teacher-directed instructional program, they read" (p. xx). The following section introduces you to an overview of major methods and strategies teachers use to ensure students exhibit mastery of the alphabetic principle.

Strategies/Methods in the Alphabetic Principle

Moats (1998) emphasized, "One of the most fundamental flaws found in almost all phonics programs, including traditional ones, is that they teach the code backwards. That is, they go from letter to sound instead of from sound to letter" (p. 44). Carnine et al. (1997) recommended teaching letter sounds before letter names as knowledge of letter names is not as useful in beginning reading as the knowledge of letter sounds. In addition, they recommended that students sound out words before they read whole word units and read words in isolation (lists) prior to reading words in stories. They included the following four guidelines for sequencing letter-sound instruction:

1. Initially introduce only the most common sound for a new letter.
2. Separate letters that are visually or auditorily similar.
3. Introduce more useful letters before less useful letters.
4. Introduce lower-case (small) letters before upper-case (capital) letters. (p. 71)

The authors explained that the most common sound for a letter is usually how it sounds in a short word, such as *fan* or *mitt*. Short vowel sounds are more common than long vowel sounds. Continuous sounds are held for one to two seconds without distorting the sound, and stop sounds are quickly pronounced. **Table 7-4** shows the most common sounds represented by each letter of the alphabet.

Separating the introduction of letters that are visually and/or auditorily similar reduces student confusion. Introducing more useful letter-sounds first enables students to decode more words because they have more useful knowledge. Finally, lower-case letters should be introduced before upper-case letters because the majority of written material is comprised of lower-case letters. An example of an acceptable sequence for introducing letters is as follows (Carnine et al., 1997):

a m t s l f d r o g l h u c b n k v e w j p y T L M F D I N A R H G B x q z J E Q

TABLE 7-4

Most Common Sounds of Single Letters

Continuous Sounds	Stop Sounds
a (fat)	b (boy)
e (bet)	c (can)
f (fill)	d (did)
i (sit)	g (got)
l (let)	h (his)
m (mad)	j (jet)
n (nut)	k (kiss)
o (not)	p (pet)
r (rat)	q (quit)
s (sell)	t (top)
u (cut)	x (fox)
v (vet)	
w (wet)	
y (yes)	
z (zoo)	

From *Direct Instruction Reading, 3rd Edition* by Carnine/Silbert/Kameenui, © 1997. Reprinted by permission of Pearson Education, Inc., Upper Saddle River, NJ.

As stated earlier, English is not a perfect phonetic-based language. Students, particularly those with disabilities and those at-risk for reading difficulties, need instruction that goes beyond simple letter-sound correspondences. Carnine et al. (1997) suggested that teaching students to decode words involves:

(a) phonic analysis skills,
(b) structural analysis skills, and
(c) contextual analysis skills.

As teachers provide students with instruction and practice in sounding out words letter by letter, students begin to see *units* of letters rather than merely individual letters. *Phonic analysis* is teaching the students the relationship between these units and their sounds. Carnine et al. recommended that during the primary grades, students learn letter combinations and a strategy to decode words that contain the VCe pattern (e.g., *lake, nose, stripe*). The format for teaching the VCe pattern is described in **Table 7-5.**

Structural analysis instruction shows students how to decode multisyllabic words by discriminating their prefixes, suffixes, and base words. In addition, activities that involve teaching students how word parts are combined will help students decode words with spelling changes (Carnine et al., 1997). For example, the word *repairing* is formed by adding the prefix *re* and the ending *ing* to the base word *pair* (re + pair + ing). Carnine et al. recommended that systematic introduction of prefixes, suffixes, and multisyllabic words should occur throughout the primary and intermediate grades. In addition, teachers can introduce the concept of *morphemes* (the smallest unit of our language that has meaning) to reinforce word structure as well as word meaning. For example, *re* means *again* and *ing* means *when you do something*. Students learn to combine *re* and *ing* to *name* and attach the meaning *when you name again*.

The English language contains *irregular words* that do not conform to phonic or structural analysis. Such words cannot be decoded because either (a) the sounds of the letters in a word

TABLE 7-5

Introductory Format for VCe Words

Teacher	Students
Teacher writes on the board: game, rope, mine, tape, note.	
1. Teacher states the rule: "An *e* at the end tells us to say the name of this (pointing to *a*) letter."	
2. Teacher guides students in applying the rule.	
a. Teacher points to game. "Is there an *e* at the end of this word?" (Signal.)	"Yes."
b. Teacher points to *a*. "So we say the name of this letter."	
c. "What's the name of this letter?" (Signal.)	"A."
d. "Get ready to tell me the word." Teacher pauses for 2 seconds, then says, "What word?" (Signal.)	"Game."
e. Teacher repeats step 2 (a–d) with the remaining 4 words.	
3. Students read all the words without guidance from the teacher.	
a. "You're going to read these words."	
b. Teacher points to *game*, pauses 2 seconds, then signals.	"Game."
c. Teacher repeats step 3(b) with remaining words.	
4. Teacher calls on individual students to read one or more words.	

From *Direct Instruction Reading, 3rd Edition* by Carnine/Silbert/Kameenui, © 1997. Reprinted by permission of Pearson Education, Inc., Upper Saddle River, NJ.

are not predictable, or (b) the words contain letter-sound correspondences unfamiliar to the student (Carnine et al., 1997). Teachers need to rely on contextual analysis, using the context of a sentence, along with phonic- and structural-analysis cues to decode such irregular words. Contextual analysis involves teaching students to rely on the *word order* (syntax) and *word meaning* (semantics) of the sentence in which the unfamiliar word appears. Word order limits the number of possible word types that can come next in the sentence. For example in the sentence, "Mary jumped over the _____" the final word might be any of several nouns (e.g., *log, stream, fence*), but could not be a verb (e.g., *licked, stripped, finished*). Word meaning further limits the number of possible word choices. For example, the noun needed to complete "Mary jumped over the _____" should make sense instead of nouns that would not make reasonable sense (e.g., *truck, canyon, moon*). In addition to word order and word meaning cues, students can use context to check for decoding errors. If a student reads, "The bunny went *hopping* down the path" as "The bunny went *hoping* down the path," he can infer he made a decoding error. The student needs to recheck *hoping* and correct the mistake (Carnine et al.).

In summary, teachers seeking well-designed programs that teach the alphabetic principle should look for the following basic features (Kameenui et al., 2001):

- explicit "sounding out" strategies and teacher modeling of critical concepts and skills
- systematic progression of simple word types (consonant-vowel-consonant), word lengths (number of phonemes), and word complexity (phonemes in words, blends, stop sounds) to more complex words
- explicit procedures to teach and review irregular words prior to their use in passages
- delays passage reading until students are proficient with letter-sound correspondences and simple word types, and
- explicit strategies for teaching students to transition from reading words in lists to reading words in connected text.

Classroom Assessment in the Alphabetic Principle

Torgesen (1998) emphasized that, "Once reading instruction begins, the best predictor of future reading growth is current reading achievement, and the most critical indicators of good progress in learning to read during the early elementary period are measures of word reading skill" (p. 37). Teachers should assess students' understanding of word reading skill, the alphabetic principle, in an on-going manner. *Informal assessments* that involve examining student's daily work, teacher-constructed tests, and oral reading probes should be administered on a frequent basis. Informal measures can be incorporated within the instructional period and use classroom materials that are readily available to the teacher and student (Mercer & Mercer, 2001).

Other commonly used diagnostic measures of word reading ability are tests that are *criterion-referenced* or *standardized* in nature. These tests measure sight word reading, phonetic reading, and word reading fluency. Torgesen (1998) provided a clear description of what these tests entail.

- *Sight word tests* require students to read standardized lists of words that gradually increase in length and complexity while decreasing in frequency of occurrence in printed English.

- *Nonword reading tests* provide the single best measure of a student's ability to apply phonetic reading. This type of test consists of a series of increasingly complex nonwords that students are asked to "sound out as best they can." These nonsense words are presented out of context, so they stress the student's ability to fully analyze and decode each word.

- *Word or nonword fluency assessments* require students to correctly recognize as many word items as possible in a given time period. These assessments measure a student's rate and accuracy of nonsense and real word production and should be administered to assess *fluency* (rate and accuracy) of alphabetic knowledge and skills.

Fluency in reading connected text (phrases and sentences), the third "big idea" in beginning reading instruction, is discussed in the next section of this chapter.

Fluency: The *Third* Big Idea

Oral reading fluency, the ability to read text quickly (rate), accurately, and with proper expression, is a critical but neglected reading skill (Fuchs, Fuchs, Hosp, & Jenkins, 2001; National Reading Panel, 2000). The NRP expressed concern that U.S. students are not achieving fluency in reading. A recent large-scale study by the National Assessment of Educational Progress (NAEP) found that 44% of a representative sample of the nation's fourth graders was low in fluency. In addition, the NAEP found a close relationship between fluency and reading comprehension as students who scored lower on measures of fluency also scored lower on measures of comprehension (Armbruster et al., 2001). While fluency is not the only skill necessary for good reading comprehension, it provides a bridge between word recognition and comprehension (Armbruster et al., 2001). Breznitz (1997) investigated the relationships between reading rate, decoding, and comprehension during student levels of reading acquisition over their first five years in school. Students' reading rate in the later grades (fourth to fifth) became a determining factor in reading performance.

Fluency develops gradually over time. Fluent reading is not a distinct stage of development in which readers can read all words quickly and easily. Fluency changes with text type and difficulty. Even fluent older readers experience slow, labored reading rates when presented with reading materials that contain unfamiliar words or highly technical material (Armbruster et al., 2001).

Fluency is comprised of *automaticity* and *prosody*. Automaticity is a performance level that can be demonstrated by individuals in other academic and non-academic areas (e.g., sports, music, math facts, etc.). Reading automaticity is the fast, effortless ability to translate letters-to-sounds-to-words (Armbruster et al., 2001; Kameenui et al., 2001). In other words, it is a combination of *reading rate* and *reading accuracy*. Many readers are able to decode accurately and efficiently, but may not read with expression. *Prosody* is the "quality" of oral reading including intonation and expression (Kameenui et al.). It is an essential component of reading fluency that promotes reading for meaning of connected text.

Students Who Have Difficulties with Fluency

Disfluent readers read in a choppy, word-by-word manner. They tend to omit, substitute, or misread words as they read aloud. In addition, they read in a monotonous, expressionless style because they do not pay attention to punctuation or phrasing in connected text. These difficulties lead to an overall inability to read for meaning.

Being able to identify those students at-risk for reading fluency difficulties can best be described in contrast to students who are fluent readers. Kameenui et al. (2001) provides the following list of skills good readers are able to perform:

- identify letter-sound correspondences accurately and quickly
- identify familiar spelling patterns to increase decoding efficiency
- apply knowledge of the alphabetic principle to identify words in isolation and connected text fluently
- rely primarily on the letters in words rather than the context or pictures
- process virtually every letter
- have a reliable strategy for decoding words, and
- practice reading words a sufficient number of times for words to become automatic.

Readers who are able to do the above-mentioned skills in an effortless manner have freed up their cognitive resources and can use those resources for the higher-level skill of text comprehension. Students who have difficulty with these skills expend a large portion of their mental energy on basic word identification, thereby limiting their cognitive resources for gaining meaning from what they read (Fuchs et al., 2001).

Finally, teacher knowledge of what constitutes the independent, instructional, and frustration levels of reading and the appropriate reading rates across grade levels are needed in order to identify students experiencing poor reading fluency. First, a student's reading level is primarily determined by *accuracy* of oral reading. Kameenui et al. (2001) described the independent reading level at 97% accuracy (no more than three errors per a 100-word passage), the instructional level at 94–97% accuracy (three to six errors per a 100-word passage), and the frustration level at or lower than 93% accuracy (more than six errors per a 100-word passage). To build fluency, materials should be at a student's instructional level or above (Kameenui et al.).

Oral reading fluency is usually described as the number of words read correctly per minute (wcpm). To date, no one acceptable reading rate standard exists for oral reading fluency (Hasbrouck & Tindal, 1992). Carnine et al. (1997) suggested desired reading rates, irrespective of accuracy, based on the instructional reading level of materials and the student's first reading of words per minute. The suggested rates for instructional materials at the end of each grade level were:

(a) 60 words per minute for grade one,
(b) 110 words per minute for grade two,

(c) 135 words per minute for grade three, and

(d) 150 words per minute for grade four and higher.

These suggested reading rates did not take into account word accuracy or reading with expression. Kameenui et al. (2001) suggested that students at the end of first grade should be able to do the following:

- read meaningful grade-level connected text accurately with no more than one error in 20 words
- read grade-level connected text fluently at a rate of one word per second, and
- read grade-level material with phrasing attending to punctuation.

Clearly, teachers need to be cognizant of a student's instructional level of reading, reading rate and accuracy, and ability to read with proper expression. Students experiencing difficulty with any of these skills, or who are falling behind their peers, need strategies and opportunities to build reading fluency.

Strategies/Methods in Fluency

Teachers should select materials and methods for improving reading fluency based on what reading skills the students have learned and what aspects of reading fluency (automaticity or prosody) are problematic for them. The National Reading Panel (2000) reported that the method of repeated and monitored oral reading improved reading fluency and for that matter overall reading achievement. Additionally, they found that repeated oral reading improved the reading ability of all students throughout the elementary grades as well as struggling readers in the higher-grade levels. It is important to note that the NRP did **not** find evidence to support instructional time spent on silent, independent reading with minimal guidance and feedback. The following instructional methods involve oral reading with teacher-directed instruction and guidance that are designed to promote the basic fluency components of automaticity and prosody.

Reading for Automaticity

Guided oral repeated readings with feedback take many forms. Samuels (1979) first developed a specific procedure that includes a preset criterion for rate and accuracy. The first time a student orally reads a passage, the listening partner or coach times the student and notes word reading errors. The correct words read per minute and the errors are charted to establish a baseline measure of oral reading performance. Coaches provide students explicit feedback and the students reread the passage up to five times. Coaches provide the student with explicit, corrective feedback at the end of each reading. When the student is ready, the coach times the student to see if the preset criterion levels were met. Teachers should be careful to select reading materials at the stu-

Partner reading involves pairing students who read aloud to each other, with the emphasis on accuracy.

dent's instructional level and passages that contain high overlap of similar words. The text students practice rereading should be relatively short, no more than 50 to 200 words, depending on the age of the students.

Another form of repeated reading is tape-assisted reading. In tape-assisted reading students read along in their books as they listen to an "expert" reader on audiotape. Reading material for this method should be at the student's independent reading level as the aim is to increase the student's reading rate while maintaining a high degree of accuracy. Reading along with the tape should be repeated until the student is able to read the passage at the expert's level independently (Armbruster et al., 2001).

Partner reading, a third form of guided oral repeated reading, involves paired students reading aloud to one another. The emphasis of this approach is on reading accuracy over reading rate. Usually, a stronger reader is paired with a less fluent reader. The stronger reader reads first, providing a model for the less fluent reader. Then the less fluent reader reads the same passage. The stronger reader provides the reader with word identification assistance or corrections of misidentified words as the less fluent reader is reading. This process continues until the less fluent reader has reread the passage for a specified number of times (Armbruster et al., 2001).

Reading for Prosody

Armbruster et al. (2001) suggested that teachers should model fluent reading, and then have the students reread the passage or text on their own. Students should have the opportunity to learn how a "reader's voice" can help written text make sense. Teachers in the primary grades can use big books, big enough so that all students can see the text. Teachers point to each word as they read the text with appropriate expression and pausing at punctuation marks. In addition, teachers should explain to students why they are reading in a certain way. Another method that increases students' opportunities to read with expression is "readers' theater." Students rehearse and perform a play. They learn to read from scripts rich in dialogue. Readers' theater provides readers with reasons to reread, or rehearse their scripts and become fluent with their lines (Armbruster et al.).

Students need opportunities for reading practice. Repeated readings and other fluency instructional procedures provide students with needed opportunities to become efficient and competent readers. In addition, having students engaged in repeated oral reading and monitoring of their own progress can be motivating (Armbruster et al., 2001). The next section discusses how teachers can assess and monitor students' reading fluency.

Classroom Assessment in Fluency

Teachers, particularly those in elementary grades or those working with older struggling readers, should assess fluency regularly. Teachers can informally assess students' reading fluency by simply listening to students orally read selected passages and make a judgment about their fluency. Formal measures of fluency assessment would include assessment of reading rate against some established norm, reading expression, and comprehension.

The easiest way to assess fluency is to take timed samples of a student's reading. Armbruster et al. (2001) offered the following procedure for calculating one-minute timed readings:

1. Select two or three brief passages from a grade-level basal text.
2. Have students individually read each passage aloud for exactly one minute.
3. Count the total number of words read for each passage. Compute the average number of words read per minute.

4. Count the number of errors the student made on each passage. Compute the average number of errors per minute.
5. Subtract the average number of errors read per minute from the average number of words read per minute. This is the average number of words read correctly per minute.
6. Repeat this assessment procedure several times during the year and graph the results.
7. Compare these results with locally established or published norms.

Teachers can use this procedure to determine students' independent, instructional, and frustration levels of reading. In addition, teachers can note what types of reading errors students are making as they read. Knowledge of students' errors can aid in the decision-making process for evaluating instruction and providing necessary remediation.

Assessing reading fluency and providing for fluency practice is critical to the overall end goal of reading for meaning. While not the only crucial skill, fluency provides students with the opportunity to be exposed to more words more often. This fact, coupled with the next "big idea," vocabulary/background knowledge, provides the foundation for successful reading comprehension.

Vocabulary Knowledge: The *Fourth* Big Idea

Vocabulary development is another critical area of concern for teachers, because students who know more word meanings are more likely to be better readers (Nagy, Anderson, & Herman, 1987). Vocabulary acquisition is a complex task that occurs in many settings. These settings range from incidental interactions to systematic and explicit instruction. Developing a working knowledge of vocabulary words and their meanings can occur in both oral and written contexts (Harmon, 1999). Explicitly teaching the meaning of words is especially necessary for students with limited background knowledge such as students with disabilities or students at-risk for reading difficulties. However, explicit instruction is also necessary when introducing difficult words or new concepts for the first time.

Assessing where to begin vocabulary instruction, on the continuum of explicit to implicit instruction, will be one of the important choices that the teacher will have to make in the vocabulary instruction process. However, researchers have noted that vocabulary knowledge can be more easily identified as an isolated skill in early primary grades versus in later grades (Simmons & Kameenui, 1990). That is, teachers of older students need to be aware that they may need to integrate vocabulary instruction into the content of the class rather than teaching isolated skills.

Vocabulary instruction for students at-risk for and with disabilities must be delivered in a manner that takes into account the individual student's background knowledge of the subject. The student's knowledge may be a result of explicit instruction on the words or life experiences related to the words. This background knowledge can be acquired through different formats, but it is paramount that the teacher conducts a pre-assessment, either formally or informally, of the student's knowledge of vocabulary words. This pre-assessment will guide the teacher to a starting point on the continuum of explicit to implicit vocabulary instruction and be an indicator for how much instructional support a student may need in the process of acquiring new vocabulary (Gunning, 1996).

The two major types of text structures that students will access and need vocabulary skills for success in are **narrative** (story type) and **expository** (factual information) texts. Generally, in the primary grades narrative text is emphasized while students are *learning to read*. In upper elementary grades and throughout secondary grades expository text is the main type of text used. Expository text is where students are *reading to learn*. For students with disabilities and students at-risk for reading difficulty, vocabulary deficits may be most evident in expository text structures, because new concepts are introduced rapidly and words may have multiple meanings (Baker, Simmons, & Kameenui, 1995). In order to increase opportunities for vocabulary acquisition and future reading success, teachers must provide explicit vocabulary instruction within both narrative and expository text structures.

Students Who Have Difficulties with Vocabulary

As was noted previously, background knowledge is a key factor in vocabulary understanding and acquisition in both narrative and expository text structures (Robbins & Ehri, 1994). Students with disabilities and students at-risk for reading difficulties need repetition, multiple exposures to vocabulary words, and sufficient practice using new words in order to expand their vocabularies (NRP, 2000). Therefore, teachers must provide an adequate number of examples and definitions of new words to ensure the student's understanding. Teachers will need to build experiential backgrounds for students by talking about concepts and ideas rather than merely teaching labels (Gunning, 1996).

Not only will teachers need to build background knowledge through discussions, but also teachers should explicitly point out how words are related by using synonyms and antonyms to connect and differentiate vocabulary. By explicitly teaching the relationships among words, teachers develop a depth of word meaning in students who may not have the requisite skills to connect new concepts to previously learned concepts (Gunning, 1996). Further, teachers should praise students who use new words in context and transfer their knowledge of new words to other unrelated tasks.

A final, but paramount issue for students at-risk for or with reading difficulties is the empirically noted relationship between reading achievement and vocabulary acquisition (NRP, 2000). To build vocabulary skills students must successfully engage in considerable amounts of *independent level* reading in order to be exposed to unknown words a sufficient number of times for the words to be learned (Baker, Simmons, & Kameenui, 1995). Moreover, lack of independent reading limits reading volume and vocabulary development, which in turn creates variability in skills (Cunningham & Stanovich, 2001) and a widening of the reading achievement gap. As Baker et al. (1995) point out, "Vocabulary acquisition is crucial for academic development. Not only do students need a rich body of word knowledge to succeed in basic skills, they also need vocabulary to learn content area material" (p. 3). Below are some specific activities that can enhance vocabulary acquisition for students at-risk for and with reading difficulties.

Strategies/Methods for Increasing Vocabulary Knowledge

Vocabulary can be acquired through several instructional approaches. Computer assisted instruction, feature analysis/semantic mapping, pre-instruction of vocabulary, contextual analysis, and the keyword method are a few approaches that have been effective in teaching vocabulary (NRP, 2000). Other approaches such as modeling, morphemic analysis, and the use of the dictionary have also been cited (Carnine et al., 1997) as strategies that may increase vocabulary knowledge. Each of these approaches is described in the following paragraphs.

Computer assisted instruction (CAI) is a student-directed approach facilitated by the use of computer technology. First, this approach allows for individualized and independent instruction. Second, some computer instructional software has an embedded data collection option allowing the teacher to analyze the student's error patterns and skill acquisition. This error analysis assessment is quite helpful in on-going progress monitoring of vocabulary acquisition. CAI can also be motivational for students who excel at computer-based activities.

Feature analysis and semantic mapping are graphic organizational tools used to show relationships among words and their meanings that belong to a particular category (e.g., types of governments, rock formations, or the nine planets). **Table 7-6** provides an example of a feature analysis of the nine planets in our solar system. As you can see, students are able to differentiate between characteristics of the planets and therefore recognize the distinct features of each planet as illustrated in the matrix. When presenting the feature analysis matrix, the teacher may assist students in determining if the concept (planet) possesses each of the features. If the students have little prior knowledge, then the teacher can directly present each concept and its features. The amount of support needed by individual students to acquire vocabulary knowledge should have been determined through a pre-assessment of familiarity with the nine planets. Depending on the amount of instructional support needed by struggling students, the benefit of the feature analysis approach is that it allows a teacher to reach a wide range of students through one teaching strategy.

A semantic map is a less structured graphic tool than the feature analysis. The semantic map allows for more elaboration on the relationships of the current concepts to previously taught concepts (see **Figure 7-2**). For example, the semantic map can be completed prior to reading an excerpt on fish, can be completed as information is presented in the text, or can be completed as a review activity after reading a selection. Once again, depending on the amount of instructional support a student or group of students may need, the teacher may complete the map with the whole group, or allow students to create a map in small groups or individually. After the semantic map is completed, a discussion of its components should be held to clarify any unclear concepts.

Pre-instruction of vocabulary is an effective approach to providing multiple exposures to new vocabulary and increasing the likelihood of word comprehension. Teachers can present new vocabulary in isolation prior to text reading (Kameenui & Carnine, 1998) or teachers can provide a context for the new vocabulary through pre-reading discussions. The teacher should introduce essential vocabulary, being careful to limit this instruction to a small number of critical words. Critical words should be carefully introduced, practiced, and reviewed in subsequent lessons (Carnine et al., 1997). By receiving pre-instruction on new or critical vocabulary terms, the student gains an idea of the content of the material yet to be covered and begins building a knowledge base for continued vocabulary growth.

In *contextual analysis,* the student uses the words in a sentence surrounding an unknown word to figure out the unknown word's meaning. While context analysis is a highly independent skill and must be taught explicitly, it is an essential skill for students reading content area texts, because these texts often have many unknown words. Many times the definition of an unknown word is given through the use of an appositive, a word or phrase defining the noun it directly follows, which may contain a synonym or definition (Carnine et al., 1997). Sometimes contextual analysis is made more difficult when the synonym or definition is separated from the unknown word.

Students must be explicitly taught *how and when* to use context clues to determine the meaning of words. Carnine et al. offer these three steps in teaching the use of context clues. The teacher

1. points out the unknown word,
2. has the students find the words that tell what the unknown word means, and
3. has the students restate the sentence substituting a synonym or description for the unknown word.

Providing adequate practice and appropriate examples in teaching contextual analysis is as important as the teaching procedure itself.

The *keyword method* is used when a student is taught to construct a visual image that connects the target vocabulary word to a familiar word that shares common features such

TABLE 7-6

Feature Analysis

		Life	Hotter than Earth	Colder than Earth	Big in Relationship to Earth	Small in Relationship to Earth	Rings	Satellites	Physical Characteristics Similar to Earth	Mostly Gaseous
Inner	Mercury	-	+	-	-	+	-	-	+	-
	Venus	-	+	-	-	-	-	-	+	-
	Earth	+	-	-	-	-	-	+	+	-
	Mars	-	-	+	-	+	-	+	+	-
Outer	Jupiter	-	-	+	+	-	+	+	-	+
	Saturn	-	-	+	+	-	+	+	-	+
	Uranus	-	-	+	+	-	+	+	-	+
	Neptune	-	-	+	+	-	-	+	-	+
	Pluto	-	-	+	-	+	-	+	+	-

From *Direct Instruction Reading, 3rd Edition* by Carnine/Silbert/Kameenui, © 1997. Reprinted by permission of Pearson Education, Inc., Upper Saddle River, NJ.

FIGURE 7-2

Example of a Semantic Map

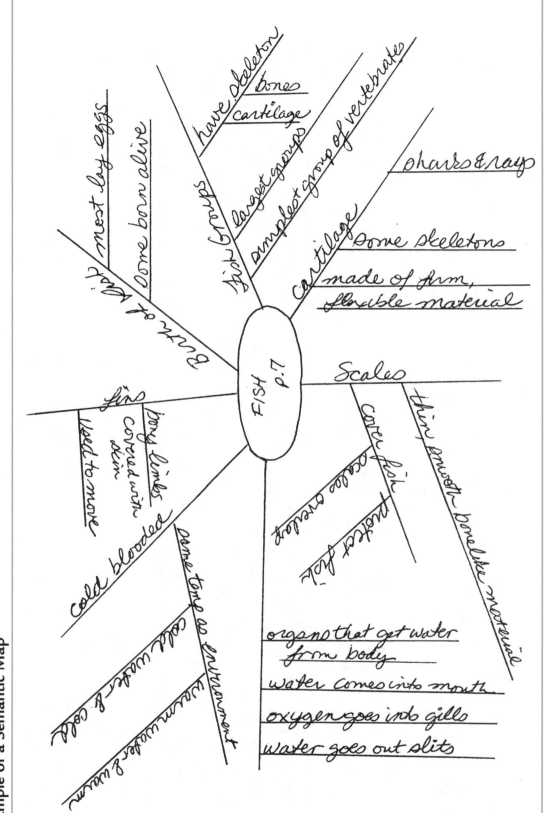

From *Direction Instruction Reading, 3rd Edition* by Carnine/Silbert/Kameenui, © 1997. Reprinted by permission of Pearson Education, Inc., Upper Saddle River, NJ.

as auditory or visual similarity. For example, in the word phoneme, which means the smallest unit of spoken language, the keyword *phone* might be used to have the student generate an image of listening to spoken sounds on a telephone (commonly referred to as the phone). When asked to recall the meaning of phoneme, the student retrieves *phone* because of its acoustic similarity to *phoneme* and then recalls the visual image and the meaning of phoneme. Critics of the keyword method have argued that it works better for concrete words (e.g., phoneme) rather than abstract words (e.g., festive). Research has demonstrated that the keyword method has been successful at teaching abstract words as well as concrete words (Mastropieri & Scruggs, 1994).

Other methods for teaching vocabulary include *modeling, morphemic analysis,* and looking up *definitions* in a dictionary (Carnine et al., 1997). *Modeling* is the verbal explanation of a new vocabulary word that includes the meaning and use of the new word (See **Table 7-7** for a modeling format). *Morphemic analysis* involves dividing a word into its component parts (morphemes—smallest unit of meaning) to figure out what it means. For example, through morphemic analysis the word unworkable can be divided into three morphemes: *un* meaning *not, work,* and *able* meaning able to. Teaching students the meaning of morphemes gives them a strategy to understand vocabulary words (Carnine et al.). Finally, finding *definitions* of new words may be done using a dictionary. However, this should be the last instructional method chosen and used only when the teacher deems that students do not have adequate language skills to understand the new vocabulary word or it is too difficult a concept to model. Using the dictionary should be the last instructional technique used in vocabulary instruction, because it is the least independent and interactive of instructional techniques for vocabulary instruction.

Classroom Assessment in Vocabulary Knowledge

After vocabulary instruction and reading activities are completed, students need the opportunity to review, apply, and synthesize the concepts they have learned. Informal teacher made activities or curriculum-based measures such as word games (e.g., crossword puzzles and cloze passages) built around story or content area vocabularies are helpful in assessing a student's command of word meaning. More formal assessments such as norm-referenced measures can be used to measure vocabulary acquisition, but may not include the array of words that have been recently introduced in the day-to-day lessons. Since curriculum-based measures relate directly to story or content area texts introduced daily, only curriculum-based assessments will be presented here. These assessments include teacher made vocabulary tests, commercially made vocabulary tests, and application of vocabulary skills in daily assignments.

The content and nature of teacher made vocabulary tests may vary greatly based on the age and skill acquisition of the students being assessed. For example, matching a pictorial image to a written word provides a measure of vocabulary knowledge for concrete vocabulary terms and is appropriate for primary level vocabulary assessment. For more abstract terms, students may match a word to a definition or provide a written definition in order to assess vocabulary knowledge (Jenkins & Dixon, 1983). Whether assessing abstract or concrete terms, using a cloze procedure may indicate whether a student can use context clues to determine the appropriate word for sentence completion. An example of a cloze procedure would be to have students use vocabulary words to complete sentences (e.g., The only planet in our solar system with identified life forms is _____.).

Commercial assessments usually accompany commercially available reading programs or content area textbooks. These assessments are curriculum-based measures. The use of commercial curriculum-based assessments is recommended in the context of teacher mediation. That is, the teacher should review the assessments and make the

TABLE 7-7

Format for Teaching Vocabulary: Modeling Example

	Object	Adjective (color)	Adverb	Adjective (texture)
Step 1: *Teacher models positive and negative examples.*	"This is a mitten" or "This is not a mitten." Examples: brown wool mitten brown wool glove red nylon glove red nylon mitten blue sock blue mitten	"This is orange" or "This is not orange." Examples: 2" red disk 2" orange disk 4 × 4 orange paper 4 × 4 brown paper	"This is writing carefully" or "This is not writing carefully." Examples: Write on board, first neatly, then sloppily Hang up coat, first carefully, then carelessly Arrange books, first carelessly, then carefully	"This is rough" or "This is not rough." Examples: red flannel shirt red silk shirt piece of sandpaper piece of paper smooth book cover rough book cover
Step 2: *Teacher tests.* Present positive and negative examples until the students make six consecutive correct responses.	"Is this a mitten or not a mitten?"	"Is this orange or not orange?"	"Is this carefully or not carefully?"	"Is this rough or not rough?"
Step 3: *Teacher tests by asking for names.* Present examples until students make six consecutive correct responses.	"What is this?" glove mitten sock mitten mitten glove	"What color is this?" orange brown orange red	"Show me how you write carefully" or "Tell me how I am writing." (carefully, slowly, quickly, etc.)	"Find the one that is rough" or "Tell me about this shirt."

From *Direct Instruction Reading, 3rd Edition* by Carnine/Silbert/Kameenui, © 1997. Reprinted by permission of Pearson Education, Inc., Upper Saddle River, NJ.

necessary modifications to be certain that these measures are appropriate for students at-risk for or with reading difficulties (See Chapter 6 for a discussion of instructional modifications). Once these assessments have been reviewed and modified, then they should be considered a viable curriculum-based vocabulary assessment.

Finally, the generalization or transfer of vocabulary knowledge to unpracticed tasks is a clear indication that students are incorporating newly learned vocabulary into their knowledge base. While teacher observations of vocabulary knowledge transfer occur in the natural process of instruction, teachers should provide more structured assessments of knowledge transfer. For example, having students use an independent application of vocabulary words to a new task can demonstrate whether sufficient instruction and acquisition has occurred. The ultimate goal of vocabulary knowledge is increased student control over independent application. Demonstrating independent knowledge of vocabulary increases the likelihood that students will comprehend written materials containing the mastered vocabulary words (NRP, 2000). Linking vocabulary to comprehension leads us to the fifth and final big idea, reading comprehension.

Comprehension: The *Fifth* Big Idea

Reading comprehension is a complex metacognitive process in which an individual derives *meaning* from printed or written materials. This process is the culmination and concurrent integration of all the "big ideas" (phonological awareness, alphabetic understanding, fluency, and vocabulary knowledge). Understanding, synthesizing, and deriving meaning from written material is the "essence of reading" (Durkin, 1993).

Whether an individual has the ability to derive meaning from text or not has implications for motivation to engage in the reading process (Collins, Dickson, Simmons, & Kameenui, 1996). Effective readers use a variety of learning strategies to ensure comprehension of text. Effective teachers employ a variety of instructional strategies to teach the reading comprehension processes. Reading strategy instruction increases the likelihood that students will comprehend textual materials (NRP, 2000). Students with disabilities and students at-risk for reading difficulties will require explicit instruction in comprehension strategies. Comprehension strategy instruction can begin early, even before students are able to read print.

Two major areas of reading comprehension are **literal** comprehension (recalling explicitly stated information such as characters or events) and **inferential** comprehension (inferring meaning based on background knowledge or conjecture about information that is not explicitly stated). Literal comprehension requires a student to recall, locate, identify, or produce specific facts that took place in a reading selection. The ability to complete a literal comprehension task may depend on several factors:

1. the degree to which items are literal,
2. the length of the passage,
3. the order in which questions are asked, or
4. the complexity of instructions (Carnine et al., 1997).

Inferential comprehension requires knowledge of relationships between objects or events based on the student's background knowledge (Carnine et al.). Inferential activities do not specify relationships, so teachers may need to lead students through information that is new or technical in nature.

Students Who Have Difficulties with Comprehension

Good readers are aware of why they are reading whereas naive readers may not be aware of their purpose in reading (Pressley, Roehrig, Bogner, Raphael, & Dolezal, 2002). Effective

The more these students read, the more vocabulary and comprehension skills they will acquire.

readers make predictions about what they are reading, figure out meanings of unknown words in context, reread sentences or passages for understanding, and self-monitor their comprehension (Pressley et al.). Naive readers may not have acquired these prerequisite metacognitive skills or even primary reading skills such as decoding or vocabulary. Naive readers use a great deal of their mental capacity on component skills and are unable to bring sufficient cognitive application to the composite metacognitive skill of comprehension (Fuchs et al., 2001). As was noted in the previous section on vocabulary acquisition, expository text structures pose great difficulty for students with disabilities and students at-risk, because these texts become increasingly more complex in secondary content areas and require significant metacognition.

Another area that limits a student's reading comprehension ability is the shear volume of text read. The more text to which an individual is exposed, the more reading vocabulary and comprehension skills may be acquired (Cunningham & Stanovich, 2001). Therefore, the very act of reading increases word recognition skills and reading comprehension. Individuals who are not exposed to a large volume of text do not develop vocabulary and comprehension skills as readily as individuals who are exposed to large volumes of text. The "Matthew Effect" is evidenced in the reading achievement gap between those who read more and those who read less.

Factors that may limit exposure to text volume and hinder reading comprehension are decoding deficits and fluency deficits. As noted earlier in this chapter, poor decoding skills lead to fluency deficits. Research has demonstrated that fluency and comprehension skills are highly correlated (NRP, 2000), but fluency-building activities are often omitted from reading instruction further limiting a student's opportunities to derive meaning from text.

Strategies/Methods in Comprehension

In order to increase comprehension at both the *literal and inferential* level, research has noted several strategies that have been effective for struggling students. These strategies include but are not limited to story mapping, the K-W-L strategy, questioning, sequencing, and summarization. Each of these reading comprehension strategies is discussed below.

Story maps are timelines showing the ordered sequence of events in a text. This strategy is appropriate for comprehending narrative (story-type) texts. Most stories have a structure that is predictable. A typical story grammar might include the setting, the goal, the plot, and the resolution. Idol (1987) used a story map to teach comprehension of narrative stories (See **Figure 7-3** for an example of a story map). In teaching story structure, it is important that students understand the purpose and form of each element of the story grammar. Completing a story map can be done as a group, in small groups, or individually depending on the amount of scaffolding students may need.

FIGURE 7-3

Story Map

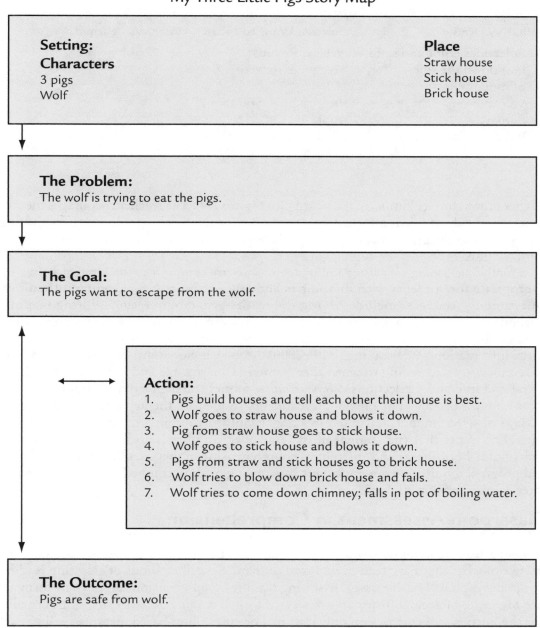

My Three Little Pigs Story Map

Setting:
Characters
3 pigs
Wolf

Place
Straw house
Stick house
Brick house

The Problem:
The wolf is trying to eat the pigs.

The Goal:
The pigs want to escape from the wolf.

Action:
1. Pigs build houses and tell each other their house is best.
2. Wolf goes to straw house and blows it down.
3. Pig from straw house goes to stick house.
4. Wolf goes to stick house and blows it down.
5. Pigs from straw and stick houses go to brick house.
6. Wolf tries to blow down brick house and fails.
7. Wolf tries to come down chimney; falls in pot of boiling water.

The Outcome:
Pigs are safe from wolf.

Adapted from Group story mapping: A comprehension strategy for both skilled and unskilled readers. By L. Idonl, 1987, *Journal of Learning Disabilities,* 20, p. 199.

The *K-W-L Strategy* is useful and easy to implement for students who are reading content area expository texts (Olson & Gee, 1991). K-W-L stands for: What I **K**now, What I **W**ant to Learn, and What I **L**earned. This strategy allows students to activate their prior knowledge, formulate questions about the topic, and summarize the information that they have learned. First, the teacher and the students identify the content area to be studied. The

FIGURE 7-4

Example of K-W-L Worksheet

Topic: Volcanoes

K	W	L
What We Know	**What We Want to Learn**	**What We Learned**
• Volcanoes erupt and send lava down the sides of mountains.	• Where are most volcanoes located?	
• Volcanoes may cause damage.	• How often do volcanoes erupt?	
• Volcanoes are very hot.	• What is the temperature inside a volcano?	

teacher draws three columns on the board (See **Figure 7-4**). The teacher encourages the students to provide as much information as they can for the first two columns by activating their prior knowledge. After reading the passage, either orally or silently, students fill in the third column.

Finally, *questioning, sequencing* and *summarization* are comprehension strategies that are appropriate for students with disabilities and students at-risk for reading difficulties. Questioning strategies include having the reader generate questions during reading. Without training, young readers are not likely to question themselves. *Questioning* should increase the reader's awareness of whether the text is being understood and connect inferential information while reading (NRP, 2000). Sequencing of events requires the ordering of several events according to when they occurred in a passage and can be used for both literal and inferential selections. *Summarization,* a brief statement that contains essential ideas about a passage, not only allows students to identify the key information from a passage or selection, but it also reduces the key information in a passage or selection to critical concepts that the student must remember. Summarization can be an effective strategy for both literal and inferential comprehension activities. On-going assessment and progress monitoring are important in ensuring reading comprehension across these three comprehension strategies.

Classroom Assessment in Comprehension

Assessing reading comprehension is important to ensure that students are deriving the essence of what they have read or had read to them. Several methods of assessing reading comprehension will be discussed. Assessing reading comprehension can be done formally (see Mercer & Mercer, 2001 for an overview of formal reading assessments) or informally. For the purposes of this section only informal or curriculum-based measures will be presented. These comprehension assessment methods include:

- picture arrangement (sequencing),
- story retell,
- informal reading inventories, and
- metacognitive assessment (e.g., think alouds and self-monitoring).

Picture arrangement (sequencing) is a very appropriate comprehension assessment for young readers. This activity involves the student arranging pictorial representations from a story or a content area selection in the order in which events occurred (Gunning, 1996). The student's sequencing of the pictures will allow the teacher to assess whether students understood the sequence and whether they can demonstrate this understanding. A higher level of this assessment would be for a student to arrange written statements in a chronological sequence to demonstrate comprehension. This assessment is especially appropriate for narrative text structures in order to measure literal comprehension.

Story retell can also provide a comprehension check. The purpose of story retell is to have the student provide an explicit linkage to the core components of a story grammar (i.e., setting, characters, goal, plot, and resolution). Students can do this orally or by using the story map. Story retell can be used to measure a student's inferential comprehension of narrative text (Rabren, Darch, & Eaves, 1999).

Informal reading inventories (IRI) are used to help teachers place students in their appropriate reading level, but IRI can also be used to assess reading comprehension progress. Assessing whether the student got the "gist" of a selection is critical. By conducting an IRI, a teacher can assess the student's independent, instructional, and frustration levels related to comprehension (Mercer & Mercer, 2001). Before leaving the instructional sequence in reading comprehension, a teacher should always measure whether the student understood the overall meaning of a selection. IRI assessment is especially critical in both literal and inferential comprehension skills assessment.

Think alouds require a reader to stop periodically to reflect on how a text is being processed and understood (Baumann, Jones, & Seifert-Kessell, 1993). When the reader stops to think aloud in an overt verbal expression of mental processes, the teacher can assess whether the student comprehends the information. This activity allows a student to monitor his progress with support from the teacher as needed. For example, the teacher models the think aloud procedure by (1) saying out loud what is going on in her mind as she reads, and (2) asking herself, "Is this making sense?" This type of assessment can be effective in both narrative and expository text activities.

Summary

Teaching reading is a complex process for all teachers especially for teachers of students with disabilities or students at-risk for reading difficulties. Reading research has defined the five big ideas of reading as *phonological awareness, alphabetic understanding, fluency, vocabulary knowledge,* and *comprehension.* Each of these ideas was presented and discussed in terms of issues for students at-risk for reading difficulties, strategies and methods to teach each big idea, and classroom assessment in each area. The importance of systematic and explicit instruction throughout the process of teaching reading was emphasized. This chapter provided an overview of the critical aspects of reading instruction and should be viewed as an initial glimpse into the complexity of the process of teaching reading.

Discussion Questions and Activities

1. Define literacy and describe the importance of reading as a part of literacy.

2. The first big idea of reading is phonological awareness. Describe two teaching activities that would promote phonological awareness skills for students with disabilities or students at-risk for reading failure. Indicate how to assess student learning as a result of the teaching activities.

3. The second big idea of reading is the alphabetic principle. Describe three areas of the alphabetic principle that a teacher should assess to determine the instructional needs of students struggling with this concept.

4. The third big idea is reading fluency. Fluency includes rate, accuracy, and reading with expression (prosody). Choose one of these areas and develop an instructional activity, which includes on-going assessment of skill acquisition. Indicate how to assess student learning as a result of instructional activity.

5. The fourth big idea of reading is vocabulary acquisition. The following words are being introduced in a science lesson on the solar system: *gaseous, satellites, meteorite, crater,* and *asteroid.* Name and describe two instructional strategies to support a student's understanding of these unfamiliar terms. Indicate how to assess student learning as a result of the strategy instruction.

6. The fifth big idea is reading comprehension. Select a narrative passage from a primary grades reading program and an expository passage from a secondary content area text. First determine if each passage is requiring literal or inferential comprehension. Next, identify an instructional method for each passage that promotes comprehension.

Internet Resources

The Big Ideas in Reading
http://reading.uoregon.edu/

The National Institute for Literacy
http://www.nifl.gov/

The National Reading Panel
http://www.nationalreadingpanel.org/

Reading Research
http://idea.uoregon.edu/~ncite/documents/techrep/reading.html

References

Adams, M. J. (1990). *Beginning to read: Thinking and learning about print.* Cambridge, MA: MIT Press.

Adams, M. J., Foorman, B. R., Lundberg, I., & Beeler, T. (1998). The elusive phoneme. *American Educator, 22(1 & 2),* 18–29.

Armbruster, B. A., Lehr, F., & Osborn, J. (2001). In C. Ralph Adler (Ed.), *Putting reading first: The research building blocks for teaching students to read.* Jessup, MD: National Institute for Literacy.

Baker, S. K., Simmons, D. C., & Kameenui, E. J. (1995). *Vocabulary acquisition: A synthesis of the research.* Retrieved from http://darkwing.uoregon.edu/~ncite/reading/reading.html.

Baumann, J. F., Jones, L. A., & Seifert-Kessell, N. (1993). Using think alouds to enhance students's comprehension monitoring abilities. *The Reading Teacher, 47,* 184–193.

Breznitz, Z. (1997). Reading rate acceleration: Developmental aspects. *The Journal of Genetic Psychology, 158,* 427–441.

Burkhardt, M. L. (1981). In R. Flesch, *Why Johnny still can't read: A new look at the scandal of our schools* (pp. xiii–xxii). New York: Harper & Row.

Carnine, D. W., Silbert, J., & Kameenui, E. J. (1997). *Direct instruction reading* (3rd ed.). Upper Saddle River, NJ: Prentice-Hall.

Chall, J. S., Jacobs, V. A., & Baldwin, L. E. (1991). *The reading crisis: Why poor students fall behind.* Cambridge, MA: Harvard University Press.

Collins, V. L., Dickson, S. V., Simmons, D. C., & Kameenui, E. J. (1996). *Metacognition and its relation to reading comprehension: A synthesis of research.* Retrieved from http://darkwing.uoregon.edu/~ncite/documents/techrep/reading.html.

Cunningham, A. C., & Stanovich, K. E. (2001). What reading does for the mind. *Journal of Direct Instruction, 1(2),* 137–149.

Durkin, D. (1993). *Teaching them to read* (6th ed.). Boston, MA: Allyn & Bacon.

ERIC Clearinghouse on Disabilities and Gifted Education. (1996). *Reading: The first chapter in education.* Retrieved February 1, 2003, from http://ericec.org

Foorman, B. R., & Torgesen, J. (2001). Critical elements of classroom and small-group instruction promote reading success in all students. *Learning Disabilities Research & Practice, 16,* 203–212.

Fuchs, L. S., Fuchs, D., Hosp, M. K., & Jenkins, J. R. (2001). Oral reading fluency as an indicator of reading competence: A theoretical, empirical, and historical analysis. *Scientific Studies of Reading, 5,* 239–256.

Gildroy, P. G. (1999). Teaching phonological awareness (Module1, Lesson 3). In B. K. Lenz & P. G. Gildroy (Eds.), *Beginning word reading* [Online]. Lawrence, KS: University of Kansas, Center for Research on Learning. Available: Onlineacademy.org

Gildroy, P. G., & Francis, S. (1999). Learning about phonemes (Module 1, Lesson 2). In B. K. Lenz, & P. G. Gildroy (Eds.), *Beginning word reading* [Online]. Lawrence, KS: University of Kansas, Center for Research on Learning. Available: Onlineacademy.org

Glaeser, B. J., Lenz, B. K., Gildroy, P. G., & McKnight, M. (2000). The development of literacy: As reading instruction begins (Module 1, Lesson 1). In *Beginning word reading* [Online]. Lawrence, KS: University of Kansas, Center for Research on Learning. Available: www.onlineacademy.org

Greene, J. F. (1998). Another chance: Help for older students with limited literacy. *American Educator, 22(1 & 2),* 74–79.

Gunning, T. (1996). *Creating reading instruction for all*. Boston: Allyn & Bacon.

Harmon, J. M. (1999). Vocabulary teaching and learning in a seventh-grade literature-based classroom. In *Reading research: Anthology The why? of reading instruction*. Consortium on Reading Excellence. Novato, CA: Arena Press.

Hart, B., & Risley, T. R. (1995). *Meaningful differences in the everyday experiences of young American students*. Baltimore: Paul H. Brookes Publishing.

Hasbrouck, J., & Tindal, G. (1992). Curriculum-based oral reading fluency norms for students in grades 2 through 5. *Teaching Exceptional Students, 24(3)*, 41–44.

Idol, L. (1987). Group story mapping. A comprehensive strategy for both skilled and unskilled readers. *Journal of Learning Disabilities, 20*, 196–205.

Jenkins, J. R., & Dixon, R. (1983). Vocabulary learning. *Contemporary Educational Psychology, 8*, 237–260.

Kameenui, E. J. (1998). The rhetoric of all, the reality of some, and the unmistakable smell of mortality. In J. Osborn & F. Lehr (Eds.), *Literacy for all* (pp. 319–338). New York: The Guilford Press.

Kameenui, E. J., & Carnine, D. W. (1998). *Effective teaching strategies that accommodate diverse learners*. Upper Saddle River, NJ: Prentice-Hall.

Kameenui, E. J., Simmons, D. C., Good, R., Harn, B., Chard, D., Coyne, M., Edwards, L., Wallin, J., & Sheehan, T. (2001). *Big ideas in beginning reading instruction*. Retrieved January 23, 2003 from http://reading.uoregon.edu/big_ideas/index.php

Lyon, R. G. (1999). *The NICHD research program in reading development, reading disorders and reading instruction*. Retrieved August 25, 1999 from http://www.ncld.org/summit99/keys99-nichd.htm

Mastropieri, M. A., & Scruggs, T. E. (1994). *Effective instruction for special education*. (2nd ed.). Austin, TX: PRO-ED.

McCardle, P., Cooper, J. A., Houle, G., Karp, N., & Paul-Brown, D. (2001). Emergent and early literacy: Current status and research directions—introduction. *Learning Disabilities Research & Practice, 16*, 183–185.

Mercer, C. D., & Mercer, A. R. (2001). *Teaching students with learning problems* (6th ed.). Upper Saddle River, NJ: Prentice-Hall.

Moats, L. C. (1998). Teaching decoding. *American Educator, 22(1 & 2)*, 42–49.

Moats, L. C. (1999, June). *Teaching reading is rocket science: What expert teachers of reading should know and be able to do*. (Item No. 372). Washington, DC: American Federation of Teachers.

Moats, L. C. (2000). *Speech to print: Language essentials for teachers*. Baltimore, MD: Paul H. Brookes Publishing.

Nagy, W., Anderson, R., & Herman, P. (1987). Learning word meanings from context during normal reading. *American Educational Research Journal, 24*, 237–270.

National Reading Panel. (2000). *Teaching students to read: An evidenced-based assessment of the scientific research literature on reading and its implications for reading instruction*. (NIH Pub. No. 00-4754). Washington, DC: National Institute of Student Health and Human Development.

Olson, M. W., & Gee, T. C. (1991). Content reading in the primary grades: Perceptions and strategies. *The Reading Teacher, 45*, 298–307.

Pressley, M., Roehrig, A., Bogner, K., Raphael, L. M., & Dolezal, S. (2002). Balanced literacy instruction. *Focus on Exceptional Students, 34*, 1–14.

Rabren, K., Darch, C., & Eaves, R. C. (1999). The differential effects of two systematic reading comprehension approaches with students with learning disabilities. *Journal of Learning Disabilities, 32*, 36–47.

Robbins, C., & Ehri, L. C. (1994). Reading storybooks to kindergartners helps them learn new vocabulary words. *Journal of Educational Psychology, 86*, 54–64.

Samuels, S. J. (1979). The method of repeated readings. *The Reading Teacher, 32*, 403–408.

Simmons, D. C., & Kameenui, E. J. (1990). The effect of task alternatives on vocabulary knowledge: A comparison of students with learning disabilities and students of normal achievement. *Journal of Learning Disabilities, 23*, 291–297.

Snow, C. E., Burns, M. S., & Griffin, P. (1998). *Preventing reading difficulties in your students*. Washington, DC: National Academy Press.

Stanovich, K. E. (1986). Matthew effects in reading: Some consequences of individual differences in the acquisition of literacy. *Reading Research Quarterly, 21*, 361–406.

Torgesen, J. K. (1998). Catch them before they fall. *American Educator, 22(1 & 2)*, 32–39.

8

Math Assessment and Instruction for Students At-Risk

David E. Houchins, Margaret E. Shippen, and Margaret M. Flores

Chapter Objectives

- to describe the principles of effective instruction for students at-risk for math failure.
- to describe the big ideas in math (i.e, mathematical awareness, mathematical conceptualization, mathematical fluency, mathematical language, and mathematical application).
- to identify and describe methods teachers can use to enhance the math curricula of students at-risk for math failure.
- to identify and describe types of math assessments for students at-risk for math failure.

Mathematics is the universal language of life. Mathematically literate people use and comprehend mathematical concepts and principles effectively on multiple levels. Practically, people use math to figure their budgets and perform daily living skills. Culturally, math is used to enjoy and participate in the visual and performing arts. Professionally, math is used in employment and serves as a marker to gauge one's success economically. Civically, math is used to pay taxes and participate in the community. Recreationally, math is used to improve physical and psychological well-being (The National Research Council, 1989). Clearly, math literacy affects every aspect of one's life.

Being mathematically literate has the power to enhance one's life. Greater mathematical knowledge is related to higher earnings (Condition of Education, 1996) and a higher quality of life. Conversely, being mathematically illiterate can diminish one's capacity to live a fulfilled and enriched life. Rivera-Batiz (1992) notes that poor math skills negatively impact one's employment, income, and work productivity. Mathematical illiteracy can be just as disabling as having reading deficits. In our data rich society, being mathematically illiterate can lead to a life characterized by confusion, anxiety, and distress.

Unfortunately, too many students are either mathematically illiterate or are at-risk for math failure (National Assessment of Educational Progress, 1997). These students have numerous deficits that make it difficult for them to achieve adequately in the classroom. Deficits in memory, attention, reasoning, language, perception, meta-cognition, and self-regulation make it difficult for them to be successful (Lucangeli, Coi, & Bosco, 1997; Miller & Mercer, 1993). Years of low math achievement often leads to increased levels of math anxiety and learned helplessness. Fortunately, there are methods that teachers can use to increase the chances these students will be successful in math.

The purpose of this chapter is to provide teachers with suggestions on what and how to teach students who are at-risk for math failure. The focus is on students who are not successful with traditional instructional approaches.

This chapter is organized around four topics related to the objectives including:

(a) explicit methods of instruction in math;
(b) the big ideas of math instruction;
(c) enhancement of math curricula; and
(d) assessment in math.

Each topic is described below. A summary with discussion questions are provided at the end of the chapter.

Explicit Methods of Instruction in Math

Two basic methods of math instruction are described in this chapter. They are **direct instruction** and **meta-cognitive instruction** (for a detailed description of each, refer to Chapter 6 of this book). Both are effective means of providing instruction for students who are at-risk for math failure. Each is briefly described below along with some common features of both instructional methods.

Direct Instruction in Math

One of the more effective means of the teaching students who are at-risk for math failure is by using direct instruction procedures. Direct instruction procedures have teachers take complex math tasks and break them down into the smaller tasks that make up the larger tasks. The teacher then teaches the smaller tasks and shows students how the smaller tasks are put together to make the more difficult task. Based on the principles of direct instruction, Stein, Silbert, and Carnine (1997) developed a set of math direct instruction steps that teachers can use. These nine steps serve as the foundation for teaching students who are at-risk for math failure.

Step One—Create long and short term math objectives for students

Based on assessment data, teachers should develop observable and measurable objectives. For example, one math objective might be "Given 100 single digit basic multiplication facts 0-9, the student will correctly answer 98 problems in four minutes three out of four attempts." Additional information on creating math objectives is found later in this chapter under the topic of math assessment.

Step Two—Develop procedural strategies

Procedural strategies are explicit cognitive routines that students will use to calculate problems. Strategies should be generalizable so students can use them in a variety of situations.

Step Three—Determine if students have the necessary prerequisite math skills to perform the given task

It is important that students have the skills necessary to answer a particular problem. Determining if students have the necessary preskills can be determined through assessment as described later in this chapter.

Step Four—Take into consideration the order the skills will be taught

Sequencing the skills correctly makes the learning process more efficient and effective. When presenting new information, the teacher should be sure to teach the prerequisite skills to a strategy. Teachers should also teach easier skills prior to teaching more difficult skills. This is obvious when skills are hierarchical (i.e., addition with regrouping is harder than addition without regrouping). It is less obvious when the skill is the same but certain aspects of teaching the skill is more difficult than another. For example, when teaching symbol identification, it is easier to teach the numbers 14, 16, 17, 18, and 19 as compared to 11, 12, 13, and 15. The reason is because the later numbers have irregular sounding names and are more difficult for students to comprehend (Stein, et al., 1997). Finally, instruction that is likely to be confused by students should be taught separately and non-consecutively. For example, the teaching of numerals 6 and 9 should be separated by lessons on other numerals.

Step Five—Select a teaching procedure

Stein et al. (1997) list three types of teaching procedures: motor, labeling, and strategy. Each is described below.

Motor tasks require the student to memorize and articulate a rule (e.g., any number minus zero is that number) or perform a particular movement (e.g., write numerals). Teachers use a four step sequence to teach motor tasks (model, lead, test, delayed test). Modeling is demonstrating how to perform the given task. Leading is the teacher performing the task with the students and allowing them to gradually demonstrate their ability to perform the task. This is also known as guided or scaffolded instruction. The goal of leading is to have students perform the given task independent of the teacher. Testing is having students answer teacher questions about the task without assistance. Delayed testing happens later after students have been given different tasks to accomplish. The time lapse is usually only minutes. If students are able to accomplish the task, the teacher should proceed to the next task. If students do not accomplish the task, the teacher should repeat the model-lead-test-delay test sequence.

Labeling tasks require students to say a word that correctly identifies an object. For example, the student says "ten" when the number 10 is presented or says "circle" when shown a picture of a circle. Teachers use a three step sequence to teach labeling tasks (model, alternating test, delayed test). When modeling, the teacher points to the object, tells the students what it is and then asks students the name of the object. Alternating testing involves showing students the given object and presenting other previously taught objects subsequently. The teacher gradually increases the number of previously taught objects. The previously taught objects should be presented in varying order. For example, if students were being taught the circle symbol, the alternating test might look like the following:

The teacher continues the testing until students respond 3 or 4 times without errors. If the student makes an error, the model-alternate testing process is repeated. After students respond correctly 3 or 4 times, the teacher conducts the delayed test where students are presented with the labeling task later in the lesson.

Strategy tasks require students to articulate and use several ordered steps that lead to the solution of a problem. The strategy is then applied to a variety of similar types of problems. Teachers use a three step sequence to teach strategy tasks (model, guided practice, test). The phases are similar to those described earlier. The main difference is that teacher asks the student more questions to encourage the student to use the strategy during the modeling phase.

Step Six—Develop and use a teaching format

Formats are teaching scripts. Formats provide teachers with specifics on what to say, how to provide students with feedback, and examples to use with students. Teaching formats

FIGURE 8-1

Motor Teaching Format Example

Format for Plus 1 Facts
PART A: NEXT NUMBER

TEACHER	STUDENTS
1. When I put my hand down, you say the next number.	
2. *(Hold up hand)* One, two, three, four, fiiive. *(Drop hand.)*	6
To correct: My turn. One, two, three, four, fiiive *(drop hand)* six.	
New problem. Tell me the next number: three, four, five, six, seven? *(Drop hand. Repeat step 2 with* 3, 4, 5 *and* 7, 8, 9.*)*	8
3. When I put my hand down, you say the next number. Siiiix. *(Drop hand.)*	7
To correct: My turn; sssiiix *(drop hand)* seven. *Repeat step 3 with* 8, 4, 9, 2, 5. *Give individual turns to several students.*)	

PART B: PLUS 1 RULE WITH STRETCH PROMPT

1. Everyone listen to the rule. When you plus one, you say the next number. My turn. Fooouur plus one equals five. Eight plus one equals nine.	
2. Get ready to tell me the answers to some plus one problems. Remember to say the next number. Five plus one, fiiive plus one equals . . . *(Signal.)* Yes, 5 + 1 = 6	6
To correct: Listen: 5. *What number comes next? So 5 plus* 1 *equals* 6	
3. Three plus one. Thhreee plus one equals? *(Signal.)* Yes, 3 + 1 = 4	4
(Present step 3 with examples like the following until students answer all + 1 problems in a row correctly: 9 + 1, 7 + 1, 2 + 1, 8 + 1, 4 + 1.*)*	

PART C: PLUS 1 RULE WITHOUT PROMPT

1. Remember, when you plus 1 you say the next number.	
2. Eight plus one equals . . . *(Pause, then signal.)* Say the whole statement: 8 + 1 = 9	9
(Repeat step 2 with the following examples: 4 + 1, 7 + 1 . . . .5 + 1, 9 + 1.*)*	

Source: Stein, M., Silbert, & Carnine, D. (1997). *Designing effective mathematics instruction: A direct instruction approach.* (3rd ed.). Upper Saddle River, NJ: Merrill.

allow teachers to provide clear and unambiguous instruction. By having a script, teachers are able to focus their attention on what the student is saying instead of focusing on what to say next. Teaching formats use various presentation techniques to keep the pace of the instruction appropriate. Teacher signals are used to convey to students when they should provide an answer. Signals might include a snap of the finger, a tap on the chalkboard, or an inflection in the teacher's voice. Student responses after the signal are usually done in unison. The teacher monitors for errors and re-teaches when necessary. **Figures 8-1, 8-2,** and **8-3** are examples of motor, labeling, and strategy formats.

FIGURE 8-2

Labeling Teaching Format Example

Format for Identification/Definition—Triangle
PART A: STRUCTURED BOARD PRESENTATION

TEACHER	STUDENTS
1. Listen to this definition: A triangle is a closed figure that has three straight sides. How many sides does a triangle have?	3
2. I'm going to point to some figures, and you tell me if they are triangles. _(Point to 6)_	
Is this a triangle?	yes
How do you know?	It has three sides
(Point to the following figures in the sequence shown.)	

PART B: LESS STRUCTURED WORKSHEET

(Give students a worksheet with problems like the ones below.)

a. Draw a circle around each triangle.

b. Write the letter R over each rectangle.
Write the letter S over each square.
Write the letter T over each triangle.
Write the letter C over each circle.

1. Look at problem "A" on your worksheet. Read the directions	Draw a circle around each triangle
2. Touch the first figure. Is that a triangle?	yes
So what are you going to do?	Draw a circle around it.
Do it.	
3. Touch the next figure. Is that a triangle?	no
So what are you going to do?	nothing
4. _(Have students complete the worksheet by themselves.)_	

Source: Stein, M., Silbert, & Carnine, D. (1997). _Designing effective mathematics instruction: A direct instruction approach._ (3rd ed.). Upper Saddle River, NJ: Merrill.

FIGURE 8-3

Strategy Teaching Format Example

NUMBER RELATIONSHIPS

a. (Draw a bug and arrow on the number line:)

0 1 2 3 4 5 6 7 8 9 10

- The arrow shows a bug problem. You can see where the bug started and how many places the bug plussed. Listen: What number did the bug start at? (Signal.) 1.
- Did the bug plus or minus? (Signal.) *Plus.* Raise your hand when you know how many places the bug plussed.
- Everybody, how many places did the bug plus? (Signal.) 4
- What number did the bug end up at? (Signal.) 5.

Source: Englemann, S., Carnine, D., Kelly, B., & Engelmann, O. (1996) *Connecting Math Concepts: Lesson sampler.* Worthington, OH: SRA/McGraw-Hill.

Step Seven—Develop appropriate examples

Developing examples prior to teaching saves valuable instruction time and increases the chances that the examples are useful to students. When developing examples, teachers should only provide examples that the student can determine using information from the current or previous lessons. Examples from previously taught lessons should be used for discrimination practice. Types of problems that are similar to the ones being taught should be used so that the student will be able to discriminate between the different types of math strategies.

Step Eight—Detail practice and review material

Teachers must teach the skills to mastery. Immediately after a skill has been taught, teachers should provide students with a significant amount of practice with the problem types until mastery is reached. Then, once mastery is reached, teachers should map-out review materials over time to ensure the student maintains the skills.

Step Nine—Monitor student progress with specific assessment procedures

Teachers should periodically check student progress to determine if long- and short-term objectives have been achieved. Mathematical assessment procedures are described in detail later in this Chapter.

Meta-Cognitive Instruction

The second method for instructing students at-risk for math failure is meta-cognitive instruction. Meta-cognitive instruction uses the principles of direct instruction, but adds information on how students can develop strategies that allow them to be more efficient and independent with solving math problems. A strategy is a student's approach to a math task. It involves how students think and act when planning, executing, and evaluating their performance on math tasks (Ellis, Deshler, Lenz, Schumaker, & Clark, 1991). Students taught meta-cognitive skills are provided with explicit instruction initially with the goal of creating independent learners. Students are taught to generalize the skills to their other classes, settings, and situations. One common feature of meta-cognitive instruction is using mnemonic devices. The use of mnemonics has been shown to be an effective means of assisting students in "chunking" information for memory purposes (Deshler, Ellis, & Lenz, 1996; Masteropieri & Scruggs, 1989). Students are taught mnemonics that incorporate the steps needed to accomplish a math task. For example, Miller and Mercer (1993) developed the **SOLVE** mnemonic device:

- **S**ee the sign.
- **O**bserve and answer (if unable to answer, keep going).
- **L**ook and draw the problem.
- **V**erify your answer.
- **E**nter your answer.

Each step starts with an action word that requires the student to perform a certain behavior. Students memorize the mnemonic device and learn why and how to apply it. The sequential steps allow students to become proficient in completing math tasks. In this case, students learn a mnemonic to compute basic facts that can be used across different types of math problems.

Common Features of Effective Math Instruction

There are several features of effective math instruction that are common across both direct and meta-cognitive based instruction. These common features are beneficial to keep in mind when planning instruction for students who are at-risk. Taking these features into consideration when planning math lessons, can provide students with quality math instruction.

A Continuum of Math Instruction

The emphasis of this chapter is on how to provide students who are at-risk for math failure with explicit math instruction. Explicit instruction is behavioral in nature. It requires the teacher to be the provider of knowledge and to give students a great deal of direct assistance. Students are led to the answer using directed discovery and task analysis (Mercer, Jordan, & Miller, 1996). Learning occurs from part to whole.

The opposite of explicit instruction is implicit instruction. Those who teach students using an implicit method of instruction believe that students actively construct knowledge. Teachers are "guides on the side" facilitating the learning process. Students are provided with opportunities to learn by engaging the environment. Self-discovery, self-regulation, and holistic learning are all aspects of implicit learning (Mercer, et al., 1996). Learning usually takes place using "whole to part" instruction.

Explicit math instructional procedures are the emphasis of this chapter because students at-risk need them to be successful in math classes. Too often, explicit math instructional procedures are not provided in general education math curricula. Students who are at-risk for math failure must be provided with explicit instruction if they are to be successful. Yet, the authors of this chapter acknowledge the need to create students who are independent math users. The goal of all instruction is to eventually produce life long learners. Students should be provided with opportunities to direct their own learning without the guidance of the teacher in real world environments. Implicit math instruction should only occur once students have been given the tools necessary to lead their own instruction. Explicit instruction principles such as teacher demonstration, mastery learning, immediate corrective feedback, fading, extensive ranges of examples, and cumulative reviews all provide students with the necessary tools that lead to independence (Bos & Vaughn, 1998). For a detailed description of the explicit to implicit continuum of instruction, see Chapter 6.

The Instructional Sequence

The second common feature of effective math instruction is associated with the order of instruction provided. Effective math instruction is delivered using a common set of eight instructional steps (Deshler, et al., 1996). These instructional steps provide teachers with a structure to develop and implement their math lesson plans effectively and efficiently. **Table 8-1** provides an overview of each of these steps.

Concrete-Semiconcrete-Abstract

The third common characteristic of effective math instruction is the use of a "concrete-semiconcrete-abstract" (CSA) learning sequence (Lambert, 1996). The CSA learning sequence is part of the modeling and demonstration phase listed above and can be used with basic fact acquisition and problem solving (Marsh & Cooke, 1996). Concepts are taught initially using concrete objects. The use of manipulatives (buttons, blocks, cuisenaire rods, or other tangible materials) is effective for students at all grade levels when new concepts are being introduced.

Once students understand the concept being taught using concrete objects, the teacher uses semiconcrete representations of those concrete objects. Semiconcrete representations might include slashes, marks, or pictures. Finally, teachers use written numbers. Written numbers are abstract and students are taught that there is a connection between the written number and the concrete and semi-concrete representations. **Figure 8-4** provides an example of how the CSA sequence can be used to teach a math skill.

Skill Hierarchy

The fourth and final common feature of effective math instruction is related to the order in which skills are presented to students. Math instruction occurs in a logical and progressive manner. Two excellent sources of math skill hierarchies are found in *Designing effective mathematics instruction: A direct instruction approach* (Stein, et al., 1997) and *Teaching students with learning problems* (Mercer & Mercer, 2001). Skills covered by these hierarchies include:

- counting
- addition
- multiplication
- problem solving
- decimals
- telling time
- measurement
- mathematics study skills: graphs, charts, maps, and statistics
- geometry.
- symbol identification and place value
- subtraction

TABLE 8-1

Math Instructional Steps

Step	Description of Step
1. Pretest	Determine the current math abilities of students by assessing their performance. For a detailed description, see the assessment section later in this chapter.
2. Obtain student commitment	Gain students' commitment to learn the math skills. The teacher and students develop short and long term math goals based on the assessment information.
3. Provide students with an advanced organizer	Students are informed of what they are going to learn and why. Connections are made with the current math lesson, previous lessons, and future lessons. Students are informed of what they will be doing during the lesson and what the teacher will be doing.
4. Model and demonstrate	Provide students with explicit instruction by demonstrating, explaining, questioning, and/or discussing the new concept. Students are actively engaged in question answering and/or discussion. Activities are presented that allow students to be active participants in the learning process. Students learn the meaning of the new math concept, not just the rote memory of it.
5. Scaffolding or guided practice with fading	Students are provided with substantial assistance to learn the new concept. The assistance may come from teachers, peers, paraprofessionals, or others. Gradually the assistance is faded as the student progressively gains a clear understanding of the concept. Students are provided with and use feedback about their performance whether supportive, corrective, or explanatory.
6. Independent practice	Students work on their own with periodic checks from the teacher. At this point students are developing mastery of the match concept (i.e., able to perform the task with a 96–98% accuracy rate). This practice may come in the form of math worksheets, board games, and computer programs.
7. Post-testing	Teachers assess student mastery of the new match concept and re-teach if necessary.
8. Generalization	Students are provided with structured opportunities to generalize the information to familiar or unfamiliar situations. Students demonstrate mastery of the new concept by using it in familiar and unfamiliar situations. The math skills generalize to other classrooms, the community, and the home.

- division
- fractions
- percent and ratio
- money

Teachers can use this skill hierarchy to determine what skills to assess, how to plan for instruction, and as a method for monitoring student progress.

FIGURE 8-4

Concrete to Semi-concrete to Abstract Representations

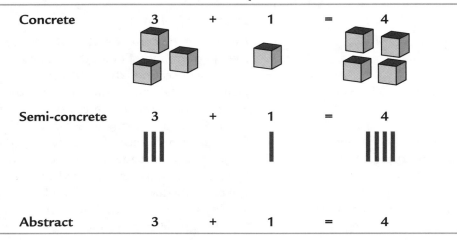

Concrete	3	+	1	=	4
Semi-concrete	3	+	1	=	4
Abstract	3	+	1	=	4

In addition to the skill hierarchy, the National Council of Supervisors of Mathematics (1988) suggest there are 12 components of essential mathematics. These components should be taken into consideration when planning instruction. They include:

1. problem solving,
2. communication of mathematical ideas,
3. application of mathematics in everyday situations,
4. alertness to the reasonableness of results,
5. estimation,
6. appropriate computational skills,
7. algebraic thinking,
8. measurement,
9. geometry,
10. statistics,
11. probability, and
12. mathematical reasoning.

Teachers can use both the skill hierarchy and the 12 components of essential mathematics when developing lessons for students.

The Big Ideas of Math Instruction

This section is organized around five big ideas or themes. These big ideas are analogous to the big ideas of reading instruction in Chapter 7. Readers should use the big ideas presented here as the foundation for determining what math skills should be taught to students who are at-risk for math failure. The five math big ideas are:

1. mathematical awareness;
2. mathematical conceptualization;
3. mathematical fluency;
4. mathematical language; and
5. mathematical application.

The math big ideas focus on *what* to teach. Under each big idea, a definition of the big idea is provided with supporting literature. Subsequently, information is provided on *how*

TABLE 8-2

A Summary of the Big Ideas in Math

Big Idea	Definition	Characteristics
1. Mathematical awareness	The ability to perceive mathematical concepts (numerical, measurement, space, size, time, volume, temperature, etc.) and associate those concepts with concrete, semiconcrete, and abstract representations.	• developmental • prerequisite skills • foundational • sensing
2. Mathematical conceptualization	The ability to form and solve mathematical problems based on rules, axioms, and principles.	• principles • rules • algorithms • axioms
3. Mathematical fluency	The effortless, automatic ability to perform mathematical operations.	• speed • accuracy • error monitoring
4. Mathematical language	The exchange of information and ideas as related to the understanding (receptive) and use of (expressive) mathematics to acquire and convey meaning.	• terminology • reading abilities • background knowledge • keywords • vocabulary
5. Mathematical application	A complex cognitive and meta-cognitive process by which a student intentionally gains meaning from situations involving math.	• problem solving • motivation • goal setting • daily living • generalization • independence

to teach each math big idea. While it is impossible to cover every method of teaching each big idea, sample direct instruction and meta-cognitive strategies are provided. See **Table 8-2** for an overview of the math big ideas.

Teachers should view the five math big ideas as interrelated. A balanced instructional approach should be used. After students are provided with a foundation in mathematical awareness, the last four big ideas have a circular and complementary relationship with changes in the level and type of instruction. Teachers should integrate mathematical conceptualization, fluency, language, and application as students are learning new math skills. Taking all the big ideas into consideration when teaching students who are at-risk for math failure increases their chances of becoming mathematically successful.

Mathematical Awareness: The *First* Big Idea

Mathematical awareness is the ability to perceive mathematical concepts (numerical, measurement, space, size, time, volume, temperature, etc.) and associate those concepts with concrete, semiconcrete, and abstract representations. This idea has also been referred to as number sense and has been compared to phonemic awareness in reading (Gersten & Chard, 1999). Mathematical awareness may be the underlying deficit that discriminates between good math students and poor math students. It appears to be an essential foundational math skill and is the prerequisite skill for all the other big math ideas. Mastery of mathematical awareness skills appears to be necessary for the thorough development of basic and more advanced math skills.

Mathematical awareness instruction should focus on the understanding of basic math concepts. Too often, special education and remedial education have focused predominately on the rote memory of mathematical operations at the expense of concept discernment, discrimination, and development (Gersten & Chard, 1999). To do so is a disservice to students. Students who do not have a sense of numbers will be hindered by this lack of knowledge as they progress toward more advanced math skills.

Teachers often report that some students "get it" (mathematical awareness) while others (those at-risk for math failure) simply do not. Upon closer examination of this phenomenon, researchers (Gersten & Chard) suggest that one difference might be environmental. Students from educationally impoverished environments may not be exposed to mathematical awareness activities. These mathematically naive students are then at a disadvantage early on in their schooling.

Other students may have visual spatial deficits that interfere with their ability to understand mathematics (Miller & Mercer, 1993). These students may have a specific math learning disability. Whether students are disadvantaged by environmental factors or have a true math learning disability, the teacher can remedy many deficits by providing students with explicit instruction in mathematical awareness.

Mathematical Awareness Skills

Mathematical awareness skills serve as the developmental foundation for future mathematical tasks (Bender, 1996; Mercer & Mercer, 2001; Piaget, 1965). The acquisition of these skills is influenced by the overall cognitive abilities of students, their background knowledge, and their understanding of oral and written language. Teachers should be alert for students who do not learn these basic concepts. Students with deficits in these areas will require direct instruction and more time to acquire the skills. Since these skills are fundamental to understanding future mathematical big ideas, teachers must take the time to ensure student comprehension of them. Some of the more important mathematical awareness skills are briefly described below (Bender, 1996; Copeland, 1979; Mercer & Mercer, 2001).

1. **Conservation** means that quantitative properties of an object or set of objects remains constant without regard to the spatial arrangement. Conservation is related to area, distance, length, number, quantity, time, volume, and weight. The classic Piagetian demonstration of this skill is the pouring of equal amounts of water into two different sized glass tubes. One tube is tall and thin while the other one is short and wide. Students who understand that the amount of water in both tubes is the same, understand the concept of conservation. Conservation can also be explained with other materials such as clay, spoons, cuisenaire rods, and other manipulatives.

2. **Classification** is related to the ability of students to discriminate between objects based on similarities and differences. Classification is mastered between ages 5 and 7. Objects are discriminated based on some attribute (texture, color, shape, size, function, weight, length, etc.). Students who can sort different colored plastic eating utensils by type (fork, spoon, knife) and by color (red, white, blue) understand classification.

3. **One-to-one correspondence** involves being able to indicate that the number of objects in one set, regardless of differing characteristics (size, shape, color, etc.), has the same numerical value as the same number of objects in another set. One-to-one correspondence is an important prerequisite skill for counting. Teachers can test their students one-to-one correspondence abilities by placing an equal number of different sized buttons in two glass jars (Mercer & Mercer, 2001). Students who can say that

there is an equal number of buttons in each jar understand the concept of one-to-one correspondence.

4. **Seriation** is characterized by being able to order objects based on some attribute (texture, color, shape, size, function, weight, length, etc.). Peg board and patterning games are examples of common preschool activities that involve seriation. Students who can arrange objects based on a particular attribute (i.e., size) without regard to other differing attributes (i.e., color), understand seriation.

If this student understands numeral recognition, he will be able to name this number.

5. **Numeral recognition** takes into consideration the student's ability to identify numbers (Bender, 1996). It is similar to the concept of the alphabetic principle in reading. Students must understand that each number represents a set of objects. Students who understand numeral recognition can name numbers written on flash cards or on the board.

6. **Numeral production** simply involves students writing numbers as they relate to corresponding objects. Writing numbers is a motor task that requires consistent modeling and practice.

7. **Counting** is stating numbers in a particular order. Students start by being able to count to ten, then to twenty, and then to one hundred. Students are then taught to count higher and with a variation on the sequence of the numbers. For example, students learn how to count by twos, fives, and tens. This skill will prepare students to calculate multiplication problems later on.

8. **Place value** is having an understanding that numerals represent different values depending on where they are located in a number. For example, in the number 3,023 the number 3 in the thousands place means something different than the 3 in the ones place. Teaching students place value starts in first grade and continues throughout elementary school. Place value is one of the most important skills students need to learn. A lack of understanding can impede the student's ability to understand regrouping, money concepts, and decimals.

9. **Expanded notation** is being aware that a number can be reduced to its component units. For example, the number 43 is comprised of four tens and three ones ($10 + 10 + 10 + 10 + 1 + 1 + 1 = 43$) (Kameenui, Carnine, Dixon, Simmons, & Coyne, 2002).

10. **Equivalency** is having an awareness that the equal sign means that both sides of it are the same. For example: $10 + 10 + 5 = 30 - 5$.

11. **Rate of composition/decomposition of numbers** focuses on the idea that we use a base 10 system. Composition refers to having an awareness that 10 ones is the same thing as one ten. Decomposition refers to having an awareness that when you remove a one from a 10 the result is 9 ones.

Teaching Mathematical Awareness

Most students acquire mathematical awareness skills informally by interacting with parents, peers, and siblings (Gersten & Chard, 1999). This is not the case of students who are at-risk for math failure. When students have not been exposed to mathematical awareness skills at home or otherwise, they must be taught in school. Teachers need to provide students with structured activities that allow them to understand numbers conceptually.

Teachers must provide students with verbally rich activities that require the student to be engaged with their environment using concrete examples. Some opportunities to teach mathematical awareness include:

- setting the lunch table;
- lining up to go to lunch;
- discriminating between and classifying toys and other objects;
- recognizing numbers in the environment (food containers, signs, computers, etc.);
- recognizing the amount of space between desks, chairs, and other items in the class;
- dividing food in the class (e.g., birthday cake);
- cooking;
- keeping track of students' heights;
- having a class store; and
- making students aware of different times of various activities in class and at home.

There are numerous other activities that teachers can use to develop students' mathematical awareness. The key to teaching these and similar activities is that teachers provide students with meaningful activities in structured environments. Students should be encouraged to explore their environments in an efficient and goal oriented manner. "Place value" and "greater than/less than" examples are provided below since they are often difficult for educators to teach.

Understanding place value is one of the more difficult math awareness tasks for students, so a detailed description of how to teach it is provided. Place value should be taught using the concrete-semiconcrete-abstract (CSA) sequence. **Figure 8-5** provides an example of how the CSA sequence can be used to teach students place value.

Once students understand place value on the concrete and semiconcrete levels, they can be taught a meta-cognitive place value strategy. The strategy is represented by the mnemonic **FIND** (Mercer & Mercer, 2001). **FIND** stands for:

- **F**ind the columns (between the numerals)
- **I**nsert the t's (the lines that form a "t" between the numbers)
- **N**ame the columns (by place value)
- **D**etermine the place value of individual numbers

For example, 65 → $\underline{\text{Tens} \mid \text{Ones}}$ "6 tens and 5 ones"
$$6 \mid 5$$

FIGURE 8-5

A Place Value Example

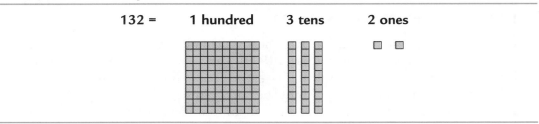

132 =   **1 hundred**   **3 tens**   **2 ones**

Another skill that can be taught at the abstract level is the concept of "greater than" and "less than." After students have been provided with concrete examples, students can be introduced to the concept using a picture of an animal with its jaws open (alligator, dog, duck, etc.). The teacher can use puppets or pictorial representations (Bernard, 1990). The teacher can tell the students that the animal has to open its mouth wider for larger amounts of food. Gradually, the teacher fades the concrete and semiconcrete representations and teaches students to associate them with the "greater than" (>) and "less than" (<) signs.

Mathematical Conceptualization: The *Second* Big Idea

Mathematical conceptualization is the ability to form and solve mathematical problems based on rules, axioms, and algorithms. As stated earlier, mathematical conceptualization should be taught after students are mathematically aware. When being taught mathematical conceptualization, students should understand the processes, not simply memorize the math skills (Miller & Mercer, 1993). Rules, axioms, and principles are all logical. The logic behind each should be formally taught to students. Verbally engaging students while providing concrete-semiconcrete-abstract representations will encourage understanding. Teachers can verbally describe (think aloud) to students about how they are solving a problem. Students can do the same so teachers can understand how the student is thinking about a problem.

Math Axioms

Math axioms are truisms or tenets. Explicitly teaching students math axioms allows them to understand the relationship between numbers and prepares them for more advanced topics such as algebra and geometry. Some of the more common math axioms include the commutative property of addition and multiplication, the associative property of addition and multiplication, inverse operations, and the distributive property of multiplication. **Table 8-3** provides a definition and example of each.

Once mathematical axioms have been taught through direct instruction for understanding using concrete and semiconcrete representations, the teacher can instruct students using meta-cognitive strategies. Allsopp (1999) provides a method of teaching students how to solve multi-operation problems that involve an understanding of the order of operations. The rule of order (**M**any **D**ogs **A**re **S**melly) stands for the basic math operations (Multiplication and Division come before Addition and Subtraction). The mnemonic used is **ORDER.**

- **O**bserve the problem—Examine the problem and highlight all operations, signs, exponents, and parentheses.
- **R**ead the signs—Verbally describe the role of the different signs in the problem.
- **D**ecide what operations to do first—Verbally describe what actions must be taken and why.
- **E**xecute the rule of order (**M**any **D**ogs **A**re **S**melly)—Cross out numbers as they are used and write the answer.
- **R**elax, you're done! Take a deep breath and realize your success.

Rules

In addition to axioms, there are math rules for addition, subtraction, multiplication, and division (Mercer & Mercer, 2001). Rules should be taught in a similar manner as axioms. Teaching rules, like axioms, can be beneficial to students in seeing the relationship

TABLE 8-3

Mathematical Axioms

Axiom	Definition	Example
1. Commutative property of addition	The order of the numbers does not change the answer.	$A + B = B + A$ $6 + 8 = 8 + 6$
2. Commutative property of multiplication	The order of the numbers does not change the answer.	$A \times B = B \times A$ $3 \times 4 = 4 \times 3$
3. Associative property of addition	The grouping arrangement does not change the answer.	$(A + B) + C = A + (B + C)$ $(2 + 3) + 4 = 2 + (3 + 4)$
4. Associative property of multiplication	The grouping arrangement does not change the answer.	$(A \times B) \times C = A \times (B \times C)$ $(2 \times 3) \times 4 = 2 \times (3 \times 4)$
5. Inverse operations	The operation reverses or undoes what another operation does.	$A + B = C, \quad C - A = B$ or $C - B = A$ $5 + 6 = 11, \quad 11 - 5 = 6$ or $11 - 6 = 5$ $A \times B = C, \quad C \div A = B$ or $C \div B = A$ $3 \times 4 = 12, \quad 12 \div 3 = 4$ or $12 \div 4 = 3$
6. Distributive property of multiplication over addition	The product of a number and a sum can be expressed as a sum of two products.	$A \times (B + C) = (A \times B) + (A \times C)$ $4 \times (9 + 5) = (4 \times 9) + (4 \times 5)$

between numbers and operations (Baroody, 1988). **Table 8-4** summarizes common math rules for basic operations.

Algorithms

Finally, students should also be taught algorithms. An algorithm is a set of rules for solving a math problem in a finite number of steps. Algorithms provide students with a means to solve a math problem. There are different methods for solving math problems. While it is beyond the scope of this chapter to present all possible algorithms, teachers should keep in mind that students solve problems differently. For example, some students approach problems from right to left while others go from left to right. Others have additional steps that reduce the level of stress caused by performing certain calculations. Regardless of what algorithm is taught to students, it is best to teach algorithms that are consistent with or similar to previously taught algorithms (Stein, Silbert, & Carnine, 1997). The more similar the algorithms, the less likely that students will be confused and the more likely that students will understand the concept.

Mathematical Fluency: The *Third* Big Idea

Mathematical fluency is the effortless, automatic ability to perform mathematical operations. Mathematical fluency takes into consideration the student's ability to compute problems quickly (speed) and with high levels of accuracy (few or no errors) at the abstract level. Mathematically fluent students do not rely on concrete and semiconcrete representations to figure math problems. The faster and more accurate students are in

TABLE 8-4

Mathematical Rules

Addition rules	Definition	Example
1. Order rule	The order of the numbers you are adding does not affect the answer. This is also known as the commutative property of addition.	$8 + 7 = 7 + 8$
2. Zero rule	A number plus zero equals the number.	$0 + 9 = 9$
3. One rule	A number plus 1 is one more than the number.	$1 + 8 = 9$
4. Nine rule	The result of adding any single-digit number greater than zero to 9 is that number minus 1 plus 10.	$9 + 5 = 14$; $5 - 1$ equals 4 plus 10 which equals 14
5. Tens rule	When adding any single-digit to 10, the result is having the 0 being changed to that number.	$10 + 3 = 13$. The zero is replaced by the 3 to make 13.

Subtraction rules	Definition	Example
1. Zero rule	A number minus zero equals that number.	$6 - 0 = 6$
2. One rule	A number minus 1 is one less. This can be taught by having the student count backwards by ones.	$9 - 1 = 8$. Counting 1 backwards from 9 is 8.
3. Same number rule	A number minus itself is zero.	$3 - 3 = 0$
4. BBB rule	If the **B**ottom number is **B**igger than the top number, you must **B**reak down the top number in the next column to the left, trade it in for a 10 units, and subtract.	$23 - 5 = 18$. The 2 is broken down into ten units and given to the 3 to make 13; then 5 is taken away from 13 and the 2 is made into a 1.

Multiplication rules	Definition	Example
1. Order rule	The order of the numbers you are multiplying does not affect the answer. This is also known as the commutative property of multiplication.	$3 \times 6 = 6 \times 3$
2. Zero rule	The result of zero times any number is zero.	$0 \times 2 = 0$
3. One rule	The result of one times any number is that number.	$1 \times 3 = 3$
4. Two rule	The result of two times any number is double that number.	2×3 is calculated by counting by 2's three times; 2 . . . 4 . . . 6.
5. Five rule	The result of five times any number is calculated by counting by five's the number of times indicated by the multiplier.	5×4 is calculated by counting by 5's four times. 5 . . . 10 . . . 15 . . . 20.
6. Nine rule	The result of nine times any number is calculated by subtracting one from the multiplier to get the tens digit and then adding up to 9. The amount you add up to 9 is the number in the ones digit.	$9 \times 6 = 54$ since $6 - 1 = 5$ for the ten's place and $5 + 4 = 9$.

continued on next page

TABLE 8-4

Mathematical Rules (continued)

Division rules	Definition	Example
1. Zero rule	Zero divided by any number is zero.	$0 \div 3 = 0$
2. One rule	A number divided by 1 is that number.	$7 \div 1 = 7$
2. Two rule	A number divided by 2 is half that number.	$10 \div 2 = 5$ since 5 is half of 10. This is reverse of nines multiplication rule. $54 \div 9 = 6$ since 6 is one more than 5.
4. Nines fact rule	The result of nine divided by a nine's fact is one more than the number in the ten's column.	
5. Multiplication and division relationship rule	The quotient times the divisor equals the dividend.	$12 \div 6 = 12$. This is calculated by asking "What number times 6 equals 2?"

Adapted from Mercer, C. D., & Mercer, A. R. (2001). *Teaching students with learning problems* (5th Ed.). Upper Saddle River, NJ: Merrill/Prentice Hall.

solving mathematical problems, the more fluent they are in math. To be fluent, students must have mastered mathematical awareness and conceptualization prerequisite skills that are associated with given skills or behaviors.

Mathematical fluency is important to all students, but is often overlooked by teachers when working with students who are at-risk for math failure. Teachers may think that these students need extended time to complete math problems. While these students may need more time to complete math tasks, if they are to be successful in solving more complex math problems they must be mathematically fluent. According to Zentall and Ferkis (1993), computational speed (math fluency) is a significant predicator of word problem behavior. Those who lack proficiency in basic number facts and have difficulty in recalling those facts, will be at a disadvantage when compared to other students.

Much of the math literature has focused on the fluency of the basic operations. This is because students must be fluent in the basic operations to efficiently solve more advanced math problems. Yet mathematical fluency is not limited to the basic operations. Mathematical fluency is also concerned with the calculation and application of more advanced math skills. These advanced skills often require students to use many different skills at one time. Take for example the skill of estimating a shopping bill. This advanced mathematical application skill (see the Fifth Big Idea) often requires students to mentally add prices taking into consideration the actual sales price, discounts, taxes, and whether they have enough money to pay for the shopping items. If the student is to shop without performing laborious calculations, he must be fluent in estimating.

Teaching Mathematical Fluency

Two essential characteristics of effectively teaching mathematical fluency are speed and accuracy. Any method used to increase fluency should be judged based on how well it increases both. Several methods of increasing a student's mathematical fluency are provided below.

Constant Time Delay ••• Constant time delay is a nearly errorless one-on-one instructional method that provides consistent opportunities for student reinforcement (Koscinski & Gast, 1993). It has been used effectively with students of all ages and in a variety of subjects including math (Whalen, Schuster, & Hemmeter, 1996). It is a structured method of using flash cards for drill and practice. Instruction is divided into two main parts. During the first part, known as the "zero time delay trial", students are presented with a math problem, read the math problem, told/shown the answer, and asked to repeat the answer and write it. Initially students only answer the problem with the correct answer being presented. Students should answer questions with 100% accuracy.

In the second part, known as the "non-zero second time delay trial", the teacher presents a math problem, asks the student the problem, and waits for a certain amount of time (often 3–5 seconds depending on student needs) to allow the student to answer the problem correctly. If the student does not answer the problem correctly or gives no answer, the teacher provides the student with the correct answer. **Table 8-5** is an example of a constant time delay data sheet.

Cover-Copy-Compare ••• The copy-cover-compare method is used with students who can be trusted to work independently (Ozaki, Williams, & McLaughlin, 1995). The procedure is rather simple. The teacher provides the student with math problems that have been answered. The student is instructed to copy the problem and cover up the answer with a note card. The student then proceeds to answer the problem without looking back. Once the student is done, she compares her answer to the correct answer. The copy-cover-compare method can be used in conjunction with instruction on error analysis as described later in this chapter. This will allow students to become aware of the types of errors they are making and correct them.

Constant time delay uses flash cards to provide consistent opportunities for student reinforcement.

Dot Math ••• Dot math (Kramer & Krug, 1973), also packaged commercially as Touch Math (Bullock, 1996), uses a multi-sensory approach to math that uses visual, auditory, and tactile modes to assist student in learning all the basic mathematical operations. Reference points (dots) are put on numbers 1–9 as follows.

Each number has a corresponding number of dots to its value (the number one has one dot, the number two has two dots, etc.). Addition is taught by having students say the number, touch the dots, and add them up. Students learn to subtract by saying the numbers and counting backwards. Both multiplication and division are taught by teaching the students skip counting. For example, with multiplication if a student was figuring 2×3 she would count by twos three times. With division, the student would calculate $12 \div 4$ by skip counting by four until she reached twelve. Each time she skipped counted, she would make a mark. The answer would be the final number of marks.

TABLE 8-5

Constant Time Delay Data Sheet Used to Develop Mathematical Fluency Skills

Time Delay Date Sheet

Student: Jacques Thibodeaux   **Skill:** Addition problems

Lesson Objective: Jacques will state the answer of addition facts using five as an addend when presented with a flashcard with a 3-second time delay with a 95% accuracy over 3 consecutive trials.

Date: 7-31-07	Delay:		Date: 8-1-07	Delay:	
Student Behavior	Zero time delay	3-second time delay	Student Behavior	Zero time delay	3-second time delay
1. $5 + 4$	+		1. $5 + 10$	+	
2. $5 + 5$	+		2. $5 + 6$	+	
3. $5 + 1$	+		3. $5 + 7$	+	
4. $5 + 2$	+		4. $5 + 4$	+	
5. $5 + 3$	0	+	5. $5 + 9$	+	
6. $5 + 8$	0	+	6. $5 + 1$	0	+
7. $5 + 10$	+		7. $5 + 2$	+	
8. $5 + 6$	0	+	8. $5 + 3$	0	+
9. $5 + 7$	+		9. $5 + 8$	+	
10. $5 + 9$	0	+	10. $5 + 5$	+	
Total # correct	6	4	Total # correct	8	2

Teachers should use dot math keeping the concrete-semiconcrete-abstract sequence of instruction in mind. The dots provide students with a semiconcrete representation of the numbers. If students are to be fluent, the teacher must systematically fade the dots.

Error Analysis ••• Error analysis is the process of examining the math mistakes of students and finding patterns. Teachers should use student mistakes as opportunities for learning. Determining student error patterns allows teachers to focus their instruction. Error analysis is part of student assessment, as discussed later in this chapter, but should be used to make students aware of the types of errors they are making. Explicitly showing students the type of errors they are making and methods for reducing those errors will ultimately increase the students' mathematical fluency. When using error analysis to improve the mathematical fluency of students, teachers should use the following steps (Stein, et al., 1997):

1. Determine student error patterns by examining the student's work.
2. Inform student of the error pattern.
3. Model the correct method of solving the problem.
4. Teach student using concrete examples if necessary.
5. Teach student using semiconcrete examples if necessary.
6. Teach student abstractly using direct instruction procedures.
7. Allow student to practice until mastery is reached.
8. Assess student mastery of skills.

There are common math errors that teachers should be aware of while grading students' work. Some of those common math errors include:

1. **Computational error:** This is one of the most common types of errors. A computational error involves not recalling basic number facts. Teachers who identify this error pattern need to teach the particular skill to mastery.
2. **Place value error:** A place value error is an indication that students lack an understanding of what each place value represents. There are two typical types of place value errors. The first one involves regrouping (e.g., in the problem 23 + 38 = 511, the student has not carried the tens). The second place value error has to do with directionality.
3. **Operation error:** An operation error occurs when students do not use the correct operation (e.g., a student subtracts when addition should be used: 45 + 12 = 33).
4. **Algorithm error:** An algorithm is a method to solve a problem. Students who make an algorithm error use a defective algorithm or do not use an effective one correctly.
5. **Order of operations error:** An order of operations error occurs when the student performs the operation in the wrong direction (e.g., in the problem 861 − 489 = 428, the student has subtracted the minuend (the top number) from the subtrahend (the bottom number)).
6. **Zero errors:** A zero error happens when the student does not put down a zero as a place holder. (e.g., in the problem 1206 ÷ 6 = 21, the student has forgotten to put a zero in the answer for the tens place).
7. **Careless response error:** A careless response error occurs when the student does not take the time to be precise (e.g., working too quickly, illegible writing).

Graphing ••• The importance of graphing student math progress cannot be emphasized too much. Graphing student academic achievement has been shown to be an effective method of motivating students, keeping track of their daily progress, and providing instructional feedback (Kerr & Nelson, 1998). While graphing is useful and beneficial with all the big ideas in math, it is even more important when developing mathematical fluency. Graphs can be used to keep track of how fast students answer problems, how many problems they get correct, and how accurate (number of errors) they are in solving the problems.

Multiplication Facts ••• A common fluency concern of teachers is instructing their students in the basic multiplication facts. There are several specific methods that teachers can use to teach multiplication. The first method focuses on teaching fact families. There are 100 basic multiplication facts using the numerals 0–9. These basic facts can be grouped into families. Families are groupings of multiplication facts based on common characteristics. For example, the "ones family" is made up of problems that have the numeral one (any number times one is that number). Another example is the "double family" that is comprised of any problem that has a two (any number times two is double that number) (Greene, 1999). Some problems fall into two families and can be taught in one or both families. Easier facts such as 0 and 1 should be taught first. Facts involving 2, 5, and 9 should be taught after mastery has been reached with 0 and 1.

A second method of teaching multiplication facts is by using pegword mnemonic instruction (Greene, 1999; Wood & Frank, 2000). Students develop mnemonic flashcards to enhance the learning and retention of multiplication facts. Greene (1999) provides an example for the problem 6 × 7 = 42. In this case, the student thinks of a word that rhymes with 6 (sticks), 7 (heaven), and 42 (warty shoe) and then draws a picture of a shoe in heaven that has 42 warts. This process can be done with all math facts or with those that are particularly problematic for students.

Mathematical Language: The *Fourth* Big Idea

Mathematical language is the exchange of information and ideas as they relate to the understanding (receptive) and use of (expressive) mathematics to acquire and convey meaning. Mathematical language takes into consideration both oral and written math expression. Similar to the other forms of language, mathematical language has its own symbols, syntax, semantics, pragmatics, and vocabulary. The understanding of mathematics may be more difficult than reading for some students because it is "conceptually dense" (Wiiig & Semel, 1984). Symbols (e.g., =, >, α, π) all represent complex ideas. Additionally, these complex ideas are often presented without contextual clues that might be available in reading. These factors make it difficult for students with language and reading difficulties to understand mathematics.

One particular aspect of mathematics language that is difficult for students is vocabulary. Mathematics has its own vocabulary. **Table 8-6** provides a list of mathematical vocabulary that is commonly used. Teachers should be aware of these words and teach their meanings and pronunciation when appropriate. The list covers basic mathematical, computational, basic geometric shapes and concepts, and banking and credit vocabulary. Each list is arranged by level of difficulty.

In addition to vocabulary, particular aspects of math language are problematic for students (Shorrocks-Taylor & Hargreaves, 1999). Some of those problems include:

- Common words often have different meanings in math. For example, the words "odd", "mean", and "product" probably mean something different to students than is generally expressed in math. Conversely, some common words such as "similar", "average", and "reflection" have the same or similar meanings in math.

- The meaning of a word can change depending on its context. For example, the word "big" means something different in the phrases "big number" and "big square."

- Mathematical symbols can be confusing. For example, 6 ÷ 2 can be expressed as "6 divided by 2", "2 goes into 6", and "6 divided into 2 parts."

- Important mathematical phrases can be difficult to understand. For example, "so that", "suppose that", and "but then" are ambiguous.

Closely related to math vocabulary is the written and oral understanding of math problems. Logically, there is a connection between a student's reading level and his ability to read math problems. If a student has problems in reading, there is a good chance he will have problems reading math problems. A student who has reading problems will probably also have difficulties using illustrations and diagrams (Noonan, 1990). Math textbooks use illustrations and diagrams to provide students with additional and often essential information. Students need to understand how to use them correctly if they are to be effective math communicators.

Additionally, students who have language problems will have difficulty understanding oral math presentations. Teachers should be aware of the language they use when presenting a math lesson. The more aware teachers are of their students' communication abilities, the greater the chances the instruction will match the students' abilities. The examples teachers use should take into consideration the students' background knowledge. Students need the prerequisite skills necessary to learn a new concept or skill. Background knowledge takes into consideration the life experiences of students. Information used in examples and problems should contain information that is familiar to students. Students' culture, socio-economic status, and language all play a part in their understanding of new concepts and skills.

Finally, students need to be taught how to express what they learn about math (Bottge, 2001). Students can use oral and written forms of communication to express their thoughts. Expression may require students to justify and explain their answers. To do so, students may use their higher order thinking skills. The more articulate students are, the greater the chances they will be able to express themselves correctly.

TABLE 8-6

Basic Mathematical Vocabulary

answer	mile	pair	ton
feet	hour	plus	yard
cent	total	foot	count
check	point	area	number
dozen	amount	equal	pint
dollar	percent	remainder	second
less than	balance	divide	figure
ounce	quart	height	width
volume	greater than	cancel	degrees
average	length	weight	round off
angle	gallon	division	minus
temperature	measure	square	inch
solve	convert	compute	numeral
increase	decrease	cubic	whole number
fraction	metric	multiply	right angle
geometric	multiplication	calculate	quantity
invert	maximum	estimate	minimum
subtract	reduce (to lowest terms)	equivalent	solution
improper fraction	solution	improper fraction	linear
percentage	denominator	subtraction	numerator
proper fraction	numbers 0–1000	first-tenth	

Computational & Problem Solving Vocabulary

addend	sum	minuend	subtrahend
multiplicand	multiplier	product	Quotient
dividend	divisor	finds	altogether
lost	remains	groups	Rows
each	cost per	share	Spent

Basic Geometric Shapes and Concepts Vocabulary

circumference	clockwise	cone	counterclockwise
cube	cylinder	90 degrees	45 degrees
135 degrees	diameter	hexagon	horizontal
octagon	parallel	perimeter	perpendicular
radius	rectangle	semicircle	Spiral
square	triangle	vertical	

Banking and Credit Vocabulary

balance	canceled check	cashier check	check stub
checking account	collateral	credit card	coins
currency	deposit slip	endorse	interest
loan	minimum payment	personal check	savings account
statement	withdrawal slip	(coin names)	

Source: Brigance, A. (1983). *Inventory of Essential Skills.* Curriculum Associates, Inc.

Teaching Mathematical Language

Math teachers should instruct students in how to effectively communicate mathematically. This instruction should not simply be left up to the reading or language arts teachers. The skills necessary to effectively communicate are similar to teaching reading. It is beyond the scope of this chapter to go into all the methods of teaching mathematical language. Please refer to Chapter 7 of this book for specifics on how to teach math vocabulary and comprehension skills to students.

Mathematical Application: The *Fifth* Big Idea

Mathematical application is a complex cognitive and meta-cognitive process by which a student intentionally gains meaning from situations involving math. The application of math skills to authentic and meaningful situations is the main reason for learning the first four big ideas. Providing students with opportunities to apply their math abilities should occur continuously and immediately as students learn new skills and concepts. Elementary as well as secondary teachers should provide students with structured opportunities for students to use newly learned skills in novel and meaningful situations.

Mathematical application is often associated with a student's ability to problem solve. Providing students with a mathematically rich environment that emphasizes problem solving skills increases the potential opportunities that they will have to participate in society (Miller & Mercer, 1993). To effectively problem solve, students must first be able to demonstrate their understanding of the problem by paraphrasing the problem or by making a representation of it. Then, they must develop an organizational plan of action for solving the problem. Next, they must execute the actual mathematical computation needed to solve a problem. During this process they must apply their strategies to monitor their actions to ensure that their actions are consistent with their plan. Finally, they must verify their work by checking the accuracy and logic of their answer.

Students at-risk for math failure have difficulties with math problem solving (Algozzine, O'Shea, Crews, & Stoddard, 1988). The interpretation and application of abstract concepts to real-life situations is a complex task. The more concrete and real teachers can make the learning experience, the greater the likelihood that students will acquire and retain their math knowledge. To effectively teach mathematical application, teachers need to provide students with systematic opportunities to generalize their math knowledge (Bos & Vaughn, 1998). Skills related to money, measurement, time, fractions, and estimation are often used. Being able to discriminate between what is and is not important (extraneous information) is a valuable skill.

Teaching Mathematical Application

Problem-solving ••• Teaching students to problem-solve is essential if they are to be successful in applying their skills to the real world. Problem-solving is usually difficult for students. It requires them to understand vocabulary, sequence data, discriminate between the relevant and irrelevant, isolate key information within problems, apply computational skills, understand similarities and differences, apply the correct strategy to solve the problem, and think abstractly (Bley & Thornton, 1995). The more hypothetical and abstract the problems, the more difficult the problem is for students. If students at-risk for math failure are to be successful problem solvers, they need incremental practice at all grade levels and explicit instruction in solving problems.

According to Montague (1997), students should be taught explicit steps to solve problems. She suggests teachers instruct students to use the following steps:

1. *Read the problem aloud.* Assistance is provided to the student with unfamiliar vocabulary. The problem can be read out loud to the student if necessary.

2. *Paraphrase the problem aloud.* The student rephrases the problem verbally.
3. *Visualize.* The student draws a representation of the problem.
4. *State the problem.* The student verbally states, "I have . . . I want to find. . . ."
Students can underline keywords in the problem.
5. *Hypothesize.* The student verbally states, "If I . . . then. . . ."
6. *Estimate.* The student estimates the potential answer and underlines it. Rounding and estimating skills are emphasized here.
7. *Calculate.* The student calculates the answer and circles it.
8. *Self-check.* The student examines each step involved in solving the problem then asks herself "Is this answer logical?" Computation calculations are checked.

Mercer and Miller (1991–1993) provide teachers with a more extensive strategy that students can use to solve math problems. They use the mnemonic **FAST DRAW** for solving math word problems. The DRAW portion of the mnemonic can be used by itself to solve problems with whole numbers or fractions. FAST DRAW can be used with basic word problems (Mercer & Mercer, 2001) and with algebra problems (Allsopp, 1999). See **Table 8-7** for details about FAST DRAW for basic math word problems.

TABLE 8-7

Fast Draw

Find what you are solving for.
- Look for the question mark.
- Underline information that tells you what you are solving for.
- Look at the keywords.
- Underline them twice.

Ask yourself, "What information is given?"
- Read the whole problem.
- Find number phrases and circle them.

Set up the equation.
- Write the equation with the number in the correct order.

Tie down the equation.
- Reread the underlined sentences.
- Check highlighted key words and operation signs.
- Say aloud the operation and what the operation means.

Discover the sign
- Find the sign (+, −, ×, ÷).
- Circle the sign.
- Say the name of the sign aloud.
- Say what the sign means.

Read the problem
- Say the problem aloud.

Answer the problem or draw tallies and/or circles.
- Draw your answers.
- Double-check your answer.

Write the answer.
- Write the answer to the problem.

Adapted from Mercer, C. D., & Mercer A. R. (2001). *Teaching students with learning problems* (5th Ed.). Upper Saddle River, NJ: Merrill/Prentice Hall.

General Problem Solving Strategies ••• In addition to teaching students problem-solving steps, teachers can instruct students in general strategies that are beneficial when solving problems (Vaughn, Bos, & Schumm, 2000). Some of those strategies include:

1. **Pattern recognition:** Patterns can be found in words, letters, shapes, and forms. Recognizing patterns can be taught using "cryptoquotes" where students decode patterns from scrambled patterns. Patterns in nature (i.e., geological formations, DNA, fingerprints, cloud formations, etc.) can be used as examples.

2. **Solving backwards:** When students are given problems with the known (costs, time, distances, etc.), they can work backwards to find the answer (time to complete a project).

3. **Draw and model:** Teaching students to make a graphic or physical representation of the problem will allow them to see it more clearly.

4. **Graphing and using tables:** Organizing and summarizing numerical and verbal data using graphs and tables can teach students relationships (more/less, sequence).

5. **Calculator usage:** Calculators allow students to focus on complex and higher-order concepts instead of being impeded by the details of routine computation (Maccini & Calvin, 2000). Calculator use after students have been taught the meaning of the operations does not negatively impact basic math skill acquisition and can improve students' attitudes toward math (Heddens & Speer, 1997; Hembree, 1986).

6. **Computer usage:** Computer usage allows students to understand place value, decimals, complex calculations, integrate relationships, and variables (Knapp & Glenn, 1996). Students must be provided with explicit instruction in how to use spreadsheets and database programs.

7. **Graphic organizers:** While teachers predominately use graphic organizers, students can be taught to use them to display relationships between math concepts (Lovitt & Horton, 1994). Teachers can provide students with graphic organizers for problems or have students develop their own.

Estimation ••• Estimating answers is an essential daily living skill that students need to solve problems. When people buy groceries or purchase a meal at a fast food restaurant, rarely do they know exactly how much money it will cost. They need to have a general understanding of whether they can or cannot afford the purchase.

Reys (1986) provides strategies that can be used to teach computational estimation. One example is the expanded notation strategy. Take for example the problem $521 \times 8 = ?$. First, the student writes the number out in expanded notation form: $500 + 20 + 1$. Then, the student multiplies each component by 8 and adds the answers together to get the estimation ($500 \times 8 = 4000$; $20 \times 8 = 160$; $1 \times 8 = 8$ thus $4000 + 160 + 8 = 4168$. Another example is the rounding strategy. The rounding strategy requires that students understand the concept of rounding. For example, if a student is adding the following numbers $170 + 523 = ?$ In this case, the student would round 170 up to 200 and 523 down to 500. The estimated answer would be 700. A variation on this strategy could occur with multiplication. For example, a sandwich might cost $3.87. If the student wants to estimate the purchase cost of three sandwiches he could round the cost up to $4.00 and then multiply by three to come up with answer of $12.00.

In addition to teaching students estimation strategies, teachers should instruct students in the vocabulary of estimation (see Big Idea: Mathematical Vocabulary in this chapter). Phrases such as "about," "close to," and "in the neighborhood" indicate that the problem is asking for an estimate. Knowing these words will cue students into using their estimation skills.

Enhancement of Math Curricula to Meet the Needs of Students At-Risk

This section provides information on how teachers can enhance their math curricula. The first part provides information on different types of math curricula and how each might impact students who are at-risk for math failure. The second half of this section provides general methods teachers can use to boost their students' math abilities by making curricula adaptations and modifications. For a detailed description of additional adaptations see Chapter 6.

Types of Math Curricula

There are several different types of math curricula. The first and probably the most common type is a **developmental spiraling curriculum.** A developmental spiraling curriculum presents many different math skills to students each year (Stein, Silbert, & Carnine, 1997). In subsequent years students are reintroduced to the same skills but at a more advanced level. On the surface the concept of a spiraling curriculum seems appropriate. The idea is that once math skills have been introduced, the student can gain more in-depth knowledge about those skills in the next grades. Unfortunately, how this approach is implemented is often not effective with students who are at-risk for math failure (Carnine, 1991; Cawley, Baker-Kroczynski, & Urban, 1992). The problem is one of mastery. Since teachers are often racing to "get through" the curriculum, students do not master the appropriate math skills at each grade level. Students only acquire a superficial knowledge of the math skills. This puts teachers in the difficult position of re-teaching the unmastered skills or progressing to the next skills.

The second type of math curricula is a **skill specific curriculum.** A skill specific math curriculum targets particular skills such as place value, addition, multiplication, or division (Stein, et al., 1997). The value of a skills specific curriculum is that it can provide students with thorough and in-depth instruction in a specific skill. Students can be given enough practice in the given skills so that mastery can be achieved. The disadvantage of a skill specific curriculum is that it lacks breadth. A full-range of skills is not taught. A skill specific curriculum might be more effective if it was used in conjunction with other curricula that cover a broad range of skills.

The third type of curricula is a **functional skills curriculum.** A functional skills curriculum focuses on daily living skills students need to succeed in life. Daily living skills are on a wide continuum from the very basic to the complex. The level of functional skills curricula depends on the needs of students and can be taught to all students. Some areas include budgeting, making change, grocery shopping, measuring, and other life skills. Functional skills curricula can be used at all grade levels but are often used at the secondary level and usually are targeted at students who are not going on to college. **Table 8-8** is a summary of some of the math curricula available.

Adaptations and Modifications in Math Curriculum and Instruction

Math curricula are often poorly written and designed (Miller & Mercer, 1997). Most do not take into consideration the needs of students at-risk for mathematical failure (Carnine, 1997). Teachers may or may not have control over what kind of curricula is used. Poorly designed math curricula can be problematic for the teacher and the student.

TABLE 8-8

Math Curricula for Students Who Are At-Risk

Curricula	Description	Source
Connecting Math Concepts	Uses a direct instruction model in a basal format. Is used with grades 1 through six.	Engelmann, Carnine, Engelmann, & Kelly (1989)
Corrective Mathematics	Uses a direct instruction model in a highly sequenced format. The focus is on remedial math skills for students in grades 3–12.	Englemann & Carnine (1982)
DISTAR Arithmetic	Uses direct instruction in a highly sequenced formal. Teaches the basic operations. Provides detailed teacher's guide, workbooks, homework activities, and student books.	Englemann & Carnine (1976)
Key Math Teach and Practice	Uses a diagnostic and prescriptive format. Provides remedial instruction. Provides teacher's guide, activities, worksheets, and student progress charts.	Connolly (1985)
Project Math	Uses a both developmental and remedial instruction. Materials are provided at reduced reading levels. Teaches sets, patterns, numbers, operations, fractions, geometry, measurement.	Cawley, Fitzmaurice, Sedlak, & Althaus (1976)
Real-Life Math Program	Uses practical materials in math. The focus is on consumer skills, homemaking, health care, auto care, and vocational skills. The target population is ages 13 to 18.	Schwartz (1977)
Saxon Math: Adaptations for Special Populations	Uses remedial instruction at the middle school level. Provides student materials and methods for teachers to adapt materials for students performing below grade level.	Saxon (2003)
Solve it!	Use meta-cognitive instruction. Provides secondary teachers with a method to teach problem solving.	Montague, Wagner, & Morgan (2000)
Strategic Math Series	Uses direct and meta-cognitive instruction in the basic operations. Provides students with a strategy to solve math problems.	Mercer & Miller, (1991–1993)

Teachers who do not have control over the curricula they use may find it necessary to enhance the math curricula to meet the needs of their students using effective teaching procedures.

Peer Tutoring

Peer tutoring is an alternative classroom arrangement where students take an instructional role in the classroom with other students (Cohen, Conway, & Gow, 1988; Vacc & Cannon, 1991). Peer tutoring in math has a stronger impact than in any other subject.

Peer-tutoring has been effective in teaching computational skills (Berine-Smith, 1991) and problem-solving skills (Allsopp, 1997). Teachers can develop their own math tutoring program or purchase packaged tutoring programs. One program that has been shown to be effective in teaching with students who are at-risk for math failure in kindergarten through grade 6 is the Peer-Assisted Learning Strategies in Math program also called PALS Math (Fuchs, Fuchs, & Karns, 2001).

Cooperative Learning

Cooperative learning is an instructional arrangement where students work in heterogeneous groups to practice or review skills and concepts (Slavin, 1991). Cooperative learning has been shown to be an effective instructional tool in math (Slavin, Madden, & Leavey, 1984; Slavin, 1991). When designing and evaluating the effectiveness of cooperative learning math groups, teachers might consider how effective students are at

- using math vocabulary correctly;
- paraphrasing word problems;
- using math rules effectively in groups;
- applying math strategies in groups;
- using the appropriate algorithms;
- making connections with previously mastered math skills and concepts;
- making math connections with other disciplines (science, social studies, etc.);
- making concrete, semiconcrete, and abstract representations of concepts; and
- applying the math concepts to real life situations (Bryant & Rivera, 1997).

A Life Skills Approach to Mathematics Instruction

Instruction can be improved by focusing on its usefulness to students in their daily lives. Life skills such as purchasing food, identifying personal body measurements, knowing how to rent an apartment, and making a realistic budget are just a few of the essential adult outcomes that are important to students as they transition from school to adult life. **Table 8-9** lists some life skills students need.

All students need life skills. This is particularly true of students who are not college-bound. One way of thinking about life skills is to ask "what math skills will students need to know to be successful when they are adults?" From this stance, teachers need to plan backwards based on the future adult outcomes of their students. While such thinking is crucial for secondary teachers, it is also important for elementary school teachers. Both groups of teachers need to focus on the future adult outcomes of students.

Cronin and Patton (1993) provide three ways all teachers (general and special education) can provide students with real-life skill instruction. Life skills instruction can occur through specific coursework, augmentation, or infusion. A life skills specific coursework approach is used when a separate course is available. This course could focus just on real-life math or incorporate life skills from a broad range of topics such as reading, science, and social studies. This type of course is typically found at the secondary level and may or may not be used toward graduation credit.

The second method of teaching life skills math instruction is by using an augmentation approach. An augmentation approach requires teachers to set aside a portion of the day for life skills instruction. Often a unit approach is used. For example, the topic of the unit might be "Math for everyday living." Again, the focus would be on the future adult outcomes of students. Like the specific coursework approach, the unit approach could incorporate more subjects than just math.

TABLE 8-9

Math Life Skills

Home

measuring food	maintaining a home	doing laundry	maintaining a car
maintaining a yard	measuring clothing	budgeting	counting calories
setting thermostat	determining medicine dosages	reading a thermometer	measuring solutions (i.e., oil for mower)
planning meals	reading recipes	using timers	reading food labels
measuring materials for home repairs	painting	weighing oneself	gauging air pressure (bike & care tires)

Leisure

estimating time	planning exercise	finding locations on a map	using first aid
playing games that require math	understanding games of chance	discriminating sizes and shapes	calculating motel & activities costs
using discount tickets	estimating traveling time and distance	splitting the bill	making online purchases

Work

planning to arrive on time	using public transportation	planning daily assignments	using a phone
telling time	using a computer	using a copier	scanning
using spreadsheets	using databases		

Financial

writing checks	filing taxes	using credit	taking out a loan
planning retirement	making change	paying taxes	comparing prices
estimating costs	paying rent/mortgage	estimating change	making purchases
using tables	counting money	paying insurance	reading bills
using graphs	determining salary	calculating wages	using coupons
using a self service grocery checkout	using an ATM	keeping financial records	using online banking services
figuring price per unit	examining bills for errors	responding to telemarketers	

The third life skills math method is an infusion approach. The infusion approach can be used in a special education classroom but is beneficial in the general education classroom where students who are at-risk are being taught. This approach allows teachers to use their current curriculum and create opportunities where real-life topics can be infused into the existing curriculum. The advantage of this approach is that it allows students who are at-risk to have access to the general education curriculum and still be taught important life skills.

Instructional Math Games

Instructional games provide students with an opportunity to increase their math fluency and maintain skills they have already learned. Well designed games can provide students with better practice than traditional worksheets (Beattie & Algozzine, 1982) and can be motivational (Lavoie, 1993). Motivational games are individualized, have some chance factors (i.e., lose a turn, skip ahead two spaces, etc.), allow students to win much more often than lose, are fast paced, and allow for few opportunities to make errors (Lavoie, 1993; Mercer & Mercer, 2001).

Self-correcting math games can be particularly beneficial to students (Mercer & Mercer, 2001). Self-correcting games give students access to the answers during the game so they can check their own work. The chief value of self-correcting games is that they provide students with immediate feedback without the teacher being present. Students can check their work without being embarrassed in front of others when they make a mistake. While self-correcting games do increase the chance that students will cheat, informing students of the benefit of the game can lessen the amount of dishonesty.

Graphic Representations

Graphic representations (webs, concept maps, graphic organizers, etc.) are visual illustrations of a math problem (Jitendra, 2002). Graphic representations allow students to see a problem conceptually. Students who are at-risk for math failure often have difficulty remembering all the important aspects of a problem. Graphic representations reduce the amount of mental resources students need to answer the problem and allow them to focus on analyzing and solving a problem. In addition to teachers using graphic representations in their classroom when presenting problems, teachers can instruct students in how to use them when solving problems. Students who use graphic representations while solving a problem have a better chance of answering the problem correctly and understanding it conceptually.

Mathematical Motivation

The affective characteristics of students at-risk has a direct impact on their ability to use math (Montague, 1997). Histories of math failure contribute to the development of mathematical learned helplessness and reduced motivation. Students who have experienced math failure over time may attribute their failure to bad luck or a personal lack of effort (Weiner, 1990). Conversely, students who believe that they can be successful in math attribute their success to their own efforts, try harder, and are more persistent (Deshler, Schumaker, & Lenz, 1984; Yasutake, Bryan, & Dohrn, 1996). Corral and Anita (1997) suggest that teachers can improve student attitudes toward math and their math performance by teaching them to use positive self-talk. They suggest that teachers use the following six steps to increase the chances students will be more successful at math.

1. Model a math strategy for students demonstrating the value of the strategy.
2. Model positive self-talk while working a problem. For example, "If I make a mistake, I can find my mistake and correct it", "If I work carefully I probably will not make as many mistakes and be more successful", and "If I'm having difficulties with a problem, I'll try harder and find the answer."
3. Model positive self-talk when mistakes are made. Make several mistakes and verbally indicate what the student should think.
4. Have students periodically reflect on their math progress using self-report or journal writing. For example, on a Likert scale, have students rate statements such as "I thought this task was . . . (very easy to very hard)" or "On this task, I think my answers were . . . (all wrong to all right)."
5. Promote students keeping records of positive self-talk while working on tasks.
6. Have students set math goals. Students who select their own math goals perform better over time (Fuchs, Bahr, & Reith, 1988). Allow students to read the math goals prior to starting an assignment or taking a test.

Assessment in Math

Assessment is an integral part of teaching math. Good math assessment helps educators improve the effectiveness and efficiency of their teaching. Math assessment can be used to monitor student progress, influence the pace of instruction, evaluate and refine math curricula, motivate students, inform parents and administrators of student math learning, and determine placement in special programs.

There are two basic types of standardized math tests: **norm-referenced** and **criterion-referenced.** Norm-referenced math tests are used to compare the math abilities of a student to a group of students (Rudner & Schafer, 2002). Norm-referenced tests typically are used to determine the achievement levels of students. Criterion-referenced math tests compare the student to a math criterion. Criterion-referenced math tests are more specific than norm-referenced tests but less specific than informal math testing. They are often used to diagnosis specific math problems. **Table 8-10** provides a summary of the more common norm- and criterion-referenced math tests.

The most specific and probably the most useful type of assessment for teachers is **informal testing.** Informal math tests provide teachers with data they can use to improve their daily instruction. Some types of informal math tests include (a) curriculum-based measurement, (b) rubrics, and (c) mathematical interviewing with error analysis. Each is described below with examples.

Curriculum-based Measurement

Curriculum-based measurement (CBM) assesses how fluent a student is in the math skill being assessed (Wright, 2002). CBM uses direct measurement techniques in the form of probes. **Table 8-11** is a sample math probe. Probes are timed samples of the academic material taken from the student's math curricula. Math probes are usually administered for 2 minutes and measure either mixed skills or single skills. Progress is graphed based on the number of digits the student answers correctly. **Table 8-12** provides the steps teachers can use to make math CBM sheets for their classroom.

Rubrics

Rubrics are systematic scoring guidelines used to evaluate students' performance based on a detailed description of what is required of the students (Wiggins, 1998). Rubrics can be either holistic (general) or analytic (specific). Holistic rubrics give teachers an overall sense of how a student is performing. Analytical rubrics show teachers the specific skills students know. In math, teachers often use rubrics to assess students' higher order thinking skills (i.e., problem solving, projects, etc.). Both kinds of rubrics use some kind of a scale to determine student performance. Student performance behaviors are put on a Likert scale indicating mastery to non-mastery of the given behaviors. Numerous rubric examples can be found on the Internet, in assessment books, and in materials developed by school systems.

Mathematical Interviewing with Error Analysis

Teachers can evaluate the math abilities of students by conducting a math interview (Kennedy & Tipps, 1994; Mercer & Mercer, 2001). The purpose of a math interview is to see how the student thinks about and figures math problems. Students at-risk for math failure often think about math problems differently than other students (Montague & Applegate, 1993). It is conducted on an individual basis. This process allows teachers to hear and see what errors students are making.

TABLE 8-10

Norm- and Criterion-referenced Math Tests

Test:	Type of Assessment and Grade/Age Level	Areas Assessed
Key Math Diagnostic Arithmetic Tests—Revised American Guidance Service	Norm-referenced Individual Preschool–Grade 6	• basic concepts (numeration, rational numbers, geometry) • operations (addition, subtraction, multiplication, division, mental computation) • applications (measurement, time, money, estimation, interpretation of data, problem solving)
Test of Early Mathematics Ability-2 PRO-ED	Criterion-referenced Individual Age 3–9	• informal mathematics (magnitude, counting, calculation) • formal mathematics (facts, calculations, base-10-concept)
Test of Mathematical Abilities PRO-ED	Criterion-referenced Individual or group Ages 8.0–18.11	vocabulary, computation, general information, story problems, attitude towards math
The Steenburgen Diagnostic-Prescriptive Math Program and Quick Math Screening Test Academic Therapy Publications	Criterion-referenced Group Ages 6–11	• levels assessed: grades 1–6
Enright Diagnostic Inventory of Basic Arithmetic Skills Curriculum Associates	Criterion-referenced Individual or group Grades 1–6	• calculations • error analysis
Brigance Diagnostic Inventory of Basic Skills (Math subtest) Curriculum Associates	Criterion-referenced Individual or group Grades K-6 & older student below level	rote counting, writing numerals, reading words, ordinal concepts, numeral recognition, writing to dictation, counting in sets, Roman numerals, fractions, decimals, measurement, geometric concepts
Kaufman Test of Educational Achievement (Math subtest) American Guidance Service	Norm-referenced Individual Grades 1–12	• mathematical computation
Peabody Individual Achievement Test—Revised (Math subtest) American Guidance Service	Norm-referenced Individual Grades K-12	• numerical recognition through trigonometry
Wechsler Individual Achievement Test (Math subtest) The Psychological Corporation	Norm-referenced Individual Ages 5–19	problem solving, geometry, measurement, statistics
Mathematical Problem Solving Assessment University of Miami, Marjorie Montague	Structured interview Individual Middle school	• affective and cognitive factors associated with problem solving

TABLE 8-11

Sample Math Probe in Addition of 2 Digits Plus 2 Digits Without Regrouping

22 + 12	43 + 23	34 + 44	68 + 11	12 + 87	10 digits
15 + 34	43 + 11	89 + 10	71 + 23	65 + 14	20 digits
45 + 53	60 + 16	33 + 22	22 + 54	11 + 88	30 digits
55 + 12	77 + 10	11 + 17	42 + 16	56 + 41	40 digits
29 + 10	38 + 11	14 + 63	53 + 35	86 + 13	50 digits

TABLE 8-12

Steps in Math Curriculum-Based Measurement (CBM)

Step 1: Determine the math skills you want to monitor

A. Examine classroom academic math record (i.e., student work samples, report cards, lesson plans, old teacher lesson plans, individualized Educational Program, etc.).

B. Look at math scope and sequence materials. Compare the classroom academic math record information to the scope and sequence information to determine where students fall on the math skills continuum.

C. Develop a worksheet comprised of several math skills the student potentially needs instruction in based on the information from "A" and "B" above. The worksheet should contain at least 3–5 problems of each skill. Give the worksheet to the student.

D. Score the worksheet. Based on the results, determine the math skill(s) that should be monitored.

E. Develop an observable and measurable math skill objective. The objective should contain the student's name, the behavior, criteria, and condition.

Step 2: Develop a measurement pool of math probes

A. For a *single skill probe,* create probes with math problems of the same skill. For example, if the student needs to develop fluency with basic multiplication facts, the probes might only have basic facts 0–9.

B. For a *mixed skill probe,* create probes with math problems with different skills. For example, if the student needs to develop fluency with addition of 1 digit plus 1 digit without regrouping and 1 digit plus 2 digits without regrouping, the probes would contain both types of problems.

C. Whether single or multiple skills probes are used, the teacher should make numerous probes with the problems arranged in different orders. Each probe should contain 80–200 problems depending on the type of problems and the abilities of the student.

TABLE 8-12

Steps in Math Curriculum-Based Measurement (CBM) (continued)

Step 3: Administer the math probes to determine baseline

A. Provide the student with specific directions such as:
   "When I say, "begin," start answering the math problems from the top of the page. (Examiner points where to start the problems & motions from right to left). These problems involve (fill in this blank with the type of problems.) Try to answer all the problems. If you come to a problem you don't know, put an "X" on it and go to the next one. Try to do your best. Do you have any questions?"
   {Wait}
   "Begin"
   Stop the student after two minutes
B. Administer three probes across three different days.
C. Score the three probes. Give the student a point for *every digit* that is correct. Count the number of errors. Count the number of digits attempted. Using
D. Plot the points on a graph. The horizontal line of the graphs should indicate the dates the probes were given. The vertical line of the graph should indicate the number of digits possible.
E. Calculate the student's math fluency by subtracting the number of errors from the number of digits attempted. Convert the answer into a percent by dividing the correct digits by the total digits attempted and multiplying by 100%. For example, say there were 45 correct digits and 50 digits attempted then 45/50 = .90 × 100% = 90%. Record this information on the graph.

Step 4: Set a performance goal for the student.

A. Determine the student's baseline by taking the middle score from the first three data points.
B. Project where the student will be over a given time period by doing the following:
   - Ask, "What is the expected rate of increase in skills for the student?
   - Estimate the weekly fluency increase.
   - Determine the number of instructional weeks.
   - Multiply estimated weekly fluency increase times the number of instructional weeks.
   - Add the baseline to the product above. The result is the performance goal.
C. Develop an aimline by connecting the baseline with the performance goal.

Step 5: Evaluate your instruction using the CBM data

The aimline can be used to determine whether the student is making satisfactory progress or not. Do this by using the 3 point rule. If 3 consecutive data points are below the aimline, intensify instruction. If 3 consecutive data points are above the aimline, adjust the aimline higher. If the points are consistently around the aimline, maintain the current instruction.

Source: Wright, J. (2002). Curriculum Based Measurement Manual. Available at: http://www.interventioncentral.org/.

Summary

The focus of this chapter was on students who are at-risk for math failure. In order to address their needs, an overview of how to use direct and meta-cognitive instruction was provided. The five big ideas of math including mathematical awareness, mathematical conceptualization, mathematical fluency, mathematical language, and mathematical application were presented and discussed. These five big ideas form the foundation for providing students with math instruction. Methods for adapting and modifying math curricula to meet the needs of students were specified. Finally, examples of how to assess the math performance of students were given.

Discussion Questions and Activities

1. Having a math deficit can have a profound impact on the lives of students. Describe three ways in which a math deficit might affect a student.

2. Imagine you are working in a school where the principal has asked you to give a presentation to the faculty about direct and meta-cognitive instruction. Describe both approaches and state why teachers should use them in their classrooms.

3. Some individuals have suggested that mathematical awareness is an underlying problem for students who have difficulties in math. What problems might a student encounter if he does not have a firm grasp of mathematical awareness? Pick three mathematical awareness skills and indicate how you could teach each of them to a student.

4. There are five big ideas in math including mathematical awareness, mathematical conceptualization, mathematical fluency, mathematical language, and mathematical application. In your own words, define each big idea. Describe how the five big ideas will impact how you teach and what you teach.

5. Describe the circular relationship among the five big ideas. Why should teachers keep this relationship in mind when planning their math instruction?

Internet Resources

National Council of Teachers of Mathematics
http://www.nctm.org/

MathVids
http://coe.jmu.edu/mathvidsr/

All kinds of minds: Understanding differences in learning
http://www.allkindsofminds.org/learningBaseCategory.aspx?categoryID=1

LD Online: Math Skills
http://www.ldonline.org/ld_indepth/math_skills/math-skills.html

PBS: Misunderstood minds
http://www.pbs.org/wgbh/misunderstoodminds/math.html

What Works Clearinghouse
http:www.whatworks.ed.gov/

Ask Dr. Math
http://mathforum.org/dr.math/

References

Algozzine, B., O'Shea, D. J., Crews, W. B., & Stoddard, K. (1988). Analysis of mathematics competence of learning disabled adolescents. *The Journal of Special Education, 21,* 97–102.

Allsopp, D. H. (1997). Using classwide peer tutoring to teach beginning algebra problem-solving skills in heterogeneous classrooms. *Remedial and Special Education, 18(6),* 367–379.

Allsopp, D. H. (1999). *Building algebra skills: Teaching beginning algebra skills to students with learning problems.* Unpublished manuscript.

Allsopp, D. H. (2003). Mathvids. Available at: http://coe.jmu.edu/mathvidsr/disabilities.htm.

Baroody, A. J. (1988). Number-comparison learning by children classified as mentally retarded. *American Journal on Mental Retardation, 92,* 461–471.

Beattie, J. U., & Algozzine, B. (1982). Improving basic academic skills of educable mentally retarded adolescents. *Education and Training of the Mentally Retarded, 17,* 255–258.

Bender, W. N. (1996). *Learning disabilities: Characteristics, identification, and teaching strategies* (2nd ed.). Boston: Allyn & Bacon.

Berine-Smith, M. (1991). Peer tutoring in arithmetic for children with learning disabilities. *Exceptional Children, 57(4),* 330–337.

Bernard, C. (1990). *Teaching mathematics in the elementary school. Childhood education mathematics games, activities, and laboratory materials.* Unpublished manuscript.

Bley, N. S., & Thornton, C. A. (1995). *Teaching mathematics to students with learning disabilities* (3rd ed.). Austin, TX: Pro-Ed.

Bos, C., & Vaughn, S. (1998). *Strategies for teaching students with learning and behavior problems.* (4th ed.). Boston, MA: Allyn & Bacon.

Bottge, B. A. (2001). Reconceptualizing mathematics problem solving for low-achieving students. *Remedial and Special Education, 22(2),* 1–11.

Bryant, B., & Rivera, D. (1997). Educational assessment of mathematics skills and abilities. *Journal of Learning Disabilities, 30(1),* 57–68.

Bullock, J., (1996). Touchmath Resource Center Set. Colorado Springs, CO: Innovative Learning Concepts.

Carnine, D. (1997). Instructional design in mathematics for students with learning disabilities. *Journal of Learning Disabilities Quarterly, 5,* 65–70.

Carnine, D. (1991). Reforming mathematics instruction: The role of curriculum materials. *Journal of Behavioral Education, 1,* 37–58.

Cawley, J. F., Baker-Kroczynski, S., & Urban, A. (1992). Seeking excellence in mathematics education for students with mild disabilities. *Teaching Exceptional Children, 24,* 40–43.

Cawley, J., Fitzmaurice, A. M., Sedlak, R., & Althaus, V. (1976). *Project Math*. Tulsa, OK: Educational Progress.

Cohen, S. J., Conway, R., & Gow, J. (1988). Mainstreaming special class students with mild handicaps through group instruction. *Remedial and Special Education, 9(5),* 34–41.

Condition of Education. (1996). *Third International Mathematics and Science Study* (NCES Publication No. 97255). Washington, DC: National Center for Educational Statistics.

Connolly, A. J. (1985). *Key Math teach and practice*. Circle Pines, MN: American Guidance Services.

Copeland, R. W. (1979). *Math activities for children: A diagnostic and developmental approach*. Upper Saddle River, NJ: Merrill/Prentice Hall.

Corral, N. & Anita, S. (1997). Self-Talk: Strategies for success in math. *TEACHING Exceptional Children, 29(4),* 42–45.

Cronin, M., & Patton, J. (1993). *Life skills instruction for all students with special needs: A practical guide for integrating real-life content into the curriculum*. Austin, TX: Pro-Ed.

Deshler, D., Ellis, E., & Lenz, K. (1996). *Teaching adolescents with learning disabilities*. (2nd ed.). Denver, CO: Love Publishing.

Deshler, D., Schumaker, J., & Lenz, B. (1984). Academic and cognitive interventions for LD adolescents: Part I. *Journal of Learning Disabilities, 41,* 108–117.

Ellis, E., Deshler, D., Lenz, K., Schumaker, J., & Clark, G. (1991). An instructional model for teaching learning strategies. *Focus on Exceptional Children, 23(6),* 1–23.

Englemann, S., & Carnine, D. (1976). *DISTAR arithmetic level II*. Chicago, IL: Science Research Associates.

Englemann, S., & Carnine, D. (1982). *Corrective mathematics program*. Chicago, IL: Science Research Associates.

Engelmann, S., Carnine, D., Engelmann, O., & Kelly, B. (1989). *Connecting Math Concepts*. Chicago, IL: Science Research Associates.

Fuchs, L. S., Bahr, C. M., & Reith, H. J. (1988). *Effects of goal structures and performance contingencies on the math performance of adolescents with learning disabilities*. Paper presented at the annual meeting of the American Association of Educational Research, New Orleans, LA.

Fuchs, L. S., Fuchs, D., & Karns, K. (2001). Enhancing kindergarteners' mathematical development: Effects of peer-assisted learning strategies. *The Elementary Scholl Journal, 101(5),* 495–510.

Gersten, R. & Chard, D. (1999). Number sense: Rethinking arithmetic instruction for students with mathematical disabilities. *The Journal of Special Education, 44,* 18–28.

Greene, G. (1999). Mnemonic multiplication fact instruction for students with learning disabilities. *Learning Disabilities Research and Practice, 14(3),* 141–148.

Heddens, J. W., & Speer, W. R. (1997). *Today's mathematics: Part II. Activities and instructional ideas* (9th ed.). Upper Saddle River, NJ: Merrill/Prentice Hall.

Hembree, R. (1986). Research gives calculators a green light. *Arithmetic Teacher, 34(1),* 18–21.

Jitendra, A. (2002). Teaching students math problem-solving through graphic representations. *TEACHING Exceptional Children, 3(4),* 34–38.

Kameenui, E., Carnine, D., Dixon, R., Simmons, D., & Coyne, M. (2002). *Effective teaching strategies that accommodate diverse learners*. (2nd ed.). Upper Saddle River, NJ: Merrill/Prentice Hall.

Kennedy, L. M., & Tipps, S. (1994). *Guiding children's learning of mathematics,* (7th ed.). Belmont, CA: Wadsworth.

Kerr, M. M., & Nelson, C. M. (1998). *Strategies for managing behavior problems in the classroom* (3rd ed.). Upper Saddle River, NJ: Merrill/Prentice Hall.

Knapp, L. R., & Glenn, A. D. (1996). *Restructuring schools with technology*. Boston, MA: Allyn & Bacon.

Kramer, T., & Krug, D. A. (1973). A rationale and procedure for teaching addition. *Education and Training of the Mentally Retarded, 8,* 140–144.

Koscinski, S. T., & Gast, D. L. (1993). Use of constant time delay in teaching multiplication facts to students with learning disabilities. *Journal of Learning Disabilities, 26(8),* 533–546.

Lambert, M. A. (1996). Mathematics textbooks, materials, and manipulatives. *LD Forum, 21(2),* 41–45.

Lavoie, R. D. (1993, March), *Batteries not included: Motivating the reluctant learner*. Paper presented at the Learning Disabilities Association International Conference, Washington, DC.

Lovitt, T. C., & Horton, S. V. (1994). Strategies for adapting science textbooks for youth with learning disabilities. *Remedial and Special Education, 15(2),* 105–116.

Lucangeli, D., Coi, G., & Bosco, P. (1997). Meta-cognitive awareness in good and poor math problem solvers. *Learning Disabilities Research and Practice, 12(4),* 209–212.

Maccini, P., & Calvin, J. (2000). Best practices for teaching mathematics to secondary students with special needs. *Focus on Exceptional Children, 32(5),* 1–22.

Marsh, L. G., & Cooke, N. L. (1996). The effects of using manipulatives in teaching math problem solving to students with learning disabilities. *Learning Disabilities, 11(1)* 58–65.

Masteropieri, M. A., & Scruggs, T. E. (1989). Constructing more meaningful relationships: Mnemonic instruction for special populations. *Educational Psychology Review, 1,* 83–111.

Mercer, C. D., Jordan, L, & Miller, S. (1996). Constructivistic math instruction for diverse learners. *Learning Disabilities Research and Practice, 11(3),* 147–156.

Mercer, C. D., & Mercer, A. R. (2001). *Teaching students with learning problems* (5th ed.). Upper Saddle River, NJ: Merrill/Prentice Hall.

Mercer, C. D. & Miller, S. P. (1991–1993). *Strategic math series* (A series of seven manuals: *Addition Facts 0 to 9; Subtraction Facts 0 to 9; Place Value: Discovering Tens and Ones; Addition Facts 10 to 18; Subtraction Facts 10 to 18; Multiplication Facts 0 to 81; Division Facts 0 to 81*). Lawrence, KS: Edge Enterprises.

Miller, S., & Mercer, C. D. (1993). Using mnemonics to enhance the math performance of students with learning difficulties. *Intervention in School and Clinic, 29,* 78–82.

Montague, M. (1997). Cognitive strategy instruction in mathematics for students with learning disabilities. *Journal of Learning Disabilities, 30(2),* 164–177.

Montague, M., & Applegate, B. (1993). Middle school students' mathematical problem solving: An analysis of think-aloud protocols. *Learning Disabilities Quarterly, 16,* 19–30.

Montague, M., Wagner, C., & Morgan, T. (2000). Solve it! Strategy instruction to improve mathematical problem solving. *Learning Disabilities Research and Practice, 15(2),* 110–116.

National Assessment of Educational Progress. (1997). *Digest of educational statistics: International comparison of education* (Publication No. 98–105). Washington, DC: Bureau of Labor Statistics.

National Council of Supervisors of Mathematics. (1988). *Twelve components of essential mathematics.* Minneapolis, MN: Author.

National Research Council (1989). *Everybody counts: A report to the nation on the future of mathematics education.* Washington, DC: National Academy Press.

Noonan, J. (1990). Readability problems presented by mathematics text. *Early Child Development and Care, 54,* 57–81.

Ozaki, C., Williams, R., & McLaughlin, T. (1995). Effects of a copy/cover/compare drill and practice procedure for multiplication facts mastery with a sixth grade student with learning disabilities. *B.C. Journal of Special Education, 20(2),* 65–74.

Piaget, J. (1965). *The Child's Conception of Number.* New York: Norton.

Reys, B. J. (1986). Teaching computational estimation: Concepts and strategies. In H. Schoen & M. Zweng (Eds.), *Estimation and mental computation* (pp. 31–44). Reston, VA: National Council of Teachers of Mathematics.

Rivera-Batiz, F. L. (1992). Quantitative literacy and the likelihood of employment among young adults in the United States. *The Journal of Human Resources, 27,* 313–328.

Rudner, L., & Schafer, W. (2002.) *What Teachers Need to Know About Assessment.* Washington, DC: National Education Association.

Saxon, J. (2003). *Saxon Math.* Norman, OK: Saxon Publishers.

Schwartz, S. E. (1977). *Real Life Math Program.* Austin, TX: Pro-Ed.

Shorrocks-Taylor, D., & Hargreaves, M. (1999). Making it clear: A review of language issues in testing with special references to the National Curriculum mathematics tests as key stage 2. *Educational Research, 41(2),* 123–136.

Slavin, R. E. (1991). Synthesis of research on cooperative learning. *Educational Leadership, 48(5),* 71–82.

Slavin, R. E., Madden, N. A., & Leavey, M. (1984). Effects of team assisted individualization on mathematics achievement of academically handicapped and non-handicapped students. *Journal of Educational Psychology, 76,* 813–819.

Slavin, R. E., Madden, N. A., & Stevens, R. J. (1990). Cooperative learning models for the 3 R's. *Educational Leadership, 47(4),* 22–28.

Stein, M., Silbert, J., & Carnine, D. (1997). *Designing effective mathematics instruction: A direct instruction approach* (3rd ed.). Upper Saddle River, NJ: Merrill/Prentice Hall.

Vacc, N. N., & Cannon, S. J. (1991). Cross-age tutoring in mathematics: Sixth graders helping students who are moderately handicapped. *Education and Training in Mental Retardation, 26,* 89–97.

Vaughn, S., Bos, C. S., & Schumm, J. S. (2000). *Teaching mainstreamed diverse, and at-risk students in general education classrooms.* Boston, MA: Allyn & Bacon.

Whalen, C., Schuster, J. W., & Hemmeter, M. L. (1996). The use of unrelated instructive feedback when teaching in a small group instructional arrangement. *Education and Training in Mental Retardation and Developmental Disabilities, 31,* 188–201.

Weiner, B. (1990). History of motivational research in education. *Journal of Learning Disabilities, 82,* 616–622.

Wiggins, G. (1998). *Educative Assessment.* San Francisco, CA: Jossey-Bass Publishers.

Wood, D., & Frank, A. (2000). Using memory-enhancing strategies to learn multiplication facts. *TEACHING Exceptional Children, 32(5),* 78–82.

Wright, J. (2002). Curriculum Based Measurement Manual. Available at: http://www.interventioncentral.org/.

Yasutake, D., Bryan, T., & Dohrn, E. (1996). The effects of combining peer tutoring and attribution training on students' perceived self-competence. *Remedial and Special Education, 17,* 83–91.

Zentall, S. S., & Ferkis, M. A. (1993). Mathematical problem solving for youth with ADHD, with and without learning disabilities. *Learning Disability Quarterly, 16(1),* 6–18.

9

Students with Moderate and Severe Mental Retardation

Paul Alberto, Melissa Alldread Hughes, and Rebecca Waugh

Chapter Objectives

- to define the specific learning characteristics of students with moderate and severe mental retardation;
- to provide an overview of an appropriate curriculum model;
- to present effective instructional strategies;
- to explore the relationship between student characteristics, curriculum, and instructional strategies;
- to describe the various settings considered appropriate for instruction; and
- to present a discussion on the post-school options available for individuals with moderate and severe mental retardation.

Students functioning at the cognitive level of moderate or severe mental retardation can and do learn. The learning of these students can be substantial, and it is shaped and advanced by instruction in the public schools and community neighborhoods. Since the 1970s, professional journals have documented the acquisition of cognitive, communication, social, motor, self-help, and vocational skills by these students. Years of research and classroom practice make it clear that student learning is a result of systematic **direct instruction.** Direct instruction is teacher directed through the selection of functional learning objectives. It involves the use of behavioral strategies (e.g., reinforcement, response prompting, shaping, fading, and task analysis), a learning environment which provides opportunities for student errorless responding, and ongoing data collection for program monitoring and adjustment. In addition to learning through direct instruction, **observational learning** was verified in these students. Observational learning employs modeling, in which correct imitation of a model by the student is reinforced. Learning through observation is one of the reasons for using group instruction. The use of adults, peers, and nondisabled peers as models is effective for social, motor, and some communication and problem solving skills (Mercer & Snell, 1977; Westling, 1986). In both direct and observational learning, instruction is targeted directly to the student. **Incidental learning,** what is learned while something else is being taught, has not proved beneficial for these students. For example, second-grade students may incidentally learn to spell their vocabulary words. What they acquire through incidental learning is often haphazard or irrelevant. Therefore, direct rather than exploratory instructional strategies must be used. These conclusions arise from the learning characteristics of students with moderate and severe mental retardation. Their learning characteristics, along with each student's post-school outcome goals, influence curriculum development to result in graduates who can actively live, work, and participate in an integrated adult community with as great a degree of independence as possible.

Characteristics

The term moderate and severe mental retardation is descriptive of students functioning at a level significantly lower than that of the typical student. The broad characteristic of students with moderate and severe mental retardation is **developmental delay.** Developmental delay implies these students go through the same stages of cognitive, communicative, social, and motor development as nondisabled peers; however, due to their disability they progress through the stages of development at a slower rate (Zigler, 1969). It needs to be emphasized that slower developmental progress is directly correlated to these students' levels of cognitive functioning. This delay in rate of progress is not a difference in stages. Common across these students are assessed IQ scores below 55 (moderate mental retardation has an IQ range of 55–40; severe mental retardation has an IQ range of 40–25, AAMR, 2002). All students with moderate and severe disabilities have as the cause of their disability either brain damage or genetic errors. These etiologies result in a heterogeneous population and in a population of students who are multiply disabled. Significant numbers of these students will have, in addition to their cognitive disability, sensory, physical, and health disabilities. These may include vision and hearing impairments, physical disabilities (e.g., cerebral palsy, spina bifida, seizures), or health impairments (e.g., coronary or respiratory problems). These various potential combinations of disabilities present a significant challenge to our educational technology and creativity.

Although this is a heterogeneous population of students, certain generalizations can be made about their learning characteristics which result from their cognitive deficits. The following characteristics frame the content of curriculum and influence strategies for instruction.

Skills Learned

Students with moderate and severe mental retardation learn fewer skills within the time available in school, require more instructional opportunities (trials) to learn those skills and therefore more time to learn, and require more time to recoup lost skills (Brown et al., 1989). These learning characteristics require the careful selection of learning objectives and those selected must have a direct effect on the student's life. For example, teaching a student to put together a peg board has little direct effect on a student's life now or in the future. However, teaching a student to set the table for morning snack has an immediate and long-term purpose.

Generalization

One of the most significant learning weaknesses of these students is their inability to apply information learned in one situation to another. This is known as a deficit in generalization (Browder, 1991; Haring, 1988). Deficits in generalization will appear when the student attempts to use newly learned skills in contexts other than the initial learning environment. Thus, they have difficulty using new skills in different settings (e.g., dressing at home and at school), with a variety of people (e.g., giving correct coins to the teacher, a cashier, and a bus driver), with various materials (e.g., learning to clean the floor in a grocery with a broom and a mop), and across time (maintenance of learned skills). Generalization also involves using skills in other environments and situations in different ways. For example, calculators can be used to do addition in situations other than just grocery shopping. Students without mental retardation would determine a variety of ways addition can be used in everyday life; whereas students with moderate and severe mental retardation would require explicit instruction (Taylor, Richards, & Brady, 2005). Context and environment are critical factors for instruction (Brown et al., 1989). To the extent possible, instruction should take place in the setting(s) in which skills are to be used with natural materials and with a variety of people.

Memory

Students with moderate and severe mental retardation may have a variety of deficits which will affect their memory ability. These deficits include impaired reception of information due to sensory deficits, inability to attend to and rehearse relevant information for storage, and ineffective grouping of information for retrieval. These deficits result in memory characterized by less reliable information storage, fragmented skill performance, and significant loss of information. This may be due to inadequate initial exposure to the learning condition, insufficient opportunity to practice or use the information or skill, or learning without appropriate context. Skills selected for instruction must be those that occur frequently in the students' lives so that they have repeated opportunities for practice. For example, reading words should be selected from directional signs encountered in the community rather than from a basal reader. Skills that are used often and in various settings will have natural reoccurrence and therefore, enhance memory functions (Ellis, 1970; Westling & Fox, 1995).

Attention

Typically, for a student with moderate or severe mental retardation, the ability to discriminate between relevant and irrelevant stimuli is overwhelmed by the quantity of information in the environment. These students have difficulty learning what in the environment or on what part of an object they should focus to get information to make a correct answer or decision (Zeaman & House, 1979). Therefore, the teacher must employ behavioral instructional strategies such as prompting in order to focus student attention. For example, a teacher would draw a student's attention to the first letter of the words "saw" and "was" by making them larger or a different color in order for the student to learn to read them correctly; a teacher would draw a student's attention to the label of a sweater by attaching a red ribbon in order for the student to learn "front" and "back" for dressing. Without such prompting, there will be long periods of trial and error by the student.

Synthesizing Information

The ability of these students to synthesize information and skills is limited (Westling & Fox, 1995). They have difficulty perceiving the relationship between parts and a whole. This can be seen in their inability to combine parts to create a story or relate a morning's series of activities. This also is demonstrated in their initial limited ability to perform self-help and vocational skills. They do not initially detect the relationship between one step in a chain and the next. Therefore, there is no anticipation of the next step. For example, during job training after spraying window cleaner, the student would not necessarily anticipate the need for wiping the window. This lack of anticipation is seen across behaviors. As a result, one cannot teach isolated skills and expect them to be organized for use. Skills must be taught within the contexts of the environment and activity in which they will be performed. In addition, the acquisition of skills requires an instructional strategy which breaks down task chains into component steps and skills so each can be taught directly.

Communication

The cognitive and physical impairments of students with moderate and severe mental retardation impact their ability to communicate effectively. The primary forms of communication used by students with moderate mental retardation range from verbal communication to the use of gesture. These are symbolic forms of communication. Words or signs are used to represent some item, person, condition, etc. Their verbal communication is characterized by a limited vocabulary pool, lack of abstractions, short sentence length, and simple grammatical structures (no compound or complex sentences). In addition to these language characteristics, a majority of these students have speech disorders (e.g., articulation and voice problems). The communication of students with severe mental retardation is 57 percent nonsymbolic and 43 percent symbolic, which increases to 80 percent symbolic at adulthood. Their nonsymbolic communication is expressed as vocalizations, body movements, and/or physical behaviors upon objects or persons in an attempt to satisfy wants and needs, e.g., grabs for a toy, pushes away a bowl of food, or strikes out at teacher when frustrated. For these students the behaviors themselves are the communication message (Mar & Sall, 1999; McLean, Brady, & McLean, 1996). Of particular concern for effective communication is the students' deficit in pragmatics. Pragmatics are the social aspects of communication in natural contexts. These students have difficulty with turn-taking and following the change of topics in conversation. They have difficulty adjusting their conversation to the status of the person to whom they are talking, whether it is peer, parent, teacher, coworker, or employer.

For students who are nonverbal, augmentative and alternative communication devices (e.g., electronic and nonelectronic language boards) are used to enhance and standardize their ability to communicate. Instruction for these students focuses on access and use of the device, vocabulary selection, and generalization across settings and individuals. (For a complete discussion of augmentative devices, see Chapter 10).

Social Skills

Social relationships are limited by these students' inability to interpret social cues and situations (Kennedy, Horner, & Newton, 1989; Sullivan, Vitrello, & Foster, 1988). Deficits in both communication and physical abilities often lead to social isolation (Gaylord-Ross & Peck, 1984) and fewer opportunities to learn appropriate social skills across individuals and settings. These social skills include conversation skills, eye contact, sharing, and control of physical contact. Systematic instruction of social skills is required to provide varied practice across individuals in integrated school and community settings.

Another influential social characteristic is the students' view that their environment is controlled by someone other than themselves. This is known as having an *external locus of control*. This view results in their waiting for others to initiate social interactions or task engagement, to look to others for cues about the correctness of their performance or behavior, or expect others to make even basic personal choices as what to wear, or to eat, or with what toy to play. In some students this is seen as learned helplessness. This tendency hinders development of a sense of self-determination and independence as the students do not realize they can or should have input into life choices (Hodapp & Zigler, 1997).

Challenging Behaviors

Many students with moderate and severe mental retardation exhibit challenging behaviors, especially those students with the most severe disabilities. These behaviors include stereotypic behavior (e.g., repetitive behaviors such as body rocking and hand flapping), self-injurious behaviors (e.g., head banging and hair-pulling), and aggressive behaviors (e.g., hitting others and throwing objects). It is generally accepted that these behaviors are attempts to communicate, resulting from an inability to communicate in a more standard manner (Carr & Durand, 1985). In most instances these behaviors serve the function of gaining a person's attention or a particular object; or escaping from a demanding task or social situation. As indicated by "best professional practice" and required by IDEA, the function of a student's challenging behavior is determined by conducting a Functional Assessment and/or Functional Analysis (Alberto & Troutman, 2003; Iwata, Dorsey, Slifer, Bauman, & Richman, 1982). Instructional implications for addressing these behaviors include instruction of alternative standard forms of communication, simplifying difficult and complex tasks by breaking them down into smaller parts, and scheduling activities which are functional throughout the day.

Figures 9-1 to **9-3** present descriptions of three students with moderate and severe mental retardation. **Figure 9-1** describes Shandra, an elementary student with severe mental retardation, without a secondary physical disability. **Figure 9-2** describes Ross, a middle school student with moderate mental retardation. He has Down syndrome. **Figure 9-3** describes Dario, a high school student with severe mental retardation and cerebral palsy.

FIGURE 9-1

Description of Shandra, an Elementary School Student with Severe Mental Retardation

Shandra is a seven-year-old female who attends the neighborhood elementary school. She is eligible for special education services for students with severe mental retardation. She has a reported IQ of 28 with severe deficits in adaptive behavior. Shandra has no sensory disabilities, but she does have grand mal seizures which occur at least twice per week while at school. She is on a toileting schedule of every hour and has few accidents. She can eat with a spoon and eat finger foods. She can put on jackets and pull-over blouses with assistance, and she can put on pants independently. However, she does require assistance with zippers and buttons. Shandra can wash her hands and face independently and is learning to brush her hair and teeth. She can make her needs and wants known through the use of one and two word phrases and gestures. However, most of her communication is responsive; she makes few social communication initiations. She is independently mobile and she likes to ride on a bicycle, but needs physical prompting to push the peddles. Shandra also is learning to play with toys appropriately and to share them with classmates. When she first entered the class, she waited for someone to direct her through her morning arrival routine, regularly laying on the floor. She now has a picture prompt system she follows which gets her through her arrival routine of entering, hanging up her coat, going to the bathroom, and finding her seat and first task. She can match by color (black, white, and red), follow one step directions, understands one-to-one correspondence (she can put one straw with each milk carton and give one cookie to each student), and is beginning to learn to "read" community logos.

Shandra tends to body rock, both when sitting and standing, when she does not know what to do next or is confronted with a task she does not know how to perform. Shandra currently is included with her nondisabled peers in music and math classes two days per week, physical education class one day per week, and the second-grade social studies class three days per week.

FIGURE 9-2

Description of Ross, a Middle School Student with Moderate Mental Retardation

Ross is a twelve-year-old male, who attends the neighborhood middle school. He is eligible for special education services for students with moderate mental retardation. He has a reported IQ of 50 with moderate deficits in adaptive behavior. Ross has Down syndrome. He has a heart murmur which restricts some of his physical activities, and he wears glasses (when he remembers to bring them to school; sometimes he throws them out the school bus window). He knows when he needs to go to the bathroom and is independent while there. He also can perform all his hygiene, dressing, and eating tasks independently and is independently mobile. He tends to be stubborn when he does not want to do a particular task. He will sit and ignore all requests from the teacher pretending he does not hear. Ross communicates verbally with a limited vocabulary. Ross is very social and has friends in the school with and without disabilities. However, he needs to work on following a conversation without going off on tangents and not monopolizing it. He enjoys participating in group games such as volleyball and T-ball and also can play simple board games with up to two peers. Ross has learned to read on a second grade level through sight-words and some initial sounds. His math skills include double-digit addition using a calculator, counting money to the next dollar, rational counting to 12, and rote counting to 25. He can write names and numbers and provide personal information when requested. One day a week, he and his classmates work at the Red Cross center where he assembles mailing materials and blood donation kits. Ross currently attends exploratory classes, art, and science classes with his nondisabled peers and is an active participant in the after school chorus.

FIGURE 9-3

Description of Dario, a High School Student with Severe Mental Retardation

Dario is an 18-year-old male who attends high school. He is eligible for special education services for students with severe mental retardation. He has a reported IQ of 38 with severe deficits in adaptive behavior. Dario has cerebral palsy which severely limits his use of his lower extremities, and mildly affects his arms and facial muscles. He uses a wheel chair and has use of both arms and hands. He wears Attends, adult undergarments, and needs to be changed at least once per day while at school. He partially participates in dressing and hygiene. Dario uses an electronic communication device to communicate his wants and needs. He has a vocabulary of 434 words which include social vocabulary, but the limited pool of words limits the length of his interactions. Dario uses switches to operate a tape recorder to listen to music and to turn on the television. He recognizes logos, understands the concepts of quantity, can rote count up to 10 and rationally knows up to 5, can match by color and size, and can make one-to-one correspondence, as well as follow two-step directions. He participates in vocational training in a local department store where he unpackages shoes. Both in school and on the job, Dario will engage in face slapping when he feels frustrated by a task or direction. While on the job site he enjoys interacting with co-workers in the break room. At school Dario attends fifth period keyboarding class where he accesses computer games with a peer. He also attends home economics class where he practices his home living, eating (drool control), and arithmetic skills. For school dances he is a member of the ticket-taking staff.

Curriculum

The goal of education for students with moderate and severe mental retardation is the same as for nondisabled students. As a result of their years in school, they will live, work, and participate in an integrated community. When typical students graduate, it is expected that they will have a range of vocational and living options, as well as a variety of social associations from which to choose. This is the same expectation for students with moderate and severe mental retardation. The purpose of curriculum is to provide students with the skills necessary to meet this goal. Because of their developmental delay, curriculum for students with moderate and severe disabilities will require significant deviations from the general education core curriculum. These students will require a curriculum based on a functional model rather than one which is developmentally or academically sequenced.

A curriculum is **functional** if its content is derived from the life skills which are performed in the integrated community settings in which these students currently, or ultimately, will live, work, and participate (Brown et al., 1979). Such a content source ensures that the behaviors to be learned are of immediate or future importance and are age-appropriate. A skill or behavior is functional if a direct line can be drawn between the skill and its use by the student in an immediate or identifiable future environment. This is more narrowly defined than for the general education student. Knowing the details of grammatic structure may be important if the student goes to college, or knowledge of the economic history of the United States may make one a more informed voter. However, for students with moderate and severe mental retardation, content must be much less inferential and have more concrete application. A functional curriculum would have students counting or sorting coins to be used in a vending machine rather than pegs to be placed in a pegboard, matching or sorting socks or silverware rather than colored cubes, stringing shoe laces rather than beads, and walking on bleachers in the gym rather than a balance beam. Given its content source, a functional curriculum would have objectives which occur often and naturally and provide opportunities for ongoing practice and improved retention. Further examples are provided in **Figure 9-4.**

A functional curriculum is developed from a "top-down" perspective rather than "bottom-up" (Brown et al., 1979). A top-down curriculum is one in which goals and objectives are defined by the skills needed in the settings in which we want the student to function. These settings include home, school, neighborhood shops and services, leisure facilities, and work settings. A bottom-up curriculum is based on a Developmental Model of learning. It follows the progression of learning of typical students for curriculum objectives. In a developmental curriculum, learning objectives based on chronological age are sequenced for each curriculum area (e.g., language, social, self-help, motor skills). Since students with moderate and severe mental retardation are developmentally delayed, they often are chronologically beyond the developmental stages at which they are seen to be performing. This may result in inappropriately teaching 19-year-old students the developmental skills of a two-year-old. This has the effect of teaching skills and tasks which are chronologically age-inappropriate, in inappropriate settings, utilizing materials typically designed for young children. This results in students leaving school without the adolescent or adult skills needed to live somewhere other than their parents' homes or state institutions, to do any kind of work in the real economy, or to participate in age-appropriate community activities.

Because a curriculum based on developmental milestones results in an inappropriate educational focus for students with moderate and severe mental retardation, educators now use a **community-referenced** curriculum. This is a curriculum based on skills

FIGURE 9-4

Examples of Functional and Nonfunctional Activities

Steps	Functional Task	Non-Functional Task
Domestic (Elementary)	• Buttoning and unbuttoning jacket for school arrival, departure, and community trips.	• Buttoning and unbuttoning on doll with dressing vest at 9:45, 3 mornings per week for 5 trials.
Leisure (High School)	• Buying a card (birthday, holiday), "signing" and mailing it at the post office.	• Teacher distributes Valentine cards and students mail them in a shoe box in the classroom.
Community (Middle School)	• Identifying the size labels on clothing in K-Mart.	• Sorting 3×5 index cards with "L", "M", "S" on them in the classroom.
Vocational (High School)	• Sorting sets of silverware and rolling them in napkins in the school cafeteria and at a local restaurant.	• Sorting pictures of silverware and paper clipping them to a napkin in the classroom.

needed for functioning in current and future environments. The objectives for a student are taken from the environmental demands of the community in which they live. These environments are those in which the student currently lives and functions and those in which it is projected the student will live. If a high school student is to live in a community group home or supervised apartment and engage in supported employment in a local discount store, the skills needed for entry into these environments are the skills which are taught. Additionally, objectives will focus on those skills needed to function in the student's high school and the current community settings in which the student and family participate. Similarly, for students in middle and elementary schools, objectives are drawn from the requirements of current and future school and community settings.

The process by which functional, community-referenced curriculum content is identified is known as **ecological assessment** (Brown et al., 1979; Falvey, 1989). Ecological assessment is the development of an ecological inventory of sequences of behaviors which reflect the skills necessary to participate in community environments (Brown et al., 1979).

An inventory is done for each of the four curriculum domains: the domestic domain (objectives for personal care and residential care), the community domain (objectives for access to services and commodities), the leisure domain (objectives for individual and group activities in the home and community settings), and the vocational domain (objectives for prevocational education and the development of a vocational training resume for entry into supported or competitive employment).

Identified in each of the domains are environments in which the student must function either now or in the future (e.g., restaurants, stores, transportation, playgrounds, libraries, instructional areas in the school, work settings). For each environment, activities are identified in which the student must engage. For example, in a store, activities include: finding the entrance, finding the cashier, paying, and exiting the store. For each activity, teachers identify the basic skills needed to perform the activity which include communication, motor, mobility, social, and academic skills. For example, to pay for an item in a store, the student must be able to wait in line, attend to the cashier, accept change, take the purchase, and exit the line. **Figure 9-5** provides examples of the steps of an ecological assessment.

Once the list of activities and skills are identified, instructional priorities among them are made by the student's IEP committee. Bases for setting instructional priorities

FIGURE 9-5

Steps in an Ecological Assessment

Domain (Curriculum Area): Community

Environment (Instructional Setting): Store (Target and WalMart)

Subenvironment (Training Site): Men's Clothing

Activity (Goal): Locate rack of socks

Skills (Objectives):   Scan displays
                            Identify display of socks
                            Walk to display of socks
                            Identify white tube socks

Activity (Goal): Select sock size 10–13

Skills (Objectives):   Pick up pair of socks
                              Identify size on label
                              Identify number 10 (match to prompt card)
                              Place in basket

Domain (Curriculum Area): Domestic-Personal Care

Environment (Instructional Setting): Public Restroom and School Restroom

Subenvironment (Training Site): Sink

Activity (Goal): Wash hands

Skills (Objectives):   Turn on water
                              Pick up soap
                              Wet hands and soap
                              Scrub hands
                              Rinse hands
                              Pull paper towel
                              Dry hands
                              Throw towel away

Adapted from: Falvey, M. (1989). Community skills, in M. Falvey (Ed.), *Community-based curriculum: Instructional strategies for students with severe handicaps* (2nd ed., pp. 100–102), Baltimore, MD: Paul H. Brookes.

include parent, student, and teacher preferences; the frequency of the activity across environments; safety concerns; age-appropriateness; and/or the time, material, appropriate settings available to teach the skills (Nietupski & Hamre-Nietupski, 1987).

Once the curriculum content is defined and specific activities are selected for instruction and incorporated into the student's IEP, direct assessment of the student's current capability to perform the activity is done. Assessment of student performance is accomplished through a **discrepancy analysis.** The teacher observes the student performing the activity and notes which skills the student can and cannot perform. For those skills the student cannot perform, it may be that he was never exposed to the activity, and direct instruction is required. It also may be that an adaptation or alternative performance strategy is needed. A determination is made whether there is a cognitive, physical, or sensory hindrance to the student performing the skills of an activity. If one is identified, the teacher must devise necessary adaptations or alternatives so that the student is able to complete the activity. For example, a young student may need to use a switch to turn on a toy, or a high school student may need to use a switch to turn on a computer.

Developing an Instructional and Evaluation Program

At this point, the teacher takes into consideration the student's learning characteristics, the skills to be learned, and the performance adaptations necessary in order to devise a combination of learning technology necessary for instruction. Often included in instructional planning are related service professionals such the physical therapist, occupational therapist, and speech-language pathologist. This team determines the nature of assistance or prompting strategies to be employed, the instructional setting, and the materials to be used. In addition, the team must decide how the effectiveness of instruction will be evaluated.

Evaluation of student performance is based on skill acquisition data collected at least twice per week (Farlow & Snell, 1994). Overall, measures are taken of the number of activities, tasks, and skills acquired, maintained, and generalized, the number of settings in which the student participates, the number of social and communicative initiations made by the student, and whether or not the IEP objectives were attained.

When setting criteria for performance, standards for accuracy must be established. Three levels of standards exist from which to choose: degree of participation, functional result, or performance equal to a nondisabled peer. The first level, the degree of participation by the student, sets the amount of an activity or task a student will be expected to perform and the student's degree of independence. For example, for a four-task morning hygiene routine (wash hands, wash face, brush teeth, brush hair) the criterion might include:

1. The number of tasks the student will perform.
2. The number of steps within a task the student will perform.
3. The number of skills within a task step the student will perform.
4. The amount of third-person assistance the student will require.

The second level is the criterion of functional result. That is, can the student achieve the desired outcome of the behavior? For example, does the student's behavior at the counter result in the clerk giving the drink wanted? The third, and strictest, criterion level is performance equal to a nondisabled peer. For this criterion, accuracy, fluency, and quality of performance are measured. This criterion is used most often in integrated settings for social skills and for vocational tasks where competitive performance is expected.

What we traditionally consider as academics are as much a part of the curriculum for students with moderate disabilities as they are for the general education student. However, academics also must meet the test of being functional. They must be identified as skills necessary to perform functional activities within each of the curriculum domains as illustrated by the following examples.

Domestic—write name, address, and phone number; set an alarm clock for work; read contents and directions on food packages; identify poison labels.

Community—identify bus; identify coins for vending machines, movies, bus ride, or paying a cashier in a store; read numbers on price labels; read size labels on clothing; read menus, signs on buildings and in the community, directions for washer and dryer; counting money for purchases and transportation.

Leisure—tell time for a TV show or movie; address greeting cards, write notes to others to convey thoughts, wishes, or needs; money skills to pay for movie, bowling.

Vocational—tell time for start and end of break; operate microwave and vending machine; read work schedules.

An important consideration in writing objectives for students with severe disabilities, especially multiple disabilities, is the concept of **partial participation** (Baumgart et al., 1982). While it acknowledges that for some students the ability to perform an entire task or chain of skills may not be cognitively or physically possible, most students can participate in a functional task by completing some of the steps in a chain independently, and/or by assisting someone else to perform it for them. This concept is important in broadening our view of instructional potential for this population of students. It refutes the once held hypotheses that long lists of prerequisite skills are needed before a student can be taught to do a task and that if a student cannot do a task with complete independence, then it should not be included in the program. (Baumgart et al., 1982).

Simply because a student cannot learn to prepare a snack independently, discuss community helpers, play a video game or soccer, or use a computer or bunsen burner, it does not mean the student cannot participate in some part of the activity and learn something cognitively or socially from the experience. It is true that participation may be partial and require using a method of engagement which is different from others. Participation may be demonstrated simply by touching, holding, or looking when using adapted materials and devices or receiving assistance from a peer or adult. Suppose, for example, that a group of third-grade students are engaged in a science lesson on how plants grow. Each student may have a particular assignment for the activity. With a severe disability, it may be difficult for a student to perform all of the activities the other students are doing, but it may be possible to participate by completing some of them. For example, the student may be unable to retrieve items from a shelf when planting seeds, but could spoon dirt into a pot and push a seed into the soil. The student may be able to make such actions alone or with the assistance of the teacher, the teacher's assistant, or another student. Regardless, this form of participation by the student can represent an important aspect of the educational experience while at the same time contributing to the group activity in a meaningful way (Westling & Fox, 1995).

Partial participation in chronologically age-appropriate environments and activities are educationally more advantageous than exclusion from such environments and activities. Students with severe disabilities, regardless of their degree of dependence or level of functioning, should be allowed to participate at least partially in a wide range of school and nonschool environments and activities. The type and degree of partial participation should be increased through direct and systematic instruction. Partial participation should result in a student being perceived by others as a more valuable, contributing, and productive member of the community. Partial participation can be reflected in IEP objectives as seen in **Figure 9-6** with Dario's dressing objective and his partial participation in the changing of his undergarments. Additional examples of IEP objectives for Dario, Shandra, and Ross are shown in **Figure 9-6.** These objectives demonstrate active participation by the student and give examples of objectives in various domains with activities in various settings.

As illustrated in **Figure 9-7,** as students get older, the curriculum focus changes to include skills needed for adult participation across each of the domains. During the preschool and primary years, the goal for students is development of personal competence. Objectives focus on the development of personal care skills, play skills, early social skills with peers, and trips into the community to familiarize the student with basic elements such as street crossing, crowds, elevators, and appropriate public social skills. During the elementary and middle school years, the goal for students is the development of competence in functioning in the local community. Objectives focus on the continuing development of personal care skills, skills required for individual and group leisure activities and play, instruction in the community in which functional academic skills are identified, and activities of prevocational instruction such as following a schedule or remaining on

FIGURE 9-6

Examples of IEP Objectives for Students with Moderate and Severe Mental Retardation

Dario

• During his scheduled trips to the bathroom, given a verbal prompt from the teacher, Dario will partially participate in changing his adult undergarments by unzipping his pants and releasing the velcro tabs, when he is assisted to a standing position, 100% of occasions for three consecutive weeks.

When told what number the big hand should be at on a clock, Dario will indicate when it is time to go to the cafeteria for lunch and time to go to his key-boarding class, within a five minute error limit, for four consecutive weeks.

When in the break room at his job training site at a local department store, Dario will match the correct coins with those on a picture prompt card in order to get a soft drink from the vending machine independently four out of five days per week for one school quarter.

Shandra

• Given natural opportunities for putting on and taking off garments requiring buttoning (e.g., putting on and taking off her sweater for school arrival and departure, community-based instructional activities, her art shirt, and recess), Shandra will independently button at least two buttons in the appropriate holes within four minutes on 90% of opportunities, for two weeks.

Given a four-step sequence of material gathering for morning and afternoon snack, Shandra will independently follow a sequence of picture prompts with only two errors in placement for one month.

When not provided immediate assistance with opening her milk carton at lunch and snack, Shandra will verbally say "need help" to seek assistance from an adult, with less than three occurrences of body rocking, for four consecutive weeks.

Ross

• Given the amount of 10 dollars entered into his calculator and a shopping list of six items, Ross will find each item, read the price label, and deduct it from the total on his calculator with 100% accuracy over six trips to the grocery store.

When at the Red Cross Center to perform his two job assignments (assembling mailing materials and blood donation kits), in the presence of a table clock, Ross will indicate when the 30 minutes allotted to each has expired, within a 5 minute error limit, for one school quarter.

During language expansion activities which focus on a specific topic, Ross will engage in turn-taking in conversations by limiting his verbalization to one sentence each time it is his turn, with 80% compliance, in each session.

---

task. During the high school years, the goal for students is the development of competence for the transition from school to adult life. Objectives focus on personal care skills which are needed for the maturing adolescent, skills in residential care, leisure skills needed to participate in community settings, continued instruction of academics like money skills, reading, arithmetic that are required for functioning in the community, and on-site job training in a variety of settings to identify vocational strengths and weakness, likes and dislikes, needed adaptations, and level of supervision required.

As legislators turn their attention to *general education academic content and/or performance standards,* increasingly educators of students with moderate and severe mental retardation are being told to incorporate curriculum choices within the framework of a state's general education curriculum and its content standards. General education content standards do not substitute for a functional curriculum's concept, content and objectives. Doing so would go against the knowledge derived from decades of research;

FIGURE 9-7

Changing Curriculum Focus Across School Years

Preschool/Primary	Elementary/Middle	Secondary
Goal: Personal Competence	**Goal:** Local Competence	**Goal:** Transition Competence
Domain Foci:	**Domain Foci:**	**Domain Foci:**
Domestic—Personal Care	**Domestic**—Personal Care	**Domestic**—Residential Care Personal Care
Leisure—Play skills, social skills	**Leisure**—Individual and group	**Leisure**—Individual and group in community
Community—Familiarity with environmental features in the community, social skills	**Community**—With functional academics, community social skills, safety skills	**Community**—With functional academics, community social skills, safety skills
	Vocational—Pre-community based vocational instruction	**Vocational**—Resume development

◄------------------------------------- **Develop, Refine, and Generalize** -------------------------------------►
Communication System
Mobility System

and would be contrary to the requirement for use of research-based educational programming. Rather there should be alignment of the functional curriculum needs of these students with the broad concepts represented by certain content standards. For example, functional cognitive and functional academic objectives can be aligned within the various traditional academic content areas in the general curriculum. At the younger grades one-to-one correspondence and basic arithmetic functions of addition and subtraction may be easily aligned. In the upper grades, a functional objective such as direction following can be aligned with science content standards in the performance of an experiment or social studies content standards in understanding maps. The functional concept of sorting by variables such as used and unused, broken and unbroken, full and not full can be aligned within academic and vocational standards. Even essential hygiene objectives can be aligned with biology in the study of identification and function of body parts, or ecology and earth science in discussions of the functions of water and how it cleanses the earth and its contents.

At younger ages there should be a considerable number of content standards, the modification of which will make them appropriate for these students. Indeed, in most instances alignment reinforces the need for skills such as literacy which has always been a part of a functional curriculum, and can be aligned throughout a student's educational career. However, as current discussions include selection of grade level equivalent standards, teachers of students with moderate and severe mental retardation may have increasing difficulty aligning content as students get older and their functional curriculum needs become more divergent from the content standards in grades 8 or 10 or 12 in the general education curriculum. Whereas, the general education curriculum content advances to algebra, the needs of these students advances to broader applications of functional objectives for maintenance and generalization. Is alignment worth the time spent on an objective that diverts from functional reading in order to access Romeo and Juliet as a modification of that content standard? The process of alignment should be a conversation which brings into focus two educational perspectives which can strengthen the purpose and goals of both (Courtade-Little & Browder, 2005). Such a conversation can encourage IEP committees to think in terms of students' functional needs along side the content prescribed for nondisabled peers; thereby providing common ground in which students have opportunities to be educated and interact together.

Literacy

Reading instruction is an example of how functional curriculum and alignment with general education content standards can be complimentary. As noted earlier, the ongoing necessity of literacy skills to be part of a student's IEP allows alignment throughout a student's educational career. The most common instructional practice and the majority of reading research conducted with students with moderate mental retardation, focuses on sight word instruction. With sight word instruction students learn through repeated practice to recognize/read words based on the configuration of the letters. A sight word approach is used because of students' articulation difficulties and the complexity of letter-sound correspondence in the English language. The words selected for instruction are functional words which will facilitate access to, and independence in, current and future environments. Students are taught words and phrases in the formats they appear in natural settings. The words and phrases provide information (e.g., signs and product labels), directions (e.g., pull, stop, exit), safety warnings (e.g., do not enter, caution), and those that affect job performance. In one study employees with moderate mental retardation who were unable to read were taught sight words that would assist them to complete job tasks and transition to new tasks at their place of employment. The employer indicated increased satisfaction with the employees, and the employees appeared to have a sense of accomplishment and pride (Browder & Minarovic, 2000).

The instructional strategies most often used to teach sight words are time delay (Gast, Ault, Wolery, Doyle, & Belanger, 1988; Gast, Wolery, Morris, Doyle, & Meyer, 1990) and picture fading (Walsh & Lamberts, 1979; Barudin & Hourcade, 1990). When using time delay, during initial teaching the student is presented with a word, asked to read it, and immediately told what the word is so the response from the student will be correct. During following instructional trials the student is asked the word and given 3 to 4 seconds to respond. If the student incorrectly identifies the word or does not respond, the teacher provides assistance (a prompt) for correct identification. Picture fading consists of pairing a picture with the written word to prompt a correct response. Over the course of instruction the teacher systematically fades the intensity of the picture or its size.

While sight word instruction can teach individual words, it does not provide word analysis skills that would allow a student to read untaught words they encounter (Browder & Lalli, 1991; Browder & Xin, 1998; Conners, 1992). For this reason it is important to consider additional approaches to reading instruction. Phonics instruction is successful with nondisabled students, students with mild mental retardation, and initial studies indicate it holds promise with some students with moderate mental retardation (Bradford, Shippen, Alberto, Houchins, & Flores, 2005; Hoogeveen, Smeets, & Van Der Houven, 1987). An example of a phonics program that has been used with success is The Distar Program. The Distar Program is a sequential, direct instruction program that requires students to master developmentally sequential skill levels. The program includes explicit step-by-step teaching procedures for student mastery, immediate feedback, practice, and gradual fading of teacher direction.

Some students with moderate mental retardation will achieve reading at the second-grade level through phonics. However, the primary purpose of phonics with this population is not to be able to read books, but rather to have a tool with which to confront untaught words and phrases in various environments, and thereby increase their independence. The overall programming of reading instruction for students with moderate mental retardation should provide opportunities at sight word and phonics instruction. Due to the complexity of the written English language and the various sound combinations the letters form, a complete phonics approach to learning to read all words may not be practical. Not all functional words in the environment conform to common phonics rules for decoding. If a phonics approach is not successful, the student will have sight words available.

Instructional Strategies

As noted previously, the learning characteristics of students with moderate and severe mental retardation influence the design of instructional strategies. Given each student's particular array of characteristics, each student will have unique learning requirements. Learning requirements will be affected by the student's particular combination of cognitive level, type and level of physical disability, and type and level of sensory disability. These will determine the extent to which tasks must be broken down into simpler parts, the need for assistance in performance, and the need for various types of technology. Despite the variety of characteristics across students, certain criteria for instruction must be maintained. Instruction must be systematic and consistent in its application. Such instruction would provide a very narrow opportunity for student error so as not to slow down the learning process. Instruction must be concrete in terms of both the skills being taught and the materials selected. Instruction must be distributed across time, with significant opportunities for ongoing practice. Most importantly, the student must be an active participant in the instructional process rather than a passive receiver of instruction. In order to meet these criteria various strategies are employed.

Activity-Based Instruction

Activity-based instruction is a strategy in which individual skills are taught in the context of an activity rather than in isolation. Within and across activities, students learn specific communication, motor, social, and academic skills in the context of the broader activity rather than in isolated half-hour-time blocks at their desks. This strategy provides students with repeated learning opportunities in functional activities scheduled across the day and week. For students with moderate disabilities such as Ross, rather than teaching coin recognition with ditto sheets or matching piles of coins at his desk, he would be taught to recognize actual coins while paying for his lunch in the cafeteria, using a public telephone, or purchasing pencils and paper in a store. In addition to learning to read by using flash cards in a classroom group lesson, he would learn to read product labels and price tags in stores and words on signs around the school building and neighborhood. For students with severe disabilities such as Shandra, rather than putting colored cubes in piles, she would be taught to sort by color when separating clothes for washing, glass for recycling, and/or colored napkins for table setting. Rather than rote recitation of numbers during circle time, she would learn to count by counting out various task materials for classmates in her special and general education class settings. An adolescent such as Dario, who is engaged in vocational training in a discount store unpacking shoes in the stock room, would have a variety of activities in which to learn and/or practice skills. When unpacking shoes, he would have an opportunity to work on sorting skills by separating the shoes from their packaging and sorting by size, counting when setting up the shoe display, and communication when he asks for assistance from co-workers using his communication device. When getting ready for work, he would practice self-help skills when dressing in his work uniform and using the restroom. During break, he would receive experience using money to purchase items from the vending machine, practice in reading words and logos when he makes his snack selection, and reinforcement of appropriate social skills when he uses his communication device to converse with his co-workers. Throughout his time at the store, Dario would have multiple opportunities to learn and practice his mobility skills as he navigates his wheelchair around the various subenvironments in the store.

Task Analysis

Many tasks performed are chains of skills rather than individual, discrete skills. For example, eating, dressing, washing, leisure tasks of playing board games, ball games, video games, vocational tasks of assembly, unwrapping and storing shoes are all tasks which combine several behaviors. Chains make use of individual skills in various combinations or series in order to achieve new behaviors. Chains may result in a complex behavior such as brushing your teeth, or a series of activities such as taking a bus to a store and returning home.

Chained tasks are taught by breaking down the chain into small steps for the student to master. The process of identifying these steps is known as **task analysis.** This allows parts of a task to be taught individually, while still in the context of the whole task. The component steps of the chain are arranged in sequence from first to last. The number of steps into which a chain is divided is determined by the student's ability level. One student may learn to wash dishes through a sequence of 10 steps, while another may need 20 steps. There should be just enough steps in the task analysis to allow efficient and systematic teaching which results in student performance over time. If a student has particular difficulty with a step, it can be further analyzed into smaller components for instruction. For example, if the step is to remove the top of the toothpaste tube, that step can be further broken-down into: (a) hold tube with left hand, (b) place right hand on cap, (c) twist cap with right hand, (d) pull cap straight up, and (e) place cap on sink-top.

Steps in a chain can be taught as individual units, in sequence, from the first step in the chain to the last **(forward chaining),** or from the last step in the chain to the first **(backward chaining).** However, the preferred procedure is known as **total task programming** (Wilcox & Bellamy, 1982). In total task programming, the student is given the opportunity to perform all the steps in the chain in ordinal sequence, and, as needed, is provided assistance by the teacher to complete steps which are difficult. This procedure has at least three advantages. First, it allows the student to perform the entire chain at each opportunity, thereby, seeing the purpose or end product of performing the chained behavior. This procedure also provides repeated motor practice in completing the entire chain, and lastly, it allows for instructional assistance as needed.

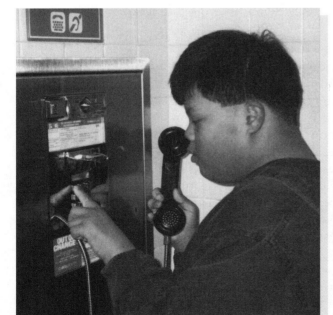

Activity based instruction teaches this student to recognize the coins he needs to use the pay phone.

FIGURE 9-8

Task Analysis for Teaching Use of Public Telephone

Step	Time Limit
1. Locate the telephone in the environment.	2 minutes
2. Find the telephone number.	1 minute
3. Choose the correct change.	30 seconds
4. Pick up the receiver using left hand.	10 seconds
5. Put receiver to left ear and listen for dial tone.	10 seconds
6. Insert first coin.	20 seconds
7. Insert second coin.	20 seconds
8–14. Dial seven-digit number.	10 seconds per number
15. Wait for a minimum of five rings.	25 seconds
16. If someone answers, initiate conversation.	5 seconds
17. If busy, hang up phone and collect money.	15 seconds

From *Behavior Modification* 14(2) by Test et al. Copyright © by Sage Publications, Inc. Reprinted by permission.

Presented in **Figure 9-8** is a task analysis appropriate for teaching Ross to use a public telephone (Test, Spooner, Keul, & Grossi, 1990). Note that for each step there is a criterion for how long it should take to perform.

Even when a task has been analyzed into its component steps, some students may still be unable to perform the entire task. This is especially true for students with the most severe mental retardation or those with complicating physical disabilities. An application of the Principle of Partial Participation differentiates competence within a chain as opposed to competence performing the entire chain (Logan, Alberto, Kana, & Waylor-Bowen, 1994). For some students, the ability to perform some of the steps is an appropriate performance criterion. For example, a student may be able to complete all the steps in putting on pants except zipping and fastening the belt. This partial completion of the activity may be the student's highest level of participation for the activity. For a student with multiple impairments, this may be considered a valid criterion level of participation because it reduces dependence on someone else.

Behavioral Prompting Strategies

In order to provide instruction which is direct, systematic, and consistent, a behavioral approach is used with this population of students. The precision of a behavioral instructional approach makes clear to the student the behavior to be performed and reduces the possible range of error. The behavioral instructional approach is summarized in the sequence of A-B-C (antecedent-behavior-consequence). For the behavior or skill to be taught, the focus is on the selection of an appropriate antecedent condition, such as materials, opportunity, cues, or environment, and a detailed definition of the expected behavior or desired outcome. This is followed by the consequence in the environment and/or an administration of a reinforcer or correction by the teacher. The relationships among these components can be seen in **Figure 9-9.**

During initial instruction, a verbal direction may not be sufficient to occasion student performance of a new behavior or skill. This is to be expected when asking students to perform responses that are not part of their behavioral repertoire. Skinner (1968) referred to this as the "problem of the first instance." This first instance must occur so

FIGURE 9-9

A-B-C Analysis of Behavior

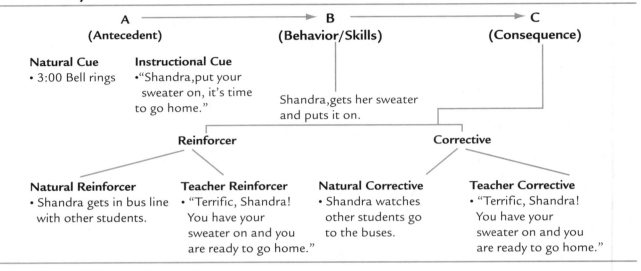

that a response can be reinforced which will increase the probability of continued performance, or so an incorrect response can be corrected, or an approximation of the response can be shaped. Performance of a new behavior can be effected by teacher assistance known as **prompting.** A prompt may be placed in relation to different components of the instructional equation. Various antecedent prompts can augment the antecedent event(s), and various response prompts can be paired with the instructional cue to assist response performance.

Antecedent prompts are alterations of, or additions to, the instructional material which focuses student attention on the natural cue(s) for making correct responses. Antecedent prompts include:

- Highlighting natural cues such as color coding the label of a sweater so the student can determine front from back, or writing initial word sounds in capital or red letters to bring them to the student's attention (relevant feature prompts).
- Teaching names of eating utensils in an array of utensils and dishes during snack and lunch rather than a random array of objects at their desks (natural context prompts).
- Teaching new words paired with pictures (associative prompts).
- Providing a model for performance before the student is asked to perform (antecedent modeling).
- Spatially arranging materials so initially correct choices are closer to the student (proximity prompts).

Response prompts are types of assistance needed for behavior performance. They require the teacher to assist the student in performing the response. These are used when a natural cue for a behavior, or an instructional cue, such as the bell ringing at the end of the school day, telling the student to put on her sweater, are not sufficient for the student to perform the behavior. Response prompts include:

- A verbal prompt which restates the instructional cue or provides the student added information or encouragement.

FIGURE 9-10

Examples of Response Prompts

Natural Cue	• The lunch bell rings. Teacher says "It's lunch time."
Instructional Cue	• "Shandra, get your lunch bag."
Verbal Prompt	• "Shandra, go to your cubby and get your lunch bag."
Gesture Prompt	• Teacher goes to student's cubby, points and says, "Shandra, get your lunch bag."
Model	• Teacher demonstrates taking out lunch bag and says, "Shandra, get your lunch bag."
Partial Physical Prompt	• Teacher assists student in getting up from her chair and says, "Shandra, get your lunch bag."
Full Physical Prompt	• Teacher takes student's hand and guides her through the entire task and says, "Shandra, get your lunch bag."

- A gesture prompt where the teacher points to or touches the material.
- A concurrent model in which the teacher demonstrates performance simultaneously with the student.
- Partial physical assistance where the teacher provides physical assistance for initiation of the behavior.
- Full physical assistance where the teacher guides the student through the entire behavior.

These types of prompts can be used individually or in various combinations. They can be used in a sequence of the most amount of assistance (full physical assistance) to the least amount (verbal assistance), or from the least to the most amount of assistance. **Figure 9-10** illustrates how these response prompts may be used with Shandra.

Prompts are not used to make the student indefinitely dependent on the teacher or some third person. Relief from such dependence is accomplished in one of two ways: prompt fading and using self-operated prompts. Prompt fading is the procedure by which antecedent prompts such as color coding of relevant features are faded slowly until they disappear after the student has acquired the skill. For example, the color code on the sweater label or the print size of the initial word sound is reduced to normal. In response prompting, the fading of the teacher assistance is built into the procedure and the amount of assistance provided is reduced until the student responds to only the natural or instructional cues. The second procedure for reduced prompt dependence is the use of self-operated prompts. There are two types of self-operated prompts: pictures as prompts (Wacker & Berg, 1983), and tape recordings as prompts (Alberto, Sharpton, Briggs, & Stright, 1986). These prompts are used most often when teaching chained behavior. For each step in a chain, either a picture is taken, or an oral direction is recorded. The student is given a booklet which contains the pictured series of steps, or a tape recording of step directions. For example, when teaching Dario to assemble the blood donation kits at the Red Cross, the teacher would take pictures of him doing each step in the assembly (e.g., a picture of him putting a donation label in the box), or the teacher would tape record the steps of the assembly (e.g., Dario, pick up one blue label and put it in the box). The number of prompts is faded as the student acquires independent task performance. However, for chains which are very complex or very long, some students may always need the prompt. This is an acceptable alternative to relying upon another person for prompting if the student is able to operate the prompts independently.

Alternative Performance Strategies

When planning instruction for students with moderate or severe mental retardation, it is important to understand the difference between the form of a behavior and the function of a behavior (White, 1980). There are a variety of ways to perform a task in order to achieve a desired outcome. If, for cognitive or physical reasons, the student cannot perform a task in the same manner as a nondisabled peer, the teacher designs an alternative performance strategy which will achieve the same functional outcome. An alternative performance strategy is a different way of engaging in a behavior (form) to achieve the same result (function). Designing an alternative form is especially important for critical activities (Brown et al., 1979). Critical activities are those which if the student cannot perform them, it will be essential for someone else to do them. This limits the student's independence. These activities typically include self-help, communication, and mobility. Alternative performance strategies are essential for reduction of dependency by these students. Examples of the use of an alternative performance strategy include:

- using matching cards for selecting the coins for bus fare
- using a picture language board to communicate
- shopping from a picture list rather than a word list
- using a pressure switch to turn on appliances

A hierarchical sequence of alternative performance strategies for purchasing items is presented in **Figure 9-11.**

The usual academic sequence approach focuses on the normal form of a behavior such as telling time, rather than on the function of the behavior which is time management. The normal form of behavior, in many cases, requires prerequisite skills quite different from those of a functional alternative. For example, being able to "tell time" on a standard watch or wall clock requires that the student be able to count by fives to 55, to count by ones from any multiple of 5 (30, 31, 32, 33, 34), and so on. In contrast, a time management strategy requires that the student be able to match-to-sample a clock and a picture of a clockface and comprehend the symbol (word, rebus, photograph) designating the target activity. A curriculum based on a usual academic sequence would clearly include instruction on the prerequisites for standard time-telling and not those required for the functional alternative (Wilcox & Bellamy, 1982).

FIGURE 9-11

Hierarchical Sequence of Alternative Performance Strategies

Task: Ordering at a candy counter, movie theater ticket booth, fast food counter, etc.
1. Student verbally orders item from memory.
2. Student verbally orders using picture card as a prompt.
3. Student points to item desired.
4. Student points to a photo of desired item in a picture booklet.
5. Student activates an electronic communication board by touching the corresponding symbol and the board "says" the word.
6. Student activates recorded audiotape (loop tape) to place order.
7. Teacher or peer gives order card to the salesperson and the student touches the card (partial participation).

FIGURE 9-12

Correlation Between Student Learning Characteristics and Curriculum/Instructional Strategies

Learning Characteristic	Curriculum/Instructional Strategy
1. Developmental delay	• Functional objectives • Age-appropriate materials and settings • Alternative performance strategies • Partial participation
2. Learn fewer skills and takes longer to learn skills	• Functional objectives based on ecological analysis • Community-based instruction • Antecedent and response prompting
3. Deficit in generalization	• Natural, integrated contexts • Activity-based instruction
4. Deficit in memory	• Functional objectives • Ongoing distributed practice • Natural contexts
5. Deficit in attention	• Antecedent prompting
6. Deficit in incidental learning	• Direct, systematic instruction
7. Deficit in information synthesis and anticipation	• Activity-based instruction • Task analysis
8. Deficit in language	• Alternative performance strategies • Natural contexts and settings
9. Deficit in social skills	• Integrated settings • Direct, systematic instruction
10. Challenging behaviors	• Alternative performance strategies • Task analysis • Prompting strategies • Partial participation

Students with moderate and severe mental retardation exhibit learning characteristics which directly influence curriculum selection and instructional strategies. These learning characteristics are summarized in **Figure 9-12.** A curriculum which focuses on specific instructional skills and strategies is necessary to enable an outcome of graduates who live, work, and participate in integrated neighborhoods with a considerable degree of independence.

Instructional Settings

In recent years, educators serving students with moderate and severe mental retardation began to examine the settings in which educational services are delivered to their students. Traditionally, instruction took place in self-contained classrooms on general education campuses where special educators were able to implement systematic instructional procedures to address specific student objectives. Although students were able to master many of the skills outlined on their IEPs in these classrooms, students had little opportunity to practice those skills in a variety of settings and few chances to interact socially with their nondisabled peers. Thus, educators now ask *"What are the most appropriate settings for students to learn and practice new skills?"* and *"Where will they have a maximum opportunity to do so with their peers?"*. Because students with moderate and severe mental retardation typically require a number of concrete experiences to master educational objectives, educators consider instructional settings beyond the self-contained special education classroom. They examine environments which not only provide students an opportunity to learn and practice new skills, but also offer the social benefit of interacting with their nondisabled peers.

General Education Settings

The legislative force behind integrated educational opportunities is the mandate for the provision of a free appropriate education in the least restrictive environment (LRE). In the 1980s, educators defined LRE as **mainstreaming.** Mainstreaming referred to the placement of students with disabilities in general education programs whenever possible (Grenot-Scheyer & Falvey, 1986; MacMillan, 1982). However, mainstreamed placements often were determined by a student's ability to acquire the skills and subject matter being taught in these classroom settings. Thus, students with moderate and severe mental retardation who lacked the cognitive skills to acquire classroom subject matter, generally were not considered for mainstreamed placements. Instead, for these students, mainstreaming often was limited to attendance at school assemblies, participation in some art, music, and physical education classes, and taking part in the regular lunch periods.

Today, the term **inclusion** is used to refer to the provision of educational services to students with disabilities in integrated settings. Instead of making the student ready for the classroom, inclusion promotes making the classroom ready for the student. Inclusive settings may include:

- regular day-care or preschool settings
- school campus settings such as the library and lunchroom
- general education classroom settings such as exploratory classes (e.g., keyboarding, woodworking) and appropriately selected academic classes
- community settings such as shopping malls, recreational centers, and vocational training sites.

Access to these settings provides students with moderate and severe mental retardation numerous opportunities to learn and generalize skills across settings, and to interact with their peers. With inclusion, instead of being concerned with the student's cognitive readiness to acquire general curriculum subject matter, educators are interested in co-mingling a student's IEP objectives within the instructional format and with the supports and instructional methods necessary to accommodate the learning needs of all students.

Inclusion Defined

Inclusion may be defined as educating all children and youth in one system of education. Characteristics of an inclusive educational system include the following principles (York-Barr, Kronberg, & Doyle, 1996):

- Students with disabilities are members of the same school community as neighbors and siblings.
- A natural proportion of students with disabilities occurs at any school site.
- A zero-rejection philosophy exists so that typically no student would be excluded on the basis of type or extent of disability.
- Students with disabilities are placed in age- and grade-appropriate school and general education classrooms.

- The focus of the instructional design and curriculum are individualized to promote independent or partial participation in current and future environments.
- Supports are provided in the context of general school and community environments which include special education and related services.

Inclusion was conceptualized with the intent of providing students with disabilities equal access to educational settings with maximum opportunities to be educated alongside and develop social relationships with their peers. However, inclusion does not mean students with disabilities spend all of their instructional time in general education classrooms, never receive one-to-one or small group instruction, or only participate in parallel instruction that is unrelated to their nondisabled classmates. Nor is the goal of inclusion for all students to learn the core curriculum or content in a given class period (York-Barr, Kronberg, & Doyle, 1996). Instead, inclusion focuses on ensuring that students with disabilities are equal members of a class, school, and community where their specific instructional needs are met in appropriate, least restrictive, and integrated settings.

Continuum of Services

When considering options for where curriculum content and IEP objectives should be taught, IEP committee members must bear in mind the mandate that ". . . to the maximum extent appropriate, children with disabilities are educated with children who are not disabled" (Least Restrictive Environment 34 CFR 300.550 (b)(2)). Therefore, initial priority is given to instruction in general education settings. IDEA also guarantees that instruction in a general education class be considered with the addition of supplementary aids and services, modifications, and personnel supports as needed to ensure access to learning. It is following consideration of general education class placement that alternative options in special education and community settings are reviewed. It is unlikely for students with moderate and severe mental retardation that all of a student's instruction will occur in any one setting. It is typical across a day or week that the student will receive instruction in various general education, special education, and community settings. Various general education classes may be determined appropriate for a student to acquire and then generalize communication and social skills among nondisabled peers. It may also be determined that a special education setting is most appropriate for instruction of certain self-care objectives. It is often the case that instruction coordinated across settings is planned. An IEP committee may decide to address money skills in a general education math class, and generalize the skills during community-based instruction in a neighborhood retail store.

In order for the IEP committee and the school system to meet the mandate of education in the least restrictive environment (LRE) a variety of modifications and personnel supports must be available for use in a general education class.

The variety of modifications and personnel supports that may be used to support a student's placement in a general education class include:

1. **Material Modifications.** Materials may be modified in many ways to facilitate student learning and participation. Using real objects and/or manipulatives will adjust the cognitive demand through making the materials more functional and concrete. Teachers may also accommodate motor or sensory requirements by changing the size, highlighting specific parts, and incorporating assistive technology. Worksheets and tests can be adapted to include more spacing, fewer items, and bold or highlighted directions.
2. **Activity Modifications.** Activities are modified to allow for access and student participation. Activity modifications may include allowing a student, who is

nonverbal, to respond by using a switch to activate a computer or an augmentative and alternative communication device. Partial participation is allowing students to participate in an activity to their maximum level of independence rather than denying access to the activity because the student could not complete the entire activity (Baumgart, et al., 1983). For example, identifying, gathering, and sorting all the necessary materials for cooking while another student actually cooks. A teacher may also reduce the number of required responses, provide additional time, or identify different outcomes. An example of requiring a different outcome would be having a student complete a picture, collage, or typed report instead of a written report. The student could use a tee to hit a ball or use a bowling ramp to participate in physical education or extracurricular activities.

3. **Instructional Modifications.** A teacher may modify the instructional setting by using large and small groups. Also, the teacher could implement peer tutors and individualized instruction. Additionally, shortening the length of a lesson or decreasing the rate at which the instruction is delivered may assist in the facilitation of learning. For example, the teacher may use vocabulary that matches the student's understanding during instruction. The teacher may also use visual aids across lessons and provide copies of overheads, class notes, and recordings of lectures to assist with note taking.

4. **Environmental Modifications.** The environment may be modified to accommodate a student's physical, sensory, academic, and behavioral needs. Teachers may implement daily schedules for students working on self-management skills, proximity seating for students who uses wheel chairs, or lamps instead of overhead lighting to reduce the glare for a student with visual impairments.

5. **Personnel Supports.** Support may also be provided through the presence of another adult outside or within the general education classroom. Support outside the classroom is typically conducted on a consultative model. A special educator or related service personnel, such as a speech-language pathologist, adaptive physical education teacher, or physical therapist, may consult with the general education teacher regarding how to address specific student IEP objectives, how to implement modifications, and how to individualize teaching strategies that promote academic, social and behavioral outcomes.

Personnel supports within the general education classroom may consist of collaboration, co-teaching, and supportive instruction models. The collaboration model is defined as a special education teacher providing direct services in the general education classroom for at least 50 percent of the course segment. Co-teaching is defined as a special education teacher and general education teacher sharing the teaching responsibilities of the general education classroom for 100 percent of the course segment. Supportive instruction is the assistance of a paraprofessional in the general education classroom either to provide direct service to one student or a group of students. Although the primary role of additional personnel is to facilitate learning and access to the general education environment for students with disabilities, their role is not limited to only assisting students with disabilities. The additional adult may work with all students during some activities and work one-to-one with a student during other activities. The goal of personnel supports is to systematically fade direct services to natural classroom conditions in which the student functions independently in the LRE.

Figure 9-13 illustrates such a continuum that emphasizes the use of modifications and supports. This continuum ranges from general education placement without modifications and supports, to placement within a separate special education class.

FIGURE 9-13

Expanded Continuum of Instructional Placement Options

1. General education classroom with no modifications or personnel supports
2. General education classroom with modifications
3. General education classroom with special education consultation
4. General education classroom with supportive instruction from paraprofessional
5. General education classroom with supportive instruction from a special educator
6. Integrated community-based instructional and vocational settings
7. Special education classroom

FIGURE 9-14A

Daily Schedule Matrix of Ross' IEP Objectives Across a Typical School Day

IEP Objectives	Reading	English	Math	Science	Social Studies	Art	Phys. Ed.
Conversational turn taking	✓	✓		✓	✓	✓	✓
Assemble item			✓	✓		✓	
Read labels	✓	✓	✓	✓	✓	✓	✓
Use a calculator			✓	✓			

Adapted from Falvey, M. (1995). Inclusive and heterogeneous schooling (p. 101). Baltimore, MD: Paul H. Brookes.

Addressing the IEP Goals and Objectives in an Inclusive Setting

When considering an age appropriate general education class, the IEP committee must determine what classes and segments are available to students at their grade level. For example, a schedule for a typical first-grade student may include calendar time, center time, reading, writing, math, recess, music, art, and physical education. Whereas, a sixth-grade student schedule may include language arts, literature, social studies, math, health, and physical education. An effective method for determining appropriate classes for implementing IEP objectives is the use of a scheduling matrix. Matrices provide a graphic view of opportunities to learn IEP objectives across a **daily schedule matrix** or within a **class schedule matrix.**

To complete a daily schedule matrix, a student's IEP objectives are listed vertically down the left column and a typical class schedule is listed horizontally across the top of the matrix. Committee members then discuss and indicate the classes in which objectives could be implemented. For example, as presented in **Figure 9-14a,** Ross's IEP indicates that he needs to work on conversational turn taking, assembling specific items in a given amount of time, reading labels, and using a calculator. When looking across the matrix at a typical sixth-grade schedule of classes, Ross's IEP committee indicates with check marks the range of options in which Ross may receive instruction in general education classes. Selecting specific classes is based on student preferences, school building schedule, scheduling of community activities, and prior experiences and training of teachers. Sixth-grade science will provide Ross multiple opportunities to address each of his IEP objectives.

FIGURE 9-14B

Class Schedule Matrix of Ross' IEP Objectives Within a General Education Classroom

	Science Class			
IEP Objectives	Roll Call and Lesson Preview	Material Distribution	Group (Lab)	Work Review of Lesson & Clean-up
Conversational turn taking	✓	✓	✓	✓
Assemble item	✓	✓	✓	✓
Read labels	✓	✓	✓	
Use a calculator			✓	✓

Adapted from Falvey, M. (1995). Inclusive and heterogeneous schooling (p. 101). Baltimore, MD: Paul H. Brookes.

Committee members also examine specific opportunities to address IEP objectives within a class. To complete a class schedule matrix, a student's IEP objectives are listed vertically down the left column. The within class schedule of activities is listed across the top of the matrix. Committee members then discuss and indicate activities in which each objective can be instructed. For example, as seen in **Figure 9-14b,** Ross's IEP objectives can be included in any and/or each of the science class activities.

Once an IEP committee determines which settings are the most appropriate for addressing a student's IEP goals and objectives, a daily schedule can be developed. For Shandra, Ross, and Dario, the following IEP objectives were developed to be addressed in their general education classroom placements:

> **Shandra:** "When given the opportunity to choose between team games in which to participate during her physical education class in the gym, Shandra will indicate which sport she would like to play and physically move to that location of the gym 100 percent of the time, with no more than one verbal prompt for six consecutive weeks."
>
> **Ross:** "During physical science class, Ross will participate in lab activities by reading and gathering the materials presented on a written list, sharing his materials with his lab partner, and assisting in putting materials away independently, two days per week for five weeks."
>
> **Dario:** "During key-boarding class, Dario will use a switch to turn his computer on and off, use his communication device to indicate which computer program he needs to use, and will type his name and social security number using an adapted keyboard with no more than two physical prompts, twice per week for six weeks."

The team of individuals involved in developing a student's daily schedule, as well as designing instructional adaptations, usually includes the classroom teacher(s), the special education teacher, related service professionals, and the student. This team generally meets on a regular basis to develop specific instructional plans for the student while at the same time completing the general classroom lesson plans. An instructional plan developed for the student with a disability might indicate the following: the specific IEP and non-IEP objectives addressed on that particular day for a student, the time(s) of day in which a student is included, the specific class, instructional support personnel, and the activity for the class period(s). In addition, this plan would indicate instructional adaptations and materials necessary to assure relevant learning opportunities are available. As illustrated in **Figure 9-15,** the instructional plan also provides the classroom teacher an

FIGURE 9-15

Example Instruction Plan for Shandra in Two General Education Classroom Placements

STUDENT: Shandra   DAY OF WEEK: Wednesday   DATE: August 16
TIME: 9:00–9:55   TIME: 1:05–2:00

Class: Physical Education
Support: Mr. Jones until 9:30

Class: Social Studies
Support: Ms. Archer

- Class Activity: Warm-up exercises, activities introduction, choosing activities, participate in chosen activity. Choices include: soccer skills, floor hockey drills, tether ball, four-square.
- IEP Obj.: 1. Choose an activity. During activity selection, the P.E. teacher will ask Shandra to select an activity in which to participate. Any prompts or reminders of which activities are available will be reviewed at this time.
2. Participate in activity. Shandra does not require physical assistance in participation in activities. However, she may require teacher and peer guidance in rule-following.
- Non-IEP Obj: 3. Share materials and equipment with her peers and teammates. Shandra may need verbal reminders for sharing.
4. Keep her shoe laces tied. Shandra is still learning to tie her shoes and may require assistance in "making loops". She also may require reminders to ask for assistance (if needed) when she needs help with her shoe laces.
- Activities completed as planned?
1. Yes
2. Yes
3. Yes
4. No
- Alternative Activities/Remediation: Although Shandra's shoe lace did come untied during the class period, she did not have an opportunity to ask for assistance nor retie her own shoe laces because a peer completed the task for her. We may need to remind Shandra's class peers of the importance for Shandra to learn to ask for help as well as tie her own shoes.

- Class Activity: Map reading, learning to read the map legend, learning to read map directions (north, south, east, west).
- IEP Obj.: 1. Locating places within the school building. Activity: Using a map of the school, Shandra and one peer will use the school map to physically locate the library, cafeteria, gym, math class, computer room, and front office. In addition, Shandra and her peer will review these places on the map in the classroom.
2. Concepts. Activity: while her peers are reading their maps, the teacher will ask questions to the class and to Shandra as to the activities conducted in various community businesses and what you might find there. For example, "at the library we check out books".
- Non-IEP Obj.: 3. Keep her personal items put away during activity time. Shandra may require verbal reminders and physical assistance in putting away her items.
- Activities completed as planned?
1. Yes
2. Yes
3. No
- Alternative Activities/Remediation: Shandra has continued to have difficulty following the verbal reminders of her teachers and peers for keeping her personal items stored during activity time. Therefore, a picture prompt system was developed and attached to the top of Shandra's desk to act as a reminder to put away items. Data on training and Shandra's ability to follow this prompting system will be taken by Ms. Archer for the first two weeks of its implementation.

opportunity to indicate whether planned activities occurred and whether alternative activities or remediations need to be implemented in future class periods.

Instructional Adaptations

The planning team which develops a student's daily class schedule also may be responsible for determining the curricular adaptations needed in order for a student to learn. Thus, team members must determine what to teach in specific curricular areas as well as how to teach activities and to evaluate student progress. If it is decided the student with a disability will be able to actively participate in a lesson without modifications while achieving the same learning outcomes as nondisabled peers, then no adaptations would be developed. For example, during recess for the second grade, Shandra is able to socialize with her peers and utilize the playground equipment independently. Therefore, no adaptations were developed for Shandra during recess. However, if adaptations are needed, then the committee may develop modifications for the teaching style, instructional format, materials, environment, or support structure. For example, in his art class, Ross was unable to complete his projects during the allotted class time without ongoing teacher attention and assistance. Therefore, the instructional format was changed, and students were assigned to work in small groups to complete a single group project. This adaptation provided Ross with immediate support in completing his projects as well as a means of addressing his social interaction skills. In Dario's key-boarding class, two adaptations were developed to assist him in utilizing the computer. First, Dario could not reach the switch on the floor to turn his computer on and off. Therefore, a tabletop switch was created for Dario's use. Second, Dario had difficulty isolating the correct keys to push on the keyboard to type his personal information. His special education teacher and occupational therapist developed a keyboard overlay highlighting specific letters for him to use when typing his personal information.

Community-Based Instruction

Community-based instruction (CBI) is an instructional model which provides students with disabilities an opportunity to learn and practice functional skills across a variety of community settings. In this model, educators present curriculum content in natural settings while addressing student deficits in generalization. It is a replication of the systematic, individualized instruction of the classroom where IEP objectives are targeted, instructional strategies are applied, and evaluation procedures are employed. The instruction which takes place in the community occurs on a regular, weekly basis. In order for CBI to be efficient, it makes use of small group instruction with no more than three to four students per adult in an instructional group.

Objectives and activities selected for instruction in the community are coordinated with classroom instruction. Skills often are taught in both settings simultaneously which provides multiple opportunities for practicing and generalizing functional skills. Those community settings selected as instructional sites influence the selection of instructional content. For example, at a shopping mall, students are required to locate various stores on the mall directory, purchase their lunches in the food court, and locate and use the restrooms. Thus, instructional content might include map reading, reading vocabulary words, math skills for using money, and self-care skills.

Various criteria are used in the selection of appropriate community sites for teaching selected student objectives. These include the opportunities available to teach targeted objectives; the opportunities available for generalizing learned skills; the age-appropriateness of the site; how often the student, nondisabled peers, or family may visit the site; the current and future appropriateness of the site for the student; and how safe the CBI setting is for the student. Once selected, the community sites are used continually throughout the school year to provide the student multiple opportunities to learn and practice new skills.

Scheduling the number of sites to be visited during a CBI session generally is based on the ages and grade levels of participating students. Initially, with young students, CBI sessions are short, with instruction taking place in no more than one community site at a time. However, as students get older or the academic year progresses, CBI often is extended to incorporate sites and activities for each of the domains of the curriculum. Chains of sites are selected and scheduled in as normal a sequence as possible for the student to experience a normal progression of a day in the community. **Figure 9-16** presents a full day expansion of CBI sessions for an elementary, middle, and high school student.

Community-based instruction contains three components:

CBI preview in the classroom
community on-site instruction
post-CBI follow-up activities in the classroom

CBI Preview in the Classroom

Prior to each CBI session, participating students receive a preview of the upcoming instructional session. Preview activities would include:

- a review of where they will be going, what activities will take place there, and the people they will encounter.
- a review of the general and location-specific vocabulary, reading/logos, and arithmetic skills required.
- behavioral expectations
- a safety review such as *"What would you do if . . . you need to go to the bathroom, don't see me, get lost, drop something, are spoken to by a stranger."*

On-site Instruction

Once in the community, teachers would implement the identified instructional objectives for each student. In addition, the teacher would employ the same systematic instructional strategies used in the classroom such as appropriate cues, prompts, consequences, task analyses, and alternative performance strategies. Because the instructional objectives may differ for each student, teachers may vary the levels of instruction or learning requirements. At a typical community site, such as a department store, the teacher would know which students are at the observation, acquisition, or generalization stages when purchasing clothing items in the following shopping activities.

1. Enter the store (mobility)
2. Take out shopping list (written or picture) (reading, motor)
3. Find the first item (reading or matching)
4. Check size labels (reading)
5. Check price tags (numbers)
6. Deduct cost from total on a calculator (arithmetic)
7. Repeat steps 3 to 6 for second and third items
8. Locate check-out register (mobility, reading)
9. Locate end of line and wait (social)
10. Hand items to cashier (communication)
11. Pay using appropriate strategy (money skills)
12. Take package and leave the store (mobility)

Expanded CBI Session Sequences for Elementary, Middle, and High School Students

Elementary
1. Pre-CBI Session.
   a. Where are we going
   b. What will we do
   c. How we behave
   d. What to do if   (20 mins.)
2. Co to school bus.
   a. Enter
   b. Find seat
   c. Buckle up
   d. Exit   (10 mins.)
3. Locate Woolworth store
   a. Enter
   b. Find paints & paper
   c. Find cashier & pay
   d. Exit   (20 mins.)
4. Locate grocery store
   a. Enter
   b. Find popcorn
   c. Find cashier &
      pay   (30 mins.)
5. Locate McDonalds
   a. Get in counter line
   b. Order
   c. Pay
   d. Find seat
   e. Eat
   f. Clear trash
   g. Use bathroom
   h. Exit   (50 mins.)
6. Stop at pet shop
   or park   (30 mins.)
7. Find bus and
   return   (10 mins.)
8. Classroom
   follow-up with
   paints & popcorn (40 mins.)

Middle School
1. Pre-CBI Session.
   a. Where and what
   b. Behavior
   c. Academics   (20 mins.)
2. Go to school bus.(10 mins.)
3. Local drug store
   a. Enter
   b. Locate 3-item list
   c. Find cashier & pay
   d. Exit   (30 mins.)
4. Locate card shop
   a. Enter
   b. Locate card
   c. Find cashier & pay
   d. Exit   (20 mins.)
5. Go to school bus (10 mins.)
6. Locate volunteer
   office and complete
   day's task   (40 mins.)
7. Go to school bus (10 mins.)
8. McDonalds
   sequence   (50 mins.)
9. Go to school bus (10 mins.)
10. Back at school
    a. Complete activity
       with card
    b. Rake school
       grounds   (40 mins.)

High School
1. Pre-CBI Session. (20 mins.)
2. Walk to corner and cross
   street
   a. Locate bus stop
   b. Identify bus
   c. Enter
   d. Deposit money
   e. Find seat
   f. Identify stop
   g. Exit bus   (20 mins.)
3. Walk to CBVI site
   a. Entrance routine
   b. Go to work area
   c. Perform job task(s)
   d. Break room
   e. Exit routine   (90 mins.)
4. Health club
   a. Change shirt
   b. Use 3 machines
   c. Exit   (30 mins.)
5. Lunch sequence in cafeteria
   style restaurant   (60 mins.)
6. Arrive at local group home
   for residential care training
   a. Complete one room
   b. Exit   (45 mins.)
7. Walk to Woolworth store
   a. Enter
   b. Complete purchasing
      routine
   c. Exit   (30 mins.)
8. Bus sequence   (20 mins.)
9. Classroom
   simulation   (40 mins.)

Post-CBI

Following each CBI session, there should be a review of the activities which took place in the community. In the classroom, students might review where they went, the activities they completed, the people they encountered (language expansion and memory activity), the functional academics used, and the behaviors they employed in certain situations (while eating, when speaking to the cashier). In addition, students may participate in carryover activities which provide closure to the instructional session. These activities might include cooking popcorn purchased at the grocery store, making a collage with art supplies purchased at a craft store, or totaling the prices of their purchases using a calculator.

Community-based instruction brings distinct advantages to the educational program. Given the proper selection of sites, it is functional by definition. Since students are taught skills in natural settings using materials which are naturally available in those settings, it is noninferential. In CBI settings, the teacher has an opportunity to use real (natural) criteria for evaluating student performance, and students have an opportunity to experience the natural sequences of events, distractions, and cues and consequences for correct and incorrect completion of activities. In addition, CBI provides multiple opportunities for the generalization of communication, mobility, and social skills with distributed practice across the various community sites.

Preparing for Post-School Options

The purpose of education for any student is preparation to be an active and contributing member of society by providing an opportunity to learn the skills necessary to live, work, and recreate in integrated community settings. For students without disabilities, this education typically consists of academic instruction in preparation for entering higher education or the military, vocational instruction in preparation for entering specific jobs or further vocational/technical training, and programming which prepares students for obtaining a job, maintaining a home, managing finances, and caring for children. For many of these students, services provided by the high school guidance counselor are sufficient for obtaining these post-school outcomes. However, for students with moderate and severe mental retardation, it is essential that systematic planning and specific instruction take place early in the student's school years to achieve desired post-school outcomes. **Transition services** is the term used to describe the systematic planning and instruction which takes place to achieve a student's desired post-school outcomes. According to IDEA, transition services are "a coordinated set of activities for a student . . . which promotes movement from school to post-school activities" (PL 105-17, Section 1401 [30][A] of IDEA). These services include "instruction, related services, community experiences, the development of employment and other post-school adult living objectives, and when appropriate, acquisition of daily living skills and functional vocational evaluation" (Section 1401 [30][C] of IDEA). Because these services require long-term planning and systematic instruction to achieve post-school goals, transition must be addressed in a student's IEP no later than age 14. With the 1997 Reauthorization of IDEA, IEP team members must begin planning for a student's transition beginning at age 14. At this time, it is the team's responsibility to develop a statement of the student's transition needs and focus on the course of study which will facilitate transition. This law further requires team members to develop "a statement of needed transition services . . . including, when appropriate, a statement of the interagency responsibilities or any needed linkages no later than age 16 for a student" (Section 1414 [vii][I] of IDEA). In addition, coordination among

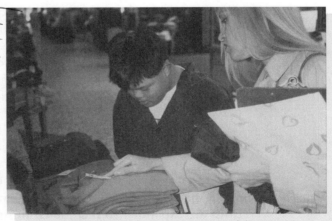

Community experiences are just one part of the transition services provided to achieve a student's desired post-school outcome.

FIGURE 9-17

Continuum of Educational Programming for Transition

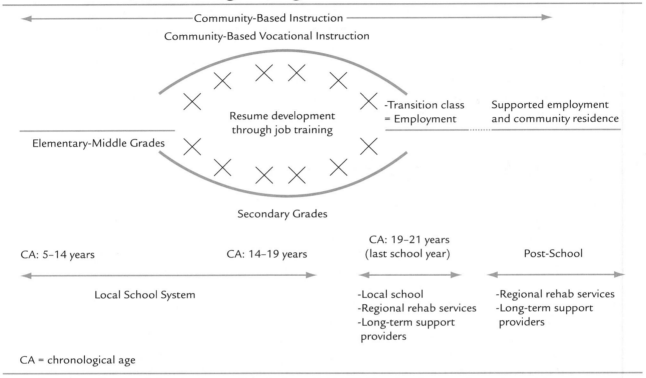

From Alberto, P., Elliott, N., Taber, T., Houser, E., & Andrews, P. (1993). Vocational content for students with moderate and severe disabilities in elementary and middle grades. *Focus on Exceptional Children, 25(9),* 1–10.

elementary, middle, secondary, and adult programs must take place to ensure that instructional programming results in each student's smooth transition to post-school activities (Alberto, Elliott, Taber, Houser, & Andrews, 1993).

For students with moderate and severe mental retardation, an educational model which leads to desired post-school outcomes is one which addresses instructional content and settings throughout a student's school career as well as the individuals and agencies who may be involved in the delivery of services. A continuum of programming which begins in the elementary grades and follows a student through the secondary level, provides a system for establishing linkages with adult agencies and an instructional foundation for the planning and delivery of educational and post-school services. As illustrated in **Figure 9-17,** students with moderate and severe mental retardation receive instructional services by educators in both school and community-based settings during the elementary and middle school grades.

The curriculum content may include instruction in domestic and self-help skills such as making a bed and grooming, community skills such as learning to cross a street or shop in a grocery store, recreation and leisure skills such as learning to play age-appropriate games and team sports, and prevocational skills such as following a schedule and remaining on task. As these students enter the secondary program, instructional settings are expanded to include **community-based vocational instruction** (CBVI) sites. CBVI is an instructional model in which students with moderate and severe disabilities experience vocational training in a variety of community businesses. These range from retail, food services, and office or clerical experiences to building maintenance, hotel guest services, and jobs in light industry. During a given school year, a student would have an opportunity to experience training in two or three vocational training settings. As preparation for future employment, students receive instruction on a variety of work-related skills and behaviors while remaining under the direct supervision of school personnel. However, they also receive training from community business employees as they begin to develop a repertoire of specific vocational skills required to obtain and maintain employment. During the final school year, students receive services from not only the local school system but also from adult agencies identified in each student's Individual Transition Plan (ITP). Once the student exits the school program, it is these agencies which continue to provide ongoing support throughout the individual's adult life.

Individual Transition Plan (ITP)

For students with moderate and severe mental retardation, the development of a comprehensive ITP is critical in planning for an individual's future. It provides a means of determining needed areas of instruction and support for working and living in an integrated community. It also provides an organized format for accessing those agencies whose support will be required for a young adult exiting a school program. Because students with moderate and severe mental retardation require extensive educational training prior to graduation and coordination with numerous post-school services from adult agencies, the development of a comprehensive ITP will take several years. Generally, the more services and supports a student requires as an adult, the earlier transition planning should occur. Thus, transition planning may need to begin well before a student's 14th birthday.

During a given school year, a student would have an opportunity to train in two or three vocational settings.

The ITP is a part of the IEP. For students with mild disabilities, transition recommendations may be incorporated in the standard IEP format. However, for students with moderate and severe disabilities requiring extensive transition planning, a separate set of pages addressing transition issues may be attached to the IEP. Regardless of where ITP recommendations are made in the IEP, they provide a foundation for developing IEP goals and objectives. For example, eighteen-year-old Dario and his family would like for him to be employed in a part-time job which provides medical and dental benefits. As part of Dario's high school program, he participated in some community-based vocational instruction (CBVI) but has yet to experience a job which he really enjoys. In his last IEP meeting, through his brother, Dario indicated that he would like to participate in training at a local movie theater. For the next school year, Dario's teacher indicated on the ITP that Dario will continue to participate in the school's CBVI program and will receive vocational training in at least three vocational sites, one being a movie theater. Thus, an IEP goal might be that Dario will participate in CBVI training at a restaurant, a pharmacy, and a movie theater over the next year. A specific objective under this goal might be as follows:

> Upon entering his vocational training site, Dario will greet his co-workers, clock-in, and collect tickets for the 1:00 movie with only verbal assistance from a co-worker, 100% of the time for three consecutive weeks.

As illustrated in **Figure 9-18,** the ITP is comprised of two major components. The first is student information, which includes the student's name and birth date as well as present skills, needs, and experiences.

This section expands the descriptive information contained in the "present levels of performance" portion of the IEP to include a concise description of the student's current skills and instructional needs in the vocational, community, domestic, and leisure domains. After completing this section, members of the IEP/ITP committee should have a clear understanding of how the student currently functions in various integrated settings and what skills remain as a needed focus for future instruction.

The second portion of the ITP identifies the specific adult outcome areas for a student and the committee recommendations for achieving those outcomes. In addition, individual and agency responsibilities are assigned and a time line is established for completing those responsibilities. For example, Dario would like to live outside the family home once he graduates from school, and his family is interested in receiving information about group homes. As noted in **Figure 9-18,** a recommendation was made regarding a group home placement following Dario's graduation. Responsibilities were assigned to each of the participating individuals and agencies who will be involved in the transition process, and a time line was established for completing assigned responsibilities. Each of the recommendations and responsibilities are then reviewed and updated in future IEP/ITP meetings.

Adult Outcome Options

In order to successfully plan for the comprehensive transition needs of students with moderate and severe mental retardation, transition team members must address a variety of adult outcome areas for a student. These areas include:

- employment preparation and placement,
- post-school community living arrangements,
- independent living skills,
- community and leisure options,
- transportation training needs,
- social behavior training,
- medical needs,
- transportation access,
- financial and other benefits,
- advocacy and legal trust,
- communication needs.

Options in each of these areas can vary from learning to use the city bus under the transportation training needs area to applying for social security benefits under the financial and other benefits section of the ITP. Although considerable planning is required for each of these areas, two areas which entail significant planning, training, and supports are the areas of employment and community living.

Employment preparation models typically available to high school students are the cooperative preparation and work-study models. Both of these training models prepare students for post-school vocational/technical training and competitive employment. Students receiving vocational training in either of these models typically require little to no support once they exit the secondary school program. However, individuals with moderate and severe mental retardation who require long-term support from an adult agency

FIGURE 9-18

Sample Portion of an ITP for Dario

Student Name: Dario Williams   Birthdate: 06/14 Date: 05/13

Summary of Student's Present Skills, Needs and Experiences: Dario is in a self-contained class for students with moderate and severe intellectual disabilities at a regular high school. He also is included in key-boarding and home economics classes. Dario uses a wheelchair and an AAC device for communication. Dario independently feeds himself and partially participates in changing his undergarments. Dario can assemble 3-part items using picture cues, wash dishes in an adapted sink, wipe tables, spray and wipe to clean, and can manipulate a variety of switches to activate items. Dario can fold paper and stuff envelopes. He accesses the community through the school CBI program and his parents taking him to grocery stores, restaurants, movies, spectator sporting events, and vocational training. Dario needs to learn to fold clothes and linens with more accuracy. Dario wants to learn to operate a drink dispenser. He also has expressed a desire to work in a movie theater. Dario needs more leisure skills and opportunities for participation in community recreational activities.

| | | Responsibilities | | | | | |
| | | Parent/Guardian | | School | | Adult Service Providers | |
A. Transition Issues for Education Planning	Recommendations	Action	Time line	Action	Time line	Action	Time line
2. Post-school Community Living Arrangements: Options and Training Needs • Group homes • Apartments • Remain at home	• It is recommended that Dario be placed on a waiting list for a group home opening.	• Contact group home closest to his present neighborhood and take care of paperwork to have Dario placed on waiting list. • Continue working on home-living and self-help skills to produce more independence.	• From present until graduation	• IEP objectives need to concentrate on shaving and washing hair for self-help. IEP goals will be written for learning to operate a washing machine and dryer and simple cooking preparation for home living to help in group home environment.	• Present–June	• Provide parents with all information concerning group homes and let parents and Dario tour group home sites	• Immediately

FIGURE 9-19

Comparison of Community-Based Vocational Instruction and Work Study Programs

Item	CBVI	Work Study
Purpose	• Job sampling for resume development and ongoing assessment	• Proficiency in a specific vocational field
Target Student Population	• Students who will be eligible for supported employment	• Students who will be eligible for competitive employment
Curriculum	• Part of IEP; clusters are identified by goals and objectives	• Part of IEP; job usually relates to vocational courses in which the student is enrolled
School Credit	• Yes	• Yes
Job Development	• Special education teacher or Job Developer for CBVI	• Special education teacher or Rehabilitation Services Counselor in cooperation with Vocational coordinator for Work Study
Transportation	• Supervised and/or provided by the school system	• Student provides own
Wages	• Non-paid	• Paid; minimum wage or more
Status	• Trainee	• Employee
Supervision	• Constant by designated school personnel	• Two visits per week by special education teacher
Evaluation	• Data collected daily; e.g., work adjustment, task analysis, level of supervision, production rate, and anecdotal notes	• Daily in the beginning tapering to monthly
Benefit to Employer	• Student does not provide benefit to employer; primary benefit is to the student	• Student does provide benefit to employer as a paid employee completing assigned tasks
Time at Site	• Average six hours per week (2 hrs/3 days), for no more than 215 hours per site.	• Daily, for two or three segments for school term
Sites Per Year	• Two to four	• One

following graduation to maintain employment may receive training in the **supported employment model.** As illustrated in **Figure 9-19,** the adult outcome for this model differs from the cooperative preparation and work study models in that the goal for individuals with moderate and severe disabilities is supported rather than competitive employment.

According to the Rehabilitation Act Amendments of 1986 (PL 99-506), supported employment is "paid employment in integrated settings" for individuals with the most severe disabilities. Individuals employed under this model receive ongoing support from an adult agency job coach for the length of their employment. Support may include assistance in locating and securing employment, on-the-job training and retraining, transportation training, and advocacy support. Students who participate in this training model receive vocational experiences across a wide range of community-based businesses in order to develop employment-related skills.

Community living is the second area for which significant transition planning and preparation is required. As illustrated in **Figure 9-20,** post-school adult options in the community living area may be divided into four levels.

FIGURE 9-20

Continuum of Community Living Options

	Level One	Level Two	Level Three	Level Four
Support Services	• Independent, only natural supports from the community and family.	• Living away from the family home with support provided by an agency that typically works with individuals with disabilities.	• Continued residence in the family home with total support from the family.	• Facility based; total support for the individual, 24 hour supervision.
Responsibilities	• Choice for all aspects of life, responsible for entire household and personal management.	• Instruction and support is provided for all areas of household responsibility such as money management, cooking, cleaning, maintenance, shopping, etc. Support is faded only when and if the individual becomes independent with these skills.	• Usually very little, some simple chores and contributions financially to household budget.	• Usually no responsibilities.
Related Curriculum Content	• Self-advocacy, self-determination; budgeting, functional academics, community skills and experiences; awareness of post-school support services, public benefits and programs.	• Self-advocacy and self-determination; community living skills and experiences; instruction in cooking, cleaning, shopping, etc.; transportation training and use of leisure time.	• Self-determination; daily living skills of personal hygiene, feeding; simple household chores such as snack preparation, dishwashing, laundry, etc.; leisure skill and activities.	• Self-determination; activities of daily living such as feeding, dressing, and bathing; leisure activities.
Examples	• Own home, apartment with a friend or spouse, live in a dormitory.	• Semi-independent living, life sharing, group homes.	• Family home with no outside agency involvement	• Personal care homes, nursing homes, institutions.
Amount of Community Integration	• Totally integrated	• Partially integrated	• Dependent on family and amount of time they spend in the community.	• Little or no integration.

Students without disabilities and the majority of students with mild disabilities will live independently and be fully integrated into the community. These individuals will receive no assistance from agencies or organizations which specialize in disabilities. Student preparation for this level of independent living may include instruction in academics related to daily living, household maintenance, self-advocacy skills, community access, and a range of leisure activities.

It is the goal of education that students with moderate and severe mental retardation be able to live in the community in supported living arrangements away from the family home. These options include semi-independent living, life sharing, and group homes. Support for individuals living in the community at this level would be provided by agencies, programs, or persons which typically assist individuals with disabilities. Student preparation for this level of community living may include instruction in functional academics related to daily living, money management, household safety, leisure activities, cooking and shopping, household maintenance and cleaning, self-advocacy, and community access skills.

Some families choose for their sons or daughters to continue to reside in the family home. The level of dependence on family members may vary significantly from complete dependence to participating and contributing to the daily household management. Instruction related to community living for individuals choosing this option may include functional academics related to daily living, household management and maintenance skills, self-advocacy, leisure activities, and community access training.

Viewed as most restrictive are community living options consisting of residing in community facilities, personal care homes, nursing homes, and public institutions which provide a great deal of structure and supervision. Individuals participating in this level are those who require constant medical care or, because of behavioral or psychiatric reasons, require intense supervision. Instructional content for these students may include: communication training, self-help skills (grooming, feeding, dressing), a range of leisure activities, self-advocacy skills, and skills leading to greater independence such as motor skills and mobility training.

Because transition planning begins early in a student's school career (no later than age 14), instructional programming may be established and implemented with specific adult outcomes in mind. In addition, educators, families, and adult service providers are able to assess future vocational, community, domestic, and leisure demands, establish early linkages with agencies which will assist a student in community participation, and provide a specific focus for a student's support, education, and on-going training. It is the responsibility of educators to serve as part of a team to assure a student has the opportunity to learn skills leading to increased independence based on real adult outcomes. It also is their responsibility to work on a team to establish a working relationship with service agencies which will assist in supporting an individual in an integrated community.

Figures 9-21 to **9-23** present descriptions of Shandra, Ross, and Dario fifteen years from now. These descriptions provide an account of how each individual obtains access to the community, where they are living and working, and the types of recreational and leisure activities in which they may participate as adults.

FIGURE 9-21

Description of Shandra at 22 Years of Age

Shandra

- At 22 years of age, Shandra continues to live at home. Over the last few years in public school, Shandra and her family expressed some interest in a group home. However, they prefer that Shandra continue to live in the family home for a while. After making several inquiries about group homes, Shandra's parents placed her name on a waiting list. It is anticipated that an opening will be available in the next few years.

   While living at home, Shandra's responsibilities increased around the house. She is responsible for helping with household chores such as setting the table, dusting furniture once a week, vacuuming the rugs, and cleaning the bathrooms. She was taught to make simple meals such as sandwiches and has learned to warm food in a microwave oven. She continues to rely on reminders to take a shower; however, she recently began using a picture schedule to complete her grooming routine which has been successful so far. Financially, Shandra contributes money for her share of groceries, new clothing, and gasoline for the car.

   After graduation, Shandra began working for a major food company. She is a supported employee who works in a small group with two other adults with severe disabilities. She also has a job coach who provides daily support on the job. She works 20 hours per week packaging and pricing snack items and folding the boxes for packing. She currently earns minimum wage, and after one year on the job she will be eligible for limited medical benefits.

   During her time away from work, Shandra enjoys shopping in the mall with her older sister. On Wednesday and Sunday evenings, Shandra sings with her church chorus during services and attends chorus practice every Thursday night. One day each week Shandra volunteers with her next-door neighbor at the local Red Cross Center. There she distributes cookies and juice to blood donors.

   Shandra's family is hesitant about allowing her to use public transportation at this time. Therefore, they provide most of the transportation for Shandra around the community. She can, however, ride a bicycle in the neighborhood and walk to neighbors' homes.

FIGURE 9-22

Description of Ross at 27 Years of Age

Ross

• At 27, Ross shares an apartment with a friend who also has mental retardation. Ross and his roommate receive support services from a local non-profit housing agency for persons with disabilities. This support allows Ross to live semi-independently in the community. The support services he receives include writing checks for bills and assistance with balancing his checkbook, developing and maintaining a budget, and morning telephone calls to ensure he is out of bed and getting ready for work. A support person from the agency also takes Ross and his roommate to the grocery store to do their weekly shopping. Ross is responsible for sharing half of the household chores and paying half of the bills.

For the past three years, Ross has worked as a stock clerk at a large retail pet store. Some of his duties include pricing items, replacing stock on the shelves, cleaning the stock room, and assembling and building store displays. Ross works 40 hours per week, receives full medical and dental benefits, and earns an hourly wage of $6.50. He receives limited supported employment services. His job coach, who initially visited him daily, now visits him on the job once a week. Most of the support Ross receives on the job comes from his co-workers.

During his time away from work, Ross has a variety of interests and activities. Ross and his roommate participate in the Parks and Recreation softball league during the spring and summer months. He also enjoys collecting and renting videos. He has an extensive Star Trek video collection and is a member of the Star Trek fan club.

Occasionally on Saturdays, you can find Ross at the local library where he enjoys reading the latest magazines. Ross also enjoys camping and hiking with his friends and family. He is currently planning an upcoming weekend camping trip which will involve primitive camping and a great deal of hiking.

Because Ross lives within two miles of his work, he usually rides his bicycle to work. On days when it rains or snows, Ross calls a co-worker to pick him up. His co-workers established a phone system for Ross on days when he needs a ride. They provided him a list of co-workers' names and phone numbers to call when he needs assistance or a ride to work. All other transportation around the community is provided by family members, friends, and support staff. No public transportation is available in the area where Ross lives.

FIGURE 9-23

Description of Dario at 33 Years of Age

Dario

• At 33, Dario lives in a group home with four other adults with disabilities and a full-time support person. At home Dario is responsible for maintaining his room, sharing in the household chores, and assisting with the grocery shopping twice each month. His household chores include washing the dishes, laundry, dusting, and keeping the kitchen counters clean. Dario also participates in some meal preparation such as making salads and operating the microwave oven.

Dario is employed part-time at a local movie theater for the past seven years. He works 30 hours per week as a ticket taker. Some of his other work responsibilities include keeping the front counters clean, stocking candy in the cases, and sweeping the front lobby with an adapted broom and dust pan. Because Dario's job responsibilities rarely change, his job coach provides only periodic visits to the job site. However, the job coach does maintain weekly phone contact with the movie theater manager. Dario has received several raises over the years and he currently earns an hourly salary of $7.50. After his first six months of employment, Dario was able to receive medical and dental benefits from the company's HMO.

During his leisure time, Dario enjoys attending basketball games at the local college, Parks and Recreation Department, and going into the city to watch the hometown professional basketball team. Every Sunday he attends religious services at his church. In addition, Dario is a member of a Unified Bowling team which bowls every Friday night. His favorite part of being a member of this bowling team is going out to eat with other team members after they are finished bowling. Twice each month Dario attends social events for adults sponsored by the local mental retardation service center. He has made several friends at these events and often calls them on the phone between social activities.

Transportation for Dario is provided by several individuals. The full-time support person at his group home provides transportation to the grocery store, shopping mall, and doctor's office. Dario rides to work with a co-worker or he uses specially equipped buses provided by the public department of transportation. He also uses the public bus to go to church on Sundays.

Summary

Students with moderate and severe mental retardation are a heterogeneous population. However, certain learning characteristics result from their significant cognitive deficits and overall developmental delay. In particular, these students exhibit deficits in the number of skills they learn, in generalization of learned skills, and in the synthesis of learned skills. These characteristics have a direct relationship to the selection of a curriculum model and a set of instructional strategies. These characteristics, and post-school goals of supported work and community living have lead to a functional curriculum model with objectives selected based on the students' ability to function in current and future environments. Instruction, based on behavioral teaching strategies, is conducted in community settings which are viewed as an extension of the classroom. Additionally, to the greatest extent possible, learning environments also should include opportunities in a variety of general education settings. This relationship among characteristics, post-school goals, and curriculum is necessary to ensure an outcome of graduates who live, work, and participate in integrated neighborhoods with a considerable degree of independence.

Discussion Questions and Activities

1. Jamie's IEP committee decided that as another step toward independence, in the cafeteria she should be required to bring her tray from the lunch line to her table. Jamie is severely mentally retarded and has a physical disability that requires her to use a four-legged walker. What adaptations and/or alternative performance strategies might be tried to enable Jamie to do this task?

2. As noted in this chapter, students with moderate and severe mental retardation may engage in challenging behaviors. One reason for these behaviors is that students become bored in class. What are potential reasons for this boredom, and what might teachers do to prevent boredom?

    p. 350 - 351 - 352

3. Conduct an ecological assessment to determine the tasks required to order an ice-cream cone in an ice-cream shop. Then, for one of the identified tasks, perform a task analysis to determine the steps that make up the task, and the skills required for performance.

4. Carol can print most of the letters of the alphabet. Her teacher wants to begin to shape her ability to print on a line. How might the teacher use antecedent prompts to teach Carol to print on a line, and to begin at the left side of the page?

5. What training would you provide a general education student who will take a turn being the peer tutor/buddy for a student with moderate mental retardation?

6. If you were the house leader of a group home for six adolescent and young adults with moderate mental retardation, what leisure skills would you program for evenings in the group home and for participation in the community?

7. Ross is a middle school student with moderate mental retardation described in this chapter (see Figure 9-2). Ross currently attends exploratory classes, art, and science classes with his nondisabled peers and is an active participant in the after school chorus. What modifications and/or supports might be employed to enable Ross to participate in the class unit on geology in the general education science class he attends?

8. Following Ross's science class, he attends art class. What skills are required for changing classes in a middle school? What supports may be put in place to assist Ross to go from his science class to his art class.

Internet Resources

American Association on Mental Retardation (AAMR)
www.aamr.org

National Transition Research Institute
www.ed.uiuc.edu/coe/sped/tri/institute.html

Office of Disability Employment Policy
www.dol.gov/odep/

The Association for Persons with Severe Handicaps (TASH)
www.tash.org

References

Alberto, P., Elliott, N., Taber, T., Houser, E., & Andrews, P. (1993). Vocational content for students with moderate and severe disabilities in elementary and middle grades. *Focus on Exceptional Children, 25(9),* 1–10.

Alberto, P., Sharpton, W., Briggs, A., & Stright, M. (1986). Facilitating task acquisition through the use of a self-operated auditory prompting system. *Journal of the Association for Persons with Severe Handicaps, 11(2),* 85–91.

Alberto, P., & Troutman, A. (2003). *Applied behavior analysis for teachers* (6th Ed.). Columbus, OH: Merrill Prentice-Hall.

American Association on Mental Retardation (AAMR). (2002). *Mental retardation: Definition, classification, and systems of supports* (10th ed.). Washington, DC: American Association on Mental Retardation.

Barudin, S., & Hourcade, J. (1990). Relative effectiveness of three methods of reading instruction in developing specific recall and transfer skills in learners with moderate and severe mental retardation. *Education and Training in Mental Retardation, 25,* 286–291.

Baumgart, D., Brown, L., Pumpian, I., Nisbet, J., Ford, A., Sweet, M., Messina, R., & Schroeder, J. (1982). Principle of partial participation and individualized adaptations in educational programs for severely handicapped students. *Journal of the Association for Persons with Severe Handicaps, 7,* 17–27.

Bradford, S., Shippen, M., Alberto, P., Houchins, D., & Flores, M. (in press). Using systematic instruction to teach decoding skills to middle school students with moderate intellectual disabilities. *Education and Training in Developmental Disabilities.*

Browder, D. (Ed.). (1991). *Assessment of individuals with severe disabilities* (2nd ed.). Baltimore: Paul H. Brookes.

Browder, D., & Lalli, J. (1991). Review of research on sight word instruction. *Research in Developmental Disabilities, 12,* 203–228.

Browder, D., & Minarovic, T. (2000). Utilizing sight words in self-instruction training for employees with moderate mental retardation in competitive jobs. *Education and Training in Mental Retardation and Developmental Disabilities, 35,* 78–89.

Browder, D., & Xin, Y. P. (1998). A meta-analysis and review of sight word research and its implications for teaching functional reading to individuals with moderate and severe disabilities. *The Journal of Special Education, 32,* 130–153.

Brown, L., Long, E., Udvari-Solner, A., Schwarz, P., VanDeventer, P., Ahlgren, C., Johnson, F., Gruenewald, L., & Jorgensen, J. (1989). Should students with severe intellectual disabilities be based in regular or in special education classrooms in home schools? *Journal of the Association for Persons with Severe Handicaps, 14(1),* 8–12.

Brown, L., McClean, M. B., Baumgart, D., Vincent, L., Falvey, M., & Schroeder, J. (1979). Using the characteristics of current and subsequent least restrictive environments in the development of curricular content for severely handicapped students. *AAESPH Review, 4(4),* 407–424.

Carr, E., & Durand, V. M. (1985). Reducing behavior problems through functional communication training. *Journal of Applied Behavior Analysis, 18,* 111–126.

Conners, F. (1992). Reading instruction for students with moderate mental retardation: Review and analysis of research. *American Journal on Mental Retardation, 96,* 577–598.

Courtade-Little, G., & Browder, D. (2005). *Aligning IEPs to academic standards.* Verona, WI: Attainment Co.

Ellis, N. (1970). Memory processes in retardates and normals. In N. Ellis (Ed.), *International review of research in mental retardation, Vol. 9.* New York: Academic Press.

Farlow, L., & Snell, M. (1994). *Making the most of student performance data.* Washington, DC: American Association on Mental Retardation.

Falvey, M. (1989). *Community-based curriculum: Instructional strategies for students with severe handicaps.* Baltimore, MD: Paul H. Brookes.

Falvey, M. (1995). *Inclusive and heterogeneous schooling.* Baltimore, MD: Paul H. Brookes.

Gast, D., Ault, M., Wolery, M., Doyle, P., & Belanger, S. (1988). Comparison of constant time delay and the system of least prompts in teaching sight words to students with moderate retardation. *Education and Training in Mental Retardation, 23,* 117–128.

Gast, D., Wolery, M., Morris, L., Doyle, P., & Meyer, S. (1990). Teaching sight word reading in a group instructional arrangement using constant time delay. *Exceptionality, 1,* 81–96.

Gaylord-Ross, R., & Peck, C. (1984). Integration efforts for students with severe mental retardation. In D. Bricker & J. Fuller (Eds.), *Severe mental retardation: From theory to practice,* (pp. 185–207). Reston, VA: Division on Mental Retardation of the Council for Exceptional Children.

Grenot-Scheyer, M., & Falvey, M. (1986). Integration issues and strategies. In M. Falvey (Ed.), *Community-based curriculum: Instructional strategies for students with severe handicaps,* (pp. 217–233). Baltimore, MD: Paul H. Brookes.

Haring, N. (Ed.). (1988). *Generalization for students with severe handicaps: Strategies and solutions.* Seattle, WA: University of Washington Press.

Hodapp, R., & Zigler, E. (1997). New issues in the developmental approach to mental retardation. In W. MacLean, Jr. (Ed.). *Ellis' handbook of mental deficiency, psychological theory, and research* (3rd ed., pp. 115–136). Mahwah, NJ: Lawrence Erlbaum Associates.

Hoogeveen, F., Smeets, P., & Lancioni, G. (1989). Teaching moderately mentally retarded children basic reading skills. *Research in Developmental Disabilities, 10,* 1–18.

Iwata, B., Dorsey, M., Slifer, K., Bauman, K., & Richman, G. (1982). Toward a functional analysis of self-injury. *Analysis and Intervention in Developmental Disabilities, 2,* 3–20.

Kennedy, C., Horner, R., & Newton, J. (1989). Social contacts of adults with severe disabilities living in the community. *Journal of the Association for Persons with Severe Handicaps, 14,* 190–196.

Logan, K., Alberto, P., Kana, T., & Waylor-Bowen, T. (1994). *Curriculum development and instructional design for students with profound disabilities,* (pp. 333–383). In L. Sternberg (Ed.), Individuals with profound disabilities. Austin, TX: PRO-ED.

MacMillan, D. (1982). *Mental retardation in school and society,* (2nd ed.). Boston: Little, Brown and Co.

Mar, H., & Sall, N. (1999). Profiles of the expressive communication skills of children and adolescents with severe cognitive disabilities. *Education and Training in Mental Retardation and Developmental Disabilities, 34,* 77–89.

Martin, R. (1993). A checklist of questions to ask in determining LRE. *The Special Educator, 8,* 2.

McLean, L., Brady, N., & McLean, J. (1996). Reported communication abilities of individuals with severe mental retardation. *American Journal on Mental Retardation, 100,* 580–591.

Mercer, C., & Snell, M. (1977). *Learning theory research in mental retardation: Implications for teaching.* Columbus, OH: Charles Merrill.

Nietupski, J., & Hamre-Nietupski, S. (1987). An ecological approach to curriculum development. In L. Goetz, D. Guess, & K. Stremel-Campbell (Eds.), *Innovative program design for individuals with dual sensory impairments.* Baltimore. MD: Paul H. Brookes.

Sacramento City Unified School District v. Holland, 18 IDELR 761 (E.D. Cal. 1992).

Skinner, B. F. (1968). *The technology of teaching.* New York: Appleton-Century-Crofts.

Sullivan, C., Vitello, S., & Foster, W. (1988). Adaptive behavior of adults with mental retardation: An intensive case study. *Education and Training in Mental Retardation, 23(1),* 76–81.

Taylor, R., Richards, S., & Brady, M. (2005). *Mental Retardation: Historical perspectives, current practices, and future directions.* Boston: Pearson/Allyn and Bacon.

Test, D., Spooner, F., Keul, P., & Grossi, T. (1990). Teaching adolescents with severe disabilities to use the public telephone. *Behavior Modification, 14(2),* 157–171.

Wacker, D., & Berg, W. (1983). Effects of picture prompts on the acquisition of complex vocational tasks by mentally retarded adolescents. *Journal of Applied Behavior Analysis, 16,* 417–433.

Walsh, B., & Lamberts, F. (1979). Errorless discrimination and picture fading as techniques for teaching sight words to TMR students. *American Journal on Mental Deficiency, 83,* 473–479.

Westling, D. (1986). *Introduction to mental retardation.* Englewood Cliffs, NJ: Prentice-Hall.

Westling, D., & Fox, L. (1995). *Teaching students with severe disabilities.* Columbus, OH: Charles Merrill.

White, O. (1980). Adaptive performance objectives: Form versus function. In W. Sailor, B. Wilcox, & L. Brown (Eds.), *Methods of instruction for severely handicapped students.* Baltimore, MD: Paul H. Brookes.

Wilcox, B., & Bellamy, G. T. (1982). *Design of high school programs for severely handicapped students.* Baltimore, MD: Paul H. Brookes.

York-Barr, J., Kronberg, R., & Doyle, M. (1996). Module 1: *A shared agenda for general and special educators. In J. York-Bar (Ed.), Creating inclusive school communities: A staff development series for general and special educators.* Baltimore, MD: Paul H. Brookes.

Zeaman, D., & House, B. (1979). A review of attention theory. In N. Ellis (Ed.), *Handbook of mental deficiency: Psychological theory and research* (2nd ed.), Hillsdale, NJ: Erlbaum.

Zigler, E. (1969). Developmental vs. differential theory of mental retardation and the problem of motivation. *American Journal of Mental Deficiency, 73(4),* 536–556.

10

Adapting Environments and Using Technology

Kathryn Wolff Heller, Mari Beth Coleman-Martin, and Jennifer Tumlin Garrett

Chapter Objectives

- to describe classroom modifications that may be required to meet the needs of students with disabilities;
- to become familiar with assistive technology devices that assist students with disabilities in school settings;
- to understand basic computer adaptations for students with disabilities;
- to describe the various components of educational software in order to effectively select appropriate software for students;
- to provide information on various technologies available to promote reading, writing, math, and notetaking; and
- to describe how teachers can use technology as a personal productivity tool.

Effective education in the schools is promoted by providing environments conducive to learning. An effective learning environment includes appropriate classroom arrangement and pertinent use of technology to help students learn. The same is true for students with disabilities. Some of the environmental arrangements and technology may be different when students have a disability, but the goal of effective learning is the same.

This chapter will discuss classroom modifications that promote learning for students with and without disabilities. Several types of assistive devices used in the classroom for students with physical, sensory, communication, and learning impairments are presented. The effective use of the computer and computer adaptations which may be made for students with disabilities also are reviewed.

Classroom Arrangement

To promote effective learning, it is important to arrange the classroom to meet the needs of the students. Classroom arrangement must take into consideration students' learning needs, as well as adaptations required for students with physical, sensory, communication, cognitive, or behavioral disabilities.

For many years, a traditional classroom arrangement was used. In this arrangement, the students' desks were in rows facing the front of the class where the teacher stood and taught the subject matter. This arrangement is teacher-centered and emphasizes such teaching formats as lecturing and questioning. It assumes that all students learn alike and at the same rate. Today, many teachers modify their classrooms to allow for differences in learning, emphasizing a more student-based approach.

Depending upon the teacher, characteristics of the students, classroom size, and subject matter, several different classroom arrangements may be used. These may include the use of small group instructional areas, individual carrels, quiet areas, and learning centers.

Small group instructional areas allow groups of students to be placed together to receive instruction on a topic or to work on special projects while the rest of the class is engaged in other activities. Quiet areas and individual carrels may be used for independent work. Learning centers can fulfill several different purposes: (a) skill centers (e.g., drill cards, practice sheets), (b) discovery and enrichment centers (e.g., advanced science activities), (c) listening centers (e.g., tapes providing additional instruction), and (d) creativity centers (e.g., music or language art activities) (Gearheart, Weishahn, & Gearheart, 1996).

Technology often can be used in a classroom to promote learning. One form of technology frequently encountered in the classroom is the computer. Computers may be placed in small group instructional areas, in learning centers, or in an area of their own in the class. Often their placement will be based on physical space as well as the types of activities for which the computers will be used.

Classroom Modifications

Classroom arrangement must take into account the needs of students with disabilities, as well as the assistive technology these students may use. Usually these modifications to classroom arrangement are minor, but the changes can make a difference to the students who need them. Classroom modifications typically occur in six areas:

1. Location of students in the classroom.
2. Position of material.
3. Use of modified furniture.
4. Furniture arrangement.
5. Environmental arrangement.
6. Assistive technology.

Each one of these areas may be considered for students with physical, sensory, communication, learning, and behavioral impairments. The special education teacher, general education teacher, and the rest of the educational team will work collaboratively to determine the appropriate classroom modifications for each student with a disability.

Location of Students

When planning the classroom arrangement, it is important to determine where and how students with disabilities will be located. In some instances, location is crucial for students to see the material effectively and participate in group discussions. In other instances, the students need to sit where they can interact easily with the teacher or paraprofessional to receive additional assistance or specialized material. Wherever students with special needs are located, it is important that they are a part of the group and not isolated from the rest of the students. The special education teacher will discuss classroom location options with the general education classroom teacher to determine the best arrangement for both the students and the teacher.

Some students with severe physical impairments may be unable to move their bodies to look around students who may be seated in front of them. This is often a problem in a traditional classroom arrangement. It may be helpful for the classroom teacher to sit where students would sit to determine any viewing obstructions. The obstruction then may be moved or an alternative placement of the student may be considered. In some instances, it is best to have the students near the front of the class so they can see the board and the teacher easily. However, students who have limited head movement may need to be farther back in the class to see the entire blackboard or the teacher when she moves around. Some students with severe physical impairments that affect arm and hand movement may need to be seated where the teacher, paraprofessional, or peer can assist them in getting and manipulating their materials.

Students with sensory impairments also may require special seating location. For students with visual impairments, the visual condition and access to materials determine seat placement. Optimal seat location allows students to use whatever vision is remaining. Students may need to be seated close to the front in order to see the blackboard (students who are nearsighted), or in the back of the class to see the blackboard (students who have tunnel vision), or to one side of the classroom (students for whom one half of the field of vision is missing in both eyes). Another consideration is access to material. Students who are blind should be sitting where the teacher, paraprofessional, or peer can hand them the material easily.

Students with hearing impairments also have seat location considerations. To use whatever hearing they have left, these students often need to be located away from air conditioning units, noisy hallways, overhead projectors, film strip projectors, or other noisy devices. Students with hearing impairments who speechread must be close to the front of the class to have a clear view of the teacher. Students using manual sign language must be seated in a location where it is easy to see the interpreter as well as the teacher.

Students with communication devices may or may not have special seating needs. When the communication device has voice output, students may be located anywhere in the classroom, provided that the voice output is loud enough to be understood. However, when there is no voice output, students must sit near the teacher, paraprofessional, or peer to let others read the output of the communication device. When students are first learning to use the communication device, it may be helpful for them to be located close to the teacher if verification of student responses is needed.

Students with learning difficulties and behavioral problems also may benefit from special seating. Students with learning difficulties may need to be near the front of the class where the teacher can provide additional assistance, or to the side where a paraprofessional can give assistance with minimal distraction. Students with behavior problems may need to be close to the front of the classroom so teachers can effectively monitor and control behavior. These students always should be seated where potential distractions are minimized.

Location and Size of Material

Materials and equipment should be placed in an accessible manner. When students have severe physical impairments that limit movement, it is important that materials are within easy reach. Math manipulatives, for example, need to be placed on the desk within the student's range of motion and books may need to be placed on bookstands for easy viewing. In order for the student to access these items, the student will be assessed by the occupational therapist to determine if items need to be placed off to one side of the desk, placed a specific distance from the student, elevated, or placed on a slant. Teachers should determine what materials students use in the classroom and if the location of these materials needs to be changed. For example, computer tables may need to be placed at a certain height to allow wheelchairs to slide under. Whiteboards and pencil sharpeners may need to be lowered to allow students in wheelchairs to use them.

Students with other types of disabilities also may need to have the location of materials changed. Students with visual impairments may need material positioned closer to them in order to see it. Students who are blind may benefit from having materials placed in a consistent, organized manner to find materials easily. Students with asthma who are allergic to animals such as guinea pigs, may need the guinea pig placed in the far corner of the room away from the student or removed from the classroom altogether.

The size of the material also must be considered when determining placement. Materials may need to be enlarged so students with visual impairments can see them more easily, especially when seated at a distant location. Students with severe physical impairments also may be better able to manipulate larger material (e.g., larger math manipulatives) more easily.

Modified Furniture

Some students will require modified furniture or adaptive equipment to assist them in the classroom. Students in wheelchairs may need a table with adjustable height and an area cut out for the wheelchair to fit underneath. Some students require special chairs to provide optimum support. In other instances, positioning devices, such as prone standers or standing frames, may be used for a few minutes a day in activities where standing would be appropriate (See **Figure 10-1**). Students who are blind and use braille, typically need larger tables or a second desk because of the size of books printed in braille and the need for a place to put the brailler when writing. Physical therapists will determine the type of modified furniture appropriate to the student and will teach proper positioning of the student in the equipment.

Although some students with physical impairments may have no positioning needs, positioning of students with severe physical impairments requires careful consideration. First, students with severe physical disabilities need to be correctly positioned in their

FIGURE 10-1

Child Positioned in a Prone Stander

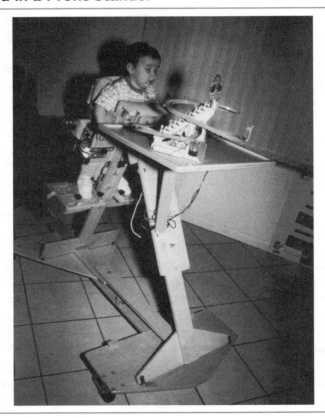

chairs or wheelchairs. Ineffective positioning can result in fatigue, restrictive arm movement, discomfort, and distraction from learning. The physical therapist will determine appropriate positioning in the chair or wheelchair and demonstrate this to the teacher. The teacher then will be able to monitor the student for proper positioning.

Furniture Arrangement

Furniture arrangement also requires special consideration. Students who have wheelchairs typically need wider aisles in the classroom to move about easily. Students with visual impairments can learn their way about the classroom independently if the location of the furniture remains fairly constant. Students with learning and behavioral disorders often learn well in small groups, so having an area for small group instruction can be beneficial. Study carrels can be helpful for students who become distracted when individual work is being done. A separate area may be designated in which students with behavior problems can calm down when they are acting inappropriately. To reinforce students when they are acting appropriately, another area with fun activities may be used.

Environmental Arrangements

Teachers also need to consider how to arrange such classroom environmental variables as lighting, color and contrast, time, and visual and auditory dimensions. Some students with visual impairments have difficulty with glare or need more or less light than other students. It often is necessary to seat students where lighting is optimal and glare is minimized. For students with hearing impairments, it is important that teachers do not lecture with the light coming from behind them (e.g., while standing in front of a window) since the glare may make it more difficult for these students to speechread.

Sometimes use of bright colors or contrasting materials will improve visual functioning in students with visual impairments. Teachers should ensure that materials being used or demonstrated in class are well contrasted with their background. For example, when the teacher holds up an item to show the class, students with visual impairments will have difficulty seeing a colorful item against a background such as a colorful bulletin board. It is better to hold a piece of contrasting paper behind the item being shown.

Part of the learning environment includes providing sufficient time for students to respond to oral or written questions. It is important to note that students with visual impairments who use large print or braille need a longer period of time to read and complete assignments. Students with physical impairments and those using augmentative communication devices also may require more time because of increased time to make the physical response and because they may experience fatigue while writing or accessing a communication device. In some situations, other modes of response may be needed (such as eye-gazing a multiple choice answer).

Students with vision or hearing impairments may need the environment arranged to compensate for the vision or hearing impairment. Students with hearing impairments who have residual hearing may perform better when background noise is minimized. Sound absorbing material in the classroom, such as a carpet and acoustic tiles, may be useful. Also, providing students with hearing impairments written information may aid learning. For example, students with hearing impairments cannot take notes and speechread or watch an interpreter at the same time. Providing a copy of another student's notes can assist these students. Students with visual impairments often need the teacher or other person to provide oral descriptions of what is being written on the board or of the video being watched. Providing more auditory information will help compensate for the visual impairment.

Assistive Technology

Modifications also need to take into account the types of assistive technology used in the classroom. Students with physical impairments often use alternate keyboards and input devices that attach to the computer. Extra space usually is needed for these items. Larger assistive devices, such as a CCTV (closed-circuit television) or an unmounted communication device, also require extra space in the classroom.

Assistive Technology Devices

Students with disabilities often use assistive technology to improve their ability to function in school, home, community, and vocational environments. According to federal legislation, an assistive device is, "any item, piece of equipment, or product system, whether acquired commercially off the shelf, modified, or customized, that is used to increase, maintain, or improve functional capabilities of individuals with disabilities" (IDEA, PL 108–446; PL 100–407). Depending upon the student and the policy of the school district, these assistive devices may be funded by any number of sources, such as the school system, insurance policies, parents, or various organizations.

There are many different types of assistive devices that may be used by individuals with disabilities. They are referred to as low technology or high technology devices. Low technology devices are simpler, less complicated types of technology. Examples of low technology include the use of an adapted switch that is pushed to turn a tape recorder on or off or the use of a clipboard to hold paper steady when writing. High technology devices are more complex forms of technology such as computers or augmentative communication devices. There are several other ways to categorize assistive devices: those that provide physical access, sensory access, access through communication devices, and access for learning and behavioral needs.

Assistive Technology for Physical Access

Students with physical impairments will vary in the type of assistive technology needed. Some students will not use assistive devices, while other students will be unable to function without them. Assistive technology for physical access can be divided into five main categories:

1. work surface modifications.
2. object modifications.
3. switch access.
4. environmental control.
5. mobility.

Students who have limited movement of their arms, such as students with severe, spastic cerebral palsy, often need work surface modifications. These modifications may include the size, position, height, and/or slant of the surface. Specialized tables may be used to accommodate individual students. Tables need to be at the proper height. Students with low muscle tone may perform better when the work area is higher, while those with higher muscle tone, may perform best if the work surface is lower (Best, Heller, & Bigge, 2005). Some students may require small boxes upon which to rest their feet to improve stability. Sometimes work surfaces are extended more on one side to benefit movement abilities. Some students may have a tray that slants on top of the desk that allows the arm to reach the surface for writing, pointing, and general access.

Simple, low technological assistive devices may be used to modify or replace objects or items used in typical classrooms. These object modifications usually involve stabilization, boundaries, grasping, or manipulation aids. Since some students with physical impairments have difficulty holding paper or material on their desk, they may use clip-boards, Velcro, clamps, a piece of tape, or any number of simple devices to prevent slip-page of material. If students have difficulty retrieving items, their work surfaces may have boundaries, such as a small wooden lip or Velcro around the edges, to prevent items from falling off the edge. For students who have difficulty with hand or arm control, there are several manipulation aids they may use. Pencils may be adapted to have a better grip through use of foam material or clay around the pencil. Some objects may be adapted with long handles to compensate for the students' decreased ability to extend and move the arm. Other objects may have Velcro attached to them, or special grasping devices may be used when the student's grasp is affected.

Some students with physical impairments may require switch access. These students have such limited movement in their arms that they are unable to turn on a tape player, turn the pages of a book, or turn on a battery operated toy. A switch is a device that con-trols the flow of power and bypasses the regular on-off control for the device (Rocklage, Peschong, Gillett, & Delohery, 1996). They can be made easily or purchased commercially to convert any battery-operated device to one that uses a switch. Electrical devices such as televisions and computers also may be converted to using a switch thorough the use of readily available special adapters. There are many types of switches. Depending upon the students' motor capability, they may use their hand, elbow, knee, or foot to activate the switch. Other types of switches may be selected in which students pull the switch, grasp the switch, blow into the switch, or contract a muscle to activate the switch. Switch selec-tion and access are determined by the occupational therapist, physical therapist, teacher of students with orthopedic impairments, and other members of the educational team. An example of a switch is shown in **Figure 10-2.**

Students with physical impairments may use environmental control systems to man-age their environment independently. An environmental control system is a device that is

FIGURE 10-2

Student Using a Switch Instead of a Keyboard to Access a Computer

activated by a switch to control almost any type of electrical appliance from a distance. Environmental control systems may be used to dial a telephone, run a CD player, turn the lights on or off, or perform many other daily activities. Environmental control systems typically operate using radio signals (like an automatic garage door opener), or infrared signals (like a television controller).

There are several types of mobility devices that may be used by students with physical impairments. The most common type of mobility device is a wheelchair. Some wheelchairs are manual; the student or someone else pushes the chair. Other wheelchairs are motorized; the student uses a joystick or switches to move the chair. Depending on the severity and type of physical impairment, wheelchairs often have straps and wedges that help the student maintain appropriate positioning. Some wheelchairs have the capability to tilt into different positions. One type of wheelchair has the capability to go from a sitting to a standing position and can move in either position. Another type of wheelchair can climb stairs.

Assistive Technology for Sensory Access

There are several different types of assistive devices that students with visual or hearing impairments use. Some of these include:

- low vision devices and magnification systems.
- braille and tactile graphics.
- mobility devices.
- hearing aids and amplification systems.
- adapted devices for daily living.

Students with visual impairments may use several different types of devices and adaptations to improve their ability to see. To better see print, students may use a low vision device or large print materials. Low vision devices (LVD) are devices that magnify items, including print (although some are used to minimize items). Optometrists trained in low vision prescribe these low vision devices. Magnifiers are used to enlarge items that are close to students, while telescopes are used to enlarge items that are farther away. A closed-circuit television (CCTV) is a device that enlarges images on a screen (such as print, maps, objects). The items are placed on a movable viewing table, and the image is projected on the screen. The control allows students to adjust the size of the image as well as the background color (See **Figure 10-3**).

Another alternative is the use of large-print materials. Books and other material may be obtained in large print, generated on a computer with a large font size, or enlarged on a copy machine. In this alternative, the material itself is actually enlarged rather than the students' image of the material, as with low vision devices. Since not all printed material students encounter is enlarged, the LVD allows students access to a range of printed material that would otherwise be too small for them to see. Regardless of the type of low vision device or enlargement strategy used, the assistive device does not correct student's vision. Typically, students will continue to have blurred vision, but the LVD or enlarged print will assist them in seeing the material.

Students who have a severe visual impairment or are blind often need information presented tactually. In the area of reading, braille is taught in the schools. Braille is a system of raised dots that represent letters, letter combinations (e.g., th), or whole words. (See **Figure 10-4**).

A teacher certified in visual impairments will teach students to read and write braille. This teacher also will adapt classroom materials into braille for the students. Students

FIGURE 10-3

Student Using a CCTV to Read

FIGURE 10-4

Braille

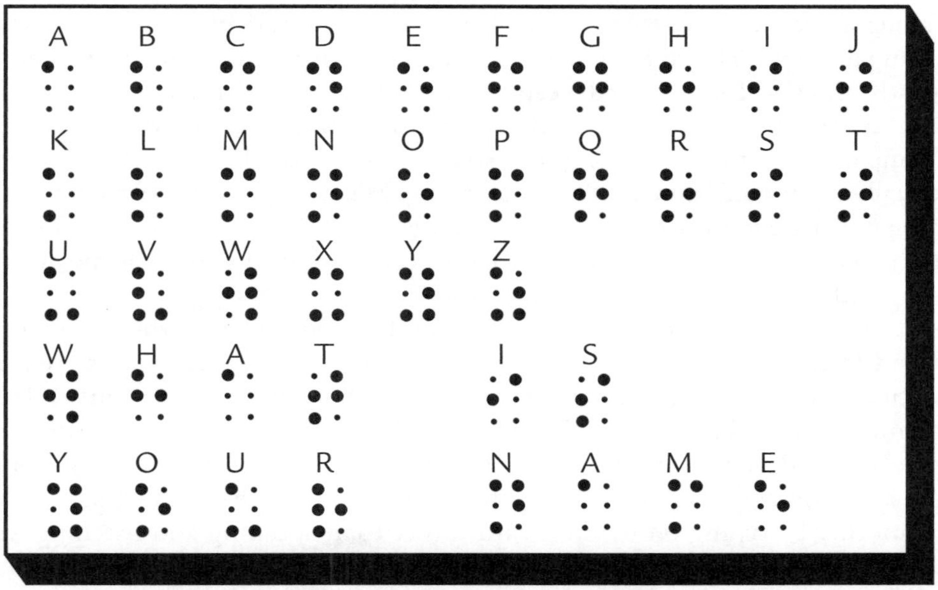

will need other materials converted into an accessible form. Materials such as graphs will need to be converted into a tactile form with the use of a wide range of materials, such as string glued over the graph or the use of a raised line drawing kit. Two-dimensional drawings or diagrams may need to be converted into tactile models that will assist students in understanding what is being taught. Close coordination between the classroom teacher and the teacher of students with visual impairments is needed to accomplish this.

Students with visual impairments may use a variety of assistive devices to help with mobility. One of the most common types of mobility devices for individuals with visual impairments is a cane. Canes provide information about objects that may be in the way or changes in elevation. Some students use electronic mobility devices that use ultrasound or laser beams to detect objects that are in the way. Electronic mobility devices provide tactile and/or auditory feedback to alert the individual to these obstacles.

Talking signs are another type of system to aid with mobility. An example is the Voice Label. This system consists of a transmitter with a recorded message and a sensory device. Upon entering a room and turning on the device, the transmitter speaks its message. This provides information regarding the presence of pay telephones, exits, elevators and other important items. Other mobility systems include the use of guide dogs and sighted guides (a technique in which one person leads another).

For students with hearing impairments, hearing aids and amplification systems are the most commonly used forms of assistive technology. As discussed in Chapter 5, hearing aids are personal amplification devices that consist of a microphone, an amplifier, and a receiver. The microphone picks up sound in the environment and converts it to an electrical signal. The intensity of the electrical signal is increased by the amplifier, and then converted back to sound by the receiver. The resulting amplified sound is directed into the ear of the hearing aid user.

In the classroom setting, students with hearing impairment often use an amplification device known as an FM (frequency modulated) system. With FM systems, the classroom teacher wears a small microphone that picks up the teacher's voice and transmits it via a radio frequency carrier wave to a special receiver worn by students in the class who have hearing impairments. The receiver sends the signal to earphones or to the students' own hearing aids, allowing for improved reception of the teacher's voice in a noisy classroom.

There are several different types of assistive devices that are used by students with sensory impairments for daily living. For students with visual impairments, daily living items usually are modified tactually or auditorily. Many items (e.g., board games, rulers, measuring cups) are modified with braille or large print. Descriptive videos also are available in which a person's voice describes what is occurring throughout the movie, without interfering with the movie's normal conversation.

For students with hearing impairments, modifications enhance the auditory signals or replace the auditory signals with visual signals. Movies and televisions are available with captions (words of the dialogue written at the bottom of the screen). Telephones may use amplification devices, or a TTY may be used. A TTY (telecommunication devices for the deaf) is a device with a keyboard, a small screen where incoming and outgoing messages are displayed, and an area to connect it to the telephone. A person communicates to another by typing on the keyboard rather than speaking and listening with the standard telephone receiver. When only one party has a TTY, a relay service may be used where the person with a hearing impairment uses the TTY, and the relay service verbally transmits the typed message to the person called. When the hearing person wants to convey a message to the person with a hearing impairment, the relay service types the message back on their TTY.

Other types of assistive devices for students with hearing impairments include alerting devices. An alerting device is one that uses lights or vibration to inform the person of an auditory sound, such as someone ringing the doorbell. Alerting devices, such as alarm clocks, often consist of putting a vibrating device under the person's pillow or on a waistband. When the alarm goes off, the device vibrates to waken or alert the person.

Assistive Technology for Communication

Some students with disabilities will be unable to effectively communicate using speech and will use augmentative and alternative communication (AAC). AAC refers to any other means of communication that is used to improve communication. It often is divided into two categories: unaided and aided (Beukelman & Mirenda, 1998).

Unaided Communication

Unaided communication refers to communication systems that use hand or body movement to communicate, but do not require any external devices. Students use a wide range of unaided communication systems: movements, facial expressions, gestures, and manual sign language. Unaided systems have the advantage of being highly portable, but many people will be unfamiliar with these systems and be unable to communicate with students who use them.

Aided Communication

Aided communication refers to those communication systems that use some type of external aid or device to communicate. Aided communication devices use objects, pictures, drawings, print, or other symbols. Students typically point to the symbol they want to communicate. Some students may be unable to point with their finger, so a head pointer, light pointer, mouthstick, eye pointer, or switch can be used to indicate a selection. In some instances, students will directly indicate their choice; in others, the device scans each selection, and students indicate when the desired choice is selected. Aided devices have the overall advantage of being more easily understood by individuals who are unaccustomed to communicating with students who use AAC. (See **Figure 10-5.**)

AAC devices may be nonelectronic or electronic. Nonelectronic devices range from a symbol on a piece of paper to symbols placed on multiple pages in a portable book. Nonelectronic devices have the advantages of being inexpensive, durable, and easy to construct. Electronic devices range from simple machines that have a few seconds of prerecorded speech to those that are highly programmable, compatible with computers, and have printed output in addition to speech output. Electronic devices have the advantages of speech output and a variety of ways to access the system (e.g., scanning, switch access). They can provide larger vocabulary selections in a more accessible format.

Often students use both nonelectronic and electronic communication devices as well as a combination of aided and nonaided approaches. This provides students with several options that can be used in different situations, for example when they encounter someone who is not familiar with them or the type of communication system they use.

The effectiveness of a student's use of an AAC device is dependent not only upon the type of device, but also appropriate vocabulary and provision of sufficient time to use the AAC device. Vocabulary specific to class topics can be added to the device to allow the student to participate in classroom discussions. If key vocabulary is lacking, the classroom teacher should notify the speech-language pathologist or teacher certified in orthopedic impairments to allow them to add the needed vocabulary. Also, it is important to realize that it may take a student longer to answer a question when using an AAC device. The teacher needs to either wait for the response, or after asking the student a question, go back for the answer after a few seconds or minutes. If the student is just learning to use the AAC device, the teacher may want to verify whether the answer given was the intended one.

FIGURE 10-5

Child Using an AAC Device to Talk to Her Brother

Assistive Technology for Learning and Behavioral Problems

Students with learning and behavioral problems may also benefit from assistive technology. Typically, the form of assistive technology for these students involves computers and certain types of software. Students with learning problems, for example, often benefit from software that provides repeated practice and immediate feedback. Word processing programs that include voice output allow students to listen to what they have written. This process may aid the student in detecting errors in sentence structure and spelling. Voice recognition programs allow students with poor motor coordination to speak rather than type when composing at the computer. Students with behavioral problems may benefit from reinforcing software that makes learning fun. These types of programs will be described in more detail later in this chapter.

Computer Adaptations

The computer has become a standard piece of equipment in most schools. For many students, computer use can help provide individualization of instruction, immediate feedback, repetition, motivation, and access to a wide range of instructional materials, including those on the Internet. However, some students may have problems using the computer due to physical, sensory, or learning difficulties. Several options exist to modify the features on the computer as well as provide alternate input and output options to address each student's specific needs.

Built-In Accessibility Features

Almost all computers have built in accessibility options that can help students with disabilities use the computer. Accessibility options involving the keyboard, mouse, and display generally are available in the control panels of Windows and Macintosh platform computers. Some accessibility options are specifically designed for students with physical disabilities. For example, when the Filter Keys option is turned on, letters will not repeat on the screen when the key is pressed too long. The keyboard also can be modified by activating the Sticky Keys option that allows students who cannot press two keys together (such as the control, alt, or shift key with another key) to press them in sequence instead of together. Often computers come with other languages, such as Dvorak, which allows the letters of the keyboard to be arranged in another sequence that may be more effective for students typing with one hand.

The mouse and screen also can be modified. The mouse usually can be changed to switch right and left clicks for individuals who are left handed. The speed of the mouse movements on the screen can also be slowed down or speeded up, depending on the needs of the student. For students with visual impairments or those who have difficulty locating the cursor, the cursor can be enlarged or changed to make a trail that is easier to find. In addition the display can be changed to a higher contrast with changes in foreground and background color to assist students with visual impairments. When a hearing impairment is present, most computers have options that can provide a visual signal to indicate when a sound is made or display captions for sounds.

Computer Input Devices

Certain students will need additional devices or software beyond those accessibility options found on most computers. In some instances it may be as easy as putting high contrast or colored labels over the keys to help students with visual or learning needs. Sometimes simple devices (such as a keyguard) are placed over the standard keyboard to assist students with physical impairments. A keyguard is a hard piece of plastic cut to fit over the computer keyboard with a hole cut out over each key. The keyguard allows a student who has difficulty with fine motor movement to isolate single keys by allowing the hand to be rested on the plastic and one finger to stick through a hole to press the intended key.

Some students may be unable to use the standard keyboard that comes with the computer. In this instance, there are numerous alternative keyboards of varying shapes, sizes, and configurations to meet the student's needs. A larger keyboard may provide easier access for individuals who have less fine motor control, who need fewer function keys and clutter for cognitive or visual reasons, or need larger labels for visual access. For example, BigKeys Plus (available from Greystone Digital Inc.) is a larger keyboard that can be purchased in standard QWERTY or ABC layout with or without color adapted keys. Another type of alternative keyboard is IntelliKeys (by Intellitools Inc.), which is a programmable "membrane" alternative keyboard. (See **Figure 10-6**). It has a flat surface over which overlays are placed for different purposes or users. Overlays can be commercially bought (e.g., ABC layout, QWERTY layout, numeric keypad, early literacy software with designed IntelliKeys overlays) or designed by the teacher using a separate software program. There are also miniature keyboards (e.g., Tash Mini by Tash Inc.) for individuals who have very limited finger mobility, who use a head pointer device to type, or who type with one hand.

On-screen keyboards are another input means for individuals who need alternate computer access. The keyboard is displayed on the screen and may be accessed by using a mouse, joystick, trackball, or other mouse alternatives. One type of alternate input device is a TouchWindow (manufactured by Edmark), which is a transparent screen that fits over the regular computer screen to allow the student to make a selection by touching the screen. Being able to directly touch what is viewed on the screen is helpful for young students and those with cognitive impairments. Another example of an alternate input device is a head controlled input device such as the Smart-NAV (manufactured by Natural Point, Inc.) in which the student places a small reflective device on the forehead and

FIGURE 10-6

Student Using an Expanded Keyboard to Access a Portable Computer

moves a cursor on the screen through head movements that are tracked by an infrared device on top of the monitor. This example of a hands free input device can allow a student to type a paper, access the Internet or use various software programs.

Some individuals who have extremely limited movements and poor head control still can access a computer through scanning. This is not to be confused with a scanner for copying documents into the computer. Switch scanning involves the computer program highlighting information on the screen and the person pressing a switch when the desired choice is highlighted. For example, some on-screen keyboard programs have options for scanning so that the upper row of keys is highlighted followed by the next row, etc. When the desired row is highlighted, the user presses a switch to select that row. The program then begins to scan by highlighting each letter across the row. The user makes the selection by activating the switch when the desired letter is highlighted. Many software programs designed for individuals with disabilities offer scanning as a built-in feature. Additionally, numerous types of switches are available to meet individual needs with regard to sensitivity (e.g., highly sensitive for individuals without much strength), size (e.g., small for a person who activates it with a head movement), and means of activation (e.g., activated by raising an eyebrow).

Some students may use speech recognition software. This type of software allows students to dictate text or commands into a microphone, and the computer types the text or performs the command (e.g., move mouse cursor, save file) that was spoken. For individuals with visual, physical or learning problems writing or keyboarding can pose difficulties. Speech recognition software may open up many possibilities for these students.

Alternative Output Devices

The standard computer usually has two primary forms of output: the screen monitor and the printer. Students with visual impairments may not be able to see the characters on the screen. Software is available that allows the letters and material on the screen to be enlarged for easier viewing. Larger monitors also may be used.

TABLE 10-1			

Summary of Input and Output Adaptations

Computer Function	Standard	Possible Adaptations	Disability Types
Input	Keyboard	Adapt the keyboard	Physical Disabilities
	Mouse	Alternative keyboard	Health Disabilities
	Trackball	TouchWindow	Visual Disabilities
	Joystick	Head controlled device	Deafblindness
		Switches	Learning Disabilities
		Voice recognition	
		Word prediction software	
Output	Printer	Braille embosser	Visual disabilities
	Monitor	Auditory output	Learning disabilities
		Enlarged print	

For students who can not see the monitor at all, the computer can be adapted to have auditory output through the use of a speech synthesizer. For software programs with speech capability, the speech synthesizer allows the computer to "talk." In some instances, specialized software (e.g., JAWS) is used that allows students to hear everything that is on the screen. Using these types of software, students can hear what is being typed as it is being typed, as well as have the full paragraph or document read. For students with hearing impairments, the volume is adjustable. Students with learning disabilities also may benefit from the use of speech synthesis. Directions for program use and help screens may be read aloud, making it easier for these students to operate programs independently. Students may listen to their own compositions, providing them with the opportunity to detect errors in word sequence and sometimes in spelling.

Printers also may be modified to meet the needs of students. Often large size fonts may be selected for students with visual impairments that result in the printing of larger letters. For students who read braille, a braille printer (also referred to as a braille embosser) can be used that prints the document in braille. Software is available that can convert the print displayed on the monitor into braille, and then print it. Another option is that some software converts the keyboard to the use of six keys, so students may type in the same manner as a braille writer. The input can be printed on a braille printer. The different input and output modifications are depicted in **Table 10-1.**

Selecting Software

There is a wide variety of software that may be used to support classroom instruction. Software can range from teaching phonics skills to Shakespeare; from identifying numerals to performing calculus. However, software programs vary not only in their content, but also in the instructional methods they use and the learning levels they target. They also have varying features and options to support a wide range of student needs. Teachers need to carefully evaluate the software they are considering to be sure it matches its intended purpose and is appropriate for their students.

When evaluating a software program to determine its suitability for a class or student, there are eight categories to consider. As seen in **Table 10-2,** these eight categories are:

1. content area,
2. developmental level,

TABLE 10-2

Evaluating Software

Categories	Example Subcategories
Content area	Numeral recognition, counting, letter-sound correspondence
Developmental level	Infant/toddler, preschool, kindergarten level
Learning level	Acquisition
	Proficiency
	Maintenance
	Generalization
	Application
Instructional Method	Discovery/Exploratory learning
	Tutorial
	Drill & Practice
	Educational Games
	Simulation
	Problem solving
Input Features	Consistency of requested input
	Appropriate motor & speed demands
	Accuracy demands (e.g., can backspace or erase input)
	Interfaces with alternate input (e.g., switch & scanning)
Presentation Features	Presented logically, accurately, with adequate repetition
	Academic demands (e.g., reading, spelling level)
	Free of stereotypes or bias
	Degree of interactivity
	Consistent presentation format and ease of use
	Presence of graphics, audio, video, animation
	Visual and/or auditory prompts and features
Presentation Options	Control presentation pace, difficulty level, lesson content
	Alternate presentation (e.g., high contrast, enlarge, scanning)
	Student, teacher or program driven starting point
Feedback to Answers	Type of feedback to correct answers (reinforces)
	Type of feedback to incorrect answers (consistency)
	Provides another opportunity when incorrect
	Provides assistance when incorrect
	Teacher controlled responses to wrong answers
	Provides reports of items issued

From Heller, K. W. (2004). Technology for Assessment and Intervention. In W. Umansky & S. R. Hooper (Eds.). *Young children with special needs (4th ed.)* Upper Saddle River, NJ: Merrill.

3. learning level,
4. instructional method,
5. input features,
6. presentation features,
7. presentation options, and
8. feedback to answers

(Bitter & Pierson, 1999; Lewis, 1993; Ray & Warden, 1995; Heller, 2004).

Content and Developmental Level

Content areas refer to the precise material being covered, whether addition or the periodic table. The content area can be presented on differing developmental levels, ranging from infant/toddler to adult. For example, some programs providing information on the periodic tables are designed for students in middle school, while others are on a high school level. It is important that the correct developmental level is selected for the student in order to avoid frustration with a program that is too advanced or too simplistic.

Learning Level

Another category to consider when evaluating software is the learning level. Learning levels are based on the stages of learning: acquisition, proficiency (or fluency), maintenance, generalization, and application (Mercer & Mercer, 2001). For example, when students are first learning a skill, such as simple addition facts, they are at the acquisition stage. Once students have achieved a high rate of accuracy and can respond quickly, they have achieved proficiency. In our addition example, this would occur when the student sees the simple addition fact and automatically says the correct answer. In the next stage, maintenance, the student retains the skill over time (e.g., the student remembers the basic addition facts a few months later). In the generalization stage, students can perform the skill with different materials, settings, people, or times. For example, a student who demonstrated proficiency on basic addition facts would demonstrate generalization if he could provide the correct answers to addition facts presented in a game. In the application stage, the student applies the skill in new situations or applications, such as using basic addition facts to determine how many cookies to buy groups of people.

Instructional Method

When evaluating software programs, it is important that the instructional method used in the program is appropriate to the student's learning level. Students at an acquisition stage should use discovery or tutorial software. Discovery software allows a student to explore the content and concepts while tutorial software gives guided instruction to teach students a new skill.

When targeting a proficiency level of learning in which speed is targeted in addition to accuracy, drill and practice software is usually selected. Drill and practice software provides students with additional practice on skills they have already learned. Often drill and practice software is presented in a game format in which a student must respond in a certain time frame to get a correct response (See **Figure 10-7**). For students who cannot respond quickly due to physical or sensory impairments, it will be important that the time for responding can be altered.

The type of software must also be considered across maintenance, generalization and application levels of learning. If the student does not retain the content being taught over time, tutorial software may again be used to reteach the skill. In the generalization stage, other software programs that present the skill using a different format may be used. In the application stage, problem solving type of software or simulation software may be selected (Blackhurst & Lahm, 2000). In problem-solving software, students are presented with problems that must be solved, drawing on higher-order thinking skills such as analysis, synthesis, and evaluation. In simulation software, the software simulates real-life situation in which the student must apply the skills learned in various situations (Ray & Warden, 1995).

FIGURE 10-7

Sample Drill and Practice Program

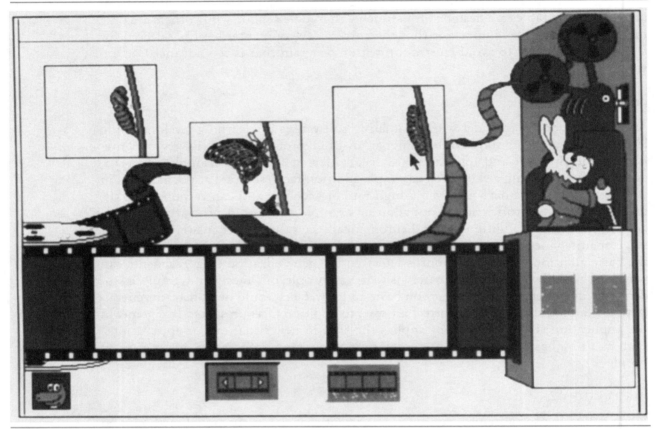

From Edmark Corporation (1995). *Sammy's science house* [Computer software]. Redmond, WA: Author.

Input Features

The method used by the student to input a response and the consistency of input should be evaluated. As seen in **Table 10-2,** input features include such areas as consistency of input and accuracy demands. Also, some students with disabilities will need alternate input in the form of a different type of keyboard, mouse, or a switch with scanning. A close examination of the software program will determine if the software will support these alternate input modalities.

Presentation Features and Options

There are many different presentation features and options that should be evaluated (See **Table 10-2**). The content should be presented in a logical manner with sufficient repetition. The academic demands (e.g., reading level) should match the student's ability. The program should have the desired degree of interactivity (e.g., few choices and predetermined order; wide variety of choices that give the student control over the order, text, sounds, graphics and content (Hutinger & Johanson, 1998.) The teacher also should evaluate the consistency of the format and the appropriateness of the graphics and audio, as well as visual and prompting features of the program.

It is often important to control the presentation pace, difficulty level, starting point in the program, and content of the lessons. Some programs will provide the teacher with the option of controlling these aspects of the presentation. In addition, it is important to determine if the presentation can be modified (e.g., high contrast) to accommodate the needs of students with specific disabilities.

Feedback to Answers

The manner in which the software program provides student feedback is critical to the software program's success. Ideally, the program should provide reinforcing feedback for correct answers. The type of feedback to incorrect answers should not be embarrassing (e.g., has auditory feedback for all to hear or make derogatory remarks). It may be desirable to have the program provide additional opportunities or guided assistance to incorrect answers. Programs that allow the teacher control over the type of feedback provided to incorrect answers offer the most flexibility and allow the teacher to tailor it to the needs of the students.

Once the software is evaluated, its feasibility to support class or student instruction can be determined. If the software meets the necessary criteria to support student learning, the software has the potential to support teacher instruction across a wide variety of academic areas (as discussed below). However, the software can be a waste of time if it does not have the proper features to meet the students' needs.

Technology for Reading

Many students have difficulties in the area of reading, whether they have a disability or not. From students who have trouble following a line of print to students who have difficulty accessing materials because of physical or sensory disabilities, technologies exist to aide these students in improving their reading abilities. Often, simple, teacher-made materials can make a large difference in a student's success. On the other hand, higher technologies may be required for students whose needs are greater.

Non-electronic Assistive Technology Options for Reading

Some students have difficulty following a line of print for cognitive, visual, or physical reasons. Reading materials for emerging readers often have larger print and fewer words to help these readers visually follow a line of print (called tracking). Once a reader's ability increases, materials typically have smaller print and an increased number of lines of print on a page. Students who have difficulty tracking may end up skipping lines or re-reading lines. This can interfere greatly with comprehension.

One strategy that can help students with trouble tracking is the use of reading guides. Reading guides are placed on the book on, under, or above the line of text that the student is reading to help stay on the line of print. Reading guides can help reduce distraction and clutter from other lines of print. Reading guides can be as simple as an index card, a ruler, or piece of construction paper. One reading guide that can be purchased commercially is The Heads Up! Reader (manufactured by HeadsUp!) This is a thin plastic sheet about the size of a 6-inch ruler that has a colored window in the middle through which a line of print is viewed. Another option for reducing the amount of text on a page presented at one time is a typoscope. The typoscope is a rectangular piece of cardboard through which a rectangular hole has been cut. The student moves the typoscope as he reads to expose one or two words at a time.

Instructional Technology for Specific Reading Skill Instruction

Numerous types of instructional software have been created to help students with reading skills. One example of a software program that provides instruction on several early reading skills is Reader Rabbit (published by the Learning Company). In *Reader Rabbit Learns to Read with Phonics,* the adult can control and track student performance in such pre-reading activities such as teaching letters, letter patterns, blending sounds, early spelling, vocabulary, sounding-out, word recognition, and word families. Reader Rabbit's graphics help engage children through interactive games and activities. Another program that is more appropriate for older students who are still working on pre-reading skills is Simon Sounds It Out (by Don Johnston, Inc.). Simon Sounds It Out offers tutorials on beginning sounds, word families, word building, spelling and word reading. There are 31 levels that automatically advance with the learner so students get an individualized lesson based on specific needs. The program tracks student progress and offers printable worksheets for further skill development. Many other software programs are available to address specific reading skills. In some instances, entire reading programs are available in software format (e.g., Attainment Company's Functional Literacy CD Series, Balanced Literacy by IntelliTools which is accessible using Intellikeys keyboard or computer switch). The teacher must carefully evaluate the software to be sure it meets the students' needs.

Text-to-Speech Technology for Reading

Text-to-speech is another type of technology that may help students learn words, master fluency, and/or concentrate on comprehension. Text-to-speech technology refers to providing speech (voice output) of the written text. A simple version of this is providing a book on tape that allows the students to read the book while listening to the text on a traditional tape player. A more advanced piece of technology aimed at helping students read words they are having difficulty with is the Quicktionary Reading Pen II (from Wiz-Com Technologies, Inc). This device is a little larger than a traditional pen and when the pen is passed over a word, the word is read aloud. The pen can also read syllables, spell words, provide definitions, and translate words for other languages.

Another type of text-to-speech technology is electronic books. Most software programs that present books on the computer screen also have the option of having the text read aloud, often while highlighting the words being said. These programs come in many forms ranging from preschool interest to high school interest levels. For example in the program, *Just Grandma and Me,* the young child can have the print read aloud as well as point to different items of the screen for actions to occur (See **Figure 10-8**). Other electronic books may have more print and provide more reading options (See **Figure 10-9**) while others may be in a format with graphics more appealing to older students.

Electronic books can be aimed at young or older students. One example for young children is the series of Living Books by The Learning Company. There is a wide selection of popular children's books available from Living Books. These books have interactive features for discovery learning. Word recognition is accomplished by the text being read with words highlighted. Living Books also offer built in activities for vocabulary development and reading comprehension. One example of electronic books for older children is Start-to-Finish books (a product of Don Johnston, Inc.). These take high-interest classic literature (e.g., *Red Badge of Courage*) and present it at a lower reading level with controlled vocabulary. Start-to-Finish books provide the student with the opportunity to hear the entire page with highlighting or to choose particular words or phrases to hear aloud.

FIGURE 10-8

Sample Screen from Electronic Book

From Broderbund (1994a). *Just grandma and me* [Computer software]. Novato, CA: Author.

Teachers can use options to control different levels of support for the student. Start-to-Finish books also offer comprehension exercises by means of graded computer quizzes, cloze reading passages, and paper quizzes. Accumulated student reports and time-on-task statistics also are available.

Another text-to-speech reading option is screen reading programs that use optical character recognition. These software programs allow books to be scanned into the computer and then provide reading support. One program that allows text to be scanned in and then read aloud is Kurzweil 3000. This sophisticated program not only reads the text, but also can highlight it and provide many options to promote study skills. Some features of Kurzweil 3000 include different settings (e.g., speed text is read, type of voice, reading a line, sentence, or paragraph at one time), onscreen text and pictures as they appear in their original form, highlighting of words and lines as it reads, ability of the user to highlight or underline text for studying, and the ability to put electronic notes by important material in the text. A less sophisticated screen reader is Read & Write (manufactured by textHELP! Systems). Read & Write highlights words as they are spoken from text within any Windows application including e-mail, web pages, and documents with

FIGURE 10-9

Sample Story Page from Little Planet Literacy Series, Ribbit Collection

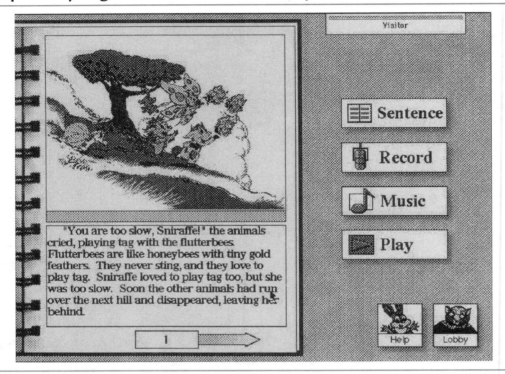

numbers. Read Please (manufactured by Read Please Corporation) is a windows-based text-to-speech program that will read any text that is copied and pasted into it. The basic version is available free, but other versions are available for a cost that offer more features.

Reading with Symbol Support

For some students, neither phonological, whole word strategies, nor audible text reading software are sufficient to foster beginning reading. Symbol support may assist these students in learning how to read or may be used to give access to reading for students who might not otherwise gain reading experience. One example of symbol software is Writing With Symbols 2000 (WWS2000). WWS2000 (by Mayer-Johnson, Inc.) is a symbol based word processing program that places a symbol above common words as they are typed. Using this program, teachers can modify reading materials by replacing the text in books with text and symbols that have been typed into WWS2000. Another way WWS2000 can foster independent reading is by students writing or dictating their own sentences or stories which they can read later with the help of symbols.

Technology for Writing

A variety of technology solutions exist for students who are having difficulty writing or who have specific disabilities that are interfering with writing. Writing can be broken down two distinct categories: using writing tools (e.g., handwriting using a writing utensil and word processing using a computer) and the development of a written product.

Using Writing Tools

Often, at-risk students and students with disabilities have accompanying fine motor difficulties that impede legible writing. Processing difficulties can make handwriting inefficient for other students. Individuals with physical disabilities often have gross and fine motor problems, contractures, spasticity, decreased muscle strength and control, or limb deficiencies that make handwriting an unavailable option for them. Handwriting for students with learning and physical disabilities can be a laborious process because they write slowly, have trouble forming letters, and often end up with messy and illegible products.

Fortunately, technology solutions exist for handwriting, ranging from low tech to high tech. Solutions as simple as using larger writing instruments or pens or pencils that have been built up with grips can assist with handwriting. Different types of writing instruments, such as felt-tip pens or magic markers can provide more resistance on the paper and therefore more feedback for some students. Pens with dark ink can provide stark contrast on paper and make the product stand out. Sometimes, simply holding the writing instrument differently is an acceptable solution. If these solutions do not work, however, students can use different body parts to hold the writing instrument. Students can use their toes or can use a mouthstick that holds the writing instrument and allows them to control writing using their mouth. Using paper with darker lines or raised lines can eliminate problems by defining the writing area more clearly. Slantboards, which provide an adjustable angled surface on which to write, are another common solution to handwriting difficulties. Often, modifying the angle of the paper will provide better access by providing a more upright visual view of the paper, as well as changing the wrist position and angle of the writing instrument.

There are several software programs designed to promote handwriting. For example, School Fonts (available through Mayer-Johnson) is a program designed to provide structured handwriting practice. The teacher can construct printable worksheets and study books, and a number of different fonts, text sizes, and colors are available. Example activities using School Fonts include using spelling words or writing stories for the students to trace over.

For students who have difficulty spelling while writing by hand, Franklin Electronic Publishers offers a number of portable products that can assist students in producing correct written work. Some spellers and dictionaries allow students to type an approximation of the word into the devise. A list of correctly spelled options will then be displayed on the screen. In addition to displaying the correct spelling, some devices will provide students with a definition. For students who cannot recognize the word by sight, some devices have auditory output and will speak both the word and the definition.

If handwriting is not feasible, software programs such as PaperPort Deluxe (manufactured by ScanSoft) can eliminate the need for handwriting. PaperPort allows the user to scan worksheets into the computer. Once the worksheet is scanned, the user can then type directly on the worksheet and print a completed copy to hand in. This allows the student to use the computer instead of having to write.

Word Processors

One option to assist with the production of written work is using a word processor. Features of word processing that can be helpful for students with and without disabilities include keyboard shortcuts, spelling and grammar check, and formatting tools that can help produce a correct and quality product. Word processors can also be used to help guide writing as well as a motivator. **Figure 10-10** provides some suggestions for using word processing with students at risk or who have disabilities.

FIGURE 10-10

Using Word Processing with Students with Mild Disabilities

Suggestions for Using Word Processing with Students with Mild Disabilities

The following is just a brief collection of ideas for how you can use the word processor as an instructional tool for students. Don't limit yourself by the ideas in this list. Use your imagination, and you will think of hundreds of ways the word processor can be a benefit to your students.

Free Writing

This first step in many writing process approaches can be enhanced by the use of a word processor. In freewriting, students are to write quickly, putting down whatever comes to mind. Using a word processor frees the student from the often difficult task of using a pencil and paper. Freewriting can be used to help students get their ideas written without concern about how the text looks on paper. A variation of freewriting is invisible writing. In invisible writing, the monitor is turned off, so the student cannot see what is written. The student is forced to concentrate only on ideas without concern for editing. Both freewriting and invisible writing are best used when students are already comfortable with the keyboard. One alternative is to have the student speak his or her ideas while the teacher or another competent typist enters them into the computer.

Prompted Writing

Teachers can use on-screen questions to prompt their students through the writing process. Students can write a sentence in response to each of the prompts. The prompts can be deleted later to leave only the student's responses in the form of a paragraph.

Add-On Stories

In an add-on story, either the teacher or a student begins a story in a new word processing file. Either a sentence or a brief paragraph can be written. Students take turns reading the previously written parts of the story and adding their own sentence or paragraph. When everyone has added a part, the entire story can be printed out and duplicated for the class. This is an excellent collaborative writing activity for students who may have difficulty completing an entire story on their own.

Journals

The daily journal is one method many teachers use to encourage their students to write. Unfortunately, for many students the act of writing with a pencil is difficult and time consuming. Using a word processing program can eliminate this frustration. Each student could be allowed 5 to 10 minutes per day to type in a journal. The journal entries could be printed and saved in a notebook, so the student can look back and reflect on his previous writings.

Reports and Projects

The word processor can be used to encourage your students to "write across the curriculum." As assignments for reports and projects are made, students can use the word processor to write their initial drafts. These can be submitted to the teacher for feedback. Revisions can be made easily on the computer, and another draft can be printed. The process of writing is supported by the ease with which revisions can be made. When final drafts are completed, students can "publish" their work in a book of class projects. They also can include the work in their writing portfolios.

Class Newspapers

Each student in the classroom can be assigned a story to write for a classroom newsletter. When the student has completed a draft of the story, another student can be assigned to read and edit it. When all of the stories have been edited, they can be copied into a new word processing document that is formatted to print in columns. The newspaper can be printed, duplicated, and distributed to parents, friends, and other teachers and students in the school.

There are several specialized word processing programs that may assist students in writing. One example is using a word processor that has auditory feedback to help students check what they have written for comprehension and flow. Write:OutLoud (manufactured by Don Johnston) is a talking word processor that will speak letters, words, sentences, and paragraphs as the student types. In addition to speaking text, Write:OutLoud has an auditory spell check that reads the word choices. It also will highlight word by word as it reads so the student can edit the work as the computer reads it back. As discussed under the section, Computer Adaptations, several alternate input and output devices may be used in conjunction with a word processing program to make using the computer accessible to students with a wide range of disabilities.

Word Prediction

Another technology solution that works along with word processing to improve written production is word prediction software. Programs such as Co:Writer (manufactured by Don Johnston) and Read & Write (manufactured by text HELP) can provide word prediction, grammar, and vocabulary support to students using the computer. When using Co:Writer, the student types in a window separate from the word processor. As the student types, Co:Writer begins predicting the word the student is trying to type and provides a list from which the correct word can be selected. The user can select the correct word by either clicking on it with the mouse or by typing the number of the corresponding word. If the correct word is not in the list, the user continues to type and the list of predicted words changes accordingly. When the user types a period or presses enter, the sentence is transferred from Co:Writer to the word processor. Co:Writer also makes provisions for phonetic spellers. As the student begins typing a word, Co:Writer predicts words consistent with the sounds of the letters. Word prediction can make typing much more efficient for individuals who are slow typists because it reduces the number of keystrokes the user has to make and provides a list of correctly spelled words from which to choose. The benefit of fewer keystrokes is the reduction of fatigue.

Speech Recognition

Speech recognition software allows students to type using their voice instead of their hands. Speech recognition software works by way of the student speaking into a microphone. As the student speaks, the software types the words onto the screen. In order to use speech recognition software, students must train the computer to recognize their voice. It is a good option for students for whom typing is slow or tiring, if motor problems or stress injuries are present, or if spelling and grammar impedes production of written work. An example of speech recognition software is Dragon NaturallySpeaking (manufactured by ScanSoft).

Development of a Written Product

Many at-risk students and students with disabilities have difficulty producing written work. A number of factors are involved in the writing process. The first step of writing is organizing thoughts and often students have difficulty with organization. Another common problem is just getting words onto paper, especially when the student is focusing on the mechanics of writing. Focusing on spelling, capitalization, punctuation, and formatting can often distract writers from communicating their message. If a student has to stop and figure out how to spell a word, the train of thought is lost.

When organizing a paper, computer-based programs can assist with the organizational process. Three examples of organizational software are Inspiration (manufactured by Inspiration Software, Inc.), Kidspiration (manufactured by Inspiration Software, Inc.) and Draft:Builder (manufactured by Don Johnston). Inspiration and Kidspiration can help writers plan out their thoughts before writing. These programs help students make diagrams and visually display relationships between thoughts and concepts. Different graphic organizer structures include concept maps, webs, and outlines. Students can type in the main topic and then associated sub-topics using text or pictures. Inspiration and Kidspiration also can be useful instructional tools for teachers. By creating diagrams, teachers can gain insight into students' prior knowledge about topics and help visually display connections between concepts

Draft:Builder is another program that helps students with organizing and constructing papers. First, it guides students through the organization of their thoughts. The student can enter topics and subtopics into an outline. While students are constructing the outline, the program simultaneously puts the outline information into a graphic format similar to a flow chart. Next, it allows students to make notes about the subtopics. For example, if writing about food groups, the student can assign a note under the dairy products category that dairy products are a good source of calcium. Finally, it allows the student to construct a paper using the outline and notes. Here, notes can be dragged into the area assigned for creating a rough draft of the paper. The paper can then be exported to a word processing program. Additionally, a variety of templates are available, ranging from book reports to 5-paragraph papers to persuasive essays. These templates provide a detailed framework for development of different types of writing. The programs discussed are only examples of software that provides structure and organization in writing. A number of other options are available.

Technology for Math

Many students have difficulty mastering mathematical concepts and skills. There are technology options available to address certain math skills ranging from electronic worksheets to software. Additional math devices are available to support various math objectives without the need to use a computer. The complexity of the math software or devices may range from teaching counting to high school calculus.

Electronic Math Worksheets

Students with fine motor deficits or those who need assistance in completing worksheets may benefit from electronic math worksheets. Electronic math worksheets, such as MathPad (by Intellitools, Inc.) provide an array of computational problems that can be easily answered on the computer. Advantages of this program is that it places the problems in a grid which helps line up place digits and navigate through multiple digit problems. Also, carrying number or borrowing can occur with prompting or by a click of a button. Font size and color are adjustable and auditory feedback can be used to let students check to see if their work is correct. Students can enter answers on the keyboard or by using the onscreen number pad. The program comes with sample problems or problems can be entered by teachers. MathPad Plus: Fractions and Decimals also allows students to perform onscreen math computations; however, this program includes features such as fraction bars, pie charts and decimal grids to allow students onscreen manipulatives for these concepts. Both MathPad programs can be customized for multiple students and allow for printing of student work. Other electronic worksheet programs are available and will require careful evaluation by the teacher.

Math Software

There is a multitude of math software that may be used to supplement math instruction in the classroom. For example, Basic Picture Math Software (available from PCI Educational Publishing) is designed to supplement any introductory math curriculum for students who have not mastered reading skills. Students using Basic Picture Math Software learn basic concepts through units in number recognition, counting, ordinal numbers, comparing amounts and patterns with recognizable onscreen displays and auditory verbal directions. Unit and final assessments are included in the program.

Students learning basic math operations may benefit from software that includes equations with visual representations of the equations. One example of this is Show Me Math (by Attainment). Show Me Math presents math questions which users answer via keyboard or by pressing onscreen numbers. Students who are struggling with the problem can choose the "Show Me!" option. The program then will provide a brief animated movie to demonstrate the equation. For example, three sheep walk onscreen to join two sheep for a total of five.

Some students may benefit from programs that include strategies for problem solving as well as multiple opportunities to practice. One example of this type of software is Destination Math (produced by Riverdeep Interactive Learning Limited). This is a comprehensive curriculum with separately available levels ranging from Pre-Primary Mathematics to Algebra. Destination Math offers teacher options for assessing student needs and tailoring the program around students' ability levels. Students participate in guided tutorials and receive step-by-step strategies for problem solving. The program is designed to manage student learning without moving on to higher levels until students have sufficient opportunities to practice skills. Practice "workouts" and real-life practice examples are provided to help students learn how to apply skills.

Some students learn mathematical operations but have difficulty generalizing these skills beyond worksheets. Software which provides various exemplars of skill application may help students learn that math skills can apply to actual life events. Sunburst Technology has a series of math software programs focusing on real-world applications of math skills. Hot Dog Stand—Top Dog is designed for younger children. Students practice math skills by simulated management of a concession stand. A few examples of the other Sunburst Technology real-world software titles are Ice Cream Truck (grades 2–6), Math Arena (grades 4–7), and My Mathematical Life (grades 6–10). Different levels of activities allow teachers to help meet individual students' skill needs. Other programs combine history and math application, such as the Oregon Trail.

Technological Devices for Math

There are several different technological devices that may be used to promote math skills. The most common are calculators. Calculators are available to help students with completing math operations as well as to prepare them for higher math functions and real-world math applications. Calculators come in many different shapes and sizes and with many different features. Most calculators are age-appropriate for older students and adults since they are used frequently by people without disabilities in an array of environments. Some students may be able to use inexpensive calculators that can be purchased in almost any store. For other students, more specialized calculators may prove beneficial. One version of a calculator that may help students who have difficulty reading numbers because of learning or visual disabilities is a talking calculator. There are various types of talking calculators. The Talking Desktop Calculator has basic operations and percentage keys. For more advanced students, the Talking Texas Instruments Scientific Calculator (by Texas Instruments) is complete with all of the same scientific functions as its non-talking counterpart. Larger calculators are available in many discount department stores (as well as from educational suppliers) and may prove useful for students with limited fine motor or visual abilities. Talking and large sized calculators can be adapted with tactile stimuli (glued on textures or Braille) for students who require these modifications.

Several small electronic devices are available to assist students in learning money skills. One such device is the Coin Abacus (produced by PCI Educational Publishing). This is a hand-held device with a row for each of the following: one-dollar bills, quarters, dimes, nickels, and pennies. Students slide the money representations from the left to right. The total amount of bills and coins on the right side is displayed on a LCD screen. Students change the displayed amount by adding and removing bills and coins. This device also features sounds, voice prompts, verbal rewards, and two different game options. Another electronic device made by PCI Educational Publishing that aids in money skill acquisition is the Coin-u-lator. The Coin-u-lator has buttons that represent a one-dollar bill and each type of coin in addition to a few function buttons. When students press a money button, the corresponding money value is displayed in the LCD screen. Students can add or subtract with the Coin-u-lator and can choose from coin counting or two different game activities. The Money Calc (another device by PCI) combines traditional calculator features with money buttons representing coins, and $1, $5, $10, and $20 bills. The Money Calc can display the dollar mark and represent numbers in money format with ending zeros displayed. This feature is helpful for students who are confused by the traditional calculator not displaying ending zeros (for example 3.50 becomes 3.5). Money Calc helps students learn to compute "change back" and has function buttons to automatically calculate tax or tip based on user-programmed percentages. Money Calc also can be used in traditional mode where it functions like a regular calculator.

Technology for Notetaking

Some students will have difficulty taking notes in class due to learning, sensory, or physical impairments. One simple solution for notetaking is the use of NCR Paper (This is paper that comes with 2 or more sheets connected and whatever is written on the top page is transferred to the bottom page). Teachers or other students can take notes and tear off the second page, providing a copy for the student who needs it. Another easy solution is the use of tape recorders. Taping lectures allows students to review the lecture at home and multiple times if necessary. Higher tech solutions for notetaking are the AlphaSmart and Dana (manufactured by AlphaSmart, Inc.) The AlphaSmart is a lightweight, portable keyboard that has word processing capabilities as well as spell check. The Dana is a lightweight alternative to a laptop computer and features a built-in Palm OS™ system. The user can hook the AlphaSmart and Dana up to a computer to transfer and print files.

Other notetaking options use specialized electronic whiteboards or software that sends what the teacher is writing on a board directly to the student's computer. A Smart-Board (manufactured by Smart Technologies, Inc.) is one example of this type of technology. It looks like a standard whiteboard, but has electronics and software to allow the figures and handwriting to be sent to the student's computer or uploaded to the internet for access from home computers. A similar device is the Mimio (manufactured by Mimio, Inc.) that attaches to the base of a white board or flip chart and sends all written information from the board or chart to the student's computer. There is an additional software program that can change the handwriting that is drawn on the white board to a standard computer font on the computer.

Technology Use for Teachers

In addition to the many ways that technology may be used with students with special needs, there are many ways that teachers can use technology every day in their classrooms. Several suggestions for teachers are provided on the following page.

Reducing Paperwork

A common problem for teachers is the amount of paperwork that teaching requires. Word processors and desktop publishing programs can be powerful time savers for teachers. Some ways that teachers can use word processing programs include class rosters, seating charts, letters to parents, test templates, classroom rules, newletters, and creating materials for students (e.g., study guides, worksheets). Remember that all of the typing needn't be done by teachers—parent volunteers often are happy to help.

Managing Information

Information management is a second way that computers can assist teachers and save time. Student information is managed easily using a database program, and grades can be maintained and averaged using a spreadsheet program. Programs are available that assist in the development and tracking of Individualized Educational Programs (IEPs) for students with special needs. Most of these programs offer a bank of instructional objectives from which teachers may choose; most programs also allow teachers to enter their own original objectives.

Assessment

Programs such as *Monitoring Basic Skills Progress: Reading, Math, Spelling* from Pro-Ed (Fuchs, Hamlett, & Fuchs, 1990) allow teachers to manage curriculum-based assessment data and make decisions regarding students' progress toward curricular goals. *The Grady Profile* from Aurbach and Associates (1995) allows teachers to scan student-produced text and graphics into computer files, making an electronic portfolio that can be saved to a disk (See **Figure 10-11**). Many test construction programs are available that allow teachers to enter questions into banks then select the questions that will appear on a test and print them out.

Many norm-referenced tests that are commonly used in special education have computerized scoring programs. For tests that are difficult and time-consuming to score (e.g., Woodcock Reading Mastery Tests-Revised, Vineland Adaptive Behaviors Scales), these programs can quickly and accurately generate standard and grade level scores from raw scores and present summaries of performance.

Database and Spreadsheet Programs

Database and spreadsheet programs allow students and teachers to manage both textual and numeric information. A database program allows teachers to manage textual information. These programs are similar to file cabinets with folders; however, they are electronic. Teachers may use a database to keep students' records. Information about students such as address, phone number, parents' names, and birthdate would be entered into the database program. At the beginning of each month, teachers can search the database for all students whose birthdays fall in that month. Each month, the birthdays can be placed on the Birthday Bulletin Board in the classroom. Students can use database programs to keep track of information for research projects, such as facts about different mammals.

FIGURE 10-11

Sample Screen from Grady Profile

Student Stack

Name: Demo-Student, Ann

Student ID: 123-45-6789   Class: 95

Sex: ○ Male ● Female   Ethnic: ☐ Caucasian

Birthdate: 5/16/81   ☐ Afro-Amer

Enrolled: 9/4/85   ☐ Hispanic

Exit date: ___   ☐ SpEd   ☒ Asian

Other: ___   ☐ Amer-Ind

Year: 93-94 Grade: 7   ☐ Other

Teacher: Miss Nelson   Scholastic History

Action	Add History	Gd.	Yr.
1st Place in Science Fair		4	91
Surreal painting - statewide exhibit		7	1993

Attendance: 0   days missed
as of 4/25/95

Reset Passwords

Student Information ▼   Show Notes

From Aurback & Associates. (1995). *Grady profile: Portfolio assessment* [Computer software]. St. Louis, MO: Author.

Spreadsheet programs allow teachers and students to manage and manipulate numeric information or data. Teachers can use a spreadsheet to calculate grades in each of their classes or to track expenses, such as for class field trips and for instructional supplies. Students can use spreadsheet programs to simulate real-life experiences such as preparing a household budget.

Making Classroom Materials

One of the most common programs found in classrooms is *The Print Shop* from Broderbund. *The Print Shop* allows teachers and students to make signs, posters, banners, greeting cards, and letterhead that incorporate both text and graphics. There are a number of calendar programs available for designing personalized classroom calendars. In addition, programs and online resources are available to design word puzzles and math fact drill sheets. Many teachers also make classroom worksheets using their word processing and desktop publishing programs.

Multimedia Presentation Tools

Multimedia presentation tools such as *Adobe Persuasion* and *Microsoft PowerPoint* allow teachers to design computer-presented lecture material. Using a computer, an overhead projector, and a computer display system, teachers can present text and graphics material to all students in the classroom at once. Full-motion video now can be saved to computer files and presented via these systems. Tools such as PowerPoint are being used by many students for instruction or for creating their own presentations for reports and projects. Interactive videodisc players may be connected to the computer system as well.

Summary

Adaptations to the classroom environment and the appropriate use of technology are two ways of improving the education of students with disabilities and those at-risk in the general education classroom. General education teachers and special education teachers must work together collaboratively to provide classroom arrangements and modifications that are conducive to the learning of all students, including those with disabilities. For many students, technology can overcome barriers to learning that are a result of learning, behavioral, sensory, or physical disabilities. With the appropriate selection of computer hardware and software, many of these students can participate successfully in the general education classroom.

Discussion Questions and Activities

1. What type of assistive technology would be easy to incorporate into the general education setting, and what type of assistive technology would be difficult? Explain why.

2. What resources are available to assist with questions, problems, or training regarding assistive technology? What is the general educator's role?

3. What types of modifications might be needed to arrange a classroom for a student with a severe physical disability who uses a wheelchair?

4. Invite a physical therapist, occupational therapist, speech-language pathologist, and teacher of students with physical disabilities into class to discuss their roles in assistive technology.

5. Observe a classroom where assistive technology is used with one or more students. What types of disabilities do(es) the student(s) have? What types of technology are in use? What are the responsibilities of the general education teacher with respect to the technology?

6. Observe a classroom where educational software is used with students with disabilities. What types of programs are used most often (tutorial, drill and practice, game, etc.)? Do students require any adaptations or special instructions to use the software?

7. John is a 12-year-old student who is entering seventh grade. He is a delightful student who is very courteous, does well in school, and enjoys being with his friends. John has a physical and visual impairment. He uses a walker to move around, but needs assistance sitting in his chair and getting up from his chair. He also has very poor fine motor skills and has used a computer for his school work since second grade. He requires an alternative keyboard which has a larger target for optimum typing accuracy. He still types rather slowly since he is unable to isolate his finger movement and must type using his right index finger. Due to his visual impairment, he needs his books close to his face and can not clearly see the blackboard from far away. He receives services from the teacher certified in orthopedic impairments and the teacher certified in visual impairments. He also receives services from the physical therapist and occupational therapist.

a) As the general education teacher, who will provide you assistance in determining the adaptations John will need in your class?

b) What are some of the questions you will have regarding room arrangement and material modification?

c) Whose responsibility do you think it is to modify materials for John to use in your class and how will this be done?

Internet Resources

Able Data
www.abledata.com

Accessible Educational Technology: RESNA Technical Assistance Project
www.resna.org/taproject/index.htm

Assistive Technology Strategies, Tools, Accommodations, and Resources (ATSTAR)
www.atstar.org

Closing the Gap
www.closingthegap.com/

Don Johnston, Corp.
www.donjohnston.com/

Mayer-Johnson Co.
www.mayerjohnson.com

The Alliance for Technology Access
www.ataccess.org

References

Adaptive Peripherals. *Co:Writer 4000* [Computer Software]. Volo, IL: Author.

Applied Learning Technologies. (1995). *Little Planet Literacy Series: Ribbit Collection* [Computer software]. Nashville, TN: Author.

Attainment Company (2004). *Functional Literacy CD Series* [Computer software] Verona, WI: Author.

Attainment Company (2005). *Show Me Math* [Computer software] Verona, WI: Author.

Aurbach & Associates. (1995). *Grady profile: Portfolio assessment* [Computer software]. St. Louis, MO: Author.

Best, S. J., Heller, K. W., & Bigge, J. L. (2005). *Teaching individuals with physical or multiple disabilities* (5th ed.). Upper Saddle River, NJ: Pearson/Merrill Prentice Hall.

Beukelman, D. R., & Mirenda, P. (1998). *Augmentative and alternative communication: Management of severe communication disorders in children and adults* (2nd ed.). Baltimore: Paul H. Brookes.

Bitter, G. C., & Pierson, M. E. (1999). *Using technology in the classroom.* Boston: Allyn and Bacon.

Blackhurst, A. E., & Lahm, E. A. (2000). Technology and exceptionality foundations. In J. D. Lindsey (Ed.), *Technology & exceptional individuals* (3rd ed., pp. 3–45). Austin, TX: Pro-Ed.

Broderbund. (1994a). *Just grandma and me* [Computer software]. Novato, CA: Author.

Broderbund. (1994b). *Where in the world is Carmen Sandiego?* (Junior Detective Edition) [Computer software]. Novato, CA: Author.

Broderbund. *The print shop* [Computer software]. Novato, CA: Encore Software.

Burkhart, L. J. (1985). *More homemade battery devices for severely handicapped children with suggested activities.* College Park, MD: Author.

Edmark Corporation. (1995). *Imagination Express: Destination Neighborhood* [Computer software]. Redmond, WA: Author.

Edmark Corporation. (1995). *Sammy's science house* [Computer software]. Redmond, WA: Author.

Fuchs, L. S., Hamlett, C. L., & Fuchs, D. (1990). *Monitoring basic skills progress.* Austin, TX: Pro-Ed.

Gearheart, B. R., Weishahn, M. W., & Gearheart, C. J. (1996). *The exceptional student in the regular classroom* (6th ed.). Englewood Cliffs, NJ: Merrill.

Haugen J. & Hernandez (2001). *Basic Picture Math Software.* San Antonio, TX: PCI Educational Publishing.

Heller, K. W. (2004). Technology for Assessment and Intervention. In W. Umansky & S. R. Hooper (Eds.). *Young children with special needs* (4th ed.). Upper Saddle River, NJ: Merrill Prentice Hall.

Hutinger, P. L., & Johanson, J. (2000). Implementing and maintaining an effective early childhood comprehensive technology system. *Topics in Early Childhood Special Education, 20* (3) 159–173.

IntelliTools, Inc. (1998). *MathPad* [Computer software] Petaluma, CA: IntelliTools.

IntelliTools, Inc. (2001). *Balanced Literacy* [Computer software] Petaluma, CA: Author.

Inspiration Software, Inc. (2005). *Inspiration* Version 7.6 [Computer Software]. Portland, OR: Author.

Inspiration Software, Inc. (2005). *Kidspiration* Version 2.1 [Computer Software]. Portland, OR: Author.

Johnston, D. (1999). *Write:OutLoud* [Computer Software]. Volo, IL: Author.

Johnston, D. (2002a). *Simon Sounds It Out* [Computer Software]. Volo, IL: Author.

Johnston, D. (2002b). *Draft:Builder.* [Computer Software]. Volo, IL: Author.

Johnston, D. (no date). *Start-to-Finish books* [Computer Software]. Volo, IL: Author.

Kurzweil Educational Systems. (2002). *Kurzweil 3000* [Computer software]. Bedford, MA: Author.

Learning Company. (1991). *The writing center* [Computer software]. Fremont, CA: Author.

Learning Company. (1998). *Reader Rabbit* [Computer software]. Novato, CA: Author.

MECC (1993). *The Oregon trail* [Computer software]. Minneapolis, MN: Author.

Mercer, C. D., & Mercer, A. R. (2001). *Teaching students with learning problems* (6th ed.). Upper Saddle River, NJ: Merrill Prentice Hall.

Microsoft. (1997). *PowerPoint* [Computer software]. Redmond, WA: Author.

Musselwhite, C. R., & St. Louis, K. W. (1988). *Communication programming for persons with severe handicaps.* Boston: College-Hill.

Ray, J., & Warden, M. K. (1995). *Technology, computers and the special needs learner.* Albany, NY: Delmar.

Riverdeep Interactive (2002). *Destination Math—Mastering Skills Concepts:* Course I–V [Computer Software]. Novato, CA: Author.

Rocklage, L. A., Preschong, L., Gillett, A. L., & Delohery, B. J. (1996). *Good junk + creativity = great low-end technology!* (Available from L. A. Rocklage, P.O. Box 971022, Ypsilanti, MI, 48197).

Rozmiarek, D. (1998). *Speech recognition software* [On-line]. Available: www.ldonline.org/ld_indepth/technology/speech_recog.html

ScanSoft, Inc. (2000). *Dragon Naturally Speaking* [Computer Software]. Peabody, MA: Author.

ScanSoft, Inc. (2000). *PaperPort Deluxe* [Computer software] Peabody, MA: Author

Smith, S., Boone, R., & Higgins, K. (1998). Expanding the writing process to the web. *Teaching Exceptional Children, 30*(5), 22–26.

Voss, K. (1997). *School Fonts* [Computer software] Solana Beach, CA: Mayer-Johnson.

Widgit Software, Ltd. (2001). *WWS2000* [Computer software] Solana Beach, CA: Mayer-Johnson.

Windows Freedom Scientific, Inc (2002). *JAWS* [Computer software] Palo Alto, CA: Author.

WINGS for Learning. (1992). *The factory* [Computer software]. Scotts Valley, CA: Author.

11

Managing Behavior for Effective Learning

L. Juane Heflin and Kristine Jolivette

Chapter Objectives

- to discuss the influence of teachers' perspectives and students' perspectives on classroom behavior;
- to identify basic classroom components that affect whether students behave appropriately or inappropriately, including the use of a comprehensive instructional approach for addressing inappropriate behavior;
- to describe a variety of evidence-based strategies that teachers can use to effectively manage behavior so all students can learn; and
- to provide information on systematically analyzing chronic problem behavior that is not responsive to general strategies by conducting a Functional Behavior Assessment (FBA) that will lead to the development of a behavior intervention plan (BIP).

Most individuals who enter the teaching profession imagine themselves dispensing knowledge and information to groups of students who are paying attention and complying with instructions out of respect for the adult who obviously knows much more than they do. Although this will be true of some students, other students will use their behavior to communicate reluctance to be in the classroom and refuse to comply with teacher directives. About one-third of teachers leave the profession within their first five years of employment (Darling-Hammond, 2003) and the behavioral climate of the school has been strongly linked to teachers quitting their jobs (Kelly, 2004) with student misbehavior cited as having a negative effect on teacher satisfaction (National Center for Education Statistics, 1997). Teachers who constantly struggle to maintain classroom control are more likely to perceive themselves as ineffective and be dissatisfied with their jobs. Teachers may be well-prepared to provide content instruction but ill-prepared to deal with students' challenging behavior, just as the students whose behaviors are challenging may be ill-equipped to deal with the academic and social demands of school.

Happy memories of their favorite teachers and fond intentions of making a difference in the lives of students are quickly overshadowed by a sense of not being in control of their classrooms as teachers discover that they are spending more time trying to restore order than they are teaching (Goodlad, 2004). There is an alternative. This chapter will:

- Describe two perspectives that come together to affect learning environments (teacher and student);
- Establish the foundation for management and learning that includes setting up physical environments that minimize misbehavior, establishing classroom expectations, linking teachers'

directions to those expectations, evaluating instructional variables under teachers' control, and developing a comprehensive instructional approach for teaching both academic and social skills;

- Identify evidence-based tools for management and learning that have been found to be effective across environments and students and give examples of each;
- Describe approaches to address more severe behavioral problems within the classroom; and
- Present a cycle of success for teachers and students.

A True Story

Ms. Connell sat wearily in her chair as the bell rang and her class fled the room noisily. It had happened again. She had prepared a good lesson and really thought she would get the students engaged in the learning opportunity. But she did not even get a chance to introduce the lesson. Milo struck again. He came into the room, announcing his intention to sit by Roger that day. After a failed negotiation to get Milo to sit in his regular seat, Ms. Connell gave up when other students started changing their seats. Trying to get the focus on the lesson, Ms. Connell used her most winsome tone to ask, "Who can remember what we were talking about yesterday?" Milo and Roger began talking about what they were going to do after school and the students who might have answered Ms. Connell slouched in their chairs, unwilling to compete with the boys' animated discussion. Recognizing the futility of continuing, Ms. Connell tried again to get Milo to go to his typical seat. After that, things are fuzzy in her memory. She remembers moving toward Milo, warning him that if he did not go sit in his seat he would not need after school plans as he would be sitting in detention. As she approached, Milo stood up quickly, knocking over his desk. Ms. Connell told him to pick up the desk and, instead, he knocked over another desk. Ms. Connell told another student to go get the principal as Milo began to yell at her for being a terrible teacher, using colorful and wholly unacceptable language for the school environment. Other students started laughing. Ms. Connell tried to reason with Milo, citing her credentials and her years of experience. But, by this time, Milo was revved up and, with a captive audience, expounded upon Ms. Connell's shortcomings until the principal appeared in the doorway. At the sight of the principal, Milo stopped as quickly as he had begun, gathered his books, and followed the principal out the door. Shaking, Ms. Connell proceeded with the lesson, but her heart was not in it. What was she doing wrong? Was she as bad a teacher as Milo said?

Because she is overwhelmed, Ms. Connell is not stopping to think about the smaller pieces that come together that contribute to an orderly learning environment in which the focus is on instruction and not on dealing with escalating misbehavior. Ms. Connell needs to stop and think about the proactive things she can use to reduce misbehavior including simple things like how she arranges the classroom, establishes classroom expectations, and uses general behavior management strategies as well as how she presents academic content. Then Ms. Connell needs to think about how she reacts to misbehavior, again through the effective use of behavior management strategies coupled with strategies to handle more disruptive and chronic behavior challenges. Before discussing the basic strategies that create the foundation for effective classroom management, it is important to recognize that whether a behavior is perceived as acceptable or unacceptable has a lot to do with the perspective from which the behavior is being evaluated.

Perspectives in the Classroom

Teaching is a social endeavor in that it involves at least two individuals interacting as a learner (student) and a facilitator of learning (teacher). When multiple individuals interact, they bring their own unique perspectives to the experience. Teachers' personalities, expectations, and tolerance levels influence their ability to facilitate learning, just as students' previous experiences and personal goals influence their ability to learn. This section will discuss these two perspectives which affect how harmoniously the students and teachers will get along.

Teacher Perspective

As would be predicted, teachers tend to respond negatively to interruptions, disruptions, and insubordination from students. However, why is it that some teachers seem to have better control over their classrooms than others? Why do some teachers send more students to an administrator's office for discipline than others? The answers to these questions may partially depend upon unique characteristics of the teacher, such as personality, tolerance levels, and expectations.

A teacher's personality may have a profound impact on reactions to students, colleagues, and parents. Indeed, classroom management styles (Martin, 1998), patterns of interaction between the teachers and students (Fisher & Kent, 1998), and even student achievement (Lessen & Frankiewicz, 1992) have been correlated with individual personality profiles. Individuals who choose to enter teaching tend to be more interested in others and tend to rely on objective data to come to logical conclusions than those who choose other fields of study (Thornton, Peltier, & Hill, 2005).

Teachers' personalities influence their expectations and levels of tolerance for student behavior. Teacher tolerance is affected by personal preference as they decide which behaviors are acceptable in their classrooms and which are unacceptable (Vitaro, Tremblay, & Gagnon, 1995). For example, some teachers are not bothered by students moving around classrooms while other teachers insist that students remain seated. These are two different reactions to the same behavior. Personalities also influence teaching styles. Teaching styles can be compared to three parenting styles that were defined by Baumrind (1966) as authoritarian, permissive, and authoritative. The first of these styles, **authoritarian,** is characterized by adults who expect conformity and obedience, are often unrealistic with their expectations, and use disciplinary approaches that are punitive and coercive. The second style, **permissive** (originally called "laissez-faire"), is a style in which adults are overly responsive to students, imposing few expectations or sanctions for inappropriate behavior. The last style is **authoritative** and is characterized by adults who have realistic expectations for students and are responsive to individual needs while using positive approaches to discipline. Pellerin (2005) found that beneficial outcomes for high schools students were associated with the last teaching style, authoritative, while schools in which professionals relied on the first style, authoritarian, have higher drop-out rates. In the same study, the lowest rates of engagement occurred in schools in which professionals adopted the permissive style. To get an idea of your own teaching style, complete the questionnaire in Appendix A. The questionnaire gives examples of how each style manifests in classrooms.

Teacher expectations have been shown to have a dramatic effect on how they interact with students. Teacher expectations for student success may be linked to socioeconomic status (Rumberger & Palardy, 2005) as well as expectations for student misbehavior (Van Acker, Grant, & Henry, 1996). Rosenthal and Jacobson (1968) demonstrated that teacher expectations for students' achievement can become self-fulfilling prophecy. Students who had been identified as bright and capable were found to perform significantly better during assessments than those whom teachers had been told were not very bright. The remarkable feature of this outcome is that the researchers misled the teachers by telling them that the lowest performing students were bright and the highest performing students were not capable of learning. In the end, the test results confirmed teachers'

FIGURE 11-1

Teacher Behavior Based on Expectations

Teachers who have low expectations for student success tend to:	Teachers who have high expectations for student success tend to:
—Give more criticism	—Do the opposite of those with low expectations PLUS
—Ask fewer questions	
—Provide less prompting	—Get in closer proximity to the student
—Give more negative feedback (including reprimands)	—Engage in more face to face interaction
—Provide less positive feedback (if any given)	—Provide more praise and signs of positive approval
	—Give redirection rather than reprimands

expectations, inciting a critical analysis of how teachers behave based on their expectations, since clearly the students' actual abilities had been misrepresented. The work of Rosenthal and Jacobson along with that of Van Acker et al. (1996) and Good and Brophy (1978), suggest that teachers interact differently with students for whom they have higher expectations. **Figure 11-1** provides a comparison of how teachers behave differently based on expectations for student achievement and appropriate behavior.

Teachers may avoid interacting with students who demonstrate negative and aggressive behavior so that they do not have to address the misbehavior. In this way, the student's inappropriate behavior modifies the teacher's behavior as the teacher seeks to avoid having to deal with the negative behavior. Teachers may react to the potential for problem behavior by not asking the students to do their work or by assigning work they think the students will find easy or fun (Carr, Taylor, & Robinson, 1991). Referred to as the "curriculum of non-instruction", teachers learn to modify their demands to avoid dealing with disruptive behavior while students learn to behave badly so that the teachers do not give them work they would rather not do (Gunter, Jack, DePaepe, Reed, & Harrison, 1994, p. 36).

The ways teachers communicate with students, particularly those who are beginning to engage in undesirable behavior may result in the behavior stopping or getting worse. Nonverbal communication constitutes the majority of any message sent to students. Angry or judgmental expressions and closed body language (e.g., arms crossed across the chest) can send the message that the teacher is frustrated by or even disinterested in the student. Paraverbal aspects of communication also influence messages sent to students. Paraverbal aspects are those related to how words are said. Paraverbal includes the tone, inflection, volume, and cadence of the spoken message. Teachers who get angry or frustrated tend to talk louder and more quickly. A good rule of thumb is: Low, Slow, and Soft. In particular, when interacting with agitated students, teachers should lower the pitch of their voice, speak more slowly, and speak quietly. It is difficult for students to continue to argue with someone who is speaking low, slow, and soft. Teachers should not allow the tone of their voice to become sarcastic or demeaning. Both of these qualities tend to make students behave worse. The actual words constitute only a small percentage of the message sent. When interacting with students, teachers are encouraged to keep their sentences brief and direct while avoiding giving advice and carefully modulating nonverbal and paraverbal communication.

In addition to teachers' personalities, interaction styles, expectations, and the monitoring of nonverbal and paraverbal aspects of communication, other aspects of the school environment can increase the risk that students will misbehave. The comfort, safety, and maintenance of the physical environment can affect student behavior (Kozol, 1991). Students in run-down school buildings that are considered unsafe tend to engage in more misbehavior. The appropriateness of the curriculum and difficulty of assigned tasks can influence student behavior (Dunlap, Dunlap, Clarke, & Robbins, 1991). If teachers ask students to complete assignments which seem irrelevant to their lives and are either boring or too hard, students tend to misbehave more. Schools that rely on punitive consequences for inappropriate behavior, including suspension and expulsion, experience higher levels of misbehavior (Walker, Ramsey, & Gresham, 2004). Aggressive behaviors are more likely to emerge when there is no system in place to recognize and reward good behavior (Wehby, Symons, & Shores, 1995). A variety of factors related to teachers and schools can set the stage for the appearance of behavior that disrupts the learning environment. There also are a number of factors related to the students which may make them more likely to misbehave.

Student Perspective

Why do some students display inappropriate or challenging behaviors during class and even in non-academic environments like the cafeteria and hallways? Many environmental factors contribute to whether or not a student engages in inappropriate behavior at school. These factors include those found in the home, school, community, and interpersonally. Any factor that negatively influences an individual's life is considered a "risk" factor. For example, home risk factors may include ineffective parental discipline, lack of parental involvement, and abuse or neglect (Walker, Stieber, Ramsey, & O'Neill, 1991). Coercive family interactions, in which the child and the parents try to out-intimidate each other, are strongly correlated with the development of aggression in children and youth (Patterson, Reid, & Dishion, 1992). School risk factors can include academic and/or social failure, not enough time devoted to instructional tasks, and the expectation that all students are the same and will learn by listening quietly (Guerra & Williams, 1996). Community risk factors may include limited opportunities to engage in socially appropriate recreation activities and few post-school employment options (Walker & Sprague, 1999). Interpersonally, individuals who are aggressive tend to distort events and think that other people are out to get them. These individuals may believe that others interact with malice of intent and that even accidents, such as bumping into someone in the hall, are deliberate acts of hostility (Dodge, Price, Bachorowski, & Newman, 1990). Intelligence levels and achievement are other interpersonal factors that may influence aggressive behavior (Huesmann, Eron, & Yarmel, 1987). Students who have been told that they are not very bright or who have not been successful at school may act out in order to hide the fact that they cannot do the assignments.

Each student will present various risk factors but no single risk factor is known to cause inappropriate behavior. It is important for teachers to understand their students' risk factors in order to plan ahead to encourage students to succeed. However, teachers should focus on school risk factors since those are the ones they have the most control over.

Students who have been exposed to multiple risk factors in school, home, and community settings may not automatically display inappropriate behavior at school. Some students become resilient to the risk factors present in their lives. Resiliency is often referred to as individuals' ability to grow up well-adjusted with appropriate social skills even when they have experienced numerous risk factors. A number of strategies that teachers can do in schools have been shown to promote resilience (Walker et al., 1996). Students who behave inappropriately often say that they feel like they do not belong and that school has nothing to offer them (Catalano, Loeber, & McKinney, 1999). Therefore, one effective way of promoting resilience is for teachers to mentor students. This mentorship could increase students' sense of belongingness when teachers: (a) spend additional time during the school day with the student by using a check-in process whereby the teacher can ask the student how things are going and what they can do to help, as well as praise the student's accomplishments; and (b) provide guidance in selecting school-related activities for the student to engage in where success is likely based on student strengths and areas of interest.

Another method teachers can employ to promote resiliency is to become educational advocates for students for both academic and social purposes (Furlong & Morrison, 2000). As an advocate, the teacher could support the student through various methods: (a) by frequently monitoring the student's academic progress and assessing areas where reteaching, adaptations, and/or accommodations in instructional practices may be required; (b) by frequently monitoring the student's social progress for predictable patterns or areas where social skills instruction or conflict resolution strategies may be needed or consequences altered; (c) by talking with the student's other teachers to discuss what is working effectively or not working and providing suggestions and resources for the teachers to use; and (d) by providing feedback to teachers regarding student progress as a means of positively affecting the academic and social expectations the teachers have for the student. Overall, no matter which risk factors are present or whether or not those factors negatively affect the student's school behavior, there are many opportunities for a teacher to promote student resiliency.

Although it is important for teachers to recognize that students who come to their classrooms may be experiencing many risk factors, it is just as important to recognize misbehavior for what it is: behavior. As such, teachers must remember that behavior is not arbitrary or incidental but purposeful and effective for accomplishing desired goals. Termed the "functions" of behavior (Iwata, Dorsey, Slifer, Bauman, & Richman, 1982/1994), the goals of behavior are either to get the individual something that is desired or to enable the individual to avoid something that is not desired. For example, college students attend class in order to gain knowledge as well as grades so that they can earn degrees and get jobs. College students also will attend class in order to avoid failing. Gaining and avoiding are powerful determinants of behavior. Toward that end, teachers should examine students' behaviors to identify what the behavior is getting for the student and/or helping the student avoid.

When students get what they want or avoid what they do not want, they are **reinforced** for their behavior. Reinforcement is a key concept in effective classroom management that will appear throughout the chapter so it needs to be defined. Anything that happens after a behavior is a consequence. For example, students who turn in their work on time are likely to get a grade. The grade is a consequence for the behavior. If the grade is one the student wants and makes the student want to turn in assignments in the future, the consequence is reinforcing. If the grade is one the student does not want and the student gives up and stops turning in assignments, then the consequence is punishing. There are no consequences that are naturally reinforcing or punishing. The only way to tell if something is reinforcing or punishing is to look at subsequent behavior. If a teacher praises a student for sitting quietly and the next day the student walks noisily around the room, then the praise was a punishment. Similarly, if a teacher yells at a student who is talking to her neighbor and the student talks to her neighbor intermittently throughout the day, then the yelling is reinforcing. Punishing consequences may stop a behavior temporarily. However, the most effective classroom management will be based on reinforcement. Sometimes the challenge for teachers is in identifying what is reinforcing.

To illustrate the functions of behavior (get or avoid) and the powerful effects of reinforcement, consider students who have difficulty completing assignments or getting along with others and who may misbehave in order to hide the fact that they are behind their peers in academic or social skills (Scott, Nelson, & Liaupsin, 2001). When these students are presented with academic and/or social tasks they think are hard or that they do not want to do, they may misbehave in order to avoid the task. These students may become noncompliant, aggressive, destructive, or run out of the room. In response, teachers typically remove students from the setting by sending them to an administrator's office or to an alternative learning environment like detention or an "opportunity room." The students are reinforced for their behavior because it kept them from doing work they did not want to do. Teachers are reinforced for sending the students out of the room because now they do not have to deal with them. However, removal from class deprives the students of needed instruction, resulting in them falling further behind in the academic or social skills needed to be successful. So, the work becomes more difficult, leading to continued use of behavior which students have learned will get them removed from class (misbehavior), allowing them to temporarily avoid failure (reinforcement) but which results in even less chance that will ever catch up academically or socially. The vicious cycle continues, showing the strong connection between academics, and specifically academic failure, and behavior (Talbott & Coe, 1997). The cycle may be seen even in achieving students who are absent for a few weeks due to illness. When they return, their behavior may communicate the frustration experienced when they discover they have fallen behind their peers in learning. **Figure 11-2** depicts the damaging cycle between misbehavior and academic failure.

In order to intervene effectively, the cycle must be broken. Students need instruction targeted at their learning levels that will improve their skill acquisition and promote academic achievement. They also will need social skills instruction to learn how to handle

FIGURE 11-2

Cycle of Failure

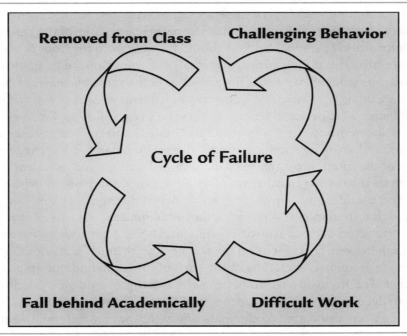

frustration and challenging situations. Breaking the cycle which perpetuates academic and behavioral failure increases the chances that students will be successful in school and after they graduate.

Foundation for Management and Learning

Students may be using misbehavior to get something they want and to avoid something they do not want in a given environment. In this way, behavioral problems may be interpreted as problems with the environment (Witt, VanDerHeyden, & Gilbertson, 2004). So, teachers must look closely at school environments, including classrooms and non-academic settings like the bus areas and gymnasiums. The critical difference between effective and ineffective teachers is not how they try to punish problem behavior but how well they change the environment to reduce the likelihood the problem behaviors will occur (McKee & Witt, 1990). Important environmental considerations include creating an environment conducive to learning, establishing clear expectations, using precision requests, analyzing instructional variables, and adopting a comprehensive instructional approach.

Creating an Environment Conducive to Learning

The physical structure of a classroom establishes the basic foundation for the learning space and can have a tremendous influence on student behavior. The way the classroom is arranged promotes or hinders students' ability to pay attention. Although teachers may not have much choice about how their classrooms have been built, simple decisions about how the environment is arranged can make a difference in whether or not teachers spend more time teaching or more time trying to squelch disruptive behavior. These simple decisions include:

1) Which way should desks face? Desks which face windows invite students to attend to things other than the teacher. Desks which face doors offer the same invitation. The desks should be positioned so that students have a clear view of chalk or dry erase boards and the teacher.

2) Where are the pencil sharpener, trash can, areas for storing personal belongings, and areas for submitting work? All of these are considered "high traffic" areas and tend to be the spots with high levels of misbehavior, particularly if out of the teacher's sight. The area for storing personal belongs should be away from the door or there will be a perpetual traffic jam during arrival, dismissal, and transitions (e.g., going to lunch or other areas) as students try to get their belongs in the same place where other students are lining up. Additionally, behavior problems may be prevented if teachers send students to get personal belongings in stages (e.g., "Group 4, can get their lunches or lunch money. . . ." followed by Group 2 and so forth). Pencil sharpeners, trash cans, and areas for submitting work should be separated by space and not in the front of the room. Most teachers allow students to go to those areas as needed and it can be distracting to other students if the pencil sharpener is behind the teacher and a student gets up to sharpen his pencil during the lesson.

3) Are distractions minimized? Also called **decontamination,** the careful storage of obvious distracters such as athletic equipment, DVDs, art materials, magazines, and so forth can help students focus on the teacher and their assignments. Cages with gerbils or other animals should be at the back of the room and not up front next to the teacher. Teachers will need to balance the amount of student work displayed and classroom decoration with the students' abilities to pay attention. The classroom also needs to be decontaminated to eliminate any items that are potential weapons. For example, years ago, teachers frequently had what looked like a nail on a base which

was used to spear pieces of paper to hold them in one place. Classrooms were decontaminated by removing such dangerous memo holders. The same is true of letter openers that look like knives. Today, preschools typically require that scissors have rounded tips. In classrooms for older students who have a history of violence, sharp scissors may be kept in a secured location. Teachers will need to carefully examine their classrooms to make sure distracting items are removed or covered and potentially dangerous items are eliminated or secured.

Once teachers have examined their classrooms to identify high traffic areas and the potential for distractions, they can decide how to arrange desks and other instructional areas. Arrangements that cluster students close together can result in problem behavior. Spacing needs are influenced by culture and mood. Some students will be more comfortable with greater distances between themselves and others, particularly when agitated or frustrated. Classroom arrangements also should allow teachers to circulate throughout the room and be close to students. This physical closeness, also known as teacher proximity to students, has a positive affect on behavior and learning (Gunter & Shores, 1995). This allows for what is called **proximity control.** When teachers can move easily among the students' desks/tables, they can use their presence to remind students of the expectations by moving closer to students who are off-task. When teachers move closer to two students who are talking, the talking typically stops. If the desks are arranged in tight rows, with student materials on the floor between the desks, teachers will not be able to use proximity control. Teacher proximity to students also has been shown to increase student participation in instruction. Additionally, when students start to argue or fight, teachers need to be able to get to the students quickly, further highlighting the need to arrange the desks/tables in ways that allow easy access to all students. **Figure 11-3** provides several possible arrangements of desk that allow for maximum proximity control.

Space constraints and class size may prevent teachers from arranging the learning space to maximize proximity control. In such situations, teachers will have to rely on other strategies to promote desirable behavior. The classroom arrangement may need to be flexible in order to accommodate a variety of instructional activities. For example, following a group lesson, teachers may want students to get in groups of four to work together. Desks will have to be rearranged to accommodate the activity.

Once the learning space is decontaminated and arranged to allow for proximity control, teachers must face the dilemma of whether to assign or not to assign seats. Deliberation should not take too long as decisions about seating arrangements have been described as the cheapest form of classroom management (Jones, 2000). Allowing students to choose their own seats will result in seating choices that are good for the students and typically bad for teachers. Many teachers will start the school year by assigning seats alphabetically (unless information provided by previous teachers would suggest otherwise). Teachers can change assigned seats at any time, although it can become confusing for students if seat assignments change too frequently. (Most college students will sit in the same seat throughout a term.) Reassignment will be based on teachers' observations that current seating is not resulting in students spending the majority of their time doing what is expected. When reassigning seats, teachers are encouraged to reassign all seats, so as not to point out (and potentially reinforce) students with problem behavior.

In addition to the important influence of the classroom arrangement, teachers will be faced with fewer problem behaviors when students know what they are expected to do during frequently occurring non-instructional tasks such as turning in assignments, submitting homework, borrowing supplies, collecting money, collecting permission slips for field trips, and so forth (Emmer & Stough, 2001). Teachers will need to identify what they expect the students to do during routines, teach the students what is expected, and have them practice the routines prior to actually using them. As an example, teachers need to

FIGURE 11-3

Desk Arrangements That Maximize Proximity Control

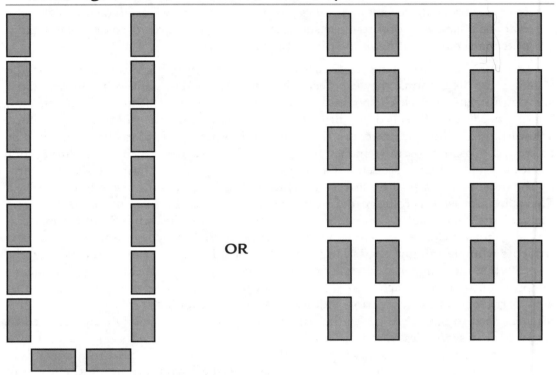

OR

OR

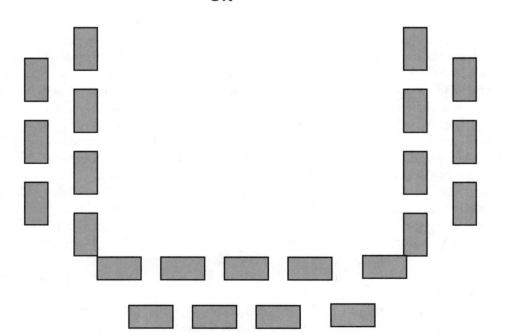

create routines for transitions such as moving from one content area to another (e.g., stop math, start science) and from one classroom to another. Students should be taught the signals for a transition, what they must do during the transition, and how to know when the transition is over. They need to be supervised during the transition and praised or reinforced for quick completion.

Teachers have control over a number of variables related to their classrooms. Teachers make simple but critical decisions about the basic parameters of working within the space they are assigned, keeping students close enough but not too close to each other, making sure they can move around to use proximity control, and assigning seats to reduce the possibility that students will misbehave. These variables, along with carefully describing, teaching, and reinforcing compliance to basic routines can have a noticeable effect on student behavior. Once the physical environment is conducive for learning, teachers are ready to establish the behavioral and psychological climate of their classrooms by developing the expectations that will govern the classroom.

Establishing Clear Expectations

Until the expectations are clear, no one in a classroom will know what they should and should not do. Years ago, the development of rules was not as important to teachers because students behaved appropriately or were not allowed in school. Now, all children and youth must attend school, even if their behavior is inappropriate, and teachers must devote time teaching students expected behavior. The most successful way to start a school year is to assume that none of the students know what to do and begin by teaching the expectations. The expectations should apply equally to adults and students. For example, if students are not allowed to chew gum in class, neither should the teacher. The basic guidelines for creating, teaching, and monitoring classroom rules and expectations are as follows:

a) 3-5 positively stated rules and expectations;
b) teaching and modeling of the rules and expectations with a rationale provided;
c) reinforcement for following the rules and displaying the expectations;
d) consistent and fair application of the rules and expectations;
e) immediate corrective feedback for breaking the rules; and
f) equitable consequences for rule violations.

Teachers should consider the needs of the students when identifying important classroom rules. These needs include aspects of age-appropriateness, links to overall school-wide expectations, and the short- and long-term goals for student behavior. When creating classroom rules and expectations, the focus is on preventing students from displaying inappropriate behavior. Such prevention can be linked to different types of rules such as those that focus on student compliance, preparation, verbalizations, engagement, and transition.

To illustrate, students in Mr. Bloomquist's sixth grade science classroom have an agreed upon set of classroom rules with specific behavioral expectations. Mr. Bloomquist teaches students with and without disabilities, including many students who engage in inappropriate behavior. At the beginning of the school year, he decided on three core classroom rules. They are 1) respect yourself, 2) respect others, and 3) respect property. Mr. Bloomquist based these rules on his prior experiences teaching students at this middle school. During the first week of school, he presented these three positively stated rules to the students, provided a rationale for why he selected them, and provided a generic example of what each rule might look like in his classroom. To increase student buy-in with the classroom rules, he had the class engage in an activity called a "chalk and talk." During this activity, the students wrote examples of what the three rules would look like to them. Students wrote: be prepared, be on time, and give your best effort as examples for "respect yourself"; raise your hand, accept correction gracefully, and follow directions as examples for "respect others"; and ask before borrowing and using materials and keep your science station clean as examples for "respect property." Mr. Bloomquist praised his students' ideas and added another example for each rule (listen during instruction, keep hands and feet to self, and return supplies where found). Then, he taught and modeled examples (what the students wrote) and non-examples of each classroom rule and discussed the consequences for violating those rules. As a class, the students practiced modeling the expected behaviors while Mr. Bloomquist provided corrective feedback and praise. In addition, Mr. Bloomquist told the class that he would reinforce students who engaged in the three rules by giving out homework passes, "sit where you want" passes, and "work with whom you want" passes. As the school year progressed and based on student feedback and performance, Mr. Bloomquist retaught the three rules, what they looked like, and reviewed the reinforcers available for following the rules and the consequences that would occur if the rules were violated.

Using Precision Requests

Establishing a set of behavioral expectations via the classroom rules, allows teachers to positively recognize students who are meeting the expectations. The emphasis should always be on the positive consequences that occur when the rules are followed. There will be students who violate the classroom expectations or fail to respond to teachers' directions. In these situations, an empirically-based strategy called **Precision Requests** (Neville & Jenson, 1984) gives teachers a structured way to intervene. To make a precision request, the teacher should be close to the student (but not in an intimidating manner), make eye contact with the student, and deliver the request with a calm, unemotional tone. The teacher gives the brief and clear request and then waits five seconds. If the student complies, the teacher provides reinforcing consequences. If the student has not complied within five seconds, the same request is given a second time. If the student complies the second time, the teacher praises the student. If the student does not reply a second time, the teacher implements a behavior reduction strategy (described more fully later).

Ms. Mozart has found that precision requests help her have more time for instruction and reduce the amount of time she spends trying to manage misbehavior. When, during a lesson, Allison begins to draw on her book, Ms. Mozart tells the class to silently identify the three main points in the next paragraph and moves close to Allison. Ms. Mozart quietly says, "Writing in your book is not respecting property. You need to stop writing in your book and look for the three main points in this (pointing) paragraph". Ms. Mozart moves away from Allison to talk quietly with the next student, but counts to five in her head. At the count of five, she looks back over at Allison who appears to be studying her book intently. Ms. Mozart goes back to Allison and says, again quietly so that only Allison hears, "Good choice for respecting property, Allison!" and then asks loudly, so that the entire class can hear, "Who has found one of the main points?"

The strategy of precision requests provides teachers with a specific sequence to follow in the event of rule violations and other inappropriate behavior. Teacher behavior within the exchange can influence the effectiveness of the request (Kauffman, Mostert, Trent, & Pullen, 2006). To avoid engaging in arguments with students in the process of the precision request, teachers should:

- Stay calm and not show any external manifestation of being upset;
- Clearly restate the expectation or response one time. In restating the expectation, remind the student of the positive consequences of meeting the expectation and the negative consequences for failing to meet the expectation;

- Move away from the student, allowing time for the student to calm down or respond appropriately;

- Ignore the student's efforts at saving face (e.g., most students will roll their eyes, mutter under their breath, or make faces as the teacher moves away). These behaviors can be addressed privately at a later time; and

- Respond immediately with a positive consequence when the student begins to engage in the expected behavior.

Analyzing Instructional Variables

Decades of research have demonstrated that engaging students in instruction is the most effective method of reducing problem behavior in classrooms. Student engagement can be increased (and misbehavior decreased) when teachers demonstrate specific behaviors, use effective instructional practices, and make sure that curricula are appropriate for the students. Over 30 years ago, Kounin (1970) identified teacher behaviors which were critical for reducing inappropriate behavior. The behaviors include:

- **Withitness,** which indicates that teachers are aware of what is going on at all times in all parts of the classroom.

- **Momentum,** describing the teacher's ability to keep a lesson moving at a fairly brisk pace, make efficient transitions among the activities, and bring the lesson to a clear conclusion. Teachers may use general management strategies (e.g., moving close to a student who is getting distracted; calling attention to a relevant point; asking students questions when attention starts to wander) to prevent potential problems.

- **Group Alerting,** which means that the teacher uses strategies to keep all students alerted to the task and involves capturing students' attention, clarifying expectations, and effectively drawing disengaged students into the lesson.

- **Student Accountability,** describing the use of strategies which elicit answers, demonstrations, and explanations from students and increase levels of engagement.

- **Overlapping,** which requires that teachers juggle a variety of activities at the same time (i.e., checking on students doing independent work while conducting a lesson with a group of students and redirecting another student to the assigned task).

Kounin recognized that effective teachers use these strategies in the context of interesting lessons and assignments that **avoid overexposure** to a particular topic. Teachers who go on and on about a particular topic, probably trying to help a few students finally understand the concepts, have created overexposure. When overexposure occurs, students often communicate their boredom with a topic by engaging in inappropriate behavior.

In addition to specific teacher behaviors, there are particular instructional practices which influence student engagement in lessons and directly influence the amount of misbehavior with which teachers will have to contend. The effective instructional practices have been summarized in an acronym, CLOCS-RAM, and are presented in **Figure 11-4.** Teachers are encouraged to evaluate their lessons according to the instructional practices represented by CLOCS-RAM.

In addition to effective instructional practices, other variables that have an effect on behavior include curricula being used and the expectations for academic performance. If the assignment does not match the student's ability level, misbehavior is more likely to occur. This holds true for work that is too easy (Umbreit, Lane, & Dejud, 2004), as well as for work that is too difficult (DePaepe, Shores, Jack, & Denny, 1996). Difficult tasks probably increase levels of off-task and disruptive behavior because students are trying to

FIGURE 11-4

Effective Instructional Practices

Keys to offering effective instruction:

1. *Clarity:* The student must know exactly what to do (i.e., have no doubt about what is expected).
2. *Level:* The student must be able to do the task with a high degree of accuracy (i.e., be able to get at least 80 percent correct), but the task must be challenging (i.e., the student should not easily get 100 percent correct repeatedly).
3. *Opportunities:* The student must have frequent opportunities to respond (i.e., be actively engaged in the task a high percentage of the time).
4. *Consequences:* The student must receive a meaningful reward for correct performance (i.e., the consequences of correct performance must be frequent and perceived as desirable by the student).
5. *Sequence:* The tasks must be presented in logical sequence so that the student gets the big idea (i.e., steps must be presented and learned in order that the knowledge or skill is built on a logical progression or framework of ideas, which is a systematic curriculum).
6. *Relevance:* The task is relevant to the student's life and, if possible, the student understands how and why it is useful (i.e., the teacher attempts to help the student see why in his or her culture the task is important).
7. *Application:* The teacher helps the student learn how to learn and remember by teaching memory and learning strategies and applying knowledge and skills to everyday problems (i.e., teaches generalization, not just isolated skills, and honors the student's culture).
8. *Monitoring:* The teacher continuously monitors student progress (i.e., records and charts progress, always knows and can show what the student has mastered and the student's place or level in a curriculum or sequence of tasks).

Source: Kauffman, J. M., Mostert, M. P., Trent, S. C., & Pullen, P. L. (2006). *Managing classroom behavior: A reflective case-based approach* (4th ed.). Boston, MA: Allyn & Bacon. (p. 17). Used with permission.

get out of work they know they cannot do (Moore & Edwards, 2003). Teachers must know students are able to do the work assigned or they will need to provide additional support. Work that is too easy can be supplemented with challenging extension tasks. In addition to ensuring assignments match students' instructional levels, relatively simple techniques have been found to have a marked effect on engagement and behavior. Students can be given a choice among acceptable alternatives for completing assignments. For example, students may be able to complete tasks involving writing by choosing to use paper and pencil, a computer, or by dictating into a tape recorder (Kern, Delaney, Clarke, Dunlap, & Childs, 2001). Amazingly enough, students will sometimes select the paper and pencil option, even though that was the one that resulted in high levels of problem behavior previously. As will be discussed in a later section, the option to make choices can influence overall student behavior.

Modifying curricula by incorporating high interest activities can promote higher levels of engagement and reduce disruptive behavior. In addition to giving students choices of which medium to use to complete a written assignment, Kern et al. (2001) modified the curriculum by allowing students to copy passages from a Sega Genesis game booklet rather than the sentences in the traditional handwriting book. If the curriculum does not match students' ability levels, interests, or expectations for production can result in misbehavior. As a part of the instructional considerations, teachers will need to examine these variables as a proactive means of providing an orderly learning environment. Chapter 6 contains additional suggestions for providing effective instruction.

Adopting a Comprehensive Instructional Approach

Behavior problems are teaching problems.
—Sigfried Engelmann

Teachers who have set-up their classrooms appropriately, developed and taught the classroom rules, are good at giving precision requests, and carefully consider instructional variables influencing student engagement, will discover that most minor misbehavior is eliminated. These proactive strategies help maintain focus on teaching and reinforcing behavior conducive to learning. Unfortunately, there will be some students who have already developed fairly ingrained patterns of inappropriate behavior. Teachers must remember that some of these students' behavioral patterns have become automatic. Without conscious thought, students have learned that inappropriate behaviors allow them to get what they want and avoid what they do not want. Van Acker and Talbott (1999) draw an analogy between these students' disruptive behaviors and driving ability. When first learning to drive, most individuals have to concentrate on each step of the process and proceed slowly. After a few times, the behaviors required to drive become more familiar and over time they become quite automatic. Few experienced drivers have to stop and think through the steps for driving a car. Indeed, most drivers do so quite automatically, thinking of many things other than driving and even engaging in other behaviors like talking on cell phones. The inappropriate behaviors of students with chronic problem behavior occur just as automatically. When a teacher corrects a student, the student may start yelling without thinking that the teacher is trying to help. Indeed, it would take considerable effort for the student not to respond automatically.

Rather than discourage, this awareness should provide reassurance to teachers. Students who are misbehaving are doing so because that is how they know to behave; it is nothing personal about the teacher. Students who are misbehaving must be taught better ways to behave—and teaching is what teachers do best. Teachers who approach classroom management proactively and plan instruction for behavioral deficits just like they do for academic learning may have fewer disruptive behaviors to address and more time and energy for the important job of teaching content (Colvin & Sugai, 1988). Unfortunately, most teachers do not think of teaching behavior like they teach academic content. When teaching academic skills, teachers assume students are trying hard and will view student errors as honest mistakes. When students make academic errors, teachers provide corrective feedback and observe as the student attempts the task again, being ready and willing to provide additional assistance. In stark contrast, when dealing with errors in behavior, teachers tend to assume that the student is not trying or is engaged in willful disobedience. Teachers then try to punish the student, which often involves sending the student out of the class. Teachers do not provide instruction or practice in the expected behavior, and carry the delusion that the student will do better in the future.

Students will not learn to behave more appropriately unless they are taught to do so. Classrooms are well managed when teachers identify and teach desirable behavior (Emmer & Stough, 2001). The comprehensive instructional approach recognizes that chronic behavior problems must be addressed just like chronic academic problems. **Figure 11-5** depicts the five steps for addressing chronic academic problems and the

FIGURE 11-5

Comparison of Procedures to Remediate Chronic Academic Problems and Chronic Behavior Problems

	Chronic Academic Problem	**Chronic Behavior Problem**
STEP 1	Identify the error pattern or misrule.	Identify functional relationships between behavior and environment.
STEP 2	Identify rule.	Identify expected or acceptable behaviors.
STEP 3	Modify examples and presentations to provide clearer focus on rule and provide less opportunity for practice of misrule.	Modify environment to allow practice of expected behaviors and remove stimuli that are likely to occasion the inappropriate behavior.
STEP 4	Provide differential feedback so that more accurate responses are more strongly reinforced.	Provide differential reinforcement so that direction of correct responding is reinforced.
STEP 5	Shape context toward target context, provide review and integrate skill with other skills.	Move toward least restrictive environment program for generalization and maintenance.

Source: Colvin, G., & Sugai, G. M. (1988). Proactive strategies for managing social behavior problems: An instructional approach. *Education and Treatment of Children, 11,* p. 347. Used with permission.

corresponding five steps for intervening with chronic behavior problems. The strategies mentioned for addressing chronic behavior problems will be described later in this chapter.

Considerable research has validated effective instructional approaches for teaching academics. This knowledge can be applied to teaching social skills and appropriate behavior. Teachers may employ the model, lead, and test approach as a means to instruct students in the use of appropriate social skills (Mercer & Mercer, 2005). The **model, lead, test** approach provides systematic and repetitious instruction with embedded error correction. For example, the teacher can **model** the appropriate skill by providing the student with a rationale for displaying the skill and showing the student how to display the skill. The teacher, along with competent and respected peers, model the skill using examples from the student's classroom and school. In addition, the teacher should model nonexamples of the skill. When doing so, the teacher can teach the student how to recognize appropriate displays of the skill and the cues in the environment that will indicate when the student should use the skill.

After modeling the skill for the student, the teacher will **lead** the student through direct applications of the skill. These applications may take the form of role plays and "think aloud" activities in which the student practices the skills while the teacher coaches and reminds the student what to do next. During the lead portion of instruction, the teacher may use small group instruction in order to keep the examples and nonexamples of the skill in a real context. While applying and practicing the skill, it is important for the teacher to reinforce the student when the student tries to do the skill, even if it is not perfect.

After multiple opportunities for the student to be led through the application of the skill, the teacher will **test** the student's independent use of the skill. The teacher may watch the student under conditions similar to those in which the model and lead were conducted or in untrained conditions. This assessment will determine whether the student can apply the skill under natural classroom and school conditions and whether the teacher needs to provide more instruction and practice.

Time and effort will be necessary to take a comprehensive instructional perspective to model-lead-test and support the development of skills and behavior that will be useful for students throughout their lives. However, these are some of the most important skills that teachers can help their students learn, so it will be well worth the effort. The comprehensive instructional approach will be more effective when the classroom setting has been carefully arranged, clear classroom expectations have been taught, and CLOCS-RAM, precision requests and other instructional components are in place. In addition to the aforementioned research-based practices, there are other evidence-based tools that can help teachers manage classroom behavior.

Evidence-Based Tools for Management and Learning

When the only tool you own is a hammer, every problem begins to resemble a nail.
—Abraham Maslow

As has been described, effective classroom management is proactive rather than reactive (Emmer & Stough, 2001). Rather than wait for students to misbehave and then react, teachers create highly engaging lessons by examining expectations and supporting students so that they can meet the expectations. Such proactive strategies include adopting a comprehensive approach to instruction in which behavioral errors are treated like errors in academic learning. By implementing proactive systems of support in which expected behaviors are identified, defined, taught, and recognized, 80% to 90% of students in school will demonstrate appropriate behavior (Lewis & Sugai, 1999). The more intensive interventions needed for the other 10% of the students will be more effective if the school environment supports the positive behavior of all students (Eber, Sugai, Smith, & Scott, 2002).

The most obvious feature of proactive interventions is reliance on positive supports to build appropriate behavior. Students are told exactly what is expected and have opportunities to practice and receive recognition when they perform as expected. This is in sharp contrast to punitive methods of control in which expectations are vague and variable and the only time students are recognized by teachers is when they have done something wrong, as in the case of negative "demerit" systems. In those negative systems, students learn they have to misbehave in order to be noticed.

Interventions which help students build repertoires of appropriate behavior exist on a continuum. **Figure 11-6** provides a diagram of this continuum. The continuum ranges from relatively easy interventions that are not intrusive to those that require more time to develop and are more intrusive. The continuum depicts a variety of tools that teachers can use to manage their classrooms. It is important to choose the tool that is appropriate for a given behavior and student. The continuum is depicted as a pyramid to stress that interventions selected from the upper levels will be less effective unless the more positive interventions on the lower levels are tried first.

All of the interventions depicted on the pyramid are considered evidence-based, meaning research supports their implementation in specific situations. The first three levels of the pyramid contain interventions that have been found universally effective and are recommended as tools that teachers can choose based on their preferences and the needs of their students. These interventions are considered **behavior enhancing** as they are positive in nature and recognize students who are behaving appropriately. The interventions on the top two levels of the pyramid are considered **behavior reducing** as they

FIGURE 11-6

Pyramid of Evidence-Based Interventions

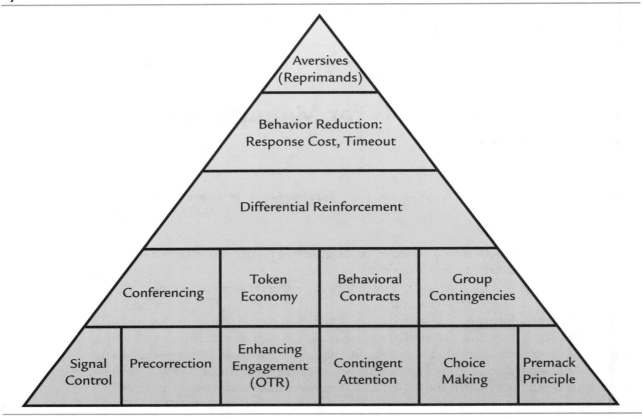

focus on providing punishing consequences for students who misbehave. Given how automatically some misbehavior occurs, behavior reducing strategies may be necessary to get students who chronically misbehave to stop and think about what they are doing. However, behavior reduction strategies do not build behavior; they are intended to stop behavior. Behavior reduction strategies must be used in conjunction with behavior enhancing strategies so that students learn behaviors to be more successful in school as well as after they graduate. The description of each of the behavior enhancing and behavior reducing strategies follows with examples of classroom application.

Behavior Enhancement Strategies

As shown in the pyramid in **Figure 11-6,** there are a wide variety of tools available that enable teachers to help students demonstrate appropriate behavior. The emphasis with behavior enhancement strategies is to teach students what is expected and then recognize them when they behave appropriately. The strategies listed on the pyramid do not include all of the behavior enhancing strategies but are inclusive of the more commonly used strategies. These include signal control, precorrection, enhancing engagement, contingent attention, choice making, Premack Principle, conferencing, token economy, behavioral contracts, group contingencies, and differential reinforcement.

Signal Control

Signals are the audible, verbal, and visual behaviors taught to students that prompt them to engage in specific behavior. Examples of audible signals include timer bells, chimes, music, whistles, clapping, and gongs. Verbal signals are phrases such as "Listen up" or the use of directions and questions. Flipping the lights off and on, holding up a certain number of fingers, changing colors on "traffic signals", and displaying written signs are all examples of visual signals. (Do not use flipping the lights off and on in classes with students with seizure disorders.) The signals notify students that certain behaviors are expected. However, the signals will not cue students' behavior unless the signals are systematically taught with opportunities to practice and the students are reinforced for behaving as expected.

Ms. Dennis realized she was losing instructional time because her students did not stop talking when it was time for the lesson to begin. Ms. Dennis knew that there would be noise as the students entered the room, chattering, retrieved their materials, and took their seats. She needed an effective way to signal the students when it was time for them to stop what they were doing and listen to her. Ms. Dennis had a small pair of chimes at home that made a pleasant but clearly audible noise when they moved. She brought the chimes to school and suspended them from the ceiling so that they hung over the area where she typically stood to teach. The next class period, after most of the students had settled, Ms. Dennis ran her hands across the chimes. Many students looked up curiously and conversations quickly faded away. Ms. Dennis told the students that she wanted to do everything she could to make sure they were prepared for the end of course exam and given how much information they needed to cover, she was going to have to use every minute of instructional time available. She then said that when the students heard the chimes, they should stop talking immediately and look at her. She informed them that each time the entire class responded by getting quiet within two seconds of the signal, she would write one of the letters of "homework" on the board. Ms. Dennis told the students that she would not assign homework on the day that the word "homework" was spelled in entirety. Ms. Dennis had the students practice by engaging in conversations with their neighbors, and after waiting a few seconds she made the chimes sound. Everyone was instantly quiet so Ms. Dennis wrote an "h" on the board. They practiced two more times and had "hom" written on the board the first day. Ms. Dennis continued to use the system and was pleased at how quickly the students responded to the signal. She noticed that many of the students even stopped talking when she moved toward the chimes to make them sound. Clearly, signal control had been established.

Precorrection

Teachers do not want students to fail academically or socially. Precorrection is one evidence-based strategy which can be used as a tool to prevent student failure (Colvin, Sugai, Good, & Lee, 1997; Colvin, Sugai, & Patching, 1993). Precorrection occurs when a teacher provides the student with a very clear cue or prompt of how to perform an expected behavior before the student displays a predictable inappropriate behavior. For example, prior to lining up for recess, the teacher says, "When you line up, please walk quietly and keep your hands to yourself", knowing that the students had a tendency to run and push each other. Precorrection typically includes seven distinct steps (Mercer & Mercer, 2005):

1. identify the context for the predictable behavior to occur;
2. explicitly identify the expected behavior;
3. modify the environment;
4. conduct a behavior rehearsal;

5. provide an effective reinforcer for expected behavior;
6. prompt the student to engage in the expected behavior; and
7. monitor the plan.

Ms. Schmidt uses precorrection with Jameson who has difficulty transitioning from whole class reading instruction to independent reading activities. The seven-steps Ms. Schmidt used for Jameson included: 1) Identifying that Jameson was noncompliant and disruptive to other students during this transition; 2) Specifying that Jameson should get his reading text, a pencil, and a piece of paper and then begin working within one-minute after the direction to begin the next activity; 3) Modifying the environment so that she stood by Jameson's desk and gave the class very clear instructions about how to transition to the next activity; 4) Rehearsing the behavior by having Jameson and another peer be the class models as she guided them through going from whole class reading instruction to independent reading activity time; 5) Reminding the students that whoever begins the independent reading activity within one minute of her prompt will receive bonus points which can be used toward their class store and then privately tells Jameson that he will receive additional bonus points if she does not have to remind him to begin; 6) Prompting the expected behavior by saying to the class "It's time to change activities" and giving bonus points to those students who begin the transition as instructed; and 7) Recording how many bonus points Jameson received, the number of points his peers received, and how long it took Jameson and the class to transition. In the above example, Ms. Schmidt used precorrection as a proactive strategy to teach, model, and reinforce Jameson and his peers to transition appropriately from one activity to the next instead of waiting for Jameson or his peers to engage in the predictable inappropriate transition behaviors.

Enhancing Engagement

Engagement, the amount of time that students spend actively participating in learning activities, has consistently been identified as critical for achievement (Greenwood, 1991; Logan, Bakeman, & Keefe, 1997). Student engagement in learning tasks is directly related to teachers' providing students with opportunities to respond (OTR). Teachers use a variety of strategies to increase OTR. Research suggests the maximum OTR are present when students are engaged in producing something (e.g., written product, project); the fewest OTR occur during teacher lectures and group discussions. Examples of strategies that increase OTR include introducing interesting materials, providing prompts (e.g., the capital of Kentucky starts with the letter "F"), and asking questions. Strategies to increase the number of opportunities to respond during lecture and group discussions include the use of choral responding and response cards.

Ms. Leslie uses a combination of choral responding and response cards during her science lessons. About every three minutes during her instruction, she will ask a recall question about something she just described. She prefaces the question by saying, "OK, this is for everyone to answer . . ." She has taught the students that this means they all should call out the answer simultaneously (choral responding). Periodically, she will say, "Write this one down . . ." and the students will write the one or two word response on their individual dry erase boards and hold them up for her to see. The combination of choral responding and short written responses interjected throughout the lesson give each student ample opportunity to respond. In addition to increasing the number of opportunities for students to respond, engagement can be facilitated through briskly paced guided practice, alternating easier with more difficult tasks, and following non-preferred activities with high interest activities.

Contingent Attention

Contingent attention is a low cost and effective strategy teachers can implement in the classroom with students at anytime. Specifically, contingent attention occurs when teachers provide immediate and genuine attention to students who have or are engaging in appropriate forms of behavior (Walker et al., 2004). For example, if a student is on-task, completes a task with high accuracy, or attempts new tasks, the teacher may provide the student with attention by: a) taking time to talk with the student and providing feedback, b) giving the student a "thumbs-up", c) looking at the student and smiling, or d) providing the student with praise. Praise is probably the most common form of contingent attention used by classroom teachers. Generically, praise is a positive statement ("good job," "nicely done," "super") provided in verbal or written form to the student. Some argue that such generic statements, although positive, are not adequate for some students who may have difficulty understanding what behavior is being praised (e.g., good job for what? what did I do that was nicely done?). Teachers may find specific praise more effective with students who display challenging behaviors (Gunter, Denny, Jack, Shores, & Nelson, 1993; Sutherland, Wehby, & Copeland, 2000) or experience academic failure (Luiselli & Downing, 1980). Specific praise pairs a generic praise statement with one that identified the appropriate social or academic behavior the teacher wants the student to display more often.

For example, Mr. Quincy is working with Anthony on his noise-making behavior during whole class instruction. During instruction, Anthony would make a clicking noise with his tongue and lips which was a distraction to his peers and Mr. Quincy. Mr. Quincy typically reprimanded Anthony or would stop his instruction and engage in discussions about the inappropriate behavior. Mr. Quincy realized that Anthony would make the inappropriate noise as soon as he began teaching again or stopped talking to Anthony. Using praise statements, Mr. Quincy began verbally attending to Anthony during instruction when he was not making the noises. This attention was provided immediately, frequently, and enthusiastically. For instance, Mr. Quincy would say "Anthony, I like the way you are sitting quietly and paying attention to the lesson" or "Anthony, I appreciate how you are quietly concentrating on your work." In addition, Mr. Quincy made a card prompting him to provide Anthony with some one-on-one time (additional attention) at the end of a lesson in which he was able to provide multiple specific praise statements. After using specific praise with Anthony for a few days, Mr. Quincy observed a decrease in his noise making. In addition, the interactions between teacher and student were more positive as Anthony made fewer noises.

Choice-Making

Making choices is a fundamental skill that can have positive effects on students' academic and social performance within the classroom (Jolivette, Wehby, Canale, & Massey, 2001; Kern, Mantegna, Vorndran, Bailin, & Hilt, 2001). A choice making opportunity occurs when a teacher selects two or more options from which the student may choose. The number of options should be based on student age and ability and on the objectives the teacher has set for the student. For example, a young child in a preschool setting who displays challenging behaviors when dropped-off by her mother may be provided with two options while a middle school aged student who is noncompliant with teacher requests may be offered a choice of three or four options. No matter the number of options, teachers should provide only options they are willing for the students to select. In addition, teachers can use choice making opportunities before, during, or after a specific task or activity in which they can predict inappropriate patterns of student behavior.

Mr. Hooper can predict that Tye will be verbally aggressive, noncompliant, and out of seat when prompted to get ready for math class. Mr. Hooper decides to provide Tye with opportunities to make choices immediately after his prompt. He says, "Tye, after you finish math class without any problems would you like to take Jerome, Steve, or Marilyn with you to the computer lab?" At first, this opportunity for Tye to make a choice was effective in that he went to math and actively and appropriately participated without incident. However, Mr. Hooper noticed that after about five weeks Tye's inappropriate behavior was occurring during math and he overheard Tye tell a friend that he really liked his new erasable pen. So, after the whole class math instruction occurred and students were getting ready to work on independent activities, Mr. Hooper praised Tye for his appropriate behavior during the lesson and then asked Tye if he would like to use a pencil or his erasable pen to complete the worksheet. Whereas Tye used to misbehave during math class, by giving Tye choices before and during the activity Mr. Hooper now observed appropriate behaviors from Tye.

Premack Principle

The Premack (1959) principle is frequently used to encourage students to engage in tasks and activities they usually would rather not do. Premack is a statement which pairs the display of an appropriate behavior with a reinforcer sought by the student and is usually phrased as "if . . . then . . ." or "after . . . then . . ." Parents may use the Premack Principle on Saturday mornings by saying "**If** you clean your room by making your bed, putting your laundry away, and putting your toys in the basket, **then** you can go outside and play with your friends." Knowing what is expected and knowing what will happen after the expectations are fulfilled promotes compliance.

In his classroom, Mr. Scott decided to use the Premack Principle with Travis, a fourth grade student who refused to legibly copy items written on the board (e.g., math problems, spelling words). When such activities took place, Mr. Scott found himself pleading with Travis to "get busy" and nagging him to do his work. Mr. Scott realized these strategies were not helping Travis get to work and were creating negative interactions between himself and Travis. Mr. Scott knew that Travis enjoyed working on the computer. The next time Travis was expected to copy his spelling words from the board, Mr. Scott discretely said to Travis "If you copy all 15 of your spelling words using your best handwriting, then you can use the computer to type in your math homework problems." Mr. Scott found that by clearly describing the behavior he expected from Travis (i.e., legibly writing all 15 spelling words) and what Travis was to get by engaging in the expected behavior (i.e., computer time), he was more focused on positive behavior, he decreased the likelihood of negatively interacting with Travis, and Travis was doing more work.

Conferencing

Teachers will need to talk to students who are stuck in automatic misbehavior. The purpose of the conference is not to lecture students or try to make them feel bad about their behavior but rather to help students see connections between their behavior and the outcomes. Conferencing provides students with a supported opportunity to think of alternatives for their misbehavior and for teachers to secure commitments from the students that they will try the alternatives. The time to conference with a student is not in the midst of misbehavior. To have a productive conference, everyone must be calm. Conferencing is usually conducted one-on-one, with just the student and teacher. Teachers should be ready for students' attempts to divert the focus of the conference. Following is an example of a productive conference:

Mr. Powell: Tell me what happened that got you sent to the principal's office.

Sylvester: It wasn't my fault. Stupid Derrick started it.

Mr. Powell: What happened first?

Sylvester: When we were working on the project, Derrick started making fun of the way I was writing. That's what happened. See it's all Derrick's fault and you should be talking to him instead of me.

Mr. Powell: What did Derrick do to make fun of your writing?

Sylvester: He started telling me that I write like a girl and that we were not going to get finished and it was all my fault 'cause I was writing so slow. Then he started laughing and singing, "Sylvester writes like a girl. Just like his sister the retard."

Mr. Powell: So Derrick tried to insult you by telling you that you write like a girl and then made a crack about your sister. That's pretty hard to hear. Derrick needs to stop doing stuff like that. What happened after he said all that stuff?

Sylvester: I made a big "X" across our project and told him that he could just finish it himself. He started yelling at me again, calling me "stupid" and "idiot" and so I tore the project in half. And then we both started yelling at each other and that's when you jumped in.

Mr. Powell: Yeah, you two were disturbing the entire class. And you didn't calm down when I asked you. Remember, we call that "belligerence". What's the rule when you're belligerent?

Sylvester: You have to go to the principal's office.

Mr. Powell: That's right, you go to the principal's office and he calls your parents.

Sylvester: But that wasn't fair because I didn't start it! Derrick started it and I was just defending myself. I have to be able to defend myself, you know!

Mr. Powell: The rule is that belligerence lands you in the principal's office, no matter who starts it.

Sylvester: That's not fair because I didn't start it. Derrick was mean and I had to stop him.

Mr. Powell: I know you wanted to stop him from saying those things and I probably would, too. But what could you do besides tear up your project when someone tries to insult you?

Sylvester: There's nothing else to do. I had to get his attention to make him stop.

Mr. Powell: But it didn't make him stop. What are some things we've talked about that you can do when someone teases you?

Sylvester: Oh, you mean like ignore him? Well, I couldn't do that because then he would get away with it.

Mr. Powell: Right! Ignoring him and pretending like you didn't hear a word he said is a good alternative. It will be hard but you could teach yourself to do it and then you wouldn't get in trouble.

Sylvester: But then Derrick gets away with it and he's mean.

Mr. Powell: You're right. Derrick needs to learn not to do those things. But when you react like you did, what happens?

Sylvester: I mess up a project we've been working on and then my parents get called. But I don't care. It was a stupid project anyway.

Mr. Powell: Right. When you react to someone's teasing by tearing up your project, then you're not going to get a good grade either. How can we work on your not losing your cool?

Sylvester: You could send Derrick to another class and make him stop being mean.

Mr. Powell: Well I can't help Derrick if he is in another class and we all need to work on respecting other people. Now, what can you and I do so that you don't lose your cool?

Sylvester: You could make Derrick shut-up when he starts talking like that.

Mr. Powell: How will I know when he's trying to insult you? I couldn't hear him when you two were working on your project.

Sylvester: I can tell you when he's being mean.

Mr. Powell: Right, you can tell me. What would you do? Would you just yell, "Mr. Powell, Derrick is being mean!" or what? How about you walk away from Derrick and come toward me and give me a signal?

Sylvester: Like what?

Mr. Powell: You could come toward me and hold up your index finger, like this. Then I would know that you are walking away from someone who is teasing you.

Sylvester: I think it would be better if I just told him to shut-up.

Mr. Powell: Well, you can certainly try that first. If it doesn't work, then you could walk away and give me the signal, and then your parents won't have to be called and you'll get your assignment finished. Can we try this?

Sylvester: I'm not sure it's going to work, but we can try.

Mr. Powell: Great. We'll give it at try.

In this conference, Mr. Powell connected what happened to Sylvester's behavior, helped Sylvester think of alternative behaviors that would have better outcomes, and secured a commitment from Sylvester to try the alternative. Mr. Powell did not respond to any of Sylvester's provocative statements or attempts to change the topic to anything other than Sylvester's behavior. Mr. Powell was empathetic and applauded Sylvester's good ideas. The conference is relatively brief, focused, and positive which will enable students to move toward more adaptive solutions to problems.

Token Economy

Token economies allow teachers to provide structured feedback for behavior and academic achievement in a systematic fashion (Kazdin, 1977). Tokens are things that are given as a consequence of behavior. They provide tangible proof that students are performing as expected. Tokens have no intrinsic value but become valuable because of how they can be used, which is to trade them for something that is valuable to the individual. Tokens include such things as grades, check marks, poker chips, tickets, marbles, and so forth. Tokens selected for use will depend upon the developmental age of the students (e.g., check marks for older students and marbles for younger students). A prime example of a token economy is teacher salary. Teachers sign a contract that they will receive a certain amount of money if they perform their duties as expected. The money is not meaningful in and of itself but is quite meaningful in terms of what it allows teachers to purchase. Similarly, grades have no intrinsic value but can be accumulated and later exchanged for a diploma or degree.

In classrooms, token economies are linked to behavioral and academic expectations. Teachers decide if students are to receive tokens in a structured or spontaneous way. To use a token economy in a structured way, teachers determine an interval that is appropriate for students. Young children and older students with poor ability to delay gratification may need to have the structured feedback given more frequently. For example, young children may earn a smiley face after each activity. The teacher will quickly talk to each child after an activity and draw or place a sticker of a smiley face in the box representing that activity on a chart. Some older students may receive tokens only at the end of the day or the end of the week.

To use a token economy in a more spontaneous fashion, teachers may intermittently award tokens when they observe students performing as expected. As with structured token economies, when awarding tokens spontaneously, teachers need to clearly describe the behavior reflecting the class rules that are being reinforced. There are many variations on spontaneous awarding of tokens. Teachers may set a timer for an undisclosed amount of time and when the timer goes off, each student who is on-task will receive a token. In another variation, students who are acknowledged for behaving as expected are given a slip of paper on which to write their names. The slips of paper are then put into a container and at the end of the day (or week) a slip is drawn and the student whose name is on the paper gets to do something special (e.g., eat lunch with teacher, get a "no homework" ticket) or receives something special (e.g., pizza coupon, bonus points). Teachers also may use token economies for the entire class. When the teacher praises the entire class for appropriate behavior or meeting an academic criteria (e.g., everyone scored above 80% on the math quiz), a token is awarded (e.g., marble placed in a container, check mark on the board) and after the accumulation of a predetermined number of tokens, the entire group gets to do or receive something special.

The keys to a token economy include that students receive feedback in the form of tokens frequently enough to make it meaningful to them and that the items for which the tokens are exchanged are things that the students want. In order to promote an understanding that the tokens are meaningful, the frequency of exchange, similar to the frequency of feedback, must match students' ability to delay gratification. In terms of the exchange items, many teachers using a token economy will have a store in which they have a variety of items with corresponding costs. The items available for the student to acquire will be determined by how many tokens the student has earned. The items available in the store do not have to be expensive or even purchased by the teacher. These items can be donated by parents, donated by the schools' business partners, or accumulated through friends (e.g., toys that come in children's meals at many fast food restaurants are popular with young children). The store also may contain activity items like passes for extra time on the computer, lunch with the principal, ice-cream at lunch, five minutes in the gym to play basketball with a peer of choice, and so forth. The cost of each item will be based on how desirable it is and how much effort should be required to earn. For example, small items like candy may be priced very low. Big ticket items like a football or pizza coupon may be priced higher. In some schools, the price for eating lunch with the janitor may be higher than the price for eating lunch with the teacher. Teachers may need to identify special interests to motivate reluctant students to participate. For example, adding a popular music CD to the class store may greatly increase the motivation of a particular student to participate.

An interesting example of a token economy is described by Cook (1999). In this token economy, the teacher duplicated enlarged photocopies of $1, $5, and $10 "behavior bucks". Students who were ready with all materials needed for the lesson (i.e., books, papers, and pencils) received behavior bucks. Raising the hand and waiting to be called on earned behavior bucks as did completed work. Students engaged in banking activities at the end of the day, completing deposit slips to bank their bucks. Students graphed their 5-day earning totals. They could write checks to purchase preferred items. In this study, the items included: hockey cards, extra computer time, time out of class to work with the librarian or custodian, special projects with the secretary to answer the phone or operate the photocopier, or extra time in the gym with a 5th grade teacher. The time in the gym with the 5th grade teacher was the big ticket item and cost $200. The token economy not only emphasized the literal value of appropriate behavior but also provided opportunities for students to learn banking, saving, and purchasing skills.

The interesting aspect of this token economy is that after a few months, the students agreed to collectively raise $10,000 in behavior bucks and use that money to help needy families. A local department store agreed to exchange the $10,000 in behavior bucks for $1,000 of store credit. Four families (not in the school community) were adopted by the class. Although their identities were never revealed, the students knew how many adults were in the family as well as the number and ages of children. After accumulating the targeted goal, the class made a field trip to the store and worked collaboratively to equitably spend the store credit to purchase items such as clothing, toys, and house wares for their adopted families. This extension of the token economy provided an opportunity to develop empathy and altruism.

Token economies will succeed only if the students' abilities are considered in terms of how often the tokens should be awarded and exchanged and if the exchange items available are things the students want. Ideas for high interest items include soda, candy bars, late to class pass, coupon to get out of detention, coupon for $2 off Friday morning breakfast, and chips of choice on Tuesday (Kehle, Bray, Theodore, Jenson, & Clark, 2000). Anticipation of reinforcement can be heightened by adding a surprise element. For example, teachers can make a pie chart with preferred items and activities written on each slice and then add a spinner. Students who meet criteria spin to discover what they have earned. Or, the preferred items and activities may be written on individual slips of paper and placed in a container for drawing when students have earned the opportunity. Unless students' behaviors warrant, token economies should not be used as a permanent strategy in a classroom for routine tasks (Van Acker, 2006). Teachers should fade the use of the artificial reinforcers used in token economies and rely as much as possible on natural reinforcers such as praise and grades. However, a token economy can be a good way to bring a classroom under control and can be used to emphasize the importance of following the class rules.

Behavioral Contracts

Some students who misbehave or who do not do their work respond positively to a written and/or verbal agreement with the teacher. Such an agreement is commonly referred to as a behavioral contract. A behavioral contract is a tool in which the teacher states which appropriate behavior the student is to display and the student identifies which reinforcer he would like to earn for displaying this behavior. Some negotiation may occur. A typical sequence of steps is followed to create a behavioral contract.

1. Based on the data the teacher has collected and what other strategies have been tried, the teacher identifies a positive academic or social behavior the student needs to demonstrate.
2. The teacher approaches the student and both discuss the behavior of concern.
3. Both the teacher and student discuss the appropriate behavior the student will display. During this discussion, the appropriate behavior needs to be clearly defined. The definition will include a) under what conditions the student should display the behavior, b) what cues or prompts the teacher may provide to the student, and

c) when the student should not display the behavior (e.g., it would not be appropriate to for a student to raise her hand on the playground to receive a turn on the slide).

4. The teacher will ask the student what type of reinforcer is preferred for when the appropriate behavior is displayed. If a student cannot name a reinforcer or the reinforcer is not appropriate (too big or costly), the teacher can ask the student to list a variety of reinforcers and then select from that list. During this discussion, the teacher and student decide how many times or how long the student needs to display the appropriate behavior before the reinforcer is given. The time element will be based on the student's age and difficulty of the behavior to be displayed. For example, some contracts may be written each day while others may span a week or more. In addition, how and by whom the reinforcer will be provided needs to be discussed. For example, will the teacher or principal deliver the reinforcement to the student at the end of the school day or as soon as the behavior is displayed?

5. At this point, the teacher and student review the appropriate behavior the student is to display, the reinforcer the student will receive for the behavior, and the time frame for delivery of the reinforcer. This step is for purposes of negotiation and detailing both the teacher and student responsibilities. If both the teacher and student are in agreement of the terms of the contract, they are ready for step 6.

6. Depending on the abilities of the student, either the student or the teacher will write the contract. The complexity of the contract will vary but it is best to keep it simple. Based on the discussion in the proceeding steps, the following are written: a) the student's and teacher's names; b) the behavior the student is to display along with the number of times and under what conditions; c) what the teacher will do to support the student; d) what the reinforcer is and when, how, and by whom it will be delivered; e) a start and end date for the contract; and f) signature lines for both the student and teacher. It is important that all aspects of the contract be written in positive terms.

Behavioral contracting can be a powerful yet simple strategy to use with students who misbehave. For example, Mr. Landis is concerned about Jason's inconsistent and often inaccurate homework completion which is negatively affecting his grades. In the past, Mr. Landis has provided Jason with reinforcers for turning in his homework but realized that it did not mean Jason had completed the assignment accurately. In addition, when Mr. Landis prompted students to turn in their homework, he and Jason often got in an argument. Mr. Landis decided to try a behavioral contract with Jason. They met privately in the back of the classroom while the other students worked on independent assignments. Mr. Landis discussed his concern regarding Jason's homework and its effect on his grades. Both agreed that homework needed to be turned in each time it was given and that Jason would receive a reinforcer (e.g., weekend homework pass, computer time) if he turned it in with 80% or higher accuracy. They decided that the duration of the contract would be one week and he had to display the appropriate behavior all five days to earn his reinforcer. A note was added to the contract that each Monday, they would sign a new contract and if Jason had earned the previous week's "weekend homework pass" that he had to display the appropriate behavior Tuesday through Friday (since he would not be turning in homework on Monday). They wrote the contract and both signed it. For the past six weeks, Jason has met his contract goal four times. Mr. Landis is pleased with Jason's goal attainment and he has seen an increase in Jason's grades as well as a positive change in his relationship with Jason during their morning routine when homework is due. If Jason was not meeting the requirements of the contract, Mr. Landis would need to reconvene a meeting with Jason to discuss changing aspects of the contract (e.g., the selected appropriate behavior, reinforcement schedule) to promote student success.

Group Contingencies

Group contingencies are programs that make getting something reinforcing dependent on the behavior of a group. Often these are expansions of token economies that use the behavior of a group as the determining factor in whether or not tokens, and ultimately, reinforcement will be given. Group contingencies can create a focus on expected behavior and students have a vested interest in prompting and encouraging appropriate behavior from their peers. In addition to being useful for getting peers involved in supporting each other, group contingencies tend to reduce students' tolerance for others who do not behave as expected, which can remove peer reinforcement of misbehavior. There are three types of group contingencies: independent, dependent, and interdependent.

In using **independent group contingencies,** the same criteria are used for all students but each student is able to access reinforcement individually. For example, the teacher may say that everyone who scores above 80% on an assignment can engage in a 5-minute free time period for talking with their friends at the end of class. The contingency applies to the entire class and each student who meets the criteria has access to the reinforcement. This type of group contingency does little to get peers to encourage each other to perform as expected since the criteria must be met individually.

With **dependent group contingencies,** the class is allowed access to a token or reinforcer based on the behavior of one individual or a small group of individuals. Modifying the example just given to be a dependent group contingency, the teacher would inform the class that if Robert earns 80% or better on his assignment, the entire class will get 5-minutes of free time to talk with their friends at the end of the class period. In this way, maximum peer pressure is exerted and students can become "heroes" in the classroom. On the other hand, the targeted student may be yelled at and snubbed if the group does not get the reinforcement. One unique variation of the dependent group contingency is evident when the teacher does not tell the class the identity of the targeted student. The teacher writes the name of a student on a piece of paper, folds it, and places it in plain sight. The "mystery" student is not revealed until the end of the class period when the teacher removes the paper and shows everyone the name that was written. Students may be motivated to meet the stated criteria in case they are revealed as the mystery student and peer encouragement is spread across the class rather than concentrated on Robert. Again, however, it is possible that if the mystery student does not earn the reinforcement for the group that others will be unkind.

The third type of group contingency is an **interdependent group contingency.** In an interdependent contingency, access to a token or reinforcement depends upon the combined performance of members of a group. The group may be an entire class or subset groups within the class. Use of subsets within a classroom adds the element of competition. Not every team will earn the reinforcement; only the team with the highest (or lowest) number of points. The competitive angle of interdependent contingencies can create high levels of animosity among classmates and should be used with caution and only when students in the class are mature enough to handle the competitive aspect.

More commonly, interdependent group contingencies are developed based on the behavior of the class as a whole. Examples of interdependent group contingencies have already appeared as parts of examples for other strategies. In the description of signal control, Ms. Dennis wrote one of the letters from the word "homework" on the board each time the entire class was quiet within two seconds of hearing the chime. In the discussion of the token economy using "behavior bucks" the students worked together toward a group contingency of $10,000. Lohrmann and Talerico (2004) describe an interdependent group contingency called "Anchor the Boat". In this group contingency, at the end of every 42-minute class period, if the number of students who got out of their seats + the number of students who did not complete the assignment + the number of students who called out was less than a specified number, a paper clip was added to the chain suspended between a picture of a boat that had been placed on the wall and the picture of an anchor that was 20 inches away (it took 10 two-inch paper clips to connect the boat to the anchor). When the boat was anchored, students could choose items from a treasure chest that included toys, bookmarks, and games. As with any contingency, after students become proficient at achieving the goal, variables can be modified to promote development of increasingly responsible behavior. In the anchor the boat game, the criteria could be systematically lowered until it was zero. Or, the anchor could be moved further away from the boat. Or small paper clips could be substituted for the large ones. In terms of the three types of group contingencies, dependent and interdependent group contingencies have been found to be more effective for increasing appropriate behavior than independent group contingencies (Gresham & Gresham, 1982).

Differential Reinforcement

Differential reinforcement must be discussed separately and appears on the third level of the pyramid because it takes a little more teacher effort to implement than strategies in which students simply earn reinforcement. As discussed previously, behaviors are followed by consequences and if the consequences result in the behavior continuing, then the consequence is reinforcing. If the consequence results in the student no longer demonstrating the behavior, then the consequence is punishing. Teachers who say, "His behavior was getting worse even though I was reinforcing him with candy" do not understand the concept of reinforcement. If the candy resulted in behavior getting worse, then it was a punisher, not a reinforcer. Some students find teacher attention and praise reinforcing, others do not. Students who continue to misbehave even though they are consistently sent to the office must be finding the trips to the office reinforcing. Some students even seem to be reinforced by teachers reprimanding them as the misbehavior continues to occur. To use differential reinforcement, teachers must first identify what the student finds reinforcing (e.g., praise, going to the office, reprimands). Then, differential reinforcement occurs when teachers reinforce appropriate behavior but withhold reinforcement when students misbehave. This is why differential reinforcement is a little harder to implement. Teachers must get very good at noticing and reinforcing appropriate behavior but must resist the urge to notice or reinforce misbehavior.

Consider the example of Ms. Long. One of her students, Michelle, wanders around the room, asks the teacher and peers questions usually not on-topic, and looks out the window when Ms. Long is trying to teach the class. This out-of-seat behavior is interfering with Michelle's ability to learn as well as the other students' learning because Ms. Long finds herself interrupting her teaching to redirect Michelle back to her seat, answering her off-topic questions, and pleading with her to sit down. The behavior usually stops when Ms. Long, totally exasperated, sends Michelle to the principal's office. Ms. Long's data suggested that Michelle spends more time out-of-seat during math class than any other class. Since math class lasts 25 minutes, Ms. Long made a data recording sheet with 5 squares and if Michelle was in her seat for the entire 5 minute segment, Ms. Long recorded a "+" and verbally reinforced Michelle (e.g., "You've earned a "+" for sitting in your seat"). Most importantly, Ms. Long ignored Michelle's out-of-seat behavior and did not interrupt her instruction to answer Michelle's questions. She also used a group contingency and put a check on the board whenever other students ignored Michelle's questions, having told the class that when they got 10 checks, they would not get math homework that day. By using differential reinforcement, Ms. Long ignored Michelle's misbehavior and reinforced her for staying in her seat. When Michelle earned 10 "+" marks, she was allowed to go to the principal's office for a visit.

The use of behavior enhancement strategies, such as the 11 described in this text, helps teachers stay focused on the positive behaviors they want students to display and allows students to receive systematic reinforcement for engaging in appropriate behavior. Teachers will find that students demonstrate less misbehavior when the emphasis is on performing as expected. Unfortunately, some students will have high levels of chronic automatic misbehavior that respond only partially to behavior enhancement strategies. For these students, teachers may have to consider temporarily adding behavior reduction strategies.

Behavior Reduction Strategies

Behavior reduction strategies, including response cost, timeout, reprimands, and aversives, may be effective but must be used with great caution because of two predictable outcomes. First, most behavior reduction strategies result in unwanted reactions from students (Sidman, 1989). Students may comply with teacher directives when faced with the prospect of punishment, but will do so grudgingly and their resentment will show in other types of resistant behavior, both overt (e.g., verbal or physical aggression) and covert (e.g., vandalism, truancy). Indeed, the use of punishment is associated with increased rates of misbehavior (Mayer, 1995) as students may want to be suspended or go to detention instead of doing their work (Atkins et al., 2002). The use of corporal punishment (an aversive), has not been shown to be effective in reducing misbehavior (Robinson, Funk, Beth, & Bush, 2005) and may actually lead to depression among those who receive it when they become adults (Turner & Muller, 2004).

Second, although behavior reduction strategies may stop misbehavior, they do nothing to teach the student what should be done instead. As has been discussed previously, errors in behavior need to be treated like errors in academics and the student should be taught the appropriate response and reinforced when it is demonstrated. Punishment does not teach, it simply suppresses, leaving a behavioral vacuum and a strong likelihood that students will repeat the misbehavior when faced with the same situation because they do not know what to do instead.

With these two cautions in mind, some behavior management plans combine strategies designed to teach appropriate behavior with those designed to reduce misbehavior. The guiding concept is to think in terms of **behavior pairs** (Kauffman et al., 2006, p. 26) in which the opposite or acceptable alternative for the misbehavior is identified. For example, if a student is out of his seat frequently and this is a problem, what is the behavior that the teacher wants to see? The behavior pair for being out of seat would be sitting in the seat. Strategies used to address the behavior should focus on increasing the time the student spends in his seat, similar to the example given of Ms. Long and differential reinforcement. If the strategies are not effective after a reasonable effort, then the teacher may want to continue to focus on motivating the student to stay in his seat but may add strategies designed to discourage him from getting out of his seat without permission. The behavior reduction strategies discussed here include: response cost and timeout. Aversive consequences also will be discussed in order to highlight why such commonly used strategies are rarely effective for long-term behavioral change.

Response Cost

Response cost procedures involve the removal or loss of something following the misbehavior in the hopes that the misbehavior will be less likely to occur in the future (Azrin & Holz, 1966). A cost is associated with the behavior. A common example of response cost is what happens when individuals are caught driving too fast. The behavior (speeding) costs something, usually literally, as the individual has to pay the speeding ticket. Response cost procedures rarely involve money in school settings. Instead, misbehavior costs students things such as lost tokens, lost privileges, lost possessions, or loss of the ability to participate in extracurricular activities. Whatever is taken away from the student must be valued by the student or the response cost procedure will not be effective.

Ms. Demming recognized that Jerry's talking-out in class was disrupting his learning and the learning of other students. She and Jerry wrote a behavioral contract that specified he would earn one minute of extra time on the computer for every five minutes in which he raised his hand and waited to be called on before talking during instruction. The strategy was somewhat effective, as Jerry did earn a few extra minutes on the computer for several days. However, his talking out was still a problem. Ms. Demming met with Jerry and modified his contract to include a loss of one minute of computer time for each instance of talking out. After Jerry experienced one day where he did not get to use the computer during free-time because the response cost procedure resulted in the loss of the available minutes, the instances of talking out were reduced to near zero. In combination, the reinforcement for raising his hand and waiting, along with the loss of minutes for talking out, was effective for reducing the misbehavior and increasing the amount of instructional time for everyone.

Timeout

Timeout is one of the most misused strategies in schools and, as such, is rarely effective. Teachers say they are using timeout when they send students away from the group to go back to their desks or to a designated area of the room. Some schools even have special timeout rooms or students may be sent to sit in the hall. Teachers must remember the full name of the strategy if it is going to be used effectively. The term "timeout" is short for "timeout from reinforcement". Timeout indicates that students are experiencing reinforcement so that losing the reinforcement during timeout is devastating. Unfortunately, students may not perceive some classrooms or academic activities as pleasurable and may prefer instead to be sent to an area away from the group where they can relax unbothered by having to do the work. Or, better yet, sent into the hall where they can talk to others who walk by. Either way, the student has been removed from a situation that was not reinforcing to one that is preferable, so there is a good chance the same behavior will occur in the future. The use of timeout may be very reinforcing for the teacher who does not have to deal with the troublesome student who is out of the room. In these examples, timeout is not effective for reducing misbehavior but may be used repeatedly because the teacher is reinforced.

When used appropriately, timeout can be effective for reducing problem behavior. As a behavior reduction strategy, it does not teach the student what to do instead of the misbehavior, so it must be accompanied by strategies to increase a behavior which is desired instead of the misbehavior. To use time-out appropriately, teachers must be sure that the academic and social demands placed on students are within their ability, so that students are not using their behavior to avoid the demands. Instruction should include high levels of reinforcement in the form of positive feedback and be engaging to students. With non-isolationary timeout, where the student remains in the classroom but may not be able to participate, teachers need to specify how much time the student will be in timeout. The length of time spent in timeout should be brief and based on the student's developmental age. The student should be expected to return to the activity that was interrupted when timeout is over, or the potential for using misbehavior to escape non-preferred activities will remain high. Teachers need to document how frequently the student goes to timeout and the duration of each timeout. Timeout is determined to be ineffective if the strategy is used for the same students multiple times each week. At this point, teachers should abandon timeout as a strategy for these students and consider alternatives.

Mr. Carlson was concerned about Andrew's use of threats and intimidation with his peers. These seemed to occur most often when Andrew thought the other students were making fun of him or not letting him have his way. Mr. Carlson implemented social skills training for the entire class during the Social Studies block. The class discussed historical and current events in which aggression erupted as a result of misunderstanding or intimidation. They then spent several days role-playing how to handle teasing and several more days addressing the steps for negotiation and compromise. Mr. Carlson was quick to encourage students to demonstrate their developing skills when opportunities presented themselves at other times during the day. Mr. Carlson commended the students whenever he saw students using the skills.

The number of threats and intimidating comments Andrew made were reduced but still occurred two or three times per week. Knowing that Andrew was reinforced by engaging in group activities, Mr. Carlson decided to implement timeout with Andrew and met with him privately. He discussed with Andrew the potential consequences for his behavior in terms of the effect on friendships and negative implications for future employment. Mr. Carlson told Andrew that if he made a threat or intimidating comment, he would be told to remove himself to a designated area and set the timer for five minutes. At the end of five minutes, Andrew could return to the group. They also discussed the consequences if Andrew refused to go to timeout and the consequences if Andrew continued to make intimidating or threatening comments while he was in timeout. Over the next few weeks, the number of times Andrew was sent to timeout decreased to zero, reflecting that Andrew was no longer making intimidating or threatening comments in class. Mr. Carlson continued to commend Andrew for using the social skills the class had learned.

Timeout which places the student in an isolated setting requires additional considerations and precautions. Isolationary timeout should be reserved only for students whose behavior has become a serious threat to personal safety or the safety and welfare of others. Districts must develop procedures and oversight for the use of isolationary timeout and teachers must be trained in the implementation of those procedures. Yell (1990) provides cautions and considerations for developing guidelines for the implementation of this restrictive form of timeout. Teachers should not attempt to isolate students in timeout unless they have been trained in the district-sanctioned procedures.

Aversives

Aversive consequences are those in which something unwanted is given or applied in the hopes the consequences will be perceived as punishing and reduce future occurrence of a particular behavior. Reprimands are the most commonly used aversive procedures in schools (e.g., "no", "stop", "don't", "quit"). Reprimands are statements made to students that inform them that they are misbehaving and need to stop. Ms. Lewis is distracted by William talking to Allison. She reprimands him by saying, "William, stop talking to Allison." As with all behavior reduction strategies, reprimands should be used with caution and by following basic guidelines. Reprimands do not teach appropriate behavior, so they will need to be used with strategies that teach and encourage the use of the behavior pair. Also, reprimands cannot be delivered without giving students attention. There are some students who seek any attention, even if it is in the form of a reprimand. If reprimands are not reducing the problem behavior, then they may be serving as reinforcement instead of punishment. Teachers tend to overuse reprimands, creating a focus on students who are misbehaving rather than those who are behaving appropriately (Shores et al., 1993). This can make the classroom more negative and actually lead to higher rates of misbehavior. To avoid this unwanted outcome, teachers should make multiple positive comments (commending students for appropriate behavior and effort) for every reprimand given.

The guidelines for the effective use of reprimands include the following (Kauffman et al., 2006):

1. Keep the reprimands brief and specific. In the example above, Ms. Lewis was brief and specific. She would have veered into lecture and shaming had she said, "I can't believe I have to tell you this again! You need to stop that incessant talking and get busy with your work, young man, or you're going to fail just like your brother did!" Those comments would constitute an inappropriate reprimand. Abramowitz, O'Leary, and Futtersak (1988) found that short reprimands (no more than two words plus the student's name) were more effective than longer reprimands for reducing off-task behavior.

2. Give reprimands as privately as possible. Get close enough to the student to be heard and deliver the reprimand quietly and firmly. Van Houten, Nau, MacKenzie-Keating, Sameoto, and Colavecchia (1982) found that reprimands delivered one meter away from elementary students were more effective for reducing disruptive behavior than those delivered seven meters away. Houghton, Wheldall, Jukes, and Sharpe (1990) found that reprimands given to secondary students privately were more effective for increasing on-task behavior than those given publicly.

3. Make sure the student is attending and attempt to establish eye contact before delivering a reprimand. If the student is not paying attention, the reprimand will probably not have the desired effect.

4. Deliver the reprimand unemotionally and matter-of-factly. Teachers who give reprimands angrily or who appear to be visibly upset have lost control of the situation. Teachers who get upset are taking the students' behavior personally. High levels of emotion will cloud good decision making. Additionally, some students want to see teachers lose control and may be reinforced when teachers get emotional. For the reprimand to deter behavior, it must be a brief, objective statement.

In addition to reprimands, the category of aversives includes other consequences which are given or applied to reduce behavior. Aversives include corporal punishment (i.e., spanking), forced activity, physical restraint, and delivery of noxious substances (e.g., hot sauce on tongue). The use of aversive procedures to reduce inappropriate behavior is rarely sanctioned in schools and then only under extenuating circumstances, after all other strategies have failed. Permission to use aversives must be given by multiple individuals including parents and district personnel. It is important to discuss the use of aversives other than reprimands; however, because some teachers use them unwittingly. For example, the teacher who makes students write "I will not talk in class" five hundred times is using an aversive procedure intended to produce fatigue. The same is true for a coach who has students run laps or do push-ups as a consequence for misbehavior. Or the teacher who has a student stand-up for 10-minutes to punish him for being out of his seat. Historically, some teachers made students sit in the corner wearing a dunce cap. This is aversive because it is intended to cause humiliation and social ostracization. All of these are examples of aversives which violate the students' rights, generate unwanted side-effects, and are not effective for behavioral change. Federal and state regulations limit the use of aversive procedures (Weiss, 2005) and teachers should recognize if they are using aversives and discontinue use of unsanctioned aversive procedures.

Addressing More Severe Behavioral Problems

For more severe misbehaviors displayed by students during academic and/or social instruction, an additional set of strategies may be employed. For students who engage in chronic or predictable misbehavior, who have a history of displaying such behavior, or when placement changes are considered due to behavior, a functional behavior assessment (FBA) may need to be conducted to determine the variables contributing to the occurrence of misbehavior. An FBA consists of four core processes and is conducted by a multi-disciplinary team which contains members who know the student and who have expertise in academic and social student difficulties (Jolivette, Scott, & Nelson, 2000; O'Neil, Horner, Albin, Sprague, Storey, & Newton, 1997). The first process, **defining the problem,** consists of the team (a) discussing the problem behavior, (b) collecting data through archival records reviews, direct observations, and interviews to determine the environments where the problem behaviors are occurring and in which environments the student behaves appropriately, and (c) reframing the problem into measurable, observable, and objective behavior.

When defining the problem, Mr. Carter states that Cecil is noncompliant. Mr. Carter defines noncompliance by stating that when he is given a direction (e.g., "Get out your Social Studies book"), Cecil a) typically says, "You can't make me", b) continues with what he was doing prior to the prompt, and c) sometimes will comply with the direction about 15 minutes after it is given. Cecil's noncompliance is reported to occur across all his classes.

Second, the team **identifies the predictable sequences of the problem behavior.** The team analyzes the data collected in terms of an observable and predictable pattern or A-B-C. The "A" is the antecedent or what happens immediately prior to the problem behavior, the "B" is the defined problem behavior, and the "C" is the consequence or what happens immediately after the problem behavior. For Cecil, his predictable pattern is as follows:

- Antecedent: Specific direction given by teacher
- Behavior: Noncompliance within expected time frame
- Consequence: Teacher continues to teach and lets Cecil do what he wants

Third, the team **creates a hypothesis** which includes the conditions (the antecedents) when the student misbehaves and what usually happens after the behavior (the consequences). After reviewing all the data collected, the team develops the following hypothesis for Cecil: During academic settings when the teacher gives a direction, Cecil does not comply with the task demand and the teacher removes the task demand.

Fourth, the team uses the prior three processes to **state the function** of the student's inappropriate or challenging behavior. As discussed previously, behavior always occurs for a reason and students are achieving a goal through their behavior. Students, who misbehave during instruction, typically do so to either get something or to avoid something. **Figure 11-7** provides typical classroom examples of what students may try to get or avoid. For Cecil, the team decides that the noncompliant behavior is being used to escape or avoid the work Mr. Carter is giving. The team also discusses how once Mr. Carter sees that Cecil is not going to do what he requested, he leaves Cecil alone, thus letting Cecil avoid any task demands he does not like.

Once an FBA has been conducted, the team has the necessary data to write a behavior intervention plan (BIP) which details the strategies the teacher(s) are to use to address the student's misbehavior during academic and social lessons. In writing a BIP, the team will

FIGURE 11-7

Classroom Examples of the Get and Escape Functions

Function	Classroom Examples
Get	
Attention from teacher	Student yells "I need help" and teacher walks over and helps.
Attention from peers	Student calls another student a "pig" and the other students sitting at the table laugh and encourage the student to continue being inappropriate.
Access to privileges	Student pushes other student so she can be at the front of the lunch line and the teacher lets her be first.
Access to items	Student grabs a puzzle box from another student during free time and the teacher allows that student to play with the puzzle.
Escape	
Avoid teacher	When the student sees Ms. Connely walking towards her desk, student says "I hate you" and Ms. Connely walks away.
Avoid peers	Student is assigned to work with a partner, student hits her partner, and student is told to work independently.
Avoid task demands	Student is asked to begin a worksheet but refuses and the teacher does not ask the student again to complete the assignment.
Avoid activities	A few minutes before the weekly timed math test, student pushes items off desk, and is sent to the office.

follow six basic steps. First, the team **decides what appropriate behaviors or replacement behaviors** the student should be displaying in place of the problem behavior. These replacement behaviors should be those which will be recognized and reinforced by the student's teachers and peers. As previously discussed, behavioral pairing is the identification of an appropriate behavior that could replace the inappropriate behavior. In Cecil's case, the behavioral pair is noncompliance and compliance. Mr. Carter wants Cecil to be more compliant to his requests by quickly responding as directed.

Second, the team will **discuss environmental signals** which will remind the student to engage in the replacement behaviors. Typically, these signals are provided verbally, visually, or gesturally by the teacher to the student in some clear manner and no longer used when the student independently engages in the replacement behaviors. As part of Cecil's BIP, the team agrees that when Mr. Carter gives a direction, he will give it to the entire class and then place a five-minute card on Cecil's desk. The card is a visual cue to remind Cecil that he has five minutes to comply. The five-minute card is replaced on Cecil's desk every minute, the next card showing "4 minutes", the next "3 minutes" and so on to "1 minute". The card provides an additional prompt for Cecil to begin the task and decreases the likelihood that Mr. Carter and Cecil will get into an argument.

Third, the team **describes any barriers which may make it hard for the student to display replacement behaviors.** Once barriers have been identified, the team will need to develop ways to get around the barriers. Mr. Carter thinks that he may forget to provide the visual cue cards and may forget to reinforce Cecil when he engages in the replacement behavior. As a means to address this potential barrier, Mr. Carter has a written prompt in his lesson plan to give Cecil the minute cards with extra cards placed near Cecil's desk and in areas from which Mr. Carter teaches.

Fourth, the team **agrees upon the consequences for the student engaging or not engaging in the replacement behaviors.** At this time, the team also will need to agree upon the short and long-term goals and objectives related to the student and the academic and/or social behavior. With Cecil, the team agrees that if he engages in the replacement behavior (follows Mr. Carter's directions within five minutes), he can earn opportunities to take a break from activities and can get homework passes. That is, Cecil can appropriately avoid work contingent upon following Mr. Carter's directions. The team also agrees that when Cecil does not follow directions that Mr. Carter will not argue with Cecil but that the work is expected to be completed and a natural consequence will be given. For Cecil, if he does not do his work in-class, then that assignment becomes homework. Thus, Cecil will no longer be reinforced with the removal of a work when he does not follow directions. A crisis management plan may be necessary for students who display extreme and unsafe challenging behavior (e.g., prolonged aggression). Each school district has a set of policies to deal with unsafe behavior and such policies should be known to all classroom teachers. If this is a concern, teachers should seek assistance and support from their school administration.

Fifth the team **creates a data collection** and sixth a **monitoring plan** to determine if the student's BIP is working to reduce the problem behavior and increase use of the replacement behavior. Data are reviewed and the plan is monitored frequently. If the student is not behaving better or if changes in the student's behavior are not occurring to the degree the team wants, the plan is modified. Embedded within the BIP process are the strategies used by the teacher to enhance student engagement, including the effective instructional practices and curricular accommodations described previously in this chapter.

With Cecil, the team decides to collect both the frequency (number of times) and latency (time between a task demand and student engagement) of Cecil's noncompliance. Using the definition of noncompliance from the first step of the FBA process, Cecil's teachers can record each time Cecil is noncompliant to their requests. In addition, the teachers can record how long it takes for Cecil to comply with their requests. The team has planned to meet in two weeks to see if Cecil's BIP is effective in producing the change desired. Two weeks later, Mr. Carter brings in his data and shares it with the team. Prior to the implementation of the BIP, Cecil was noncompliant an average of 15 times per day and spent on average 45 minutes per day not engaged in the tasks asked of him. Since implementing the BIP, Cecil has been noncompliant an average of 6 times per day and spent on average 15 minutes per day not engaged in the tasks. The team is initially pleased with these data which suggest that Cecil has decreased his noncompliant behavior and when he is noncompliant, he is quicker to engage in the task. Mr. Carter reported that Cecil is motivated by earning homework passes and short breaks from tasks. In addition, Mr. Carter stated that he is praising Cecil more often and he has heard Cecil say "I might as well do this dumb thing so I don't have to do it tonight at home." The team decides to continue monitoring Cecil's BIP by reconvening in another two weeks. If Cecil's data suggest that the BIP is no longer effective (e.g., increases in noncompliance, the reinforcers are longer as powerful) adaptations to the plan will be made.

Legal Issues Related to Managing Behavior

Since its inception as the Education for the Handicapped Act in 1975, the Individuals with Disabilities Education Act (IDEA, now IDEA 2004) has contained provisions to ensure students with disabilities who also have challenging behaviors continue to receive a free, appropriate public education (FAPE). IDEA 2004 continues this tradition with few changes. Teachers who have students with disabilities who misbehave during instruction need to know the discipline aspects of IDEA 2004. For improved clarity, related discipline subsections have been grouped together. The discipline aspects are described below.

Free Appropriate Public Education (FAPE)

As described in Chapter 2, this provision of IDEA mandates that all school-age students with disabilities receive an education at public expense to promote success within society. For students with disabilities who misbehave, FAPE is provided no matter where students receive educational services. For example, if a student with disabilities is suspended for more than 10 days or is expelled because of misbehavior, the school must continue to provide FAPE. This may mean the student's educational services are provided in an in-school suspension program or at-home. The only major change regarding discipline in IDEA 2004, is that greater authority is given to school personnel to temporarily change a student's placement if the student violates the student code of conduct.

Interim Alternative Educational Setting (IAES)

Under IDEA (2004), if a student causes serious bodily injury, brings drugs or weapons to school or school functions, the student can be placed in an IAES for up to 45 school days regardless of whether or not the student's behavior is a manifestation of the disability. In addition, the student with a disability can be placed in IAES for 10 or fewer school days if the student violates the school code of conduct.

Manifestation Determination

The purpose of a manifestation determination is to ensure that schools do not circumvent due process safeguards when students with disabilities engage in inappropriate behavior. The "stay-put" provision requires that students with disabilities remain in their current placements to avoid wrongful removal while teams decide how and where to provide services to the student. In fact, IDEA 2004 stresses the importance of schools being proactive and preventative in the educational programming provided to students with disabilities when behavioral challenges may be an issue. Under IDEA 2004, when students display inappropriate behavior and the team decides that the inappropriate behavior was a manifestation of their disability, then an FBA needs to be conducted and a BIP written and implemented. If an FBA and BIP already exist, the team is to review, modify, and re-implement the BIP. If the team decides that the student's inappropriate behavior was not a manifestation of the disability, then FAPE needs to be provided; however, the team can place the student in an IAES. With these changes, the classroom teacher will want to make sure that an FBA is conducted and a BIP written and implemented for a student who has a history of inappropriate behavior, displays consistent inappropriate behavior, or has the potential to display inappropriate behavior. Of note, IDEA 2004 does not provide a specific detailed process for teams to follow when conducting FBAs and writing BIPs. However, by following the research-based FBA and BIP processes as described in this chapter, classroom teachers will be better able to address the challenging behaviors presented by some students with disabilities as well as decrease future occurrence of such behaviors.

Cycle of Success

Teachers can adapt their instructional practices within classrooms in order to be proactive in reducing the possibility of student misbehavior. Teachers have many skills and tools they can use to break the cycle of failure illustrated at the beginning of the chapter

Cycle of Success

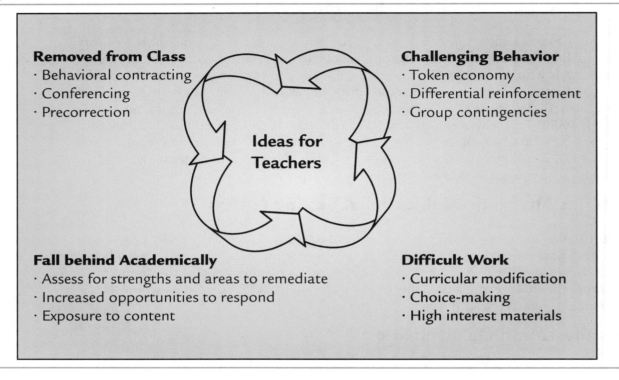

Removed from Class
· Behavioral contracting
· Conferencing
· Precorrection

Challenging Behavior
· Token economy
· Differential reinforcement
· Group contingencies

Ideas for Teachers

Fall behind Academically
· Assess for strengths and areas to remediate
· Increased opportunities to respond
· Exposure to content

Difficult Work
· Curricular modification
· Choice-making
· High interest materials

in Figure 11-2. Examples of just a few of the interventions that can be used are depicted in **Figure 11-8.**

Teachers can evaluate students' academic and social strengths to determine if students are behind their same-age peers. Teachers can modify which assignments are given and how they are presented by embedding strategies such as precorrection, the model-lead-test approach, choices, and curricular modification. Teachers can implement a comprehensive set of instructional, classroom, and behavioral strategies to address misbehavior. The encouraging message is that teachers can intervene in students' cycles of failure at various points and implement a wide variety of instructional and behavioral strategies that have been proven to be effective.

Summary

Classroom teachers may be able to minimize misbehavior in school settings by embedding multiple and varied instructional and behavioral strategies into their daily instruction. Teachers who set up their classrooms so that students are better able to attend, define and teach clear behavioral expectations, use precision requests, consider instructional influences such as CLOCS-RAM, and adopt a comprehensive instructional approach to addressing behavioral errors are applying skills associated with an authoritative style of teaching. Teachers who exhibit behaviors consistent with having high expectations for students by providing more prompting, giving less criticism, asking more questions, and giving more praise may enhance levels of student performance. In addition, teachers who rely on evidence-based strategies such as choice making, group contingencies, and differential reinforcement to increase students' demonstrations of appropriate behavior, and create positive environments conducive to learning will discover they have fewer problem behaviors to address. However, because of the automaticity of some students' chronic behavior problems, teachers may need to develop more structured behavior intervention plans (BIPs) after behavioral function has been identified through a functional behavioral assessment (FBA) process. In addition to being necessary to develop effective BIPs, FBAs are mandated by law for students with disabilities whose behavior poses a threat to others. Regardless of the potential for harm, students with disabilities who demonstrate challenging behavior are guaranteed access to FAPE. These students need to be in schools to learn better patterns of behavior and acquire skills necessary for post-school success.

Discussion Questions and Activities

1. Develop 3-5 positively stated behavioral expectations for your classroom. Give three examples three non-examples for each of the expectations. Then, create a model, lead, test plan to teach one of your behavioral examples.

2. Give an example of how each of the elements of CLOCS-RAM has been (or could be) incorporated into an instructional lesson.

3. Describe how you would use signal control in your classroom.

4. Reflect on your personality. What aspects of your personality are well-suited to being a teacher? What aspects of your personality could interfere with your effectiveness as a teacher? According to the styles described by Baumrind (authoritative, authoritarian, permissive), which one best describes your approach to teaching? What student behaviors are you likely to find the most annoying? What behaviors do you think others might find annoying that would not be troublesome for you? Compare your descriptions and lists to those of other teachers.   *p 449*

   Individual answers

5. With respect to behavior pairs, identify at least one appropriate behavior to pair with the following misbehaviors:
   —gets out of seat without permission

   —calls out in class

   —interrupts others

   —does not come to class on time

   —fails to bring necessary materials to class

   —sleeps during class

   —writes on desk

   —hits others

—bites others

—leaves class without permission

—does not turn in homework

—makes inappropriate comments to peers and teachers

6. Develop a behavioral contract to increase the appropriate behavior from one of the behavior pairs created in #5.

7. Create a group contingency plan for elementary age students who are not turning in their homework and one for high school students who are talking during instruction.

8. Read two position statements on the use of aversives/punishment from professional organizations (e.g., Council for Exceptional Children, Council for Children with Behavioral Disorders, National Association of School Psychologists, The Association for Persons with Severe Disabilities). Describe your personal position on the use of aversives/punishment in schools.

9. Think of a student who is demonstrating inappropriate behavior. How would you modify your instructional strategies, classroom management, and behavioral strategies to promote the demonstration of more appropriate behavior?

10. Considering the academic-behavior failure cycle, identify one proactive and preventative action you could take to interrupt the cycle at each of the four points.

Internet Resources

Websites

Council for Children with Behavioral Disorders
www.ccbd.net

The National Technical Center on Positive Behavioral Interventions and Supports
www.pbis.org

The National Center on Education, Disability, and Juvenile Justice
www.edjj.org

Oregon Social Learning Center
www.OSLC.org

Positive Behavior Support in Georgia
www.pbsga.org

What Works Clearinghouse
www.whatworks.ed.gov

Printed Resources

Jenson, W. R., Rhode, G., S. Reavis, H. K. (1995). *The tough kid tool box.* Longmont, CO: Sopris West.

Liaupsin, C. J., Scott, T. M., & Nelson, C. M. (2000). *Functional behavioral assessment: An interactive training module.* Longmont, CO: Sopris West.

O'Neill, R. E., Horner, R. H., Albin, R. W., Sprague, J. R., Storey, K., & Newton, J. S. (1997). *Functional assessment and program development for problem behavior: A practical handbook* (2nd ed.). Pacific Grove, CA: Brooks/Cole Publishing.

Rhode, G., Jenson, W. R., & Reavis, H. K. (1996). *The tough kid book: Practical classroom management strategies.* Longmont, CO: Sopris West.

Scott, T. M., Liaupsin, C. J., & Nelson, C. M. (2001). *Behavior intervention planning.* Longmont, CO: Sopris West.

References

Abramowitz, A. J., O'Leary, S. G., & Futtersak, M. W. (1988). The relative impact of long and short reprimands on children's off-task behavior in the classroom. *Behavior Therapy, 19,* 243–247.

Atkins, M. S., McKay, M. M., Frazier, S. L., Jakobsons, L. J., Arvanitis, P., Cunningham, T., Brown, C., & Lambrecht, L. (2002). Suspensions and detentions in an urban, low-income school: Punishment or reward? *Journal of Abnormal Child Psychology, 30,* 361–371.

Azrin, N. H., & Holz, W. C. (1966). Punishment. In W. K. Honig (Ed.), *Operant Behavior: Areas of Research and Applications* (pp. 380–447). NY: Appleton-Century-Crofts.

Baumrind, D. (1966). Effects of authoritative parental control on child behavior. *Child Development, 37,* 887–207.

Carr, E. G., Taylor, J. C., & Robinson, S. (1991). The effects of severe behavior problems in children on the teaching behavior of adults. *Journal of Applied Behavior Analysis, 24,* 523–535.

Catalano, R. F., Loeber, R., & McKinney, K. C. (1999). School and community interventions to prevent serious and violent offending. *Juvenile Justice Bulletin,* 1–12.

Christle, C. A., Jolivette, K., & Nelson, C. M. (2000). *Youth aggression and violence: Risk, resilience, and prevention.* ERIC EC E602 Digest. Reston, VA: Council for Exceptional Children.

Colvin, G., & Sugai, G. M. (1988). Proactive strategies for managing social behavior problems: An instructional approach. *Education and Treatment of Children, 11,* 341–348.

Colvin, G., Sugai, G., Good, R. H., & Lee, Y. Y. (1997). Using active supervision and precorrection to improve transition behaviors in an elementary school. *School Psychology Quarterly, 12(4),* 344–363.

Colvin, G., Sugai, G., & Patching, B. (1993). Precorrection: An instructional approach for managing predicable problem behaviors. *Intervention in School and Clinic, 28(3),* 143–150.

Cook, D. (1999). Behavior bucks: A unique motivational program. *Intervention in School & Clinic, 34,* 307–309.

Darling-Hammond, L. (2003). Keeping good teachers: Why it matters, what leaders can do. *Educational Leadership, 60,* 6–13.

DePaepe, P. A., Shores, R. E., Jack, S. L., & Denny, R. K. (1996). Effects of task difficulty on the disruptive and on-task behavior of students with severe behavior disorders. *Behavioral Disorders, 21,* 216–225.

Dodge, K. A., Price, J. M., Bachorowski, J., & Newman, J. P. (1990). Hostile attributional biases in severely aggressive adolescents. *Journal of Abnormal Psychology, 99,* 385–392.

Dunlap, G., Dunlap, L. K., Clarke, S., & Robbins, F. R. (1991). Functional assessment, curricular revision, and severe behavior problems. *Journal of Applied Behavior Analysis, 24,* 387–397.

Eber, L., Sugai, G., Smith, C. R., & Scott, T. M. (2002). Wraparound and positive behavioral interventions and supports in the schools. *Journal of Emotional and Behavioral Disorders, 10,* 171–180.

Emmer, E. T., & Stough, L. M. (2001). Classroom management: A critical part of educational psychology, with implications for teacher education. *Educational Psychology, 36,* 103–112.

Fisher, D., & Kent, H. (1998). Associations between teacher personality and classroom environment. *Journal of Classroom Interaction, 33,* 5–13.

Furlong, M., & Morrison, G. (2000). The school in school violence: Definitions and facts. *Journal of Emotional and Behavioral Disorders, 8,* 71–82.

Good, T., & Brophy, J. (1978). *Looking in classrooms.* New York: Harper and Row.

Goodlad, J. I. (2004). *A place called school: Twentieth Anniversary Edition.* NY: McGraw-Hill.

Greenwood, C. R. (1991). A longitudinal analysis of time, engagement, and academic achievement in at-risk vs. non-risk students. *Exceptional Children, 57,* 521–535.

Gresham, F. M., & Gresham, G. N. (1982). Interdependent, dependent, and independent group contingencies for controlling disruptive behavior. *The Journal of Special Education, 16,* 101–110.

Guerra, N. G., & Williams, K. R. (1996). *A program planning guide for youth violence prevention.* Boulder, CO: Center for the Study and Prevention of Violence.

Gunter, P. L., Denny, R. K., Jack, S. L., Shores, R. E., & Nelson, C. M. (1993). Aversive stimuli in academic interactions between students with serious emotional disturbance and their teachers. *Behavioral Disorders, 18,* 265–274.

Gunter, P. L., Jack, S. L., DePaepe, P., Reed, T. M., & Harrison, J. (1994). Effects of challenging behaviors of students with EBD on teacher instructional behavior. *Preventing School Failure, 38,* 35–39.

Gunter, P. L., & Shores, R. E. (1995). On the move: Using teacher/student proximity to improve student's behavior. *Teaching Exceptional Children, 28,* 12–14.

Houghton, S., Wheldall, K., Jukes, R., & Sharpe, A. (1990). The effects of limited private reprimands and increased private praise on classroom behaviour in four British secondary school classes. *British Journal of Educational Psychology, 60,* 255–265.

Huesmann, L. R., Eron, L. D., & Yarmel, P. (1987). Intellectual functioning and aggression. *Journal of Personality and Social Psychology, 52,* 232–240.

Individuals with Disabilities Education Improvement Act of 2004, 20 U. S. C. § 1400 *et seq.* (2004) (reauthorization of the Individuals with Disabilities Act of 1990)

Iwata, B. A., Dorsey, M. F., Slifer, K. J., Bauman, K. E., & Richman, G. S. (1982/1994). Toward a functional analysis of self-injury. *Journal of Applied Behavior Analysis, 27,* 197–209.

Jolivette, K., Scott, T. M., & Nelson, C. M. (2000). *The link between assessment and intervention: FBAs and BIPs.* ERIC EC Digest E592. Reston, VA: Council for Exceptional Children.

Jolivette, K., Wehby, J. H., Canale, J., & Massey, N. G. (2001). Effects of choice making opportunities on the behaviors of students with emotional and behavioral disorders. *Behavioral Disorders, 26,* 131–145.

Jones, F. H. (2000). *Tools for teaching: Discipline-Instruction-Motivation.* Santa Cruz, CA: Fredric H. Jones & Associates.

Kauffman, J. M., Mostert, M. P., Trent, S. C., & Pullen, P. L. (2006). *Managing classroom behavior: A reflective case-based approach* (4th ed.). Boston, MA: Allyn & Bacon.

Kazdin, A. E. (1977). *The token economy.* NY: Plenum Press.

Kehle, T. J., Bray, M. A., Theodore, L. A., Jenson, W. R., & Clark, E. (2000). A multi-component intervention designed to reduce disruptive classroom behavior. *Psychology in the Schools, 37,* 475–481.

Kelly, S. (2004). An event history analysis of teacher attrition: Salary, teacher tracking, and socially disadvantaged schools. *Journal of Experimental Education, 72,* 195–220.

Kern, L., Delaney, B., Clarke, S., Dunlap, G., & Childs, K. (2001). Improving the classroom behavior of students with emotional and behavioral disorders using individualized curricular modifications. *Journal of Emotional & Behavioral Disorders, 9,* 239–247.

Kern, L., Mantegna, M. E., Vorndran, C. M., Bailin, D., & Hilt, A. (2001). Choice of task sequence to reduce problem behaviors. *Journal of Positive Behavior Interventions, 3,* 3–10.

Kounin, J. S. (1970). *Discipline and group management in classrooms.* New York: Holt, Rinehart, & Winston.

Kozol, J. (1991). *Savage inequalities: Children in America's schools.* NY: Crown.

Lessen, E., & Frankiewicz, L. (1992). Personal attributes and characteristics of effective special education teachers: Considerations for teacher educators. *Teacher Education and Special Education, 15,* 124–32.

Lewis, T. J., & Sugai, G. (1999). Effective behavior support: A systems approach to proactive school-wide management. *Focus on Exceptional Children, 31*(6), 1–24.

Logan, K. R., Bakeman, R., & Keefe, E. G. (1997). Effects of instructional variables of engaged behavior of students with disabilities in general education classrooms. *Exceptional Children, 63,* 481–497.

Lohrmann, S., & Talerico, J. (2004). Anchor the boat: A classwide intervention to reduce problem behavior. *Journal of Positive Behavior Intervention, 6,* 113–120.

Luiselli, J. K., & Downing, J. N. (1980). Improving a student's arithmetic performance using feedback and reinforcement procedures. *Education and Treatment of Children, 3,* 45–49.

Martin, N., (1998). Construct validation of the attitudes & beliefs on classroom control inventory. *Journal of Classroom Interaction, 33,* 6–15.

Mayer, G. R. (1995). Preventing antisocial behavior in the schools. *Journal of Applied Behavior Analysis, 28,* 467–478.

McKee, W. T., & Witt, J. C. (1990). Effective teaching: A review of instructional, and environmental variables. In T. B. Gutkin & C. R. Reynolds (Eds.), *The handbook of school psychology* (pp. 823–847). New York: John Wiley & Sons.

Mercer, C. D., & Mercer, A. R. (2005). *Teaching students with learning problems* (7th ed.). Upper Saddle River, NJ: Pearson.

Moore, J. W., & Edwards, R. P. (2003). An analysis of aversive stimuli in classroom demand contexts. *Journal of Applied Behavior Analysis, 36,* 339–348.

National Center for Education Statistics. (1997). *Job satisfaction among America's teachers: Effects of workplace conditions, background characteristics, and teacher compensation.* Washington, D.C.: Author.

Neville, M. H., & Jenson, W. R. (1984). Precision command and the "Sure I will" program: A quick and efficient compliance training sequence. *Child & Family Behavior Therapy, 6,* 61–65.

O'Neil, R. E., Horner, R. H., Albin, R. W., Sprague, J. R., Storey, K., & Newton, J. S. (1997). *Functional assessment and program development for problem behavior* (2nd ed.). Pacific Grove, CA: Brooks/Cole Publishing.

Patterson, G. R., Reid, J. B., & Dishion, T. J. (1992). *Antisocial boys.* Eugene, OR: Castalia Press.

Pellerin, L. A. (2005). Applying Baumrind's parenting typology to high schools: Toward a middle-range theory of authoritative socialization. *Social Science Research, 34,* 283–303.

Premack, D. (1959). Toward empirical behavior laws: I. Positive reinforcement. *Psychological Review, 66,* 219–233.

Robinson, D. H., Funk, D. C., Beth, A., & Bush, A. M. (2005). Changing beliefs about corporal punishment: Increasing knowledge about ineffectiveness to build more consistent moral and informational beliefs. *Journal of Behavioral Education, 14,* 117–139.

Rosenthal, R., & Jacobson, L. (1968). *Pygmalion in the classroom: Teacher expectation and pupils' intellectual development.* New York: Hold, Rinehart & Winston.

Rumberger, R. W., & Palardy, G. J. (2005). Does segregation still matter? The impact of student composition on academic achievement in high school. *Teachers College Record, 107,* 1999–2045.

Scott, T., M., Nelson, C. M., & Liaupsin, C. J. (2001). Effective instruction: The forgotten component in preventing school violence. Education and Treatment of Children, 24, 309–322.

Shores, R. E., Jack, S. L., Gunter, P. L., Ellis, D. N., DeBriere, T. J., & Wehby, J. H. (1993). Classroom interactions of children with behavior disorders. *Journal of Emotional and Behavioral Disorders, 1,* 27–29.

Sidman, M. (1989). *Coercion and its fall-out.* Boston: Authors Cooperative.

Sutherland, K. S., Wehby, J. H., & Copeland, S. R. (2000). Effect of varying rates of behavior-specific praise on the on-task behavior of students with emotional and behavioral disorders. *Journal of Emotional and Behavioral Disorders, 8,* 2–8.

Talbott, E., & Coe, M. G. (1997). A developmental view of aggression and achievement. In T. E. Scruggs & M. A. Mastropieri (Eds.), *Advances in learning and behavioral disabilities,* (Vol. 11, pp. 87–100). Greenwich, CT: JAI Press.

Thornton, B., Peltier, G., & Hill, G. (2005). Do future teachers choose wisely: A study of pre-service teachers' personality preference profiles. *College Student Journal, 39,* 489–496.

Turner, H. A., & Muller, P. A. (2004). Long-term effects of child corporal punishment on depressive symptoms in young adults: Potential moderators and mediators. *Journal of Family Issues, 25,* 761–782.

Umbreit, J., Lane, K. L., & Dejud, C. (2004). Improving classroom behavior by modifying task difficulty: Effects of increasing the difficulty of too-easy tasks. *Journal of Positive Behavioral Intervention, 6,* 13–20.

Van Acker, R. (2006). Effective classroom-level disciplinary practices: Redefining the classroom environment to support student and teacher success. In L. M. Bullock, R. A. Gable, and K. J. Melloy (Eds.), *Effective disciplinary practices: Strategies for maintaining safe schools and positive learning environments for students with challenging behaviors* (pp. 23–31). Arlington, VA: Council for Exceptional Children.

Van Acker, R., Grant, S. B., & Henry, D. (1996). Teacher and student behavior as a function of risk for aggression. *Education and Treatment of Children, 19,* 316–334.

Van Acker, R., & Talbott, E. (1999). The school context and risk for aggression: Implications for school-based prevention and intervention efforts. *Preventing School Failure, 44,* 12–20.

Van Houten, R., Nau, P. A., MacKenzie-Keating, S. E., Sameoto, D., & Colavecchia, B. (1982). An analysis of some variables influencing the effectiveness of reprimands. *Journal of Applied Behavior Analysis, 15,* 65–83.

Vitaro, F., Tremblay, R. E., Gagnon, C. (1995). Teacher ratings of children's behaviors and teachers' management styles: A research note. *Journal of Child Psychology & Psychiatry & Allied Disciplines, 36,* 887–898.

Walker, H. M., Horner, R. H., Sugai, G., Bullis, M., Sprague, J. R., Bricker, D., & Kaufman, M. J. (1996). Integrated approaches to preventing antisocial behavior patterns among school-age children and youth. *Journal of Emotional and Behavioral Disorders, 4,* 194–209.

Walker, H. M., Ramsey, E., & Gresham, F. M. (2004). *Antisocial behavior in school: Evidence-based practices.* Belmont, CA: Wadsworth/Thomson Learning.

Walker, H. M., & Sprague, J. R. (1999). Longitudinal research and functional behavioral assessment issues. *Behavioral Disorders, 24,* 335–337.

Walker, H. M., Stieber, S., Ramsey, E., & O'Neill, R. E. (1991). Longitudinal prediction of the school achievement, adjustment, and delinquency of antisocial versus at-risk boys. *Remediation and Special Education, 12,* 43–51.

Wehby, J. H., Symons, F. J., & Shores, R. E. (1995). A descriptive analysis of aggressive behavior in classrooms for children with emotional and behavioral disorders. *Behavioral Disorders, 20,* 87–105.

Weiss, N. R. (2005). Eliminating the use of behavioral techniques that are cruel and dehumanizing. *Exceptional Parent, 35(10),* 42–43.

Witt, J. C., VanDerHeyden, A. M., & Gilbertson, D. (2004). Troubleshooting behavioral interventions: A systematic process for finding and eliminating problems. *School Psychology Review, 33,* 363–383.

Yell, M. L. (1990). The use of corporal punishment, suspension, expulsion, and timeout with behaviorally disordered students in public schools: Legal considerations. *Behavioral Disorders, 15,* 100–109.

What Is Your Classroom Management Profile?

Answer these 12 questions and learn more about your classroom management profile. The steps are simple:

- Read each statement carefully.
- Write your response, from the scale below, on a sheet of paper.
- Respond to each statement based upon either actual or imagined classroom experience.
- Then, follow the scoring instructions below. It couldn't be easier!

1. = Strongly Disagree
2. = Disagree
3. = Neutral
4. = Agree
5. = Strongly Agree

(1) If a student is disruptive during class, I assign him/her to detention, without further discussion.
(2) I don't want to impose any rules on my students.
(3) The classroom must be quiet in order for students to learn.
(4) I am concerned about both what my students learn and how they learn.
(5) If a student turns in a late homework assignment, it is not my problem.
(6) I don't want to reprimand a student because it might hurt his/her feelings.
(7) Class preparation isn't worth the effort.
(8) I always try to explain the reasons behind my rules and decisions.
(9) I will not accept excuses from a student who is tardy.

(10) The emotional well-being of my students is more important than classroom control.

(11) My students understand that they can interrupt my lecture if they have a relevant question.

(12) If a student requests a hall pass, I always honor the request.

To score your quiz,

Add your responses to statements 1, 3, and 9. This is your score for the *authoritarian style*.

Statements 4, 8 and 11 refer to the *authoritative style*.
Statements 6, 10, and 12 refer to the *laissez-faire style*.
Statements 2, 5, and 7 refer to the *indifferent style*.

The result is your classroom management profile. Your score for each management style can range from 3 to 15. A high score indicates a strong preference for that particular style. After you have scored your quiz, and determined your profile, read the descriptions of each management style. You may see a little bit of yourself in each one.

As you gain teaching experience, you may find that your preferred style(s) will change. Over time, your profile may become more diverse or more focused. Also, it may be suitable to rely upon a specific style when addressing a particular situation or subject. Perhaps the successful teacher is one who can evaluate a situation and then apply the appropriate style. Finally, remember that the intent of this exercise is to inform you and arouse your curiosity regarding classroom management styles.

Authoritarian

The authoritarian teacher places firm limits and controls on the students. Students will often have assigned seats for the entire term. The desks are usually in straight rows and there are no deviations. Students must be in their seats at the beginning of class and they frequently remain there throughout the period. This teacher rarely gives hall passes or recognizes excused absences.

Often, it is quiet. Students know they should not interrupt the teacher. Since verbal exchange and discussion are discouraged, the authoritarian's students do not have the opportunity to learn and/or practice communication skills.

This teacher prefers vigorous discipline and expects swift obedience. Failure to obey the teacher usually results in detention or a trip to the principal's office. In this classroom, students need to follow directions and not ask why.

At the extreme, the authoritarian teacher gives no indication that he\she cares for the students. Mr. Doe is a good example of an authoritarian teacher. His students receive praise and encouragement infrequently, if at all. Also, he makes no effort to organize activities such as field trips. He feels that these special events only distract the students from learning. After all, Mr. Doe believes that students need only listen to his lecture to gain the necessary knowledge.

Students in this class are likely to be reluctant to initiate activity, since they may feel powerless. Mr. Doe tells the students what to do and when to do it. He makes all classroom decisions. Therefore, his style does little to increase achievement motivation or encourage the setting of personal goals.

One Middle-school pupil reacts to this teaching style:

I don't really care for this teacher. He is really strict and doesn't seem to want to give his students a fair chance. He seems unfair, although that's just his way of getting his point across.

Authoritative

The authoritative teacher places limits and controls on the students but simultaneously encourages independence. This teacher often explains the reasons behind the rules and decisions. If a student is disruptive, the teacher offers a polite, but firm, reprimand. This teacher sometimes metes out discipline, but only after careful consideration of the circumstances.

The authoritative teacher is also open to considerable verbal interaction, including critical debates. The students know that they can interrupt the teacher if they have a relevant question or comment. This environment offers the students the opportunity to learn and practice communication skills.

Ms. Smith exemplifies the authoritative teaching style. She exhibits a warm and nurturing attitude toward the students and expresses genuine interest and affection. Her classroom abounds with praise and encouragement. She often writes comments on homework and offers positive remarks to students. This authoritative teacher encourages self-reliant and socially competent behavior and fosters higher achievement motivation. Often, she will guide the students through a project, rather than lead them.

A student reacts to this style:

I like this teacher. She is fair and understands that students can't be perfect. She is the kind of teacher you can talk to without being put down or feeling embarrassed.

Laissez-faire

The laissez-faire teacher places few demand or controls on the students. "Do your own thing" describes this classroom. This teacher accepts the student's impulses and actions and is less likely to monitor their behavior.

Mr. Jones uses a laissez-faire style. He strives to not hurt the student's feelings and has difficulty saying no to a student or enforcing rules. If a student disrupts the class, Mr Jones may assume that he is not giving that student enough attention. When a student interrupts a lecture, Mr. Jones accepts the interruption with the belief that the student must surely have something valuable to add. When he does offer discipline, it is likely to be inconsistent.

Mr. Jones is very involved with his students and cares for them very much. He is more concerned with the students' emotional well-being than he is with classroom control. He sometimes bases classroom decisions on his students' feelings rather than on their academic concerns.

Mr. Jones wants to be the students' friend. He may even encourage contact outside the classroom. He has a difficult time establishing boundaries between his professional life and his personal life.

However, this overindulgent style is associated with students' lack of social competence and self-control. It is difficult for students to learn socially acceptable behavior when the teacher is so permissive. With few demands placed upon them, these students frequently have lower motivation to achieve.

Regardless, students often like this teacher. A Middle School student says:

This is a pretty popular teacher. You don't have to be serious throughout the class. But sometimes things get out of control and we learn nothing at all.

Indifferent

The indifferent teacher is not very involved in the classroom. This teacher places few demands, if any, on the students and appears generally uninterested. The indifferent teacher just doesn't want to impose on the students. As such, he/she often feels that class preparation is not worth the effort. Things like field trips and special projects are out of the question. This teacher simply won't take the necessary preparation time. Sometimes, he/she will use the same materials, year after year.

Also, classroom discipline is lacking. This teacher may lack the skills, confidence, or courage to discipline students.

The students sense and reflect the teacher's indifferent attitude. Accordingly, very little learning occurs. Everyone is just "going through the motions" and killing time. In this aloof environment, the students have very few opportunities to observe or practice communication skills. With few demands placed on them and very little discipline, students have low achievement motivation and lack self-control.

According to one student:

This teacher can't control the class and we never learn anything in there. There is hardly ever homework and people rarely bring their books.

Ms. Johnson is a good example of an indifferent teacher. She uses the same lesson plans every year, never bothering to update them. For her, each day is the same. She lectures for the first twenty minutes of class. Sometimes she will show a film or a slideshow. When she does, it becomes a substitute for her lecture, not a supplement. If there is any time left (and there always is) she allows students to study quietly and to talk softly. As long as they don't bother her, she doesn't mind what they do. As far as she is concerned, the students are responsible for their own education.

The classroom management styles are adaptations of the parenting styles discussed in *Adolescence,* by John T. Santrock. They were adapted by Kris Bosworth, Kevin McCracken, Paul Haakenson, Marsha Ritter Jones, Anne Grey, Laura Versaci, Julie James, and Ronen Hammer.

Source: Used with permission from *Teacher Talk: A Publication for Secondary Education Teachers, 1*(2). Available under the "Resources" link at www.indiana.edu/~cafs/

12

Collaboration with Families and Professionals

Peggy A. Gallagher and Debra Schober-Peterson

Chapter Objectives

- to define the meaning of collaboration;
- to describe the members of a team for students with special needs;
- to define and describe team models;
- to explain the process of team building and characteristics of effective teams;
- to discuss family roles in the development of students with disabilities; and
- to provide strategies for building collaboration among professionals and families.

Historically, teaching has been an isolated profession with teachers remaining in their own classrooms with their students for most of the day. Recent educational reforms, however, have emphasized that teachers also must be involved in interactions with others outside the walls of their classrooms. Federal law requires that a team approach be used for several aspects of the special education process. In many states, for example, a Student Support Team (SST), consisting of general education teachers and special education teachers, meets to plan modifications for students having difficulty in the general education classroom setting. If these modifications are unsuccessful, a team of school professionals and the student's family meet to discuss assessment information and the student's eligibility for special education services. Rethinking how to provide the best special education services to students has encouraged teachers to work more closely with each other, with administrators, with support personnel, and with family members. Collaboration is a crucial part of making this teamwork successful.

Mrs. Weber, the school principal, has called an all school meeting to work on discipline problems throughout Ellis Elementary School. Miss Lamkin is a new general education teacher, in her first year of teaching. She is worried about what will happen at the meeting. She fears that some of her students are the reason Mrs. Weber called this meeting. Miss Lamkin has tried to keep Monica, a student with a learning disability and an attention deficit disorder, from running in the lunch room, but when she sees all her friends from her neighborhood, Monica gets excited and shouts. Peter, another of Miss Lamkin's students, spends most of his day in her room, but lately Mrs. Spivey, Peter's speech-language pathologist, has reported that Peter is teasing other students and doesn't seem to get along well with other students.

Could a collaborative school atmosphere help Miss Lamkin feel more comfortable? What if the school meeting turned into a small group problem-solving session that involved parents, teachers, and students? What if Miss Lamkin had the support and guidance from her fellow teachers, her principal, and the families of her students?

What Is Collaboration?

Collaboration has different meanings for different people and situations. The American Heritage College Dictionary (2002) defines collaboration as an effort to work jointly with others especially in an intellectual endeavor. Collaboration in the schools is a process in which school personnel and family members work together to provide effective services for students. It is an interactive process that enables people with diverse experiences and expertise to mutually define problems, set goals, and create solutions. In addition, collaboration encourages effective communication and respect for the knowledge of others. In all cases, collaboration results in a team of people making decisions, whether the team consists of two individuals or twenty.

Collaboration defines how individuals interact with each other when working as a team. In collaboration, school personnel should approach interactions with others by conveying a willingness and desire to work together. But, collaboration is more than cooperation; it requires a style of interacting that uses the ideas and contributions of others as a way of affecting one's own thoughts (Coufal, 1993). Individuals who successfully collaborate must consider a variety of viewpoints, take risks, and try new ideas. Collaboration often is confused with the terms consultation and co-teaching, but these activities may or may not be collaborative, depending on the interactions and background of the participants.

Consultation is a model for providing information to others. It has been used often when students with special needs attend general education classes at least part of the school day. In its usual implementation it is not collaborative because it involves special education professionals consulting with their peers in general education by giving them suggestions on how to improve their classrooms or work with students. Not surprisingly, consultants' ideas often are not implemented because the general education teacher has not asked for the advice or does not believe that the consultant giving suggestions understands the classroom or the other students in the class. This model often is labeled the "expert" model because one individual attempts to tell another what to do without considering the other's level of knowledge and skill in teaching and working with students. The expert model may not be effective largely because it is not an interaction where two persons respect and learn from each other. Consultation can be collaborative if the professionals providing information shift from an expert model of interaction to a model of joint problem solving.

Co-teaching, or **team teaching,** is another term that often is used interchangeably with collaboration. In some cases, co-teaching is collaborative; but, in other cases it is not. Team teaching involves two or more teachers teaching together, but not necessarily on an equal basis. For instance, Mr. Carley, the special education teacher, is helping to teach the eighth-grade history class so that Jane, a student with a learning disability, can attend. Though Ms. Burroughs, the history teacher, is very friendly, Mr. Carley doesn't feel he can actively participate in the class. He doesn't feel comfortable that he can make decisions concerning student behaviors and he has not yet taught any of the course content. Ms. Burroughs has never had another teacher in her class and is not sure of Mr. Carley's responsibilities in the classroom. In this instance, team teaching is not collaborative. On the other hand, two kindergarten teachers, Ms. Burbank and Ms. Houze, are co-teaching their kindergarten class collaboratively this year. [Ms. Houze is a general education

TABLE 12-1

Highlights of the Collaborative Process

1. Common mission and purpose.
2. Powerful and skilled leadership.
3. Recognized partnerships with persons considered as equal contribution members.
4. Mutual respect of others based on the philosophy that all participants have something valuable to contribute.
5. Sincere commitment.
6. Constant communication, including evaluation and respect for conflict and creativity.
7. Cooperative decision making.
8. Belief that joint efforts are more powerful than those accomplished alone.
9. Sufficient resources, including time.

teacher and Ms. Burbank is a special education teacher.] They have 28 children in the class, six of whom have special needs. They teach as co-teachers in every sense of the word with equal responsibility for every aspect of the class. They have set aside planning time on a daily basis to work on their collaborative teaching activities. When they teach, they are both in the classroom at the same time, working with the class as a whole or with small groups together. They have decided beforehand how to adapt assignments for the students with varying special needs. The most important component of co-teaching in a collaborative manner is that both teachers assume responsibility for all students in the classroom. They plan assignments together, teach together, and determine how to assess the students together.

A summary of the highlights of the collaborative process is presented in **Table 12-1** (Correa, Jones, Thomas & Morsink, 2005; Friend & Cook, 2003; Kontos & File, 1993; Malone, 1993; Pugach & Johnson, 2002).

Collaboration and the Law

IDEA 2004 provides guidelines for the team procedures to be used in the special education process. Specifically, the law requires that two teams be formed, the multidisciplinary evaluation team and the IEP (Individualized Education Program) planning team. The multidisciplinary team evaluates students referred for special education services by general education teachers or parents and determines the students' eligibility for services. Parental consent must be obtained before conducting an initial evaluation for placement in a special education program. Although the composition of the multidisciplinary team varies according to the needs of the student, it must include a teacher or other specialist with knowledge in the suspected area of disability. It also should include the student's family and other school professionals with knowledge of the student's academic performance. Once a student is deemed eligible for special education services, IDEA 2004 requires that a meeting to develop the IEP be held within 30 calendar days of the determination that the student has a disability and requires special education and related services. The IEP team develops, reviews, and revises the student's IEP. The required participants in IEP meetings include the following:

1. Parents (or guardians or surrogate parents).
2. At least one general education teacher if the student is, or may be, participating in the general education environment.

3. At least one special education teacher or, if appropriate, a special education provider.
4. A representative of the local school system who:
   - is qualified to provide or supervise the provision of specially designed instruction to meet the needs of students with disabilities.
   - has knowledge of the general curriculum.
   - has knowledge of the resources of the local school system.
5. An individual who can interpret the instructional implications of evaluation results.
6. Other individuals who have knowledge or special expertise regarding the student, including related services personnel, at the discretion of the parent or local school system or state operated program.

The general education teacher who attends a student's IEP meeting should be the one who will be implementing the IEP. The school system designates one general education teacher who should attend the IEP meeting if more than one teacher is working with the student. Input from other general education teachers who do not attend should be sought by the IEP team. General education teachers who do not attend the meeting should receive a copy of any instructional modifications and behavior management plans which they will be responsible for implementing. Any teacher who works with a student with an IEP may receive a copy of the IEP.

While participating in an IEP meeting, the general education teacher should serve on the team in the following ways:

1. Participate as a team member in the development, review, and revision of the IEP.
2. Assist in the determination of appropriate positive behavioral interventions and strategies.
3. Assist in the determination of supplementary aids and services, program modifications, and supports for school personnel.
4. Assist in the determination of the accommodations needed, if any, to allow the student to participate in the general curriculum.

In addition to the responsibilities of school personnel, the law emphasizes the involvement of parents in the development of the IEP to ensure that they are active participants in decision making regarding their child's educational program (Bateman & Linden, 1998; Correa, et al., 2005; Strickland & Turnbull, 1993). Parents must be members of any group that makes decisions on the educational placement of their child. The IEP and placement must be reviewed at least annually, but can be reviewed more often if requested by the parent or teacher. Specific requirements for parental involvement in the IEP process include the following:

1. Notifying the parents regarding the purpose, time, location, and participants at the meeting so that they have an opportunity to attend.
2. Scheduling the meeting at a mutually agreed upon time and place.
3. Ensuring that the parents understand the purpose and tasks of the meeting and that an interpreter is present for parents who are deaf or whose native language is one other than English.
4. Providing a copy of the IEP, including the placement meeting minutes, to the parents. Minutes must be taken at every IEP meeting. If parents do not attend the meeting, a copy of the IEP and the minutes must be provided to the parents before the IEP is implemented.

Parents must be afforded every opportunity to participate in the IEP process for their child. If a parent cannot attend the IEP meeting, parents and the local education agency may agree to use alternative means of meeting participation such as video conferencing or a conference call. An IEP meeting can be conducted without the parents present only if the parents have rejected all attempts by the school system to involve them. The school system must document all efforts to arrange a convenient time and place, including detailed records of telephone calls and responses, visits to the parent's home or place of work, and mailings concerning the IEP meeting (Strickland & Turnbull, 1993).

IDEA 2004 also requires that a description of how the student's parents will be regularly informed of the student's progress be included in the IEP. Annual goals on the student's IEP must be addressed in the progress report. These reports must be as frequent as reports received by parents of students without disabilities.

As a result of IDEA 2004, schools have moved toward the development of collaborative teams that include general education teachers, special education teachers, and families. There are many reasons school personnel should strive to interact collaboratively in all aspects of their work with students with disabilities. Probably the most important benefit of a collaborative process is that the student receives the best educational programming possible. Because school personnel, family members, and in many cases the student, provide input into decision making, there is a greater likelihood that plans will be carried out effectively and enthusiastically. In addition, the student's needs are viewed as a whole rather than as separate, possibly unrelated, needs. Families also may feel a stronger connection with their child's school program and be better able to assist in helping their child achieve goals. Collaboration also facilitates effective communication because it fosters an atmosphere of trust and respect among team members. Finally, another important outcome of collaboration for many students is the creation of programs that enable students with disabilities to interact positively with their peers in general education classrooms.

In summary, collaboration is a process that involves mutually agreed upon goals, joint problem solving, respect for others, and effective communication skills. Collaboration for students with disabilities involves many individuals, including their general education teachers and the family members with whom the child lives on a daily basis. Collaboration takes effort and time on the part of school personnel, but the rewards are well worth it.

Building Collaborative Teams

Caris is in the third grade at Oakview Elementary. Her IEP meeting has been scheduled and her mother, Mrs. Hickson, is worried that she will not get to have a say about what type of classroom Caris will go to for the next school year. Mrs. Hickson is never sure what she is supposed to do at the IEP meetings. She has an older daughter, Pharra, who went to Oakview, and she feels that she has a good understanding of the type of program that would best meet the goals she has for Caris. The IEP meeting occurs on schedule, and Mrs. Hickson is pleasantly surprised. Caris's classroom teacher, Ms. Walters, explained the meeting to her ahead of time and told her what the room would be like and who would be there. No one had ever done that before. Mrs. Hickson met with Ms. Walters, the school principal, the director of special education, the speech-language pathologist who works with Caris, and the occupational therapist who might work with her in the future. They all seemed to like Caris and have her best interests at heart. Together, they discussed and decided what Caris needed and how they would each help meet those needs. They even decided to get Caris's ideas as well. Mrs. Hickson felt that her views were heard as Caris's classroom for next year was decided. Ms. Walters thought that the occupational therapist and the principal finally understood the importance of helping Caris improve her fine motor skills so she can participate fully in cursive writing and art. Everyone came away from the meeting with a sense of hope and expectation for Caris and a sense of enthusiasm for working together as a group.

For collaboration to occur there must be a team of people. Let's turn now to a discussion of what is meant by the term team, who team members may be, and how a team develops and communicates within the educational setting.

Definition of Team

A **team** is two or more individuals who work and communicate in an interdependent and coordinated manner to reach a mutually agreed upon goal (Abelson & Woodman, 1983; Correa, et al., 2005; Friend & Cook, 2003). An effective team is one that collaborates. Teams are used in a variety of fields, including education, to bring together people who have differing perspectives and expertise. Team members work together on a problem or issue to develop mutually agreed upon suggestions and solutions. Schools can use teams in many ways. For example, teachers might form a team to revise a seventh-grade science curriculum. A preschool teacher may team with a speech-language pathologist to co-teach language lessons in their special needs preschool classroom. Similarly, a special education teacher and a general education teacher might form a team to determine successful ways to include students with learning disabilities in a general education math class. While teams are mandated by law to meet for multidisciplinary evaluations and IEP meetings, it is hoped that they also will form for many other reasons. School personnel who embrace collaboration likely will be involved in a variety of teams that enhance their teaching and the services they provide to students with disabilities.

The use of a collaborative team approach acknowledges that the student with disabilities has needs that cannot be met by any one person or discipline alone. A team effort, including family members, is most conducive to achieving the best progress for a student with disabilities.

Team Members

Team members vary depending on the purpose of the team and the special educational needs of the student. Some teams are large, while others have only three or four members. Let's discuss the people who may be involved in teams for a student with special needs.

1. **General Education Teacher.** The general education teacher is a valuable member of the team for the student with disabilities who will spend any portion of the day in a general education classroom. The teacher has knowledge of general education curriculum and can share input on programming issues. Even for those students who do not spend time in general education classrooms, those teachers can be a valuable source of support. They can encourage their students to play and interact positively with students with disabilities during informal times such as on the playground, in the lunchroom, and at bus time.

2. **Special Education Teacher.** The special education teacher plays a critical role in monitoring and providing services for the student with disabilities. The special educator is mandated by law under Part B of IDEA to be part of the team process to assess and design programs best suited for the student with a disability. Special educators are trained in special education and should be knowledgeable in the areas of assessment, teaching methods, curriculum, and behavior management for students with special needs.

3. **Principal.** The school principal is a valuable ally and important team member. This individual controls the scheduling of classes and rooms and plays a leading role in fostering the climate of the school. The principal can set the stage for collaborative team interactions by allowing time for teams to meet and encouraging team input and group decision making.

4. **Paraprofessional or Aide (Paraeducator).** The paraprofessional or aide may work in the general education classroom or in the special education classroom. This individual can be a critical player in the school life of students with disabilities for it is often the aide who accompanies students to classes and activities in the general education environment. While aides often are not thought of as formal members of a team, they can be valuable players in assuring consistency across programming efforts for the student with special needs.

5. **Psychologist.** A psychologist performs a major part of the assessment of a student's cognitive (IQ testing) and behavioral abilities (attentional or adaptive skills). Various procedures such as interviews, standardized IQ and achievement tests, and/or behavioral assessments are used to determine the student's level of functioning and potential.

6. **Audiologist.** As discussed in Chapter Five, an audiologist focuses on a student's hearing. This individual assesses hearing, fits and monitors hearing aids, and provides therapy services related to a diagnosed hearing loss. Audiologists assist the team in making decisions about assistive listening devices and classroom modifications.

7. **Occupational Therapist (OT).** OTs are involved in helping to teach activities of daily living, especially those skills requiring fine motor movements of the arms, fingers, and trunk. An OT's evaluation involves assessing the muscles for strength and tone, as well as monitoring reflexes, posture, and joint motion of the upper extremities and trunk. The OT also assesses self-help skills such as feeding and dressing, and perceptual motor skills such as drawing and prevocational skills for the older student. The OT provides therapeutic services to students with fine motor deficits and assists teachers in modifying classroom activities to facilitate fine motor development.

8. **Physical Therapist (PT).** The physical therapist evaluates and provides treatment for the student's motor skills, particularly gross motor skills. The PT is involved in evaluating the student's overall motor function through observing the student's muscle strength and endurance, muscle tone, and posture. The PT is involved with other team members in designing and implementing programs to improve motor skills. They may work with medical personnel to recommend assistive devices such as braces, wheelchairs, or other seating devices.

9. **Speech-Language Pathologist (SLP).** As discussed in Chapter Five, the SLP is concerned with the critical area of communication. A speech-language pathologist evaluates communication by taking a history of communication milestones, assessing language, articulation, voice, and fluency skills, and conducting an examination of the speech mechanism. SLPs provide therapy services if a speech or language problem is diagnosed. SLPs use a variety of techniques in therapy and may assist students in the use of alternative forms of communication such as sign language, communication boards, or computer-assisted devices. They also may be involved in evaluating and treating feeding and swallowing problems. SLPs can be important team members in helping to create classroom environments that foster speech and language development.

10. **Social Worker.** The social worker helps determine family strengths and resources and the family's need for support services to be able to help their child learn and develop. In early intervention programs, a social worker often serves as a service coordinator offering information to parents regarding community resources, coordinating evaluations, and facilitating the development and implementation of the service plan.

11. **Vocational Rehabilitation Counselor.** Vocational rehabilitation counselors are responsible for working with eligible students with disabilities on job training opportunities. Vocational counselors consult with school officials to make and evaluate training arrangements so that persons with disabilities learn effective job skills. They also can facilitate arrangements with other rehabilitation services to obtain job-related equipment such as prosthetic devices.

12. **School Counselor.** The school counselor, also called guidance counselor, assists students with personal and/or behavior problems. In high school, the school counselor also advises students in relation to college, career, and job finding skills. School counselors may provide individual or group counseling and consult with parents, teachers and others regarding student adjustment issues.

13. **Medical Personnel.** Medical personnel such as the school nurse, a developmental pediatrician, a neurologist, or a psychiatrist, also have important roles on the team for the student with disabilities. The medical community often has been involved with the student and family long before the school. They will be involved in diagnosis, treatment from a medical perspective (medications), and monitoring of ongoing health concerns.

14. **Family Members.** In the collaborative team concept, it is important to emphasize a true partnership between all participants including the child's family members. Family members are a critical part of the team for a student with special needs. Family members know the child in important ways outside of the classroom. Family members who might have input in team decisions include the parents, brothers and sisters, grandparents, cousins, and aunts and uncles, as well as other significant persons who may not be blood relatives but are considered family.

Team Models

Besides having a variety of possible members on a team, teams can function in many ways. Three team models may be used for students in special education: the multidisciplinary team approach, the interdisciplinary team approach, and the transdisciplinary team approach. Not all of these team approaches are truly collaborative. Most schools have moved from a multidisciplinary approach to an interdisciplinary approach. In addition, recent trends in early intervention and vocational transition have encouraged the use of the transdisciplinary approach for providing services to students with disabilities. The following is a description of each type of team that illustrates how team members function in the team models.

The Multidisciplinary Team

A multidisciplinary approach brings professionals together on a team for diagnostic and planning meetings, but professionals' discrete identities tend to overshadow any real team identity (Malone, 1993; Friend & Cook, 1993 Correa, et al., 2005). Information may be shared among team members, but recommendations are not made in a shared fashion. Rather, professionals make recommendations specific to their areas of expertise. Interaction among team members is not stressed since members are responsible primarily for their own particular discipline's program design and implementation. In the multidisciplinary approach, the student or family receiving service typically is not included in the development of the service plan (Malone, 1993; Friend & Cook, 1993). In most cases, a multidisciplinary team is not a collaborative one because team members function independently. In the school environment, IEP teams should never function in a multidisciplinary manner. General education teachers and families must be included in the development of goals and objectives and in placement decisions. See **Table 12-2** for highlights of the multidisciplinary team process and a comparison with the other types of teams.

TABLE 12-2

Characteristics of Teams (Malone, 1993)

Multidisciplinary	Interdisciplinary	Transdisciplinary
1. Focus is on discipline identity.	1. Focus on team identity and coordinated effort.	1. Focus on student's program plan.
2. Professionals work independently.	2. Professionals work together as a team.	2. Professionals and family work together as a team.
3. Information is not integrated.	3. Information is integrated.	3. Needs of student and family dictate team goals.
4. No input from student or family.	4. Input provided from student and family.	4. Professional boundaries are dissolved.
	5. Interrelationship of student/family needs.	5. One person actually assesses and/or delivers services to student.

The Interdisciplinary Team

The interdisciplinary approach differs from the multidisciplinary approach in that while discipline representatives still come together for diagnostic and planning meetings, their focus is on the development of a coordinated plan of providing services for the student with disabilities. This coordinated plan acknowledges the interrelated needs of students with disabilities and their families (Malone, 1993; Friend & Cook, 1993; Correa, et al., 2005). Team members share goals and work interdependently; this sharing and acknowledgment of contributions by team members is extended to the student and/or family for whom services and supports are being developed. Interaction processes are vital since the team, not the individual disciplines, is primarily responsible for program design and implementation. Most schools use an interdisciplinary model to provide services to students with disabilities. By definition, interdisciplinary teams should function collaboratively because the team is focused on joint, coordinated decision-making. Refer to **Table 12-2** for highlights of the interdisciplinary team process and a comparison with the other types of teams.

The Transdisciplinary Team

Another team approach that has developed recently is the transdisciplinary approach (Correa, et al., 2005). This approach carries the interdisciplinary principles one step further. This transdisciplinary process encourages the development of a mutual exchange of knowledge, information, and skills among the team members. In the transdisciplinary approach, professionals share knowledge about their respective disciplines among themselves. Problem-solving, follow-through, and support for the student are enhanced by such an approach which requires that each member of the team be knowledgeable about the other areas as well. **Role release** is integral to the transdisciplinary approach and is the process of transferring information and skills from one discipline to another (Linder, 1993).

The transdisciplinary model (TD) grew out of a consideration for families and their desire to have fewer people working directly with them and their child. Families also wanted greater continuity in programming and more integration of parent participation (Raver, 1999). In the TD model, a variety of professionals can evaluate a student during an observational group process with only one professional actually interacting with the student. Likewise, in programming, members of the team meet regularly to discuss and review the student's progress, with only one team member primarily working with the child.

The TD model implies integration of therapy and services to support the student's development and education (Linder, 1993). Thus each team member must be knowledgeable enough about the other disciplines to be able to follow through effectively on program recommendations (Linder, 1993). Members of a TD team must commit to teaching and learning from each other, assume interchangeable roles and responsibilities, and allow the needs of the student and family to dictate their team goals. Team leadership usually rotates but a coordinator is typically designated.

The TD approach is gaining popularity, particularly in the fields of early intervention and early childhood special education. However, implementing the TD model can be difficult (Bruder & Bologna, 1993) due to professional licensing requirements and reimbursement requirements. Refer to **Table 12-2** for highlights of the transdisciplinary process and a comparison with the other types of teams.

Effective Collaboration with Team Members

Teams meet for a variety of reasons and can use any of the three team models just described as they interact. If an interdisciplinary team or a transdisciplinary team hopes to be collaborative, members of the team must be willing to work together. Teams will develop general characteristics that influence their effectiveness (Malone, 1993). Teams with a healthy "personality" that understand and practice cooperation, democracy, coordination, team identity, and team goals, can be extremely successful in providing quality services. Those teams with a less than healthy composition in which conflict and ambiguity are common, may not be productive in delivering services. Understanding those characteristics that contribute to productive teamwork can help team members as they coordinate their efforts on a team. The next section will focus on the qualities of effective, exemplary teams.

The Exemplary Balanced Team

In describing a truly collaborative team, Malone (1993) has outlined the characteristics of an exemplary, balanced team. The exemplary team is one that is well-organized. All team members have a clear understanding of both the team role and the roles of the individuals who make up the team. All team members are equal in power and influence. This results in efficient team functioning and a high level of productivity. In a balanced, well-organized team, there is a designated leader whose role is to facilitate and not rule the team process. The team leader acts as one member of the team and provides guidance as needed. Discussion of issues and decision making are based on objective information and not differences in personality among team members. A team with these characteristics has reached the stage where members are comfortable with the individual and team roles and efforts are directed toward achieving the team goals.

Qualities of Effective Teams

Briggs (1993) suggests a number of characteristics of effective teams. They include:

1. An overall mission, purpose, and goals that members understand and accept.
2. Sufficient resources.
3. Appropriate training and skills for team members.
4. Open communication to encourage diversity and manage conflict.

5. Sufficient time to develop team values and beliefs and to foster the growth of the team as a whole.
6. Use of effective problem solving strategies.
7. Use of high standards to evaluate individual roles and responsibilities.
8. A climate of trust and support.
9. Designated leadership (either one individual or shared).
10. Organizational support for the team.

For teams to be collaborative, members of the team must embrace the underlying principles of effective teamwork. Raver (1999; pp. 40–44) outlines the following personal, professional, and administrative characteristics that enhance the success of a team.

Personal Characteristics

Team members who are open, cooperative, and willing to share and listen, as well as to take risks, are important in the team process. Members must be willing to acknowledge that they need each other. Briggs (1993) suggests that in order to effect systemic change within a team, individuals must consider ways in which they themselves should change and not attempt to change others. People change only as a result of their own desire or need to, not as the result of someone else's wish that they change. Such self-evaluation can be effective in leading to internal change which in turn will enhance an individual's skills and ultimately benefit the whole team.

Professional Characteristics

In the best interest of the family and student, all team members should work together with the family to contribute to the solution of problems. For example, the psychologist, the special educator, the general education teacher, and the social worker may all believe they can best help to solve a student's behavior problem. Turf protection is a common conflict on teams. Disciplines may overlap and professionals must be willing to share common ground with others.

Administrative Characteristics

Administrators must allow time for teams to plan, practice, and work together. Teams should meet regularly and face-to-face with all team members in attendance. Thus, communication between all members becomes a habit (Bruder & Bologna, 1993). Agendas distributed before a meeting are helpful in preparing members for the meeting. Team facilitation can be coordinated by a designated team leader or can rotate. Facilitators and recorders keep the meeting moving and maintain a record of actions and recommendations.

Administrators also influence teams through hiring practices and the tone they set. Persons who understand, appreciate, and have experience with the collaborative process will make effective team members. A spirit of trust and a willingness to take risks often set the tone for effective group collaboration.

The complex needs of students with disabilities and their families are best addressed through teamwork in which professionals from key disciplines work together with individuals with disabilities, family members, friends, and others to plan and provide coordinated services and supports. Such teams pass through similar developmental stages and share certain common characteristics, regardless of the age, nature, or severity of disabilities of the students they serve. Understanding the characteristics that contribute to productive teamwork can help team members as they coordinate their efforts on a team. Communication skills also are an important component of team-building.

Team members should strive to improve their ability to participate on collaborative teams. This includes being open to the ideas of others and viewing your work as overlapping with the work of others. Using a team approach requires time for meetings with other school professionals so that services to a student with a disability are coordinated and integrated. One cannot assume that some one else will take care of something; every team member is responsible to ensure that all of a student's needs are met.

Communication Skills for Team Effectiveness

Briggs (1993) outlines a number of communication skills used by effective teams. Both nonverbal skills and the actual words used in a team process are important. Nonverbal skills that lead to effective communication include attending to the speaker and listening actively (acknowledging the speaker's words or ideas perhaps through head nods or other natural expressions of listening). Verbal strategies which promote effective communication include encouraging, clarifying, checking as to whether agreement or consensus was achieved, neutral questioning such as opening up a discussion with an idea, and summarizing.

Briggs (1993) also has identified barriers to effective communication in the collaborative team process. These include making judgments or evaluating others, acting "superior," acting like a "know it all," controlling or manipulating, warning or threatening, lecturing or arguing, and ridiculing or stereotyping. In other words, any communication that expresses nonacceptance of feelings, a desire to change another, a lack of trust, or a judgment that someone is wrong will create a block to effective interactions (Briggs, 1993). Teams must be especially sensitive to the feelings and behaviors of new team members and to family members.

Working with School Personnel

The ideas already discussed regarding the elements of an effective team provide the framework for collaborative interaction with anyone, including collaboration among school personnel. First and foremost, school personnel have to embrace the idea of working interdependently rather that independently. The primary function of collaborative educational teams is to support students to achieve successful relationships with others and to lead productive lives. That is, to prepare students to participate in social interactions, to make choices, to engage in community activities, and to work or contribute to society in some way. Rainforth, York, and Macdonald (1992) suggest a variety of ways school personnel can support each other including:

- resource support, such as materials or funding.
- moral support, such as listening and encouraging.
- technical support, such as instructional strategies or adaptations.

For any support to be real, the recipient of the support must feel supported. Support does not mean conducting an observation and depositing your notes in a teacher's mailbox, giving opinions but leaving before a discussion can occur, or telling another teacher what to do. Rather support means working together and acknowledging the efforts of team members to meet the needs of students. For school personnel to be effective collaborators, they must have time to meet together as a team as often as necessary.

A specific kind of collaborative teaming now often seen in schools is co-teaching. This usually involves a regular educator and a special educator teaching together in the same classroom. Co-teaching provides ready access to the general curriculum for students with special needs. There are a variety of co-teaching models (Friend & Cook, 2003). These include:

a) one teach-one assist model in which one teacher primarily instructs and the other primarily observes and helps individual students as needed;

b) station teaching occurs when teachers divide the content and students move from teacher to teacher for content and delivery;

c) parallel teaching has both teachers teaching half of the class the same content;

d) alternative teaching in which a small group receives intensive instruction from one of the teachers;

e) team teaching when both teachers teach the content together to all students at the same time. An example of team teaching is when one teacher is speaking and the second is drawing a graph of the materials on the overhead or when both are presenting different sides of an argument.

While co-teaching has many benefits for students and teachers, it requires extra time and effort to plan, teach, grade, share space, and work together (Correa et al, 2005). Teachers must be flexible and willing to openly communicate with another adult if they are to have success as a co-teacher (Friend & Cook, 2003). They should discuss issues such as philosophy and beliefs, classroom routines, ideas on disciplines, how to give and receive feedback, and any specific habits they may have as teachers so that the relationship can be a positive and fruitful one for the teachers and students (Friend & Cook, 2003).

Professional development is crucial to school personnel who engage in collaborative interactions. Professional development means learning new information to develop your competency as a team member. Three of the most widely used types of professional development for teams are:

1. Knowledge sharing.
2. Skill development through coaching and/or reflection.
3. Team development (Correa et al., 2005).

One way to empower team members is to provide them with new information, either formally or informally. This can be done through traditional workshops or through informal presentations. In addition, skill development can be done through peer coaching and individual reflection in which team members observe each other and share ideas. Moreover, professional development can occur as the team learns about the process of team building.

Collaboration should occur among all members of a team. General education teachers, special educators, paraprofessionals, therapists, and others must move beyond discipline-specific thinking to optimize student achievement. Collaboration is a challenging endeavor, but it is crucial to providing the best services possible for students with disabilities.

Families and the Child with Special Needs

Maria, 14 years old, and Sara, 7 years old, and their family recently moved to a small U.S. community from Mexico. Both parents work full-time but on different shifts so that one of them is always home when the children are there. Their grandmother also lives with them. Maria and Sara recently started school. Maria brought some letters home from school which Señor and Señora Gomez signed as Maria told them they were from her teachers. But, the letters were in English and the Gomez parents are not yet fluent in reading English.

Maria did not always go to school in Mexico because she didn't always understand what her teachers wanted her to do and she didn't really like school.

Another letter has just come in the mail from the school, and Señor Gomez took it to work to ask a friend of his to read the English for him. He found out that there will be a meeting which he is supposed to attend regarding Maria's class. He tries to get off work to go to it but is unable to reschedule his shift. The Gomez family is unsure about what is going on at school or if they can say anything about it.

How could a more successful collaboration among school professionals and the family alleviate this situation? What are the school's responsibilities regarding interactions with families so that they understand their rights in the special education process?

Developing a healthy partnership with families is an important goal for schools. Without an active and positive partnership with families, schools can never achieve full collaboration. Students are first and foremost members of their families before being members of their school. Families have a lasting and powerful influence on their children.

Past traditional views of families pictured a working husband, an at-home wife, and several children. The basic family unit has changed drastically over the last several decades with increases in divorce rates, single parent families, married women working outside of the home, and blended families encompassing two adults and children from different unions and extended families (Johnson, Pugach & Hawkins, 2004). Today, there is no longer a "typical" family; as a result, school personnel must be prepared to work with a variety of family structures and cultures. All schools are affected by the increasing number of culturally and linguistically diverse children in our society.

The family's role in the development of a child with disabilities has gained increasing attention in recent years. The focus has shifted from viewing the development of the child alone to looking at the development of the child as a part of the family and community. This ecological perspective views the family as part of a broader system; as part of an extended family, a community, a state, and a nation (Bronfenbrenner, 1977). As a general education teacher, you need to be familiar with four theoretical approaches that can be used to examine the family of a child with disabilities. They include family systems theory, grieving cycles, family stress theory, and a family empowerment model. Each of these approaches is reviewed. They should influence your understanding of families and their needs.

Family Systems Theory

A family systems approach views families who have a child with special needs first and foremost, like all other families with the same needs, wants, and desires. In this perspective, all families need special help and support at various times. As Fewell and Vadasy (1986) note, there are differences among families in terms of their family interactions, their capacity to meet the family's basic needs or functions, and the life cycle stage of the family unit (e.g., just married, children finishing high school, etc.). In addition, these differences may be influenced greatly by the family's cultural background. These concepts combined with a broad understanding of the family's dynamics and makeup are the basis for a family systems approach (Turnbull, Brotherson, & Summers, 1985; Turnbull, Summers, & Brotherson, 1984; Turnbull, Turnbull, Erwin & Soodak, 2006). As a system, the family is composed of members. If any outside force affects one member of the family, it will in turn have an effect on the rest of the family system. For example, an economic recession causes a father to lose his job. This in turn creates additional stress in the home that might impact the student's behavior in school. Similarly, a teacher's request that parents spend additional time with a child on homework or self-help skills may put additional stress on an already overworked family system (Pugach & Johnson, 1995).

In family systems theory, a variety of sub-systems exist within a family system. They may include a husband-wife system, a parent-child system, a sibling-sibling system, grandchild-grandparent system, and others. The interaction of these subunits helps to define the family's functioning. All of these subsystems can be a source of support or stress for the family. For instance, if grandparents live in the home and are helpful with child care, they may be viewed as a source of support. If they live elsewhere and arrive unannounced for extended visits, they may create a source of stress for the family.

Family Needs and Stresses

The basic tasks that families undertake to meet their needs are called family functions. Turnbull et al. (2006) describe eight family functions: economic, daily care, socialization, recreation, self-esteem, affection, spiritual and education/vocational. Family needs are complex, and all of these functions are important, not only the educational ones. Think about these functions and consider how they influence a family with a child with disabilities. A discussion of each of these family functions follows (Turnbull et al., 2006). Think of ways you can assist families in carrying out the functions.

Economic Needs

A child with a disability can create additional stress on the financial needs of a family. For example, parents may need to pay the costs of additional health care, physical or occupational therapy, adaptive devices, or specialized after school care. Schools can help by providing resource information on financial planning, having social workers who can link families with available resources (including other families in similar circumstances), or planning parent programs on topics such as estate planning or budgeting.

Daily Care Needs

Parents may be so exhausted from the daily demands of caring and planning for a child with a disability that they neglect their own needs for rest or adequate nutrition. The parent who must transport a child to various medical or therapy appointments on the bus or by car can be overwhelmed by the process of daily living. Schools can help by allowing access to the school nurse for families that need it, being supportive in providing therapy in the classroom/school setting, providing information on adequate nutrition, and again, linking families in similar circumstances so they can discuss their ideas and circumstances with others in a similar situation.

Socialization and Recreation Needs

Families that have a child with special needs may limit their own opportunities to socialize because of the child's disability or behavior. For instance, a family may feel uncomfortable taking their six-year-old son with autism to his older sister's school play because he may run off, scream, and interrupt the play. Schools can be helpful in providing links to respite care agencies which offer child care on an as-needed basis using qualified providers. Schools might facilitate workshops on behavior management so that families can feel more comfortable in social settings with their child. Schools also can encourage brothers or sisters who have similar siblings to meet each other and share common experiences and strategies. For example, brothers and sisters might want to talk about what to do when they have friends over or when no one at the fast food restaurant can understand what their sister is saying.

Self-Esteem Needs

Confidence and self-worth are linked to a person's or family's definition of self. The self-identity of the parents is tied strongly to the self-identity of the children regardless of their special needs. Thus, parents who have a good sense of self-worth and feel competent as parents will make strong parents for their children. Family support groups sponsored by the school often can be helpful to parents of children with special needs as they allow families the chance to meet others who share their feelings. Groups also can be helpful in giving parents specific strategies to use with their children with special needs, such as feeding or behavioral techniques.

Affection Needs

The needs for love and physical intimacy are expressed through verbal and nonverbal means. Family members may have a hard time "reading" a child's facial expressions if the child has autism. Or, they may have difficulty understanding a child's speech if she has cerebral palsy, and thus some of the spontaneous give and take of affection may be lost. Teachers and therapists can be good sources of input on reading the child's cues or helping the child to communicate, either verbally or nonverbally. Most schools think of affection needs as being beyond their scope but may offer counseling or support groups as needed for students or their parents.

Spiritual Needs

Spirituality is displayed in a variety of ways across cultures, often through family values. Teachers can honor the cultural traditions of families by listening to their interpretations of religion and honoring them. This can serve as a valuable source of support for the family.

Educational/Vocational Needs

Schools help families meet their children's educational and vocational needs by encouraging and facilitating their involvement in the school. Schools must pay particular attention to the needs of parents of children with special needs when encouraging parental involvement. For instance, some schools have students with special needs who travel further than their other students to get to school. When a PTA meeting is planned, parents of the students with special needs may need careful directions and perhaps child care to be able to come to evening meetings. Families should be encouraged to choose their own level of involvement with the schools and feel supported in doing so. Some parents, for instance, may work full-time and not have extra time to spend at school but may have a grandparent who can come in to read to the students with special needs on a regular basis.

In addition to the family functions just discussed, issues related to the siblings of a child with a disability also must be considered. Siblings who are typically developing often will be in the same school with their brother or sister with a disability. Specific sibling concerns that may arise include competition, serving in a "caregiver" role, and a lack of understanding of special education (Gallagher, Powell, & Rhodes, 2006). General education and special education teachers can play an important role in working with siblings to address any special problems that may arise. They should recognize the sibling as a unique individual, help explain special education to all students in the school, involve siblings as appropriate in IEP or other meetings, and be available to talk to the siblings about concerns as needed. Siblings express special concerns related to their brother or sister with a disability such as the cause of the disability, the prognosis, inconsistent parental expectations, their own health and relationship to their brother or sister, how to inform their friends about the disability, how to react to teasing, and how to foster community acceptance of their brother or sister (Gallagher, et al., 2006).

Grieving Cycle

A second way of viewing families of children with disabilities is to examine stages in the grieving cycle (Kubler-Ross, 1969). Family members have sometimes been labeled as being in shock or denial, or as being rejecting or overprotecting as a defense against the crisis of having a child with a disability. Gartner, Lipsky, and Turnbull (1991) note that variations in family responses often are more a function of such factors as culture or economic situations rather than just a function of having a child with a disability. In fact, all families go through feelings of hate and love, acceptance, and rejection with all of their children at various times. Families of children with special needs may in fact feel grief at certain points in time, but may experience it and express it in a variety of ways (Blacher, 1984; Wright, Granger, & Sameroff, 1983). While the grieving cycle theory has been proposed to describe how families adjust to having a child with a disability, research does not support the notion that families go through a set series of emotional reactions such as shock, denial, sadness, anxiety, and anger in a specific order before adapting to their child with a disability (Gallagher, Fialka, Rhodes, & Arceneaux, 2002; Turnbull & Turnbull, 2001). Rather, families may experience some or all of the emotions in any order and at various times.

Family Stress Theory

A third way to view a family's adjustment to having a child with disabilities is to examine family stress theory. This model suggests that a potentially stressful event such as the birth or diagnosis of a child with special needs does not necessarily precipitate a family crisis (Hill, 1949; 1958). The model shows that the resources a family brings to a situation and their response to the situation will vary across families.

It is important for teachers to realize that families react to and cope with a child with disabilities in different ways and that their strategies for coping may change as the life cycle of the family changes. For instance, one mother with two other younger children consistently worked with her eight-year-old son at home to practice his language processing skills. She realized that he had special needs and being a former teacher, was happy to work with Jason every evening on special assignments from school. They had been making great progress and sent notes back and forth to the teacher regarding what they should work on next. When the mother had twins, however, and her husband in the military was shipped to an overseas assignment, she was overwhelmed and no longer able to find the time or energy to help Jason with anything the teacher sent home. Additional stress minimized her time and energy to work with her son with special needs, even though his particular needs were not the contributing factor to her stress.

Family Empowerment Model

The family empowerment model regards the family as the determiner of services, rather than the traditional recipient of services (Dunst, Trivette, & Deal, 1988). In a family empowerment model, for instance, families would initiate and plan a school wide parent meeting rather than teachers and school personnel setting dates and determining meeting agendas. Such an approach acknowledges the capability of families to generate their own solutions and reinforces collaborative relationships. These relationships must involve mutual respect among family members and school personnel. A family empowerment model demands that parents and family members have adequate information so that they can participate as equals in the collaboration process.

Families are essential for meeting the basic needs of students. The four models discussed present critical perspectives that should influence and affect your understanding of families. In turn, they should help you determine successful ways to develop collaborative partnerships with families and make educational services more effective for students. It is important to remember that the family members consist of more than just parents. Brothers and sisters, for instance, are an important part of the family and may need support as they play key roles in the development of their brothers and sisters with disabilities. (Gallagher et al., 2006). Grandparents may play an important caregiving role in the life of the child with a disability. Families can play a crucial role on many of the teams established in schools. Let's look more closely at how families can be involved in the special education process.

Working with Families

Working with families of students with disabilities can be a very meaningful experience for professionals. Family involvement is mandated by law as discussed previously, but its importance is also common sense. After all, parents are the child's first and most important educators. The home setting is a critical factor in the child's success.

Research on the importance of parental involvement in the schools shows that such involvement enhances a child's chances of school success (Epstein, 1989) and significantly improves student achievement (Dettmer, Thurston, & Dyck, 1993; Henderson, 1987; Kroth & Scholl, 1978). Parents also benefit from being involved in their child's education through improved feelings of self-worth and self-satisfaction (Murphy, 1981). Teachers benefit by having more information about their students and their backgrounds and home life.

Traditional approaches to involving parents of children with special needs in schools often have been limited to "rubber stamping" the recommendations of the professionals. Parents were expected to go home and carry out the ideas and recommendations provided by the "experts." In the past, many programs were directive in their interactions with families, demanding that families comply with the school's views on parental involvement instead of working to understand families' desires regarding their own involvement.

Recently, the focus of family involvement has shifted to a **family-centered approach** which views families as competent decision makers who can contribute as equal team members in making decisions regarding educational programs for their child with a disability (Correa et al., 2005). Such a family-centered approach is guided by family members who are fully informed and focuses on the strengths and capabilities of families. While involving parents in early intervention and special education programs may seem like a logical and natural thing to do, forming partnerships between parents and professionals is not always an easy, simple process.

The American Heritage College Dictionary (2002) defines a "partner" as one who is united with others in an activity or sphere of common interest. When we think of a partnership, we think of an agreement between two or more parties, involving active participation by all groups. Developing partnerships with families is essential for optimal success of a student in school; however, developing these partnerships is not always easy. Team members must be aware of cultural and ethnic differences among families that may influence their participation in team decision-making.

Edmondson (1994) points out three potential barriers to successful collaboration with families:

1. Most professionals have been taught to provide services in a traditional "expert" model. Moving into interdisciplinary or transdisciplinary models where professionals

work together with parents may require that professionals serve in different roles from those they have experienced. It also demands effective communication.

2. Traditionally, parents have played a somewhat passive role in decision making involving their child with special needs, primarily being the recipients of services provided by professionals. With recent legislation, however, many parents are playing a more active role in their child's education and need information and knowledge of systems and services as well as effective communication skills to be effective partners.

3. The development of a parent-professional partnership implies a collaborative relationship. Most parents and professionals hopefully agree that collaboration will result in better services, but acting in a collaborative manner to form effective partnerships involves some particular personal qualities such as mutual respect, trust, listening skills, honesty, openness, sensitivity, and empathy.

Johnson et al. (2004) also have outlined several barriers to family participation. These three barriers were identified by parents and include logistical problems, communication problems, and a lack of understanding of schools.

1. **Logistical Problems.** Situations leading to a lack of transportation or child care, or getting time away from work to attend school conferences have been identified as logistical problems families may face. Team members may need to brainstorm and be open to alternative meeting locations such as the family's home or conference calls. In addition, team members may need to consider a variety of possible times for meetings, including meetings scheduled before work, during lunch, or in the evening. These issues may be particularly critical for single parent families or those having inflexible work schedules.

2. **Communication Problems.** Families may come from cultural or socioeconomic backgrounds different from school personnel which can lead to problems in communicating. Teachers often use professional jargon which may intimidate some parents. In turn, teachers don't understand the style of communication used by the family. School personnel must successfully develop rapport and show empathic understanding with all families.

3. **Lack of Understanding of Schools.** Schools have a complex set of written and unwritten operating rules. Families may not understand, for instance, what occurs at an IEP meeting or who will be there or why. If schools are to become more family-focused, all families must understand these rules and be a part of what is happening in the schools. This may mean preparing families for who will be at a meeting, their roles, and the process that will occur. It also may mean teaching families how to access the resources of the school and accepting all families as an educational resource for the school.

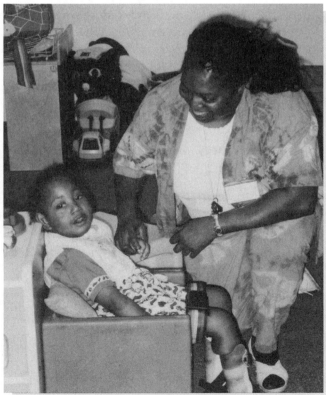

Most parents want to be involved in their child's life at school.

One of the most important components to successful family involvement is keeping the family informed. It is the school's responsibility to help families understand their child's life at school. Teachers are a crucial source of information for the family and are essential to establishing and maintaining open lines of communication.

Sometimes professionals talk about parents who don't seem to want to be involved in the child's school or who seem angry at the schools. While a few parents may be apathetic or indifferent about their involvement in the schools, most are truly interested in what is happening in their children's lives. Most parents, regardless of their background or economic status, do want to be involved but may be waiting for an invitation and an opportunity to become a team member. Teachers often misinterpret a lack of involvement as apathy, particularly with respect to families of cultures different from their own (Pugach & Johnson, 2002). Some reasons for a seeming lack of involvement or a negative attitude on the part of parents may be:

- Parents' own experiences with schools may not have been positive and they thus avoid further interactions thinking they too will be negative.

- Parents may not believe they have any influence or power over what happens in schools and therefore don't even try to make a difference.

- Certain norms from various cultures may dictate that the teacher knows best, and therefore, families have little to add.

- Parents may be exhausted from meeting all of the other family needs and do not have the time or energy to be involved with the schools.

- Parents may have interacted with teachers or school administrators in the past who were not responsive to mutually agreed upon meeting times or having parents closely involved in the IEP development, and thus think the schools don't want their input and support.

- Parents may fear that they will be blamed for their child's behavior or learning problems. Educators may blame or criticize parents (often unconsciously) for the actions of their child. Any such posture of blame or criticism should be abandoned so that collaboration and problem-solving can occur.

- Parents may become frustrated after listening to negative reports about their child year after year and feel that there is not much hope that their involvement will make a difference for their child.

How Teachers Can Help

To overcome this perceived indifference and other barriers, teachers must be responsive to demands for child care, transportation, and time away from work. Meetings can be scheduled in family homes or local community centers in the evenings with child care provided, if needed. Suggestions for meetings at times that are more convenient for families, such as evenings or weekends, may conflict directly with teachers' own times to be with their families. Creative ways of getting families and teachers together have to be developed.

Teachers also can help family members become equal members of a team by giving them information. Teachers can help prepare family members for the IEP process—who will be there and why, what some of the words that are likely to be used may mean, how long the meeting will last, what will occur, etc. so that they can be active participants in the process. **Table 12-3** presents suggestions for working with families.

Additionally, as Johnson et al. (2004) note, teachers have to be honest about their own sincere desire to have families involved. Teachers have not always valued input from families, particularly when meeting the needs of students with disabilities. Teachers often

TABLE 12-3

Suggestions for Working with Families

1. Spend more time listening than talking.
2. Keep an open mind and be free of judgements.
3. Stress that you are a member of the team.
4. Avoid comparing families and situations.
5. Find something genuinely nice to say about the child you are teaching.
6. Don't make promises that you may not be able to keep.
7. Refrain from patronizing families with statement such as, "I don't know how you cope so well."
8. Be sensitive to the impression that you project, both verbally and nonverbally.
9. Do not discount family members' problems or feelings about issues discussed.
10. Do not argue with families.

From: ASHA's Infant Project (1991) and Simpson, R. L. (1996).

characterize families as trouble makers when they "rock the boat" and don't agree with the school's ideas or suggestions. Teachers need to treat families as equal members of the team for true collaboration to occur. More importantly, families need to begin to see schools as family-centered with positive feelings and outcomes. Families need to be involved as real school decision makers and see that their participation is valued. The parent's plea provided in **Figure 12-1** helps us understand that families and teachers should be on the same side—the child's side.

Patrikakou, Weissberg, Hancock, Rubenstein, and Zeisz (1997) outline four essential ingredients to creating effective interactions between teachers and parents. They describe these strategies as the four Ps:

1. Be positive. Discuss strengths and provide praise and encouragement, not just concerns.
2. Be personalized. Write personal notes rather than using "form" letters to provide feedback to parents.
3. Be proactive. Contact parents well in advance of upcoming events and school policies and expectations. Discuss a concern immediately, don't wait and allow the problem to become more severe.
4. Develop a partnership. Encourage parents to respond to notes or questions. Show appreciation of feedback.

A collaborative attitude on the part of a teacher can go along way in creating an effective relationship with parents. Simple strategies can be very beneficial.

Communicating with Families

Teachers can facilitate interactions with family members in a variety of ways. It is important that in communication you have with families whose first language is other than English, a translator is present for face to face or telephone contact, and that all written materials have been translated. Provided below are several ideas regarding fostering successful communication with families.

FIGURE 12-1

"A Parent's Plea" by Susan Stokes

I am a parent with a special needs child. If you are involved in the treatment of my child please . . .

Treat me with respect.
I am a human being deserving of the same respect you deserve from me.

Treat me as an individual.
Give me and the other members of my family the benefit of the doubt. My child and each member of our family is unique. Don't judge or make generalizations.

Explain.
I need to understand the rationale for your recommendations as well as the recommendations themselves. If I don't understand or agree with your recommendations, it is unlikely I will follow them or otherwise support them.

Be honest.
Honestly builds trust. I need to be able to trust you to make appropriate decisions for my child. If you are less than honest or if I get the impression you are less than honest to me, just once, there is little chance I will ever trust you again.

Be direct.
I do not necessarily have the time or the patience required to guess what you are trying to say.

Be kind.
If my child is having difficulties, I suffer with him. Please consider my feelings, the high level of stress I may be feeling, and how your decisions and recommendations may affect the rest of my family.

Listen.
I am the best expert there is on the behavior of my child. I have valuable experience and insights that can be very helpful in your treatment recommendations. I will also be more likely to support your recommendations if I am involved in the planning process.

Remember, we're supposed to be on the same side . . .
We all want what is best for my child.

Reprinted by permission of the author.

Family Conferences

The most common form of communication is the family-teacher conference. This time can be an opportunity to solidify collaborative relationships with families. Turnbull and Turnbull (2001) see four main reasons for the family conference including:

1. Exchanging information about home and school.
2. Working together to help the student progress.
3. Developing rapport and mutual commitment to the student's development.
4. Cooperating in solving problems and concerns.

Family-teacher conferences should have three phases (Turnbull & Turnbull, 2001):

1. preconference planning including notification, preparation and planning of the agenda, and arranging the environment;

2. implementation—conducting the conference; and
3. postconference follow-up.

Preconference planning includes notification of the meeting and preparing parents for what will happen at the meeting. Notification should be translated into the native language of the family. Parents should know that they can bring someone with them to the meeting if that would be helpful. If parents know what to expect at a meeting, be it an information conference or an IEP meeting, they will be more likely to participate. It also may be helpful to provide parents with a preview of the child's progress on IEP goals or other information before the meeting so that they can be prepared with questions and comments at the meeting.

The teacher should review folders, gather examples of the student's work and progress on IEP goals and objectives, and make an outline of the meeting agenda with the parents if at all possible. Parents should prepare in a similar manner by reviewing the child's progress. The meeting room arrangements also should be addressed. A quiet meeting room with adult sized chairs and scheduled at a time convenient for everyone involved is ideal.

Communication skills are the basis for conducting the conference. Be sure that parental concerns are clarified and stick to the agenda, being flexible as new issues are raised. The conference follow-up should summarize and provide written copies of plans for everyone involved. Follow-up phone calls to family members or other team members are made as needed.

Phone Calls, E-mails, and Unplanned Conferences

These should be a necessary part of interaction with family members for all students. While calls frequently are made when there is a problem, it's important to make calls regarding good things as often as possible. Teachers should keep a log of all phone calls and take notes during these exchanges. This is also true of e-mail interactions. If you don't have the information at the time of the interaction, say so and get back to parents in a reasonable period of time. Give the family member a date by which you will respond but don't promise to do it immediately. For example, you might say: *"I'm glad you took the time to talk to me. I want to be sure I get the correct information, and I'll get back to you by _____."* Give yourself enough time to gather the information and review it before calling back or responding by e-mail.

If the family member is angry during your exchange, talk to the person in a calm voice, listening, and not interrupting, and indicate you'll get back with more information by a specific date. Remember that not all families have telephones or home computers, and some may not be comfortable communicating through these media. It is useful if it is convenient and acceptable to the family.

Traveling Notebooks

An excellent way to communicate frequently and in a more informal way with families and professionals is through the use of a traveling notebook. The notebook can go back and forth among all the school personnel with whom the student interacts and be sent home on a daily or weekly basis. Family members and professionals write brief messages to each other to keep everyone informed about the student's current progress and needs. The traveling notebook can be an important place to share ideas or ask questions. This may not be a feasible option if family members are not literate or fluent in English.

Observation in the Classroom

Another way to collaborate with families is to encourage family members to spend time observing or participating in their child's classroom. This could be a once-a-year experience or as frequent as a weekly experience. This type of opportunity allows the family to learn more about the student's school day and to see their child's performance on various school tasks. Observations also help parents be more active team members, especially regarding goal setting and program implementation for the student.

Reference Books

Strickland and Turnbull (1993) suggest the development and use of a reference book for parents and families. A reference notebook is a good way for parents to gather and maintain information about their child. It might include sections on legal references, names of local or national parent support groups, and names of school or community contacts.

In addition to these ideas, teachers can provide all families with calendars, announcements, or newsletters about what is happening in the classroom. In some schools, websites provide good information about school events and the school calender. Open houses and orientation programs for new parents also may be helpful in facilitating communication with families. Moreover, including families of children with disabilities as volunteers for field trips and other school events will help them feel connected with the general education classroom in which their child participates. Clearly, to foster the best communication possible between families and schools, teachers must encourage frequent communication and be receptive to family input.

Future Challenges and Perspectives

Collaboration can be a meaningful process for accomplishing positive interactions among professionals and family members for the good of a student with disabilities. It involves time and effort on the part of all involved but can be effective and well-worth the time and energy involved. Schools are now beginning to look beyond collaboration within the school setting to collaborative efforts with those outside the school setting. School personnel have become more involved in collaboration with the medical and health community, the broader disability community (e.g., Developmental Disabilities Council), the family services community (Family Support; Family Preservation), and the college and university community. Such efforts can broaden and expand the impact of the collaborative process for students with disabilities.

As our society continues to change, school personnel will continue to face challenges in implementing a collaborative model of service for students. For example, scheduling meetings outside of regular school hours may become even more challenging as the number of students raised by single parents and working parents continues to grow. As more families become familiar with and participate in early intervention programs, they will have more experience in family-centered services and will expect to continue to actively participate in programming decisions for their children with special needs once they enter the public school system. As teachers continue to face challenges, it is important to remember that change is essential for meeting the needs of all students with disabilities.

Summary

This chapter has discussed the role of the family and school professionals in providing the educational services to students with disabilities. Emphasis has been placed on developing a collaborative model of interaction. Collaboration in the schools is defined as an interactive process that enables people with diverse experiences and expertise to mutually develop goals, define problems, and create solutions. Discussion has focused on the impact of a child with a disability on the family and the family's role in decision-making for their child with special needs. Members of the educational team have been outlined along with types of teams and methods for facilitating effective collaboration among team members. Finally, ideas for fostering successful collaboration among families and school personnel have been discussed.

Name: _____   Date: _____

Discussion Questions and Activities

1. Divide the class into small groups of 5–6 persons. Ask each group to list all the teams or groups in which they have been involved over the years. Limit the time to 5 minutes. Let each group share their list to demonstrate how much "collaborative" experience many of us have.

2. As individuals or groups, discuss why a team or club of which you were a member was "collaborative" or not.

3. Take a moment and jot down a description of your family as you were growing up. Now take a moment and describe another family in your neighborhood. How were the two families similar? How were they different?

4. Think of a family you know in which there is a child with special needs. Describe the effect of this child on the family. Which theoretical approach might be most helpful in explaining this family's reaction to their situation?

5. Role play one of the barriers to family participation outlined in the chapter. Describe suggested solutions to overcome the barrier. *p. 499 – 500*

6. Read "A Parent's Plea" (see Figure 12-1 in the chapter). What is your reaction to the "plea"? *p. 502*

7. What are five strategies you could use as a teacher to foster communication between yourself and the families of students in your class? *p. 501*

8. Think about a friend or colleague who is from a different cultural background than your own. How might the two of you approach a problem differently?

Internet Resources

Center for Effective Collaboration and Practice
http:/cecp.air.org

Children, Youth and Family Consortium Electronic Clearinghouse
http://cyfc.umn.edu

Directory of Parent Centers
http://www.fcsn.org/ptis/ptilist.htm

Educators for Parents
http://educatorsforparents.com

Family Village
http://familyvillage.wisc.edu

Family Voices
http://www.familyvoices.org

Federation of Families for Children's Mental Health
http://www.ffcmh.org

National Coalition for Parent Involvement in Education
http://www.ncpie.org

Parent Resources by University of Texas, Austin
http://www.tenet.edu/parents/specialpop.html

Teacher-to-Teacher Collaboration
http://teachnet.edb.utexas.edu

The Sibling Support Project
http://thearc.org/siblingsupport

References

Abelson, M., & Woodman, R. (1983). Review of research on team effectiveness: Implications for teams in schools. *School Psychology Review, 12,* 125–136.

American Heritage College Dictionary (4th ed.). (2002). Boston: Houghton Mifflin.

ASHA's Infant Project, (1991). Rockville, MD: American Speech-Language-Hearing Association.

Bateman, B. D., & Linden, M. A. (1998). *Better IEPs.* Longmont, CO: Sopris West.

Blacher, J. (1984). Sequential stages of parental adjustment to the birth of a child with handicaps: Fact or artifact. *Mental Retardation, 2 (2),* 55–68.

Briggs, M. H. (1993). Team talk: Communication skills for early intervention teams. *Journal of Childhood Communication Disorders, 15,* 33–40.

Bronfenbrenner, U. (1977). Toward an experimental ecology of human development. *American Psychologist, 32,* 513–531.

Bruder, M. B., & Bologna T. (1993). Collaboration and service coordination for effective early intervention. In W. Brown, S. K. Thurman, & L. F. Pearl (Eds.), *Family-centered early intervention with infants and toddlers* (pp. 103–127). Baltimore, MD: Paul H. Brookes.

Correa, V., Jones, H., Thomas, C. & Morsink, C. (2005) *Interactive Teaming: Enhancing Programs for Students with Special Needs.* Upper Saddle River, NJ: Pearson Prentice Hall.

Coufal, K. (1993). Collaborative consultation for speech-language pathologists. *Topics in Language Disorders, 14(1),* 1–14.

Dettmer, P., Thurston, L. P., & Dyck, N. (1993). *Consultation, collaboration, and team work.* Boston: Allyn & Bacon.

Dunst. C., Trivette, C., & Deal, A. (1988). *Enabling and empowering families.* Cambridge, MA: Brookline Books.

Epstein, J. L. (1989). Building parent-teacher partnerships in inner-city schools. *Family Resource Coalition Report, 8:7.*

Fewell, R. R., & Vadasy, P. F. (1986). *Families of handicapped children: Needs and supports across the life span.* Austin, TX: PRO-ED.

Friend, M., & Cook, L. (2003). *Interactions: Collaboration skills for school professionals* (4th ed.). Boston: Allyn & Bacon.

Gallagher, P. A., Fialka, J., Rhodes, C., & Arceneaux, C. (2002). Working with families: Rethinking denial. *Young Exceptional Children, 5(2),* 11–17.

Gallagher, P. A., Powell, T. H., & Rhodes, C. A. (2006). *Brothers and sisters: A special part of exceptional families* (3rd ed.). Baltimore, MD: Paul H. Brookes.

Gartner, A., Lipsky, D. K., & Turnbull, A. P. (1991). Families and a child with a disability. In A. Gartner, D. K. Lipsky, & A. P. Turnbull (Eds.), *Supporting families with a child with a disability* (pp. 57–96). Baltimore, MD: Paul H. Brookes.

Henderson, A. T. (1987). *The evidence continues to grow: Parent involvement improves student achievement.* Silver Springs, MD: National Citizens Committee in Education.

Hill, R. (1949). *Families under stress: Adjustment to the crisis of war and separation.* New York: Harper & Row.

Hill, R. (1958). Social stress in the family. *Social Casework, 39,* 139–150.

Johnson, L. J., Pugach, M. C., & Hawkins, A. (2004). School-Family Collaboration: A Partnership. *Focus on Exceptional Children, 36(4),* 1–12.

Kontos, N., & File, N. (1993). Staff development in support of integration. In C. A. Peck, S. L. Odom, & D. D. Bricker (Eds.), *Integrating young children with disabilities into community programs: Ecological perspectives on research and implementation* (pp. 169–186). Baltimore, MD: Paul H. Brookes.

Kroth, R. L., & Scholl, G. T. (1978). *Getting schools involved with parents.* Arlington, VA: Council for Exceptional Children.

Kubler-Ross, E. (1969). *On death and dying.* New York: Macmillan.

Linder, T. (1993). *Transdisciplinary play-based intervention.* Baltimore, MD: Paul H. Brookes.

Malone, D. M. (1993). UAP core curriculum: *Team process module.* Athens, GA: UAP at University of Georgia.

McGonigel, M. J., & Garland, C. W. (1988). The individualized family service plan and the early intervention team: Team and family issues and recommended practices. *Infants and Young Children, 1,* 10–21.

Murphy, A. G. (1981). *Special children, special parents: Personal issues with handicapped children.* Englewood Cliffs, NJ: Prentice Hall.

Patrikakou, E., Weissberg., R., Hancock, M., Rubenstein, M., & Zeisz, J. (1997). *Positive communication between parents and teachers.* Philadelphia, PA: Laboratory for Student Success (LSS). Retrieved from http://www.temple.edu/LSS.

Pugach, M. C., & Johnson, L. J. (2002). *Collaborative practitioners; collaborative schools.* (2nd. ed.). Denver, CO: Love.

Rainforth, B., York, J., & Macdonald, C. (1992). *Collaborative teams for students with severe disabilities: Integrating therapy and educational services.* Baltimore, MD: Paul H. Brookes.

Raver, S. A. (1999). *Strategies for teaching at-risk and handicapped infants and toddlers: A transdisciplinary approach.* New York: Merrill.

Rich, D. (1987). *Schools and families: Issues and actions* Washington, DC: National Education Association. *American Psychologist, 32,* 513–531.

Simpson, R. L. (1996). *Working with families of exceptional children and youth.* Austin, TX: Pro-Ed.

Strickland, B. B., & Turnbull, A. P. (1993). *Developing and implementing Individualized Education Programs.* New York: Macmillan.

Turnbull, A., Turnbull, R., Erwin, E., & Soodak, L. (2006). *Families, Professionals and Exceptionality* (5th ed.) Columbus, OH: Pearson/Merrill Prentice Hall.

Turnbull, A. P., Brotherson, M. J., & Summers, J. A. (1985). The impact of deinstitutionalization on families: A family systems approach. In R. H. Bruininks & K. C. Lakin (Eds.), *Living and learning in the least restrictive environment* (pp. 115–140). Baltimore, MD: Paul H. Brookes.

Turnbull, A. P., Summers, J. A., & Brotherson, M. J. (1984). *Working with families with disabled members: A family systems approach.* Lawrence, KS: University of Kansas, Kansas University Affiliated Facility.

Turnbull, A. P., & Turnbull, H. R. III (2001). *Families, professionals, and exceptionality* (4th ed.). Columbus, OH: Merrill.

13

Students Who Are Talented and Gifted

John E. Kesner and Teresa Pawlik

Chapter Objectives

- to provide an overview of the history of gifted education;
- to describe the characteristics of students who are talented or gifted;
- to review the ways in which students are assessed and identified as talented or gifted;
- to describe the service delivery models used by schools for students who are talented and gifted; and
- to present instructional strategies classroom teachers can use to address the needs of these students.

The distribution of talents and abilities in our society varies widely. If we accept that some individuals have abilities below the norm, we are forced to recognize that some individuals will be blessed with talents and abilities far above the norm. Recognition of those gifted individuals is difficult because in our efforts to attain an egalitarian society, we confuse equality of individuals with equality of opportunity. Striving for an egalitarian society does not mean that all are equal in ability, but rather that all should be afforded the same opportunities to develop to their full potential.

Students who are talented and gifted have been viewed by some as being handicapped, because their abilities lie outside the norm and their needs are not met in regular education curricula (Coleman & Cross, 2001). If the myriad of problems facing mankind are to be solved, the talents and abilities of these students are our brightest hope. Too often, however, they are met with suspicion, ridicule and even scorn. In our efforts to help those with abilities below the norm, gifted students are often forgotten or relegated to programs on the margin of the educational spectrum. The No Child Left Behind (NCLB) legislation which has become the national educational obsession is a prime example. NCLB has the laudable goals of bringing all students to proficiency, yet does little to assist those students above the median (Colangelo, Assouline, & Gross, 2004). Although considered by many as special education, programs for students who are gifted and talented are not subject to the same state and federal regulations that govern other special education services.

We believe that students who are talented and gifted have special needs that are not fully met by the general education curriculum in most schools. It is important that schools identify and nurture these students to ensure they have the opportunity to develop to their fullest potential. Due to limited resources in many schools, this often becomes the responsibility of the classroom teacher. This chapter will review the history of gifted education and examine the ways in which giftedness is defined and identified. In addition, we will provide suggestions for teachers to assist them in enriching the curriculum and meeting the needs of their students who are talented or gifted.

History of Gifted Education

Historically, concern for individuals who are gifted is as old and varied as mankind. The Greeks and the Romans believed that exceptionally competent individuals should be identified and educated to become future leaders of the state. The Ottoman Empire sent scouts to locate gifted students and bring them to Constantinople to be educated. Thomas Jefferson believed that gifted students should be identified and educated at state expense (Coleman & Cross, 2001).

Sir Francis Galton is credited with the first scientific investigation of giftedness. Galton's 1869 treatise, *Hereditary Genius,* provided a systematic exposition using statistical methods to identify giftedness. Galton concluded from his studies that intelligence is an inherited trait. Today, although most psychologists agree heredity is a major contributor to intelligence, disagreement continues as to the relative role of nature (genetics) and nurture (environment) in its development. Current pioneering research seems to indicate the experiences of childhood aid in forming the brain's circuits for language, mathematics, music, and emotion. Sir Francis Galton's conclusions had an effect on educational and social policies from the mid-nineteenth to the mid-twentieth centuries. His belief that eugenics or selective breeding could improve the general level of intellectual development is open to challenge in a democratic society.

French psychologist Alfred Binet raised interest in measuring intelligence when he constructed the first developmental scale for children in the early 1900s. He developed the scale by observing children of various ages and their ability to perform specific tasks. Children then could be identified as developmentally advanced or delayed by comparing their performance on these tasks to what was expected given their chronological age. Lewis Terman further refined Binet's scale and adapted it for use in the United States. This test, renamed the Stanford-Binet Intelligence Scale, became the most often used test of individual intelligence until a series of tests developed by Wechsler came to be the standard throughout most of the developed world. Terman began using the term intelligence quotient (IQ) and his test allowed the examiner to calculate a person's aptitude for performing cognitive tasks (IQ score).

Terman (1925) conducted a longitudinal study of more than 1,500 children with Stanford-Binet IQ scores of 140 and above. The Terman study followed these subjects into adulthood, examining their physical characteristics, personality attributes, and educational and career achievements. Terman found bright children become bright adults. These individuals enjoyed better health and adjusted better to the problems of life than did others. Also, they were more productive than their average colleagues. Terman's research stimulated interest in the systematic study of giftedness.

In the U.S., interest in educating students who are talented and gifted has waxed and waned. In 1957, the launching of the Soviet Union's Sputnik satellite triggered concern that the United States was no longer the world leader in science and technology. Public and private funds were allocated to establish programs to develop the talents of students who were gifted in this country. In 1958 the National Defense Education Act (P.L. 85-864) was passed to support the development of math, science and foreign language talent. In addition, the Association for the Gifted, an affiliate of the Council for Exceptional Children, was created (Clark, 2002). In 1965 provisions for the development of model gifted programs and funding for state personnel in gifted education were contained in the Elementary and Secondary Education Act (P.L. 89-10). Federal recognition of the need for educating gifted and talented students was established in the Elementary and Secondary Education Act of 1970 (P.L. 91-230, Section 306).

Interest was heightened following the publication of *Education of the Gifted and Talented* by Sidney Marland (Marland, 1972). This congressionally mandated a national survey of gifted programs and needs. The Marland Report noted that only a small number of students who were talented or gifted were receiving special services. The report emphasized three main areas of concern relative to gifted programming:

1. The need to develop curricula emphasizing high level thinking processes and concepts.
2. The need to develop appropriate teaching strategies to accommodate the learner who is gifted.
3. The need to develop educational delivery systems and administrative procedures adequate to provide differential educational services for specific groups of students who are gifted.

As a result of the Marland Report (Marland, 1972), the U.S. Office of Gifted and Talented was created, with a budget of $2.5 million. The first federal definition of giftedness was adopted, and funds for training, technical assistance, and continuing education continued to increase until they peaked at $6.2 million in 1980 (Jenkins-Friedman & Nielsen, 1990).

In the 1980s, during the Reagan administration, gifted education funding was cut and the Office of Talented and Gifted eliminated. Fortunately, the 100th Congress re-established the Office and provided funding for teacher training and technical assistance to school districts (Jenkins-Friedman & Nielsen, 1990). Passage of Public Law 100-297, the Jacob K. Javits Gifted and Talented Students Education Act of 1988, its reauthorization in 1994 reflected the national concern that the talents and gifts of students were not being recognized and developed.

Currently there is no federal requirement to provide gifted programs in the schools, as gifted education is only mentioned once in the Individuals with Disabilities Education Improvement Act of 2004. Consequently, little federal or state money is targeted for students with gifts and talents. In fact, the Javits Gifted and Talented Grants program, the only federal program that directly funds programming for gifted and talented children, is facing elimination due to funding cuts in fiscal year 2006 (Council for Exceptional Children, 2005).

The No Child Left Behind Act (P.L. 107-110; Elementary and Secondary Education Amendments of 2001) has created quite a stir in the educational community. This "comprehensive" law is designed to ensure that all students achieve at a higher level, especially those at-risk for academic failure. It is generally agreed that NCLB ignores the needs of gifted and talented students. Its "high stakes testing" requirements ensure that curricula will be replaced with instruction designed to enable students to do well on these tests. Testing will be done at a basic conceptual level, thus not providing the necessary intellectual challenge for gifted and talented students (Gallagher, 2004).

With the trend toward inclusive classrooms and the popularity of the teaching strategy of cooperative learning, students who are gifted often remain in the general education classroom and may be expected to assist their less able peers. These methods may be highly effective teaching strategies for many students, but they do little to challenge students who are gifted and ensure they have the opportunity to reach their maximum potential (Colangelo & Davis, 1997). The controversy remains as to whether separate programs are necessary for these students.

Definition

Defining giftedness and talent is not a simple task, yet it has a significant impact on both the identification of students and the types of services and special programs provided. A close examination of attempts to define giftedness reveals tremendous variety. This variety is most likely the result of influences such as the values of the person making the definition, the social climate of the time, and the impact of new knowledge of human intelligence (Coleman & Cross, 2001). Prior to systematic attempts, defining giftedness relied on ex post facto definitions (Lucito, 1963). That is, a person was considered gifted after making some outstanding and novel contribution to society. Initial systematic attempts at defining giftedness focused on measuring intelligence. For example, students having an IQ score of above 130 or those who ranked in the upper five percent on academic achievement tests would be labeled gifted and often placed in special classes or provided an advanced curriculum. Despite their widespread popularity in defining giftedness, intelligence tests are only modestly correlated to school performance. Students with high IQs often do not do well in school, leading some to propose that definitions of giftedness that stress academic achievement might better serve gifted students (Gallagher & Gallagher, 1994). However, such definitions excluded students who exhibited outstanding talent in other areas such as music, art, dance, athletics, and leadership. In the 1950s, Guilford (1950, 1959) proposed that intelligence was not a single ability or capacity that could be measured by an IQ score. Rather he viewed intelligence as a diverse range of intellectual and creative abilities. Other researchers (Cattell, 1971; Renzulli, 1978; Torrance, 1965; Sternberg, 1981, 1982, 1988; Gardner, & Hatch, 1989) championed the concept of giftedness as a multidimensional construct that requires the use of multidimensional assessments. As a result, the definitions of these terms began to be more inclusive of creativity and performance talents.

Although there is no universally accepted definition for this group of students, the definition included in the Jacob K. Javits Gifted and Talented Students Education Act of 1988 (PL 100-297) often is used by states and school systems:

> The term 'gifted and talented students' means children and youth who give evidence of high performance capability in areas such as intellectual, creative, artistic, or leadership capacity, or in specific academic fields, and who require services or activities not ordinarily provided by the school in order to fully develop such capabilities.(Section 4103)

Another widely accepted definition created by a group of experts commissioned by the U.S. Department of Education's Office of Educational Research and Improvement (1993) states:

> Children and youth with outstanding talent perform or show the potential for performing at remarkably high levels of accomplishment when compared with others of their age, experience, or environment.
>
> These children and youth exhibit high performance capability in intellectual, creative and/or artistic areas, possess an unusual leadership capacity, or excel in specific academic fields. They require services or activities not ordinarily provided by the schools. Outstanding talents are present in children and youth from all cultural groups, across all economic strata, and in all areas of human endeavor (p. 26).

Unlike early definitions, this includes students with talents in the arts and leadership as well as those who are intellectually gifted. In addition, they also emphasize performance rather than just the potential for high achievement.

The research of Renzulli and his colleagues (Renzulli, 1978; Renzulli, Reis, & Smith, 1981; Renzulli & Smith, 1980) has influenced the thinking of professionals about the definition of giftedness. They suggest that giftedness is an interaction of three traits and that all three must be present to be truly gifted. These traits or behaviors are:

1. Above-average intellectual ability, as indicated by the student achieving in the upper five to ten percent of the class.
2. A high level of task-commitment, as demonstrated by clear evidence of persistence and achievement.
3. A high level of creativity, as evidenced in original ways of thinking which lead to new solutions or new definitions of problems.

Other researchers (Gardner, 1983; Gardner & Hatch, 1989; Ramos-Ford & Gardner, 1997) view giftedness based on a theory of multiple intelligences. This theory proposes that there are at least eight areas in which intelligence manifests itself:

- logical-mathematical,
- linguistic,
- musical,
- spatial,
- bodily-kinesthetic,
- naturalist,
- interpersonal, and
- intrapersonal.

Individuals might exhibit special gifts or talents in any one or more of these areas. These multiple intelligences are described in **Table 13-1.**

Characteristics

Misperceptions and stereotypes of individuals who are talented and gifted can lead to a misunderstanding of these students. As late as the late 1800s, some experts viewed giftedness as being linked to emotional imbalance and were concerned that it might lead to society's decline (Henson, 1976). Early research in giftedness (MacKinnon, 1962; Terman, 1925) sought to identify the characteristics of gifted individuals. This initial research used a restricted population of subjects which included few girls or individuals from diverse ethnic or racial groups. The result was a stereotypical profile of gifted individuals which did not control for gender, socioeconomic, or cultural variables. It is important to remember that the talented and gifted are a heterogeneous group with differences and similarities as great as any other group of students. They exhibit a wide range of specific aptitudes, abilities, and interests which makes it difficult for researchers to reduce giftedness to a recognizable set of characteristics.

Clark (2002) synthesized the work of previous researchers to develop a list of the differentiating characteristics of the gifted as shown in **Table 13-2.** It is unlikely that gifted students will manifest all of these characteristics, but they will most likely exhibit more of these characteristics when compared to their peers. It is important that teachers are familiar with these characteristics because teacher nomination for gifted programs plays a significant role in the identification process in most schools today. However, teachers must remember that these characteristics can be observed in students who do not necessarily have the best grades or highest academic performance. Some students who are talented or gifted may not be performing at their highest potential. Teachers need to be alert to the possible display of gifted characteristics in any of their students.

It is an interesting paradox that some of the behaviors exhibited by students who are gifted can be misinterpreted as behavior problems as shown in **Table 13-3.** Because these students learn new skills more easily and rapidly than their peers, they may irritate teachers by shouting out answers, showing impatience to move on to the next task, or engaging in

TABLE 13-1

Gardner's Multiple Intelligences*

Intelligence	Processing Operations	End-State Performance Possibilities
Linguistic	Sensitivity to the sounds, rhythms, and meaning of words and the functions of Language	Poet, journalist
Logico-mathematical	Sensitivity to, and capacity to detect, logical or numerical patterns; ability to handle long chains of logical reasoning	Mathematician
Musical	Ability to produce and appreciate pitch, rhythm (or melody), and aesthetic quality of the forms of musical expressiveness	Instrumentalist, composer
Spatial	Ability to perceive the visual-spatial world accurately, to perform transformations on those perceptions, and to re-create aspects of visual experience in the absence of relevant stimuli	Sculptor, navigator
Bodily-kinesthetic	Ability to use the body skillfully for expressive as well as goal-directed purposes; ability to handle objects skillfully	Dancer, athlete
Naturalist	Ability to recognize and classify all varieties of animals, minerals, and plants	Biologist
Interpersonal	Ability to detect and respond appropriately to the moods, temperaments, motivations, and intentions of others	Therapist, salesperson
Intrapersonal	Ability to discriminate complex inner feelings and to use them to guide one's own behavior; knowledge of one's own strengths, weaknesses, desires, and intelligences	Person with detailed, accurate self-knowledge

*Gardner also has proposed a possible spiritual intelligence (gift for religion, mysticism, or the transcendent), existential intelligence (concern with "ultimate" issues, such as the significance of life and death), and moral intelligence (capacity to recognize and reason about moral issues). However, these potential intelligences are less well defined and more controversial than the eight intelligences listed above.

From Berk, L. (2003). *Child Development* (6th ed.). Boston, MA: Allyn & Bacon.

off-task behaviors when they are bored with the regular curriculum. So too, peers may become annoyed when gifted students dominate class discussions, consistently score the highest on exams, or receive special attention from the teacher.

Identification

As with the lack of clarity on a definition, identification of students who are talented and gifted is equally vague. Many claim that an ideal identification system does not exist (Feldhusen, Hoover, & Sayler, 1990), and given the political incorrectness of labeling one student superior to another in any area suggests that one is not likely to be devised. Identification must be based on a value-free universally accepted definition of giftedness.

TABLE 13-2

Common Characteristics of Highly and Exceptionally Gifted Individuals

- An extraordinary speed in processing information
- A rapid comprehension of the whole idea or concept
- An unusual ability to perceive essential elements and underlying structures and patterns in relationships and ideas
- A need for precision in thinking and expression, resulting in need to correct errors and argue extensively
- An ability to relate to a broad range of ideas and synthesize commonalities among them
- A high degree of ability to think abstractly that develops early
- Appreciation of complexity; finding myriad alternative meanings in even the most simple issues or problems
- An ability to learn in an integrative, intuitively nonlinear manner
- An extraordinary degree of intellectual curiosity
- An unusual capacity for memory
- A long concentration span
- A fascination with ideas and words
- An extensive vocabulary
- An ability to perceive many sides of an issue
- Argumentativeness
- Advanced visual and motor skills
- An ability from an early age to think in metaphors and symbols and a preference for doing so
- An ability to visualize models and systems
- An ability to learn in great intuitive leaps
- Highly idiosyncratic interpretations of events
- An awareness of detail
- An unusual intensity and depth of feeling
- A high degree of emotional sensitivity
- Highly developed morals and ethics and early concern for moral and existential issues
- Unusual and early insight into social and moral issues
- An ability to empathetically understand and relate to ideas and other people
- An extraordinarily high energy level
- A need for the world to be logical and fair
- A conviction of correctness and personal ideas and beliefs

From Clark, B. (2002). *Growing up gifted* (6th ed.). NJ: Prentice Hall.

Historically, identification procedures have relied heavily on measures of intellectual ability. IQ scores were regularly used to identify students for gifted programs. However, many students, for a variety of reasons, do not perform well on IQ and other standardized tests of mental ability, thus these gifted students were excluded from these programs. More recently, a number of states have moved to a multi-modal method for assessing giftedness. In Georgia, for example, students are assessed on mental ability, achievement, creativity, and motivation in determining eligibility for gifted services. However, many state assessments still rely on standardized tests.

As previously discussed, not all gifted students are identified and served in gifted programs. Certain minorities and students from low socioeconomic backgrounds are overrepresented in remedial programs and underrepresented in programs for the gifted.

TABLE 13-3

Possible Behaviors of Students Who Are Gifted

Positive	Not-So-Positive
1. Persistent, goal-directed behavior	1. Stubbornness
2. Power of concentration	2. Resistance to interruption
3. Large vocabulary; highly verbal	3. Escape into verbalism
4. Ability to see relationships	4. Difficulty in accepting the illogical
5. Willingness to examine the unusual	5. Possible gullibility
6. Power of critical thinking; skepticism	6. Critical of others
7. High expectations for self	7. Critical of self
8. High energy, alertness, eagerness	8. Frustration with lack of progress or inactivity
9. Independence in work and study	9. Possible difficulty working in groups
10. Self-reliance; need for freedom	10. Possible rebellion against constraints
11. Likes new ways of doing things	11. Dislike of routine and drill
12. Diversity of interests and abilities	12. Need to build basic competencies in major interests
13. Sensitivity, intuitiveness, empathy	13. Need for success and recognition; sensitive to criticism, vulnerable to peer group rejection

African American and Hispanic students are far more likely to be participating in remedial programs than in programs for the gifted. However, this is not true of all minority groups. Asian and Pacific Americans are commonly perceived as being overrepresented in programs for the gifted (Kitano & Dijiosia, 2002). Educators are encouraged to consider the following abilities as described in the Marland Report (1972) when assessing students who are potentially gifted.

General Intellectual Ability

Usually measured by individually or group administered mental abilities tests, this generally gives teachers an indication of how well the student will adapt to the academic environment. Often, high performance in this area requires special learning provisions for the student.

Specific Academic Aptitude

Regularly measured by outstanding performance on standardized achievement tests, this relates to high aptitude in a specific subject area which allows the student to exceed beyond peers and requires a special program in that particular content field.

Creative/Productive Thinking

Tests of creative/productive thinking are helpful in finding this population of original thinkers. Opportunities allowing students with this ability to think divergently and manipulate information to arrive at new and unique solutions to problems are important needs.

Leadership Ability

Performance in social settings both in and out of the classroom, positions of responsibility held in clubs and organizations, sociograms, and personality inventories are some of the tools used as possible indicators of leadership ability.

Visual and Performing Arts

Expert opinion, performance, portfolio assessment, and, if available, valid and reliable standardized instruments can be useful in locating students with ability in the arts. Special opportunities in school should be provided for these youngsters to excel.

It is important to remember that students who are gifted and talented are found at all grade levels in the schools. Some aspects of giftedness may emerge early in a child's development (e.g., an exceptionally large vocabulary or self-taught reading ability at a young age) and be identified by parents. Other aspects may not appear until the student matures (e.g., exceptional academic performance, athletic skills, or artistic abilities) and may be noted first by classroom teachers, counselors, or even peers. To appropriately determine an individual's giftedness at any age, a multidimensional assessment should be performed. Such an assessment might include teacher nominations, developmental inventories, mental ability tests, achievement tests, creativity tests, newly developed information-processing tests, student interview and observation, motivation assessment, and student portfolios (Benbow & Minor, 1990; Sowell, Bergwall, Zeigler, & Cartwright, 1990). These expanded criteria will be helpful in locating a broader range of students who are gifted including those who often do not score highly enough on tests of mental abilities and/or standard achievement tests to be included in typical gifted programs. Several of these assessment strategies are discussed below.

Teacher Nomination

The accuracy of teachers as identifiers of students who are potentially gifted has been questioned, particularly with younger children and students from diverse ethnic, cultural, or linguistic populations (Baldwin, 1991; Kitano, 1989). A study by Pegnato and Birch (1959) of an entire junior high school population indicated teachers missed 55 percent of the eligible students when asked to nominate the gifted students in their classes. Teachers tend to identify the stereotypical student who is gifted (see **Figure 13-1**). This means that students who are bright, cooperative, task-oriented, and well adjusted to school will be nominated for gifted programs. Students who are bright, but disruptive, bored with routine tasks, nonconforming, underachievers, or who exhibit unusual skills and abilities are often overlooked. **Figure 13-2** provides a description of a student who is gifted, but not identified.

Teachers may receive no specific criteria to use when asked to nominate students for gifted programs, however their observations tend to improve when they are made familiar with the behavior characteristics of students who are gifted. Scales such as the Scales for Rating the Behavioral Characteristics of Superior Students (Renzulli, Smith, White, Callahan, & Hartman, 1976) can improve teacher judgment. This scale, as shown in **Figure 13-3,** allows the teacher to rate a student's performance in areas of learning, motivation, and creativity.

Frasier (1994) also has developed rating scales including the Frasier Talent Assessment Profile (FTAP), a comprehensive assessment system to facilitate the use of information from multiple sources, to help classroom teachers assess and summarize student performance. The information gained from such scales as these is useful for both identification and educational planning. In addition, Kitano (1989) offers suggestions for teachers to improve their accuracy in identifying gifted students. These are presented in **Table 13-4.**

Intelligence Tests

Individual IQ tests are considered the single most reliable indicator of intellectual giftedness. The Stanford-Binet Intelligence Scale IV and the Wechsler Intelligence Scale for Children–Fourth Edition (WISC–IV) are the most widely used individual tests. Scores

FIGURE 13-1

Description of a Stereotypical Student Who is Gifted

David's parents did not realize that their first child was exceptional until he started school. He was clearly inquisitive and eager to learn. He wanted to be read to and often woke his mother early in the morning to read his favorite Richard Scarry book. He would follow his father as he went about his chores and attempted to help. At age four he tried to "wire" his house by using ropes and cords to connect outlets and appliances. His parents were supportive of this activity and allowed the "wires" to remain until David found a new interest. As a result of his investigations, he was able to write a book explaining electricity for his kindergarten class.

David was reading when he entered kindergarten, but it was not just his ability to read but also his keen memory and wealth of knowledge which alerted his teacher to his special abilities. David's mathematical ability was well above his age peers. He could not only add and subtract, but could multiply and divide as well. With his parents' permission, David's kindergarten teacher referred David for the gifted program.

David scored a school ability index of 150/99th percentile. On the instrument that was used, David did not answer a single question incorrectly. It was not necessary to do further testing, and David was found to be eligible for the gifted program.

David was accelerated in mathematics in the third grade by receiving instruction with fourth graders. In his last year of elementary school, David received individual mathematics instruction from an administrator with a doctorate in mathematics education.

David, though profoundly gifted in mathematics, achieved beyond his age expectations in all areas of school. Although a quiet and serious young man, David was well liked by his peers and was always selected for team or group work. His work habits were recognized by his peers, and he was voted the most outstanding gifted student.

In middle school, David continued to develop his mathematics ability. He took all gifted math classes and worked with a teacher after school as part of a math team. David also continued to excel in other academic areas, but his mathematical abilities were truly outstanding. He earned a perfect score on the American Junior High School Mathematics Examination, won numerous prizes with Mathcounts and Mathematics League, and participated in mathematics competitions on the state and national level.

In high school, David continued his outstanding achievement. He was ranked first in his class and was valedictorian of an extremely large class. While in high school David earned enough advanced placement credits that will enable him to earn both a bachelor's and a master's degree in four years.

David has stated that his curiosity drove him to investigate and learn independently. He felt that he was self-motivated and learned for the joy of learning. He said that he was inspired by teachers who were enthusiastic about learning and the material they were teaching.

derived from these two instruments are useful in pinpointing strengths and weaknesses of students, but these tests may only be administered by a licensed psychologist. Consequently, many school systems rely on results from group tests such as the Otis-Lennon School Ability Test and the Cognitive Abilities Test for referral and placement in gifted programs. These tests may be administered by classroom teachers or administrators.

There are many reasons that IQ scores derived from these measures should not be the sole selection criterion for gifted programs. These scores are predictors of school related abilities not measures of innate ability. Their accuracy is questionable in measuring the abilities of students who have disabilities or come from diverse ethnic, cultural, or linguistic groups. IQ tests are a predictor of school performance and may be biased in favor of individuals from middle- and upper-class socioeconomic groups. Lyman (1997) states

FIGURE 13-2

Description of a Student Who Is Gifted but Not Identified

Joe's parents are very concerned about him. He has always been a difficult child, having very intense feelings and views about things. He seems to be on a roller coaster in terms of his emotions, and gets very upset when others don't agree with his point of view. He expects that everyone sees the world as he does. Other times he seems to have blinders on, only focusing on what he is doing and oblivious to others and the world around him. He is frequently argumentative with peers and other adults, claiming that they don't know anything. He is disorganized and has trouble making friends.

Not surprisingly, Joe is having difficulty at school. He has been diagnosed with Attention Deficit Hyperactivity Disorder (ADHD) and is on Ritalin. Joe's teachers believe that although he is extremely bright, he is not working up to his potential. They claim that he often fails to try new things because he is afraid he won't do well. Surprisingly, he usually scores in the 90th percentile or higher on standardized achievement tests, but his schoolwork is often sloppy and his grades are poor.

His teachers echo his parents' concerns that he has trouble making and keeping friends. They worry that his challenging authority will escalate as he gets older, causing him further, more serious problems. They all agree that Joe is "different" from his classmates. He sees the world differently and has trouble fitting in with the group. He seems to relish being a nonconformist which further alienates him from his peers. The school counselor thinks that Joe is depressed and overly anxious and worries that he is becoming a loner. Her attempts to counsel Joe have been met with resistance and resentment. Joe says that he is picked on because he is different. Without the proper intervention, the outlook for Joe is bleak.

FIGURE 13-3

Sample Statements from the Scales for Rating the Behavioral Characteristics of Superior Students

	Seldom or Never	Occasionally	Considerably	Almost Always
• Carries responsibility well; can be counted on to do what he has promised and usually does it well.	❏	❏	❏	❏
• Adapts readily to new situations; is flexible in thought and action and does not seem disturbed when the normal routine is changed.	❏	❏	❏	❏
• Arrives at unique, unconventional solutions to artistic problems as opposed to traditional, conventional ones.	❏	❏	❏	❏
• Shows a sustained interest in music— seeks out opportunities to hear and create music.	❏	❏	❏	❏
• Modifies and adjusts expression of ideas for maximum reception.	❏	❏	❏	❏
• Is good at games of strategy where it is necessary to anticipate several moves ahead.	❏	❏	❏	❏

Renzulli, Smith, White, Callahan, & Hartman, 1976

TABLE 13-4

Suggestions for Teachers to Identify Students Who Are Gifted

- Consider all students as potential candidates for giftedness. For example, a hyperactive, disruptive, or unkempt youngster may also be gifted.
- Recognize that "negative traits" . . . do not disqualify a student from consideration as gifted. Although gifted and average students may display negative behaviors, gifted students will also demonstrate their strengths when provided opportunities to do so.
- Look for and analyze the strengths exhibited by all students, including those who do not display stereotypical achieving, cooperating, and conforming behaviors. For example, the individual who touches expensive equipment after being admonished not to touch may be exhibiting extreme curiosity rather than defiance.
- Provide opportunities for and encourage students to express their abilities. For example, the teacher can informally assess reading and writing skills by inviting students to read to them at the book center and encouraging volunteer efforts to write.
- Use parents as informants. Parents serve as effective identifiers of gifted individuals and they can provide accurate observations about what their children can and cannot do. (p. 60).

From Kitano, M. K. (1989). The K-3 teacher's role in recognizing and supporting young gifted children. *Young Children, 44(3)*, 57–63.

that no intelligence test gets at all cognitive functions. Because of this, critics point out that IQ tests are unable to assess adequately many of the higher mental processes that characterize the thinking and learning of individuals who are gifted. Because they were not developed to do so, IQ tests do not assess such abilities as creativity, leadership, and specific talents. As Kaufman (1992) stresses, the appropriate use of IQ tests to screen or identify students who are gifted, or potentially gifted, demands that they be used in conjunction with other tests and selection criteria.

Achievement Tests

Critics of the typical identification process for students who are potentially gifted also warn teachers about the limitations of academic achievement tests. Although these tests may identify students who are bright, have received outstanding instruction, and are adept at taking standardized tests, some students who are potentially gifted may be missed because they have received inadequate instruction, are bored by routine tests, have extreme test anxiety, or purposely score poorly because they don't want to stand out from their peers. In addition, it is important to realize that achievement tests are not designed to measure the true achievement of students who are academically gifted. These tests have a restricted range of test items which prevents some students from demonstrating their achievement at higher levels beyond the limits of the test range. Like IQ tests, academic achievement tests cannot assess such abilities as creativity, leadership, or artistic talents.

Creativity Tests

As the definition of giftedness has expanded, there have been increased attempts to measure the wider range of abilities and capacities included in the newer definition, particularly in the area of creativity. As Davis and Rimm (1989) note, this is a formidable task.

The nature of creativity and the many ways in which it can be expressed have made it difficult to develop tests to determine its presence and magnitude. Callahan (1991) recommends that multiple measures of creativity be used to demonstrate a student's exceptionality. These measures could include analysis of a student's creative products or performances as well as direct observation of the student's behavior. Tests designed to assess creative or divergent thinking include the Torrance Tests of Creative Thinking (Torrance, 1966) and Thinking Creatively in Action and Movement (TCAM), (Torrance, 1981). Clasen, Middleton, and Connell (1994) have developed tests of problem solving and drawing to identify students who exhibit creativity in these areas. Although creativity tests may offer insight into a student's thinking and reasoning style or artistic ability, they are more subjective than most other tests to assess the intellectual ability of students who are potentially gifted.

Neglected Gifted

Given the traditionally narrow definition placed on giftedness, there are many neglected students who are talented and gifted who are not included in gifted education programs. The U.S. Department of Education (1993) described several groups of neglected gifted: underachievers, students with disabilities, students from certain minority and ethnic groups, and girls. More recently a new category of neglected gifted students has emerged—the "tough bright" child (Peterson, 1997). In addition, there is evidence that a lack of diversity among gifted program participants is a continuing national concern. For example, Pfeiffer (2003) solicited views from a national panel of experts in the field of gifted education to get their perspective on recent and emerging concerns and trends in gifted education. Among the most frequent categories mentioned was the need to develop new identification procedures to decrease the under-representation of gifted minority students in programs. Specifically, the concern was with the disproportionate number of potentially gifted students of color, economic disadvantage, or both and students who are female, linguistically different, handicapped, or from rural communities who were not being adequately identified and served.

Underachievers

The gifted underachiever presents a paradox. High ability students not performing to their abilities represent an enormous loss of potential, as well as immense potential for change (Davis & Rimm, 1998). Van Tassel-Baska (1998) reports that as many as 63 percent of gifted students are underachievers. Gifted underachievers can be defined as those students who have a significant discrepancy between their intelligence or standardized tested abilities (scoring in the gifted range on these tests) and their performance in class (average or even failing grades). There is no single cause for the underachievement of some students who are gifted. The many possible factors related to this problem include poor study skills or habits, a lack of motivation for academic achievement, low self-esteem, the absence of a supportive or nurturing environment at home or school, and a boring or nonchallenging curriculum. Just as there is no single cause for underachievement, there is no single solution to this problem. It is a generally accepted fact, however, that these students will need special services to develop to their fullest potential (Emerick, 1992). The strategies found to be effective for some students include counseling, acceleration (subject or grade skipping), using noncompetitive learning strategies (mastery learning, cooperative learning, contracts), school-sponsored community service or work-study programs, and the integration of personal interests into school work (Covington, 1984; Feldhusen, 1989; Rimm & Lovance, 1992).

Students with Disabilities

Students with disabilities often are overlooked as potential candidates for gifted programs for several reasons. The nature of the disability may mask the true talents or abilities of the student. Individuals with severe physical impairments or hearing impairment may not have the exceptional communication skills parents and teachers generally associate with giftedness. Identification of the gifted students with these disabilities is equally problematic. The usual identification procedures and protocols may be wholly inappropriate for students with physical or hearing impairments (Willard-Holt, 1994). Teachers may be so focused on the student's disability (attention deficit/hyperactivity disorder, learning disability, etc.) and its effect on the student's classroom performance, that they overlook the individual's abilities or special talents. In some cases, the disability may not be readily apparent. Many gifted students suffer from learning disabilities. Baum (1990) describes three types of learning disabilities that may affect gifted students:

"1. identified gifted students who have subtle learning disabilities,
  2. unidentified students whose gifts and disabilities may be masked by average achievement, and
  3. identified learning disabled students who are also gifted."

For some students with disabilities, restrictions in their home or school environment may have resulted in limited opportunities to demonstrate their talents. Johnson, Karnes, and Carr (1997) note that gifted programs must pay special attention to include and meet the needs of students with disabilities.

Students from Minority Cultures

Individuals who are gifted and talented exist in every cultural and linguistic group. The situation in our schools today, however, is that students from certain minority groups (African American, Latino, and Native American) are not identified as gifted in numbers reflecting their proportion in the general population (Kitano & Dijosia, 2002). The U.S. Department of Education reports that in 2000–2001 approximately two-thirds of public school children were non-white (U.S. Department of Education, 2001). Given these statistics, it is logical to assume that more minority students would be involved in gifted programs. Numerous reasons for this disproportional representation have been cited. Many students from minority groups live in poverty or come from families with low socioeconomic status which limit the student's opportunities for enrichment and learning in the home environment.

Educators and policy makers have long been concerned about the lack of diversity in gifted programs (Borland & Wright, 1994; Ford & Harris, 1990; Van Tassel-Baska, Patton, & Prillaman, 1989). This lack of diversity is particularly evident in the limited number of students from minority, socio-economically deprived, and/or limited English proficiency backgrounds who participate in gifted programs. The U.S. Department of Education reports that in 2000–2001 approximately two-thirds of public school children were non-white (U.S. Department of Education, 2001). Given these statistics, it is logical to assume that more minority students would be involved in gifted programs. However, in 1991, the U.S. Department of Education report from a study of eighth grade gifted programs (USDOE, 1991) indicated that students whose families' socioeconomic status placed them in the top quartile of the population were about five times more likely to be in gifted programs than were students from the bottom quartile Numerous reasons for this disproportional representation have been cited. Many students from minority groups live in poverty or come from families with low socioeconomic status which limit the students' opportunities for enrichment and learning in the home environment. Ambrose (2002) stated that an awareness of the suppressive effects of socioeconomic deprivation on talent development puts the responsibility on all who influence public policy to ensure that all children, especially those who are deprived, have access to adequate primary goods such as educational opportunities and adequate health care. He further advised that educators of the gifted must recognize that deprivation does indeed stunt aspiration development which, in turn, undermines talent development. Consequently, they must work harder to find potential within children by alternative methods of identification for these children's motivation to achieve is often undermined by oppressive outside forces.

Some claim that traditional standardized tests used to identify gifted students are unfair and biased to students from minority cultures requiring a familiarity with the dominant culture. Research has indicated that there is validity to this argument; however, not all minority groups seem to be adversely affected by this bias. Recent research suggests that Asian and Pacific Americans may in fact be overrepresented in gifted programs (Kitano & Dijosia, 2002). It is unlikely that students from this minority group are more familiar with the dominant culture, thus this argument needs further research. Schools in some districts have attempted to maximize the likelihood that students from diverse cultures will be appropriately identified by using a variety of selection criteria for gifted programs. These include flexible cut-off scores on standardized tests and the use of checklists for parents and teachers to rate students' behaviors and skills in areas other than academic performance. In addition, it is important for all teachers to have an awareness and understanding of the cultural differences of their students and how these may affect students' performance and behavior in the classroom (see Chapter 1). When designing gifted programs for students from minority cultures, Feldhusen (1989) has recommended increased parental involvement, the use of experiential learning strategies, and the inclusion of mentors and role models.

Women

Although males and females do not differ in intellectual ability, significant differences exist in their achievement and their identification for gifted programs. Girls score higher than boys on achievement tests until puberty, when boys begin to excel, particularly in math and science (Kerr, 1997). Differences in enrollment in gifted programs by gender may be due to a variety of factors. The gender-role socialization that girls receive can impact on the way they behave and perform in school. Some behaviors associated with giftedness (competitiveness, risk taking, independence) typically are not encouraged in girls. Traditional cultural and societal expectations regarding educational performance and occupational choices still influence girls' behavior. Many families place a higher value on academic achievement in boys than in girls. Females frequently disguise their abilities and limit their achievement to what are perceived as socially acceptable levels (Parke, 1989). Some girls deliberately sabotage their own grades (leaving answers blank on exams, not turning in assignments) to avoid being identified as smarter or different from their peers. Terwilliger and Titus (1995) found that when nominated for accelerated programs, girls who are gifted do not accept enrollment as often as boys. Widespread discrimination against females from teachers, texts, and tests (American Association of University Women, 1992) also may affect their enrollment in gifted programs. Teachers pay less attention to girls than boys (Sadker & Sadker, 1985) and underestimate their female students' mathematical abilities (Kimball, 1989). Some tests remain biased against girls, and textbooks used in schools often stereotype or ignore women (American Association of University Women, 1992). Tremendous strides have been taken in recent years; however, the expectations of society continue to have a negative effect on the achievement of many women who are gifted (Pendarvis, 1993). Walker, Reis, and Leonard (1992) noted that when women who are gifted were questioned about their perception of the problem of underachieving women, the issues raised were a lack of role models for such females, the denial of giftedness, the lack of organized mentoring, and lower expectations for women.

Many barriers still exist to the identification and inclusion of neglected students who are gifted in schools today. The approach of using multiple criteria to identify gifted populations as discussed in the previous section of this chapter is one way schools can begin to address this problem. Using peer nomination and parent nomination, considering broader ranges of scores, including assessments by persons other than educational personnel, and obtaining information provided by adaptive behavior assessments can help to locate those students not readily identifiable by traditional methods (Robinson, Bradley, & Stanley, 1990).

Program Delivery Models

Because students spend over 15,000 hours of life in school, it is crucial that educational programming be appropriately stimulating and challenging for all students including students who are gifted. In an age of standards-based reform, school systems are becoming more aware of the need to develop content-based approaches to curriculum for gifted learners (VanTassel-Baska, 2005). No longer can gifted programs survive if they are not fundamentally connected to the business of schools, that is preparing all students for proficiency in key areas of learning. There are a variety of administrative arrangements for service delivery of gifted programs. These administrative arrangements are used to varying degrees throughout the country with each school system generally responsible for selecting the arrangement it implements. These arrangements can include special schools, resource classrooms, special classes, cluster grouping, collaboration, mentorships, joint enrollment options and inclusion within the general education classroom. These models deliver either direct or indirect services.

Direct Services

Special Schools

Typical schools may be unable to offer the number of advanced courses and the diverse curriculum needed to challenge students identified as gifted. Establishing special schools for these students allows for the development of a wide range of advanced courses and a unique educational experience. Such schools also offer students a supportive climate for unlimited interaction with others of similar ability. Some school systems have developed special schools, often called magnet schools, to provide unique learning opportunities in specific fields for students with superior ability in those areas (e.g., language arts, music, math, science). The New York School of Performing Arts (commonly known as the Fame school) is an example of this type institution.

There is a growing trend to develop special residential high schools for students who are gifted and talented (Kolloff, 1997). These schools offer students an educational experience designed for them, taught by expert faculty, with peers who have similar interests and comparable abilities. The programs often incorporate mentorships, internships, and opportunities for independent study. Some residential schools are located on university campuses which allow the students access to university classes, laboratory facilities, and cultural events.

Resource Model

The resource model generally is a "pull-out" program where students are grouped with other students who are gifted and talented for part of their school day. Resource models can also include options for weekend programs, summer programs, workshops, and special programs sponsored by national or state agencies such as Odyssey of the Mind or Future Problem Solving. In most school systems this is the model used at the elementary level.

Special Classes

When students who are gifted are taken out of the general education classroom and placed together in a special class for part or all of the school day in the school setting, a school-within-a-school concept has been created. These special classes are designed primarily to provide a variety of educational opportunities above and beyond those of the typical school curriculum. Activities may extend from academic acceleration to cultural enrichment. Honors courses, electives, mentoring programs, and the study of topics generally not available to the rest of the student body are examples of special class strategies. Offering special classes before or after school, on weekends, or during summers are other alternatives used by schools. High schools often offer special advanced placement classes which have strict content area and requirements and can assist the student in receiving college credit through examination.

Cluster Grouping

In a cluster grouping model, identified gifted students are placed as a group into an otherwise heterogeneous general education classroom. The general education teacher must have the gifted endorsement and must document curriculum modifications made for the gifted students such as separate lesson plans and individual student contracts.

Indirect Services

Collaborative Teaching

In this model, a teacher with a gifted education teaching endorsement, the classroom teacher, and the gifted student (when appropriate) collaborate in the development of challenging assignments that substitute for or extend core curriculum objectives. Direct instruction may be provided by the classroom teacher, but there must be collaborative planning between this teacher and the gifted specialist. In addition, teacher-partners document curriculum modifications through separate lesson plans, student contracts, and collaborative planning time logs.

Mentorship/Internship

In a mentorship or internship model, identified gifted students work with mentors to explore professions of interest. The teacher with gifted endorsement supervises these experiences by collaborating with the student and mentor in documenting student contracts for work to be done, learning objectives, assessment strategies, and data logs.

Joint Enrollment/Postsecondary Options

In this option, students who have completed the secondary curriculum in a specific content area in a school can opt to attend a college or university near the school on a part-time basis. There should be a demonstrated need for an advanced curriculum not offered otherwise and the experience should be monitored by the gifted specialist in the secondary school.

Inclusion

Presently, the most frequently offered educational experience for students who are gifted involves attending a special resource class for a period of time that may range from forty-five minutes to five or more hours each week. When these students are in the general education classroom, it is the responsibility of the classroom teacher to make adaptations in the curriculum.

The classroom teacher should make no assumptions about the knowledge base of a student who is identified as academically gifted. Classroom adaptations can be made for those who excel in a particular area, but regular instruction may meet the needs of those who need instruction in some basic skills. Students may have academic gifts and talents in only one area of the curriculum. They can be extremely gifted in one area and average in another. Teachers should familiarize themselves with test results to determine the strengths and weaknesses of those students in their classroom. With this model, the gifted education specialist can be of invaluable assistance in helping the classroom teacher modify the curriculum for the gifted student.

Including gifted students in the general education classroom imposes some administrative challenges. Effective inclusion requires flexible scheduling, and the collaboration of other school personnel requires coordination of schedules. Without proper administrative support, these challenges can make including gifted students in the classroom impossible, even though it may be the most financially efficient way to deliver programming for students who are talented and gifted (Coleman & Cross, 2001).

Within these varied models the approach taken for delivery of the services can be offered as enrichment or acceleration or a combination of the two. The term **enrichment** refers to richer, more varied educational experiences and can apply to both service delivery and curriculum (Schiever & Maker, 1997). **Acceleration** involves increasing the pace of teaching and learning and also can apply to service delivery (grade skipping) as well as curriculum (completing two years of the math curriculum in a single year) (Schiever & Maker, 1997).

Enrichment and Acceleration in the General Education Classroom

Schools that rely on resource room instruction for a portion of the school day must ensure that the general education classroom teacher and the teacher of the gifted collaborate to develop and implement a plan to supplement resource room instruction with enrichment or acceleration of content in the general classroom. The resource room delivery model allows these students to be academically challenged and remain with their same-age peers while participating in other school activities. Enrichment and acceleration are methods by which general education can be modified to meet the needs of students with gifts and talents.

Enrichment

Typically, enrichment is viewed as a supplement to the school's general education curriculum, adding depth and breadth to the normally studied content. The classroom teacher dispenses lessons and materials distinctive to students who are gifted as they remain in the classroom for most or all of the school day. Independent study projects, investigations of a unit in more depth and breadth than other students in the class, Internet contacts with authorities in fields of interest to the student, special high-level materials and activities supplementing the class content being studied, and pursuit of special topics under the guidance of the classroom teacher, a mentor, or the teacher of the gifted are some ways enrichment may be accomplished.

Program coordination among elementary, middle, and secondary schools is important to the expansion and long-range planning of content offered in an enrichment program. Doing this helps eliminate the add-on nature of many enrichment programs that offer fragmented or non-intellectually challenging subject matter to students as they move through the school experience. Offerings of enrichment should be above and beyond the general school curriculum, yet supplemental to it. Enrichment content should include the application of acquired knowledge to actual situations, breaking down a problem or situation into its component parts and analyzing each for its relevance to a solution, combining information in new and unique ways, and evaluating the value a process or product possesses when compared to established criteria. Renzulli and Reis (1997) offer a school-wide enrichment model which incorporates a triad of activities and strategies. The first component is the use of general exploratory activities to expose students to disciplines, topics, persons, places, and other content typically not included in the general education curriculum. The second part of the triad involves the development of specific skills in creative thinking, problem solving, and communication related to various disciplines, topics, persons, places, and other content typically not included in the general education curriculum. The third component is the self-selected investigation of real life problems by individuals and small groups with the possible development of an original product. This enrichment triad is a widely used approach for instruction of students who are gifted because it provides opportunities to stimulate and encourage their natural curiosity, interests, and abilities.

Acceleration

With acceleration, students who are gifted move through the general education curriculum at a faster rate than their grade-level peers. Academic achievement is a major factor in a program emphasizing acceleration. Strategies for acceleration include:

- Early admission to school at the primary, secondary, or college level;
- Skipping grades;
- Telescoping or compacting the curriculum typically covered in two or more grades into one year; and
- Taking high school courses for credit in middle school, or college courses for credit in high school.

Advanced placement courses often are used at the high school level as well as credit by exam allowing the student to test-out of courses, units, or grades and in some cases to graduate early. Acceleration for some students may involve the entire curriculum, but for others acceleration may be appropriate in only one or two subjects. Many school systems allow cross-grade placement (i.e., a fourth-grade student is enrolled in grade-level social studies and language arts and in sixth-grade math and science) or joint enrollment between high school and college.

Enrichment and Acceleration Opportunities for Gifted and Talented Students Outside the General Education Classroom

In the continuing debate over how best to serve the educational needs of students, current popular thinking suggests that inclusion in the general education classroom is best for most, if not all, students. However, research generally suggests that homogeneous grouping of gifted and talented students is more advantageous. Recent reviews of the research on grouping clearly suggest that homogeneous grouping of gifted and talented students has a significant positive effect on academic achievement (Shields, 2002). Homogeneous grouping can vary from situations where students spend a few hours each week in a gifted classroom, to placement in full-time gifted classrooms, to attendance at a special school for the gifted and talented.

Controversies Associated with Enrichment and Acceleration

There is long-standing controversy surrounding the issue of acceleration and enrichment. Some parents and teachers may express concern about acceleration and resist its implementation due to possible negative effects on students' social-emotional development. VanTassel-Baska (1994) found no such negative effects and noted higher achievement rates in students who were accelerated than those who were not. Kulik (1992) also reported that students from accelerated classes outperform their non-accelerated peers on achievement tests.

Some educators claim that true enrichment does not exist and that many enrichment activities are often pointless and unrelated to each other (Stanley & Benbow, 1986). Stanley (1978) suggested that enrichment without acceleration is potentially dangerous to the gifted student. Others argue that acceleration is simply allowing students to progress at their own natural rate through curriculum without predetermined institution-imposed parameters as to when and at what rate students should learn certain academic material. This debate notwithstanding, acceleration and enrichment can often be complementary pieces in a gifted education program. Allowing students to progress at their own rate and receive enrichment will lead to greater knowledge and skills as well as develop creativity and other cognitive skills. Regardless of the model or approach chosen, Coleman and Cross (2001) suggest that program planners base their program on several premises. These premises should form the foundation for all program planning:

1. The child's strengths are to be encouraged and developed.
2. The learning environment should provide opportunities for expanding one's knowledge, and building more effective cognitive, affective and creative capabilities.
3. Arrangements must be made to accommodate individual differences, such as interests, abilities, learning rates, and learning styles.
4. Contact with other gifted children promotes social-emotional development.
5. A program should be responsive to the community it serves and involve families of children.
6. The curricula should promote these premises.
7. Evaluation is an indispensable part of effective program planning.

Davis and Rimm (1998) propose that any program serving the needs of gifted students must contain four core components. Based in part on Treffinger's model, they suggest that program planners should attend to these four components:

1. Program philosophy and goals. Key questions:
   a. What is our attitude toward gifted children?
   b. Why are we doing this?
   c. What do we wish to accomplish?
2. Definition and identification. Key questions:
   a. What do we mean by "gifted and talented"?
   b. Which categories of gifts and talents will this program serve?
   c. How will we select them?
3. Instruction-grouping, acceleration, and enrichment. Key questions:
   a. What are students' needs?
   b. How can we best meet those needs?
   c. How can we implement our instructional plans?
4. Evaluation and modification. Key questions: Was the program successful? How do we know?
   a. What did we do right?
   b. What did we do wrong?
   c. What changes shall we make?

It is important that while planning instructional activities teachers include activities for those who finish their work early. These should be meaningful activities which would benefit all students not just those who have been identified gifted. Kennedy (1995) proposes the suggestions listed in **Table 13-5** to promote the well being of gifted students in the general education classroom. These suggestions are important for every classroom teacher to understand and implement as they teach gifted students.

Recent reforms in education have stressed the inclusion of all students in the general education classroom and have resulted in a reduction of the number of special classes found in schools. The limited number of special classes and resource room programs for students who are gifted concerns some educators and parents for several reasons. They believe that classroom teachers must focus on the typical students in their classes and are unable to provide the enrichment and acceleration needed by students who are gifted. Westberg, Archabault, Dobyns, and Slavin (1993) observed third-and fourth-grade general education classrooms in which students identified as gifted were placed and found the majority of these students were not receiving instruction or curriculum appropriate to their abilities. Grouping students who are gifted allows for increased opportunities for interaction and accelerated learning which can have positive effects on both their achievement and their attitudes (Barnett & Durden, 1993; Sowell, 1993).

Instructional Strategies

While avoiding the controversy of whether the identification of students who are talented and gifted is elitist, it is important to recognize that gifted students are "differently abled" (Morelock, 1996, p. 11) and thus require different instructional strategies. Students who exhibit exceptional intellectual abilities must be allowed to develop and demonstrate those abilities in the classroom. If they are not provided with appropriate opportunities, they could become underachievers or behavior problems. Core content areas are important for instructional focus for these students and the general education curriculum should not be abandoned. A classroom teacher can differentiate the curriculum by taking into account the characteristics, educational needs and interests of the student, and then modifying the standard curriculum appropriately. Techniques that will help teachers modify instructional strategies and make curriculum adaptations for students with gifts and talents include curriculum

TABLE 13-5

Promoting the Well Being of Gifted Children in Regular Classrooms

1. Resist policies requiring more work of those who finish assignments quickly and easily. Instead, explore ways to assign different work, which may be more complex, more abstract, and both deeper and wider. Find *curriculum compacting* strategies that work, and use them regularly.

2. Seek out supplemental materials and ideas which extend, not merely reinforce, the *curriculum*. Develop inter-disciplinary units and learning centers that call for higher level thinking. Don't dwell on comprehension-level questions and tasks for those who have no problems with comprehension. Encourage activities that call for analysis, synthesis, and critical thinking, and push beyond superficial responses.

3. De-emphasize grades and other extrinsic rewards. Encourage learning for its own sake, and help perfectionists establish realistic goals and priorities. Try to assure that the self-esteem of talented learners does not rest solely on their products and achievements.

4. Encourage intellectual and academic risk-taking. The flawless completion of a simple worksheet by an academically talented student calls for little or no reward, but struggling with a complex, open-ended issue should earn praise. Provide frequent opportunities to stretch mental muscles.

5. Help all children develop social skills to relate well to one another. For gifted children this may require special efforts to see things from other viewpoints. Training in how to "read" others and how to send accurate verbal and nonverbal messages may also be helpful. Tolerate neither elitist attitudes nor anti-gifted discrimination.

6. Take time to listen to responses that may at first appear to be off-target. Gifted children often are divergent thinkers who get more out of a story or remark and have creative approaches to problems. Hear them out, and help them elaborate on their ideas.

7. Provide opportunities for independent investigations in areas of interest. Gifted children are often intensely, even passionately, curious about certain topics. Facilitate their in-depth explorations by teaching research skills as needed, directing them to good resources, and providing support as they plan and complete appropriate products.

8. Be aware of the special needs of gifted girls. Encourage them to establish realistically high-level educational and career goals, and give them additional encouragement to succeed in math and science.

From Kennedy, D. M. (1995). Plain talk about creating a gifted-friendly classroom. *Roeper Review, 17(4)*, 232–234.

compacting, flexible grouping, tiered assignments, questioning techniques, independent study centers or projects, and interest centers.

Curriculum compacting, a strategy which allows students to identify content that they already know, is an effective method for modifying instruction for students who are gifted. Curriculum compacting allows students to move at a more rapid pace and "buy" time for individual projects of interest. Winebrenner (1992) suggests the following guidelines for teaching students who are gifted in the general education classroom:

- First, find out what they already know.
- Give them "credit" for the concepts they have mastered.
- Don't have them repeat grade level work if they show they know it.
- Provide alternate challenging activities for them to do instead of drill and practice or already mastered work. Provide opportunities for them to work with complex and abstract ideas.

- Discover what their interests are, and build their projects around their interests.
- Allow them flexibility in the way they use the time they "buy back" by mastering a concept early.
- Allow them to learn at a faster pace than their age peers.
- Use discovery-learning techniques often.
- Trust students to learn in nontraditional ways.
- Help them find students just like themselves. Try not to judge their social skills solely on the way they interact with their age peers.
- Give them lots of experience with setting their own goals and evaluating their own work.
- Offer choice, choices, and more choices! (p. 138).

In **flexible grouping,** students are grouped for instruction within the classroom by demonstrated strengths. Thus an identified gifted student might be in a high-level group for math but in an average group for reading. However, as the students demonstrate their strengths it is important to include opportunities to move in and out of groups so that students receive appropriate instruction.

Tiered assignment strategy includes large group instruction with differing activities depending on the ability of the students. Thus, a class may be studying the Civil Rights movement in a social studies class; however, they may be assigned different projects appropriate for their instructional level. If there are book assignments on a topic for instance, different students might be assigned different books to read and discuss. Also, important considerations should be that the assignments should never make the gifted students feel as though they are being punished for being smart by the amount of work expected of them nor should the assignments for the gifted students look like too much fun to the students in the other groups. Much thought needs to go into the development of activities in order to avoid these pitfalls.

Questioning techniques is another appropriate strategy for differentiating instruction in the classroom. When asking questions about material in the content area, the classroom teacher takes care to ask more probing questions, designed to encourage the development of higher order thinking skills. It is important to make sure students have understood the material taught, but it is equally important to ask them questions which require them to analyze, synthesize, and evaluate what they have learned. To ask a student to predict what happened after Goldilocks woke up and ran away or to compare and contrast different versions of the Cinderella story are the kinds of questions which may stimulate thoughtful responses in students who have never had to think like that before. Finally, open-ended questions such as the one for the Goldilocks story encourage students to be risk-takers and realize that there are sometimes no "right" answers to problems.

Independent study projects can be used to stimulate gifted students because they allow a degree of ownership in choosing and designing the project. Gifted students, in particular, can be encouraged through this strategy to take risks and explore topics in more depth than they would be able to in the classroom setting. Also, at the end of the project, students should present their projects affording them the opportunity to develop poise and self-confidence.

A final strategy in differentiating instruction for gifted learners within the general education classroom is through the use of **interest centers.** In the beginning of the school year, students are asked to fill out an interest inventory, not unlike the "Interest-a-lyzer" developed by Dr. Joseph Renzulli. Using this inventory as a guide, the teacher would set up interest centers in the classroom for student use. Thus, all the students, including the gifted students, have the opportunity to explore subject matter beyond the scope of the general education classroom curriculum. The result of the interest centers is much like that of the independent project strategy in that students have ownership of their projects, but with the bonus result that they may also discover a new area of interest and become passionate about it.

Although the above techniques are considered to be appropriate differentiation strategies for modifying the curricular experiences for gifted students, the following points should be considered as any and/or all of the techniques are employed:

- Differentiation can occur with respect to one, two, or all of the following:
  - content (the subject matter or body of knowledge to be acquired)
  - process (mastery of skills, development of concepts, thinking)
  - product (the way in which the learning is demonstrated).
- Differentiation may also occur in the way the curriculum is presented (e.g., separate setting, itinerant teacher, integrated classroom).
- One approach to differentiating curriculum is to extend or study in depth an existing curriculum area. Another approach is to shift to curriculum that arises out of the student's own interests and concerns. Both concepts are important, and both emphasize the processes of learning, thinking, applying, and creating.
- Working together to develop this curriculum, student and teacher share the responsibility for the following levels of a chosen area of study:
  - planning (independent study contract)
  - implementation (student independent study log)
  - evaluation (student self-evaluation)
- The teacher's role in this partnership involves:
  - serving as a mentor or facilitator of learning and thinking rather than as a dispenser of information
  - creating a learning environment that is both secure and stimulating
  - helping the student receive a good balance of learning experiences
  - keeping the focus on the quality of the learning experience.
- Discussions, brainstorming sessions, and related follow-up activities can promote the development of higher-level thinking skills. Higher-level thinking involves analyzing, synthesizing, and evaluating information as opposed to simple knowledge gathering.
- Skills work in the basic subject areas should be an integral part of the gifted student's differentiated curriculum:
  - Basic skills can be taught by using materials that are at the student's instructional level and adapting them so there is less repetition and more opportunity for creative application and critical thinking
  - Independent study provides an ideal vehicle for incorporating basic skills work with the development of higher-level thinking skills.
- Independent study enables the gifted student to become involved in selecting, structuring, executing, and judging his or her work in partnership with the teacher. Sharing the results of this study with others can be beneficial to the gifted students and to others in the class.[1]

---

[1]From the Council for Exceptional Children (1981). *Gifted and Talented Multi-Media Kit, Meeting the Needs of Gifted and Talented Students.* Reston, VA: Author.

Particularly in the early grades, teachers may need to assist students to become independent learners by defining a continuum of skills from the totally dependent to the totally independent learner and the variety of study, research, and communication skills used at each step. It is possible to move them towards becoming totally independent learners.

Task commitment, according to Renzulli (1978), is one of three components constituting giftedness. In many schools, students are identified as gifted because of above average intelligence, but little or nothing is done regarding the area of task commitment. Often students who are gifted have a wide variety of interests and find it difficult to stay focused on one. By being a guide and helping students acquire and maintain task commitment, teachers will be providing them a great service.

Students who are gifted need opportunities to go beyond what is already known to generate new ideas, judge long-held assumptions, and solve complex problems. For these students curriculum and its adaptations should be developed in accord with individualized aims and objectives to parallel their mental abilities and talents, and in accord with the role these students can be expected to play in society. The curriculum for gifted and talented should differ from that for other students in degree of challenge, depth, rigor, sophistication, and required excellence.

Traditionally, curriculum for students who are gifted has been differentiated in three ways: content, process, and product (Howley, Howley, & Pendarvis, 1986; Kaplan, 1974). Differentiated content may include courses the student ordinarily would not encounter until a later date and time. For example, the student may be taking an advanced mathematics class a year or two sooner than same age peers. Differentiated process may include expanding the breadth and depth of the content being studied. For instance, when studying The Great Depression, students may compare and contrast it to other historical depressions and examine them at a higher and more abstract level than just knowledge and understanding. Differentiated product would be using the most acceptable and creative form to report the results of a student's study. For example, if a video would be the best method to convey the results of a student's study of videography, then that should be the product form used. **Table 13-6** presents a guide for modifications in the curriculum.

As noted previously in this chapter, creativity is considered a key component of giftedness. Creative individuals are curious and adventurous. They are able to speculate and generate many different ideas or solutions to problems and questions. Their responses are unusual, unique, or clever and evidence both imagination and knowledge. Hammer (1961) defines creativity as "the unique innovation, the unique configuration, whether it be artistic, philosophical, or scientific. It must be new, fresh and original, and it must be worthwhile, important or highly valued. If it is creativity in the arts as opposed to creativity in the sciences, it must have richness of communicated emotion" (p. 18). Creativity is natural in many students who are gifted, however, the classroom climate, instructional strategies, activities, and curricular approaches must support and enhance that creativity (Daniels, 1997). Gallagher (1985) emphasizes that a person engages in different activities or different ways of treating products during the stages of the creative process. These stages and characteristics are presented in **Table 13-7.**

Gallagher (1985) discusses the problem of our educational programs concentrating on the encouragement of students in the stages of preparation and verification and not in the stages of incubation and illumination. For example, compositions may be evaluated for neatness and organization and not for divergent thinking. How often do teachers encourage the efforts of students whose ideas are in the incubation period, by accepting confusing and sloppy work?

Give students opportunities to develop their creative abilities. Allow them to be original, divergent thinkers. Brainstorming and creative problem solving techniques foster

TABLE 13-6

Curriculum Modifications

Content Modifications

- Abstractness: Factual information is used for illustration, not the focus. The emphasis is on studying abstract concepts.
- Complexity: Ideas discussed need to be as complex as possible.
- Variety: A large variety of topics other than standard curriculum are studied and offered for individual study.
- Organization and Economy: Content should be organized around a few key concepts that serve to unify the diverse special topics studied.
- Study of People: Biographies and stories of how other individuals have faced and solved problems to become creative people are studied.
- Study of Methods: The methods of inquiry and methodologies of disciplines should serve as the focus of study.

Process Modifications

- Higher-Level Thinking: Use of knowledge rather than acquisition of knowledge is the emphasis.
- Open-Endedness: The general atmosphere should contribute to further inquiry, divergent thought, and student-centered interaction.
- A sense of discovery in the learning process increases interest, builds on natural curiosity, and increases self-confidence and independence in learning.
- Evidence of Reasoning: Students should be encouraged to evaluate both the process and product of reasoning.
- Freedom of Choice: A wide variety of topics and activities should be available for individual choice.
- Group Interaction and Simulations: Cooperative learning experiences and group problem solving are important both cognitively and affectively.
- Pacing and Variety: Rapid pacing maintains interest and provides a challenge.

Product Modifications

- Real Problems: Solutions to actual personal, societal, scientific, and artistic problems that adults face should be sought.
- Real Audiences: Appropriate audiences such as journals, newspapers, and public presentations for products of learning should be sought.
- Transformation: The focus should be on transforming existing knowledge rather than merely summarizing existing knowledge.
- Evaluation: Products should be evaluated by appropriate audiences such as professionals in the field or real consumers of the product.

fluency, flexibility, elaboration, and originality, the four creative cognitive processes. Programs such as Odyssey of the Mind and Future Problem Solving encourage this behavior. Recognize that students have individual styles for generating creative ideas. Creativity might best occur while walking rather than while sitting, when working in short segments rather than in a long session, with background noise or music rather than in silence, and in cooperation with another rather than alone. Remember that creativity comes in a variety of forms, not only in the arts, but also in an unusual way to display a model aircraft collection, or a working heart made from sandwich bags and drinking straws. Be accepting of the possibility that a student who is creatively gifted may choose

TABLE 13-7

The Stages of the Creative Process

Stage of Creative Process	Expected Form	Predominant Thinking Operation	Personality Factor or Aptitude
• Preparation	• Well organized and well stated.	• Cognitive • Memory	• Studiousness and sustained attention.
• Incubation	• Often confused and sloppy.	• Divergent Thinking	• Intellectual freedom and risk taking.
• Illumination	• Incoherent		• Tolerance of failure and ambiguity.
• Verification	• Neat, well organized, clearly following a logical sequence.	• Convergent Thinking	• Intellectual

to discard what appears to be a perfectly acceptable, wonderfully creative idea. Some of the most important things you can provide these students are an environment conducive to creativity free from too much structure, the necessary resources and materials to work creatively, and support and encouragement to continue even when students initially fail.

Students demonstrate various types of creative behaviors at different ages. The type and level of their creativity depend on their experience, their physical development, and also their cognitive development (Amabile, 1989). Very young children may show their creativity through singing inventive songs, drawing, building while experimenting with different materials, and experimenting with sounds and instruments. As young children mature, their creativity may be seen through dancing, painting or combining colors in new ways, playing with sounds and meanings of words, and inventing and playing imaginary characters as they play.

Amabile (1989) further asserted that problem solving involves the creativity process in all four steps, beginning with problem finding. Once the problem has been defined, resources and data are gathered which will help solve the problem. The next stage of problem-solving is the generation of many ideas and possibilities, no matter how wild and seemingly impractical. Since judgment of ideas is withheld in this stage, creative talent is allowed free rein. Finally, the validation stage of problem-solving proceeds with testing the various possibilities and ideas produced. Young children can be encouraged and observed demonstrating their engagement in the creative process especially when they are in a flexible classroom that encourages independence, acceptance, and creativity.

One of the dangers in recognizing creativity in young children, according to Cramond (2001), is that many of the behaviors that identify creativity in these children also can be used to identify learning and/or behavior problems. The child who is different may be misdiagnosed as having Attention Deficit Hyperactivity Disorder (ADHD). Both highly creative children as well as ADHD children tend to daydream, be impulsive, take risks, and have poor social skills and generally difficult personalities. Both groups also demonstrate high energy levels and higher levels of sensation seeking behavior.

The early childhood teacher who is in tune with this conundrum in the overlapping of creative behavior and ADHD behavior will do the highly creative child (or any child for that matter) a great service simply by being careful not to place an ADHD label on the child too quickly. Also, the most important thing that the teacher can do for this child is simply to recognize and encourage creativity. Offering a safe haven for the highly creative child to express new ideas and to take risks without fear of rejection or ridicule is vital to this child's self-esteem and builds confidence. The creative child learns to accept his different feelings as valuable in an adult's eyes.

Researchers (Getzels & Jackson, 1962; Torrance, 1984) have indicated that many teachers consider students who are high on intelligence but low on creativity to be more ambitious, more studious, and more hard working than the highly creative student. They tell us teachers best like students who work industriously on teacher designated tasks, obey authority and rules readily and without conflict, and retain knowledge well. So, attempt to be accepting of your students who are creatively gifted and supportive of their ability. **Table 13-8** offers suggestions for encouraging creativity.

TABLE 13-8

Suggestions for Encouraging Creativity

- To stimulate students' powers of close examination, inquisitiveness, and alertness, ask them to look out the school bus window on a field trip and record only things that are living, or things of a certain color, or shape, etc. You may ask them to mentally record their observations while traveling and later make a written list. On the return trip, they can check to see what they overlooked or missed.
- To stimulate fluency, ask students to propose as many uses as possible for everyday items such as a cereal box, a pliers, a nail clipper, a shopping bag, etc. You can ask them to list as many things as they can that are shiny, sharp, slimy, or dry; round, square, or rectangular; black, white, yellow, or blue; etc.
- To stimulate inventiveness and imagination, ask students what they think would happen if:
  — animals wore clothes
  — we were born with wheels on our feet
  — we all lived in the trees
  — there were no electrical appliances
  — everyone became some kind of animal/flower/bird/fish/insect
  — we were transported to Ancient Egypt/Merry Old England/Prehistoric times.
- Try brainstorming by proposing a question affecting the entire school, such as where to go on a field trip. Have your students generate as many ideas as possible for answering the question or solving the problem, no matter how bizarre, and record them on paper or a computer. When the list is complete, select the best responses and elaborate on them.
- Do "pass it on" stories. Begin an extemporaneous story that each student must continue as the previous student stops. For instance, you may begin a story by saying, *"One day, a boy and girl were strolling through a deep woods when they saw a . . ."* and at this point pass the story on to the next participant. This procedure continues for as long as you choose. Sometimes it's fun to tape record the stories for later listening.
- Try play-making by acting out fictitious scenes, such as playing basketball against Michael Jordan, interviewing Columbus on his return to Spain, or pretending to have a conversation between Rosa Parks and Harriet Beecher Stowe.
- Expose your creatively gifted students to other creative individuals. This might include reading comic strips such as "Calvin and Hobbs" or "The Far Side" together; viewing videotapes about Edison, Van Gogh, Martin Luther King Jr., etc.; visiting museums and art institutes to encounter first hand the works of creative masters in various fields; reading biographies and autobiographies of highly creative individuals; and viewing and discussing films and videotapes produced by highly creative people such as Disney, Spielberg, Lee, and Lucas. Use the work of such creative individuals to intrigue and encourage exploration, not as a model to be emulated.

Although many students who are gifted are natural leaders and will assume many leadership roles, they must understand there also will be occasions when they must be part of a team effort. Classroom teachers can foster leadership skills by providing opportunities for students to serve as both leaders and followers in the classroom and to participate as members of teams. Allowing students the opportunity to be followers teaches them that a good leader must, at times, be willing to follow. Encourage your students who are gifted to participate in a variety of school organizations and activities (band, athletic teams, drama club, etc.) so they can encounter the diverse talents of others. Participating in an organization gives students the opportunity to encounter a variety of leadership role models. Provide your students with information about leaders in the fields in which they have an interest and discuss the characteristics and attributes these individuals possessed to become leaders.

Technology, the Internet and Gifted Education

The recent advances in technology have offered opportunities for enhanced educational experiences for all students. These technological advances have significant implications for the education of gifted and talented students, particularly disadvantaged students. The proliferation of computer software for students and teachers has made learning and facilitating learning easier and more interesting. The use of email and distance learning can offer those disadvantaged students learning opportunities that were previously inaccessible. However, there remains a "digital divide" that separates students who have access to technology and the internet from those who do not. Typically these divisions occur along economic, racial and geographic lines (Roach, 2002).

For gifted and talented students the internet offers opportunities that were previously unavailable. At the touch of a button, vast amounts of information are available to the gifted learner. No longer are teachers bound by the physical resources on hand (maps, textbooks, encyclopedias, trade books, etc.), they can tailor an individualized education plan for the gifted student in their classroom. Online and distance learning allows gifted students the opportunity for acceleration and enrichment as they move through curriculum at their own pace and pursue topics in depth.

Suggestions for Classroom Teachers

In the section that follows, suggestions for classroom activities are presented by subject area.

Art

1. Write a numeral, a letter of the alphabet, or a squiggly line and use it as a part of a larger drawing. Try to disguise your choice of letter, numeral, or squiggly line so it will be difficult for others to find it without a search.
2. Given several objects such as string, a paper clip, an empty paper towel roll, rubber band, glue, coat hangers, construction paper, scissors, etc., construct a mobile.
3. Given four letters of the alphabet and/or numerals, randomly invent a variety of monogram designs for your school, your name, your state, etc.
4. Design your own recreational vehicle and describe the function of each major feature.
5. Design the ideal bedroom you would like to have and describe the function of each major feature of the room.
6. Design a clothing outfit you would like to own. Be original with color, material, style, etc.
7. Design a school you think would be more fun to attend. Describe the function of each major feature and how it would improve your learning.

8. Using items such as construction paper, paper clips, paper towel rolls, rubber bands, tape, glue, post-it notes, etc., make something no one else will think of doing.
9. Brainstorm many different uses for a shoe string.
10. Design a new cage for a gerbil.

Language Arts

1. Orally describe in class what you would do with a **pumglitz** if given one. What would it look like; smell like; do? What can be done with it? Write a two person play with a partner about the day you were given a **pumglitz** and the adventures you had with it. Perform the play in class with your partner.
2. You are an "object." Tell your life story in a short story format, illustrations optional, using all the features a good short story should possess. An alternate project would be to create an illustrated story book using the same theme. Possible objects may include: a mirror, a foreign coin, a well travelled penny, one of Michael Jordan's shoes, etc.
3. Name three occupations that would well fit someone with the following names:
   Hy Pancake
   Sally Forth
   Noel Belle
   Ben Fender
   Create a children's story about one of your choices.
4. If you could create a new television show, about what would it be? Who would be the main characters? What actors would you cast to play these roles? What would be the title of the show? Write a five minute script for the introductory show.
5. What could you do if you were 12 feet tall you now can't do? Write a short story about your imaginary experiences.
6. To what uses other than wearing to play football can a football helmet be put?
7. Create an idea for a web site that has not been done but you think would be a success.
8. Women's dress hats are no longer fashionable. Develop a strategy to return them to popularity. What will be the main medium you will use in your effort (e.g., television, newspapers, magazines, point-of-purchase display, motion pictures, etc.)? In what ways will you use this medium?
9. Write four new cheers for your school's athletic team. Will they be humorous, musical, rhyming, tough, friendly, congratulatory, encouraging, etc.? Will they follow a particular presentation style such as rap, hip-hop, etc.?
10. Brainstorm designs to make a computer table more useful, practical, and/or portable. Select ten improvements you like best and add as many of these as possible to a drawing or a model of your improved computer table. Style, practicality, aesthetics, and utility should be important considerations in your plan.
11. What are seven new ideas for the use of post-it notes. Try to think of uses other than those of anyone else. If possible, demonstrate in class the new use for this product.
12. What major lead news story might be hidden in:
    a circus parade
    a howling dog
    a jack-o-lantern
    a man's stocking
13. Invent a snack food you think would be well-liked but is different from anything with which you are familiar on today's market. What research and marketing steps must you follow before your new product is mass produced?

14. Write five equally effective headlines for the lead story in today's sports section of the newspaper. Try to make your headline four words or fewer yet descriptive of the sporting event that occurred. Try to make it provocative so readers will choose to complete the article. Without reading the newspaper article, write one of your own describing the sporting event. Read the newspaper article and compare and contrast your work with the newspaper's. Did you cover all pertinent information? Did you use a writing style conducive to newspaper articles, etc.?

15. Design, name, and develop a magazine ad for a cartoon character who represents a sport's shoe company. Decide on the major advertising approach you will use (e.g., propaganda, celebrity endorsement, prestige, etc.). Learn the characteristics of a good magazine advertisement and incorporate as many as possible into your ad. If you have access to a computer program and/or VCR and/or camcorder allowing animation do an animated commercial in lieu of a magazine advertisement.

16. What would be a suitable name for a home for retired NASCAR drivers? Write a newspaper article about the home's dedication ceremony and residents by succinctly answering the questions who, what, when, where, why, how, and how many.

17. Create a single word to describe each of the following:

   - hometown fans who throw back onto the field an opposing team's home run ball.

   - a curved foot long hot dog containing bacon, three cheeses, special sauce, onion rings, french fries, tomato, lettuce, pickle, mustard, jalapeno peppers, and catsup served on a croissant roll.

18. What is the title of your favorite book, magazine, movie, or television show? Propose five other titles you think would be equally or more effective.

19. Make a list of things that go up and down.

20. Make a list of things that are round.

Science

1. Create an invention that demonstrates the principle of the simple pulley using a soda straw, a cup, two yard's length of string, a stapler, a piece of cardboard three feet long, two feet wide and a minimum of 1/4 inch thick, two empty soda pop bottles, transparent tape, a scissors, four empty spools, a small saw, and two 3 foot dowels. You may alter the materials as desired and do not need to use all of the listed items in your final invention. Some of the items may serve only as tools. Explain and demonstrate your invention to the class.

2. Classify the following gibberish words into as many categories as possible:

hmda	kmor	ftam	ecto	wyrr
belk	cvst	arf	turr	reg
xel	jul	sdo	ghak	botts

3. Create original similes using content you studied in science (biology, zoology, chemistry, physics, etc.):

flexible as . . .	twinkling like . . .	odorous as . . .	clear as . . .
strong as . . .	screaming like . . .	blue as. . .	elusive as . . .
bright as . . .	treacherous as . . .	mild as . . .	elegant as . . .

   Explain your choices to the class.

4. Create a unique name for a store selling together the following: pharmaceuticals, playground equipment, electric appliances, exotic animals, and Harley-Davidson motorcycles. Design a layout for the store and indicate where the various merchandise would be located and how they would be displayed. What considerations must be made to insure the merchandise does not interfere one with the other?

5. List seven things we encounter regularly that operate on the principle of the simple incline.

6. Make a thorough drawing or a scale model of an invention for:
   tying a bow tie
   a practical total home car wash
   an inflatable playhouse
   Detail is important as are the scientific principles needed to be considered to successfully complete a life-size prototype of this invention.

7. Brainstorm ways to reduce the ozone pollution in your town. What things will you need to know when you complete generating possible solutions to the problem before you can decide which solutions are best? What may be helpful to know before you begin your brainstorming session?

8. Describe five ways in which a simple telescope, microscope, Bunsen burner, barometer, tachometer, etc. may be improved to make it more effective and useful.

9. Of what new and useful functions can you think for a Hummer? Draw or make a model of your favorite idea and demonstrate it to your class. To your knowledge, are there things not yet invented necessary to the actual completion of your idea? Can you name the genius from the Renaissance era who created a model of the helicopter, but could not successfully complete a manned aircraft because other discoveries had not yet been made making this possible?
   Can the new functions for your Hummer help in:
   environmental research
   medical assistance
   oceanographic research
   space exploration
   wildlife conservation?
   If so, how? If not, what will be the vehicle's primary use? What will you need to know prior to starting this exercise?

10. List five items to which Vitamin E may be added to increase their marketability. What information will you need to gain about the items and Vitamin E before you can make cogent recommendations for their combining? Prepare a defense for your favorite choice to present to your class.

11. Using your ideas as a guide, decorate a van or truck for your store.

12. Invent a new cereal for children. Consider taste, uniqueness, and health.

13. Create a chain reaction to a) wash a dog, b) crack an acorn, c) wake a person up in the morning.

14. Develop an underground city, a city in the ocean, or a city on the moon.

Social Studies

1. If you were an individual with truly super powers, how would you use them? Generate a list of super powers you would like to possess. From this list, choose three powers you would most want. Generate a list of things you could do with these combined powers. Choose the one you best like and create a comic book about your exploits. Will it benefit mankind? Will it benefit the environment? Will it benefit wildlife? Will it benefit you? Or, will your super powers be used in other ways?

2. Many fairy tales have universal similarity. Although some of the details may differ, the basic plot is the same. Locate as many cultures as possible having a Cinderella story. Try to find translations of the original tale from each country. Compare and contrast those tales with the version told in the Walt Disney movie/video. What assumptions can be drawn about the various cultures based upon their version of Cinderella?

Compare and contrast your assumptions about the various cultures. Do you think your assumptions accurately describe the culture as a whole? Why or why not?

3. Premiums given with the purchase of a product are intended to enhance that product's sale. Yet, to the seller, the premium cannot be of great cost compared to the original product's cost.

   For instance, a fast food chain may offer a pressed plastic model, of very little cost to them, as their prize with the sale of their childrens' meal. Oftentimes, these premiums have tie-ins to movies or TV shows the sellers hope will be popular with their primary user. Extensive demographic information is collected and analyzed when premium choices are made. Develop a survey instrument asking anonymous, non-threatening information about your school mates. Tabulate this information and develop a profile of demographic information about the student body in your school. Next, develop a questionnaire asking a representative group of your classmates to list the premiums most motivating in their hypothetical purchase of:
   a man's cologne
   a hair dryer
   a woman's high school graduation ring
   a dune buggy
   a Recreational Van
   Establish the criteria a response from your pilot group must meet to be reasonable to include in a list to be presented to the total school body. Tabulate your lists and develop a questionnaire containing the most reasonable responses asking the total school to prioritize the three premiums they would most like for the purchase of each of the products.

4. How might our country and/or world be different if:
   Columbus had landed on the west coast of America
   Elvis Presley had been an opera singer
   George Washington had been born in England
   Adolph Hitler had been accidentally killed as a youth
   Abraham Lincoln had not been assassinated
   JFK's brother, Joseph Kennedy, had not been killed in World War II

5. Pretend you are an archeologist in the year 3000 A.D. having just completed an excavation of a room in your house without having any prior knowledge of what the things in it actually were or how they were used. Develop an imaginary log of what you, as a future archeologist, may think the things in the room of your choice were and how they were used. Be creative. The wilder the better!

6. What is the name of your town? How did it get that name? Was it originally called what it is today? If you were asked to rename your town, what would you call it? Why?

7. Compare and contrast the nonviolent protest movement of Gandhi and Martin Luther King, Jr.

Mathematics

1. Measure the length of one of your paces and record it using the metric and/or U.S. measurement system. Pace-off a selected area such as a parking lot, a hallway, a gymnasium, etc. Translate the number of your paces into linear measure. Next, measure the same area with an accurate measuring device. Is there a difference? If so, what is it? How could using pacing instead of accurate measurement effect some of your school sporting events?

2. Given an answer to a problem, brainstorm the number of ways in which that answer may be arrived.
3. Amount of shelf space in a supermarket is important to product manufacturers. Contact a manufacturer and ask about the mathematics involved in designing packages for optimum usage of shelf space. Ask about things such as volume, weight, size, product type, package shape, etc.
4. Discover how mathematics is used in the following occupations:
   animator
   veterinarian
   chiropractor
   film and/or video tape editor
   NASCAR mechanic and/or pit crew boss
5. Design a geodesic house using geometric principles.

Summary

Students who are talented and gifted can be found in every school and their identification is the first step in ensuring that they have the opportunity to develop to their fullest potential. Because the classroom teacher plays an important role in that process, this chapter has provided a description of the characteristics of students who are gifted and a review of the ways in which they are assessed and identified. Although differentiated services for these students are not mandated by federal law, their unique abilities require special attention in the schools. Unfortunately, programming for these students typically receives less funding and focus than programming for other students who have special needs. As a result of the limited funding and the trend toward inclusive classrooms, the primary responsibility for the education of students who are gifted may be delegated to the classroom teacher. While some school districts do provide resource room or special class placements for these students, many of them will continue to remain in the general education classroom for at least part of their educational experience. The instructional strategies presented in this chapter will assist classroom teachers as they nurture and encourage the development of these students' unique abilities.

Discussion Questions and Activities

1. Generate a list of individuals you consider to be gifted. Would these individuals qualify for placement in a gifted program using the definitions in this chapter? In your state or school district?

2. Discuss inclusion. Should students who are gifted be served only by an inclusion model? What would be the advantages of this service delivery model? The disadvantages?

3. Gina does not have an IQ score above 130. She is an extremely motivated and creative young lady. If she has above grade-level achievement, could she qualify for gifted placement in some states? What about in your state or district?

4. Gifted education has been controversial over the years. Why? What is the controversy?

5. Discuss the difference between the two types of IQ tests described in this chapter. Why would a district or school system choose to use one over the other?

6. Discuss the neglected gifted. Why do you suppose that these groups are underrepresented?

No standardized criteria

No federal mandate

No funding

7. Administrative models for gifted programs vary from state to state. Should there be a national norm for service and/or identification procedures for gifted education? Why or why not?

Probably — need mandates for identification & service

Internet Resources

Center for Talent Development
www.ctd.northwestern.edu/index.html

Council for Exceptional Children
http://www.cec.sped.org/

Educational Resources Information Center (ERIC)
http://www.ericec.org/

Gifted and Talented Resources List
http://www.isd77.k12.mn.us/resources/g&tresources.txt

Center for Talented Youth
http://www.jhu.edu/~gifted/

National Research center on the Gifted and Talented
http://www.gifted.uconn.edu/nrcgt.html

National Association For Gifted Children
http://www.nagc.org/

Providing Curriculum Alternatives to Motivate Gifted Students
http://www.kidsource.com/education/motivate.gifted.html

Prufrock Press
http://www.prufrock.com/

Blending Gifted Education and School Reform
http://www.kidsource.com/kidsource/content/Blending_Gifted_Ed.html

Ten Tips for Parents of Gifted Children
http://www.hoagiesgifted.org/ten_tips.htm

World Council for Gifted and Talented Children
http://www.worldgifted.org/

References

Amabile, T. M. (1989). *Growing up creative: Nurturing a lifetime of creativity*. New York: Crown Publishers, Inc.

Ambrose, D. (2002). Socioeconomic stratification and its influence on talent development: Some interdisciplinary perspectives. *Gifted Child Quarterly, 46 (3)*, 170–180.

American Association of University Women (1992). *How schools short-change girls*. Washington, DC: AAUW Educational Foundation.

Baldwin, A. Y. (1991). Ethnic and cultural issues. In N. Colangelo & G. A. Davis (Eds.), *Handbook of gifted education* (pp. 416–427). Boston: Allyn & Bacon.

Barnett, L., & Durden, W. (1993). *Education patterns of academically talented youth*. Gifted Child Quarterly, 37, 161–168.

Baum, S. (1990). *Gifted but learning disabled: A puzzling paradox*. Reston, VA: Council for Exceptional Children (ERIC Digest E479).

Benbow, C. P., & Minor, L. L. (1990). Cognitive profiles of verbally and mathematically precocious students: Implications for identifications of the gifted. *Gifted Child Quarterly, 34(1)*, 21–26.

Berk, L. (2003). *Child Development* (6th ed.). Boston: Allyn & Bacon.

Borland, J. H., & Wright, L. (1994). Identifying young, potentially gifted, economically disadvantaged students. *Gifted Child Quarterly, 38*, 164–171.

Callahan, C. M. (1991). The assessment of creativity. In N. Colangelo & G. A. Davis (Eds.), *Handbook of gifted education* (pp. 219–235). Boston: Allyn & Bacon.

Cattell, R. B. (1971). *Abilities: Their structure, growth, and action*. Boston: Houghton Mifflin.

Clark, B. (2002). *Growing up gifted* (6th ed.). Englewood Cliffs, NJ: Prentice Hall.

Clasen, D. R., Middleton, J. A., & Connell, T. J. (1994). Assessing artistic and problem-solving performance in minority and nonminority students using a nontraditional multidimensional approach. *Gifted Child Quarterly, 38*, 27–32.

Colangelo, N., Assouline, S. G., & Gross, M. (2004). *A nation deceived: How schools hold back America's brightest students.* Connie Belin & Jacqueline N. Blank International Center for Gifted Education and Talent Development, Iowa City, Iowa.

Colangelo, N., & Davis, G. A. (1997). Introduction and overview. In N. Colangelo & G. A. Davis (Eds.), *Handbook of gifted education* (2nd ed., pp. 3–9). Boston: Allyn & Bacon.

Coleman, L. J., & Cross, T. L. (2001). *Being Gifted in School: An introduction to development, guidance, and teaching.* Waco, TX: Prufrock Press.

Council for Exceptional Children (1981). *Gifted and talented multi-media kit, Meeting the needs of gifted and talented students.* Reston, VA: Author.

Council for Exceptional Children (2005). Tell the Senate to Fund Grants to Students with Gifts and Talents! [on-line] *http://www.cec.sped.org/pp/*

Covington, M. V. (1984). The self-worth theory of academic motivation: Findings and applications. *Elementary School Journal, 85,* 5–20.

Cramond, B. (2001). Fostering creative thinking. In F. Karnes & S. Bean (Eds.). *Methods and materials for teaching the gifted,* (pp. 399–406). Waco, TX: Prufrock Press.

Daniels, S. (1997). Creativity in the classroom: Characteristics, climate, and curriculum. In N. Colangelo & G. A. Davis (Eds.), *Handbook of gifted education* (2nd ed., pp. 292–307). Boston: Allyn & Bacon.

Davis, G. A., & Rimm, S. B. (1989). *Education of the gifted and talented.* Englewood Cliffs, NJ: Prentice-Hall.

Davis, G. A., & Rimm, S. B. (1998). *Education of the gifted and talented* (4th ed.). Boston: Allyn & Bacon.

Emerick, L. J. (1992). Academic underachievement among the gifted: Students' perceptions of factors that reverse the pattern. *Gifted Child Quarterly, 36,* 140–146.

Feldhusen, J. F. (March, 1989). Synthesis of research on gifted youth. *Educational Leadership,* 6–11.

Feldhusen, J. F., Hoover, S. M., & Sayler, M. F. (1990). *Identifying and educating gifted students at the secondary level.* New York: Trillium Press.

Ford, D. Y., & Harris, J. J. (1990). On discovering the hidden treasures of gifted and talented African-American children. *Roeper Review, 13,* 27–32.

Frasier, M. M. (1994). *Frasier Talent Assessment Profile—Revised.* Athens, GA: The University of Georgia.

Gallagher, J. J. (1985). *Teaching the gifted child* (3rd ed.). Boston: Allyn & Bacon.

Gallagher, J. J., & Gallagher, S. A. (1994). *Teaching the gifted* (4th ed.). Boston: Allyn & Bacon.

Galton, F. (1869). *Hereditary genius.* London: Macmillan.

Gardner, H. (1983). *Frames of mind: The theory of multiple intelligences.* New York: Basic Books.

Gardner, H., & Hatch, T. (1989). Multiple intelligences go to school: Educational implications of the theory of multiple intelligences. *Educational Researcher, 18(8),* 6.

Gearhart, B. R., Weishahn, M. W., & Gearhart, C. J. (1996). *The exceptional student in the regular classroom* (6th ed.). Englewood Cliffs, NJ: Merrill.

Getzels, J. W., & Jackson, P. W. (1962). *Creativity and intelligence.* New York: Wiley.

Guilford, J. P. (1950). *Creativity. American Psychologist, 5,* 444–454.

Guilford, J. P. (1959). Three faces of intellect. *American Psychologist, 14,* 469–479.

Hammer, E. F. (1961). *Creativity.* New York: Random House.

Henson II, F. O. (1976). *Mainstreaming the gifted.* Austin, TX: Learning Concepts.

House, E. R., Steele, J. M., & Kerins, T. (1970). *Advocacy in a non-rational system.* Springfield, IL: Illinois Department of Program Development for Gifted Children.

Howley, A., Howley, C. B., & Pendarvis, E. D. (1986). *Teaching gifted children.* Boston: Little Brown.

Jenkins-Friedman, R., & Nielsen, M. E. (1990). Gifted and talented students. In E. L. Meyen (Ed.), *Exceptional children in today's schools* (2nd ed., pp. 451–493). Denver, CO: Love.

Johnson, L. J., Karnes, M. B., & Carr, V. W. (1997). Providing services to children with gifts and disabilities: A critical need. In N. Colangelo & G. A. Davis (Eds.), *Handbook of gifted education* (2nd ed., pp. 516–527). Boston: Allyn & Bacon.

Kaplan, S. (1974). *Providing programs for the gifted and talented: A handbook.* Ventura, CA: Office of the Ventura County Superintendent of Schools.

Kaufman, A. S. (1992). Evaluation of WISC-R and WIPSI-R for gifted children. *Roeper Review, 15,* 154–158.

Kennedy, D. M. (1995). Plain talk about creating a gifted-friendly classroom. *Roeper Review, 17(4),* 232–234.

Kerr, B. (1997). Developing talents in girls and young women. In N. Colangelo & G. A. Davis (Eds.), *Handbook of gifted education* (2nd ed., pp. 483–497). Boston: Allyn & Bacon.

Kimball, M. (1989). A new perspective on women's math achievement. *Psychological Bulletin, 105,* 198–214.

Kitano, M. K. (1989). The K-3 teacher's role in recognizing and supporting young gifted children. *Young Children, 44(3),* 57–63.

Kitano, M. K., & Dijiosia, M. (2002). Are Asian and Pacific Americans over represented in programs for the gifted? *Roeper Review, 24(2),* 76–80.

Kolloff, P. B. (1997). Special residential high schools. In N. Colangelo & G. A. Davis (Eds.), *Handbook of gifted education* (2nd ed., pp. 198–206). Boston: Allyn & Bacon.

Kulik, J. A. (1992). *An analysis of the research on ability grouping: Historical and contemporary perspectives.* Research-Based Decision Making Series. Storrs, CT: National Research Center on the Gifted and Talented, University of Connecticut.

Lucito, L. (1963). Gifted children. In L. Dunn (Ed.), *Exceptional children in the schools* (pp. 179–238). New York: Holt, Rinehart and Winston.

Lyman, H. (1997). *Test scores and what they mean* (6th ed.). Boston: Allyn and Bacon.

MacKinnon, D. W. (1962). The nature and nurture of creative talent. *American Psychologist, 17(7),* 484–495.

Maker, C. J. (1982). *Curriculum development for the gifted.* Rockville, MD: Aspen.

Marland, S. (1972). *Education of the gifted and talented.* Report to the Subcommittee on Education, Committee on Labor and Public Welfare, U.S. Senate. Washington, DC: GPO.

Morelock, M. (1996). The nature of giftedness and talent: Imposing order on chaos. *Roeper Review, 19(1),* 4–12.

Parke, B. N. (1989). *Gifted students in regular classrooms.* Boston: Allyn & Bacon.

Pegnato, C. C., & Birch, J. W. (1959). Locating gifted children in junior high school. *Exceptional Children, 25,* 300–304.

Pendarvis, E. D. (1993). Students with unique gifts and talents. In A. E. Blackhurst & W. H. Berdine (Eds.), *An introduction to special education* (3rd ed., pp. 563–599). New York: Harper Collins.

Peterson, J. S. (1997). Bright, tough, and resilient—and not in a gifted program. *Journal of Secondary Gifted Education, 8(3),* 121–136.

Pfeiffer, S. I. (2003). Challenges and opportunities for students who are gifted: What the experts say. *Gifted Child Quarterly, 47(2),* 161–169.

Ramos-Ford, V., & Gardner, H. (1997). Giftedness from a multiple intelligence perspective. In N. Colangelo & G. A. Davis (Eds.), *Handbook of gifted education* (2nd ed., pp. 54–66). Boston: Allyn & Bacon.

Renzulli, J. S. (1978). What makes giftedness? Reexamining a definition. *Phi Delta Kappan, 60(3),* 180–184, 261.

Renzulli, J. S., & Reis, S. M. (1997). The schoolwide enrichment model: New directions for developing high-end learning. In N. Colangelo & G. A. Davis (Eds.), *Handbook of gifted education* (2nd ed., pp. 136–154). Boston: Allyn & Bacon.

Renzulli, J., Reis, S., & Smith, L. (1981). *The revolving door identification model.* Mansfield Center, CT: Creative Learning Press.

Renzulli, J., & Smith, L. (1980). An alternative approach to identifying and programming for gifted and talented students. *Gifted/Creative/Talented, 15,* 4–11.

Renzulli, J. S., Smith, L. H., White, A. J., Callahan, C. M., & Hartman, R. K. (1976). *Scales for rating the behavior characteristics of superior students.* Mansfield Center, CT: Creative Learning Press.

Richert, E. S. (1997). Excellence with equity in identification and programming. In N. Colangelo & G. A. Davis (Eds.), *Handbook of gifted education* (2nd ed., pp. 75–88). Boston: Allyn & Bacon.

Rimm, S. B., & Lovance, K. J. (1992). The use of subject and grade skipping for the prevention and reversal of underachievement. *Gifted Child Quarterly, 36,* 100–105.

Roach, R. (2002). Report touts federal role in solving digital divide. *Black Issues in Higher Education, 19(12),* 23–27.

Robinson, A., Bradley, R. H., & Stanley, T. D. (1990). Opportunity to achieve: Identifying mathematically gifted Black students. *Contemporary Educational Psychology, 15(1),* 1–2.

Sadker, M., & Sadker, D. (1985). Sexism in the schoolroom in the '80s. *Psychology Today, 19,* 54–57.

Samara, J., & Curry, J. A. (1993). *Gifted education unit: Curriculum guide for the education of gifted students*. Atlanta, GA: State Superintendent of Schools.

Schiever, S. W., & Maker, C. J. (1997). Enrichment and acceleration: An overview and new directions. In N. Colangelo & G. A. Davis (Eds.), *Handbook of gifted education* (2nd ed., pp. 113–125). Boston: Allyn & Bacon.

Shields, C. M. (2002). A comparison study of student attitudes and perceptions in homogeneous and heterogeneous classrooms. *Roeper Review, 24(3),* 115–119.

Sowell, E. (1993). Programs for mathematically gifted students: A review of empirical research. *Gifted Child Quarterly, 37,* 124–132.

Sowell, E. J., Bergwall, L. K., Zeigler, A. J., & Cartwright, R. M. (1990). Identification and description of mathematically gifted students: A review of empirical research. *Gifted Child Quarterly, 34(4),* 147–154.

Stanley, J. C. (1978). Identifying and nurturing the intellectually gifted. In R. E. Clasen & B Robinson (Eds.), *Simple Gifts*. Madison, WI: University of Wisconsin Extension.

Stanley, J. C., & Benbow, C. P. (1986). Youths who reason exceptionally well mathematically. In R. J. Sternberg & J. E. Davidson (Eds.), *Conceptions of giftedness* (pp. 361–387). New York: Cambridge University Press.

Sternberg, R. J. (1981). A componential theory of intellectual giftedness. *Gifted Child Quarterly, 25,* 86–93.

Sternberg, R. J. (1982). Lies we live by: Misapplication of tests in identifying the gifted. *Gifted Child Quarterly, 26,* 157–161.

Sternberg, R. J. (1988). A triarchic theory of intellectual giftedness. In R. J. Sternberg & J. E. Davidson (Eds.), *Conceptions of Giftedness* (pp. 223–243). New York: Cambridge University Press.

Terman, L. M. (1925). *Genetic studies of genius*. Vol. 1. Mental and physical traits of a thousand gifted children. Stanford, CA: Stanford University Press.

Terwilliger, J. S., & Titus, J. C. (1995). Gender differences in attitudes and attitude changes among mathematically talented youth. *Gifted Child Quarterly, 39,* 29–35.

Torrance, E. P. (1965). *Rewarding creative behavior*. Englewood Cliffs, NJ: Prentice-Hall.

Torrance, E. P. (1966). *Torrance tests of creative thinking*. Princeton, NJ: Personnel.

Torrance, E. P. (1981). *Thinking creatively in action and movement*. Bensonville, IL: Scholastic Testing Services.

Torrance, E. P. (1984). *Mentor relationships*. Buffalo, NY: Bearly Limited.

Tyler-Wood, T., & Carrie, L. (1991). Identification of gifted children: The effectiveness of various measures of cognitive ability. *Roeper Review, 14,* 63–64.

U. S. Department of Education's Office of Educational Research and Improvement (1993). *National Excellence: A case for developing America's talent*. Washington D.C.: U.S. Government Printing Office.

U.S. Department of Education's National Center for Education Statistics (2001). *State Nonfiscal Survey of Public Elementary/Secondary Education 2000–01*. Washington D.C.: U.S. Government Printing Office.

VanTassel-Baska, J. (1994). *Comprehensive curriculum for gifted learners* (2nd ed.). Boston: Allyn & Bacon.

VanTassel-Baska, J. (1998). Appropriate curriculum for the talented learner. In J. Van Tassel-Baska (Ed.), *Excellence in educating gifted and talented learners* (3rd ed., pp. 339–361). Denver, CO: Love.

VanTassel-Baska, J. (2005). Politics and children with high potential. *Parenting for High Potential*, September, 3.

VanTassel-Baska, J., Patton, J., & Prillaman (1989). Disadvantaged gifted learners at risk for educational attention. *Focus on Exceptional Children, 22(3),* 1–15.

Vaughn, S., Bos, C., & Schumm, J. (1997). *Teaching mainstreamed, diverse, and at-risk students in the general education classroom*. Boston: Allyn and Bacon.

Walker, B. A., Reis, S. M., & Leonard, J. S. (1992). A developmental investigation of the lives of gifted women. *Gifted Child Quarterly, 36,* 201–206.

Wallach, M. A. (1976). Tests tell us little about talent. *American Scientist, 64,* 57.

Westberg, K., Archambault, F., Dobyns, S., & Slavin, T. (1993). The classroom practices observation study. *Journal for the Education of the Gifted, 16,* 120–146.

Willard-Holt, C. (1994). Strategies for individualizing instruction in regular classrooms. *Roeper Review, 17(1),* 43–45.

Winebrenner, S. (1992). *Teaching gifted kids in the regular classroom*. Minneapolis, MN: Free Spirit Publishing Inc.

Glossary

ABC model: A behavioral model encompassing antecedents, behaviors, and consequences with a focus on observable actions.

Ability grouping: Homogeneous placement of students based on their perceived ability or their performance in meeting established criteria required for participation in a gifted program.

Academic learning time: Time during which students are making a high rate of correct responses.

Acceleration: Instructional strategy for students who are gifted that emphasizes advanced subject matter content to be learned and mastered at a faster than usual rate. Included in this are practices such as credit by examination, grade-skipping, advanced placement, joint enrollment, and telescoping grade levels.

Advance organizer: Used to assist students in learning content-area material. Assists students in identifying their prior knowledge about a topic and provide information about the goals of the lesson, the activities that will take place during the lesson, and the teacher's expectations of the students.

Aided communication: Communication systems that use some type of external device to communicate. May be as simple as objects, pictures, or drawings or as complex as an electronic system with voice output.

Allocated time: The amount of time scheduled for academic skill areas.

Alternative performance strategy: A manner of performing a behavior (form), other than that usually done by a nondisabled person, which achieves the same result (function).

Antecedent: An event preceding a behavior and serving as a cue or inhibition of a response.

Assistive technology devices: Items or equipment designed to increase, maintain, or improve the functional capabilities of individuals with disabilities.

Autism spectrum disorders: Current term being used to refer to the diverse population of individuals with autism and autism related disorders (i.e., Asperger's, Rett's, Childhood Disintegrative disorder, and pervasive developmental disorders). This term reflects that each individual with autism is uniquely affected and can be impaired on a continuum from mild to severe.

Basic psychological processes: Functions that the brain performs in order to interpret, apply, and store stimuli and information. This term includes short or long term memory; auditory, visual, and haptic discrimination; sequencing; attention; organization; psychomotor skills and visual motor integration; conceptualization and reasoning; and social perception.

Behavioral intervention plan: A plan mandated in the IDEA 1997 Amendments for any special education student exhibiting behavioral difficulties. The behavioral intervention plan is to be based upon the results of a functional behavioral assessment and should have a positive orientation. The behavioral intervention plan must also address contingencies and supports for the student and teachers in addressing behavioral difficulties.

Blind: A term to describe individuals who are totally without vision or who have only light perception and use other senses (i.e., hearing and touch) as primary channels for receiving information.

Bloom's Taxonomy: A cognitive model developed by Benjamin S. Bloom and his colleagues providing a hierarchy of thinking processes helpful in working with students who are intellectually gifted. It moves from the very concrete through the more abstract levels of thinking (knowledge, comprehension, application, analysis, synthesis, and evaluation).

Braille: A system of raised dots that represents letters or whole words that allows individuals who have severe visual impairments or who are blind to read.

Central hearing loss: A type of hearing loss caused by damage to the auditory cortex of the brain.

Childhood Disintegrative disorder: Also known as Heller's Syndrome, this condition occurs when a child who was developing normally suddenly loses previously acquired skills and abilities and demonstrates behaviors consistent with autism. The regression usually occurs around age two but can happen anytime before age ten.

Cluster grouping: Gathering groups of students with similar abilities together in the regular classroom for learning opportunities suited to their aptitudes.

Collaboration: Working jointly with others in an endeavor.

Communication disorder: An impairment in the ability to receive, send, process, and comprehend concepts or verbal, nonverbal, and graphic symbol systems.

Community-based instruction (CBI): An instructional model which uses community settings as an extension of the classroom. Community-based instruction provides the opportunity for the student to learn and/or practice skills directly in the settings in which performance is required.

Conduct disorders: A diagnosis in the DSM-IV, conduct disorders describe anti-social patterns of rule-violating behavior, often directed with the intent to harm others or property. Some authorities describe conduct disorders as failing to have an emotional basis and describe those who have conduct disorders as making a conscious choice to engage in the behaviors, thereby differentiating conduct disorders from emotional disturbances.

Conductive hearing loss: A type of hearing loss caused by damage to the outer or middle ear. It usually is treatable by medication or surgery.

Congenital: A condition or disorder that is existing at birth.

Consequence: An event following a behavior and strengthening or weakening the chance of the behavior occurring again in the future.

Consultation: Providing advice, an opinion, or information to another individual.

Contingency: A planned or structured relationship between antecedents and consequences.

Convergent thinking: The tendency of thinking toward a restricted or single answer or solution to a question or problem.

Cooperative learning: Heterogeneous groups of students work together to achieve a common goal. Groups are rewarded based on the progress of the entire group.

Co-teaching: Two or more teachers teaching together with both taking responsibility for lesson development and implementation. Also termed team teaching.

Creativity: The process of sensing gaps or missing elements; forming ideas or hypotheses; testing these hypotheses; and communicating the results, possibly modifying and retesting the hypotheses.

Curriculum: The set of instructional knowledge, skills, and activities that comprise a school's program of study. Typically, the curriculum is a reflection of the texts and materials used.

Curriculum compacting: An instructional strategy for students who are gifted that allows for faster acceptable mastery of the necessary and required content components in a subject area to provide time to work with that content in a more enriching way.

Deaf/deaf: Individuals who have a hearing loss and use sign language as their primary mode of communication.

Delivery of service: The organizational pattern for grouping students for instruction. Includes placement in general or special education as well as grouping patterns within a class, i.e., whole class instruction, small group, or one-to-one instruction.

Discrepancy analysis: The format of direct observation of students performing functional skills to identify current performance capabilities and skills which require instruction.

Divergent thinking: Independent or liberal thinking. It includes producing original work, being open-minded and intellectually curious, and considering many approaches or possible solutions to a problem.

Ecological assessment: Observation of individuals in community settings to identify tasks performed in particular settings. The results of this assessment contribute to the content of a functional curriculum.

Educational games: Software programs that are designed to make learning fun. May teach thinking skills, provide extra practice on academic skills, or serve as a leisure activity or reward.

Eligibility team: Those who determine a student's eligibility for special education services, including a school psychologist, special educator, general educator, and parents. Other professionals may be included.

Emotional/behavioral disorders: Preferred name for the federal category of emotional disturbances.

Engaged time: The portion of the scheduled time during which students are actually working. Same as time-on-task.

Enrichment programs: A supplement to the regular curriculum offerings for students who are gifted to expand depth and breadth of understanding. Offerings include independent study programs and electives.

Etiology: The cause of a disability or condition, usually related to biologic or environmental factors.

Event recording: Recording each occurrence of a target behavior, such as each time students talked out without raising their hand.

Explicit instruction: Model of teaching that includes three main components: (a) demonstration and modeling, (b) guided practice, and (c) independent practice.

Externalizing disorders: When an emotional/behavioral disorder is directed outward at others, it is called externalizing (e.g., aggression, bullying, harassment, cruelty to animals, vandalism).

Family centered approach: The view that families are competent decision makers who must be equal team members in the decision making process for a child with special needs.

Functional behavioral assessment: An assessment to determine the function of a special education student's disruptive behavior through an analysis of the antecedents and consequences surrounding the behavior. Specific functions of behavior could include escape (i.e., getting out of an assignment) or attention (either peer or adult). A functional behavioral assessment is the initial step in the development of a behavioral intervention plan as specified by IDEA 97.

Functional curriculum: A curriculum model for students with moderate and severe disabilities. Content is selected based on identified skills needed for functioning in current and future integrated community, residential, and vocational environments.

Functional vision exam: An exam performed by a teacher certified in visual impairments to determine how well a student is using vision and what modifications and adaptations are needed.

Grieving cycle: The view that families with a child with special needs respond by progression through the stages of grieving such as shock, denial, and anger.

Guided practice: Students work directly under the teacher's supervision on tasks that are new and difficult. Teacher may assist students in producing correct responses through additional models, prompts, or cues.

Hard of hearing: A term to describe individuals who have some amount of hearing loss, but still rely on hearing and listening to communicate and learn.

Health impairments: Chronic or acute health problems that limit an individual's strength, vitality, or alertness.

Hearing impairments: A generic term used to described any type or amount of hearing loss.

High technology devices: Complex forms of assistive technology such as computers or augmentative communication devices.

Hyperactivity: Excessive motor movement given the child's age and gender.

IEP team: Those who develop and monitor the Individualized Education Program. It includes at least a special educator, general educator, and parent or guardian. Other specialists and the student may be included.

Impulsivity: Lack of self-control and inhibition that results in acting before thinking and poor choice making.

Inattention: Inability to focus on relevant information or sustain a focus that would be expected for a student of a particular age.

Inclusion: The process of educating students with disabilities in the general education setting.

Independent practice: Practice that students complete without direct teacher supervision. Students should not independently practice new skills until they are performing them accurately under guided practice conditions.

Individualized Education Program (IEP): The formal plan that teachers and parents develop to meet the educational needs of a student who is eligible for special education services. The IEP includes a description and management plan for the special services provided by the general and special educators.

Individualized Family Service Plan (IFSP): The formal plan that describes the child's and family's needs and the services to be provided for children with disabilities from birth through age three.

Individualized Transition Program (ITP): The plan developed by teachers, parents, and often the student which specifies what special activities will occur to prepare the student for work, leisure, and independent living after leaving school. It is required for students with disabilities age 14 and above.

Interdisciplinary team: A model of team interaction in which professionals develop a coordinated plan for providing services and take mutual responsibility for implementing goals.

Interim Alternative Education Setting (IAES): An educational placement designated by the IEP team for a special education student after involvement in a weapons or illicit substance violation at school. The IAES can be determined from a number of options including alternative school placement or after-school program placement and have a duration of 45 calendar days.

Internalizing disorders: When an emotional/behavioral disorder is directed inward at one's self instead of outward at others, it is called internalizing (e.g., depression, self-mutilation, anorexia, bulimia, drug/alcohol abuse).

Language disorders: Difficulty with the comprehension or use of spoken or written language. The term includes disorders of morphology, syntax, semantics, and pragmatics.

Least restrictive environment (LRE): The policy mandated by IDEA that students with disabilities be educated in the general school environment with their nondisabled peers to the greatest extent possible and appropriate.

Legal blindness: Central visual acuity of 20/200 or less in the better eye with best correction, or widest diameter of visual field subtending an angle of no greater than 20 degrees.

Low technology devices: Simple, less complicated forms of assistive technology, such as adapted switches and adapted grips for utensils.

Low vision: This term refers to individuals who have significant visual impairments with best correction, but still have usable vision.

Low vision devices: Devices that magnify items, including print.

Low vision exam: An exam performed by an optometrist to determine if an individual would benefit from the use of low vision devices (e.g., magnifiers, telescopes, etc.).

Manifestation determination: An IEP team decision indicating if an offense, such as weapons possession, was related to the handicapping condition of a student in special education.

Mastery learning: Instructional delivery model in which students demonstrate mastery of content in an area before moving on to new material.

Mediation: A formal process for resolving disputes between parents and schools.

Mediational strategies: Cognitive processes that create images, organize, classify, and attach meaning to new information.

Mixed hearing loss: The term used to describe a hearing loss that has both conductive and sensorineural components.

Modeling: Showing the students exactly what to do. Same as demonstration.

Modified instruction: Using the same type of instruction and materials, but at a slower pace, in smaller steps, or with more careful teaching.

Multidisciplinary team: A model of team interaction in which each professional makes decisions in a specific area of expertise and is responsible discipline specific program design and implementation.

Multimedia: Software programs that link graphics, text, sound, and full-motion video via computer systems. Common examples include multimedia encyclopedias and electronic books.

Orthopedic impairments: Disorders that are the result of diseases or conditions which interfere with the normal functioning of muscles or bones.

Partial participation: The curriculum and instruction philosophy which states that for students with severe disabilities it is desirable and appropriate for the development of curriculum objectives which target participation within a task in lieu of the ability to independently perform a task.

Peer tutoring: A student who is competent in an area serves as a teacher/monitor of another student who needs additional practice.

Perinatal: The period of time during labor and delivery.

Permanent product recording: Recording the evidence of a behavior, such as a spelling test grade.

Permanent records: The accumulation of school information about a student, including attendance records, achievement test scores, grades, and comments from teachers.

Perseveration: Repeating the same actions, thoughts, or behaviors, without functional purpose (e.g., turning on/off the light switch over and over, talking about rabbits in every conversation, refusing to step on the cracks in sidewalks). Commonly associated with autism and obsessive compulsive disorders.

Pervasive developmental disorder (PDD): The umbrella term used in the DSM-IV which includes subcategories of autism spectrum disorders (i.e., Autism, Asperger's, Rett's, Childhood Disintegrative disorder, Pervasive developmental disorders-Not otherwise specified).

Physical impairments: Another term for orthopedic impairments.

Postnatal: The period of time following birth.

Prenatal: The period of time between conception and birth.

Prereferral team: A group of educators, typically general education teachers, who implement and monitor instructional and behavioral modifications for students prior to a formal referral for a formal assessment to evaluate eligibility for possible special education services.

Problem-solving software: Software programs in which students are presented with problems that must be solved. Designed to build higher-order thinking skills, such as analysis, synthesis, and evaluation.

Proximity control: The visual and physical monitoring of a classroom by a teacher to reduce disruptive behavior.

Reading comprehension: The ability to gain meaning from text. Requires fluent decoding, knowledge of semantics and syntax, and activation of prior knowledge about the topic of the text.

Reading decoding: The ability to accurately identify unknown words when reading.

Reading fluency: The ability to decode words accurately at an efficient word per minute rate.

Response prompts: Assistance provided by the teacher to initiate and/or guide student performance of a behavior. Types of response prompts include: verbal, gesture, model, and physical prompts.

Role release: Professionals transfer information and skills from one discipline to another.

Semantics: Knowledge of word meaning, vocabulary.

Sensorineural hearing loss: A type of hearing loss caused by damage to the inner ear. It usually is a permanent hearing loss for which individuals will be fit with hearing aids.

Severe discrepancy: According to federal law, to qualify for special education as having a learning disability, there must be a significant difference between IQ scores and achievement scores. Individual states define severe discrepancy, which usually means a difference of 20 or more points.

Signal control: The use of teacher cue either audibly, visually, or kinesthetically to prompt students to perform or cease actions (i.e., rapping the desk 3 times to indicate the class should stop talking).

Significantly subaverage intellectual functioning: Refers to intellectual ability at least two standard deviations below the mean as measured by a standardized IQ test.

Simulation: Software programs that allow students to experience real-life situations that may be difficult, dangerous, or impossible to reproduce in the classroom.

Special education: The instruction and services designed to meet the unique learning needs of students with disabilities.

Specialized instruction: Use of a different curriculum and methods than those used with average students. Often used in special education classrooms.

Speech disorders: Difficulty with the production of oral language. The term includes disorders of articulation, voice, and fluency.

Speech synthesizer: Allows voice output from a computer.

Stages of learning: Three stages through which students move as they learn new skills. Acquiring—student knows little or nothing about the skills; Practicing—student performs skill accurately, but needs to build rate; Generalizing—student can perform skill in circumstances other than those used during teaching (e.g., with different persons, in different settings, or when skill is embedded in another task).

STORCH: An acronym for the maternal infections of Syphilis, Toxoplasmosis, Other, Rubella, Cytomegalovirus, and Herpes.

Story map: A strategy for teaching reading comprehension in which students identify the structural components of a story (e.g., plot, setting, characters, etc.) and place them on a story diagram.

Student-directed strategies: Students take responsibility of monitoring and recording their own progress. Also called self-management strategies.

Syntax: Knowledge of grammar; structure of sentences.

Task analysis: The process of breaking down a complex task into its component steps. This allows for analysis of student competence in performance of each step and for structuring instruction.

TDD: Telecommunications Device for the Deaf. A keyboard and small screen are used to carry incoming and outgoing text messages through telephone lines.

Team teaching: Two or more teachers teaching together with both taking responsibility for lesson development and implementation. Also termed co-teaching.

Time delay: An instructional strategy in which a prompt is always available to assist the student in making a correct response.

Time-on-task: The portion of the scheduled time during which students are actually working. Same as engaged time.

Time sampling: Intermittent recording of behavior rather than continuous recording. For example, recording behaviors that occur in the first minute, third minute, and eighth minute of a 20 minute observation period across several separate observations.

Total communication (TC): A communication system used by individuals with a hearing loss that incorporates both auditory/oral communication and manual communication.

Transdisciplinary team: A model of team interaction in which professionals work together to develop an integrated plan of service and then one person delivers the services.

Unaided communication: Communication systems that use hand or body movement to communicate, but do not require any external devices.

Visual acuity: A term that describes how clear or sharp a visual image appears.

Index